ARISTOTLE

Nicomachean Ethics

ARISTOTLE

Nicomachean Ethics

THIRD EDITION

Translated, with Introduction, Notes, and Glossary, by

Terence Irwin

Hackett Publishing Company, Inc.
Indianapolis/Cambridge

22 21 20 19   1 2 3 4 5 6 7

For further information, please address
  Hackett Publishing Company, Inc.
  P.O. Box 44937
  Indianapolis, Indiana 46244-0937

  www.hackettpublishing.com

Cover design by Listenberger Design & Associates
Composition by Aptara, Inc.

Library of Congress Cataloging-in-Publication Data

Names: Aristotle, author. | Irwin, Terence, translator.
Title: Nicomachean ethics / Aristotle ; translated with introduction, notes,
    and glossary by Terence Irwin.
Other titles: Nicomachean ethics. English
Description: Third Edition. | Indianapolis : Hackett Publishing Company,
    Inc., 2019. | Includes bibliographical references.
Identifiers: LCCN 2019010477 | ISBN 9781624668159 (pbk.) |
    ISBN 9781624668166 (cloth)
Subjects: LCSH: Ethics.
Classification: LCC B430.A5 N5313 2019 | DDC 171/.3—dc23
LC record available at https://lccn.loc.gov/2019010477

CONTENTS

Preface   ix

Abbreviations and Conventions   x

Introduction   xiii

NICOMACHEAN ETHICS

Book I

    1. [Ends and goods]   1

    2. [The highest good and political science]   1

    3. [The method of political science]   2

    4. [Common beliefs]   3

    5. [The three lives]   4

    6. [The Platonic Form of the Good]   5

    7. [An account of the human good]   8

    8. [Defence of the account of the good]   11

    9. [How is happiness achieved?]   13

    10. [Can we be happy during our lifetime?]   14

    11. [How happiness can be affected after one's death] 17

    12. [Praise and honour]   17

    13. [Introduction to the virtues]   18

Book II

    1. [How a virtue of character is acquired]   21

    2. [Habituation]   22

    3. [The importance of pleasure and pain]   23

    4. [Virtuous actions contrasted with virtuous character] 25

    5. [Virtue of character: its genus]   26

    6. [Virtue of character: its differentia]   27

    7. [The particular virtues of character]   30

    8. [Relations between mean and extreme states]   32

    9. [How can we reach the mean?]   33

Book III

    1. [Voluntary action]   35

    2. [Decision]   39

    3. [Deliberation]   40

    4. [Wish]   43
    5. [Virtue and vice are in our power]   43
    6. [Bravery: its scope]   47
    7. [Bravery: its characteristic outlook]   48
    8. [Conditions that resemble bravery]   50
    9. [Feelings proper to bravery]   52
  10. [Temperance: its scope]   53
  11. [Temperance: its outlook]   55
  12. [Intemperance]   56

Book IV

    1. [Generosity]   58
    2. [Magnificence]   63
    3. [Magnanimity]   66
    4. [The virtue concerned with small honours]   71
    5. [Calmness]   71
    6. [Friendliness]   73
    7. [Truthfulness]   75
    8. [Wit]   77
    9. [Shame]   78

Book V

    1. [Varieties of justice]   79
    2. [Special justice contrasted with general]   82
    3. [Justice in distribution]   84
    4. [Justice in rectification]   85
    5. [Justice in exchange]   87
    6. [Political justice]   90
    7. [Justice by nature and by law]   92
    8. [Justice, injustice, and the voluntary]   93
    9. [Puzzles about justice and injustice]   95
  10. [Decency]   98
  11. [Injustice to oneself]   99

Book VI

    1. [The mean and the virtues of thought]   101
    2. [Thought, desire, and decision]   102
    3. [Scientific knowledge]   103
    4. [Craft knowledge]   104
    5. [Prudence]   105
    6. [Understanding]   106
    7. [Wisdom contrasted with prudence]   107

8. [Types of prudence]   108
9. [Good deliberation]   110
10. [Comprehension]   111
11. [Practical thought and particulars]   112
12. [Puzzles about prudence and wisdom]   113
13. [Prudence and virtue of character]   115

Book VII

1. [Virtue, vice, and incontinence]   117
2. [Puzzles about incontinence]   118
3. [Incontinence and ignorance]   120
4. [Simple incontinence]   123
5. [Bestiality and disease]   125
6. [Incontinence and related conditions]   127
7. [Incontinence, intemperance, and softness]   128
8. [Why intemperance is worse than incontinence]   130
9. [Continence]   132
10. [Answers to further questions about incontinence]   133
11. [Disputed questions about pleasure]   134
12. [Pleasure and good]   135
13. [Pleasure and happiness]   137
14. [Bodily pleasures]   138

Book VIII

1. [Common beliefs and questions]   141
2. [The object of friendship]   142
3. [The three types of friendship]   143
4. [Comparison between the types of friendship]   145
5. [State and activity in friendship]   147
6. [Characteristic activities in the different types of friendship]   148
7. [Friendship between unequals]   150
8. [Giving and receiving in friendship]   151
9. [Friendship in communities]   152
10. [Political systems]   154
11. [Friendships in political systems]   155
12. [Friendships in families]   156
13. [Disputes in friendships between equals]   158
14. [Disputes in friendships between unequals]   161

Book IX

1. [Friends with dissimilar aims]   162
2. [Conflicts between different types of friendships]   164

3. [Dissolution of friendships]   166
4. [Self-love and friendship]   167
5. [Goodwill and friendship]   169
6. [Friendship and concord]   170
7. [Active benevolence and friendship]   171
8. [Self-love and selfishness]   173
9. [Why do we need friends?]   175
10. [How many friends are needed?]   178
11. [Friends in good and ill fortune]   179
12. [Shared activity in friendship]   180

Book X

1. [The right approach to pleasure]   181
2. [Arguments about pleasure]   182
3. [Pleasure is a good, but not the good]   184
4. [Pleasure is an activity]   186
5. [Pleasures differ in kind]   189
6. [Conditions for happiness]   191
7. [Happiness and theoretical study]   193
8. [Theoretical study and the other virtues]   195
9. [Moral education]   198

Notes   204
Glossary   361
Appendix   404
Further Reading   440

PREFACE

This translation seeks to make Aristotle's terse and concentrated Greek fairly intelligible to those who read him in English. Some readers will want to read through the *Ethics* in order to grasp the main outlines of Aristotle's position. They need a translation that is fairly intelligible without constant reference to detailed explanations, and I have tried to keep the needs of these readers in mind. But I have also tried to help those who want to study the *Ethics*, and not merely to read through it. To learn more about what to expect, readers should consult sections 17–20 of the Introduction before turning to the translation. They will also want to consult the Notes and Glossary to help them towards a fuller understanding of the text.

I have tried to present the text without too much editorial intervention (though, like other translators, I have marked the chapters into which previous editors have divided the work). The headings in the translation are mine, with no authority in Aristotle. Readers should consult the last section of the Introduction before they turn to the translation or Notes. At every stage, I have benefited from the work of previous translators and commentators, and especially from the commentaries by Stewart and by Gauthier and Jolif.

In this third edition I have revised the translation, in the hope of making it both more accurate and more readable. The Notes now try to give the reader a clearer idea of alternative possibilities of translation and interpretation. The Glossary has been expanded and rearranged. The Introduction has also been expanded in order to give readers some idea of the main questions that they might pursue in studying the translation and Notes.

A new feature of this edition is the Appendix, which includes a few supplementary texts from other works of Aristotle. I hope it will be convenient for readers to have these few passages in the same volume as the *Ethics*.

At different times over a number of years, I have benefited from comments by reviewers, and from the help of John Cooper, Daniel Devereux, Gail Fine, Richard Kraut, Anthony Long, Alexander Nehamas, Susan Sauvé Meyer, Jennifer Whiting, Katherine Woolfitt, and Donald Zeyl.

Hackett Publishing Company has made a significant contribution to philosophical publishing and to philosophical education, and I am fortunate to have been associated with it.

T. H. Irwin
Oxford, 2019

ABBREVIATIONS AND CONVENTIONS

Works of Aristotle

The works of Aristotle are cited by abbreviations of their conventional Latin (or Greek) or English titles.

APo	Analytica Posteriora	Posterior Analytics
APr	Analytica Priora	Prior Analytics
[Ath. Pol.]	Athenaiôn Politeia	Constitution of Athens
Catg.	Categoriae	Categories
DA	De Anima	On the Soul
DC	De Caelo	On the Heavens
DI	De Interpretatione	On Interpretation
EE	Ethica Eudemia	Eudemian Ethics
EN	Ethica Nicomachea	Nicomachean Ethics
GA	De Generatione Animalium	Generation of Animals
GC	De Generatione et Corruptione	Generation and Corruption
HA	Historia Animalium	History of Animals
IA	De Incessu Animalium	Progression of Animals
MA	De Motu Animalium	Movement of Animals
Met.	Metaphysica	Metaphysics
Metr.	Meteorologica	Meteorology
MM	Magna Moralia	Great Ethics
PA	De Partibus Animalium	Parts of Animals
Phys.	Physica	Physics
PN	Parva Naturalia	Short Natural Treatises
Poet.	De Arte Poetica	Poetics
Pol.	Politica	Politics
[Probl.]	Problemata	Problems
Rhet.	Rhetorica	Rhetoric
Top.	Topica	Topics

The *Problems* is generally regarded as spurious. The *Ath. Pol.* is often regarded as a work done under Aristotle's supervision, though not by Aristotle himself.

Dialogues of Plato are cited by abbreviated title and standard Stephanus pages.

Other abbreviations

For full details see Further Reading.

ROT	The Revised Oxford Translation
OCD	*Oxford Classical Dictionary*

OCT	Oxford Classical Text, ed. Bywater
DK	Diels-Kranz, *Fragmente der Vorsokratiker*
Kaibel	Kaibel, G., ed., *Comicorum Graecorum Fragmenta* (Berlin, 1899)
Kock	Kock, T., ed., *Comicorum Atticorum Fragmenta* (Leipzig, 1880–1888)
Page	Page, D. L., ed., *Lyra Graeca Selecta* (Oxford, 1968)
TGF	Nauck, A., ed., *Tragicorum Graecorum Fragmenta* (ed. 2, Leipzig, 1899)
West	West, M. L., ed., *Delectus ex Elegis et Iambis Graecis* (Oxford, 1980)
CAG	*Commentaria in Aristotelem Graeca* (Berlin, various dates)

Other marks in the translation

{{ . . . }}	indicates the conjectural place for a passage transposed from its place in the mss.
[[. . .]]	indicates the place in the mss. from which a passaged marked by {{ . . . }} has been moved.
/	an oblique line marks the beginning of every fifth line of a Bekker page.

Other Conventions in the Notes and Glossary

c5 (etc.) Chapter 5 (etc.) of the same book.

[Or . . .] Another possible translation or interpretation.

CAPITALS indicate a reference to an entry in the Glossary.

An obelus (†) refers to a selection included in the Appendix.

A reference to another passage in *EN* should be taken to include any note on that passage.

INTRODUCTION

1. Aristotle's life

Aristotle was born in Stagira in Macedon (now part of northern Greece; see 1094b10, 1134b23) in 384 BC. In his lifetime the kingdom of Macedon, first under Philip and then under his son Alexander ('the Great'), achieved hegemony over the Greek cities in Europe and Asia, and then went on to conquer the Persian Empire. The Macedonian rulers tried to present themselves as Greeks. They did not entirely succeed, and many Greeks (e.g., Demosthenes in Athens) regarded them as foreign invaders. Though Aristotle spent much of his adult life in Athens, he was not an Athenian citizen; he was closely linked to the kings of Macedon (cf. 1150b9–12), and he was affected by the volatile relations between the Greek cities, especially Athens, and Macedon.

Aristotle was the son of Nicomachus, a doctor who had been attached to the Macedonian court. (See MEDICINE.[1]) In 367 Aristotle came to Athens, and was a member of PLATO's Academy until the death of Plato in 347. Plato's successor as head of the Academy was his nephew SPEUSIPPUS. At that time Aristotle left Athens, first for Assos (in Asia Minor), where the pro-Macedonian TYRANT Hermeias was a patron of philosophical studies. Aristotle married Pythias, a niece of Hermeias; they had a daughter, also called Pythias. After Hermeias was killed by the Persians, Aristotle travelled further (cf. 1155a21–2); he moved on to Lesbos in the eastern Aegean (cf. 1137b30), and then to Macedon. He was a tutor of Alexander. In 334 he returned to Athens and founded his own school, the Lyceum. After the death of Pythias, Aristotle formed an attachment to Herpyllis, and they had a son Nicomachus (named, following the Greek custom, after his grandfather). In 323 Alexander died; in the resulting outbreak of anti-Macedonian feeling in Athens Aristotle left for Chalcis, on the island of Euboea (cf. 1167b7), where he died in 322. In his will Aristotle directed that Pythias' bones were to be placed in his grave, in accordance with her wishes; he also made provision for the support of Herpyllis and Nicomachus.[2]

---

1. Words in CAPITALS refer to entries in the Glossary. Numbers in square brackets refer to items listed in Further Reading. For abbreviations see the list of Abbreviations and Conventions.
2. Aristotle's will; see ROT p. 2464.

2. Aristotle's works

The modern English translation of Aristotle (in ROT) fills about 2,450 pages. Many of his works, however, have been lost, and those that survive complete are probably quite different in character from many of the lost works.[3] Among the lost works are dialogues, which may have been similar in character to some of Plato's dialogues, and other treatises designed for publication. Aristotle may refer to some of the lost works when he speaks of his POPULAR writings.

The Aristotelian Corpus, as we have it, largely consists of works that appear to be closely related to Aristotle's lectures. Sometimes he seems to refer (1107a33) to 'visual aids' of the sort that might be present in a classroom. Sometimes the grammatically incomplete sentences and compressed allusions suggest notes that a lecturer might expand.

We cannot tell how many of his treatises Aristotle regarded as 'finished'. They may be 'files' that he revised, expanded, summarized, or combined, either for teaching or when new ideas struck him.

In the Greek manuscripts, the Corpus is arranged as follows:[4]

1. *Catg., DI, APr, APo, Top.* These are traditionally known as the 'Organon' (i.e., 'instrument') because they deal with logic (in Aristotle's broad sense), which is an instrument of philosophical thinking, not a discipline with its own specific subject matter.
2. *Phys., DC, GC, Metr., DA, PN, HA, PA, MA, IA, GA.* These belong to natural philosophy, dealing with different aspects of NATURE.
3. *Met.* This deals with 'first philosophy' the study of reality in general. (*EN* i 6 discusses metaphysical topics.)
4. *EN, MM, EE, Pol.* These belong to 'practical' philosophy, which deals with ACTION rather than PRODUCTION.
5. *Rhet., Poet.* These deal with PRODUCTION rather than ACTION.[5]

Aristotle presents ETHICS as a distinct discipline, relatively independent of other areas of philosophy (1096b30–1, 1155b8–9; cf. *EE* 1216b35–1217a10†). Nonetheless, he often refers to, or relies on, his other philosophical doctrines. See ACTIVITY, CAPACITY, CAUSE, ETHICS, FUNCTION, HUMAN BEING, SCIENCE, SOUL. Readers will read the *EN* with more understanding if they also read the most immediately relevant parts of Aristotle's other works. For a

---

3. Ancient lists of titles of Aristotle's works are printed in ROT p. 2386.
4. This list excludes (a) works generally agreed to be spurious that have been included in the Aristotelian Corpus; (b) the lost works; (c) the *Constitution of Athens* (probably not by Aristotle himself), which was discovered after the standard arrangement of Aristotle's works was established. All of (a) and (c), and some surviving fragments, or supposed fragments, of (b), are included in ROT.
5. Aristotle's own division of disciplines: *PA* 640a1, *Met.* 982b11, 993b20, vi 1.

start, they might try *Catg.* 1–9 (the doctrine of categories); *APo* i 1–3, ii 19 (on SCIENCE); *Top.* i (on the dialectical method practised in ETHICS); *Phys.* ii, iii 1 (on NATURE, CAUSE, and MOVEMENT); *DA* i 1, ii 1†–4 (on SOUL), ii 5–11 (on PERCEPTION), iii 4 (on UNDERSTANDING), iii 9–11† (on DESIRE and ACTION); *PA* i 1 (on NATURE); *MA* 9† (on practical INFERENCE); *Met.* i 1 (on SCIENCE), 6, 9 (on SOCRATES and PLATO), iv 1–2, ix 1–8 (on CAPACITY and ACTIVITY), xii (on GOD).

3. The ethical treatises

Aristotle's ethical theory is mostly contained in three treatises: the *MM*, the *EE*, and the *EN*.

At some time in antiquity *MM* was written on two papyrus rolls that were larger than the standard size; hence it was called 'the large rolls [*biblia*] on ethics'. It is probably Aristotle's first major work on ethics. Some critics, however, regard it as post-Aristotelian. It covers roughly the same topics as *EE* and *EN*. Usually, but not always, it is briefer than the other two works. (See Appendix.)

The titles of *EE* and *EN* may reflect a tradition that Eudemus (a member of the Lyceum) and Nicomachus (the son of Aristotle and Herpyllis) edited Aristotle's lectures. The *EE* is now widely agreed to be authentic. It is usually (not universally) and reasonably taken to be earlier than the *EN*. *MM* and *EE* are generally more similar to each other than either is to *EN*. (See Appendix.)

The three books *EN* v–vii are also, according to manuscripts of *EN* and *EE*, the three books *EE* iv–vi. Stylistic and doctrinal evidence suggests that these books were originally part of the *EE*. Aristotle, however, may have intended the current version of them to be part of the *EN*. If the *EE* is earlier than the *EN*, he may have used these books, perhaps revised, in his new course of lectures. See 1128b33–5, 1152b1–3, 1176a30–2.

4. Outline of the *Ethics*

We can gain some idea of the contents and structure of the *EN* from this outline:

   A. i 1–12. HAPPINESS, the ultimate human good.
   B. i 13–ii 9. Happiness requires VIRTUES of character and of thought. Virtues of character.
   C. iii 1–5. Preconditions of virtue: VOLUNTARY action and responsibility.
   D. iii 6–v 11. The individual virtues of character.
   E. vi 1–13. Virtues of thought.
   F. vii 1–10. INCONTINENCE and related conditions.
   G. vii 11–14. PLEASURE.
   H. viii–ix. Friendship.

I. x 1–5. Pleasure.

J. x 6–8. Happiness and theoretical STUDY.

K. x 9. Ethics, moral education, and politics.

We can follow the development of Aristotle's argument if we examine the main themes. This introduction presents the main themes briefly, to orient readers who have not yet studied the text in detail. It does not go into all the relevant questions of interpretation. The Notes take up some of these questions.

5. Method

Aristotle sets out to examine the most widespread and plausible of common views about happiness (1095a28–30). These views form the starting point that is 'known to us' (1095b2–8). He tries to find the most plausible objections and puzzles that can be raised against these common views, with the aim of finding a resolution that resolves apparent contradictions and conflicts.[6] Sometimes we find that the contradictions are only apparent. But in other cases we find genuine contradictions and puzzles, In these cases our resolution seeks to maintain the 'most and the most important' (1145b5–6) of our views, and revises our initial views in order to fit the most and most important.[7]

Aristotle describes this method in vii 1. The procedure of examining the common beliefs corresponds to his description of dialectic (*Topics* i 2). When we are looking for the basic principles of a discipline, we cannot argue deductively from principles that we have not yet found; we have to look for the principles by examining the relevant common beliefs. (Cf. *EE* i 3.) This method is closely related to the Socratic dialogue, without the overt form of a dialogue.[8]

Aristotle conceives the discipline that he calls 'ethics' (*MM* 1181a24–1182a1; *Pol.* 1322a7) as a part of political science; it is the part concerned with finding the good for an individual and a community (*EN* 1094b5–10). He treats the *EN* and the *Politics* as parts of a single inquiry (*EN* 1181b12–23).

In Aristotle's view, ethics is a distinct discipline that does not depend on a general metaphysical theory of reality. The attempt to derive ethical conclusions from a general metaphysical theory is one of the errors, in his view, that underlie Plato's Theory of Forms (criticized in i 6). He rejects the intrusion of alien principles into ethics (1155b8–9).

Ethics is not wholly isolated, however, from Aristotle's other philosophical inquiries: (1) His account of the human good (i 7) relies on the account of SOUL that is set out more fully in *De Anima* ii 1. (2) The analysis of the virtues

---

6. On puzzles (*aporiai*), cf. *Top.* 145b16–20.

7. See, e.g., i 8; 1143b36; 1144b32–4; viii 1; 1168a28–b13; 1169b3–8.

8. *Top.* 100a18–21.

relies on the division of the soul into rational and non-rational parts, found both in the *De Anima* and in Plato's *Republic*. (3) The account of the intellectual virtues in Book vi relies partly on Aristotle's theory of SCIENCE, as set out in the *APo*. (4) Aristotle's views about the nature and value of pure intellectual activity (STUDY) are connected with his conception of GOD, set out most fully in *Met*. xii.

6. The ultimate good: happiness

Ethics tries to discover the good for an individual and a community (i 2), and so it begins with an examination of the ultimate good for a human being. This is a good (1) which we pursue only for its own sake, not for the sake of anything else; (2) for the sake of which we pursue all the other goods we pursue; and (3) which includes all the other goods that we pursue for their own sakes (1094b6).

Why does Aristotle believe in this ultimate and all-embracing good? He tells us that the main task of political science is to select, control, and adjust the different activities and pursuits that go on in a community, because it has some conception of what the point of each of them is. We have a conception of our final good, then, insofar as we rationally select, control, and adjust our different pursuits.

To see why such a conception is rationally required, consider what we would be like without it. If we have no idea of what we care about for its own sake and what we care about simply for the sake of other things, we cannot make reasonable decisions about what to do. Similarly, if we simply have a list of things that we care about for their own sakes but we have no idea of their relative importance, we cannot make reasonable decisions. A conception of a final good is a conception of the relative weight of the different things that we care about for their own sake.

We all aim at an ultimate good, then, not because we all have an explicit conception of it, but because we implicitly rely on some views about it when we consider the relative importance of different non-instrumental goods.

What, then, is this ultimate good? Aristotle's first answer, drawn from the unanimous agreement of common views, is that it is HAPPINESS (*eudaimonia*) or living well or doing well (1095a17–20.) These equivalents for *eudaimonia* show us why 'happiness' may be a misleading translation. Aristotle does not mean that we all agree that the ultimate good is a feeling of pleasure or satisfaction. He means that we agree that the ultimate good consists in the best kind of life for a human being. To achieve *eudaimonia* is to be well off over one's life as a whole. But we still want to know what kind of life is the one that achieves the ultimate good.

7. What is the ultimate good?

Aristotle argues that the ultimate good is complete and self-sufficient (1097a15–b21).[9] If it were incomplete, it would be wrong to use it to choose other goods, because it might leave out some consideration that should matter to us. If it is self-sufficient, leaving out nothing that it is reasonable to pursue, it must be suitable for human nature, and especially for the nature of a human being as a political animal. Aristotle states briefly an important claim that he develops later (ix 9).

To find a better account of the human good, Aristotle introduces the human FUNCTION. He explains his claim by referring to the functions of craftsmen and organs. The function of a craftsman, an artifact, or an organ is the goal-directed activity that makes it the kind of thing it is, and is essential to it as that kind of thing. Something is an axe insofar as it has a function of cutting; and when it loses this, it no longer serves as an axe. Its carrying out that function is essential to its being an axe.

Aristotle assumes that the essential human function is some kind of life. It is plainly not the life of plants or of animals, but a distinctively human life. This is the activity of the SOUL expressing reason. In the *De Anima* Aristotle describes the soul as the form of the living body, so that it is what makes the living body alive. The human good is determined by the human function insofar as it is determined by the human form—the life and activity that distinguish human beings from other things.

When Aristotle claims that it is essential to human beings, in contrast to other animals, that they guide their actions by reason, he does not mean that the human good consists primarily in thinking or reasoning, but that it consists in a life that expresses reason in controlling and guiding our lives. He does not deny the importance of other human activities besides reasoning, but he insists on the essential role of rational reflexion in human life. Since virtues are the states that cause us to exercise practical reason well, the human good is activity in accordance with the virtues.

Aristotle derives his account of the good from his account of the human essence because he assumes that if we want to find out what is good for a certain kind of thing, we need to know what kind of thing that is. If we did not know that a knife is for cutting, we would not know that it's good for it to be protected from rust. If we did not know what kind of life a normal tiger lives, we would not know whether it is good for a tiger to be kept in a cage or to be given more freedom to run. Similarly, if we do not know what sort of life is characteristic of a human being, we do not know what sort of thing is good for a human being.

---

9. More precisely: If we think some good G is to be identified with happiness, but then find that we can add some further good H to G, so that the total of G + H is a greater good than G alone, then G cannot be identified with happiness.

Aristotle remarks later that no one would choose to go back to the life of a child, even if one could gain the greatest pleasures of the sort that appeal to a child. The good for adult humans beings depends on our use of our rational capacities to guide our lives.

This outline of happiness (1098a20–2) rules out some serious errors and points us in the right direction. (1) We must reject the life devoted purely to pleasure (1095b19–20), for reasons that Aristotle makes clear only in x 2–5. This life is incomplete because it allows no essential role to rational activity; and mere pleasure without rational activity is not the good for a rational agent (cf. 1174a1–4). Since a life of pleasure can be improved on in this way, pleasure cannot be the good (1172b28 32). Hence Aristotle rejects hedonism. (2) SOCRATES' view that virtue is sufficient for happiness conflicts with common beliefs (1096a2). Virtue alone does not constitute a complete and self-sufficient life. For external misfortunes impede rational activity (1100b29–30, 1153b14–25), and therefore preclude happiness (1100a5–9). (3) Still, whatever misfortunes we suffer, we have better reason to choose virtue than we have to choose any combination of other goods that are incompatible with it (1100b30–1101a8).

Some critics argue, however, that when Aristotle identifies happiness with activity in accord with the best and most COMPLETE (or most perfect?) virtue, and not with activity in accord with all the virtues (see 1097a30, 1098a17–18, 1099a30–1), he anticipates his argument in Book x, which discusses the place of STUDY in happiness. (See §10 below.)

8. Virtue of character

If virtuous activity controls happiness, we need to know what the relevant virtues are (i 13). Since Aristotle recognizes both rational and non-rational DESIRES, he argues that the excellent and virtuous condition of the soul will include virtues of both the rational and the non-rational parts. The virtues of the rational part are the virtues of thought, discussed in Book vi. The virtues of character are the various ways in which the non-rational elements co-operate with reason, so that human beings fulfil their function well and in accordance with complete virtue. Aristotle discusses these virtues in Books ii–v.

He defines a virtue of character as a STATE, as distinct from a CAPACITY and a FEELING (ii 5). I may have a capacity without using it properly on the right occasions; for instance, I may have medical skill even if I do not bother to use it at all, or if I use it to poison my patients. Similarly, I may have a feeling (of sympathy, hatred, anger, etc.) without guiding it properly to the right objects. To be a generous person, I must not only know how to give money on the right occasions, and have generous impulses; I must also direct my capacities and feelings to the right goals, so that I act from the right desires, for the right reasons, and on the right occasions (cf. *Met.* 1025a1–13).

Aristotle does not treat virtues as merely instrumental means to virtuous action. Actions may be virtuous even though they are not done for the virtuous person's reasons (1105a26–b9, 1144a11–20). But agents are not virtuous unless they do the virtuous action because they have decided to do it for its own sake. Aristotle assumes that in praising and valuing virtuous people we do not value simply their reliable tendency to produce virtuous actions; we also value the state of character that they display in their actions. He agrees with Kant's view that the morally good will not only produce the right actions, but also produce the right actions for the right reason (*Grundlegung* Akad. p. 397–8). The discussion of VOLUNTARY action shows us the circumstances in which the praiseworthy state is displayed in actions.

A virtue of character is a 'mean' or an 'intermediate' state, which aims at the 'mean' or 'intermediate' in acting and being affected. Aristotle does not recommend moderation, as we usually understand it, in actions or in feelings. He does not suggest, for instance, that if we achieve the mean in relation to anger, we will never be more than moderately angry; on the contrary, the virtuous person will be extremely angry on the occasions when extreme anger is called for. (He discusses anger more fully in iv 5.)

The doctrine of the mean rejects attempts to reduce the virtues to patterns of action that can be expressed in simple behavioural rules. We might notice that it is often bad to give way to anger, and so we might form the mistaken view that we ought to eliminate or repress anger altogether. If we notice that the pursuit of honour sometimes has bad results, we might reject the pursuit of honour. But if we also notice that it is sometimes bad to suppress anger, we might mistakenly go to the other extreme and advocate the expression of anger. If we notice that people are sometimes worse off if they are indifferent to honour, we might mistakenly go to the other extreme and advocate the unrestrained pursuit of honour. Aristotle replies that these unqualified rules are misleading. We need to say that anger and the pursuit of honour should be cultivated to the right degree, so that we act on these impulses on the right occasions. This cultivation is neither of the extreme solutions (suppression and indulgence), and in that respect it is intermediate. But it does not simply split the difference between the extremes. A virtue achieves the right adjustment of different aims and impulses. (See 1106a24–6.)

In claiming that a mean state in relation to non-rational impulses and appetites is possible and desirable, Aristotle rejects other possible treatments of them. Possible treatments of such impulses would be these: (1) Indulgence, leaving them completely unchecked; (2) Suppression, as far as possible (1104b24–6); (3) Control or continence (cf. 1102b13–20), as far as possible; (4) Harmony and agreement with the rational part. In treating a virtue as a mean, Aristotle signals his adherence to the fourth solution, as opposed to any of the other three. He thinks it should be intermediate between the extremes of excess (leaving anger, say, totally unchecked) and the extreme of deficiency (complete suppression of anger).

Virtuous people, therefore, allow reasonable satisfaction to their appetites; they do not suppress all their fears; they do not disregard all their feelings of pride or shame or resentment (1126a3–8), or their desire for other people's good opinion. Brave people are appropriately afraid of serious danger (1115b10–20), and if the cause is not worth the danger, they withdraw; but when the cause justifies their standing firm, their fear is not so strong that they have to struggle against it.

When Aristotle spells out the sense of his claim that virtue aims at a mean in acting and being affected, he says that virtuous people do what they ought, when they ought, in the circumstances where they ought to, and so on. Later he adds that we do what we ought to, when we ought to, etc., insofar as we do what is FINE. More details on these specifications of the mean are provided in the section on the individual virtues.

In claiming that the virtuous person makes a DECISION (iii 2–3) to do the virtuous action for its own sake, Aristotle implies that a certain pattern of desire and deliberation (1113a2–12, 1139a21–b5) is characteristic of the virtuous person.

In claiming that the mean is determined by the PRUDENT person, he refers to the intellectual virtue that is responsible for good deliberation (1140a24–31). These aspects of his definition of virtue of character imply that it is inseparable from virtue of intellect.

Aristotle illustrates and explains these different aspects of virtue of character in Books iii–vii.

9. Voluntary action and responsibility

The last part of the general account of virtue of character is a discussion of VOLUNTARY action and conditions for moral responsibility. Aristotle wants to show how his account of the nature of virtue supports the common belief that we are justly praised and blamed both for virtuous and vicious actions and for being virtuous and vicious people. The proper objects of praise and blame are the things that we ourselves, rather than necessity or fortune, are responsible (*aitios*) for (*EE* 1223a9–15†), and we are responsible for our virtuous and vicious actions and characters.

Aristotle argues that voluntary actions are those that are caused neither by force nor ignorance, but have their 'PRINCIPLE in us', insofar as we know the particular circumstances of the action (1111a22–4). Even if we act under certain kinds of duress or compulsion, we act voluntarily because it is in our power to act or to refrain.

Aristotle draws two conclusions: (1) According to these criteria, voluntary actions are appropriate for praise and blame. (2) According to these criteria, non-rational animals act voluntarily (1111a24–6). These non-rational agents, however, are not open to praise or blame. These conclusions seem to create a difficulty for Aristotle, because he also seems to believe that (3) non-rational animals are not open to the sort of praise and blame that would make them candidates for virtue.

Aristotle can perhaps reconcile all these claims, if he maintains that ordinary human voluntary action is open to praise and blame because its principle is in us as rational agents (1110a17–18, 1111a22–4, 1113b20–1). A bodily process, such as ageing, that has (in one respect) an internal principle and that we are aware of is nonetheless not voluntary, because we have no rational control over it, and therefore it has no principle in us as rational agents (1135a31–b2). Voluntary action is in our control as rational agents; hence we are justly praised and blamed for it. To understand this rational control, we need to examine Aristotle's analysis of DECISION.

10. Decision, deliberation, character, and responsibility

Since Aristotle claims that the virtuous person decides on the virtuous action for its own sake, and that virtue is a state that decides, his conception of the virtuous character depends on his account of DECISION. Decision is a deliberative desire that results from (1) the rational WISH for some end and (2) DELIBERATION about how to achieve the end. A doctor wishes to produce health in the patient, discovers by inquiry into various medicines and their effects on patients of different kinds that some specific medicine will restore this patient to health, and so decides to prescribe this medicine.

To see how this pattern applies to ethical deliberation and decision, we need to understand Aristotle's claim that deliberation is not about ends, but about means to ends. 'Means' include two ways of achieving ends: (1) Instrumental means are causally separate from the ends that are their effects, as buying fish is a means to cooking fish, which is a means to eating dinner. (2) Constituent or component means are not causally separate from but are parts of the ends that they achieve, as eating the main course is a means to, but not separate from, eating dinner (since it is a part of eating dinner). Aristotle's expression *ta pros to telos* (literally 'things towards the end' or 'things promoting the end') may be used for both instrumental means and constituents.

The wide scope of deliberation makes it clearer why decision is an essential element in virtue and why Aristotle claims—surprisingly at first sight—that we can decide on an action for its own sake, even though decision is always about means to ends. The virtuous person's decision is the result of deliberation about the composition of the good; and this deliberation results in specific claims about which actions are non-instrumentally good components of happiness. These are the actions that the virtuous person decides on, both for their own sakes and for the sake of happiness.

The actions we are responsible for reflect our character, decisions, and hence (given the nature of decision) our deliberation about the good. For similar reasons, characters and outlook are also open to justified criticism, because we are responsible for our characters. Aristotle implies that it is in our rational control (when, presumably, we pass beyond the pure habituation of early childhood) to affect the way our character develops (1114a4–9); that is why we are justly held responsible for the resulting state of character. Rational deliberation and decision are the source of responsibility for character no less than for action.

Aristotle's discussion of voluntary action and responsibility considers some of the questions that mediaeval and modern philosophers treat as questions about free will and determinism. Should we say that Aristotle discusses problems about free will? Different answers might be given:

1. No. Aristotle has no term that corresponds exactly to 'free will', and he does not discuss the question whether the truth of causal determinism is incompatible with free will. He discusses arguments about how the past might necessitate the present (*De. Int.* ch. 9; *Met.* vi 3), but these are not exactly about the problems raised by causal determinism.

2. Yes. He holds that human beings and their choices are PRINCIPLES (i.e., beginnings, origins; *archai*), and that this is why we are responsible for our actions. If our actions and choices were all causally determined, they would not be genuine origins, since something else would be their origins. Moreover, since the truth of causal determination would imply that our actions are necessitated by the past, they would not meet Aristotle's conditions for being up to us and in our power. Therefore Aristotle believes that causal determination is incompatible with free will, and affirms an indeterminist doctrine of free will.

3. Yes. Aristotle affirms free will, as later philosophers understand it, insofar as he affirms that we are justly held responsible for some of our actions because of freedom that belongs to us (hence he speaks of actions being 'up to us', *eph' hêmin*). In his view, facts about our desires, choices, and character justify the attribution of responsibility to us (see 1113b19–20). Since he does not suggest that causal determination of our choices and actions would rule out responsibility, he implcitly affirms the compatibility of freedom and determinism.

11. The individual virtues of character

From Book iii 6 to the end of Book v, Aristotle describes the different virtues of character that he has discussed in general terms in Book ii and in Book iii 1–5. He divides the virtues into different groups: (1) Bravery and temperance are the virtues that direct the impulses of the SPIRITED and APPETITIVE parts towards the right goals. (2) Generosity, proper pride, and their two large-scale counterparts, magnificence and magnanimity, aim at the right use of EXTERNAL goods. (3) Mildness, friendliness, and wit regulate social intercourse for the right ends. (4) Justice is the aspect of virtue that is directed to the good of another. It is divided into general justice, which is virtue as a whole, and special justice, which is the part of justice that is concerned with distribution, correction, and exchange.

Some of these virtues are discussed at length (bravery, temperance, generosity, magnanimity, and justice), others more briefly. But some common themes run through these books:

1. They provide concrete details to illustrate the doctrine of the mean. A brave person is not distracted from pursuit of his rational plans by excessive fears; nor, however, is he so recklessly overconfident that he fears nothing, or so indifferent to his own life that he does not care if he loses it. Bravery does not eliminate fears altogether. It modifies and shapes the non-rational part so that our fears are directed towards what deserves to be feared. Similarly, temperance controls and shapes basic biological appetites for food, drink, and sex. It does not eliminate them or stop us enjoying them; it regulates and shapes our enjoyments so that we have them on the right occasions. A temperate person is not distracted from his rational plans by excessive attachment to particular appetites and enjoyments; but he is not so unaware of these appetites that he is indifferent to the pleasure of satisfying them in the right circumstances. In each case, rational agents benefit from the harmony of their rational and non-rational desires. Virtuous people do not act virtuously with reluctance as a result of struggle against non-rational impulses. They even take pleasure in facing the dangers that brave people have to face, and in avoiding the misguided pleasures that temperate people avoid.

2. In some cases we might have thought Aristotle is wrong to assert that the virtue in question is a mean. We might, for example, suppose that the point of generosity is to encourage us to give freely and not to be stingy or grasping. Aristotle disagrees. In his view, generosity is the right use of wealth, and we can go wrong by indiscriminate giving, just as we can go wrong by reluctance to give on the right occasions. Similarly, the right attitude to anger is not suppress it, since it sometimes has a place in a virtuous person's response to some circumstances. In all these cases, we identify the virtue with the right use of a particular impulse, not with its renunciation.

3. Aristotle sometimes remarks that people's failure to recognize that virtue is a mean explains why some virtues have no name of their own. Since we tend to think that the pursuit of honour is good or bad, we assume that the only options are the competitive pursuit of honour or the rejection of competition. We do not see that the pursuit of honour should be modified and corrected, but not suppressed, and so we do not see that there is a mean in relation to honour. The same is true of anger and of the attitudes that are regulated by the virtue he calls friendliness.

4. The mean at which the virtues aim is described as doing what one ought, when one ought, et cetera. Aristotle repeats these formulations in the descriptions of

the individual virtues and also clarifies them. He often remarks that the virtuous person does FINE actions, and does them for the sake of the fine. He does not explain in detail what makes an action fine, but he offers some indication by saying that it is characteristic of virtue to benefit others and to use external goods for the common benefit of the community (as the magnificent person does in spending large amounts). Since this is the character of fine actions, it is reasonable for Aristotle to say that when everyone strains to do fine actions, the common good is promoted (1169a8–11).

5. This essential connexion between the virtues and the fine supports the claim that they are moral virtues. If we assume that morality and moral virtue are essentially concerned with the good of others, some Aristotelian virtues do not seem to be moral virtues. Some of them seem to be largely self-regarding (e.g., temperance, magnanimity); some seem to involve good manners or good taste rather than strictly moral qualities (e.g., magnificence, truthfulness, wit), and only some seem to deal with the good of others (bravery, mildness, generosity). Only one virtue—justice (in its general form)—is clearly focussed on the good of others in its own right (1129b25–1130a5).

This description of the virtues, however, underestimates ways in which the virtues of character as a whole display the impartial concern for others that is often ascribed to morality. The virtuous person decides on the virtuous action because it is fine; and fine action is fine because it promotes the common good. This is why Aristotle takes general justice, which maintains happiness and its parts for the political community, to be nothing more than the exercise of the other virtues of character (1130a10–13).

Happiness, as Aristotle conceives it, requires activity in accordance with complete virtue (1098a16–18). Why should complete virtue require concern for the good of others? In Aristotle's view, a human being is a political animal insofar as human capacities and aims are completely fulfilled only in a community; the individual's happiness must involve the good of fellow-members of a community (1097b8–11, 1169b16–19).

12. Prudence and virtue

In Book vi Aristotle discusses the intellectual virtues. These belong to the good exercise of the human function that achieves the human good because they are excellent conditions of the rational SOUL. In contrast with the virtues of character, they simply aim to understand the different aspects of the cosmos. They include the different forms of STUDY that seek the truth about the natural world. WISDOM is the theoretical SCIENCE that studies the divine reality in the cosmos, and Aristotle eventually argues, in Book x 6–8, that the exercise of wisdom is the supreme element in human happiness.

One intellectual virtue, however, namely PRUDENCE, is inseparably connected with virtue of character, and in Book vi Aristotle explores the different aspects of prudence that make it necessary for achieving the human good:

1. Prudence deliberates about what promotes living well as a whole. It finds the actions that promote happiness insofar as they are parts of the happy life. Such actions are (a) to be chosen for their own sake, as being their own end, rather than (b) to be chosen simply as instrumental means to some further end. Aristotle identifies (a) as *praxis* ('ACTION' or 'activity') and (b) as *poiêsis* ('PRODUCTION') (1140b4–7). He draws a closely connected distinction between (a) *energeia* ('activity') and *kinêsis* ('process') (1174a14–b14).

2. Prudence also grasps the correct end for virtuous action (1142b33). Since it deliberates about means to living well as a whole, and since these means are actions that are ends in themselves, it grasps an end that is a part of happiness. The conclusions reached by prudence, therefore, will result in the virtuous person's decision to do the virtuous action for its own sake.

3. Since prudence is deliberative, and deliberation requires a grasp of the relevant particulars that affect one's eventual decision, prudence also grasps the relevant features of a particular situation. The right moral choice requires experience of particular situations, since practical rules, which are USUALLY true, cannot be applied to particular situations without further moral judgment (1103b34–1104a11). Aristotle describes this aspect of prudence as a sort of perception or intuitive understanding of the right aspects of particular situations (1143a32–b5).

4. Through these features of prudence Aristotle justifies his claim that the mean achieved by the virtues is determined by the reason by which the prudent person would determine it (1107a1).

5. Prudence is both necessary and sufficient for virtue of character. Aristotle explains their relation in Book vi 12–13, especially in his discussion of full virtue (*kuria aretê*).

13. Incontinence

After describing the virtues of character and thought, Aristotle discusses the problem of incontinence (vii 1–10). Incontinence (or 'weakness of will') is usually taken to consist in knowing that x is better than y, but choosing y nonetheless. SOCRATES, as Aristotle understands him, denies the possibility of incontinence; and to explain apparently incontinent behaviour as the result of ignorance of the good, in i 13 and iii 2, Aristotle suggests an account of incontinence much closer to the one that Plato offers in *Republic* iv: incontinence results when an agent's non-rational desires are stronger than his rational desire and overcome it.

His full account of incontinence, however, includes both Socratic and Platonic elements in a rather puzzling combination. This is one of the most difficult parts of the *EN*; the Notes on vii 3 mention some of the questions of interpretation.

Aristotle disagrees with Socrates over the possibility of incontinence. Since he assumes an irreducible difference between rational and non-rational desires, he rejects Socrates' view that only ignorance of what is better and worse underlies apparent incontinence; he asserts that the Socratic view evidently conflicts with the appearances (1145b27–8).

In Aristotle's view, incontinents make the right decision (1152a17), and act against it (1148a13–17, 1151a5–7). Their failure to stick to their decision is the result of strong appetites; in Aristotle's example, we recognize that we ought to avoid eating this sweet thing, but our recognition that it is sweet actually triggers our appetite for sweet things, which causes us to eat it after all.

Aristotle, however, also accepts part of the Socratic account because he thinks incontinent action must be explained by some sort of ignorance. This ignorance results from disordered non-rational desires; it is not ignorance of general principles (e.g., that we ought not to steal), but of the application of these principles to particular cases. Aristotle seems to suggest that the incontinent is someone who agrees that he ought not to overindulge his appetites, agrees that eating these six cakes would be overindulgence, and hence makes the correct decision not to eat them, but nonetheless, when he eats them, fails to recognize that this is really a case of overindulgence. Though he admits that incontinents have the right decision and act against it because of appetite, he believes it is impossible for them to act against a correct decision that they fully accept at the very moment of incontinent action (1147b15–17).

In Aristotle's view, incontinent people's appetite causes them to lose part of the reasoning that formed their correct decision. They retain the right general principles, but they do not acknowledge that these apply to their present situation, and even though they say they know they are wrong to do what they are doing, they are just saying the words without really meaning them (1147b9–12). To this extent Aristotle thinks Socrates is right to appeal to ignorance—though he disagrees with Socrates about the kind of ignorance that is relevant.

14. Pleasure

To begin with, Aristotle describes the life of pleasure as the life that is devoted to gross sensual pleasures (i 5; see §5 above). But he also attributes a more positive role to pleasure. His requirement that the virtuous person should decide on the virtuous action for its own sake is connected with the requirement that the virtuous person should take pleasure in virtuous action as such (1099a7–21, 1104b3–11). Aristotle relies on his views about the nature of pleasure and its role in happiness.

Books vii and x contain two distinct discussions of the nature of pleasure and the different value of different types of pleasure (see end of §3 above). Aristotle believes that true judgments about pleasure imply that the virtuous person's life is also the pleasantest life. In both vii and x, he argues that pleasure is a good (i.e., one good thing above others), but he does not say it is the good (i.e., the ultimate good) or the only good. Book x offers a fuller positive account of what pleasure is (x 4), and a more definite rejection of the view that pleasure is the ultimate or the only good. (See Notes.)

He rejects the view that pleasure is some uniform sensation to which different kinds of pleasant action are connected only causally and externally (in the way that reading many boring books might induce the same feeling of boredom). Instead he argues that the specific pleasure taken in x rather than y is internally related to doing x rather than y, and essentially depends on pursuing x for x's own sake. In that case, different pleasures—for instance, the pleasure of lying on the beach in the sun and the pleasure of solving a crossword puzzle—are not two instances of the same sensation that just happen to have different causes. The two different objects (i.e., the activities we take the pleasure in) are essential to the character of the pleasures themselves.

Aristotle tries to express this relation of a pleasure to the activity that is its object by describing the pleasure as a 'supervenient end' (1174b31–3) resulting from an ACTION or ACTIVITY, not from a PRODUCTION or PROCESS, as such. As Plato argues in the *Philebus* (see PLATO), the value of the pleasure depends on the value of the activity on which the pleasure supervenes (1176a3–29). Aristotle infers both that the virtuous person has the pleasantest life and that the pleasantest life cannot be the one devoted exclusively to the pursuit of pleasure.

15. Virtue and friendship

If the virtues of character are states that aim at the fine and the common good, rather than the good of the individual agent, how do they belong to the individual's happiness? Aristotle's answer relies on his claim that a human being's happiness depends on the human function and on human nature. A human being, he claims, is a political animal insofar as human capacities and aims are completely fulfilled only in a community; the individual's happiness must involve the good of fellow-members of a community.[10] We lack a complete life that fulfils human nature if we lack any concern for the good of other people. If we are indifferent to the good of others, we deny ourselves the relations of co-operation and mutual concern and trust that are necessary for the fulfilment of human capacities.

---

10. Self-sufficiency: 1097b7–15.

Aristotle defends this claim in his discussion of FRIENDSHIP. He distinguishes three kinds—concerned, respectively, with advantage, pleasure, and goodness. The first two kinds are relatively easy to understand from a purely self-interested point of view. Often we advance our own interests more efficiently if we can rely on help from other people; we might make bargains with them for our mutual advantage. We might also take an interest in other people because we enjoy their company; our concern depends on what we enjoy, not on any concern for the other person herself. The third kind of friendship is different from the other two, because it involves concern for the other person because of herself and for her own sake, not simply as a source of advantage or pleasure. Aristotle argues that this sort of concern for others also promotes one's own good.

In the best sort of friendship the friend is 'another himself' (1170b5–7), so that if A and B are friends, A takes the attitudes to B that A also takes to A. Aristotle uses this feature of friendship to explain why friendship is part of a complete and self-sufficient life (ix 9). Friendship involves 'living together' (i.e., sharing the activities one counts as especially important in one's life; 1157b17–19), and especially the sharing of reasoning and thinking. Friends co-operate in deliberation, decision, and action; and the thoughts and actions of each provide reasons for the future thoughts and actions of the other. If A regards B as another self, then A will be concerned about B's aims and plans, and pleased by B's successes no less than by A's own. The co-operative aspects of friendship with B more fully realize A's own capacities as a rational agent, and so promote A's happiness more fully.

When we act on this concern, we are capable of concerns, achievements, and co-operative activities that would otherwise be denied to us. I will not derive much enjoyment from playing in a team, or in an orchestra, or working on some collaborative project, if I care only about my own success. If I care about the success of others too, I can take pleasure in their success, and in collective successes, not simply in my own.[11]

For this reason Aristotle thinks that the full development of a human being requires concern for the good of others. He defends his claim initially for friendship between individuals, but also for the type of friendship that forms a CITY, the 'complete COMMUNITY' (*Pol.* 1252a1–7†, b27–30†) that achieves the complete life that is identified with happiness.

16. Two conceptions of happiness?

In Book x 6–8, Aristotle returns to the discussion of happiness. He argues that the human FUNCTION is especially realized by the pure intellectual activity of STUDY—the contemplation of scientific and philosophical truths apart from any attempt to apply them to practice. Since human happiness consists in the

---

11. Friendship: 1156b7–12.

fulfilment of the human function, study is a supremely important element in happiness. For it is the highest fulfilment of our nature as rational beings; it is the sort of rational activity that we share with the gods, who are rational beings with no need to apply reason to practice. Aristotle infers that study is the happiest life available to us, insofar as we have the rational intellects we share with gods (see notes to x 7).

One might conclude that Aristotle actually identifies study with happiness: study is the only non-instrumental good that is part of happiness, and the moral virtues are to be valued—from the point of view of happiness—simply as means to study. It is natural to take x 6–8 in this way; if one does, it is tempting to understand the argument in i 7 from the human FUNCTION as an argument to show that happiness is to be identified with the theoretical reasoning involved in study.

If this is Aristotle's view, however, two difficulties arise: (1) It is difficult to see how the purely instrumental status that seems to be ascribed to virtue of character in x 6–8 is compatible with Aristotle's repeated claims in the rest of the *EN* that virtues and virtuous actions are to be chosen for their own sake. (2) It is difficult to see how the virtues of character are even the best instrumental means to happiness. Even if some virtuous actions are instrumental means to study, the motives demanded of the virtuous person do not seem useful for those who aim at study.

In the light of these difficulties, some readers who are convinced that x 6–8 identify happiness with study have inferred that Books i–ix defend a 'comprehensive' conception of happiness (explained in i 7), and that x 6–8 defends an incompatible conception of happiness as study. One might argue that these are two alternative conceptions of happiness; perhaps happiness as study is for those who are capable of it and in the conditions that allow single-minded devotion to it, and happiness as the exercise of the virtues of character is the best available to those who are less well endowed or are in less favourable circumstances.

Is it clear, however, that in x 6–8 Aristotle identifies happiness with study? One might take Aristotle to mean that happiness is 'theoretical' because it is characterized by *theoria*, not because it consists entirely of *theoria* (just as a chocolate biscuit does not consist entirely of chocolate). According to this view, study is the best component of happiness, but not the whole of happiness. If we were pure intellects with no other desires and no bodies, study would be the whole of our good. Since, however, we are not in fact merely intellects, our good is the good of the whole human being. Since study is not the complete good for a human being (1178b5–7), it is not our complete good. For Aristotle has argued that happiness must be complete, and for this reason he argues that neither virtue alone nor pleasure alone can be happiness. He should not, then, agree that study is happiness just because it is invulnerable and self-contained.

If this is Aristotle's view, study fits into the account of happiness that we seem to find in the rest of the *EN*. According to this account, the virtues of character, and the actions that accord with them, deserve to be chosen for their own sakes as components of happiness. In the virtuous person, they regulate the choice of other goods, and so they also regulate choices about study. Admittedly, Aristotle does not explain how we should decide on particular occasions whether to pursue study or to prefer one of the other components of happiness; but he does not seem to retreat from his conception of happiness as a compound of rational activities that assigns a central and dominant place to the moral virtues. The *Politics* may be taken to develop this conception of happiness, since it sets study in the context of a social order that is regulated by the virtues of character (see esp. *Pol.* vii 3–4, 9, 13).

17. The Greek text

Modern editions of the Greek text of the *EN* are based on Greek manuscripts copied in the Byzantine period (from the tenth to the fifteenth centuries)[12] from manuscripts derived indirectly from the edition of Aristotle's works produced by Andronicus in the first century BC. The transmitted text is usually fairly sound; but numerous variations and imperfections in the manuscripts require decisions by editors and translators. I have taken the OCT (see [8]) as the basis of the translation, and have mentioned deviations (on points other than punctuation) in the notes. These deviations express different judgments (a) about which reading is to be preferred in cases where the manuscripts differ, or (b) about how to emend the manuscript reading, in cases where it does not seem to give satisfactory sense, or (c) about whether some words are intrusions into the manuscripts, not part of what Aristotle actually wrote, or (d) about whether something has fallen out of the manuscripts and needs to be supplied, or (e) about whether the manuscripts have the text in the right order.

18. Divisions of the text

The division of books into chapters does not go back to antiquity. Modern editions of the Greek text of *EN* print two capitulations (both of mediaeval origin). I have included the first (marked by Roman figures in OCT) for reference. Where the second capitulation differs, I have left a blank line.

Modern editions also print the division of chapters (according to the first numeration) into sections (which go back at least to the edition by Carl Zell in 1820). I have also reproduced these sections (marked by §), since they reflect a generally sensible view of the structure of Aristotle's argument. In cases where my paragraphs diverge from the marginal sections, it may be useful to readers to

---

12. On ancient manuscripts, see OCD, s.v. 'Books, Greek and Roman', 'Palaeography', 'Textual criticism'.

compare the two divisions. The marginal line numbering is derived from Immanuel Bekker's edition of Aristotle (1831).[13]

The headings to each chapter are mine and have no authority in the manuscripts.

19. Translating Aristotle

This translation is intended for readers who want to understand the *EN* in detail, and not merely to acquire a general impression of it. Any translator who wants to be reasonably accurate in details that matter to the philosophical reader has to face some difficulties presented by the *EN*:

1. Aristotle's writing is often compressed and allusive; to convey in English the impression made by Aristotle's Greek, a translator would have to produce a version that would be hard to understand without a detailed commentary. A translator who tries to make Aristotle readily intelligible to the English reader must sometimes expand, interpret, and paraphrase. I have used bracketed supplements in cases where it seemed reasonable to point out to the reader that no precise equivalent for the bracketed words appears in the Greek text. Readers should by no means suppose that everything not enclosed in brackets indisputably corresponds to something in Aristotle's text. If they consult the Notes, they should be able to see where my rendering is controversial.

2. Some of Aristotle's central philosophical terms cannot easily be translated uniformly; see, e.g., PRINCIPLE, REASON. But one's choice of rendering often requires a decision about the course of the argument. (See, e.g., 1096a30–b9, 1098a33–b8.)

3. Aristotle has come to us through mediaeval Latin philosophy, and some English equivalents to Latin terms (such as 'substance', 'essence', 'incontinence') have come to be standard renderings for some of Aristotle's Greek terms. These English terms, however, no longer convey in modern English what the mediaeval Latin terms conveyed, and so they may be misleading. Still, an attempt to purge a translation of these terms derived from Latin would conceal an important thread in the history of philosophy; see PRUDENCE, VOLUNTARY. I have been reluctant to discard these traditional renderings (though sometimes I have overcome this reluctance); though they may mislead readers who do not study the terms in their context (with the help of the Glossary), they are probably no

---

13. '1094a10', for instance, refers to line 10 of the left-hand column of page 1094 of Bekker's edition. Since Bekker's pagination is continuous, a Bekker page and line uniquely identify a particular passage. These Bekker pages and lines are standardly used to refer to passages in Aristotle. Since they refer to pages and lines of the Greek text, they correspond only roughly to an English translation.

more misleading than the superficially more contemporary renderings that one might choose instead.

4. Greek tolerates longer sentences than English; hypotactic constructions (with several long subordinate clauses) are common. The paratactic character of modern English encourages the translator to break one complex Greek sentence into two or more English sentences. Sometimes, however, the structure of an argument can be more clearly expressed in a long sentence forming a logical unit; that is why some sentences in the translation are more complex than a contemporary English sentence would normally be.

5. It is characteristic of Greek to begin sentences with connecting particles. Concern for English style would require omitting many of these particles in a translation. Omission, however, sometimes removes useful information. When Aristotle connects two clauses or sentences with 'for', he normally indicates that the second clause gives some reason for what has been said in the first clause; such information about the structure of the argument is useful to the philosophical reader. Hence the translation includes more connectives ('for', 'but', 'however', and so on) than are usual in contemporary English, and also marks Aristotle's repeated use of a given connective with a special force.

20. How to use this edition

As they read through the *EN*, readers may want to read through a section of this Introduction before turning to the more detailed discussion in the Notes and Glossary. The Notes provide different sorts of information that may be useful in trying to understand the text:

1. They suggest alternative translations (in some important passages) or more literal translations (in some cases where expansion or paraphrase is needed for the sake of intelligibility; see, e.g., note to i 7.§8).

2. They contain brief discussion of the course of Aristotle's argument, and of some passages that seem both difficult and important.

3. They list departures from the OCT.

4. They give the sources for Aristotle's references to other authors.

5. They include a few comments on historical events, proper names (Priam, Thales, Sparta, etc.), and so on. Readers must be prepared to look these up in reference books, among which OCD is especially useful. A few references to OCD are included.

The Glossary should be constantly consulted by readers who want to understand Aristotle's philosophical vocabulary. If we understand the philosophical assumptions that underlie his central ethical terms, we understand a good bit of his philosophy. It is useful to look up the passages cited in the entries in the Glossary and to examine them in their context. We need to keep two complications in mind:

1. In line with his method in ethical inquiry (see §5 above), Aristotle does not use many technical terms (i.e., terms that are explicitly defined for a specific theoretical purpose). His main terms (e.g., 'happiness', 'virtue', 'decision') are ordinary Greek words used in their ordinary senses. Aristotle, however, sometimes disagrees with ordinary usage about what these terms apply to, or with the criteria that should be used in applying them (so that, e.g., not everything that might normally count as a decision counts as a DECISION by Aristotle's standards). The Glossary tries to point out some of these complex relations between Aristotle's usage and ordinary Greek.

2. The relevant Greek terms often correspond only partially to natural English renderings. 'Happiness', 'voluntary', 'prudence', for instance, may mislead us about Aristotle's terms, unless we keep in mind the assumptions that underlie his use of the relevant Greek terms. Moreover, several English terms are sometimes needed to translate one Greek term in different contexts. It is often useful to bear in mind that Aristotle uses the same term without equivocation because its sense coincides only partially with any one English term (see, e.g., PRINCIPLE).

A superscript number in the translation marks the end of a passage that is discussed in the Notes. A word in capital letters in the notes refers to the relevant entry in the Glossary. Aristotle's works are cited throughout by the abbreviated titles given in the list of Abbreviations and Conventions.

NICOMACHEAN ETHICS

Book I
[Happiness]

1
[Ends and goods]

/ §1 Every craft and every discipline, and likewise action and decision, seems to seek some good[1]—that is why some people were right
to describe the good as what everything seeks.[2] §2 But the ends
appear to differ; for some are activities, and others are / products 5
apart from the activities.[3] And where there are ends apart from the
actions, the products are by nature better than the activities.

§3 Now since there are many actions, crafts, and sciences, the
ends turn out to be many as well; for health is the end of medicine,
a boat of boat building, victory of generalship, and wealth of household management. §4 But some / of these pursuits are subordinate 10
to some one capacity; for instance, bridle making and every other science producing equipment for horses are subordinate to horseman-
ship, while this and every action in warfare are in turn subordinate to
generalship, and in the same way[4] other pursuits are subordinate to
further ones.[5]

In all such cases, then,[6] the ends of the ruling sciences are / more 15
choiceworthy than all the ends subordinate to them, since the lower
ends are also pursued for the sake of the higher. §5 Here it does not
matter whether the ends of the actions are the activities themselves,
or something apart from them, as in the sciences we have mentioned.

2
[The highest good and political science]

§1 If, then, the things achievable by action have some end that we
wish for because of itself, and we wish for the other things because
of this end, and we do not / choose everything because of something 20
else (for if we do, it will go on without limit, so that desire will prove
to be empty and futile), it is clear that, this end will be the good, that
is to say, the best good.[1]

§2 Then surely knowledge of this good also carries great weight
for one's way of life, and if we know it, we are more likely, like archers
25   who have a target to aim at, to hit the right mark.[2]   §3 If / so, we
should try to grasp, in outline at any rate, what the good is, and which
is its proper science or capacity.[3]

§4 Now it seems proper to the most controlling <science>—
the highest ruling <science>.[4]   §5 And this appears characteristic of political science.[5]   §6 For it prescribes which of the sciences
1094b1   ought to be studied in cities, / and which ones each class in the city
should learn, and how far; indeed we see that even the most honoured capacities—generalship, household management, and rhetoric,
for instance—are subordinate to it.   §7 And since it uses the other
5   sciences concerned with action,[6] / and moreover legislates what must
be done and what avoided, its end will include the ends of the other
sciences,[7] and so this will be the human good.

§8 For even if the good is the same for a city as for an individual, still the good of the city is apparently a greater and more complete good to acquire and preserve.[8] For while it is satisfactory to
10   acquire and preserve the good even for an individual, / it is finer and
more divine to acquire and preserve it for a people and for cities.[9]

And so our discipline aims at these things,[10] being a sort of political science.[11]

3

[The method of political science]

But our discussion will be adequate if we make things perspicuous
enough to accord with the subject matter; for we should not seek the
same degree of exactness in all sorts of arguments alike, any more than
15   in the products of different crafts.[1]   §2 Now fine and just things, /
which political science examines, differ and vary so much[2] as to seem
to rest on convention only, not on nature.[3]   §3 But goods also vary in
the same way, because they result in harm to many people—for some
have been destroyed because of their wealth, others because of their
20   bravery.[4]   §4 And so, since this is our subject / and these are our premisses, we shall be satisfied to indicate the truth roughly and in outline, and
since our subject and our premisses are things that hold good usually, we
shall be satisfied to draw conclusions of the same sort.

Each of our claims, then, ought to be accepted in the same way.
For the educated person seeks exactness in a given area to the extent

that the / nature of the subject allows; for apparently it is just as mis-   25
taken to demand demonstrations from a rhetorician as to accept
\<merely\> persuasive arguments from a mathematician.[5] §5 Further, each person judges rightly what he knows, and is / a good judge   1095a
about that; hence the good judge in a given area is the person educated in that area, and the unqualifiedly good judge is the person educated in every area.

This is why a youth is not a suitable student of political science;
for he lacks experience of the actions in life, which are the subject
and premisses of our arguments. §6 Moreover, since he tends to
follow his feelings, his / study will be futile and useless, since the goal   5
is action, not knowledge.[6] §7 And it does not matter whether he is
young in years or immature in character, since the deficiency does
not depend on age, but results from following his feelings in his life
and in a given pursuit; for an immature person, like an incontinent
person, gets no benefit from his knowledge. / But for those who fol-   10
low reason in forming their desires and in their actions, knowledge of
these things \<political science\> will be of great benefit.

§8 These are the preliminary points about the student, about the
way our claims are to be accepted, and about what we propose to do.[7]

4
[Common beliefs]

[c2] Let us, then, begin again.[1] Since every sort of knowledge and
decision[2] / pursues some good, what is the good that we say political   15
science seeks, and what is the highest of all the goods achievable in
action?

§2 As far as its name goes, most people practically agree; for both
the many and the cultivated call it happiness, and they suppose that
living well and doing well are the same as / being happy.[3] But about   20
what happiness is they disagree, and the many do not give the same
answer as the wise.[4]

§3 For the many think it is one of the obvious and evident things,
such as pleasure, or wealth, or honour. Some take it to be one thing,
others another. Indeed, the same person often changes his mind; for
when he has fallen ill, he thinks happiness is health, and when he has
fallen into poverty, he thinks it is wealth. And when they are con-
scious of their own ignorance, / they admire anyone who speaks of   25
something grand and above their heads.

Some, however, some used to think that besides these many goods there is some other good that exists in its own right and that causes all these goods to be goods.[5]

30 §4 Presumably, then, it is rather futile to examine all these beliefs, and it is enough to examine those that are most current / or seem to have some argument for them.

§5 We must notice, however, the difference between arguments from principles and arguments towards principles.[6] For Plato also was right to be puzzled about this, when he used to ask if <the argu-
1095b ment> set out from the principles or led towards / them[7]—just as on a race course the path may go from the starting line to the far end,[8] or back again. For we should begin from things known, but things are known in two ways;[9] for some are known to us, some known without qualification. Presumably, then, *we* ought to begin from things known to *us*.

5 §6 That is why we need to have been brought up in fine habits / if we are to be adequate students of fine and just things, and of political questions generally.   §7 For the <belief> that <something is true> is the beginning, and if this is apparent enough to us, we will not need <, at this stage, to know> why <it is true> as well;[10] and someone who is well brought up has the beginnings, or would easily acquire them.[11]
10 Someone who neither has them nor can acquire them / should listen to Hesiod:[12] 'He who grasps everything himself is best of all; he is noble also who listens to one who has spoken well; but he who neither grasps it himself nor takes to heart what he hears from another is a useless man.'

5

[The three lives]

[c3] But let us begin again from the point from which we digressed.[1] For, it would seem, people, not unreasonably, reach their concep-
15 tion of the good / and of happiness, from the lives.   §2 For there are roughly three most favoured lives—the lives of gratification, of political activity, and, third, of study.[2]

The many, the most vulgar, would seem to conceive the good and happiness as pleasure, and hence they also like the life of gratifica-
20 tion.   §3 In this they appear completely slavish, / since the life they decide on is a life for grazing animals.[3] Still, they have some argument in their defence, since many in positions of power feel as Sardanapallus[4] felt, <and choose this life>.

§4 But the cultivated people, those who are active <in politics>, conceive the good as honour, since this is more or less the end <normally pursued> in the political life. This, however, appears to be too superficial to be what we are seeking;[5] for it seems to / depend   25
more on those who honour than on the one honoured, whereas we intuitively believe that the good is something of our own and hard to take from us.[6] §5 Further, it would seem, they pursue honour to convince themselves that they are good; at any rate, they seek to be honoured by prudent people, among people who know them, and for virtue. It is clear, then, that, in / their view at any rate, virtue is supe-   30
rior <to honour>.

§6 Perhaps, indeed, one might conceive virtue more <than hon-our> to be the end of the political life. However, this also is apparently too incomplete <to be the good>. For it seems possible for someone to possess virtue but be asleep or inactive / throughout his life, and,   1096a
moreover, to suffer the worst evils and misfortunes, but if this is the sort of life he leads, no one would count him happy, except to defend a philosopher's paradox.[7] Enough about this, since it has been ade-quately discussed in the popular works[8] as well.

§7 The third life is the life of study, which / we shall examine in   5
what follows.[9]

§8 The moneymaker's life is in a way forced on him <not chosen for itself>;[10] and clearly wealth is not the good we are seeking, since it is <merely> useful, <choiceworthy only> for some other end. Hence one would be more inclined to suppose that <any of> the goods mentioned earlier is the end, since they are liked for themselves. But apparently they are / not <the end> either; and many arguments have   10
been presented against them.[11] Let us, then, dismiss them.

6
[The Platonic Form of the Good]

[c4] Presumably, though, we had better examine the universal good, and go through the puzzles about what is meant in speaking of it.[1] This sort of inquiry is, to be sure, unwelcome to us, because those who introduced the Forms were friends[2] of ours; still, it presumably seems better, indeed only right, / to destroy even what is close to us   15
if that is the way to preserve truth. And we must especially do this as philosophers, <lovers of wisdom>; for though we love both the truth and our friends, reverence is due to the truth first.

§2 Those who introduced this view did not mean to produce an Idea for any <series> in which they spoke of prior and posterior; that was why they did not mean to establish an Idea for numbers either.[3]/ But the good is spoken of both in what-it-is <i.e., substance>, and in quality and relative; and what exists in its own right, i.e., substance, is by nature prior to the relative,[4] since a relative would seem to be an appendage and coincident of being. And so there is no common Idea over these.

§3 Further, good is spoken of in as many ways as being is spoken of:[5] in what-it-is, as god and / mind;[6] in quality, as the virtues; in quantity, as the measured amount; in relative, as the useful; in time, as the opportune moment; in place, as the <right> situation; and so on. Hence it is clear that the good cannot be some common and single universal; for if it were, it would be spoken of in only one of the predications, not in them all.

§4 Further, if a number of things have / one Idea, there is also one science of them; hence <if there were an Idea of Good> there would also be one science of all goods. But in fact there are many sciences even of the goods under one <type of> predication; for the science of the opportune moment, for instance, in war is generalship, in disease medicine. And similarly the science of the measured amount in food is medicine, in exertion gymnastics.[7]

§5 One might be puzzled about what they / really mean in speaking of the So-and-So Itself,[8] since Man / Itself and man[9] have one and the same account of man; for insofar as each is man, they will not differ at all. If that is so, then neither will they differ at all insofar as each is good.[10]

§6 Moreover, Good Itself will be no more of a good by being eternal; for a white thing is no whiter if it lasts a long / time than if it lasts a day.

§7 But the Pythagoreans would seem to have a more plausible view about the good, since they place the One in the column of goods. Indeed, Speusippus seems to have followed them.[11] §8 But let us leave this for another discussion.

A dispute emerges, however, about what we have said, because the arguments / <for the Idea> are not concerned with every sort of good. Rather, goods pursued and liked in their own right are spoken of as one species of goods, whereas those that in some way tend to produce or preserve these goods, or to prevent their contraries, are spoken of as goods because of these and in a different way. §9 Clearly, then, goods are spoken of in two ways, and some are goods in their own right, and others goods because of these.[12] Let us, then, separate / the goods in their own right from the <merely> useful goods, and consider whether goods in their own right correspond to a single Idea.

§10 But what sorts of goods would one take to be goods in their own right? Are they the goods that are pursued even on their own—for instance, prudence, seeing, some types of pleasures, and honours?[13] For even if we also pursue these because of something else, we may nonetheless take them to be goods in their own right. Alternatively, is / nothing except the Idea good in its own right, so that the Form will be futile?[14] §11 But if these other things are also goods in their own right, then the same account of good will have to turn up in all of them, just as the same account of whiteness turns up in snow and in chalk.[15] In fact, however, honour, prudence, and pleasure have different and dissimilar accounts, / in the respect in which they are goods. Hence the good is not something common corresponding to a single Idea.

§12 But how, then, is good spoken of, since it is not like homonyms resulting from chance?[16] Is it spoken of from the fact that goods derive from one thing or all contribute to one thing? Or is it spoken of more by analogy? For as sight is to body, so understanding is to soul, and so on for other cases.[17]

§13 / Presumably, though, we should leave these questions for now, since their exact treatment is more appropriate for another <branch of> philosophy.[18] And the same is true about the Idea. For even if there is some one good predicated in common,[19] or some separable good, itself in its own right, clearly that is not the sort of good a human being can achieve in action or possess; but that is the sort / we are looking for now.

§14 Perhaps, however, someone might think it is better to get to know / the Idea with a view to the goods that we can possess and achieve in action, for if we have this as a sort of pattern, we shall also know better about the goods that are goods for us, and if we know about them, we shall hit on them.[20] §15 This argument certainly has some plausibility, but it would seem to clash with the sciences. / For each of these, though it aims at some good and seeks to supply what is lacking, leaves out knowledge of the Idea; but surely it would not be reasonable for all craftsmen to know nothing about such an important aid, and not even to look for it.

§16 Moreover, it is a puzzle to know what the weaver or carpen-
10 ter will gain for his own craft from knowing this Good / Itself, or how anyone will be better at medicine or generalship from having viewed the Idea Itself. For what the doctor appears to consider is not even health, but human health, and presumably the health of this human being even more, since he treats one particular patient at a time.[21]

So much, then, for these questions.

7

[An account of the human good]

15 [c5] / But let us return once again to the good we are looking for, and consider just what it could be. For it is apparently one thing in one action or craft, and another thing in another; for it is one thing in medicine, another in generalship, and so on for the rest. What, then, is the good of each action or craft? Surely it is that for the sake of which
20 the other things are done. In medicine this is health, in generalship / victory, in house building a house, in another case something else, but in every action and decision it is the end, since it is for the sake of the end that everyone does the other actions.[1] And so, if there is some end of everything achievable in action, the good achievable in action will be this end, but if there are more ends than one, it will be these ends.[2]

§2 Our argument, then, has followed a different route to reach the
25 same conclusion.[3] / But we must try to make this still more perspicu-ous.[4] §3 Since there are apparently many ends, and we choose some of them (for instance, wealth, flutes, and, in general, instruments) because of something else, it is clear that not all ends are complete.[5] But the best good is apparently something complete. And so, if only one end is complete, what we are looking for will be this end, but if more
30 ends than one are complete, / it will be the most complete of these.[6]

§4 Now we say that an end pursued in its own right is more com-plete than an end pursued because of something else, and that an end that is never choiceworthy because of something else is more complete than ends that are choiceworthy both in their own right and because of this end. Hence an end that is always choiceworthy in its own right,[7] never because of something else, is complete without qualification.

§5 Now happiness, more than anything else, seems complete with-
1097b out qualification.[8] / For this we choose always because of itself,[9] never

because of something else. But honour, pleasure, understanding, and every virtue we choose because of themselves also—since we would choose each of them even if it had no further result—but we also choose them for the sake of happiness, / supposing that through them we shall be happy.[10] Happiness, however, no one ever chooses for their sake, or for the sake of anything else at all.

§6 The same conclusion[11] also appears to follow from self-sufficiency. For the complete good seems to be self-sufficient.[12] But what we count as self-sufficient is not what suffices for a solitary person by himself, living an isolated life, but what suffices also for / parents, children, wife, and in general for friends and fellow-citizens, since a human being is a naturally political <animal>.[13] §7 (Here, however, we must impose some limit; for if we extend the good to parents' parents and children's children and to friends of friends, we shall go on without limit; but we must examine this another time.) But we take what is self-sufficient to be whatever all / by itself makes a life choiceworthy and lacking nothing; and that is what we think happiness does.

§8 Moreover, we think happiness is most choiceworthy of all goods, <since> it is not counted as one good among many. <If it were> counted as one among many, then, clearly, we think it <would be> more choiceworthy if the smallest of goods <were> added;[14] for the good that is added becomes an extra quantity of goods, and the larger of two goods is always more choiceworthy. / Happiness, then, is apparently something complete and self-sufficient, since it is the end of the things achievable in action.[15]

§9 [c6] But presumably the remark that the best good is happiness is apparently something <generally> agreed, and we still feel the need of a clearer statement of what the best good is.[16] §10 Perhaps, then, we shall find this if we first grasp the function of / a human being. For just as the good, i.e., <doing> well, for a flautist, a sculptor, and every craftsman, and, in general, for whatever has a function and <characteristic> action, seems to depend on its function,[17] the same seems to be true for a human being, if a human being has some function.

§11 Then do the carpenter and the leatherworker have their / functions and actions, but has a human being no function?[18] Is he by nature idle, without any function?[19] Or, just as eye, hand, foot, and, in general, every <bodily> part apparently has its function, may we likewise ascribe to a human being some function apart from all of these?[20]

§12 What, then, could this be? For living is apparently shared with
1098a   plants, but what we are looking for is the special function / of a human
being; hence we should set aside the life of nutrition and growth.²¹
The life next in order is some sort of life of sense perception; but this
too is apparently shared with horse, ox, and every animal.²²

§13 The remaining possibility, then, is some sort of life of action²³
of the <part of the soul> that has reason.²⁴ One <part> of it has rea-
5   son as obeying reason; the other has it as / itself having reason and
thinking.²⁵ Moreover, life is also spoken of in two ways <as capacity
and as activity>, and we must take <a human being's special function
to be> life as activity, since this seems to be called life more fully.²⁶
We have found, then, that the human function is activity of the soul
in accord with reason or requiring reason.²⁷

§14 Now we say that the function of a kind of thing, such as a
harpist, is the same in kind as the function of an excellent individual
10   of the kind, such as an excellent / harpist. And the same is true without qualification in every case, if we add to the function the superior
achievement in accord with the virtue; for the function of a harpist is
to play the harp, and the function of a good harpist is to play it well.²⁸
Moreover, we take the human function to be a certain kind of life, and
take this life to be activity and actions of the soul that involve reason;
15   hence the function of the excellent man is to do this well and / finely.

§15 Now each function is completed well by being completed in
accord with the virtue proper <to that kind of thing>. And so the
human good proves to be activity of the soul in accord with virtue,²⁹
and indeed in accord with the best and most complete virtue, if there
are more virtues than one,³⁰ and, further,   §16 in a complete life³¹—
for one swallow does not make a spring, nor does one day, nor, simi-
20   larly, does / one day or a short time make us blessed and happy.

§17 [c7] Let this, then, be our sketch of the good; for, presumably,
we must draw the outline first, and fill it in later.³² If the sketch is
good, it would seem to be everyone's task³³ to advance and articulate
it, and in such cases time discovers more, or is a good partner in dis-
25   covery. That is also how the crafts / have improved; for it is everyone's
task to supply what is lacking.

§18 But we ought also to remember our previous remarks, and not
to look for the same degree of exactness in all areas, but the degree

that accords with a given subject matter and is proper to a given discipline.[34] §19 For the inquiries of the carpenter and of the geometer / about the right angle are also different; for the carpenter restricts himself to what helps his work, but the geometer inquires into what, or what sort[35] of thing, the right angle is, since he studies the truth. We must do the same, then, in other areas too,[36] so that digressions do not overwhelm our main task.

§20 Nor should we make the same demand for / an explanation in all cases. On the contrary, in some cases it is enough to prove rightly that <something is true>. This is so, for instance, with principles, where the fact that <something is true> is the first thing and the principle.[37]

§21 Now among principles some are studied by means of induction, some by means of perception, some by means of some sort of habituation, and others by other means.[38] §22 And in each case / we should try to find them out by means suited to their nature, and work hard to define them rightly. §23 For they carry great weight[39] for what follows; for the principle seems to be more than half the whole,[40] and makes evident the answer to many of our questions.

8

[Defence of the account of the good]

[c8] We should examine the principle, however, not only from the conclusion and / premisses, but also from the things said about it;[1] for all the facts harmonize with a true account, whereas the truth soon clashes with a false one.

§2 Goods are divided, then, into three types, one type called external, another goods of the soul, and another goods of the body.[2] We say that the goods of the soul are goods most fully, and / more than the others, and we take actions and activities of the soul to be <goods> of the soul. And so our account <of the good> is right, to judge by this belief anyhow—and it is an ancient belief, and accepted by philosophers.

§3 Our account is also correct in saying that some sort of actions and activities are the end; for in that way the end turns out to be a good of the soul, / not an external good.

§4 The belief that the happy person lives well and does well also agrees with our account, since we have practically said that the end is a sort of living well and doing well.

§5 [c9] Further, all the features that people look for in happiness appear to belong to the good we have described.³   §6 For to some
25   people happiness seems to be virtue; to others prudence;⁴ / to others some sort of wisdom; to others again it seems to be these, or one of these, including pleasure or requiring it;⁵ others add in external prosperity as well.   §7 Some of these views are traditional, held by many, while others are held by a few men who are widely esteemed. It is reasonable for each group not to be completely wrong, but to be correct on one point at least, or even on most points.

30   §8 / First, our account agrees with those who say happiness is virtue or some type of virtue; for activity in accord with virtue is proper to virtue.   §9 Presumably, though, it matters quite a bit whether we suppose that the best good consists in possessing or in using—that is to say, in a state or in its activity.⁶ For someone may be in a state that
1099a   / achieves no good—if, for instance, he is asleep or inactive in some other way—but this cannot be true of the activity; for it will necessarily act and act well. And just as Olympic prizes are not for the finest and strongest, but for /
5   the contestants—since it is only these who win—the same is true in life; among the fine and good people, only those who act correctly⁷ win the prize.

§10 Moreover, the life of these active people is also pleasant in itself.⁸ For being pleased is a condition of the soul, Further, each type of person finds pleasure in whatever he is called a lover of; a horse, for
10   instance, pleases the horse lover, a spectacle the / lover of spectacles. Similarly, what is just pleases the lover of justice, and in general what accords with virtue pleases the lover of virtue.

§11 Now the things that please most people conflict,⁹ because these things are not pleasant by nature, whereas the things that please lovers of the fine are pleasant by nature. Actions in accord with virtue are pleasant by nature, so that they are pleasant both to lovers of
15   the fine and / in their own right.

§12 Hence these people's life does not need pleasure to be added <to virtuous activity> as some sort of extra decoration; rather, it has its pleasure within itself.¹⁰ For besides the reasons already given, someone who does not enjoy fine actions is not good; for no one would call a person just, for instance, if he did not enjoy doing just
20   actions, or generous if he did not enjoy / generous actions, and similarly for the other virtues.

§13 If this is so, actions in accord with the virtues are pleasant in their own right. Moreover, these actions are good and fine as well as pleasant; indeed, they are good, fine, and pleasant more than anything else is, since on this question the excellent person judges rightly, and his judgment agrees with what we have said.

§14 Happiness, then, is best, finest, and most pleasant, and / these   25 things are not distinguished, as the Delian inscription says they are: 'What is most just is finest; being healthy is most beneficial; but it is most pleasant to win our heart's desire.'[11] For all three features are found in the best activities, and we say happiness is these activities, or <rather> one of them, the best one.[12]

§15 Nonetheless, happiness evidently also needs external goods to be added, as we said; for we cannot, or cannot easily, do fine actions if we lack the resources.[13] For, first of all, in many actions / we use friends,   1099b wealth, and political power just as we use instruments.   §16 Further, deprivation of certain <externals>—for instance, good birth, good children, beauty—mars our blessedness. For we do not altogether have the character of happiness[14] if we look utterly repulsive or are ill-born, solitary, or childless; and we have it / even less, presumably,   5 if our children or friends are totally bad, or were good but have died.

§17 As we have said, therefore, happiness would seem to need this sort of prosperity added also. That is why some people identify happiness with good fortune, and others identify it with virtue.

9
[How is happiness achieved?]

[c10] This also leads to a puzzle: Is happiness acquired by learning, or habituation, or by some / other type of cultivation? Or is it the result   10 of some divine fate, or even of fortune?[1]

§2 First, then, if the gods give any gift at all to human beings, it is reasonable for them to give us happiness more than any other human good, insofar as it is the best of human goods.   §3 Presumably, however, this question is more suitable for a different inquiry.

But even if it is / not sent by the gods, but instead results from virtue   15 and some sort of learning or cultivation, happiness appears to be one of the most divine things, since the prize and goal of virtue appears to be the best good, something divine and blessed.   §4 Moreover <if happiness comes in this way> it will be widely shared; for anyone who

is not deformed <in his capacity> for virtue will be able to achieve
20   happiness through some sort of learning / and attention.

§5 And since it is better to be happy in this way than because of
fortune, it is reasonable for this to be the way we become happy. For
whatever is natural is naturally in the finest state possible.   §6 The
same is true of the products of crafts and of every other cause, especially the best cause; and it would be seriously inappropriate to entrust
what is greatest and finest to fortune.[2]

25   §7 / The answer to our question is also evident from our account.
For we have said that happiness is a certain sort of activity of the soul
in accord with virtue.[3] Of the other goods, some are necessary conditions of happiness, while others are naturally useful and co-operative
as instruments.

§8 Further, this conclusion agrees with our opening remarks. For
30   we took / the goal of political science to be the best good; and most of
its attention is devoted to the character of the citizens, to make them
good people who do fine actions.[4]

§9 It is not surprising, then, that we regard neither ox nor horse
1100a   nor any other kind of animal as happy; for none of / them can share
in this sort of activity.   §10 For the same reason a child is not happy
either, since his age prevents him from doing these sorts of actions.
If he is called happy, he is being congratulated <simply> because of
anticipated blessedness; for, as we have said, happiness requires both
5   complete virtue / and a complete life.[5]

§11 It needs a complete life because life includes many reversals
of fortune, good and bad, and the most prosperous person may fall
into a terrible disaster in old age, as the Trojan stories tell us about
Priam.[6] If someone has suffered these sorts of misfortunes and comes
to a miserable end, no one counts him happy.

10
[Can we be happy during our lifetime?]

10   [c11] / Then should we count no human being happy during his lifetime, but follow Solon's advice to wait to see the end?[1]   §2 But if we
agree with Solon, can someone really be happy during the time after
he has died? Surely that is altogether strange, especially when we say
happiness is an activity.

15   §3 / We do not say, then, that someone is happy during the time he
is dead, and Solon's point is not this, but rather that when a human

being has died, we can safely pronounce <that he was> blessed, on
the assumption that he is now finally beyond evils and misfortunes.[2]
But this claim is also disputable. For if a living person has good or
evil of which he is not aware, a dead person also, it seems, has good
or evil, if, / for instance, he receives honours or dishonours, and his   20
children, and descendants in general, do well or suffer misfortune.[3]

§4 However, this conclusion also raises a puzzle. For even if someone has lived in blessedness until old age, and has died appropriately,
many fluctuations of his descendants' fortunes may still happen to him;
for some may be / good people and get the life they deserve, while the   25
contrary may be true of others, and clearly they may be as distantly
related to their ancestor as you please. Surely, then, it would be a strange
result if the dead person's condition changed along with the fortunes
of his descendants, so that at one time he would turn out to have been
happy <in his lifetime> and at another time he would turn out to have
been miserable.[4]   §5 But / it would also be strange if the condition of   30
descendants did not affect their ancestors at all or for any length of time.

§6 But we must return to the previous puzzle, since that will perhaps also show us the answer to our present question.   §7 Let us
grant that we must wait to see the end, and must then count someone blessed, not as now being blessed <during the time he is dead>
but because he previously was blessed. Would it not be strange, then,
if, at the very time when he is happy, / we refused to ascribe truly to   35
him the happiness he has?[5] Such refusal results from / reluctance to   1100b
call him happy during his lifetime, because of its ups and downs; for
we suppose happiness is enduring and definitely not prone to fluctuate, but the same person's fortunes often turn to and / fro.[6]   §8 For   5
clearly, if we take our cue from his fortunes, we shall often call him
happy and then miserable again, thereby representing the happy person as a kind of chameleon, insecurely based.

§9 But surely it is quite wrong to take our cue from someone's fortunes. For his doing well or badly does not rest on them.[7] A human
life, as we said, needs these added, but / activities in accord with   10
virtue control happiness, and the contrary activities control its contrary.   §10 Indeed, the present puzzle is further evidence for our
account <of happiness>. For no human achievement has the stability
of activities in accord with virtue, since these seem to be more enduring even than our knowledge of the sciences.[8] / Indeed, the most hon-   15
ourable among the virtues themselves are more enduring than the

other virtues, because blessed people devote their lives to them more fully and more continually than to anything else—for this continual activity would seem to be the reason we do not forget them.

§11 It follows, then, that the happy person has the <stability> we are looking for and keeps the character he has throughout his life. For always, or more than anything else, he will do / and study the actions in accord with virtue, and will bear fortunes most finely, in every way and in all conditions appropriately, since he is truly 'good, four-square, and blameless'.[9]

§12 Many events, however, are subject to fortune; some are minor, some major. Hence, minor strokes of good or ill fortune clearly will not carry any / weight for his life. But many major strokes of good fortune will make it more blessed; for in themselves they naturally add adornment to it, and his use of them proves to be fine and excellent.[10] Conversely, if he suffers many major misfortunes, they oppress and spoil his blessedness, since they involve pain and impede / many activities. And yet, even here what is fine shines through, whenever someone bears many severe misfortunes with good temper, not because he feels no distress, but because he is noble and magnanimous.[11]

§13 And since it is activities that control life, as we said, no blessed person could ever become miserable, since he will / never do hateful and base actions. For a truly / good and prudent person,[12] we suppose, will bear strokes of fortune suitably, and from his resources at any time will do the finest actions, just as a good general will make the best use of the forces available to him in war, and a good shoemaker / will make the finest shoe from the hides given to him, and similarly for all other craftsmen.

§14 If this is so, the happy person could never become miserable. Nor will he be blessed if he falls into misfortunes as bad as Priam's.[13] Nor, however, will he be inconstant and prone to fluctuate, since he will neither be easily shaken from his happiness / nor shaken by just any misfortunes.[14] But he will be shaken from it by many serious misfortunes, and from these a return to happiness will take no short time. At best, it will take a long and complete length of time that includes great and fine successes.

§15 Then why not say that the happy person is the one whose / activities accord with complete virtue, with an adequate supply of external goods, not for just any time but for a complete life? Or should we add that he will also go on living this way and will come

to an appropriate end, since the future is not apparent to us, and
we take happiness to be the end, and altogether complete in every
way? §16 Given these facts, we shall say that / a living person who   20
has, and will keep, the goods we mentioned is blessed, but blessed
as a human being is.[15] So much for a determination of this question.

11
[How happiness can be affected after one's death]

Still, it is apparently rather unfriendly and contrary to the <com-
mon> beliefs to claim that the fortunes of our descendants and all
our friends contribute nothing. §2 But since they can find themselves in many and various circumstances, some / of which affect us   25
more, some less, it is apparently a long, indeed endless, task to dif-
ferentiate all the particular cases. Perhaps a general outline will be
enough of an answer.

§3 Misfortunes, then, even to the person himself, differ, and
some have a certain gravity and weight for his life, whereas others /   30
would seem to be lighter. The same is true for the misfortunes of his
friends; §4 and it matters whether they happen to living or to dead
people—much more than it matters whether lawless and terrible crimes
are committed before a tragic drama begins or in the course of it.[1]

§5 In our reasoning, then, we should also take account of this difference, / but even more account, presumably, of the puzzle about whether   35
/ the dead share in any good or evil. For if we consider this, anything   1101b
good or evil penetrating to the dead would seem to be weak and unimportant, either without qualification or for them. Even if the good or
evil is not so weak and unimportant, still its importance and character are not enough to make people happy who / are not already happy,   5
or to take away the blessedness of those who are happy. §6 And so,
when friends do well, and likewise when they do badly, it appears to
contribute something to the dead, but of a character and size that
neither makes happy people not happy nor anything of this sort.

12
[Praise and honour]

[c12] / Now that we have determined these points, let us consider   10
whether happiness is something praiseworthy, or instead something
honourable; for clearly it is not a capacity.[1]

§2 Whatever is praiseworthy appears to be praised for its character and its state in relation to something.² We praise the just and the
15   brave person, for instance, and in general the good / person and virtue,
because of their actions and achievements; and we praise the strong
person, the good runner, and each of the others because he naturally
has a certain character and is in a certain state in relation to something
good and excellent.   §3 This is clear also from praises of the gods; for
20   these praises appear ridiculous because they are referred to us, but /
they are referred to us because, as we said, praise depends on such a
reference.

§4 If praise is for these sorts of things, then clearly for the best
things there is no praise, but something greater and better. And
indeed this is how it appears. For the gods and the most godlike³ of
25   men are <not praised, but> congratulated for / their blessedness and
happiness. The same is true of goods; for we never praise happiness,
as we praise justice, but we count it blessed, as something better and
more godlike <than anything that is praised>.

§5 Indeed, Eudoxus seems to have used the right sort of argument in defending the supremacy of pleasure.⁴ By not praising pleasure though it is a good, we indicate—so he thought—that it is supe-
30   rior / to everything praiseworthy; <only> the god and the good have
this superiority since the other goods are <praised> by reference to
them.   §6 For praise is given to virtue, since it makes us do fine
actions; but celebrations are for achievements, either of body or of
35   soul.   §7 But an exact treatment of this is presumably more proper /
1102a   for specialists in celebrations. For us, anyhow, it is clear / from what
has been said that happiness is something honourable and complete.

§8 A further reason why this would seem to be correct is that happiness is a principle; for <the principle> is what we all aim at in all
our other actions;⁵ and we take the principle and cause of goods to be
something honourable and divine.

13
[Introduction to the virtues]

5   [c13] / Since happiness is a certain sort of activity of the soul in
accord with complete virtue, we must examine virtue; for that
will perhaps also be a way to study happiness better.¹   §2 Moreover, the true politician² seems to have put more effort into virtue
10   than into anything else, since he wants to make / the citizens good

and law-abiding.   §3 And we find an example of this in the Spartan and Cretan legislators[3] and in any others who share their concerns.   §4 Since, then, the examination of virtue is proper for political science, the inquiry clearly fits our decision at the beginning.[4]

§5 Now it is clear that the virtue we must examine is human virtue, since we are also seeking the human good and human / happiness.   §6 Now by human virtue we mean virtue of the soul, not of the body, since we also say that happiness is an activity of the soul.   §7 If this is so, it is clear that the politician must in some way know about the soul, just as / someone setting out to heal the eyes must know about the whole body as well.[5] This is all the more true to the extent that political science is better and more honourable than medicine; even among doctors, the cultivated ones devote a lot of effort to finding out about the body. Hence the politician as well <as the student of nature> must study the soul.[6]   §8 But he must study it for his specific purpose, / far enough for his inquiry <into virtue>; for a more exact treatment would presumably take more effort than his purpose requires.[7]

§9 <We> have discussed the soul sufficiently in <our> popular works as well <as our less popular>,[8] and we should use this discussion. We have said, for instance, that one <part> of the soul is non-rational, while one has reason.   §10 But are these distinguished as parts / of a body and of everything divisible into parts are? Or are they two <only> in definition, and inseparable by nature, as the convex and the concave are in a surface? It does not matter for present purposes.[9]

§11 Consider the non-rational <part>. One <part> of it, i.e., the cause of nutrition and growth, would seem to be plantlike and / shared <with all living things>: for we can ascribe this capacity of the soul to everything that is nourished, including embryos, and the same capacity to full-grown living things, since this is more reasonable than to ascribe another capacity to them.[10]   §12 Hence the virtue of this capacity is apparently shared, not <specifically> human. For this part and this capacity more than / others seem to be active in sleep, and here the good and the bad person are least distinct; hence happy people are said to be no better off than miserable people for half their lives.   §13 This <lack of distinction> is not surprising, since sleep is inactivity of the soul insofar as it is called excellent or base, unless to some small extent some movements penetrate / <to our awareness>,

15

20

25

30

1102b

5

10

and in this way the decent person comes to have better images <in dreams> than just any random person has.   §14 Enough about this, however, and let us leave aside the nutritive part, since by nature it has no share in human virtue.

§15 Another nature in the soul would also seem to be non-rational, though in a way it shares in reason. For in the / continent and the incontinent person we praise their reason and the <part> of the soul that has reason, because it exhorts them correctly and towards whatever is best; but they evidently also have in them some other <part> that is by nature something apart from reason, clashing and struggling with reason. For just as uncontrolled[11] parts of a body, when we decide to / move them to the right, do the contrary and move off to the left, the same is true of the soul; for incontinent people have impulses in contrary directions.   §16 In bodies, admittedly, we see the part go astray, whereas we do not see it in the soul; nonetheless, presumably, we should suppose that the soul also has something apart from reason, countering and opposing / reason. The <precise> way it is different does not matter.   §17 However, this <part> as well <as the rational part> appears, as we said, to share in reason. At any rate, in the continent person it obeys reason; and in the temperate and the brave person it presumably listens still better to reason, since there it agrees with reason in everything.[12]

§18 The non-rational <part>, then, as well <as the whole soul> apparently has two parts. For while the plantlike <part> shares / in reason not at all, the <part> that has appetites and in general desires[13] shares in reason in a way, insofar as it both listens to reason and obeys it. This is the way in which we are said to 'listen to reason' from father or friends, as opposed to the way in which <we 'give the reason'> in mathematics.[14] The non-rational part also <obeys and> is persuaded in some way by reason, as is shown by correction, and by every sort / of reproof and exhortation.

§19 If, then, we ought to say that this <part> also has reason, then the <part> that has reason, as well <as the non-rational part>, will have two parts. One will have reason fully, by having it within itself; the other will have reason by listening to reason as to a father.[15]

The division between virtues accords with this difference. / For some virtues are called virtues of thought, others virtues of character. Wisdom, comprehension, and prudence are called virtues of thought, generosity and temperance virtues of character.[16] For when we speak

of someone's character we do not say that he is wise or has good comprehension, but that he is gentle or temperate. And yet, we also praise the wise person for his state, / and those states that are praiseworthy   10
we call virtues.

Book II
[Virtue of character]

1
[How a virtue of character is acquired]

Virtue, then, is of two sorts, virtue of thought and virtue / of charac-   15
ter.[1] Virtue of thought arises and grows mostly from teaching; that is why it needs experience and time. Virtue of character <i.e., of *êthos*> results from habit <*ethos*>; hence its name 'ethical', slightly varied from 'ethos'.[2]

§2 Hence it is also clear that none of the virtues of character arises in us naturally. / For if something is by nature in one condition, habit-   20
uation cannot bring it into another condition. A stone, for instance, by nature moves downwards, and habituation could not make it move upwards, not even if you threw it up ten thousand times to habituate it; nor could habituation make fire move downwards, or bring anything that is by nature in one condition into another condition.   §3 And so the virtues arise in us neither by nature nor against / nature. Rather, we are by nature able to acquire them, and we are   25
completed through habit.[3]

§4 Further, if something arises in us by nature, we first have the capacity for it, and later perform the activity. This is clear in the case of the senses; for we did not acquire them by / frequent seeing or   30
hearing, but we already had them when we exercised them, and did not get them by exercising them. Virtues, by contrast, we acquire, just as we acquire crafts, by having first performed the actions. For we learn a craft by producing the same product that we must produce when we have learned it; we become builders, for instance, by building, and we become harpists by playing the harp. Similarly, then, we become just / by doing just actions, temperate by doing temperate   1103b
actions, brave by doing brave actions.[4]

§5 What goes on in cities is also evidence for this. For the legislator makes the citizens good by habituating them, and / this is the wish   5 of every legislator; if he fails to do it well he misses his goal.[5] Correct habituation distinguishes a good political system from a bad one.

§6 Further, the sources and means that develop each virtue also ruin it, just as they do in a craft. For playing the harp makes both
10   good and bad harpists, and it is analogous in the / case of builders and all the rest; for building well makes good builders, and building badly makes bad ones. §7 Otherwise no teacher would be needed, but everyone would be born a good or a bad craftsman.

It is the same, then, with the virtues. For what we do in our deal-
15   ings / with other people makes some of us just, some unjust, and what we do in terrifying situations, and the habits of fear or confidence that we acquire, make some of us brave and others cowardly. The same is true of situations involving appetites and anger; for one or another
20   sort of conduct in these situations / makes some people temperate and calm, but other people intemperate and irascible. To sum it up in a single account: a state <of character> results from <the repetition of> similar actions.[6]

§8 That is why we must perform the right actions, since differences in these imply corresponding differences in the states.[7] It is not unimportant, then, to acquire one sort of habit or another,
25   right from our youth. On the contrary, it is / very important, indeed all-important.

2
[Habituation]

[c2] Our present discussion does not aim, as our others do, at study; for the purpose of our examination is not to know what virtue is, but
30   to become good, since otherwise the inquiry / would be of no benefit to us.[1] And so we must examine the right ways of acting; for, as we have said, the actions also control the sorts of states we acquire.

§2 First, then, actions should accord with the correct reason.[2] That is a common <belief>,[3] and let us assume it. We shall discuss it later, and say what the correct reason is and how it is related to the other virtues.

1104a   §3 / But let us take it as agreed in advance that every account of the actions we should do[4] has to be stated in outline, not exactly. As we also said at the beginning, the type of accounts we demand should accord with the subject matter; and questions about actions and expediency, like questions about health, have no fixed answers.[5]

§4 /While this is the character of our general account, the account ₅ of particular cases is still more inexact. For these fall under no craft or profession; the agents themselves must consider in each case what the opportune action is, as doctors and navigators do.⁶ §5 / The ₁₀ account we offer, then, in our present inquiry is of this inexact sort; still, we must try to offer help.⁷

§6 First, then, we should observe that these sorts of states naturally tend to be ruined by excess and deficiency. We see this happen with strength and health (for we must use evident cases as witnesses to things that arc / not evident).⁸ For both excessive and deficient ₁₅ exercise ruin bodily strength, and, similarly, too much or too little eating or drinking ruins health, whereas the proportionate amount produces, increases and preserves it.

§7 The same is true, then, of temperance, bravery, and the / other ₂₀ virtues. For if, for instance, someone avoids and is afraid of everything, standing firm against nothing, he becomes cowardly; if he is afraid of nothing at all and goes to face everything, he becomes rash. Similarly, if he gratifies himself with every pleasure and abstains from none, he becomes intemperate; if he avoids them all, as boors do, he becomes / some sort of insensible person. Temperance and brav- ₂₅ ery, then, are ruined by excess and deficiency, but preserved by the mean.⁹

§8 But these actions are not only the sources and causes both of the emergence and growth of virtues and of their ruin; the activities of the virtues also consist in these / same actions.¹⁰ For this is also true ₃₀ of more evident cases; strength, for instance, arises from eating a lot and from withstanding much hard labour, and it is the strong person who is most capable of these very actions.   §9 It is the same with the virtues. For abstaining from pleasures makes us become temperate, / ₃₅ and once we have become temperate we are most capable / of abstain- ₁₁₀₄ᵇ ing from pleasures. It is similar with bravery; habituation in disdain for frightening situations and in standing firm against them makes us become brave, and once we have become brave we shall be most capable of standing firm.

3
[The importance of pleasure and pain]

But we must take the pleasure or pain that supervenes on his / actions ₅ to be a sign of the state <of character>.¹ For if someone who abstains from bodily pleasures enjoys this <abstinence> itself, he is temperate; but if he is grieved by it, he is intemperate.² Again, if he stands firm against terrifying situations and enjoys it, or at least does not find it painful, he is brave; but if he finds it painful, he is cowardly. For virtue of character is about pleasures and pains.³

10   / For pleasure causes us to do base actions, and pain causes us to abstain from fine ones.   §2 That is why we need to have had the appropriate upbringing—right from early youth, as Plato says⁴—to make us find enjoyment or pain in the right things; for this is the correct education.

§3 Further, virtues are about actions and feelings; but every feel-
15   ing and every action implies pleasure or / pain;⁵ hence, for this reason too, virtue is about pleasures and pains.   §4 Corrective treatments also indicate this, since they use pleasures and pains; for correction is a form of medical treatment, and medical treatment naturally oper-ates through contraries.

§5 Further, as we said earlier, every state of soul is naturally related
20   to and about whatever naturally makes / it better or worse; and plea-sures and pains make people base, from pursuing and avoiding the wrong ones, at the wrong time, in the wrong ways, or whatever other distinctions of that sort are needed in an account. These <bad effects of pleasure and pain> are the reason why people actually define the
25   virtues as ways of being unaffected / and undisturbed <by pleasures and pains>.⁶ They are wrong, however, because they speak of being unaffected without qualification, not of being unaffected in the right or wrong way, at the right or wrong time, and the added qualifications.

§6 We assume, then, that virtue is the sort of state that does the best actions concerning pleasures and pains, and that vice is the con-trary state.

30   §7 The following will also make it evident that virtue / and vice are about the same things. For there are three objects of choice—fine, expedient, and pleasant—and three objects of avoidance—their con-traries, shameful, harmful, and painful.⁷ About all these, then, the
35   good person is correct and the bad person is in error, and especially /
1105a   about pleasure. For pleasure is shared with animals, and implied / by every object of choice, since what is fine and what is expedient appear pleasant as well.

§8 Further, pleasure grows up with all of us from infancy on. That is why it is hard to rub out this feeling that is dyed into our lives. We

also estimate actions <as well as feelings>, some / of us more, some   5
less, by pleasure and pain.   §9 For this reason, our whole discussion must be about these; for good or bad enjoyment or pain is very important for our actions.

§10 Further, it is more difficult to fight pleasure than to fight spirit—and Heracleitus tells us <how difficult it is to fight spirit>.[8] Now both craft and virtue in every case are about / what is more   10
difficult, since a good result is even better when it is more difficult. Hence, for this reason also, the whole discussion, for virtue and political science alike, must consider pleasures and pains; for if we use these well, we shall be good, and if badly, bad.

§11 To sum up: virtue is about pleasures and pains; the / actions   15
that are its sources also increase it or, if they are done badly, ruin it; and its activity is about the same actions as those that are its sources.

4
[Virtuous actions contrasted with virtuous character]

[c3] Someone might be puzzled, however, about what we mean by saying that we become just by doing just actions and become temperate by doing temperate actions.[1] For <one might suppose that> if we do grammatical or musical actions, we / are grammarians or musi-   20
cians, and, similarly, if we do just or temperate actions, we are thereby just or temperate.

§2 Or are actions insufficient in the case of crafts as well?[2] For it is possible to produce a grammatical result by chance, or by following someone else's instructions. To be grammarians, then, we must both produce a grammatical result and produce / it grammatically—   25
that is to say, produce it in accord with the grammatical knowledge in us.

§3 Moreover, in any case, what is true of crafts is not true of virtues.[3] For the products of a craft determine by their own qualities whether they have been produced well; and so it suffices that they have the right qualities when they have been produced.[4] But for actions in accord with the virtues to be done temperately or justly it does not suffice that / they themselves have the right qualities.[5]   30
Rather, the agent must also be in the right state when he does them. First, he must know <that he is doing them>[6]; secondly, he must decide on them, and decide on them for themselves; and, thirdly, he must also do them from a firm and unchanging state.

1105b   As conditions for / having a craft, these three do not count, except
for the bare knowing.[7] As a condition for having a virtue, however, the
knowing counts for nothing, or <rather> for only a little, whereas the
other two conditions are very important, indeed all-important. And

5   we achieve these other two conditions / by the frequent doing of just
and temperate actions.

§4 Hence actions are called just or temperate when they are the
sort that a just or temperate person would do. But the just and temperate person is not the one who <merely> does these actions, but
the one who also does them in the way in which just or temperate
people do them.

10   §5 / It is correct, then, to say that a person comes to be just from
doing just actions and temperate from doing temperate actions; for
no one has the least prospect of becoming good from failing to do
them.

§6 The many, however, do not do these actions. They take refuge
in arguments, thinking that they are doing philosophy, and that this is

15   the way to become excellent people. They / are like a sick person who
listens attentively to the doctor, but acts on none of his instructions.
Such a course of treatment will not improve the state of the sick person's body; nor will the many improve the state of their souls by this
attitude to philosophy.[8]

5
[Virtue of character: its genus]

20   [c4] Next we must examine what virtue is. Since there are three /
conditions arising in the soul—feelings, capacities, and states—virtue
must be one of these.[1]

§2 By feelings I mean appetite, anger, fear, confidence, envy, joy,
love, hate, longing, jealousy, pity, and in general whatever implies
pleasure or pain. By capacities I mean what we have when we are said

25   to / be capable of these feelings—capable of being angry, for instance,
or of feeling pain, or of feeling pity. By states I mean what we have
when we are well or badly off in relation to feelings.[2] If, for instance,
our feeling is too intense or slack, we are badly off in relation to anger,
but if it is intermediate, we are well off; the same is true in the other
cases.

30   §3 First, then, neither virtues nor vices are feelings.[3] For / we
are called excellent or base insofar as we have virtues or vices, not

insofar as we have feelings. Further, we are neither praised nor blamed insofar as we have feelings; for we do not praise the angry or the frightened person, and do not / blame the person who is   1106a simply angry, but only the person who is angry in a particular way. We are praised or blamed, however, insofar as we have virtues or vices.[4]   §4 Further, we are angry and afraid without decision; but the virtues are decisions of some kind, or require decision.[5] Besides, insofar as / we have feelings, we are said to be moved; but insofar as   5 we have virtues or vices, we are said to be in some condition rather than moved.

§5 For these reasons the virtues are not capacities either; for we are neither called good nor called bad, nor are we praised or blamed, insofar as we are simply capable of feelings. Further, while we have / capacities by nature, we do not become good or bad by nature; we   10 have discussed this before.[6]

§6 If, then, the virtues are neither feelings nor capacities, the remaining possibility is that they are states. And so we have said what the genus of virtue is.

6

[Virtue of character: its differentia]

[c5] But we must say not only, as we already have, that it is / a state,   15 but also what sort of state it is.[1]

§2 It should be said, then, that every virtue causes its possessors to be in a good state and to perform their functions well.[2] The virtue of eyes, for instance, makes the eyes and their functioning excellent, because it makes us see well; and similarly, / the virtue of a horse   20 makes the horse excellent, and thereby good at galloping, at carrying its rider, and at standing steady in the face of the enemy.   §3 If this is true in every case, the virtue of a human being will likewise be the state that makes a human being good and makes him perform his function well.

§4 / We have already said how this will be true, and it will also be   25 evident from our next remarks, if we consider the sort of nature that virtue has.[3]

In everything continuous and divisible we can take more, less, and equal, and each of them either in the object itself or relative to us; and the equal is some intermediate between excess and deficiency.   §5 /   30 By the intermediate in the object I mean what is equidistant from each extremity; this is one and the same for all. But relative to us the intermediate is what is neither superfluous nor deficient; this is not one, and is not the same for all.⁴

§6 If, for instance, ten are many and two are few, we take six as
35 intermediate in the object, since it exceeds <two> and is exceeded / <by ten> by an equal amount, <four>. §7 This is what is interme-
1106b diate by numerical proportion. But that is not how / we must take the intermediate that is relative to us. For if, ten pounds <of food>, for instance, are a lot for someone to eat, and two pounds a little, it does not follow that the trainer will prescribe six, since this might also be either a little or a lot for the person who is to take it—for Milo <the athlete> a little, but for the beginner in gymnastics a lot; and the
5 same is / true for running and wrestling. §8 In this way every scientific expert avoids excess and deficiency and seeks and chooses what is intermediate—but intermediate relative to us, not in the object.

§9 This, then, is how each science produces its product well, by concentrating on what is intermediate and making the product
10 / conform to that.⁵ This, indeed, is why people regularly comment on well-made products that nothing could be added or subtracted; they assume that excess or deficiency ruins a good <result>, but the mean preserves it. Good craftsmen also, we say, concentrate on what
15 is intermediate when they produce / their product. And since virtue, like nature, is better and more exact than any craft, it will also aim at what is intermediate.⁶

§10 By virtue I mean virtue of character; for this is about feelings and actions, and these admit of excess, deficiency, and an intermediate condition. We can be afraid, for instance, or be confident, or have appetites, or get angry, or feel pity, and in general have plea-
20 sure / or pain, both too much and too little, and in both ways not well. §11 But having these feelings at the right times, about the right things, towards the right people, for the right end, and in the right way, is the intermediate and best condition, and this is proper to virtue. §12 Similarly, actions also admit of excess, deficiency, and an intermediate condition.

25 / Now virtue is about feelings and actions, in which excess is in error and deficiency is blamed,⁷ whereas the intermediate condition is praised and is correct, which are both proper to virtue. §13 Virtue, then, is a mean, insofar as it aims at what is intermediate.

§14 Moreover, there are many ways to be in error—for badness /   30
is proper to the indeterminate, as the Pythagoreans pictured it, and
good to the determinate. But there is only one way to be correct. That
is why error is easy and correctness is difficult, since it is easy to miss
the target and difficult to hit it. And so for this reason also excess and
deficiency are proper / to vice, the mean to virtue; 'for we are noble in   35
only one way, but bad in all sorts of ways.'[8]

§15 [c6] Virtue, then, is a state that decides, consisting in / a mean,   1107a
the mean relative to us, which is defined by reference to reason, that is
to say, to the reason by reference to which the prudent person would
define it.[9] It is a mean between two vices, one of excess and one of
deficiency.

§16 It is a mean for this reason also: Some vices miss what is right
because they are deficient, others because they are / excessive, in feel-   5
ings or in actions, but virtue finds and chooses what is intermediate.

§17 That is why virtue, as far as its essence and the account stating
what it is are concerned, is a mean, but, as far as the best <condition>
and the good <result> are concerned, it is an extremity.

§18 Now not every action or feeling admits of the mean.[10] For / the   10
names of some automatically include baseness—for instance, spite,
shamelessness, envy <among feelings>, and adultery, theft, murder,
among actions.[11] For all of these and similar things are called by these
names because they themselves, not their excesses or deficiencies, are
base. Hence in doing these things we can never be correct, but / must   15
invariably be in error. We cannot do them well or not well—by committing adultery, for instance, with the right woman at the right time
in the right way. On the contrary, it is true without qualification that
to do any of them is to be in error.

§19 <To think these admit of a mean>, therefore, is like thinking
that unjust or cowardly or intemperate action also admits / of a mean,   20
an excess and a deficiency. If it did, there would be a mean of excess,
a mean of deficiency, an excess of excess, and a deficiency of deficiency. §20 On the contrary, just as there is no excess or deficiency of
temperance or of bravery (since the intermediate is a sort of extreme),
so also there is no mean of these vicious actions either, but whatever
way anyone does them, he is in error. For in general there is no mean /   25
of excess or of deficiency, and no excess or deficiency of a mean.

7

[The particular virtues of character]

[c7] However, we must not only state this general account but also
apply it to the particular cases. For among accounts / concerning
actions, though the general ones are common to more cases, the specific ones are truer, since actions are about particular cases, and our
account must accord with these.[1] Let us, then, find these from the
chart.[2]

§2 First, then, in feelings of fear and confidence the mean is / bravery. The excessively fearless person is nameless (indeed many cases
are nameless), and the one who is excessively confident is rash. The
one who is excessive in fear and deficient in confidence is cowardly.

§3 / In pleasures and pains—though not in all types, and in pains
also, \<but\> less than in pleasures—the mean is temperance and the
excess intemperance. People deficient in pleasure are not often found,
which is why they also lack even a name; let us call them insensible.

§4 In giving and taking money the mean is generosity, / the excess
wastefulness, and the deficiency ungenerosity. Here the vicious people have contrary excesses and defects; for the wasteful person is
excessive in spending and deficient in taking, whereas the ungenerous person is excessive in taking and deficient in spending. §5 At
the moment we are speaking in / outline and summary, and that is
enough; later we shall define these things more exactly.

§6 In questions of money there are also other conditions. Another
mean is magnificence; for the magnificent person differs from the
generous by being concerned with large matters, while the generous
person is concerned with small. The / excess is ostentation and vulgarity, and the deficiency is stinginess. These differ from the vices
related to generosity in ways we shall describe later.

§7 In honour and dishonour the mean is magnanimity, the excess
something called a sort of vanity, and the deficiency pusillanimity. §8 / And just as we said that generosity differs from magnificence in its concern with small matters, similarly there is a virtue
concerned with small honours, differing in the same way from magnanimity, which is concerned with great honours. For honour can
be desired either in the right way or more or less than is right. If
someone desires it to excess, he is called an honour-lover, and if
his desire is deficient / he is called indifferent to honour, but if he is
intermediate he has no name. The corresponding conditions have

no name either, except the condition of the honour-lover, which is
called honour-loving.

This is why people at the extremes lay claim to the intermediate
area. Moreover, we also sometimes call the intermediate person an
honour-lover, and sometimes call him indifferent to honour; and sometimes we praise the honour-lover, sometimes the person indifferent to
/ honour.³ §9 We will mention later the reason we do this; for the   1108a
moment, let us speak of the other cases in the way we have laid down.

§10 / Anger also admits of an excess, deficiency, and mean. These   5
are all practically nameless; but since we call the intermediate person calm, let us call the mean calmness. Among the extreme people
let the excessive person be irascible, and his vice irascibility, and let
the deficient person be a sort of inirascible person, and his deficiency
inirascibility.

§11 / There are also three other means, somewhat similar to one   10
another, but different. For they are all concerned with common dealings in conversations and actions, but differ insofar as one is concerned with truth-telling in these areas, the other two with sources
of pleasure, some of which are found in amusement, and the others
in daily life in general. Hence we should also discuss these states, so
that we can better / observe that in every case the mean is praisewor-   15
thy, whereas the extremes are neither praiseworthy nor correct, but
blameworthy. Most of these cases are also nameless, and we must try,
as in the other cases also, to supply names ourselves, to make things
clear and easy to follow.

§12 / In truth-telling, then, let us call the intermediate person truth-   20
ful, and the mean truthfulness; pretence that overstates will be boastfulness, and the person who has it boastful; pretence that understates
will be self-deprecation, and the person who has it self-deprecating.

§13 In sources of pleasure in amusements let us call the intermediate person witty, and the condition wit; the excess / buffoonery and   25
the person who has it a buffoon; and the deficient person a sort of
boor and the state boorishness.

In the other sources of pleasure, those in daily life, let us call
the person who is pleasant in the right way friendly, and the mean
state friendliness. If someone goes to excess with no <ulterior> aim,
he will be ingratiating; if he does it for his own advantage, a flatterer.
The deficient person, / unpleasant in everything, will be a sort of   30
quarrelsome and ill-tempered person.

§14 There are also means in feelings and about feelings. Shame, for instance, is not a virtue, but the person prone to shame as well as <the virtuous people we have described> receives praise. For here also one person is called intermediate, and another—the person excessively prone to shame, who is ashamed about everything—is
35 called excessive; the / person who is deficient in shame or never feels shame at all is said to have no sense of disgrace; and the intermediate
1108b / one is called prone to shame.

§15 Proper indignation is the mean between envy and spite; these conditions are concerned with pleasure and pain at what happens to our neighbours. For the properly indignant person feels pain when
5 someone does well undeservedly; the / envious person exceeds him by feeling pain when anyone does well, while the spiteful person is so deficient in feeling pain that he actually enjoys <other people's misfortunes>.[4]

§16 There will also be an opportunity elsewhere to speak of these.[5] We must consider justice after these. Since it is spoken of in more than one way, we shall distinguish its two types and say how each of
10 them is a mean. / Similarly, we must also consider the virtues that belong to reason.

8

[Relations between mean and extreme states]

[c8] Among these three conditions, then, two are vices—one of excess, one of deficiency—and one—the mean—is virtue. In a way each of them is opposed to each of the others, since each extreme is contrary both to the intermediate condition and to the other extreme,
15 while the intermediate is contrary / to the extremes.

§2 For, just as the equal is greater in comparison to the smaller, and smaller in comparison to the greater, so also the intermediate states are excessive in comparison to the deficiencies and deficient in comparison
20 to the excesses—both in feelings and in actions. / For the brave person, for instance, appears rash in comparison to the coward, and cowardly in comparison to the rash person; the temperate person appears intemperate in comparison to the insensible person, and insensible in comparison with the intemperate person; and the generous person appears wasteful in comparison to the ungenerous, and ungenerous in comparison to the wasteful person.[1]   §3 That is why each of the extreme
25 people tries to push the intermediate / person to the other extreme, so

that the coward, for instance, calls the brave person rash, and the rash person calls him a coward, and similarly in the other cases.

§4 Since these conditions of soul are opposed to each other in these ways, the extremes are more contrary to each other than to the intermediate. For they are further from each other than from the intermediate, just as the large is further from / the small, and the small from the large, than either is from the equal.

§5 Further, sometimes one extreme—rashness or wastefulness, for instance—appears somewhat like the intermediate state—bravery or generosity. But the extremes are most unlike one another; and the things that are furthest apart from each other / are defined as contraries. And so the things that are further apart are more contrary.

§6 / In some cases the deficiency, in others the excess, is more opposed to the intermediate condition. For instance, cowardice, the deficiency, not rashness, the excess, is more opposed to bravery, whereas intemperance, the excess, not insensibility, the deficiency, is more opposed / to temperance.

§7 This happens for two reasons: One reason is derived from the object itself. Since sometimes one extreme is closer and more similar to the intermediate condition, we oppose the contrary extreme, more than this closer one, to the intermediate condition.[2] Since rashness, for instance, seems to be closer and more similar to bravery, / and cowardice less similar, we oppose cowardice more than rashness to bravery; for what is further from the intermediate condition seems to be more contrary to it. This, then, is one reason, derived from the object itself.

§8 The other reason is derived from ourselves. For when we ourselves have some natural tendency to one extreme more than to the other, this extreme appears more opposed to the intermediate condition. Since, for instance, we have more of a natural / tendency to pleasure, we drift more easily towards intemperance than towards orderliness. Hence we say that an extreme is more contrary if we naturally develop more in that direction; and this is why intemperance is more contrary to temperance, since it is the excess <of pleasure>.

9
[How can we reach the mean?]

[c9] / We have said enough, then, to show that virtue of character is a mean and what sort of mean it is; that it is a mean between two vices,

30

35

1109a

5

10

15

20

one of excess and one of deficiency; and that it is a mean because it aims at the intermediate condition in feelings and actions.

§2 That is why it is also hard work to be excellent. For in each case 25 / it is hard work to find the intermediate; for instance, not everyone, but only one who knows, finds the midpoint in a circle. So also getting angry, or giving and spending money, is easy and everyone can do it; but doing it to the right person, in the right amount, at the right time, for the right end, and in the right way is no longer easy, nor can 30 everyone do it.[1] Hence / doing these things well is rare, praiseworthy, and fine.

§3 That is why anyone who aims at the intermediate condition must first of all steer clear of the more contrary extreme, following the advice that Calypso also gives—'Hold the ship outside the spray and surge.'[2] For one extreme is more in error, the other less. §4 Since, therefore, it is hard to hit the intermediate extremely accurately,[3] the 35 second-best tack, as they say, is / to take the lesser of the evils. We shall 1109b succeed best in this / by the method we describe.

We must also examine what we ourselves drift into easily. For different people have different natural tendencies towards differ- 5 ent goals, and we shall come to know our own tendencies / from the pleasure or pain that arises in us. §5 We must drag ourselves off in the contrary direction; for if we pull far away from error, as they do in straightening bent wood, we shall reach the intermediate condition.

§6 And in everything we must beware above all of pleasure and its sources; for we are already biased in its favour when we come to judge 10 it. Hence we must react to it as the elders / reacted to Helen, and on each occasion repeat what they said; for if we do this, and send it off, we shall be less in error.[4]

§7 In summary, then, if we do these things we shall best be able to reach the intermediate condition. But presumably this is difficult, 15 especially in particular cases, since it is not easy to / define the way we should be angry, with whom, about what, for how long. For sometimes, indeed, we ourselves praise deficient people and call them calm, and sometimes praise quarrelsome people and call them manly.

§8 Still, we are not blamed if we deviate a little in excess or defi- 20 ciency from / doing well, but only if we deviate a long way, since then we are easily noticed. But how great and how serious a deviation receives blame is not easy to define in an account; for nothing else perceptible is easily defined either. Such things are among particulars, and the judgment depends on perception.[5]

§9 This is enough, then, to make it clear that in every case the intermediate / state is praised, but we must sometimes incline towards   25
the excess, sometimes towards the deficiency; for that is the easiest way to hit the intermediate and good condition.

Book III
[Preconditions of virtue]

1
[Voluntary action]

/ Virtue, then, is about feelings and actions. These receive praise or   30
blame if they are voluntary, but pardon, sometimes even pity, if they are involuntary.[1] Hence, presumably, in examining virtue we must define the voluntary and the involuntary. §2 This is also useful to legislators, both for / honours and for corrective treatments.[2]   35

§3 / It seems, then, that things coming about by force or because   1110a
of ignorance are involuntary.[3]

What is forced has an external principle, the sort of principle in which the agent, or <rather> the victim,[4] contributes nothing[5]—if, for instance, a wind or people who have him in their control were to carry him off.

§4 But what about actions done because of fear of greater / evils,   5
or because of something fine?[6] Suppose, for instance, a tyrant tells you to do something shameful, when he has control over your parents and children, and if you do it, they will live, but if not, they will die.[7] These cases raise dispute about whether they are voluntary or involuntary.

§5 However, the same sort <of unwelcome choice> is found in throwing / cargo overboard in storms.[8] For no one willingly throws   10
cargo overboard, without qualification,[9] but anyone with any sense throws it overboard to save himself and the others.

§6 These sorts of actions, then, are mixed,[10] but they are more like voluntary actions. For at the time they are done they are choiceworthy, and the goal of an action accords with the specific occasion; hence we should also call the action voluntary or involuntary on the occasion when he / does it. Now in fact he does it willingly. For in   15 such actions he has within him the principle of moving the limbs that are the instruments <of the action>; but if the principle of the actions is in him, it is also up to him to do them or not to do them.[11] Hence actions of this sort are voluntary, though presumably the actions without <the appropriate> qualification are involuntary, since no one would choose any such action in its own right.

20   §7 / But for such actions people are also sometimes praised, whenever they endure something shameful or painful as the price of great and fine results. And if they do the reverse, they are blamed; for it is a base person who endures what is most shameful for nothing fine or for only some moderately fine result. But in some cases there is no 25 praise, but there is pardon, / whenever someone does a wrong action because of conditions of a sort that overstrain human nature, and that no one would endure.[12]

§8 But presumably there are some things that we cannot be compelled to do, but instead we should suffer the most terrible consequences and accept death. For the things that <allegedly> compelled Euripides' Alcmaeon to kill his mother appear ridiculous.[13]

30   §9 / It is sometimes difficult, however, to judge what <goods> should be chosen at the price of what <evils>, and what <evils> should be endured as the price of what <goods>. It is even more difficult to abide by our judgment, since the results we expect <when we endure> are usually painful, and the actions we are compelled <to 1110b endure, when we choose> are usually / shameful. That is why those who have been compelled or not compelled receive praise or blame.

§10 What sorts of things, then, should we say are forced? Perhaps we should say that something is forced without qualification whenever its cause is external and the agent contributes nothing. Other things are involuntary in their own right, but choiceworthy on this 5 occasion and as the price of these / <goods>, and their principle is in the agent. These are involuntary in their own right, but, on this occasion and as the price of these <goods>, voluntary.[14] But they are more like voluntary actions, since the actions are particulars, and these particulars are voluntary. But what sort of thing should be chosen as the price of what <good> is not easy to answer, since there are many differences in particular <conditions>.

10   §11 But what if someone says that pleasant things and fine / things force us, on the ground that they are outside us and compel us? For him, then, everything must be forced, since everyone in every action

aims at something fine or pleasant. Moreover, if we are forced and unwilling to act, we find it painful; but if something pleasant or fine is its cause, we do it with pleasure. Further, it is ridiculous for him to hold external causes responsible, / and not himself as being easily snared by such things;[15] and ridiculous to hold himself responsible for his fine actions, but pleasant things responsible for his shameful actions.

§12 What is forced, then, would seem to be what has its principle outside the person forced, who contributes nothing.

§13 [c2] Everything caused by ignorance is non-voluntary, but what is involuntary also involves pain and regret. For if someone's / action was caused by ignorance, but he now has no objection to the action, he has done it neither willingly, since he did not know what it was, nor unwillingly, since he now feels no pain.[16] Hence, among those who act because of ignorance, the agent who now regrets his action seems to be unwilling, but the agent with no regrets may be called non-willing, since he is another case—for since he is different, it is better if he has his own special name.

§14 / Further, action caused by ignorance would seem to be different from action done in ignorance. For if the agent is drunk or angry, his action seems to be caused by drunkenness or anger, not by ignorance, though it is done in ignorance, not in knowledge. Certainly every vicious person is ignorant of the actions he must do or avoid, and this sort of error makes people unjust, and / in general bad.

§15 <This> ignorance of what is beneficial is not taken to make action involuntary. For the cause of involuntary action is not <this> ignorance in the decision, which causes vice; it is not <in other words> ignorance of the universal, since that is a cause for blame.[17] / Rather, the cause is ignorance of the particulars which the action consists in and is concerned with,[18] since these allow both pity and pardon. For an agent acts involuntarily if he is ignorant of one of these particulars.

§16 Presumably, then, it is not a bad idea to define these particulars, and say what they are, and how many. They are who is doing it; what he is doing; about what or / to what he is doing it; sometimes also what he is doing it with—with what instrument, for example; for what result—safety, for example; in what way—gently or hard, for example.

§17 Now certainly no one could be ignorant of *all* of these unless they were mad. Nor, clearly, could one be ignorant of who is doing it, since one could hardly be ignorant of oneself. But one might be ignorant of what one is doing, as when someone says that <the secret> slipped out while he was speaking, or, as Aeschylus said about the mysteries, that he did not know it was forbidden to reveal it; or,

10 like the / person with the catapult, that he let it go when he <only> wanted to demonstrate it. Again, he might think that his son is an enemy, as Merope did;[19] or that the barbed spear has a button on it, or that the stone is pumice stone. By giving someone a drink to save

15 his life we might kill him; / and wanting to touch someone, as they do in sparring, we might wound him.

§18 Since an agent may be ignorant of any of these particular constituents of his action, someone who was ignorant of one of these seems to have acted unwillingly, especially if he was ignorant of the most important; these seem to be what he is doing, and the result for which he does it.[20]

§19 Hence the agent who acts involuntarily is the one who acts in

20 accord with this specific sort of ignorance, / who must also feel pain and regret for his action.[21]

§20 [c3] Since involuntary action is either forced or caused by ignorance, voluntary action seems to be what has its principle in the agent himself, knowing the particulars that constitute the action.[22]

25 §21 For, presumably, it is not / right to say that action caused by spirit or appetite is involuntary.[23] §22 For, first of all, on this view none of the other animals will ever act voluntarily; nor will children.[24] §23 Next, among all the actions caused by appetite or spirit do we do none of them voluntarily? Or do we do the fine actions voluntarily and the shameful involuntarily? Surely <the second answer> is ridiculous, given that one and the same thing <i.e., appetite or

30 spirit> causes <both fine and shameful actions>. §24 / And presumably it is also strange to say <as the first answer implies> that things we ought to desire[25] are involuntary. Indeed, we ought both to be angry at some things and to have appetite for some things—for health and learning, for instance. §25 Again, what is involuntary seems to be painful, whereas what accords with appetite seems to be pleasant. Moreover, how are errors in accord with spirit any less vol-

1111b untary than those in accord with rational calculation? For / both sorts of errors are to be avoided. §27 Besides, non-rational feelings seem to be no less human than rational calculation; and so actions resulting from spirit or appetite are also proper to a human being. It is strange, then, to regard them as involuntary.

2
[Decision]

[c4] / Now that we have defined the voluntary and the involuntary,   5
the next task is to discuss decision; for decision seems to be most proper to virtue, and to distinguish characters from one another better than actions do.[1]

§2 Decision, then, is apparently voluntary, but not the same as the voluntary, which extends more widely. For children and the other animals share in voluntary action, but not in decision; and the actions we do on the spur of the moment / are said to be voluntary, but not   10
to accord with decision.[2]

§3 Those who say decision is appetite or spirit or wish or some sort of belief would seem to be wrong.

For decision is not shared with non-rational animals, but appetite and spirit are shared with them.   §4 Again, the incontinent person acts on appetite, not on / decision,[3] but the continent person does   15
the reverse, by acting on decision, not on appetite.   §5 Again, appetite is contrary to decision, but not to appetite. Besides, the object of appetite is what is pleasant or painful, whereas neither of these is the object of decision.[4]

§6 And still less is spirit decision; for actions caused by spirit seem least of all to accord with decision.

§7 / But further, it is not wish either, though it is apparently close   20
to it.[5] For we do not decide on impossible things, and anyone who claimed to decide on them would seem a fool;[6] but we do wish for impossible things—for immortality, for instance—as well as possible things.   §8 Further, we wish <not only for results we can achieve>, but also for results that are <possible, but> not achievable through our own agency[7]—victory for some actor or / athlete, for instance.[8]   25
But what we decide on is never anything of that sort, but what we think would come about through our own agency.   §9 Again, we wish for the end more <than for the means to it>, but we decide on means to the end.[9] We wish, for instance, to be healthy, but we decide to do things that will make us healthy; and we wish to be happy, and say so, but we could not appropriately / say we decide to be happy,   30

since in general the things we decide on would seem to be things that are up to us.

§10 Nor is it belief.[10] For belief seems to be about everything, no less about things that are eternal and things that are impossible <for us> than about things that are up to us. Moreover, beliefs are divided into true and false, not into good and bad, but decisions are divided *1112a* into good and bad more than into true and false. §11 / Now presumably no one even claims that decision is the same as belief in general. But it is not the same as any kind of belief either. For our decisions to do good or bad actions, not our beliefs, form the characters we have. §12 Again, we decide to take or avoid something 5 good or bad. / We believe what it is, whom it benefits or how; but we do not exactly believe to take or avoid. §13 Further, decision is praised more for deciding on what is right, or <in other words> for being made correctly, but belief is praised for believing truly.[11] Moreover, we decide on things that we most of all know to be good;[12] but we believe things that we do not altogether know. §14 Again, those who make the best decisions do not seem to be the same as those with 10 the best beliefs; on the contrary, / some seem to have better beliefs, but to make the wrong decisions because of vice. §15 We may grant that decision follows or implies belief. But that is irrelevant, since it is not the question we are asking; our question is whether decision is the same as some sort of belief.

§16 Then what, or what sort of thing, is decision, since it is none of the things mentioned? Well, apparently it is voluntary, / but not 15 everything voluntary is decided. §17 Then perhaps what is decided is what has been previously deliberated. For decision involves reason and thought, and even the name itself would seem to indicate that <what is decided, *prohaireton*> is chosen <*haireton*> before <*pro*> other things.[13]

3
[Deliberation]

[c5] Do we deliberate about everything, and is everything a matter for 20 deliberation? Or is there no deliberation about some / things? §2 By 'a matter for deliberation', we should mean, presumably, that someone with some sense, not some fool or madman, would deliberate about it.

§3 Now no one deliberates about eternal things—about the universe, for instance, or about the incommensurability of the sides

and the diagonal; §4 nor about things that are in movement but
always come about the same way, either from necessity or by / nature   25
or by some other cause—the solstices, for instance, or the rising of
the stars; §5 nor about what happens in different ways at different
times—droughts and rains, for instance; nor about what results from
fortune—the finding of a treasure, for instance. [[§6 / But we do not   28
... political system.]] / For none of these results could be achieved   30
through our agency.

§7 We deliberate about what is up to us, that is to say, about the
actions we can do; and this is the remaining possibility. For causes
seem to include nature, necessity, and fortune, / but besides them   33
mind and everything <operating> through human agency.

{{ §6 / But we do not deliberate about all human affairs;   28
/ no Spartan, for instance, deliberates about how the Scythians might   29
have the best political system.[1] }} / Rather, each group of human   33
beings deliberates about the actions that they themselves can do.

§8 / There is no deliberation about the sciences that are exact and   1112b
self-sufficient, as, for instance, about letters, since we are in no doubt
about how to write them <in spelling a word>. Rather, we deliberate about what comes about through our agency, but comes about in
different ways on different occasions—about, for instance, / medicine   5
and moneymaking. We deliberate about navigation more than about
gymnastics, to the extent that it is less exactly worked out, and similarly with other <crafts>.   §9 And we deliberate about beliefs more
than about sciences,[2] since we are more in doubt about them.

§10 Deliberation is about things that happen usually, where the
outcome is unclear and where it is / indeterminate. And we enlist   10
partners in deliberation on large issues when we distrust our own
ability to discern.

§11 We deliberate not about ends, but about means to ends.[3] A
doctor, for instance, does not deliberate about whether to cure, or an
orator about whether to persuade, or a politician about whether to
produce good order, or / any other <expert> about the end <that the   15
science aims at>. Rather, we lay down the end, and then examine the
ways and means[4] to achieve it.

If it appears that any of several means will reach it, we examine
which of them will reach it most easily and most finely;[5] and if only
one means reaches it, we examine how that means will reach it, and
how the means itself is reached, until we come to the first cause,

20   the last thing to be discovered. / For a deliberator would seem to inquire and analyse in the way described, as though analysing a diagram— §12 for, apparently, all deliberation is inquiry, though not all inquiry—in mathematics, for instance—is deliberation. And the last thing in the analysis would seem to be the first that comes into being.[6]

25   §13 / If we encounter something impossible—for instance, we need money but cannot raise it—we desist; but if the action appears possible, we undertake it.[7] What is possible is what we could achieve through our agency—for what our friends achieve is, in a way, achieved through our agency, since the principle is in us.   §14 <In crafts> we

30   sometimes look for instruments, sometimes for / the proper way to use them; so also in other cases we sometimes look for the means to the end, sometimes for the proper use of the means, or for the means to that proper use.

§15 As we have said, then, a human being would seem to be a principle of action. Deliberation is about the actions he can do, and actions are for the sake of other things; §16 for we deliberate about

1113a   means to an end, not about the end. / Nor do we deliberate about particulars, about whether this is a loaf, for instance, or is cooked the right amount; for these are questions for perception, and if we keep on deliberating at each stage we shall go on without end.

§17 What we deliberate about is the same as what we decide to do, except that by the time we decide to do it, it is definite; for

5   what we decide to do is what we have judged <to be right> / as a result of deliberation. For each of us stops inquiring how to act as soon as he traces the principle to himself, and within himself to the guiding part; for this is the part that decides.   §18 This is also clear from the ancient political systems described by Homer; there the kings would first decide and then announce their decision to the people.[8]

10   §19 / We have found that what we decide to do is whatever action, among those up to us, we deliberate about and <consequently> desire to do. Hence also decision will be deliberative desire to do an action that is up to us; for when we have judged <that it is right> as a result of deliberation, we desire to do it in accord with our wish.[9]

§20 We have said in outline, then, what sorts of things decision is about, and <specifically> that we decide on means to ends.

4

[Wish]

[c6] / Wish, we have said, is for the end. But some think that wish is   15
for the good, others that it is for the apparent good.

§2 For those who say the good is the object of wish,[1] it follows that
what someone wishes if he chooses incorrectly is not an object of wish
at all. For if it is an object of wish, then <on this view> it is good; but
what he wishes is in fact bad, if it turns out that / way. <Hence what   20
he wishes is not an object of wish.>

§3 But for those who say the apparent good is <the> object of
wish, it follows that nothing is by nature an object of wish. Rather, for
each person <the object of wish> is what seems <good to him>; but
different things, and indeed contrary things, if it turns out that way,
appear good to different people.[2]

§4 If, then, these views do not satisfy us, should we say that, without qualification and in reality, <the> object of wish is the good, but
for each person it is the apparent good? / For the excellent person,   25
then, it is the <object of wish> in reality, but for the base person it
is whatever it turns out to be <that appears good to him>. Similarly
in the case of bodies, really healthy things are healthy to people in
good condition, while other things are healthy to sickly people; and
the same is true of what is bitter, sweet, hot, heavy, and so on.[3] / For   30
the excellent person judges each sort of thing correctly, and in each
case what is true appears to him.

§5 For each state <of character> has its own distinctive <view of>
fine and pleasant things. Presumably, then, the excellent person is
far superior because he sees what is true in each case, being himself a sort of standard and measure.[4] In the many, however, pleasure would seem to cause deception, / since it appears good when   1113b
it is not. §6 They choose what is pleasant, therefore, because they
assume it is good, and avoid pain because they assume it is evil.

5

[Virtue and vice are in our power]

[c7] We have found[1] that we wish for the end, and deliberate and
decide on the means to it; hence the actions / concerned with these   5
<means to the end> are in accord with decision and are voluntary.

The activities of the virtues are concerned with these <means to the end>.²

§2 Hence virtue is also up to us, and so also, in the same way, is vice. For when acting is up to us, so is not acting, and when no is up to us, so is yes. And so if acting, when it is fine, is up to us, not acting,
10 when it is shameful, is also up / to us; and if not acting, when it is fine, is up to us, then acting, when it is shameful, is also up to us. §3 But if doing, and likewise not doing, fine or shameful actions is up to us, and if, as we saw, <doing or not doing them> is <what it is> to be a good or bad person, being decent or base is up to us.³

15 §4 /The claim that 'no one is willingly bad or unwillingly blessed'⁴ would seem to be partly true but partly false. For while certainly no one is unwillingly blessed, vice is voluntary.

§5 If this is not so, we must dispute what has been said, and we must deny that a human being is a principle, begetting actions as
20 he begets children. §6 But if what we have said appears true, / and we cannot refer back to other principles apart from those that are up to us,⁵ those things that have their principle in us are themselves up to us and voluntary.

§7 There would seem to be evidence in favour of our view not only in what each of us does as a private citizen, but also in what legislators themselves do. For they impose corrective treatments and penalties
25 on anyone who does vicious / actions, unless his action is forced or is caused by ignorance that he is not responsible for;⁶ and they honour anyone who does fine actions. In all this they assume that they will encourage the second sort of person, and restrain the first. But no one encourages us to do anything that is not up to us and voluntary; people assume it is pointless to persuade us not to get hot or distressed or hungry or anything else of that sort, since persuasion will not stop it happening to us.

30 §8 / Indeed, legislators also impose corrective treatments for the ignorance itself, if the agent seems to be responsible for the ignorance.⁷ A drunk, for instance, pays a double penalty; for the principle is in him, since he controls whether he gets drunk, and his getting drunk causes his ignorance.⁸ They also impose corrective treatment on someone who <does a vicious action> in ignorance of some provision of law that he is required to know and that is not hard <to
1114a know>. §9 / And they impose it in other cases likewise for any other ignorance that seems to be caused by the agent's inattention; they

assume it is up to him not to be ignorant, since he controls whether he pays attention.

§10 But presumably he is the sort of person who is inattentive.[9] Still, he is himself responsible for becoming this sort of person, because he has lived / carelessly. Similarly, an individual is   5 responsible for being unjust, because he has cheated, and for being intemperate, because he has passed his time in drinking and the like; for each type of activity produces the corresponding sort of person.[10] §11 This is clear from those who train for any contest or action, since they continually practise the appropriate activities. §12 / <Only> a totally insensible person would not know   10 that a given type of activity is the source of the corresponding state. {{ / §13 <Hence> if someone does what he knows will make him   12 unjust, / he is willingly unjust.[11] }}   13

/ Further, it is unreasonable for someone doing injustice not to   11 / wish to be unjust, or for someone doing intemperate action not to   12 / wish to be intemperate.[12] §13 [[<Hence ... unjust.]] §14 This   13 does not mean, however, that if he is unjust and wishes to stop, he will thereby stop and be just.[13] / For neither does a sick person recover his   15 health <simply by wishing>. And if it turned out that way, he is sick willingly, by living incontinently and disobeying the doctors.[14] At that time, then, he was free not to be sick, though no longer free once he has let himself go, just as it was up to someone to throw a stone, since the principle was up to him,[15] though he can no longer take it back once he has thrown it. / Similarly, then, the person who is unjust or   20 intemperate was originally free not to acquire this character, so that he has it willingly, though once he has acquired the character, he is no longer free not to have it.[16]

§15 It is not only vices of the soul that are voluntary. Vices of the body are also voluntary for some people, and we actually censure them. For we never censure someone if nature causes his ugliness; but if his lack of training or attention / causes it, we do censure him.   25 The same is true for weakness or maiming; for everyone would pity someone, not reproach him, if he were blind by nature or because of a disease or a wound, but would censure him if his heavy drinking or some other form of intemperance made him blind. §16 Hence bodily vices that are up to us are censured, while / those not up to us   30 are not censured. If so, then in the other cases also the vices that are censured will be up to us.

1114b   §17 But someone may say that everyone aims at the apparent / good, and does not control how it appears, but, on the contrary, his character controls how the end appears to him.[17] <We reply that> if each person is in some way responsible for his own state <of character>, he is also himself in some way responsible for how <the end> appears.[18]

5   Suppose, on the other hand, that no one[19] is responsible for acting badly, but one does so because one is ignorant of the / end, and thinks this is the way to gain what is best for oneself. In that case, one's aiming at the end is not one's own choice; one needs a sort of natural, inborn sense of sight to judge finely and to choose what is really good. Whoever by nature has this sense in a fine condition has a good nature; for <according to this view> this sense is the greatest and finest thing, given that one cannot acquire it or learn it from another, but

10   its natural / character determines <one's> later condition, and when it is naturally good and fine, that is true and complete good nature.[20] If all this is true, then, surely virtue will be no more voluntary than

15   vice.[21]   §18 For how the end appears is laid down, by / nature or in whatever way, for the good and the bad person alike; they trace all the other things back to the end in doing whatever actions they do.

           §19 Let us suppose, then, that nature does not make the end appear however it appears to each person, but something also depends on him.[22] Alternatively, let us suppose that <how> the end <appears> is natural, but virtue is voluntary because the virtuous person does the

20   other things voluntarily.[23] In either / case, vice will be no less voluntary than virtue; for the bad person, no less than the good, is responsible for his own actions, even if not for <how> the end <appears>.[24]

           §20 Now the virtues, as we say, are voluntary. For in fact we are ourselves in a way jointly responsible for our states of character, and the sort of character we have determines the sort of end we lay down.[25]

25   Hence the vices will / also be voluntary, since the same is true of them.

           §21 [c8] We have now discussed the virtues in common. We have described their genus in outline; they are means, and they are states. Certain actions produce them, and they cause us to do these same actions in accord with the virtues themselves. They are up to us and voluntary, and in the way that correct reason prescribes.[26]

30   §22 / But actions and states are not voluntary in the same way. For we are in control of actions from the beginning to the end, when we know

1115a   the particulars. With states, however, / we are in control of the beginning,

46

but do not know, any more than with sicknesses, what the cumulative effect of particular actions will be. Nonetheless, since it was up to us to exercise a capacity either this way or another way, states are voluntary.[27]

[The individual virtues of character]

§23 [c9] Let us now take up the virtues again, and discuss them one by one. Let us say what they are, / what sorts of thing they are concerned with, and how they are concerned with them. It will also be clear at the same time how many of them there are.[28]

6
[Bravery: its scope]

First let us discuss bravery. We have already made it apparent that there is a mean about feelings of fear and confidence.[1] §2 What we fear, clearly, is what is frightening,[2] and such things are, speaking without qualification, bad things; hence people define fear as expectation of something bad.[3]

§3 / Certainly we fear all bad things—for instance, bad reputation, poverty, sickness, friendlessness, death—but they do not all seem to concern the brave person. For fear of some bad things, such as bad reputation, is actually right and fine, and lack of fear is shameful; for if someone fears bad reputation, he is decent and properly prone to shame, and if he has no fear of it, he has no feeling of disgrace. Some, however, / call this fearless person brave, by a transference of the name; for he has some similarity to the brave person, since the brave person is also a type of fearless person.

§4 Presumably it is wrong to fear poverty or sickness or, in general, <bad things> that are not the results of vice or caused by ourselves; still, someone who is fearless about these is not thereby brave. He is also called brave by similarity; / for some people who are cowardly in the dangers of war are nonetheless generous, and face with confidence the <danger of> losing money.[4]

§5 Again, if someone is afraid of committing wanton aggression on children or women,[5] or of being envious or anything of that sort, that does not make him cowardly. And if someone is confident when he is going to be whipped for his crimes, that does not make him brave.

§6 / Then what sorts of frightening conditions concern the brave person? Surely the most frightening; for no one stands firmer against

terrifying conditions. Now death is most frightening of all, since it is a
boundary, and when someone is dead nothing beyond it seems either
good or bad for him any more.   §7 Still, not even death in all conditions—on the sea, for instance, or in sickness, seems to be the brave
person's concern.

30   §8 In what conditions, then, is death his concern? Surely in / the
finest conditions. Now such deaths are those in war, since they occur
in the greatest and finest danger.[6]   §9 This judgment is endorsed
by the honours given in cities and by monarchs.   §10 Hence someone is called fully brave if he is intrepid in facing a fine death and the
35   immediate / dangers that bring death. And this is above all true of the
dangers of war.

1115b   §11 / Certainly the brave person is also intrepid on the sea and in
sickness, but not in the same way as seafarers are. For he has given up
hope of safety, and objects to this sort of death <with nothing fine in
it>, but seafarers' experience makes them hopeful.   §12 Moreover,
5   we act like brave men on occasions / when we can use our strength,
or when it is fine to be killed; and neither of these is true when we
perish on the sea.

7

[Bravery: its characteristic outlook]

[c10] Now what is frightening is not the same for everyone. We say,
however, that some things are too frightening for a human being to
resist;[1] these, then, are frightening for everyone, at least for everyone
with any sense. What is frightening, but not irresistible for a human
10   being, varies in / its seriousness and degree; and the same is true of
what inspires confidence.

     §2 The brave person is unperturbed, as far as a human being can
be. Hence, though he will fear even the sorts of things that are not irresistible, he will stand firm against them, in the right way, as reason prescribes, for the sake of the fine, since this is the end aimed at by virtue.[2]

     §3 It is possible to be more or less afraid of these frightening
15   things, and also possible to be afraid of what is not frightening / as
though it were frightening.   §4 The cause of error may be fear of the
wrong thing, or in the wrong way, or at the wrong time, or something
of that sort; and the same is true for things that inspire confidence.

     §5 Hence whoever stands firm against the right things and fears
the right things, for the right end, in the right way, at the right time,

and is correspondingly confident, is the brave person; for the brave person's actions and feelings accord with what something is worth, and follow what reason prescribes.

§6 / Every activity aims at actions in accord with the state of char-   20
acter. Now to the brave person bravery is fine; hence the end it aims at is also fine, since each thing is defined by its end.[3] The brave person, then, aims at the fine when he stands firm and acts in accord with bravery.

§7 Among those who go to excess / the excessively fearless per-   25
son has no name—we said earlier that many cases have no names.[4] He would be some sort of madman, or incapable of feeling distress, if he feared nothing, neither earthquake nor waves, as they say about the Celts.[5]

The person who is excessively confident about frightening things is rash. §8 The rash person also seems to be a boaster, / and a pre-   30
tender to bravery.[6] At any rate, the attitude to frightening things that the brave person really has is the attitude that the rash person wants to appear to have; hence he imitates the brave person where he can. §9 That is why most of them are also rash cowards; for, rash though they are on these <occasions for imitation>, they do not stand firm against anything frightening. {{ §12 / Moreover, rash people are   1116a7
impetuous, / and wish for dangers before they arrive, but shrink from   8
them / when they come. Brave people, on the contrary, are eager   9
when in action, but keep quiet until then.[7] }}

§10 / The person who is excessively afraid is the coward, since   1115b34
/ he fears the wrong things, and in the wrong way, and so on.   35
/ Certainly, he is also deficient in confidence, but his excessive pain   1116a
distinguishes him more clearly. §11 Hence, since he is afraid of everything, he is a despairing sort. The brave person, on the contrary, is hopeful, since <he is confident and> confidence is proper to a hopeful person.

§12 / Hence the coward, the rash person, and the brave person are   5
all concerned with the same things, but have different states related to them; the others are excessive or defective, / but the brave person has   7
the intermediate and right state. [[Moreover, ... until then.]]

§13 [c11] / As we have said, then, bravery is a mean about what   10
inspires confidence and about what is frightening in the conditions we have described; it chooses and stands firm because that is fine or

because anything else is shameful. Dying to avoid poverty or erotic passion or something painful is proper to a coward, not to a brave person. For shirking / burdens is softness, and such a person stands firm <in the face of death> to avoid an evil, not because standing firm is fine.[8]

8

[Conditions that resemble bravery]

Bravery, then, is something of this sort. But five other sorts of things are also called bravery.[1]

The bravery of citizens comes first, since it looks most like bravery. For citizens seem to stand firm against dangers with the aim of avoiding reproaches and legal penalties and / of winning honours; that is why the bravest seem to be those who hold cowards in dishonour and do honour to brave people.   §2 That is how Homer also describes them when he speaks of Diomede and Hector: 'Polydamas will be the first to heap disgrace on me', and / 'For sometime Hector speaking among the Trojans will say, "The son of Tydeus fled from me."'[2]   §3 This is most like the <genuine> bravery described above, because it results from a virtue; for it is caused by shame and by desire for something fine, namely honour,[3] and by aversion from reproach, which is shameful.

§4 / In this class we might also place those who are compelled by their superiors. However, they are worse to the extent that they act because of fear, not because of shame, and to avoid pain, not disgrace. For their commanders compel them, as Hector does: 'If I / notice anyone shrinking back from the battle, nothing will save him from being eaten by the dogs.'[4]   §5 Commanders who strike any / troops who give ground, or who post them in front of ditches and suchlike, do the same thing, since they all compel them.[5] The brave person, however, must be moved by the fine, not by compulsion.

§6 Experience about a given situation also seems to be bravery; / that is why Socrates actually thought that bravery is scientific knowledge.[6] Different people have this sort <of apparent courage> in different conditions. In wartime <professional> soldiers have it. For there seem to be many groundless alarms in war, and the professionals are the most familiar with these;[7] hence they appear brave, since others do not know that the alarms are groundless.   §7 Moreover, their experience makes them most capable in / attack and defence,

50

since they are skilled in the use of their weapons, and have the best weapons for attack and defence.   §8 The result is that in fighting non-professionals they are like armed troops against unarmed, or trained athletes against ordinary people; for in these contests also the best fighters are the strongest and physically fittest, not / the bravest.   15

§9 <Professional> soldiers, however, turn out to be cowards whenever the danger overstrains them[8] and they are inferior in numbers and equipment. For they are the first to run, but the citizen troops stand firm and get killed; this was what happened at the temple of Hermes.[9] For the citizens find it / shameful to run, and find   20 death more choiceworthy than safety at this cost. But the <professionals> from the start were facing the danger on the assumption of their superiority; once they learn their mistake, they run, since they are more afraid of being killed than of doing something shameful. That is not the brave person's character.

§10 Spirit is also counted as bravery; for those who act on /   25 spirit also seem to be brave—as beasts seem to be when they attack those who have wounded them—because brave people are also full of spirit.[10] For spirit is most eager to run and face dangers; hence Homer's words, 'put strength in his spirit', 'aroused strength and spirit', and 'his blood / boiled'.[11] All these would seem to signify the   30 arousal and the impulse of spirit.

§11 Now brave people act because of the fine, and their spirit co-operates with them. But beasts act because of pain; for they attack only because they have been wounded or frightened (since they keep away from us in a forest). They are not brave, then, since distress and spirit drives / them in an impulsive rush to meet danger, foresee-   35 ing none of the terrifying prospects. For if they were brave, hungry /   1117a asses would also be brave, since they keep on feeding even if they are beaten;[12] and adulterers also do many daring actions because of lust. [[The <bravery> ... the goal.]]

§12 / Human beings as well as beasts find it painful to be angered,   5 and pleasant to exact a penalty. But those who fight for these reasons are not brave, though they are good fighters; for they fight because of their feelings, not because of the fine nor as reason prescribes. Still, they have something similar <to bravery>. / {{ The <bravery> caused   4 by spirit would seem to be the most natural sort, and to be / <genuine>   5 bravery once it has also acquired decision and the goal.[13] }}

9 §13 / Hopeful people are not brave either; for their many
10 / victories over many opponents make them confident in dangers.
They are somewhat similar to brave people, since both sorts are confident. But whereas brave people are confident for the reason given
earlier, the hopeful are confident because they think they are stron-
15 ger and nothing could happen to / them; §14 drunks do the same
sort of thing, since they become hopeful. When things turn out differently from how they expected, they run away. The brave person,
on the contrary, stands firm against what is and appears frightening
to a human being; he does this because it is fine to stand firm and
shameful to fail.

§15 Indeed, that is why someone who is unafraid and unperturbed
in emergencies seems braver than <someone who is unafraid only>
20 when he is warned in advance; for / his action proceeds more from
his state of character, because it proceeds less from preparation.¹⁴ For
if we are warned in advance, we might decide what to do <not only
because of our state of character, but> also by reason and rational
calculation; but in emergencies <we must decide> in accord with our
state of character.¹⁵

§16 Those who act in ignorance also appear brave, and indeed
they are close to hopeful people, though inferior to them insofar as
25 they lack the self-esteem of hopeful people. / That is why the hopeful stand firm for some time, whereas if ignorant people have been
deceived and then realize or suspect that things are different, they
run. That was what happened to the Argives when they stumbled on
the Spartans and took them for Sicyonians.¹⁶

§17 We have described, then, the character of brave people and of
those who seem to be brave.

9

[Feelings proper to bravery]

30 [c12] / Bravery is about feelings of confidence and fear—not, however, about both in the same way, but more about frightening things.
For someone is brave if he is undisturbed and in the right state about
these, more than if he is in this state about things inspiring confidence.

§2 As we said, then, standing firm against what is painful makes
us call people brave; that is why bravery is both painful and justly
35 praised, since / it is harder to stand firm against something painful
1117b than to refrain from something pleasant. §3 / Nonetheless, the end

that bravery aims at seems to be pleasant, though obscured by its surroundings. This is what happens in athletic contests. For boxers find that the end they aim at, the crown and the honours, is pleasant, but, being / made of flesh and blood, they find it distressing and painful to 5 take the punches and to bear all the hard work; and because there are so many of these painful things, the end, being small, appears to have nothing pleasant in it.

§4 And so, if the same is true for bravery, the brave person will find death and wounds painful, and suffer them unwillingly, but he will endure them because that is fine or because failure is shameful.[1] / Indeed, the truer it is that he has every virtue and the happier he is, 10 the more pain he will feel at the prospect of death. For this sort of person, more than anyone, finds it worthwhile to be alive, and knows he is being deprived of the greatest goods, and this is painful. But he is no less brave for all that; presumably, indeed, he is all the braver, because he / chooses what is fine in war at the cost of all these goods.   §5 It 15 is not true, then, in the case of every virtue that its active exercise is pleasant; it is pleasant only insofar as we attain the end.

§6 But presumably it is quite possible for brave people, given the character we have described, not to be the best <professional> soldiers.[2] Perhaps the best will be those who are less brave, but possess no other good; for they are ready to face / dangers, and they sell their 20 lives for small gains.

§7 So much for bravery. It is easy to grasp what it is, in outline at least, from what we have said.

10
[Temperance: its scope]

[c13] Let us discuss temperance next; for bravery and temperance seem to be the virtues of the non-rational parts.[1] / Temperance, then, 25 is a mean concerned with pleasures, as we have already said; for it is concerned less, and in a different way, with pains. Intemperance appears in this same area too. Let us, then, now distinguish the specific pleasures that concern them.

§2 First, let us distinguish pleasures of the soul from those of the body. Love of honour and of learning, for instance, are among the pleasures of the soul; for though a lover of one of / these enjoys it, 30 only his thought, not his body, is at all affected. Those concerned with such pleasures are called neither temperate nor intemperate. The

same applies to those concerned with any of the other non-bodily
35   pleasures; / for lovers of tales, storytellers, those who waste their days
1118a on trivialities, are called babblers, but not intemperate. Nor / do we
call people intemperate if they feel pain over money or friends.

§3 Temperance, then, will be about bodily pleasures, but not
even about all of these. For those who find enjoyment in objects of
5   sight, such as colours, shapes, a painting, are / called neither temperate nor intemperate, even though it would also seem possible to
enjoy these either rightly or excessively and deficiently.   §4 The
same is true for hearing; no one is ever called intemperate for excessive enjoyment of songs or playacting, or temperate for the right
enjoyment of them.

10   §5 Nor is this said about someone enjoying smells, except / coincidentally.[2] For someone is called intemperate not for enjoying the
smell of apples or roses or incense, but rather for enjoying the smell
of perfumes or cooked delicacies. For these are the smells an intemperate person enjoys because they remind him of the objects of his
15   appetite.[3]   §6 And / we can see that others also enjoy the smells of
food if they are hungry.[4] It is the enjoyment of the things <that he is
reminded of by these smells> that is proper to an intemperate person,
since these are the objects of his appetite.

§7 Nor do other animals find pleasures from these senses, except
20   coincidentally. What a / hound enjoys, for instance, is not the smell of
a hare, but eating it; but the hare's smell made the hound perceive it.
And what a lion enjoys is not the sound of the ox, but eating it; but
since the ox's sound made the lion perceive that it was near, the lion
appears to enjoy the sound. Similarly, what pleases him is not the
sight of 'a deer or a wild goat',[5] but the prospect of food.

25   §8 The pleasures that concern temperance and intemperance / are
those that are shared with the other animals, and so appear slavish
and bestial.[6] These pleasures are touch and taste.[7]

§9 However, they seem to deal even with taste very little or not at
all. For taste discriminates flavours—the sort of thing that wine tast-
30   ers and cooks savouring food do; but / people, or intemperate people
at any rate, do not much enjoy this. Rather, they enjoy the gratification that comes entirely through touch, in eating and drinking and in
what are called the pleasures of sex.   §10 That is why a glutton actu-
1118b ally prayed for his throat to become longer than a crane's, showing /
that he took pleasure in the touching.[8] And so the sense that concerns

54

intemperance is the most widely shared, and seems justifiably open to reproach, since we have it insofar as we are animals, not insofar as we are human beings.

§11 To enjoy these things, then, and to like them most of all is bestial. For indeed the most civilized / of the pleasures coming through 5 touch, such as those produced by rubbing and warming in gymnasia, are excluded from intemperance, since the touching that is proper to the intemperate person concerns only some parts of the body, not all of it.

11
[Temperance: its outlook]

Some appetites seem to be shared <by everyone>, while others seem to be additions that are distinctive <of different people>. / The appe- 10 tite for nourishment, for instance, is natural, since everyone who lacks nourishment, dry or liquid, has an appetite for it, sometimes for both; and, as Homer says, the young in their prime <all> have an appetite for sex.[1] Not everyone, however, has an appetite for a specific sort of food or drink or sex, or for the same things. §2 That is why an appetite of this type seems to be distinctive of <each of> us. Still, this also includes a natural element, since different sorts of people find different sorts of things pleasanter, and there are some things that are pleasanter for everyone than things chosen at random would be.

§3 / In natural appetites few people are in error, and only in one 15 direction, towards excess. Eating indiscriminately or drinking until we are too full is exceeding the quantity that accords with nature; for <the object of> natural appetite is the filling of a lack. That is why these people are called 'gluttons', / showing that they glut their bel- 20 lies past what is right;[2] that is how especially slavish people turn out.

§4 With the pleasures that are distinctive of different people, many make errors and in many ways; for people are called lovers of something if they enjoy the wrong things, or if they enjoy something in the wrong way. And in all these / ways intemperate people go to excess. 25 For some of the things they enjoy are hateful, and hence wrong; distinctive pleasures that it is right to enjoy they enjoy more than is right, and more than most people enjoy them.

§5 Clearly, then, with pleasures excess is intemperance, and is blameworthy. With pains, however, we are not called temperate, as we are called brave, for standing firm against / them, or intemperate for 30 not standing firm. Rather, someone is intemperate because he feels more pain than is right at failing to get pleasant things; and even this pain is produced by the pleasure <he takes in them>. And someone is temperate because he does not feel pain at the absence of what is pleasant, or at refraining from it.

1119a §6 [c14] / The intemperate person, then, has an appetite for all pleasant things, or rather for the pleasantest of them, and his appetite leads him to choose these at the cost of the other things. That is why he also feels pain both when he fails to get something and when
5 he has an appetite for it, since appetite / involves pain. It would seem absurd, however, to suffer pain because of pleasure.

§7 People who are deficient in pleasures and enjoy them less than is right are not found very much. For that sort of insensibility is not human; indeed, even the other animals discriminate among foods, enjoying some but not others. If someone finds nothing pleasant, or
10 preferable to anything / else, he is far from being human. The reason he has no name is that he is not found much.

§8 The temperate person has an intermediate state in relation to these <bodily pleasures>. For he finds no pleasure in what most pleases the intemperate person, but finds it disagreeable; he finds no pleasure at all in the wrong things. He finds no intense pleasure in any <bodily pleasures>, suffers no pain at their absence, and has no appe-
15 tite for them, or / only a moderate appetite, not to the wrong degree or at the wrong time or anything else at all of that sort.[3] If something is pleasant and conducive to health or fitness, he will desire this moderately and in the right way; and he will desire in the same way anything else that is pleasant, if it is no obstacle to health and fitness, does not deviate from the fine, and does not exceed his means. For
20 the opposite sort of person likes these pleasures more / than they are worth; that is not the temperate person's character, but he likes them as correct reason prescribes.

12
[Intemperance]

[c15] Intemperance is more like a voluntary condition than cowardice; for it is caused by pleasure, which is choiceworthy, whereas cowardice is caused by pain, which is to be avoided.[1] §2 Moreover, pain disturbs and ruins the nature of the sufferer, while pleasure does

nothing of the sort; intemperance, / then, is more voluntary. That is   25
why it is also more open to reproach. For it is also easier to acquire
the habit of facing pleasant things, since our life includes many of
them and we can acquire the habit with no danger; but with frightening things the reverse is true.

§3 However, cowardice seems to be more voluntary than particular
cowardly actions. For cowardice itself involves no pain, but the particular actions disturb us because of the pain / <that causes them>,   30
so that people actually throw away their weapons and do all the other
disgraceful actions. That is why these actions even seem to be forced
<and hence involuntary>.²

§4 For the intemperate person the reverse is true. The particular
actions are the result of his appetite and desire, and so they are voluntary; but the whole condition is less voluntary <than the actions>,
since no one has an appetite to be intemperate.

§5 We also apply the name of intemperance to the errors of / chil-   1119b
dren, since they have some similarity.³ Which gets its name from
which does not matter for our present purposes, but clearly the posterior is called after the prior.

§6 The name would seem to be quite appropriately transferred.
For the things that need to be tempered are those that desire shameful / things and tend to grow large. Appetites and children are most   5
like this; for children also live by appetite, and desire for the pleasant
is found more in them than in anyone else.

§7 If, then, <the child or the appetitive part> is not obedient and
subordinate to its rulers, it will go far astray. For when someone lacks
understanding, his desire for the pleasant is insatiable and seeks
indiscriminate satisfaction. The <repeated> active exercise of appetite increases the appetite / he already had from birth, and if the appe-   10
tites are large and intense, they actually expel rational calculation.
That is why appetites must be moderate and few, and never contrary
to reason.   §8 This is the condition we call obedient and temperate.
And just as the child's life must follow the instructions of his guide,
so too the appetitive part must / follow reason.⁴   15

§9 Hence the temperate person's appetitive part must agree with
reason; for both <his appetitive part and his reason> aim at the fine,
and the temperate person's appetites are for the right things, in the
right ways, at the right times, which is just what reason also prescribes.
So much, then, for temperance.

Book IV

1

[Generosity]

Next let us discuss generosity. It seems, then, to be the mean about wealth; for the generous person is praised not in conditions of war, nor in those in which the temperate / person is praised, nor in judicial verdicts, but in the giving and taking of wealth, and more especially in the giving.[1] §2 By wealth we mean anything whose worth is measured by money.

§3 Both wastefulness and ungenerosity are excesses and deficiencies about wealth. Ungenerosity is always / ascribed to those who take wealth more seriously than is right. But when wastefulness is attributed to someone, several vices are sometimes combined. For incontinent people and those who spend money on intemperance are called wasteful. §4 That is why wasteful people seem the basest— for these people have many vices at the same time, they make wasteful people seem the basest. These people, however, are not properly called wasteful.[2] §5 For the wasteful person is meant to have the single / vicious feature of ruining his property; for someone who causes his own destruction <'lays waste' to himself, and so> is wasteful, and ruining one's own property seems to be a sort of self-destruction, on the assumption that our living depends on our property. This, then, is how we understand wastefulness.

§6 / Whatever has a use can be used either well or badly; riches are something useful; and the best user of something is the person who has the virtue concerned with it. Hence the best user of riches will be the person who has the virtue concerned with wealth; and this is the generous person.[3]

§7 Using wealth seems to consist in spending and giving, whereas taking and keeping seem to be possessing rather / than using. That is why it is more proper to the generous person to give to the right people than to take from the right sources and not from the wrong sources.[4]

For it is more proper to virtue to do good than to receive good, and more proper to do fine actions than not to do shameful ones;[5] §8 and clearly <the right sort of> giving implies doing good and doing fine actions, / while <the right sort of> taking implies receiving well or not doing something shameful. Moreover, thanks go to the one who gives, not to the one who fails to take, and praise goes more <to the giver>.   §9 Besides, not taking is easier than giving, since people part with what is their own less readily than they avoid taking what is another's.   §10 / Further, those who are called generous are those who give <rightly>. Those who avoid taking <wrongly> are not praised for generosity, though they are praised nonetheless for justice, while those who take <rightly> are not much praised at all.   §11 Besides, generous people are loved more than practically any others who are loved because of their virtue; that is because they are beneficial; and they are beneficial in their giving.

§12 [c2] Actions in accord with virtue are fine, and aim at the fine. Hence the generous person will also / aim at the fine in his giving, and will give correctly;[6] for he will give to the right people, the right amounts, at the right time, and all the other things that are implied by correct giving.   §13 Moreover, he will do this with pleasure,[7] or at any rate without pain; for action in accord with virtue is pleasant or at any rate painless, and least of all is it painful.

§14 If someone gives to the wrong people, or does not aim at the fine, but gives for some other reason, he will not be called generous, but some other sort of person. Nor will he be called / generous if he finds it painful to give; for such a person would choose wealth over fine action, and that is not how the generous person chooses.

§15 Nor will the virtuous person take wealth from the wrong sources; since he does not honour wealth, this way of taking it is not for him.   §16 Nor will he be ready to ask for favours; since he is the one who benefits others, receiving benefits readily is not for him.[8]

§17 He will, however, acquire wealth from the right sources / — from his own possessions, for instance—regarding this not as fine, but as necessary to provide something to give. Nor will he neglect his own possessions, since he wants to use them to assist people. And he will avoid giving to just anyone, so that he will have something to give to the right people, at the right time, and where it is fine.

§18 It is also very definitely proper to the generous person to / exceed so much in giving that he leaves less for himself, since it is proper to a generous person not to look out for himself.   §19 In speaking of generosity, however, we refer to what accords with one's means. For what is generous does not depend on the quantity of what

20

25

30

1120b

5

is given, but on the state <of character> of the giver, and the generous state gives in accord with one's means. Hence one who gives less than
10　　another may still be more generous, if he / has less to give.[9]

§20 Those who have not acquired their means by their own efforts, but have inherited it, seem to be more generous; for they have had no experience of shortage, and, besides, everyone likes his own work more than <other people's>, as parents and poets do.[10]

15　　It is not easy for a generous person to grow rich, since he / is ready to spend, not to take or keep, and honours wealth for the sake of giving, not for itself.　§21 Indeed, that is why fortune is denounced, because those who most deserve to grow rich actually do so least. This is only to be expected, however, since someone cannot possess wealth, any more than other things, if he pays no attention to possessing it.

20　　§22 / Still, he does not give to the wrong people, at the wrong time, and so on. For if he did, he would no longer be acting in accord with generosity, and if he spent his resources on the wrong sort of giving, he would have nothing left to spend for the right purposes.　§23 For, as we have said, the generous person is the one who spends in accord with his means, and for the right purposes, whereas the one who exceeds his means is wasteful. That is why tyrants are not called
25　　wasteful, since it seems they / will have difficulty exceeding their possessions in giving and spending.

§24 Since generosity, then, is a mean concerned with the giving and the taking of wealth, the generous person will both give and spend
30　　the right amounts for the right purposes, in / small and large matters alike, and do this with pleasure. He will also take the right amounts from the right sources. For since the virtue is a mean about both giving and taking, he will do both in the right way; for decent giving implies decent taking, and the other sort of taking is contrary to the decent sort. Hence the states that imply each other are present at the
1121a　　same time in the same subject, whereas the contrary states / clearly are not.

§25 If the generous person finds that his spending deviates from what is fine and right, he will feel pain, but moderately and in the right way; for it is proper to virtue to feel both pleasure and pain in the right things and in the right way.[11]

§26 The generous person is also an easy partner to have common
5　　dealings / with matters of money;　§27 for he can easily be treated unjustly, since he does not honour money, and is more grieved if he

has failed to spend what it was right to spend than if he has spent what it was wrong to spend—here he does not please Simonides.[12]

§28 [c3] The wasteful person is in error here too, since he feels neither pleasure nor pain at the right things or in the right way; this will be more evident as we go on.

§29 / We have said, then, that wastefulness and ungenerosity are 10 excesses and deficiencies in two things, in giving and taking—for we also count spending as giving. Now wastefulness is excessive in giving and not taking, but deficient in taking. / Ungenerosity is deficient in 15 giving and excessive in taking, but in small matters.

§30 Now the different aspects of wastefulness are not very often combined; for it is not easy to take from nowhere and give to everyone, since private citizens soon outrun their resources in giving, and private citizens are the ones who seem to be wasteful. §31 However, such a person seems to be quite a lot / better than the ungen- 20 erous person, since he is easily cured, both by growing older and by poverty, and is capable of reaching the intermediate condition.[13] For he has the features proper to the generous person, since he gives and does not take, though he does neither rightly nor well. If, then, he is changed, by habituation or some other means, so that he does them rightly and well, he will be generous; for then he will / give to the 25 right people and will not take from the wrong sources. This is why the wasteful person seems not to be base in his character; for excess in giving without taking is proper to a foolish person, not to a vicious or ignoble one. §32 Someone who is wasteful in this way seems to be much better than the ungenerous person, both for the reasons just given and because he benefits many, whereas the ungenerous person benefits no one, not even himself.[14]

§33 / Most wasteful people, however, as we have said, <not only 30 give wrongly, but> also take from the wrong sources, and to this extent are ungenerous.[15] §34 They become acquisitive because they wish to spend, but cannot do this readily, since they soon exhaust all they have; hence they are compelled / to provide from elsewhere. At 1121b the same time they care nothing for the fine, and so take from any source without scruple; for they have an urge to give,[16] and the way or source does not matter to them.

§35 This is why their ways of giving are not generous either, since they are not fine, do not aim at the fine, and are / not done in the right way. 5

Rather, these people sometimes enrich people who ought to be poor, and would give nothing to people with sound characters, but would give much to flatterers or to those providing some other pleasure. That is why most of these people are also intemperate. For since they part with money readily, they also spend it lavishly on / intemperance; and because their lives do not aim at the fine, they decline towards pleasures.

§36 If, then, the wasteful person has been left without a guide, he changes into this;[17] but if he receives attention, he might reach the intermediate and the right state.

§37 Ungenerosity, however, is incurable,[18] since old age and every incapacity seem to make people ungenerous.[19] And it comes more naturally to human beings than wastefulness; / for the many are money-lovers rather than givers.   §38 Moreover, it extends widely and has many species, since there seem to be many ways of being ungenerous. For it consists in two conditions, deficiency in giving and excess in taking; but it is not found as a whole in all cases. Sometimes / the two conditions are separated, and some people go to excess in taking, whereas others are deficient in giving.

§39 For the people called misers, tightfisted, skinflints,[20] and so on, are all deficient in giving, but they do not go after other people's goods and do not wish to take them. With some people the reason for this is some sort of decency in them, and a concern to avoid what is shameful. For / some people seem—at least, this is what they say— to hold on to their money so that they will never be compelled to do anything shameful.[21] These include the cheeseparer, and everyone like that; he is so called from his excessive refusal to give anything. Others keep their hands off other people's property because they / are afraid,[22] supposing that it is not easy for them to take other people's property without other people taking theirs too; hence, they say, they are content[23] if they neither take from others nor give to them.

§40 Other people, by contrast, go to excess in taking, by taking anything from any source—those, for instance, who work at degrading occupations,[24] pimps and all such people, and usurers / who lend small amounts at high interest; for all of these take the wrong amounts from the wrong sources.

§41 Shameful love of gain is apparently their common feature, since they all put up with reproaches for some gain—more precisely, for a small gain.   §42 For those who take the wrong things from / the wrong sources on a large scale, such as tyrants who sack cities

and plunder temples, are called wicked, impious, and unjust, but not ungenerous. §43 The ungenerous, however, include the gambler and the robber,[25] since these are shameful lovers of gain. For in pursuit of gain both go to great efforts and put up with reproaches; / the   10
robber faces the greatest dangers to get his haul, while the gambler takes his gains from his friends, the very people he ought to be giving to. Both of them, then, are shameful lovers of gain, because they wish to acquire gains from the wrong sources; and all these methods of acquisition are ungenerous.

§44 It is plausibly said that ungenerosity is contrary to generosity. / For it is a greater evil than wastefulness; and error in this direction   15
is more common than the error of wastefulness, as we have described it. §45 So much, then, for generosity and the vices opposed to it.

2
[Magnificence]

[c4] Next in order, it seems appropriate to discuss magnificence as well <as generosity>. For it seems to be, like generosity, a virtue concerned with / wealth, but it does not extend, as generosity does, to   20
all the actions to do with wealth, but only to those to do with heavy expenses. In these it exceeds generosity in its large scale. For, just as the name <*megaloprepeia*> itself suggests, magnificence is expenditure that is fitting <*prepousa*> in its large scale <*megethos*>. §2 But large scale is large relative to something; for the expenses of the captain of a warship and of the / leader of a delegation are not the same.[1] Hence   25
what is fitting is also relative to oneself, the circumstances, and the purpose.

§3 Now someone is called magnificent only if he spends the worthy amount on a large purpose, not on a trivial or an ordinary purpose like the one who 'gave to many a wanderer';[2] for the magnificent person is generous, but generosity does not imply magnificence.[3]

§4 / The deficiency falling short of this state is called stinginess.   30
The excess is called vulgarity, poor taste, and such things. These are excesses not because they spend an excessively large amount on the right things, but because they show off in the wrong circumstances and in the wrong way.[4] We shall discuss these vices later.

§5 The magnificent person, in contrast to these, is like a scientific / expert, since he is able to observe what will be the fitting amount,   35
and to spend large amounts in an appropriate way. §6 / For, as we   1122b

63

said at the start, a state is defined by its activities and its objects; now the magnificent person's expenditures[5] are large and fitting; so also, then, must the results be, since that is what makes the expense large

5   and fitting to the result. Hence the result must be / worthy of the expense, and the expense worthy of, or even in excess of, the result.

§7 In this sort of spending the magnificent person will aim at the fine; for that is a common feature of the virtues.[6] §8 More-over, he will spend gladly and readily, since it is stingy to count every penny. §9 He will think more about the finest and most fitting way

10   to spend than about the / cost or about the cheapest way to do it.

§10 Hence the magnificent person must also be generous; for the generous person will also spend what is right in the right way. But it is in this spending that the large scale of the magnificent person, his greatness, is found, since his magnificence is a sort of large scale of generosity in these things; and from an expense that is equal <to a non-magnificent person's> he will make the result more magnificent.

15   / For a possession and a result have different sorts of excellence; the most honoured <and hence most excellent> possession is the one that is worth most, for example, gold, but the most honoured result is the one that is great and fine, since that is what is admirable to behold.[7] Now what is magnificent is admirable, and the excellence of the result consists in its large scale.[8]

20   §11 [c5] This sort of excellence is found in the expenses / that are called honourable, such as expenses for the gods—dedications, tem-ples, sacrifices, and so on, for everything divine—and in expenses that provoke a good competition for honour, for the common <good>,[9] if, for instance, some city thinks a splendid chorus or warship or a feast for the city must be provided.

25   §12 But in all cases, as we have said, we fix the right amount / by reference to the agent <as well as the task>—by who he is and what resources he has; for the amounts must be worthy of these, fitting the producer as well as the result.

§13 That is why a poor person could not be magnificent; he lacks the means for large and fitting expenditures. If he tries to be mag-nificent, he is foolish; for he spends more than what is worthy and

30   right for him, whereas correct spending accords with virtue. §14 / Large spending befits those who have the means, acquired through their own efforts or their ancestors or connexions, or are well-born or

reputable, and so on; for each of these conditions includes greatness and reputation for worth.

§15 This, then, above all is the character of the magnificent person, and magnificence is found in these sorts of expenses, as / we have said, since these are the largest and most honoured.   35

It is found also in those private expenses that arise only / once, 1123a such as a wedding and the like, and in those that concern the whole city, or the people in it with a reputation for worth—the receiving of foreign guests and sending them off, gifts and exchanges of gifts. For the magnificent person spends / money on the common <good>, not   5 on himself, and the gifts have some similarity to dedications.

§16 It is also proper to the magnificent person to build a house befitting his riches, since this is also a suitable adornment.[10] He spends more readily on long-lasting results, since these are the finest. In each case he spends on what is fitting.   §17 For / what suits gods does not   10 suit human beings, and what suits a temple does not suit a tomb.

. And since each great expense is great in relation to a particular kind of object, the most magnificent will be a great expense on a great object, and <what is magnificent> in a particular area will be what is great in relation to the particular kind of object.[11]   §18 Moreover, greatness in the results is not the same as greatness in the expense, since the finest ball / or oil bottle has the magnificence proper to a gift   15 for a child, but its value is small and paltry.[12]   §19 That is why it is proper to the magnificent person, in whatever area he produces some result, to produce it magnificently, since this is not easily exceeded, and to produce a result that is worthy of the expense.

§20 This, then, is the character of the magnificent person.

[c6] The vulgar person who exceeds <the mean> exceeds by /   20 spending more than is right, as has been said. For in small expenses he spends a lot, and puts on an inappropriate display. He gives his club a dinner party in the style of a wedding banquet,[13] and when he supplies a chorus for a comedy, he brings them onstage dressed in purple, as they do at / Megara.[14] In all this he aims not at the fine, but   25 at the display of his wealth and at the admiration he thinks he wins in this way. Where a large expense is right, he spends a little, and he spends a lot where a small expense is right.[15]

§21 The stingy person will be deficient in everything. After spending the largest amounts, he will refuse a small amount, and so destroy

30   a fine result. Whatever he does, while he is / doing it he will hesitate
and consider how he can spend the smallest possible amount; he will
even moan about spending this, and will always think he is doing
something on a larger scale than is right.

§22 These states, vulgarity and stinginess, are vices. But they do
not bring reproaches, since they do no harm to one's neighbours[16]
and are not too disgraceful.

3
[Magnanimity]

35   [c7] Magnanimity seems, even if we go simply by the name, to be /
1123b   concerned with great things.[1] Let us see first the sorts of things / it
is concerned with.   §2 It does not matter whether we consider the
state itself or the person who acts in accord with it.

§3 The magnanimous person, then, seems[2] to be the one who
thinks himself worthy[3] of great things and is really worthy of them. For
if someone is not worthy of them but thinks he is, he is foolish, and no
virtuous person is foolish or senseless; hence the magnanimous per-
5   son is the one we have mentioned. /   §4 For if someone is worthy of
little and thinks so, he is temperate, but not magnanimous;   §5 for
magnanimity is found in greatness, just as beauty is found in a large
body, and small people can be attractive and well-proportioned, but
not beautiful.[4]

§6 Someone who thinks he is worthy of great things, but is not
worthy of them, is vain; but not everyone who thinks he is worthy of
greater things than he is worthy of is vain.

10   /   §7 Someone who thinks he is worthy of less than he is worthy
of is pusillanimous,[5] whether he is worthy of great or of moderate
things, or of little and thinks himself worthy of still less. The one who
seems most pusillanimous is the one who is worthy of great things; for
consider how little he would think of himself if he were worthy of less.

§8 The magnanimous person, then, is at the extreme insofar as he
makes great claims. But insofar as he makes them rightly, he is inter-
15   mediate; for what he thinks he is worthy / of accords with his real
worth, whereas the others are excessive or deficient. {{ §12 The
pusillanimous person is deficient both in relation to himself <i.e., his
25   worth> / and in relation to the magnanimous person's estimate of his
own worth.   §13 The vain person makes claims that are excessive for
him, but not for the magnanimous person.[6] }}

§9 If, then, he thinks he is worthy of great things, and is worthy of them, especially of the greatest things, he has one concern above all. §10 Worth is said to <make one worthy of> external goods; and we would suppose that the greatest of these is the one we award to the gods, the one above all that is the aim of people with a reputation for worth, the prize for the finest / <achievements>. All this is true of honour, since it is the greatest of external goods. Hence the magnanimous person has the right concern with honours and dishonours. §11 And even without argument it appears that magnanimous people are concerned with honour; for the great think themselves worthy of honour most of all, but in accord with their worth.[7] [[§12–13 The pusillanimous … magnanimous person.]]

§14 Since the magnanimous person is worthy of the greatest things, he is the best person. For in every case the better person is worthy of something greater, and the best person is worthy of the greatest things; and hence the truly magnanimous person must be good.[8]

/ Greatness in each virtue also seems proper to the magnanimous person.[9] §15 Surely[10] it would not at all fit a magnanimous person to run away <from danger when a coward would>, swinging his arms <to get away faster>, or to do injustice. For what goal will make him do shameful actions, given that none <of their goals> is great to him? And if we examine particular cases, we can see that the magnanimous person appears altogether ridiculous if he is not good. / Nor would he be worthy of honour if he were base; for honour is the prize of virtue, and is awarded to good people.

§16 / Magnanimity, then, would seem to be a sort of adornment[11] of the virtues; for it makes them greater, and it does not arise without them. That is why it is difficult to be truly magnanimous, since it is not possible without being fine and good.

§17 / The magnanimous person, then, is concerned especially with honours and dishonours.[12] When he receives great honours from excellent people, he will be moderately pleased, thinking he is getting what is proper to him, or even less. For there can be no honour worthy of complete virtue; but still he will accept honours <from excellent people>, since they have nothing greater to award him. / But if he is honoured by just anyone, or for something small, he will altogether make light[13] of it; for that is not what he is worthy of. And similarly he will make light of dishonour; for it will not be justly attached to him.

§18 As we have said, then, the magnanimous person is concerned especially with honours. Still, he will also have a moderate attitude to riches and power and every sort of good / and bad fortune, however it turns out. He will be neither excessively pleased by good fortune nor excessively distressed by ill fortune, since he does not even regard honour as the greatest good. For positions of power and riches are choiceworthy for their honour—at any rate their possessors wish to be honoured on account of them—but the one who counts honour for little will also count these other goods for / little; that is why he seems arrogant.[14]

§19 [c8] The results of good fortune, however, also seem to contribute to magnanimity. For the well-born and the powerful or rich are thought worthy of honour, since they are in a superior position, and everything superior in some good is more honoured. That is why these things also make people more magnanimous, since some people honour their possessors for these goods.[15] / In reality only the good person is honourable, §20 but anyone who has both virtue and these goods is more readily thought worthy of honour.

Those who lack virtue but have these other goods are not justified in thinking themselves worthy of great things, and are not correctly called magnanimous; that is impossible without complete virtue. §21 They become arrogant and / wantonly aggressive when they have these other goods.[16] For without virtue it is difficult to bear the results of good fortune / suitably, and when these people cannot do it, but suppose they are superior to other people, they think less of everyone else, and do whatever they please. They do this because they are imitating the magnanimous person though they are not really like him. They imitate him where they can; hence they do not act in accord with virtue, / but they think less of other people. §22 For the magnanimous person is justified whenever he thinks less of others, since his beliefs are true; but the many think less of others with no good reason.[17]

§23 He does not face dangers in a small cause; he does not face them frequently, since he honours few things; and he is no lover of danger.[18] But he faces dangers in a great cause, and whenever he faces them he is unsparing of his life, since he does not think life is worth living at all costs.

§24 / He is the sort of person who does good but is ashamed when   10
he receives it; for doing good is proper to the superior person, but
receiving it is proper to the inferior.[19] He returns more good than he
has received; for in this way the original giver will be repaid, and will
also have incurred a new debt to him, and will be the beneficiary.

§25 Magnanimous people seem to remember the good they do, but
not what they receive, since the recipient is inferior to the giver, and the
magnanimous person wishes to be superior. / And they seem to find   15
pleasure in hearing of the good they do, and none in hearing of what
they receive—that also seems to be why Thetis does not tell Zeus of the
good she has done him,[20] and the Spartans do not tell of the good they
have done the Athenians, but only of the good received from them.[21]

§26 Again, it is proper to the magnanimous person to ask for nothing, or hardly anything, but to help eagerly.

When he meets people with good fortune or a reputation / for worth,   20
he displays his greatness,[22] since superiority over them is difficult and
impressive, and there is nothing ignoble in trying to be impressive
with them. But when he meets ordinary people[23] he is moderate, since
superiority over them is easy, and an attempt to be impressive among
inferiors is as vulgar as a display of strength against the weak.

§27 He stays away from what is commonly honoured, and from
areas where others lead; he is inactive and a delayer, except / for   25
some great honour or achievement. His actions are few, but great and
renowned.[24]

§28 Moreover, he must be open in his hatreds and his friendships,
since concealment is proper to a frightened person.[25] He is concerned
for the truth[26] more than for people's opinion. He is open in his speech
and actions, since his thinking less of other people makes / him speak   30
freely. And he speaks the truth, except <when he speaks less than
the truth> to the many, <because he is moderate>, not because he is
self-deprecating.[27]

§29 / He cannot let anyone else, except a friend, determine his life.   1125a
For that would be slavish; and this is why all flatterers are servile and
inferior people are flatterers.[28]

§30 He is not prone to marvel, since he finds nothing great, or to
remember evils, since it is proper to a magnanimous person not to
nurse memories, especially not of evils, but to / overlook them.   5

§31 He is no gossip. For he will not talk about himself or about
another, since he is not concerned to have himself praised or other

people blamed. Nor is he given to praising people. Hence he does not speak evil even of his enemies, except <when he responds to their> wanton aggression.²⁹

10 §32 / He especially avoids laments or entreaties about necessities or small matters, since these attitudes are proper to someone who takes these things seriously.

§33 He is the sort of person whose possessions are fine and unproductive rather than productive and advantageous, since that is more proper to a self-sufficient person.

§34 The magnanimous person seems to have slow movements, a deep voice and calm speech. For since he takes few things seriously,
15 he is in no hurry, and since he counts nothing great, / he is not strident; and these <attitudes he avoids> are the causes of a shrill voice and hasty movements.³⁰

[c9] This, then, is the character of the magnanimous person. §35 The deficient person is pusillanimous, and the person who goes to excess is vain. <Like the vulgar and the stingy person> these also seem not to be evil people—since they are not evildoers—but to be in error.
20 / For the pusillanimous person is worthy of goods, but deprives himself of the goods he is worthy of, and would seem to have something bad in him because he does not think he is worthy of the goods. Indeed he would seem not to know himself; for if he did, he would aim at the things he is worthy of, since they are goods. For all that, such people seem hesitant rather than foolish. But this belief of theirs
25 actually seems to make them worse. / For each sort of person seeks what <he thinks> he is worth; and these people hold back from fine actions and practices, and equally from external goods, because they think they are unworthy of them.

§36 Vain people, by contrast, are foolish and do not know themselves, and they make this obvious. For they undertake commonly
30 honoured exploits, but are not worthy of them, / and then they are found out. They adorn themselves with clothes and ostentatious style and that sort of thing; and since they want everyone to know how fortunate they are, they talk about it, thinking it will bring them honour.

§37 Pusillanimity is more opposed than vanity to magnanimity; for it arises more often, and is worse.³¹
35 §38 Magnanimity, then, / as has been said, is the virtue concerned with honour, and <specifically> with great honour.³²

4

[The virtue concerned with small honours]

[c10] / But, as we said in the first discussion, <just as there is a virtue   1125b
for small-scale giving>, there would also seem to be a virtue concerned with honour; it seems to be related to magnanimity in the way
that generosity is related to magnificence.[1] For it abstains, just as generosity does, from anything great, / but forms the right attitude in us   5
on medium and small matters.

§2 Just as the taking and giving of money admits of a mean, an
excess and a deficiency, so also we can desire honour more or less
than is right, and we can desire it from the right sources and in the
right way.[2] §3 / For we blame the honour-lover for aiming at hon-   10
our more than is right, and at honour from the wrong sources; and we
blame someone indifferent to honour for deciding not to be honoured
even for fine things. §4 Sometimes, however, we praise the honour-lover for being manly and a lover of the fine; and again we praise
the indifferent person for being moderate and temperate, as we said
in the first discussion.

Clearly, since we speak in several ways of loving something, what
we refer to as love of honour is not the / same attitude in every case.[3]   15
When we praise it, we refer to loving honour more than the many do.
When we blame it, we refer to loving honour more than is right. Since
the mean has no name, the extremes look like the only contestants, as
though they had the field to themselves.[4] Still, if there is excess and
deficiency, there is also an intermediate condition.

§5 Since people desire / honour both more and less than is right,   20
it is also possible to desire it in the right way. This state, therefore, a
nameless mean concerned with honour, is praised. In relation to love of
honour, it appears as indifference to honour; in relation to indifference,
it appears as love of honour; in relation to both, it appears in a way as
both. §6 The same would seem to be true of / the other virtues too;   25
but in the case of this virtue the extreme people appear to be opposed
<only to each other> because the intermediate person has no name.

5

[Calmness]

[c11] Calmness is the mean about anger. Since the mean is nameless, and the extremes are practically nameless too, we call the

intermediate condition calmness, inclining towards the deficiency,
30 which is also nameless.¹   §2 The excess might be / called a kind of
irascibility; for the relevant feeling is anger, though its sources are
many and varied.

§3 The person who is angry at the right things and towards the
right people, and also in the right way, at the right time, and for the
right length of time, is praised. This, then, will be the calm person, if
calmness is praised.² For <if calmness is something to be praised,>
35 being a calm person means being undisturbed, not led / by feeling,
1126a but complaining wherever reason prescribes, and / for the length of
time it prescribes.   §4 And he seems to err more in the direction
of deficiency, since the calm person is ready to pardon, not eager to
exact a penalty.

5 §5 The deficiency—a sort of inirascibility or whatever it is—is /
blamed. For people who are not angered by the right things, or in the
right way, or at the right times, or towards the right people, all seem
to be foolish.   §6 For such a person seems to be insensible and to
feel no pain, and since he is not angered, he does not seem to be the
sort to defend himself. Such willingness to accept insults to oneself
and to overlook insults to one's family and friends is slavish.³

10 §7 The excess arises in all these ways—in anger towards the /
wrong people, at the wrong times, more than is right, more hastily
than is right, and for a longer time—but they are not all found in the
same person. For they could not all exist together; for evil destroys
itself as well as other things, and if it is present as a whole it becomes
unbearable.

§8 Irascible people get angry quickly, towards the wrong people,
15 at the wrong times, and more than is right; but they stop / soon, and
this is their best feature. They do all this because they do not contain
their anger, but their quick temper makes them pay back the offence
without concealment, and then they stop.

§9 Choleric people are quick-tempered to extreme, and irascible
about everything and at everything; that is how they get their name.

20 §10 / Bitter people are hard to reconcile, and stay angry for a long
time, since they contain their <angry> spirit. It stops when they pay
back the offence; for the exaction of the penalty produces pleasure in
place of pain, and so puts a stop to the anger. But if this does not happen, they hold their grudge. For no one else persuades them to get
25 over it, / since it is not obvious; and digesting anger in oneself takes

time. This sort of person is most troublesome to himself and to his closest friends.

§11 The people we call complainers are those who complain about the wrong things, more strongly, and for longer than is right, and are not reconciled until <the offender has suffered> a penalty and corrective treatment.[4]

§12 We regard the excess as more opposed than the deficiency / to calmness. For it is more widespread, since it comes more naturally to human beings[5] to exact a penalty from the offender <than to overlook an offence>; and, moreover, complainers are harder to live with.

§13 These remarks also make clear a previous point of ours. For it is hard to define how, against whom, about what, and how long we should be angry, and up to what point someone is acting correctly or in error. / For someone who deviates a little towards either excess or deficiency is not blamed; for sometimes we praise deficient / people and say they are calm, but sometimes we say that people who complain are manly because we think they are capable of ruling others.[6] How far, then, and in what way must someone deviate to be open to blame? It is not easy to answer in a <general> account; for the judgment depends on particular cases, and <we make it> by perception.[7]

§14 / This much at least, however, is clear: The intermediate state is praiseworthy and in accord with it we are angry towards the right people, about the right things, in the right way, and so on. The excesses and deficiencies are blameworthy, lightly if they go a little way, more if they go further, and strongly if they go far. Clearly, then, we must keep to the intermediate state. §15 / So much, then, for the states concerned with anger.

6

[Friendliness]

[c12] In meeting people, living together, and common dealings in conversations and actions, some people seem to be ingratiating; these are the ones who praise everything in order to please us, and never cross us, but think they must cause no pain to those / they meet.[1] §2 In contrast to these, people who oppose us on every point and do not care in the least about causing pain are called cantankerous and quarrelsome.

§3 Clearly, the states we have mentioned are blameworthy, and the state that is intermediate between them is praiseworthy; in accord

with it one accepts or objects to things when it is right and in the
20   right way.   §4 / This state has no name, but it would seem to be most
like friendship; for the character of the person in the intermediate
state is just what we mean in speaking of a decent friend, except that
the friend is also fond of us.

§5 It differs from friendship in not including any <specific> feeling[2] or any fondness for the people we meet. For this person takes
each thing in the right way because that is his character, not because
25   he is a friend or an enemy. / For he will behave this way to new and
old acquaintances, to familiar companions and strangers without distinction, except that he will also do what is suitable for each; for the
proper ways to spare or to hurt the feelings of familiar companions
are not the proper ways to treat strangers.[3]

§6 We have said, then, that in general he will treat people in the
right way in his dealings with them. He will aim to avoid causing pain
or to share pleasure, but will always refer to the fine and the benefi-
30   cial.[4]   §7 / For he would seem to be concerned with the pleasures
and pains that arise in meeting people; and if it is not fine, or it is
harmful, for him to share one of these pleasures, he will object and
will decide to cause pain instead. Further, if the other person will suffer no slight disgrace or harm from doing an action, and only slight
pain if he is crossed, the virtuous person will object to the action and
not accept it.

35   §8 / When he meets people with a reputation for worth, his atti-
1127a   tude will be different from his attitude to just anyone; he / will take
different attitudes to those he knows better and those he knows less
well; and similarly with the other differences, according what is suitable to each sort of person. What he will choose in itself is to share
5   pleasure and avoid causing pain.[5] / But he will be guided by consequences, if they are greater—that is to say, by the fine and the expedient;[6] and to secure great pleasure in the future he will cause slight
pain.

§9 This, then, is the character of the intermediate person, though
he has no name.

Among those who share pleasure the person who aims to be pleasant with no ulterior purpose[7] is ingratiating; the one who does it for
10   some advantage in money and what / money can buy is the flatterer.
The one who objects to everything is, as we have said, the cantankerous and quarrelsome person. However, the extremes appear to be

opposite <only> to each other, because the intermediate condition has no name.[8]

7

[Truthfulness]

[13] The mean that corresponds to boastfulness is also concerned with practically these same <conditions of social life>; and it too is nameless. / It is a good idea to examine the nameless virtues as well as the others. For if we discuss particular aspects of character one at a time, we will acquire a better knowledge of them; and if we survey the virtues and see that in each case the virtue is a mean, we will have more confidence in our belief that the virtues are means.[1] As concerns social life, then, having discussed those who aim at giving pleasure or pain when they meet people, let us now discuss those who are truthful and false, both in words / and in actions, that is to say, in their claims <about themselves>.

§2 The boaster[2] seems to claim qualities that win reputation, but he either lacks them altogether or has less than he claims. §3 The self-deprecator, by contrast, seems to disavow or to belittle his actual qualities. §4 The intermediate person is straightforward, and therefore truthful in what he says and / does, acknowledging the qualities he has without exaggerating or belittling.[3]

§5 Each of these things may be done with or without an ulterior purpose; and someone's character determines what he says and does and the way he lives, if he is not acting for an ulterior purpose. §6 Now in itself <when no ulterior purpose is involved>, falsehood is base and blameworthy, and truth is fine and praiseworthy; in this way the truthful person, like / other intermediate people, is praiseworthy, and both the tellers of falsehoods are blameworthy, the boaster to a higher degree. Let us discuss each type of blameworthy person; but first let us discuss the truthful person.

§7 For we do not mean someone who is truthful in agreements in matters of justice and / injustice, since these concern a different virtue. We mean someone who is truthful both in what he says and in how he lives, when nothing about justice is at stake, simply because that is his state of character. §8 Someone with this character seems to be a decent person. For a lover of the truth who is truthful even when nothing / is at stake will be still more concerned to tell the truth when something is at stake, since he will avoid falsehood as shameful <when something is at stake>, having already avoided it in itself <when nothing was at stake>. This sort of person is praiseworthy. §9 He inclines to tell less, rather than more, than the truth; for this appears more suitable, since excesses are oppressive.

10   §10 / If someone claims to have more than he has, with no ulterior purpose, he certainly looks as though he is a base person, since otherwise he would not enjoy telling falsehoods; but apparently he is pointlessly foolish[4] rather than bad. §11 Among those who do it with an ulterior purpose, the one who does it for the reputation or honour is not to be blamed too much as a boaster.[5] But the one who does it for money or for means to making money is more disgraceful.

15   §12 It is not a person's capacity, but his decision, that makes / him a boaster; for his state of character makes a person a boaster, just as it makes a person a liar.[6] And <boasters differ in their states of character>; one is a boaster because he enjoys telling falsehoods in itself, another because he pursues reputation or gain.

    §13 Boasters who aim at reputation, then, claim the qualities that win praise or win congratulation for happiness. Boasters who aim at
20 profit claim the qualities that gratify other people / and that allow someone to avoid detection when he claims to be what he is not—a wise diviner or doctor,[7] for instance. That is why most <boasters> claim these sorts of things and boast about them; for they have the features just mentioned.

    §14 Self-deprecators underestimate themselves in what they say, and so appear to be more cultivated in their characters. For they seem
25 to be avoiding bombast, not looking for profit, / in what they say. The qualities that win reputation are the ones that these people especially disavow, as Socrates also used to do.[8]

    §15 Those who disavow small qualities that they obviously have are called humbugs, and people more readily think less of them. Sometimes, indeed, this even appears a form of boastfulness, as the
30 Spartans' <austere> dress / does; for the extreme deficiency, as well as the excess, is boastful.[9] §16 But those who are moderate in their self-deprecation and confine themselves to qualities that are not too commonplace or obvious appear sophisticated.

    §17 It is the boaster <rather than the self-deprecator> who appears to be opposite to the truthful person, since he is the worse <of the two extremes>.

8
[Wit]

[c14] Since life also includes relaxation, and in this we pass our / time   1128a
with some form of amusement, here also it seems possible to behave
appropriately in meeting people, and to say and listen to the right
things and in the right way. The company we are in when we speak
or listen also makes a difference.   §2 And, clearly, in this case also
it is possible to exceed the intermediate condition or to be deficient.[1]

§3 / Those who go to excess in raising laughs seem to be vulgar   5
buffoons.[2] They stop at nothing to raise a laugh, and care more about
that than about saying what is seemly and avoiding pain to the victims
of the joke. Those who would never say anything themselves to raise
a laugh, and even object when other people do it, seem to be boorish
and stiff. / Those who joke in appropriate ways are called witty, or, in   10
other words, agile-witted. For these sorts of jokes seem to be movements of someone's character, and characters are judged, as bodies
are, by their movements.

§4 Since there are always opportunities at hand for raising a laugh,
and most people enjoy amusements and jokes more than they should,
/ buffoons are also called witty because they are thought cultivated;   15
nonetheless, they differ, and differ considerably, from witty people, as
our account has made clear.

§5 Dexterity[3] is also proper to the intermediate state. It is proper
to the dexterous person to say and listen to what suits the decent and
civilized person. For some things are suitable / for this sort of person   20
to say and listen to by way of amusement; and the civilized person's
amusement differs from the slavish person's.   §6 This can also be
seen from old and new comedies; for what people used to find funny
was shameful abuse, but what they now find funny instead is innu-
endo, which is / considerably more seemly.[4]   25

§7 Then should the person who jokes well be defined by his making remarks not unsuitable for a civilized person, or by his avoiding
pain and even giving pleasure to the hearer? Perhaps, though, this
<avoiding pain and giving pleasure> is indefinable, since different
people find different things hateful or pleasant.[5]   §8 The remarks he
is willing to hear made are of the same sort, since those he is prepared
to hear made seem to be those he is prepared to make himself.[6]

§9 Hence he will not go to every length. For / since a joke is a type   30
of abuse, and legislators prohibit some types of abuse, they would

presumably be right to prohibit some types of jokes too.   §10 Hence the cultivated and civilized person, as a sort of law to himself,[7] will take this <discriminating> attitude. This, then, is the character of the intermediate person, whether he is called dexterous or witty.

35   The buffoon cannot resist raising a laugh, and spares / neither himself nor anyone else if he can cause laughter, even by making remarks
1128b   that the sophisticated person would never / make, and some that the sophisticated person would not even be willing to hear made.

The boor is useless when he meets people in these circumstances. For he contributes nothing himself, and objects to everything;   §11 but relaxation and amusement seem to be necessary in life.

5   §12 / We have spoken, then, of three means in life, all concerned with common dealings in certain conversations and actions. They differ insofar as one is concerned with truth, the others with what is pleasant. One of those concerned with pleasure is found in amusements, and the other in our behaviour in the other aspects of life when we meet people.

9
[Shame]

10   [c15] / It is not appropriate to treat shame as a virtue; for it would seem to be more like a feeling than like a state <of character>.[1] It is defined, at any rate, as a sort of fear of disrepute.   §2 Its expression is similar to that of fear of something terrifying; for a feeling of disgrace makes people blush, and fear of death makes them turn pale.
15   Hence both <types of fear> / appear to be in some way bodily <reactions>, which seem to be more characteristic of feelings than of states.

§3 Further, the feeling of shame is suitable for youth, not for every time of life. For we think it right for young people to be prone to shame, since they live by their feelings,[2] and hence often go astray,
20   but are restrained by shame; and hence / we praise young people who are prone to shame. No one, by contrast, would praise an older person for readiness to feel disgrace, since we think it wrong for him to do any action that causes a feeling of disgrace.

§4 For a feeling of disgrace is not proper to the decent person either, if it is caused by base actions; for these should not be done.   §5 If some actions are really disgraceful and others are base
25   <only> in <his> belief, that does not matter, / since neither should

be done, and so he should not feel disgrace. §6 On the contrary; being the sort of person who does any disgraceful action is proper to a vicious person.

If someone's state <of character> would make him feel disgrace if he were to do a disgraceful action, and because of this he thinks he is decent, that is absurd. For shame is concerned with what is voluntary, and the decent person will never willingly do base actions.

§7 Shame might, however, be / decent on an assumption; if one were to do <disgraceful actions>, one would feel disgrace; but this does not apply to the virtues.³ If we grant that it is base to feel no disgrace or shame at disgraceful actions, it still does not follow that to do such actions and then to feel disgrace at them is decent.

Continence is not a virtue either. It is a sort of mixed state. / We will explain about it in what we say later.⁴ Now let us discuss justice.

Book V
[Justice]

1
[Varieties of justice]

/The questions we must examine about justice and injustice are these: What sorts of actions are they concerned with? / What sort of mean is justice? What are the extremes between which justice is intermediate? §2 Let us investigate them in accordance with the same discipline¹ as in the previous questions.

§3 We see that the state everyone means in speaking of justice is the state that makes us just agents—that makes us do justice and wish what is just.² In the same way they / mean by injustice the state that makes us do injustice and wish what is unjust. That is why we also³ should first assume these things as an outline.

§4 For what is true of sciences and capacities is not true of states. For while one and the same capacity or science seems to have contrary activities,⁴ a state that is a contrary has no / contrary activities. Health, for instance, only makes us do healthy actions, not their contraries; for we say we are walking in a healthy way if <and only if> we are walking in the way a healthy person would.

§5 Often one of a pair of contrary states is recognized from the other contrary;⁵ and often the states are recognized from their

20 subjects. For if, for instance, the good state is evident, the bad / state becomes evident too; and moreover the good state becomes evident from the things that have it, and the things from the state. For if, for instance, the good state is thickness of flesh, the bad state must be thinness of flesh, and the thing that produces the good state must be what produces thickness of flesh.

25 §6 If one of a pair of contraries is / spoken of in more ways than one, it follows, usually, that the other is too. If, for instance, the just is spoken of in more ways than one, so is the unjust.

§7 [c2] Now it would seem that justice and injustice are both spoken of in more ways than one, but since their homonymy is close, the difference is unnoticed, and is less clear than it is with distant hom-
30 onyms where / the distance in appearance is wide (for instance, the bone below an animal's neck and what we lock doors with are called keys homonymously).[6]

§8 Let us, then, find the number of ways an unjust person is spoken of. Both the lawless person and the overreaching and unfair[7] person seem to be unjust; and so, clearly, both the lawful and the fair
1129b person will be just. Hence the just / will be both the lawful and what is fair, and the unjust will be both the lawless and the unfair.

§9 Since the unjust person is an overreacher, he will deal with goods—not with all goods, but only with those involved in good and bad fortune, goods which are, <considered> without qualification, always good, but for this or that person not always good.[8] Though
5 human beings pray for these and pursue / them, they are wrong; the right thing is to pray that what is good without qualification will also be good for us, but to choose <only> what is good for us.

§10 Now the unjust person <who chooses these goods> does not choose more in every case; in the case of what is bad without qualifi-
10 cation he actually chooses less. But since what is / less bad also seems to be good in a way, and overreaching aims at more of what is good, he seems to be an overreacher.   §11 In fact he is unfair; for unfairness includes <all these actions>, and is a common feature <of his choice of the greater good and of the lesser evil>.

§12 [c3] Since, as we saw, the lawless person is unjust and the lawful person is just, it clearly follows that whatever is lawful is in some way just; for the provisions of legislative <science> are lawful, and we

say that each of them is just.[9] / §13 Now in every matter that they   15
speak about, the laws aim[10] either at the common benefit of all, or at
the benefit of those in control, whose control rests on virtue[11] or on
some other such basis. And so in one way what we call just is whatever produces and maintains happiness and its parts for a political
community.[12]

§14 / Now the law instructs us to do the actions of a brave person—   20
not to leave the battle line, for instance, or to flee, or to throw away our
weapons; of a temperate person—not to commit adultery or wanton
aggression; of a mild person—not to strike or revile another; and similarly requires actions in accord with the other virtues, and prohibits
actions in accord with / the vices. The correctly established law does   25
this correctly, and the less carefully framed one does this worse.

§15 This type of justice, then, is complete virtue, not complete virtue without qualification, but complete virtue in relation to another.[13]
And that is why justice often seems to be supreme among the virtues,
and 'neither the evening star nor the morning star is so marvellous',
and the proverb says 'And in justice / all virtue is summed up.'[14]   30

Moreover, justice is complete virtue to the highest degree because
it is the complete exercise of complete virtue.[15] And it is the complete
exercise because the person who has justice is able to exercise virtue
in relation to another, not only in what concerns himself; for many
are able to exercise virtue in their own concerns but unable in what
relates to another.

§16 / That is why Bias seems to have been correct in saying that   1130a
ruling will reveal the man; for a ruler is automatically related to
another, and in a community.[16]   §17 That is also why justice is the
only virtue that seems to be another person's / good, because it is   5
related to another; for it does what benefits another, either the ruler
or the fellow-member of the community.[17]

§18 The worst person, therefore, is the one who exercises his vice
towards himself and his friends as well \<as towards others\>.[18] And
the best person is not the one who exercises virtue \<only\> towards
himself, but the one who \<also\> exercises it in relation to another,
since this is a difficult task.[19]

§19 This type of justice, then, is the whole, not a part, of virtue, /   10
and the injustice contrary to it is the whole, not a part, of vice.

§20 Our discussion makes clear the difference between virtue
and this type of justice. For virtue is the same as justice, but what

it is to be virtue is not the same as what it is to be justice.[20] Rather, in the respect that virtue is related to another, it is justice, and in the respect that it is a certain sort of state without qualification, it is virtue.

2
[Special justice contrasted with general]

15   [c4] / But we are looking for the type of justice, since we say there is one, that consists in a part of virtue, and correspondingly for the type of injustice that is a part of vice.

§2 A sign[1] that there is this type of justice and injustice is this: If someone's activities accord with the other vices—if, for instance, cowardice made him throw away his shield, or irritability made him revile someone, or ungenerosity made him fail to help someone with
20   money—what he does is unjust, but / not overreaching. But when someone acts from overreaching, in many cases his action accords with none of these vices—certainly not all of them; but it still accords with some type of wickedness, since we blame him, and <in particular> it accords with injustice.[2]   §3 Hence there is another type of injustice that is a part of the whole, and a way of being unjust that is a part of the whole that is contrary to law.

25   §4 / Further, if one person commits adultery for profit and makes a profit, but another commits adultery because of his appetite, and spends money on it to his own loss, the second seems intemperate rather than overreaching, but the first seems unjust, not intemperate. Clearly, then, this is because the first acts to make a profit.

30   §5 Further, we can refer every other unjust action to some / vice— to intemperance if someone committed adultery, to cowardice if he deserted his comrade on the battle line, to anger if he struck someone. But if he made an <unjust> profit, we can refer it to no other vice except injustice.

§6 It is evident, then, that there is another type of injustice, special injustice, apart from injustice as a whole, and that it is synony-
1130b   mous[3] with injustice as a whole, since the definition is in the / same genus. For both have their area of competence in relation to another, but special injustice is concerned with honour or wealth or safety (or whatever single name will include all these), and aims at the pleasure that results from making a profit, whereas the concern of injustice as
5   a whole is / whatever concerns the excellent person.[4]

§7 [c5] Clearly, then, there is more than one type of justice, and there is another type besides <the type that is> the whole of virtue. But we must still grasp what, and what sort of thing,[5] it is.

§8 The unjust is divided into the lawless and the unfair, and the just into the lawful and the / fair.[6] The injustice previously described,   10
then, is concerned with the lawless. §9 But the unfair is not the same as the lawless, but it is related to it as part to whole, since whatever is unfair is lawless, but not everything lawless is unfair. Hence also the unfair type of injustice and the unfair way of being unjust are not the same as the lawless type, but differ / as parts from wholes.   15
For unfair injustice is a part of the whole of injustice, and similarly fair justice is a part of the whole of justice. Hence we must describe special as well as general justice and injustice, and equally this way of being just or unjust.

§10 / Let us, then, set aside the type of justice and injustice that   20
accords with the whole of virtue, justice being the exercise of the whole of virtue, and injustice of the whole of vice, in relation to another.[7] And it is evident how we must distinguish the way of being just or unjust that accords with this type of justice and injustice.[8] For most lawful actions, we might say, are those produced by virtue as a whole;[9] for the law prescribes living in accord with each virtue, and forbids living in accord with each vice.[10] §11 / Moreover,   25
the actions producing the whole of virtue are the lawful actions that the laws prescribe for education promoting the common good. We must wait till later, however, to determine whether the education that makes an individual an unqualifiedly good man is a task for political science or for another science; for, presumably, being a good man is not the same as being every sort of good citizen.[11]

§12 / Special justice, however, and the corresponding way of being   30
just have one species that is found in the distribution of honours or wealth or anything else that can be divided among members of a community who share in a political system; for here it is possible for one member to have a share equal or unequal to another's. / A second   1131a
species concerns rectification in transactions.

§13 This second species has two parts, since one sort of transaction is voluntary, and one involuntary. Voluntary transactions (for instance, selling, buying, lending, pledging, renting, depositing, hiring out) / are so called because their principle is voluntary. Among   5
involuntary transactions some are secret (for instance, theft, adultery,

poisoning, pimping, slave-deception, murder by treachery, false witness), whereas others involve force (for instance, imprisonment, murder, plunder, mutilation, slander, insult).

3
[Justice in distribution]

10   [c6] / Since the unjust person is unfair, and what is unjust is unfair, there is clearly an intermediate between the unfair <extremes>.[1] §2 This is the fair; for in any action where too much and too little are possible, the fair is also possible.   §3 And so, if the unjust is unfair, the just is fair (*ison*), as seems true to everyone even without argument. And since the equal (*ison*) <and fair> is intermediate, the just is some sort of intermediate.

15   §4 Since / the equal involves at least two things <equal to each other>, it follows that the just must be intermediate and equal, and related to something, and for some people. In the respect that it is intermediate, it must be between too much and too little; in the respect that it is equal, it involves two things; and in the respect that it is just, it is just for some people.   §5 Hence the just requires
20   four things at least; the people for whom it is just are two, and / the <equal> things involved are two.

§6 Equality for the people involved will be the same as for the things involved, since <in a just arrangement> the relation between the people will be the same as the relation between the things involved. For if the people involved are not equal, they will not <justly> receive equal shares; indeed, whenever equals receive unequal shares, or unequals equal shares, in a distribution, that is the source of quarrels and accusations.

25   §7 This is also clear from considering what accords with worth. / For all agree that the just in distributions must accord with some sort of worth, but what they call worth is not the same; supporters of democracy say it is free citizenship, some supporters of oligarchy say it is wealth, others good birth, while supporters of aristocracy say it is virtue.[2]

§8 Hence the just <since it requires equal shares for equal people>
30   / is in some way proportionate. For proportion is special to number as a whole, not only to numbers consisting of units,[3] since it is equality of ratios and requires at least four terms.   §9 Now divided proportion clearly requires four terms. But so does continuous propor-
1131b   tion, since here we use one term / as two, and mention it twice. If, for

instance, line A is to line B as B is to C, B is mentioned twice; and so if
B is introduced twice, the terms in the proportion will be four.[4]

§10 The just also requires at least four terms, with the / same ratio   5
<between the pairs>, since the people <A and B> and the items <C
and D> involved are divided in the same way.   §11 Term C, then,
is to term D as A is to B, and, taking them alternately, B is to D as A
is to C. Hence there will also be the same relation of whole <A and
C> to whole <B and D>; this is the relation in which the distribution
pairs them, and it pairs them justly if this is how they are combined.

§12 [c7] Hence the combination of term A with C and of B with /   10
D is the just in distribution, and this way of being just is intermediate,
whereas the unjust is contrary to the proportionate. For the proportionate is intermediate, and the just is proportionate.

§13 This is the sort of proportion that mathematicians call geometrical, since in geometrical proportion the relation of whole to whole is
the same as the relation of each <part> to / each <part>.   §14 But   15
this proportion <involved in justice> is not continuous, since there is
no single term for both the person and the item. The just, then, is the
proportionate, and the unjust is the counter-proportionate. Hence
<in an unjust action> one term becomes more and the other less; and
this is indeed how it turns out in practice, since the one doing injustice has more of the good, and the victim has / less.   20

§15 With an evil the ratio is reversed, since the lesser evil, compared to the greater, counts as a good;   §16 for the lesser evil is
more choiceworthy than the greater, what is choiceworthy is good,
and what is more choiceworthy is a greater good.

§17 This, then, is the first species of the just.

4

[Justice in rectification]

/ The other species is rectificatory, found in transactions both volun-   25
tary and involuntary.   §2 This way of being just belongs to a different species from the first.

For the just in distribution of common assets will always accord
with the proportion mentioned above; for <just> distribution / from   30
common funds will also accord with the ratio to one another of different people's deposits. Similarly, the way of being unjust that is
opposed to this way of being just is what is counter-proportionate.

85

1132a   §3 The just in / transactions, by contrast, though it is a sort of equality (and the unjust is a sort of inequality), accords with numerical proportion, not with the \<geometrical\> proportion of the other species. For here it does not matter if a decent person has taken from a base person, or a base person from a decent person, or if a decent or a base person has committed adultery. Rather, the law looks only at differences in the harm \<inflicted\>, / and treats the people involved as equals, if one does injustice while the other suffers it, and one has done the harm while the other has suffered it.

    §4 And so the judge tries to restore this unjust situation to equality, since it is unequal.[1] For \<not only when one steals from another but\> also when one is wounded and the other wounds him, or one kills and the other is killed, the action and the suffering are unequally divided \<with profit for the offender and loss for / the victim\>; and the judge tries to restore the \<profit and\> loss to a position of equality, by subtraction from \<the offender's\> profit.[2]

    §5 For in such cases, stating it without qualification, we speak of profit for the attacker who wounded his victim, for instance, even if that is not the proper word for some cases; and we speak of loss for the victim who suffers the wound.   §6 At any rate, when what was suffered has been measured, one part is called the \<victim's\> loss, and the other the \<offender's\> profit. Hence the equal is / intermediate between more and less. Profit and loss are more and less in contrary ways, since more good and less evil is profit, and the contrary is loss. The intermediate area between \<profit and loss\>, we have found, is the equal, which we say is just. Hence the just in rectification is the intermediate between loss and profit.

    §7 / That is why parties to a dispute resort to a judge, and an appeal to a judge is an appeal to the just; for the judge is intended to be a sort of living embodiment of the just.[3] Moreover, they seek the judge as an intermediary, and in some cities they actually call a judge a 'mediator', assuming that if they are awarded an intermediate amount, the award will be just. If, then, the judge is an intermediary, the just is in some way intermediate.

    §8 / The judge restores equality, as though a line \<AB\> had been cut into unequal parts \<AC and CB\>, and he removed from the larger part \<AC\> the amount \<DC\> by which it exceeds the half \<AD\> of the line \<AB\>, and added this amount \<DC\> to the smaller part \<CB\>.[4] And when the whole \<AB\> has been halved \<into AD and

DB>, then they say that each person has what is properly his own, when he has got an equal share.

§9 The equal <in this case> is intermediate, by numerical / proportion, between the larger <AC> and the smaller line <CB>. This is also why it is called just (*dikaion*), because it is a bisection (*dicha*), as though we said bisected (*dichaion*), and the judge (*dikastes*) is a bisector (*dichastes*). §10 For when <the same amount> is subtracted from one of two equal things and added to the other, then the one part exceeds the other by the two parts; for if a part had been / subtracted from the one, but not added to the other, the larger part would have exceeded the smaller by just one part. Hence the larger part exceeds the intermediate by one part, and the intermediate from which <a part> was subtracted <exceeds the smaller> by one part.

§11 In this way, then, we will recognize what we must subtract from the one who has more and add to the one who has less <to restore equality>; for to the one who has less we must add the amount by which the intermediate exceeds what / he has, and from the greatest amount <held by the one who has more> we must subtract the amount by which it exceeds the intermediate. §12 Let lines AA', BB' and CC' be equal; let AE be subtracted from AA' and CD be added to CC', so that the whole line DCC' will exceed the line EA' by the parts CD and CF <where CF equals AE>; it follows that DCC' exceeds BB' by CD.[5]

§13 / These names 'loss' and 'profit' are derived from voluntary exchange. For having more than one's own share is called making a profit, and having less than what one had at the beginning is called suffering a loss, / in buying and selling, for instance, and in other transactions permitted by law. §14 And when people get neither more nor less, but precisely what belongs to them, they say they have their own share and make neither a loss nor a profit. Hence the just is intermediate between a certain kind of loss and profit, since it is having the equal amount both / before and after <the transaction>.[6]

5

[Justice in exchange]

[c8] Some people, however, think reciprocity is also just without qualification. This was the Pythagoreans' view, since their definition stated without qualification that what is just is reciprocity with another.

25   §2 The truth is that reciprocity suits neither distributive nor / rectificatory justice, §3 though people take even Rhadamanthys' \<primitive\> conception of justice to describe rectificatory justice: 'If he suffered what he did, upright justice would be done.'[1] §4 For in many cases reciprocity conflicts \<with rectificatory justice\>. If, for instance, a ruling official \<exercising his office\> wounded someone

30   else, he must not be wounded in retaliation, / but if someone wounded a ruling official, he must not only be wounded but also receive corrective treatment. §5 Moreover, the voluntary or involuntary character of the action makes a great difference.

§6 In communities for exchange, however, this way of being just, reciprocity that is proportionate rather than equal, holds people together; for a city is maintained by proportionate reciprocity.

1133a   For people seek to return either evil for evil, / since otherwise \<their condition\> seems to be slavery,[2] or good for good, since otherwise there is no exchange; and they are maintained \<in a community\> by exchange. §7 Indeed, that is why they make a temple of the Graces prominent, so that there will be a return of benefits received. For this is what is special to grace; when someone has been gracious to us, we

5   must do a service for him in return, and / also ourselves take the lead in being gracious again.[3]

§8 It is diagonal combination that produces proportionate exchange. Let A be a builder, B a shoemaker, C a house, D a shoe.

10   The builder must receive the shoemaker's product / from him, and give him the builder's own product in return. If, then, first of all, proportionate equality is found, and, next, reciprocity is also achieved, the proportionate return will be reached. Otherwise it is not equal, and the exchange will not be maintained, since the product of one may well be superior to the product of the other. These products, then, must be equalized.

15   §9 This is true of the other crafts also; for they would have / been destroyed unless the producer produced the same thing, of the same quantity and quality as the thing affected underwent. For no community \<for exchange\> is formed from two doctors. It is formed from a doctor and a farmer, and, in general, from people who are different and unequal and must be equalized.[4]

20   §10 This is why all items for exchange must be comparable / in some way. Currency came along to do exactly this, and in a way it becomes an intermediate, since it measures everything, and so

measures excess and deficiency—for instance, how many shoes are equal to a house.[5] Hence, as builder is to shoemaker, so must the number of shoes be to a house; for if this does not happen, there will /   25
be no exchange and no community.   §11 But proportionate equality will not be reached unless they are equal in some way. Everything, then, must be measured by some one measure, as we said before.

In reality, this measure is need, which holds everything together; for if people needed nothing, or needed things to different extents, there would be either no exchange or not the same exchange.[6] And currency has become a sort of / pledge of need, by convention; in fact it   30
has its name (*nomisma*) because it is not by nature, but by the current law (*nomos*), and it is in our power to alter it and to make it useless.[7]

§12 Reciprocity will be secured, then, when things are equalized, so that the shoemaker's product is to the farmer's as / the farmer is to   1133b
the shoemaker. However, they must be introduced into the figure of proportion not when they have already exchanged and one extreme has both excesses, but when they still have their own; in that way they will be equals and members of a community, because this sort of equality can be produced in / them.[8] Let A be a farmer, C food, B a   5
shoemaker, and D his product that has been equalized; if this sort of reciprocity were not possible, there would be no community.

§13 Now clearly need holds <a community> together as a single unit, since people with no need of each other, both of them or either one, do not exchange, as they exchange whenever another requires what one has oneself, such as wine, when they / allow the export of   10
corn. This, then, must be equalized.

§14 If an item is not required at the moment, currency serves to guarantee us a future exchange, guaranteeing that the item will be there for us if we need it; for it must be there for us to take if we pay. Now the same thing happens to currency <as other goods>, and it does not always count for the same; still, it tends to be more stable. Hence everything / must have a price; for in that way there will always   15
be exchange, and then there will be community.

Currency, then, by making things commensurate as a measure does, equalizes them; for there would be no community without exchange, no exchange without equality, no equality without commensuration. And so, though things so different cannot become commensurate in reality, they / can become commensurate enough in relation to our   20
needs.

§15 Hence there must be some single unit fixed <as current> by a stipulation. This is why it is called currency; for this makes everything commensurate, since everything is measured by currency. Let A, for instance, be a house, B ten minae, C a bed. A is half of B if
25   a house is worth five minae or equal to them; / and C, the bed, is a tenth of B. It is clear, then, how many beds are equal to one house— five.   §16 This is clearly how exchange was before there was currency; for it does not matter whether a house is exchanged for five beds or for the currency for which five beds are exchanged.

30   §17 [c9] We have now said what it is that is unjust and just. / And now that we have defined them, it is clear that doing justice is intermediate between doing injustice and suffering injustice, since doing injustice is having too much and suffering injustice is having too little.[9]
1134a   Justice is a mean, not as the other virtues are, but because / it is about an intermediate condition,[10] whereas injustice is about the extremes.[11] Justice is the virtue in accord with which the just person is said to do what is just in accord with his decision, distributing good things and bad, both between himself and others and between others.
5   He does not award too much of / what is choiceworthy to himself and too little to his neighbour (and the reverse with what is harmful), but awards what is proportionately equal; and he does the same in distributing between others.

§18 Injustice is related in the same way to the unjust. What is unjust is disproportionate excess and deficiency in what is beneficial or harmful; hence injustice is excess and deficiency because it is
10   about excess / and deficiency. The unjust person awards himself an excess of what is beneficial without qualification, and a deficiency of what is harmful, and, speaking as a whole, he acts similarly <in distributions between> others, but deviates from proportion in either direction. In an unjust action getting too little good is suffering injustice, and getting too much is doing injustice.
15   §19 / So much, then, for the nature of justice and the nature of injustice, and similarly for just and unjust in general.

6
[Political justice]

[c10] Since it is possible to do injustice without thereby being unjust, what sort of injustice must someone do to be unjust by having one of

the different types of injustice, by being a thief or adulterer or brig-
and, for instance?[1]

Perhaps it is not the type of action that makes the difference
<between merely doing injustice and being unjust>. / For someone   20
might lie with a woman and know who she is, but the principle might
be feelings rather than decision.   §2 In that case he is not unjust,
though he does injustice—not a thief, for instance, though he stole,
not an adulterer though he committed adultery, and so on in the
other cases.

§3 Now we have previously described the relation of reciprocity /   25
to the just.[2]   §4 But we must recognize that what we are inquiring
into is both the just without qualification and the politically just.[3]
The latter belongs to those who share in common a life aiming at
self-sufficiency, who are free and either proportionately or numerically equal.[4.] Hence those who lack these features have nothing politically just in their relations, though they have something just insofar
as it is similar to the politically just.

/ For the just belongs to those who have law in their relations. Law   30
belongs to those among whom injustice is <possible>; for the judicial process is judgment that distinguishes the just from the unjust.
Where there is injustice there is also doing injustice, though where
there is doing injustice there need not also be injustice.[5] And doing
injustice is awarding to oneself too many of the things that are good
without qualification, and too few of the things that are bad[6] without
qualification.

§5 / That is why we allow only reason, not a human being, to   35
/ be ruler.[7] For a human being awards himself too many goods and   1134b
becomes a tyrant, but a ruler is a guardian of the just, and hence of
the equal.[8]

§6 If a ruler is just, he seems to profit nothing by it. For since
he does not award himself more good without qualification,[9] if it is
not proportionate to him, he / seems to labour for another's benefit.   5
That is why justice is said, as we also remarked before, to be another
person's good.[10]   §7 Hence some payment <for ruling> should be
given; this is honour and privilege. The people who are not satisfied
with these rewards are the ones who become tyrants.[11]

§8 The just for a master and a father is similar to this, / not the   10
same. For there is no unqualified injustice in relation to what is one's
own; one's own possession, or one's child until it is old enough and

separated, is as though it were a part of oneself.[12]   §9 Now no one decides to harm himself. Hence there is no injustice in relation to them,[13] and so nothing politically unjust or just either. For we found that the politically just must accord with law, and belong to those who
15   / are naturally suited for law, and hence to those who have equality in ruling and being ruled.[14] <Approximation to this equality> explains why relations with a wife more than with children or possessions allow something to count as just;[15] for that is the just in households. Still, this too is different from the politically just.

7

[Justice by nature and by law]

One part of the politically just is natural, and the other part legal. The
20   natural has the same validity everywhere / alike, not by its seeming so or not. The legal originally makes no difference <whether it is done> one way or another, but makes a difference whenever people have laid down the rule—that a mina is the price of a ransom, for instance, or that a goat rather than two sheep should be sacrificed. The legal also includes laws passed for particular cases (for instance, that sacrifices should be offered to Brasidas)[1] and enactments by decree.
25   §2 Now some people think everything just is merely / legal. For the natural is unchangeable and equally valid everywhere—fire, for instance, burns both here and in Persia—whereas they see that the just changes <from city to city>.
       §3 This is not so, though in a way it is so. With us, though presum-
30   ably not at all with the gods,[2] there is such a thing / as the natural, but still all is changeable. Nonetheless one sort of things is natural and one sort is not.
       §4 Then what sort of thing, among those that admit of being otherwise,[3] is natural, and what sort is not natural, but legal and conventional, if both natural and legal are changeable? It is clear in other cases also, and the same distinction will apply;[4] for the right hand is
35   naturally superior, even / though it is possible for everyone to become ambidextrous.[5]
       §5 The sorts of things that are just by convention and expediency / are like measures. For measures for wine and for corn are not
1135a   of equal size everywhere, but in wholesale markets they are bigger, and in retail smaller. Similarly, the things that are just by human
5   <enactment> and not by nature differ / from place to place, since

political systems also differ.[6] Still, only one system is by nature the best everywhere.[7]

§6 Each <type of> just and lawful <action> is related as a universal to the corresponding particulars; for the <particular> actions that are done are many, but each <type> is one, since it is universal.[8]

§7 An act of injustice is different from the unjust, and an act of justice from the just. For the unjust is unjust / by nature or enactment; when this has been done, it is an act of injustice,[9] but before it is done it is only unjust. The same applies to an act of justice <in contrast to the just>. Here, however, the general <type of action contrary to an act of injustice> is more usually called a just act, and what is called an act of justice is the <specific type of just act> that rectifies an act of injustice.

Later we must examine each of these actions, to see what sorts of species, and how many, they have, and what they / are concerned with.

8

[Justice, injustice, and the voluntary]

Given this account of just and unjust actions, one does injustice or does justice whenever one does them willingly. Whenever one does them unwillingly, one neither does justice nor does injustice, except coincidentally, since the actions one does are coincidentally just or unjust.[1]

§2 / An act of injustice and a just act are defined by the voluntary and the involuntary. For when the action is voluntary, the agent is blamed, and thereby also it is an act of injustice. And so something will be unjust without thereby being an act of injustice, if it is not also voluntary.

§3 As I said before, I say that an action is voluntary just in case it is up to the agent, who does it in knowledge, and <hence> not in ignorance / of the person, instrument, and goal (for instance, whom he is striking, with what, and for what goal),[2] and <does> each of these neither coincidentally nor by force[3] (if, for instance, someone seized your hand and struck another <with it>, you would not have done it willingly, since it was not up to you). But <a further distinction must be drawn about knowledge. For> it is possible that the victim is your father, and you know he is a human being or a bystander, but do not / know he is your father.[4] The same distinction must be made for the goal and for the action as a whole.

Actions are involuntary, then, if they are done in ignorance; or they are not done in ignorance, but they are not up to the agent; or they are done / by force. For we also do or undergo many of our natural <actions and processes>, such as growing old and dying, in knowledge, but none of them is either voluntary or involuntary.[5]

§4 Both unjust and just actions may also be coincidental in the same way. For if someone returned a deposit unwillingly / and because of fear, we ought to say that he neither does anything just nor does justice, except coincidentally.[6] Similarly, if someone is under compulsion and unwilling when he fails to return the deposit, we should say that he coincidentally does injustice and does something unjust.

§5 In some of our voluntary actions we act on a previous decision, / and in some we act without previous decision. We act on a previous decision when we act on previous deliberation, and we act without previous decision when we act without previous deliberation.[7]

§6 Among the three ways of inflicting harms in a community, actions done with ignorance are errors if someone does neither the action he supposed, nor to the person, nor with the instrument, nor for the result he supposed. For he thought, for instance, that he was not hitting, or not hitting this person, or / not for this result; but coincidentally the result that was achieved was not what he thought (for instance, <he hit him> to graze, not to wound), or the victim or the instrument was not the one he thought.

§7 If, then, the infliction of harm violates reasonable expectation, the action is a misfortune. If it does not violate reasonable expectation, but is done without vice, it is an error. For someone is in error if the principle of the cause is in him, and unfortunate when it is outside.[8]

§8 / If he does it in knowledge, but without previous deliberation, it is an act of injustice; this is true, for instance, of actions caused by spirit and other feelings that are natural or necessary for human beings. For when someone inflicts these harms and commits these errors, he does injustice and these are acts of injustice; but he is not thereby unjust or wicked, since it is not vice that causes him to inflict the harm. / But whenever his decision is the cause, he is unjust and vicious.[9]

§9 That is why it is right to judge that actions caused by spirit do not result from forethought <and hence do not result from decision>, since the principle is not the agent who acted on spirit, but the person who provoked him to anger.[10] §10 Moreover the dispute is not about whether <the action caused by anger> happened or not, but

about whether it was just, since anger is a response to apparent injustice. / For they do not dispute about whether it happened or not, as   30
they do in commercial transactions, where one party or the other must
be vicious, unless forgetfulness is the cause of the dispute. Rather <in
cases of anger> they agree about the fact and dispute about which
action was just; but <in commercial transactions> the <cheater> who
has plotted against his victim knows very well <that what he is doing
is unjust>.[11] / Hence <in cases of anger the agent> thinks he is suf-   1136a
fering injustice, while <in transactions the cheater> does not think so.

§11 If <the cheater's> decision causes him to inflict the harm, he
does injustice, and this is the sort of act of injustice that makes an
agent unjust,[12] if it violates proportion or equality. In the same way, a
person is just if his decision causes him to do justice; one <merely>
does justice if one merely does it voluntarily.

§12 / Some involuntary actions are to be pardoned, and some are   5
not. For if someone's error is not only committed in ignorance, but
also caused by ignorance, it is to be pardoned. But if, though committed in ignorance, it is caused not by ignorance but by some feeling
that is neither natural nor human, it is not to be pardoned.[13]

9
[Puzzles about justice and injustice]

[c11] / If we have adequately defined suffering injustice and doing   10
injustice, some puzzles might be raised.

First of all, are those bizarre words of Euripides correct, where
he says: "'I killed my mother—a short tale to tell.' / 'Were both of   15
you willing or both unwilling?'"?[1] Is it really possible to suffer injustice willingly, or is it always involuntary, as doing injustice is always
voluntary? And is it always one way or the other, or is it sometimes
voluntary and sometimes involuntary?

§2 The same question arises about receiving justice. Since doing
justice is always voluntary <,as doing injustice is>, it is / reasonable   20
for the same opposition to apply in both cases, so that both receiving
justice and suffering injustice will be either alike voluntary or alike
involuntary. But it seems absurd in the case of receiving justice as well
<as in the case of suffering injustice> for it to be always voluntary,
since some people receive justice, but not willingly.

§3 We might also raise the following puzzle: Does everyone who
has received something unjust suffer injustice, or is it / the same with   25

receiving as it is with doing? For certainly it is possible, in the case both of doing and of receiving, to have a share in just things coincidentally; and clearly the same is true of unjust things, since doing something unjust is not the same as doing injustice, and suffering something unjust is not the same as suffering injustice. The same is true of / doing justice and receiving it; for it is impossible to suffer injustice if no one does injustice and impossible to receive justice if no one does justice.

§4 Now if doing injustice is simply harming someone willingly (and doing something willingly is doing it with knowledge of the victim, the instrument, and the way), and the incontinent person harms himself willingly, he suffers injustice willingly. Hence someone can do injustice to himself; and one of our puzzles / was just this, whether someone can do injustice to himself. §5 Further, someone's incontinence might cause him to be willingly harmed by another who is willing, so that it would be possible to suffer injustice willingly.

Perhaps, however, our definition <of doing injustice> was incorrect, and we should add to 'harming with knowledge of the victim, the instrument, and the way', the further condition / 'against the wish of the victim'. §6 If so, someone is harmed and suffers something unjust willingly, but no one suffers injustice willingly. For no one wishes it, not even the incontinent, but he acts against his wish; for no one wishes for what he does not think is excellent, and what the incontinent does is not what he thinks it is right <and hence excellent> to do.[2]

§7 And if someone gives away what is his own, as Homer / says Glaucus gave to Diomede 'gold for bronze, a hundred cows' worth for nine cows' worth',[3] he does not suffer injustice. For it is up to him to give them, whereas suffering injustice is not up to him, but requires someone to do him injustice.

§8 Clearly, then, suffering injustice is not voluntary.

[c12] / Two further questions that we decided to discuss still remain: If A distributes to B more than B deserves, is it A, the distributor, or B, who has more, who does injustice? And is it possible to do injustice to oneself?

§9 For if the first alternative is possible, and A rather than B does injustice, it follows that if A knowingly and willingly distributes / more to B than to himself, A does injustice to himself. And indeed this is what a moderate person seems to do; for the decent person tends to take less than his share.

Perhaps, however, it is not true without qualification that he takes less. For perhaps he overreaches for some other good,[4] such as reputation or the unqualifiedly fine. Moreover, our definition of doing injustice allows us to solve the puzzle. For since he suffers nothing against his own wish, he does not suffer injustice, at least not from his / distribution, but, at most, is merely harmed.   25

§10 But it is evidently the distributor who does injustice, and the one who has more does not always do it. For the one who does injustice is not the one who has an unjust share, but the one who willingly does what is unjust, that is to say, the one who has the principle of the action; this is the distributor, not the recipient. / §11 Besides, doing   30 is spoken of in many ways, and in a way inanimate things, or hands, or servants at someone else's order, kill; the recipient, then, does not do injustice, but does something that is unjust.

§12 Further, if the distributor judged in ignorance, he does not do injustice in violation of what is legally just, and his judgment is not unjust; in a way, though, it is unjust, since what is legally just is different from what is primarily just. If, however, he judged unjustly, and did it knowingly, / he himself as well <as the recipient> is overreach-   1137a ing—for gratitude or to exact a penalty.

§13 And so someone who has judged unjustly for these reasons has also got more, exactly as though he got a share of the <profits of> the act of injustice. For he gave judgment about some land, for instance, on this condition <that he would share the profits>, and what he got was not land, but money.

§14 [c13] / People think doing injustice is up to them; that is why   5 they think that being just is also easy. But it is not. For lying with a neighbour's wife, wounding a neighbour, bribing, are all easy and up to us, but being in a certain state when we do them is not easy, and not up to us.[5]

§15 / Similarly, people think it takes no wisdom to know the things   10 that are just and unjust, because it is not difficult to comprehend what the laws speak of. But these are not the things that are just, except coincidentally. Knowing how actions must be done, and how distributions must be made, if they are to be just, takes more work than it takes to know about healthy things. And even in the case of healthy things, knowing / about honey, wine, hellebore, burning, and cutting   15 is easy, but knowing how these must be distributed to produce health, and to whom and when, takes all the work that it takes to be a doctor.

§16 For the same reason they think doing injustice is no less proper to the just than to the unjust person, because the just person is no less, and even more, able to do each of the / actions.[6] For he is able to lie with a woman, and to wound someone; and the brave person, similarly, is able to throw away his shield, and to turn and run this way or that. But doing acts of cowardice or injustice is not doing these actions, except coincidentally; it is being in a certain state when one does them. Similarly, practising medicine or healing is not cutting or not cutting, giving / drugs or not giving them, but doing all these things in a certain way.

§17 Just things belong to those who have a share in things that, <considered> without qualification, are good, who can have an excess or a deficiency of them.[7] Some (as, presumably, the gods) can have no excess of them; others, the incurably evil, benefit from none of them, but are harmed by / them all; others again benefit from these goods up to a point; and this is why the just is something human.[8]

10

[Decency]

[c14] The next task is to discuss how decency is related to justice and how the decent is related to the just.[1] For on examination they appear as neither the same without qualification nor as states of different kinds.

Sometimes we / praise what is decent and the decent person, so that even / when we praise someone for other things we transfer the term 'decent' and use it instead of 'good',[2] making it clear that what is more decent is better.

Sometimes, however, when we reason about the matter, it appears absurd for what is decent to be something apart from what is just, and still praiseworthy. For <apparently> either what is just is not excellent or what is decent is not excellent,[3] / if it is something other than what is just; or else, if they are both excellent, they are the same.

§2 These, then, are roughly the claims that raise the puzzle about the decent. But they are all correct in a way, and none is contrary to any other. For the decent is better than one way of being just, but it is still just, and not better than the just by being a different kind of thing. / Hence the same thing is just and decent; while both are excellent, what is decent is superior.

§3 The puzzle arises because the decent is just, but is not the legally just, but a rectification of it.   §4 This is because all law is universal, but in some areas no universal <rule> / can be correct; and   15 so where a universal <rule> has to be made, but cannot be correct, the law chooses the <universal rule> that is usually <correct>, well aware of the error being made. And the law is no less correct on this account; for the source of the error is not the law or the legislator, but the nature of the object itself, since that is what the subject matter of actions is bound to be like.[4]

§5 / Whenever, therefore the law makes a universal <rule>, but in   20 this particular case what happens violates the <intended scope of> the universal <rule>, on this point the legislator falls short, and has made an error by making an unqualified <rule>. Then it is correct to rectify the deficiency; this is what the legislator would have said himself if he had been present there, and what he would have prescribed, had he known, in his legislation.

§6 That is why the decent is just, and better than a certain way / of   25 being just—not better than the just without qualification,[5] but better than the error that results from the omission of any qualification <in the rule>. And this is the nature of the decent—rectification of law insofar as the universality of law makes it deficient.[6]

This is also why not everything is guided by law. For on some matters legislation is impossible, and so a decree is needed.   §7 For the standard applied to the indefinite / is itself indefinite, as the lead stan-   30 dard is in Lesbian building, where it is not fixed, but adapts itself to the shape of the stone;[7] similarly, a decree is adapted to fit its objects.

§8 It is clear from this what is decent, and clear that it is just, and better than a certain way of being just. It is also evident / from this   35 who the decent person is. For he is the one / who decides on and does   1138a such actions, not an exact stickler for justice in the bad way, but taking less than he might even though he has the law on his side. This is the decent person. His state is decency; this is a sort of justice, and not some state different from it.

11
[Injustice to oneself]

[c15] Whether it is possible to do injustice to oneself or not is evident from what has been said.[1]

5   / First of all, some just actions are the legal prescriptions in accord with each virtue; we are legally forbidden, for instance, to kill ourselves.[2] §2 Moreover, if someone illegally and willingly inflicts harm on another, not returning harm for harm, he does injustice (a
10   person acting willingly is one who knows / the victim and the instrument). Now if someone murders himself because of anger, he does this willingly, in violation of correct reason, when the law forbids it; hence he does injustice. §3 But injustice to whom? Surely to the city, not to himself, since he suffers it willingly, and no one willingly suffers injustice. That is why the city both penalizes him and inflicts further dishonour on him for destroying himself, on the ground that he does injustice to the city.[3]

15   §4 Now consider the type of injustice that belongs to / an agent who is only unjust, not base generally. Clearly the corresponding type of unjust action is different from the first type. For this second type of unjust person is wicked in the same <special> way as the coward is, not by having total wickedness; hence his acts of injustice do not accord with total wickedness either. In this case also one cannot do injustice to oneself. For if one could, the same person could lose and get the same
20   thing at / the same time. But this is impossible; on the contrary, what is just or unjust must always involve more than one person.

§5 Moreover, doing injustice is voluntary, and results from a decision,[4] and strikes first; for a victim who retaliates does not seem to do injustice. But if someone does injustice to himself, he does and suffers the same thing at the same time. Further, on this view, it would be possible to suffer injustice willingly.

25   §6 Besides, no one does injustice without doing one of the / particular acts of injustice. But no one commits adultery with his own wife, or burgles his own house, or steals his own possessions.

And in general the puzzle about doing injustice to oneself is also solved by the distinction about voluntarily suffering injustice.

30   §7 It is also evident that both doing and suffering injustice / are bad, since one is having more, one having less, than the intermediate amount, just as in the case of health in medicine and fitness in gymnastics <both more and less than the intermediate amount are bad>.[5] But doing injustice is worse; for it is blameworthy, involving vice that is either complete and unqualified or close to it (since not all voluntary doing of injustice is combined with <the state of> injus-
35   tice).[6] Suffering injustice, however, involves / no vice or injustice.

§8 / In its own right, then, suffering injustice is less bad; and   1138b
though it might still be coincidentally a greater evil, that is no concern
of a craft. Rather, the craft says that pleurisy is a worse illness than a
stumble, even though a stumble might sometimes coincidentally turn
out worse—if, for instance, someone / stumbled and by coincidence   5
was captured by the enemy or killed because he fell.

§9 It is possible for there to be a sort of justice, by similarity and
transference, not of a person to himself, but of certain parts of a
person—not every kind of justice, but the kind that belongs to masters or households. For in these discussions the part of the soul that
has reason is distinguished from the non-rational part. People look at
these and it seems to them that there is injustice to oneself, because in
these parts it is possible to suffer something against one's own desires.
Hence it is possible for those parts to be just to each other, as it is for
ruler and ruled.[7]

§10 / So much, then, for our definitions of justice and the other   10
virtues of character.[8]

Book VI
[Virtues of thought]

1
[The mean and the virtues of thought]

Since we have said previously that we must choose the intermediate
condition, not the excess or the deficiency, and / that the intermedi-   20
ate condition is as correct reason says, let us now determine what it
says.[1] For in all the states of character we have mentioned, as well as
in the others, there is a target that the person who has reason focuses
on and so tightens or relaxes; and there is a definition of the means,
which we say are between / excess and deficiency because they accord   25
with the correct reason.

§2 To say this is admittedly true, but it is not at all clear.[2] For in other
pursuits directed by a science it is equally true that we must labour and
be idle neither too much nor too little, but the intermediate amount
prescribed by correct reason. / But knowing only this, we would know   30
nothing more about, for instance, the medicines to be applied to the
body, if we were told we must apply the ones that medical science prescribes and in the way that the medical scientist applies them.

§3 That is why our account of the states of the soul, in the same way, must not only be true as far as it has gone. We must also determine what the correct reason is, that is to say,[3] what its definition[4] is.

35   §4 [c2] / After we divided the virtues of the soul we said that some
1139a / are virtues of character and some of thought. And so, having finished our discussion of the virtues of character, let us now discuss the others as follows, after speaking first about the soul.

5   §5 Previously, then, we said there are two parts of the soul, / one that has reason, and one non-rational.[5] Now we should divide in the same way the part that has reason. Let us assume there are two parts that have reason: with one we study beings whose principles do not admit of being otherwise than they are, and with the other we study beings whose principles admit of being otherwise.[6] For if the beings
10 are of different kinds, the parts of the soul naturally / suited to each of them are also of different kinds, since the parts possess knowledge by being somehow similar and appropriate <to their objects>.

§6 Let us call one of these parts the scientific part, and the other the rationally calculating part; for deliberating is the same as rationally calculating, and no one deliberates about what cannot be other-
15 wise. Hence the rationally calculating part / is one part of the part of the soul that has reason.

§7 Hence we should find the best state[7] of the scientific part and the best state of the rationally calculating part; for this state is the virtue of each of them. Now a thing's virtue is relative to its own proper function, <and so we must consider the function of each part>.[8]

2

[Thought, desire, and decision]

There are three <capacities> in the soul—sense perception, understanding, desire[1]—that control action and truth. §2 Of these three sense perception is clearly not the principle of any action, since beasts
20 have / perception, but no share in action.[2]

As assertion and denial are to thought, so pursuit and avoidance are to desire. Now virtue of character is a state that decides; and decision is a deliberative desire. If, then, the decision is excellent,
25 the reason must be true and the / desire correct, so that what reason asserts is what desire pursues. This, then, is thought and truth concerned with action. §3 The thought concerned with study, not with

action or production, has its good or bad state in being true or false; for truth is the function of whatever / thinks. But the function of what   30 thinks about action is truth agreeing with correct desire.[3]

§4 Now the principle[4] of an action—the source of motion, not the goal[5]—is decision. But the principle of decision is desire and goal-directed reason.[6] That is why decision requires understanding and thought, and also a state / of character; for acting well or badly   35 requires both thought and character.[7]

§5 Thought by itself moves nothing, but goal-directed thought concerned with action <moves us>.[8] / For this thought is also the principle   1139b of productive thought; for every producer in producing aims at some <further> goal,[9] and the unqualified goal is not the product, which is only the <qualified> goal of some <production>, and aims at some <further> goal. <An unqualified goal is> what we achieve in *action*, since acting well is the goal, and desire is for the goal. That is why[10] decision is either understanding / combined with desire or desire combined   5 with thought;[11] and this is the sort of principle that a human being is.

§6 We do not decide to do what is already past; no one decides, for instance, to have sacked Troy. For neither do we deliberate about what is past, but only about what will be and admits of being or not being; and what is past does not admit of not having happened. That is why Agathon is correct to say 'Of / this alone even a god is   10 deprived—to make what is all done to have never happened.'[12]

The function of each of the understanding parts, then, is truth. And so the virtues of each part will be the states that best direct it towards the truth.[13]

3

[Scientific knowledge]

[c3] Then let us begin again, and discuss these states of / the soul.[1]   15 Let us say, then, that there are five states in which the soul grasps the truth in its affirmation or denials. These are craft, scientific knowledge, prudence, wisdom and understanding; for belief and supposition admit of being false.

§2 What science is is evident from the following, if we ought to speak exactly and not be guided by <mere> similarities.[2] / For we   20 all suppose that what we know scientifically does not even admit of being otherwise. But whenever what admits of being otherwise escapes observation, we do not notice whether it is or is not, <and

hence we do not know about it>. Hence what is known scientifically is by necessity. Hence it is everlasting; for the things that are by
unqualified necessity are all everlasting, and everlasting things are
ingenerable and indestructible.

25   §3 / Further, every science seems to be teachable, and what is
scientifically knowable is learnable. But all teaching is from what
is already known,³ as we also say in the analytics;⁴ for some teaching
is through induction, some by deduction, <which both require previous knowledge>. Induction <leads to> the principle, i.e., the univer-
30 sal,⁵ but deduction proceeds from the universal. Hence / deduction
has principles from which it proceeds and which are not <reached>
by deduction. Hence they are <reached> by induction.

      §4 Scientific knowledge, then, is a demonstrative state, and has all
the other features that in the analytics⁶ we add to the definition. For
one has scientific knowledge whenever one has the appropriate sort
of confidence, and knows the principles; for if one does not know
35 them better / than the conclusion, one will have scientific knowledge
<only> coincidentally.⁷

      [c4] So much for a definition of scientific knowledge.

4
[Craft knowledge]

1140a   / What admits of being otherwise includes what is produced and what
is achieved in action.¹   §2 Production and action are different; about
them we rely also on <our> popular discussions. Therefore the state
involving reason and concerned with action is different from the state
5   involving reason and concerned / with production. Nor is one included
in the other;² for action is not production, and production is not action.

      §3 Now building, for instance, is a craft, and is essentially a certain
state involving reason concerned with production; there is no craft
that is not a state involving reason concerned with production, and
10 no such state that is not a craft. Hence a / craft is the same as a state
involving true reason concerned with production.

      §4 Every craft is concerned with coming to be, and the exercise of
the craft is the study³ of how something that admits of being and not
being comes to be, something whose principle is in the producer and
not in the product. For a craft is not concerned with things that are
15 or come to be by necessity; / nor with things that are by nature, since
these have their principle in themselves.⁴

§5 Since production and action are different, craft must be concerned with production, not with action.

In a way craft and fortune are concerned with the same things. As Agathon says: 'Craft was fond of fortune, and fortune / of craft.'[5]   20

§6 A craft, then, as we have said, is a state involving true reason concerned with production. Lack of craft is the contrary state involving false reason and concerned with production. Both are concerned with what admits of being otherwise.

5
[Prudence]

[c5] / To grasp what prudence is, we should first study the sort of   25
people we call prudent.[1] It seems proper to a prudent person to be able to deliberate finely[2] about things that are good and beneficial for himself, not about some restricted area[3]—about what sorts of things are means to health or strength, for instance—but about what sorts of things are means to living well altogether.[4]

§2 A sign of this is the fact that we call people prudent about some <restricted area> whenever they calculate well about means to / some   30
excellent end, in an area where there is no craft.[5] Hence where <living well> as a whole is concerned, the deliberative person will also be prudent.

§3 Now no one deliberates about things that cannot be otherwise or about things that cannot be achieved in his action. Hence, if science involves demonstration, but there is no demonstration of anything whose principles admit of being otherwise / (since every such   35
thing itself admits of being otherwise); and / if we cannot deliberate   1140b
about things that are by necessity; it follows that prudence is not science nor yet craft knowledge. It is not science, because what is achievable in action admits of being otherwise; and it is not craft knowledge, because action and production belong to different kinds.

§4 The remaining possibility, then, is that prudence is a / state   5
grasping the truth, involving reason, concerned with action about things that are good or bad for a human being. For production has its end in something other than itself, but action does not, since its end is acting well itself.[6]

§5 That is why Pericles and such people are the ones whom we regard as prudent, because they are able to study what is / good for   10
themselves and for human beings. We think that household managers and politicians are such people.[7]

This is also how we come to give temperance (*sôphrosunê*) its name, because we think that it preserves prudence (*sôzousan tên phronêsin*).[8] §6 It preserves the <appropriate> sort of supposition. For the sort of supposition that is corrupted and perverted by the pleasant or painful is not every sort—/ not, for instance, the supposition that the triangle does or does not have two right angles—but suppositions about what is achievable in action. For the principles of things achievable in action are the end for the sake of which <we act>,[9] but if someone is corrupted because of pleasure or pain, no <appropriate> principle can appear to him, and it cannot appear[10] that this is the end, nor that for the sake of this and because of this one ought to choose and perform every action; for vice corrupts the principle.[11] And so prudence must be a state grasping the truth, involving reason, and concerned with action about human goods.[12]

§7 Moreover, there is virtue <or vice in the use> of craft, but not <in the use> of prudence. Further, in a craft, someone who makes errors voluntarily is more choiceworthy; but with prudence, as with the virtues, the reverse is true. Clearly, / then, prudence is a virtue, not a craft.[13]

§8 There are two parts of the soul that have reason. Prudence is a virtue of one of them, of the part that has belief; for belief is concerned, as prudence is, with what admits of being otherwise.

Moreover, it is not only a state involving reason. A sign of this is the fact that such a state can be forgotten, but prudence cannot.[14]

6
[Understanding]

[c6] / Scientific knowledge is supposition about universals, things that are by necessity. Further, everything demonstrable and every science have principles, since scientific knowledge involves reason. Hence there can be neither scientific knowledge nor craft knowledge nor prudence about the principles of what is scientifically / known. For what is scientifically known is demonstrable, <but principles are not>; and craft and prudence / are about things that admit of being otherwise. Nor is wisdom <exclusively> about principles;[1] for it is proper to the wise person to have a demonstration of some things.

§2 <The states of the soul> by which we always grasp the truth and never make mistakes, about things that can be / otherwise or those that cannot be otherwise, are scientific knowledge, prudence, wisdom, and understanding. But none of the first three—prudence, scientific knowledge, wisdom—is possible about principles. The remaining possibility, then, is that understanding is about principles.²

7
[Wisdom contrasted with prudence]

[c7] We ascribe wisdom in crafts to the people who have the / most   10
exact expertise in the crafts.¹ For instance, we call Pheidias a wise stone-worker and Polycleitus² a wise bronze-worker; and by wisdom we signify precisely virtue in a craft. §2 But we also think some people are wise in general, not wise in some <restricted> area, or in some other <specific> way / (as Homer says in the *Margites*: 'The   15
gods did not make him a digger or a ploughman or wise in anything else').³ Clearly, then, wisdom is the most exact <form> of scientific knowledge.

§3 Hence the wise person must not only know what is derived from the principles of a science, but also grasp the truth about the principles. Therefore wisdom is understanding plus scientific knowledge; it is scientific knowledge of the most honourable things that has received <understanding as> its coping stone.⁴

/ For it would be absurd for someone to think that political science   20
or prudence is the most excellent science;⁵ for the best thing in the universe is not a human being <and the most excellent science must be of the best things>.

§4 Moreover,⁶ if what is good and healthy for human beings and for fish is not the same, whereas what is white or straight is always the same, everyone would also say that the / content of wisdom is the   25
same in every case, but the content of prudence⁷ is not. For the agent they would call prudent is the one who studies well each question about his own <good>, and he is the one to whom they would entrust such questions.⁸ That is why prudence is also ascribed to some of the beasts, the ones that are evidently capable of forethought about their own life.⁹

It is also evident that wisdom is not the same as political / sci-   30
ence.¹⁰ For if people are to say that science about what is beneficial to themselves <as human beings> counts as wisdom, there will be many types of wisdom <corresponding to the different species of animals>. For if there is no one medical science about all beings, there is no one

science about the good of all animals, but a different science about each specific good.[11] It does not matter if human beings are the best
1141b   among the animals; for there are other beings of a far more divine / nature than human beings—most evidently, for instance, the beings composing the universe.[12]

§5 What we have said makes it clear that wisdom is both scientific knowledge and understanding about the things that are by nature
5   most honourable. That is why people say that Anaxagoras / or Thales[13] or that sort of person is wise, but not prudent, whenever they see that he is ignorant of what benefits himself. And so they say that what he knows is extraordinary, amazing, difficult, and divine, but useless, because it is not human goods that he looks for.

10   §6 [c8] Prudence, by contrast, is about human concerns, about / things open to deliberation. For we say that deliberating well is the function of the prudent person more than anyone else[14]; but no one deliberates about things that cannot be otherwise, or about things lacking any goal that is a good achievable in action.[15] The unquali- fiedly good deliberator is the one whose aim accords with rational calculation in pursuit of the best good that is achievable in action for a human being.[16]

15   §7 / Nor is prudence about universals only. It must also acquire knowledge of particulars, since it is concerned with action and action is about particulars.[17] That is why in other areas also some people who lack knowledge but have experience are better in action than others who have knowledge. For someone who knows that light meats are digest-
20   ible and <hence> healthy,[18] but / not which sorts of meats are light, will not produce health. Rather, the one who knows that bird meats are light and healthy[19] will be better at producing health. And since prudence is concerned with action, it must possess both <the universal and the particular knowledge> or the <particular> more <than the universal>. Here too, however, <as in medicine> there is a ruling <science>.[20]

8

[Types of prudence]

Political science and prudence are the same state, but their being is not the same.[1]
25   §2 / One type of prudence about the city is the ruling part; this is legislative science. The type concerned with particulars[2] is given the

name 'political science' that is common <to both types>.[3] This type is concerned with action and deliberation, since the decree[4] is to be acted on as the last thing <reached in deliberation>. That is why only these people are said to be politically active; for only these put <political science> into practice, as handcraftsmen put <a craft> into practice.[5]

§3 / Similarly, prudence concerned with the individual himself   30
seems most of all to be counted as prudence; and this <type of prudence> is given the name 'prudence' that is common <to all types>. Of the other types one is household science, another legislative, another political, one type of which is deliberative and another judicial.

§4 [c9] In fact knowledge of what is <good> for oneself is one species <of prudence>.[6] But there is much difference <in opinions> about it.[7] / The one who knows about himself, and spends his time   1142a on his own concerns, seems to be prudent, while politicians seem to be too active.[8] Hence Euripides says, 'Surely I cannot be prudent, since I could have been inactive, / numbered among all the many in   5 the army, and have had an equal share. . . . For those who go too far and are too active. . . .'[9] For people seek what is good for themselves, and suppose that this <inactivity> is the right action <to achieve their good>. Hence this belief has led to the view that these are the prudent people.[10] Presumably, however, one's own welfare requires household / management and a political system. Further, <another   10 reason for the difference of opinion is that> it is unclear, and should be examined, how one must manage one's own affairs.

§5 A sign of what has been said is the fact that whereas young people become accomplished in geometry and mathematics, and wise within these limits, prudent young people do not seem to be found.[11] The reason is that prudence is concerned with particulars as well as universals, and particulars become / known from experience, but a   15 young person lacks experience, since some length of time is needed to produce it.

§6 Indeed we might also consider why a child can become accomplished in mathematics, but not in wisdom or natural science.[12] Is it because mathematical objects are reached through abstraction,[13] but in these other cases the principles[14] are reached from experience? Young people, then, / have no real conviction in these other sciences,   20 but only say the words,[15] whereas the nature of mathematical objects is clear to them.

§7 Further, deliberation may be in error about either the universal or the particular.[16] For <we may wrongly suppose> either that all sorts of heavy water are bad or that this water is heavy.

§8 It is apparent that prudence is not scientific knowledge; for, as

25 / we said, it concerns the last thing <i.e., the particular>, since this is what is achievable in action.[17]   §9 Hence it is opposite to understanding.[18] For understanding is about the <first> terms,[19] <those> that have no account of them; but prudence is about the last thing, an object of perception, not of science. This is not the perception of special objects,[20] but the sort by which we perceive that the last among mathematical objects[21] is a triangle; for it will stop there too.[22] This is

30 another / species <of perception than perception of special objects>; but it is still perception more than prudence is.[23]

9

[Good deliberation]

[c10] Inquiry and deliberation are different, since deliberation is a type of inquiry. We must also grasp what good deliberation is,[1] and see whether it is some sort of scientific knowledge, or belief, or good guessing, or some other kind of thing.

1142b   §2 First of all, then, it is not scientific knowledge. For we / do not inquire for what we already know;[2] but good deliberation is a type of deliberation, and a deliberator inquires and rationally calculates.

Moreover, it is not good guessing either. For good guessing involves no reasoning, and is done quickly; but we deliberate a long

5 time, and it is said that we must act quickly on / the result of our deliberation, but deliberate slowly.[3]   §3 Further, quick thinking is different from good deliberation, and quick thinking is a kind of good guessing.

Nor is good deliberation just any sort of belief. Rather, since the bad deliberator is in error, and the good deliberator deliberates correctly, good deliberation is clearly some sort of correctness.

10   But it is not correctness in scientific knowledge or in belief. / For there is no correctness in scientific knowledge,[4] since there is no error in it either; and correctness in belief consists in truth.[5] Further, everything about which one has belief is already determined.[6]

However, good deliberation requires reason; hence the remaining possibility is that it belongs to thought. For thought is not yet assertion;[7] <and this is why it is not belief>. For belief is not inquiry, but

already an assertion; but in deliberating, / either well or badly, we   15
inquire for something and rationally calculate about it.

§4 But good deliberation is a certain sort of correctness in deliberation. That is why we must first inquire what <this correctness> is and what it is <correctness> about.[8]

Since there are several types of correctness, clearly good deliberation will not be every type.[9] For the incontinent or base person will use rational calculation to reach what he proposes to see,[10] and so will have deliberated correctly,[11] / but will have got himself a great evil.[12]   20
Having deliberated well, however, seems to be some sort of good; for the sort of correctness in deliberation that makes it good deliberation is the sort that reaches a good.[13]

§5 However, we can reach a good by a false inference, as well <as by correct deliberation>, so that we reach the right thing to do, but by the wrong steps, when the middle term / is false.[14] Hence neither   25
is this type of deliberation, leading us by the wrong steps to the right thing to do, enough for good deliberation.

§6 Further, one person may deliberate a long time before reaching the right thing to do, while another reaches it quickly. Nor, then, is the first condition enough for good deliberation; good deliberation is correctness that accords with what is beneficial, about the right thing, in the right way, and at the right time.

§7 Further, our deliberation may be either good without qualification or good only to the extent that it is a means to some <limited> end.[15] / Hence unqualifiedly good deliberation is the sort that is a cor-   30
rect means to promotes the unqualified end <i.e., the highest good>, while the <limited> sort is the sort that is a correct means to some <limited> end.[16] If, then, having deliberated well is proper to a prudent person, good deliberation will be the type of correctness that accords with what is expedient as a means to the end about which prudence is true supposition.[17]

10
[Comprehension]

[c11] Comprehension, i.e., good comprehension, makes people, / as   1143a
we say, comprehend and comprehend well.[1] It is not the same as scientific knowledge in general. Nor is it the same as belief, since, if it were, everyone would have comprehension. Nor is it any one of the specific sciences, in the way that medicine is about what is healthy or

geometry is about magnitudes. For comprehension is neither about
what always is and / is unchanging nor about just anything that comes
to be. It is about what we might be puzzled about and might deliberate about. That is why it is about the same things as prudence, but
not the same as prudence.

§2 For prudence is prescriptive, since its end is what action we
ought or ought not to do, but comprehension only / judges.[2] (For
comprehension and good comprehension are the same—for, similarly, people with comprehension[3] and with good comprehension are
the same.) Comprehension is neither having prudence nor acquiring
it.

§3 Rather, it is similar to the way learning is called comprehending
when someone applies scientific knowledge. In the same way comprehension consists in the application of belief to judge someone
else's remarks on a question that concerns / prudence, and moreover
it must judge them finely since judging well is the same as judging
finely. §4 That is how the name 'comprehension' was attached to
the comprehension that makes people have good comprehension. It
is derived from the comprehension that takes place in learning; for we
often call learning comprehending.[4]

11
[Practical thought and particulars]

The <state> called consideration makes people, as we say, / considerate and makes them have consideration; it is the correct judgment of
the decent person.[1] A sign of this is our saying that the decent person
more than others is considerate, and that it is decent to be considerate
about some things. Considerateness is the correct consideration that
judges what is decent; and correct consideration judges what is true.

[c12] §2 / It is reasonable that all these states tend in the same
direction.[2] For we ascribe consideration, comprehension, prudence,
and understanding to the same people, and say that these have consideration, and thereby understanding, and that they are prudent and
comprehending. For all these capacities are about the last things,
i.e.,[3] particulars. Moreover, someone has comprehension and good
consideration, or has considerateness, / in being able to judge about
the matters that concern the prudent person; for the decent is the
common concern of all good people in relations with other people.

§3 Now all the things achievable in action are particular and last things.⁴ For the prudent person also must recognize <things achievable in action>, while comprehension and consideration / are con-   35
cerned with things achievable in action, and these are last things.

§4 Understanding is also concerned with the last things, and in both directions.⁵ For there is understanding, not a rational account, both about the first terms and about the last.⁶ / In demonstrations   1143b
understanding is about the unchanging terms that are first. In <prem-isses> about action understanding is about the last term, the one that admits of being otherwise, and <hence> about the minor premiss.⁷ For these last terms are beginnings of the <end> to be aimed at, since universals are / reached from particulars.⁸   5

§5 We must therefore have perception of these particulars, and this perception is understanding.⁹ {{ §6 / That is why / understanding   9, 10
is both beginning and end; for demonstrations <begin> from these things and are about them.¹⁰ }}

§5 / That is why these states actually seem to grow naturally,¹¹ so   6
that, whereas no one seems to have natural wisdom,¹² people seem to have natural consideration, comprehension, and judgment.   §6 A sign <of their apparent natural character> is our thinking that they also correspond to someone's age, and the fact that understanding and consideration belong to a certain age, as though nature were the cause.   §6 / [[That is why ... about them]] And so we must attend   9
to the undemonstrated remarks and beliefs of experienced and older people or of prudent people, no less than to demonstrations. For these people see correctly because experience has given them their eye.

§7 / We have said, then, what prudence and wisdom are; what each   15
is about; and that each is the virtue of a different part of the soul.¹³

12
[Puzzles about prudence and wisdom]

[c13] One might, however, go through some puzzles about what use they are.¹

/ For wisdom is not concerned with any sort of coming into being,   20
and hence will not study any source of human happiness.

Admittedly prudence will study this; but what do we need / it for?   25
/ For knowledge of what is healthy or fit (i.e., of what results from   26
the state of health, not of what produces it) makes us no readier to act appropriately if we are / already healthy; for having the science of   27

21 medicine or / gymnastics makes us no readier to act appropriately. Similarly, prudence is the science of what is just and what is fine, and what is good for a human being; but this is how the good man acts;

25 and if we are already / good, knowledge of them makes us no readier to act appropriately, since virtues are states.[2]

28 §2 / If we concede that prudence is not useful[3] for this, should we

30 say it is useful for becoming good? In that case it will / be no use to those who are already excellent.[4] Nor, however, will it be any use to those who are not. For it will not matter to them[5] whether they have it themselves or take the advice of others who have it. The advice of others will be quite adequate for us, just as it is with health: for we wish to be healthy, but still do not learn medical science.

35 §3 Besides, it would seem absurd for prudence, inferior as / it is to wisdom, to control it—for the science that produces also rules and prescribes about each thing.[6]

We must discuss these questions; for so far we have only raised the puzzles about them.

1144a §4 / First of all, let us state that both prudence and wisdom must be choiceworthy in themselves, even if neither produces anything at all; for each is the virtue of one of the two <rational> parts <of the soul>.[7]

§5 Secondly, they do produce something. Wisdom produces hap-

5 piness, not in the way that medical science produces / health, but in the way that health produces <health>.[8] For since wisdom is a part of virtue as a whole, it makes us happy because it is a state that we possess and activate.

§6 Further, we fulfil our function[9] insofar as we have prudence and virtue of character; for virtue makes the goal correct, and pru-

10 dence makes the means to it <correct>.[10] / The fourth part of the soul, the nutritive part, has no such virtue,[11] since no action is up to it to do or not to do.

§7 To answer[12] the claim that prudence will make us no better at achieving[13] fine and just actions, we must begin from a little further back <in our discussion>. We begin here: we say that some people

15 who / do just actions are not yet thereby just, if, for instance, they do the actions prescribed by the laws either unwillingly or because of ignorance or because of some other end, not because of the actions themselves, even though they do the right actions, those that the excellent person ought to do.[14] Equally, however, it would seem to be

possible for someone to do each type of action in the state that makes him a good person, that is to say, because / of decision and for the sake of the actions themselves.[15] 20

§8 Virtue, therefore, makes the decision correct.[16] But the actions that are naturally to be done to fulfil <the decision> do not belong to virtue, but to another capacity.[17] We must grasp them more perspicuously before continuing our discussion.

§9 There is a capacity, called cleverness, which is such as / to be able to do the actions that are means to the goal that is assumed[18] and to attain them.[19] If, then, the goal is fine, cleverness is praiseworthy, and if the goal is base, cleverness is unscrupulousness. That is why both prudent and unscrupulous people are called clever.[20] 25

§10 Now prudence is not cleverness,[21] though not without this capacity. But <prudence>, / this eye of the soul, acquires its state only with virtue,[22] as we have said and as is clear. For inferences about actions have a principle, 'Since the end and the best good is this sort of thing' (whatever it actually is—let it be any old thing for the sake of argument).[23] And this <best good> is not apparent, except to the good person; / for vice perverts us and produces false views about the principles of actions. Evidently, then, we cannot be prudent without being / good. 30

1144b 35

13
[Prudence and virtue of character]

We must, then, also examine virtue over again.[1] For virtue is similar <in this way> to prudence; as prudence is related to cleverness, not the same but similar, so natural virtue is related to full virtue.[2] For each of us seems to possess his type of character to / some extent by nature; for we are just, brave, prone to temperance, or have another feature, immediately from birth. But still we look for some further condition to be full goodness, and we expect these features to belong to us in another way. For these natural states belong to children and to beasts as well <as to adults>, but without understanding they are / evidently harmful.[3] At any rate, this much would seem to be clear: just as a heavy body moving around unable to see suffers a heavy fall because it has no sight, so it is with virtue.[4] 5

10

§2 But if someone acquires understanding, he improves in his actions, and the state he now has, though still similar <to the natural

condition>, will be fully virtue. And so, just as, in the part of the soul
that has belief, there are two sorts of conditions, cleverness / and
prudence, so also there are two in the part that has character, natural virtue and full virtue. And of these full virtue cannot be acquired
without prudence.[5]

§3 That is why some say that all the virtues are <cases of> prudence, and why the inquiries Socrates used to undertake[6] were in one
way correct, and in another way in error. For insofar as he thought
/ all the virtues are <cases of> prudence,[7] he was in error; but insofar as he thought they all require prudence, what he used to say was
right.

§4 Here is a sign of this: whenever people now define virtue, they
all say what state it is and what it is related to, and then add that it
is the state in accord with correct reason.[8] Now the correct reason is
the reason in accord with prudence; it would / seem, then, that they
all in a way intuitively believe that the state in accord with prudence
is virtue.

§5 But we must make a slight change. For it is not merely the state
in accord with the correct reason,[9] but the state involving the correct
reason,[10] that is virtue. And it is prudence that is correct reason in this
area. Socrates, then, used to think the virtues are <cases of> reason
because he thought they / are all <cases of> knowledge, but we think
they involve reason.

§6 What we have said, then, makes it clear that we cannot be fully
good without prudence, or prudent without virtue of character. And
in this way we can also solve the dialectical argument that someone
might use to show that the virtues are separated from one another.[11]
For, <it is argued>, since the same person / is not naturally best
suited for all the virtues, someone will already have one virtue before
he has got another. This is indeed possible in the case of the natural
virtues. It is not possible, however, in the case of the <full> virtues
that someone must / have to be called good without qualification;
for one has all the virtues if and only if one has prudence, which is a
single state.[12]

§7 And it is clear that, even if prudence were useless in action,
we would need it because it is the virtue of this part <of the soul>,[13]
and because the decision will not be correct without / prudence or
without virtue[14]—for <virtue> makes us achieve the end, whereas
<prudence> makes us achieve the means to the end.[15]

§8 Moreover, prudence does not control wisdom or the better part of the soul, just as medical science does not control health.[16] For medical science does not use health, but only aims to bring health into being; hence it prescribes for the sake of health, / but does not 10 prescribe to health. Besides, <saying that prudence controls wisdom> would be like saying that political science rules the gods because it prescribes about everything in the city.

Book VII
[Incontinence]

1
[Virtue, vice, and incontinence]

/ Let us now make a new start, and say in the area of character there 15 are three conditions to be avoided—vice, incontinence, and bestiality. The contraries of two of these are clear; we call one virtue and the other continence.

The contrary to bestiality is most suitably called virtue that is superior to us, / a heroic, indeed divine, sort of virtue. Thus Homer 20 made Priam say that Hector was remarkably good; 'nor did he look as though he were the child of a mortal man, but of a god.'[1] §2 If, therefore, human beings become gods, as they are said to do, because of exceedingly great virtue, this is clearly the sort of state that would be opposite / to the bestial state. For indeed, just as a beast has nei- 25 ther virtue nor vice, so neither does a god; but the god's state is more honourable than virtue, and the beast's belongs to some other kind than vice.[2]

§3 Now it is rare that a divine man exists. (This is what the Spartans habitually call him; whenever they very much admire some- one, they say 'divine man'.[3]) Similarly, the / bestial person is also 30 rare among human beings. He is most often found in foreigners; but some bestial features also result from diseases and deformities. We also use 'bestial' as a term of reproach for people whose vice exceeds the human level.

§4 We must make some remarks about this condition later. / We 35 have discussed vice earlier. We must now discuss incontinence, soft- ness, and self-indulgence, and also continence / and resistance; for we 1145b must not suppose that continence and incontinence are concerned with the same states as virtue and vice, or that they belong to a different kind.

§5 As in the other cases we must set out the appearances,[4] and first

5   of all go through the puzzles. In this way we must prove / the common beliefs about these ways of being affected[5]—ideally, all the common beliefs, but if not all, most of them, and the most important.[6] For if the objections are solved, and the common beliefs are left, it will be an adequate proof.

§6 [c2] Continence and resistance, then, seem to be good and

10 praiseworthy conditions, but incontinence and softness seem to / be base and blameworthy conditions.[7] The continent person seems to be the same as one who abides by his rational calculation; and the incontinent person seems to be the same as one who abandons it. The incontinent person knows that his actions are base, but does them because of his feelings, whereas the continent person knows that his appetites are base, but because of reason does not follow them.

15 People think the temperate person is continent and resistant. / Some think that every continent and resistant person is temperate; others deny it. Some people say the incontinent person is intemperate and the intemperate incontinent, with no distinction; others say they are different.

§7 Sometimes it is said that a prudent person cannot be incontinent; but sometimes it is said that some people are prudent and clever, but still incontinent.

20 / Further, people are called incontinent about spirit, honour, and gain.

These, then, are the things that are said.

2

[Puzzles about incontinence]

[c3] We might be puzzled about what sort of correct supposition someone has when he acts incontinently.[1]

First of all, some say he cannot have knowledge <at the time he acts>. For it would be terrible—Socrates used to think[2]—for knowl-

25 edge to be in someone, but mastered by something else, / and dragged around like a slave.[3] For Socrates used to oppose the account <of incontinence> altogether, in the belief that there is no incontinence. For no one, in Socrates' view, supposes while he acts that his action

conflicts with what is best; on the contrary, our action conflicts with what is best only because we are ignorant <of the conflict>.[4]

§2 This argument, then, contradicts things that appear manifestly,[5] and we ought to ask if ignorance causes this way of being affected, what type of ignorance / it proves out to be. For it is evident, at any 30 rate, that before he is affected the one who acts incontinently does not think <he should do the action he eventually does>.[6]

§3 Some people concede some of <Socrates' points>, but reject some of them. For they agree that nothing is superior to knowledge, but they deny the claim that no one's action conflicts with what has seemed better to him. That is why they say that when the incontinent person is overcome by pleasure he has only / belief, not 35 knowledge.

§4 If, however, he has belief, not knowledge, / and the supposi- 1146a tion that resists is not strong, but only a weak one, such as people have when they are in doubt, we will pardon failure to abide by these beliefs against strong appetites. In fact, however, we do not pardon vice, or any other blameworthy condition <including incontinence>.

§5 / Then is it prudence that resists, since it is the strongest? But 5 that is strange. For on this view the same person will be both prudent and incontinent; but no one would say that the prudent person is the sort who does the worst actions willingly. Besides, we have shown earlier that the prudent person acts <on his knowledge>, since he is concerned with the last things, <i.e., particulars>, and that he has the other virtues.[7]

§6 / Further,[8] if the continent person must have strong and base 10 appetites, the temperate person will not be continent nor the continent person temperate. For the temperate person is not the sort who has either excessive or base appetites, but <the continent person> must have both. For if his appetites are good, the state that prevents him from following them must be base, so that not all continence / 15 is excellent. If, however, the appetites are weak and not base, continence is nothing impressive; and if they are base and weak, it is nothing great.

§7 Further, if continence makes someone prone to abide by every belief, it is bad, if, for instance, it makes him abide by a false as well <as a true> belief. And if incontinence makes someone prone to abandon every belief, there will be an excellent type of incontinence. / Take, for instance, Neoptolemus in Sophocles' *Philoctetes*.[9] For he is 20 praiseworthy for his failure to abide by <his promise to tell the lies> that Odysseus had persuaded him <to tell>; <he breaks his promise> because he feels pain at lying.

§8 Further, the sophistical argument is a puzzle. For <the sophists> wish to refute an <opponent, by showing> that his views have paradoxical results,[10] so that they will be clever in encounters.[11]

25 Hence the inference that results is a puzzle; / for thought is tied up, whenever it does not want to stand still—because the conclusion is displeasing—but it cannot advance—because it cannot solve the argument.[12]   §9 A certain argument, then, concludes that foolishness combined with incontinence is virtue. For incontinence makes

30 someone act contrary to what he supposes <is right>; but since / he supposes that good things are bad and that it is wrong to do them, he will do the good actions, not the bad.

§10 Further, if someone who acts in pursuit of pleasant things because this is what he is persuaded and decides to do,[13] he seems to be better than someone who acts not because of rational calculation, but because of incontinence. For the first person is the easier to cure, because he might be persuaded to act otherwise; but the incontinent

35 person illustrates / the proverb 'If water chokes us, how are we to wash
1146b / it down?' For if he had been persuaded to do the action he does, he would have stopped when he was persuaded to act otherwise; but in fact, though already persuaded to act otherwise, he still acts <wrongly>.

§11 Further, is there incontinence and continence about everything? If so, who is simply incontinent?[14] For no one has all the types

5 of incontinence, but we say that some people / are simply incontinent.

§12 [c4] These, then, are the sorts of puzzles that arise.[15] We must undermine some of these claims, and leave others intact; for the solution[16] of the puzzle is the discovery <of what we are seeking>.

3
[Incontinence and ignorance]

First, then, we must examine whether the incontinent has knowledge

10 or not, and in what way he has it. Second, what / should we take to be the range of incontinence and continence—every pleasure and pain, or some definite subclass? Are the continent and the resistant person the same or different? Similarly we must deal with the other questions that are relevant to this study.

§2 / We begin[1] by examining whether continence and inconti- 15
nence differ from other things by their range or by their attitudes.[2]
In other words, is the incontinent person incontinent because of a
specific range of actions, or because of a specific attitude, or because
of both? Next, is there incontinence and continence about everything, or not?

For the simply incontinent person is not incontinent about everything, / but he has the same range as the intemperate person.[3] Nor is 20
he incontinent simply by being related to these <pleasures>—for that
would make incontinence the same as intemperance.[4] No; he is incontinent by being related to them in this way. For the intemperate person
acts on decision when he is led on, since he thinks it is right in every
case to pursue the pleasant thing at hand. The incontinent person, however, thinks it is wrong to pursue this pleasant thing, yet still pursues it.[5]

§3 [c5] / Now on the question whether the incontinent person's 25
action conflicts with true belief, not with knowledge:[6] whether it is
knowledge or belief does not matter for this argument. For some who
have belief are in no doubt, but think they have exact knowledge.

§4 If, then, it is the weakness of their conviction that makes people
with belief, not people with knowledge, act in conflict with their supposition, it follows that knowledge will <for these purposes> be no
different from belief; for, as Heracleitus / makes clear,[7] some people's 30
convictions about what they believe are no weaker than other people's
convictions about what they know.

§5 But we speak of knowing in two ways; we ascribe it both to
someone who has it without using it and to someone who is using
it.[8] Hence it will matter whether someone has the knowledge that
his action is wrong, without attending[9] to his / knowledge, or he both 35
has it and attends to it. For this second case seems extraordinary,
but wrong action when he does not attend to his knowledge does not
seem extraordinary.

§6 / Further, since there are two types of premisses, someone's 1147a
action may well conflict with his knowledge if he has both types of
premisses, but uses only the universal premiss and not the particular
premiss.[10] For it is particulars that are achievable in action.[11] There
are also different types of universal,[12] one type referring to the agent
himself, / and the other referring to the object. Perhaps, for instance, 5
someone knows that dry things benefit every human being, and that

he himself is a human being, or that this sort of thing is dry; but he either does not have or does not activate the knowledge that this particular thing is of this sort. These ways <of knowing and not knowing>, then, make such a remarkable difference that it seems not at all strange <if someone acting against his knowledge> has the one sort of knowledge, but astounding if he has the other sort.[13]

§7 / Further, human beings may have knowledge in a way different from those we have described. For we see that having without using includes different types of having; hence some people, such as those who are asleep or mad or drunk, both have knowledge in a way and do not have it.[14] Moreover, this is the condition of those affected by strong / feelings.[15] For spirited reactions, sexual appetites, and some conditions of this sort clearly <both disturb knowledge and> disturb the body[16] as well, and even produce fits of madness in some people. Clearly, then <since incontinents are also affected by strong feelings>, we should say that they have knowledge in a way similar to these people.

§8 Now saying the words that come from knowledge is no sign <of fully having it>.[17] For some who are affected in these ways even / go through demonstrations and recite verses of Empedocles. And those who have just learnt something do not yet know it, though they string the words together; for it must grow into them, and this takes time.[18] We must suppose, therefore, that those who are acting incontinently also say the words in the way that actors do.[19]

§9 Further, we may also look at the cause in the following / way, referring to <human> nature.[20] For one belief is universal; the other is about particulars, and therefore perception controls them. And in the cases where these two <beliefs> result in one <belief>,[21] it is necessary, in one case, for the soul to affirm what has been concluded,[22] but, in the case of beliefs about production, to act at once <on what has been concluded>. If, for instance, everything sweet must be tasted, and this, / some one particular thing, is sweet, it is necessary for someone who is able and unhindered also to act on this at the same time.[23]

§10 Suppose, then, that someone has the universal <belief> hindering him from tasting;[24] he has the second <belief>, that everything sweet is pleasant and this is sweet,[25] and this <belief> is active;[26] but it turns out that appetite is present in him.[27] The <belief>, then, / <that is formed from the previous two beliefs> tells him to avoid this,[28] but

10

15

20

25

30

35

appetite leads him on—for each of the parts <of the soul> is capable of initiating motion.[29]

/ The result, then, is that in a way reason and belief make him act   1147b
incontinently. The <second> belief is contrary to correct reason, but only coincidentally, not in its own right.[30]   §11 For the appetite, not the belief, is contrary <in its own right to correct reason>. That is also why beasts are not incontinent, because they have no / universal sup-   5
position, but <only> appearance and memory of particulars.[31]

§12 How is the ignorance resolved, so that the incontinent person recovers his knowledge?[32] The same account that applies to some-one drunk or asleep applies here too, and is not special to this way of being affected. We must hear it from the naturalists.[33]

§13 Since the last premiss is a belief about something / percepti-   10
ble,[34] and controls action, this is what the incontinent person does not have when he is being affected.[35] Or <rather> the way he has it is not knowledge of it, but, as we saw, saying the words,[36] as the drunk says the words of Empedocles.[37]

And since the last term does not seem to be universal, or expressive of knowledge in the same way as the universal / term,[38] the result Soc-   15
rates was looking for would seem to come about as well. §14 For the knowledge that is present when someone is affected by incon-tinence is not the sort that seems to be fully knowledge, nor is this dragged about because he is affected, but only perceptual knowl-edge[39] is present.

So much, then, for knowing and not knowing, and for how it is possible to know and still to act incontinently.

4

[Simple incontinence]

[c6] / Next we must say whether anyone is simply incontinent, or all   20
incontinents are incontinent in some particular way; and if someone is simply incontinent, we must say what sorts of things he is inconti-nent about.

First of all, both continence and resistance and incontinence and softness are evidently about pleasures and pains.

§2 Some sources of pleasure are necessary; others are choice-worthy / in their own right, but can be taken to excess.[1] The nec-   25
essary ones are the bodily conditions, i.e., those that concern food, sexual intercourse, and the sorts of bodily conditions that we took

temperance and intemperance to be about. Other sources of pleasure
30   are not necessary, but are choiceworthy / in themselves, such as victory, honour, wealth, and similar good and pleasant things.

When people go to excess, against the correct reason in them, in the
pursuit of these sources of pleasure, we do not call them simply incontinent, but add the qualification that they are incontinent about wealth,
gain, honour, or spirit, and not simply incontinent. For we assume that
35   they are different, and called incontinent because of / a <mere> simi-
1148a   larity, just as the Olympic victor named Human[2] was / different, since
for him the common account <of human being> was only a little different from his special one, but it was different nonetheless.

A sign in favour of what we say is the fact that incontinence is
blamed not only as an error but as a vice, either unqualified or partial,[3] while none of these conditions is blamed as a vice.

5   §3 / Now consider the people concerned with the bodily gratifications, those that we take temperance and intemperance to be about.
Some of these people go to excess in pursuing these pleasant things
and avoiding painful things—hunger, thirst, heat, cold, and all the
objects of touch and taste—not, however, because they have decided
10   on it, but against their decision and thought. / These are the people
called simply incontinent, not with the added condition that they are
incontinent about, for instance, anger.

§4 A sign of this is the fact that people are also called soft about
these <bodily> pleasures, but not about any of the non-necessary
ones.

This is also why we include the incontinent and the intemperate
person, and the continent and the temperate person, in the same
15   class, but do not include any of those who / are incontinent in some
particular way. It is because incontinence and intemperance are, in a
way, about the same pleasures and pains. In fact they are about the
same things, but not in the same way; the intemperate person decides
on them, but the incontinent person does not.[4] That is why, if someone has no appetites, or slight ones, for excesses, but still pursues
them and avoids moderate pains, we will take him to be more intem-
20   perate than the person who / does it because he has intense appetites.
For think of the lengths he would go to if he also acquired vigorous
appetites and felt severe pains at the lack of necessities.

§5 Some pleasant things are naturally choiceworthy, some naturally
the contrary, some in between, as we divided them earlier. Hence some

appetites and pleasures are for fine and / excellent kinds of things, such   25
as wealth, profit, victory, and honour. About all these and about the
things in between people are blamed not for feeling an appetite and
love for them, but for doing so in a particular way, namely to excess.

Some people are overcome by, or pursue, some of these / naturally   30
fine and good things to a degree that goes against reason; they take
honour, or children, or parents (for instance) more seriously than is
right. For though these are certainly good and people are praised for
taking them seriously, still excess about them is also possible. It is
excessive if one fights, as Niobe did <for her children>, even with the
gods, / or if one regards his father as Satyrus, nicknamed the Father-   1148b
lover, did—for he seemed to be excessively silly about it. There is no
vice[5] here, for the reason we have given, since each of these things is
naturally choiceworthy for itself, though excess about them is bad
and to be avoided.

§6 Similarly, / there is no incontinence here either, since inconti-   5
nence is not merely to be avoided, but also blameworthy.[6] But because
this way of being affected is similar to incontinence, people call it
incontinence, adding the qualification that it is incontinence about
this or that. Just so they call someone a bad doctor or a bad actor,
though they would never call him simply bad, / since each of these   10
conditions is not vice, but only similar to it by analogy. It is clear,
likewise, that the only condition we should take to be continence or
incontinence is the one concerned with what concerns temperance
and intemperance. We speak of incontinence about spirit because of
the similarity <to simple incontinence>, and hence add the qualification that someone is incontinent about spirit, as we do in the case
of honour or gain.

5

[Bestiality and disease]

/ Some things are naturally pleasant, and some of these are pleasant   15
without qualification, while others correspond to differences between
kinds of animals and of human beings. Other things are not naturally
pleasant, but deformities or habits or base natures make them pleasant; and we can see states that are about each of these that are similar
to <states that are about naturally pleasant things>.

§2 / By bestial states I mean, for instance, the female human being[1]   20
who is said to tear pregnant women apart and devour the children; or

the pleasures of some of the savage people around the Black Sea who are reputed to enjoy raw meat and human flesh, while some trade their children to each other to feast on; or what is said about Phalaris.[2]

25 §3 These states are bestial. / Other states result from attacks of disease, and in some cases from fits of madness—for instance, the one who sacrificed his mother and ate her, and the one who ate the liver of his fellow-slave. Others result from diseased conditions or from habit—for instance, plucking hairs, chewing nails, even coal and earth, and besides these sexual intercourse between males. For in

30 some / people these result from <a diseased> nature, in others from habit, as, for instance, in those who have suffered wanton <sexual> assault since their childhood.

§4 If nature is the cause, no one would call these people incontinent, any more than women would be called incontinent for being mounted rather than mounting.[3] The same applies to those who are in a diseased state because of habit.

1149a §5 / Each of these states, then, is outside the limits of vice, just as bestiality is. If someone who has them overcomes them or is overcome by them, that is not simple <continence or> incontinence, but the type so called from similarity, just as someone who is overcome by spirit should be called incontinent in relation to his feeling, but not

5 <simply> incontinent. / For among all the excesses of foolishness, cowardice, intemperance, and irritability some are bestial, some diseased.

§6 If, for instance, someone's natural character makes him afraid of everything, even the noise of a mouse, he is a coward with a bestial sort of cowardice. Another person was afraid of a weasel because of an attack of disease. Among foolish people also those who natu-

10 rally lack reason / and live only by sense perception,[4] as some races of distant foreigners do, are bestial. Those who are foolish because of attacks of disease, such as epilepsy, or because of fits of madness, are diseased.

§7 Sometimes it is possible to have some of these conditions without being overcome—if, for instance, Phalaris had an appetite to / eat a

15 child or for some bizarre sexual pleasure, but restrained it. It is also possible to be overcome by these conditions and not merely to have them.

§8 One sort of vice is human, and this is called simple vice; another sort is called vice with an added condition, and is said to be bestial or diseased vice, but not simple vice. Similarly, then, it is also clear that one sort of incontinence is bestial, another diseased, but only

the incontinence corresponding / to human intemperance is simple   20
incontinence.

§9 [c7] It is clear, then, that incontinence and continence apply
only within the range of intemperance and temperance, and that for
other things there is another form of incontinence, so called by transference[5] of the name, and not simply.

6
[Incontinence and related conditions]

Moreover, let us observe that incontinence about spirit is / less   25
shameful than incontinence about appetites. For spirit would seem to
hear reason a bit, but to mishear it. It is like overhasty servants who
run out before they have heard all their instructions, and then carry
them out wrongly, or dogs who bark at any noise at all, before looking to see if it is a friend. In the same / way, since spirit is naturally   30
hot and hasty, it hears, but does not hear the instruction, and rushes
off to exact a penalty. For reason or appearance has shown that we
are being slighted or wantonly insulted; and spirit, as though it had
inferred that one ought to fight this sort of thing, is irritated / at once.[1] 35
Appetite, however, only needs reason or perception to say that this is
pleasant, and it rushes off for gratification.[2]

/ And so spirit follows reason in a way, but appetite does not.   1149b
Therefore <incontinence about appetite> is more shameful. For if
someone is incontinent about spirit, he is overcome by reason in a
way; but if he is incontinent about appetite, he is overcome by appetite, not by reason.

§2 Further, it is more pardonable to follow natural desires, / since   5
it is also more pardonable to follow those natural appetites that are
common to everyone and to the extent that they are common.[3] Now
spirit and irritability are more natural than the excessive and unnec-
essary appetites. It is just as the son said in his defence for beating his
father: 'Yes, and he beat his father, and his father beat his own father
before that'; / and pointing to his young son, he said, 'And he will beat   10
me when he becomes a man; it runs in our family.'[4] Similarly, the
father being dragged by his son kept urging him to stop at the front
door, since that was as far as he had dragged his own father.

§3 Further, those who plot more are more unjust. Now the spirited
person does not plot, and neither does spirit; / it is open.[5] Appetite,   15

however, is like what they say about Aphrodite, 'trick weaving Cypris',[6] and what Homer says about her embroidered girdle: 'Blandishment, which steals the wits even of the very prudent.'[7] If, then, incontinence about appetite is more unjust and more shameful than incontinence
20 about spirit, it is simple / incontinence, and vice in a way.

§4 Further, no one feels pain when he commits wanton aggression; but whatever someone does from anger, he feels pain when he does it, whereas the wanton aggressor does what he does with pleasure. Now if whatever more justly provokes anger is more unjust, incontinence caused by appetite is more unjust, since spirit involves no wanton aggression.

25 §5 It is clear, then, how incontinence about appetites is more / shameful than incontinence about spirit, and that continence and incontinence are about bodily appetites and pleasures.

§6 Now we must grasp the varieties of these appetites and pleasures.[8] As we said at the beginning, some appetites are human and
30 natural in kind and degree, some bestial, some caused / by deformities and diseases. Temperance and intemperance are concerned only with the first of these. This is also why we do not call beasts either temperate or intemperate, except by transference of the name, if one kind of animal exceeds another altogether in wanton aggression,
35 destructiveness, and ravenousness. For beasts have / neither decision
1150a nor rational calculation, but are outside / <rational> nature, as the madmen among human beings are.[9]

§7 Bestiality is less grave than vice, but more frightening; for the best part is not corrupted, as it is in a human being, but absent altogether.[10] Hence a comparison between the two is like a comparison between an
5 inanimate and an animate being / to see which is worse. For in each case the badness of something that lacks an internal principle of its badness is less destructive than the badness of something that has such an internal principle; and understanding is such an internal principle.[11] It is similar, then, to a comparison between the injustice <of a beast> and an unjust human being; for in a way each <of these> is worse, since a bad human being can do innumerably more bad things than a beast.

7

[Incontinence, intemperance, and softness]

[c8] Let us now consider the pleasures and pains arising through
10 touch / and taste, the appetites for these pleasures, and the aversions

from these pains. Earlier we defined temperance and intemperance as being about these. Now it is possible for someone to be in the state in which he is overcome, even by <pleasure and pains> which most people overcome; and it is possible to overcome even those that overcome most people.[1] The person who is prone to be overcome by pleasures is incontinent; the one who overcomes is continent; the one overcome by pains is soft; and the one who overcomes them / is resis- 15
tant. The state of most people is in between, though indeed they may lean more towards the worse states.

§2 Now some pleasures are necessary and some are not. <The necessary ones are necessary> to a certain extent, but their excesses and deficiencies are not. The same is true for appetites and pains. One person pursues excesses of pleasant things because / they are excesses 20
and because he decides on it,[2] for themselves and not for some fur-ther result. He is intemperate; for he is bound to have no regrets, and hence he is incurable, since someone without regrets is incurable.[3] The one who is deficient is his opposite, while the intermediate one is temperate. The same is true of the one who avoids bodily pains not because he is overcome, but because he decides on it.

§3 / One of those who do not <act on what they> decide is led 25
on because of pleasure. The other is led on because he is avoiding the pain that comes from appetite. Hence these two differ from each other.[4]

Now it would seem to everyone that someone who does a shameful action from no appetite or a weak one is worse than if he does it from an intense appetite; and, similarly, that if he strikes another not from anger, he is worse than if he / strikes from anger.[5] For <if he can do 30
such evil when he is unaffected by feeling>, what would he have done if he had been strongly affected? That is why the intemperate person is worse than the incontinent.

One of the states mentioned <i.e., the decision to avoid pain> is more a species of softness, but the other person is intemperate.[6]

§4 The continent person is opposite to the incontinent, and the resistant to the soft.[7] For resistance consists in / holding out, and con- 35
tinence in overcoming, but holding out is different from overcoming, just as not being defeated differs from winning. That is why conti-nence is also more choiceworthy than resistance.

§5 / Someone who is deficient in withstanding what most people 1150b
withstand, and are capable of withstanding, is soft and self-indulgent;[8]

for self-indulgence is a kind of softness. This person trails his cloak
5   to avoid the labour and pain of lifting / it,[9] and imitates an invalid,
though he does not think he is miserable—he is <merely> similar to
a miserable person.

§6 And the same is true of continence and incontinence. For it
is not surprising if someone is overcome by strong and excessive
pleasures or pains; indeed, this is pardonable, provided he strug-
10   gles against them—like Theodectes' / Philoctetes bitten by the snake,
or Carcinus' Cercyon in the *Alope*, and like those who are trying to
restrain their laughter and burst out laughing all at once, as happened to Xenophantus.[10] But it is surprising if someone is overcome
by what most people can resist, and is incapable of withstanding it,
15   not because of his hereditary nature or because of disease (as, / for
instance, the Scythian kings' softness is hereditary, and as the female
is distinguished <by softness> from the male).

§7 The lover of amusements also seems to be intemperate, but in
fact he is soft. For amusement is a relaxation, since it is a release, and
the lover of amusement is one of those who go to excess here.

20   §8 One type of incontinence is impetuosity, while another is /
weakness. For the weak person deliberates, but then his feeling makes
him abandon what he reached by deliberation; but the impetuous
person is led on by his feelings because he has not deliberated.[11] For
some people are like those who do not get tickled themselves if they
tickle someone else first; if they see and notice something in advance,
and rouse themselves and their rational calculation, they are not
25   overcome / by feelings, no matter whether something is pleasant or
painful.[12] Quick-tempered and volatile people are most prone to be
impetuous incontinents. For in quick-tempered people the appetite
is so fast, and in volatile people so intense, that they do not wait for
reason, because they tend to follow appearance.[13]

8
[Why intemperance is worse than incontinence]

30   [c9] The intemperate person, as we said, is not prone to regret, / since
he abides by his decision. But every incontinent is prone to regret.
That is why the truth is not what we said in raising the puzzles, but
in fact the intemperate person is incurable, and the incontinent curable.[1] For vice resembles diseases such as dropsy or consumption,
but incontinence is more like epilepsy; for vice is a continuous bad

condition, but incontinence is not. / {{ For the incontinent / is simi-   1151a3, 4
lar to those who get drunk quickly from a / little wine, and from less   5
than it takes for most people.[2] }} / And in general incontinence and   1150b35
vice are of different kinds; for the vicious person does not recognize
that he is vicious, but the incontinent person recognizes that he is
incontinent.

§2 / Among the incontinent people themselves, those who aban-   1151a
don themselves are better than those who have reason but do not
abide by it.[3] For the second type are overcome by a less strong feeling,
and do not act without having deliberated, as the first type do. [[For
the incontinent . . . most people.]]

§3 / Evidently, then, incontinence is not a vice, though presum-   5
ably it is one in a way. For incontinence is against one's decision, but
vice accords with decision. Still, incontinence is similar to vice in its
actions, as Demodocus says against the Milesians: 'The Milesians are
not stupid, but they do what / stupid people would do';[4] in the same   10
way incontinents are not unjust, but will do injustice.

§4 Moreover, the incontinent person is the sort to pursue excessive bodily pleasures against correct reason, but not because he is persuaded <it is best>. The intemperate person, however, is persuaded,
because he is the sort of person to pursue them. Hence the incontinent person is easily persuaded out of it, while the intemperate person is not.

/ For virtue preserves the principle, whereas vice corrupts it; and   15
in actions the end we act for is the principle, as the assumptions are
the principles in mathematics.[5] Reason does not teach the principles
in either case, but virtue, either natural or habituated, teaches correct
belief about the principle.[6] The sort of person <who has this virtue>
is temperate, and the / contrary sort intemperate.   20

§5 But there is also someone who because of his feelings abandons himself against correct reason. They overcome him far enough
so that his actions do not accord with correct reason, but not so far
as to make him the sort of person to be persuaded that it is right to
pursue such pleasures without restraint. This, then, is the incontinent
person. He is better than the intemperate person, / and is not bad   25
without qualification, since the best thing, the principle, is preserved
in him.[7] Another sort of person is contrary to him. <This is the continent person> who abides <by reason> and does not abandon himself, not because of his feelings at least. It is evident from this that

the continent person's state is excellent, and the incontinent person's state is base.

9
[Continence]

30 [c10] Then is someone continent if he abides by just any sort / of reason and any sort of decision, or must he abide by the correct decision?[1] And is someone incontinent if he fails to abide by just any decision and any reason, or must it be reason that is not false, and the correct decision? This was the puzzle raised earlier.

Perhaps in fact the continent person abides, and the incontinent fails to abide, by just any decision coincidentally, but abides by the
35 true reason and the correct decision in its own right.[2] / For if someone
1151b chooses or pursues one thing because / of a second, he pursues and chooses the second in its own right and the first coincidentally. Now when we speak of something without qualification, we speak of it in its own right. Hence in one way <i.e., coincidentally> the continent person abides by just any belief, and the incontinent abandons it; but, <speaking> without qualification, the continent person abides by the true belief and the incontinent person abandons it.

5 §2 / Now there are some other people who tend to abide by their belief.[3] These are the people called stubborn, who are hard to persuade of something and not easy to persuade out of it. These have some similarity to continent people, just as the wasteful person has to the generous, and the rash to the confident. But they are different on many points. For the continent person is not swayed because of feeling and appetite; <but he is not inflexible about everything,> since
10 he / will be easily persuaded whenever it is appropriate. But stubborn people are not swayed by reason; for they acquire appetites, and many of them are led on by pleasures.

§3 The stubborn include the opinionated, the ignorant and the boorish. The opinionated are as they are because of pleasure and
15 pain. For they find enjoyment in winning <the argument> / if they are not persuaded to change their views, and they feel pain if their opinions are voided, like decrees.[4] Hence they are more like incontinent than like continent people.

§4 There are also some people who do not abide by their resolutions, but not because they are incontinent—Neoptolemus, for instance, in Sophocles' *Philoctetes*.[5] Though certainly it was pleasure

that made him abandon his resolution, it was / a fine pleasure; for   20
telling the truth was pleasant to him,[6] but Odysseus had persuaded
him to lie. <He is not incontinent;> for not everyone who does something because of pleasure is either intemperate or base or incontinent, but only someone who does it because of a shameful pleasure.[7]

§5 [c11] There is also the sort of person who enjoys bodily things
less than is right, and does not abide by reason; hence / the continent   25
person is intermediate between this person and the incontinent.[8] For
the incontinent fails to abide by reason because of too much <enjoy-
ment>; the other person fails because of too little; but the continent
person abides and is not swayed because of too much or too little. If
continence is excellent, then both of these contrary states / must be   30
base, as indeed they appear. However, the other state is evident in
only a few people on a few occasions; and hence continence seems
to be contrary only to incontinence, just as temperance seems to be
contrary only to intemperance.

§6 Now many things are called by some name because of similarity <to genuine cases>; this has happened also to the continence of
the temperate person, because of similarity.[9] / For the continent and   35
the temperate person are both the sort to do nothing against reason because of bodily pleasures, / but the continent person has base   1152a
appetites, whereas the temperate person lacks them. The temperate
person is the sort to find nothing pleasant against reason, but the
continent is the sort to find such things pleasant but not to be led by
them.[10]

The incontinent and the intemperate person are similar too; /   5
though they are different, they both pursue bodily sources of pleasure. But the intemperate person <pursues them because he> also
thinks it is right, while the incontinent person does not think so.

10
[Answers to further questions about incontinence]

Nor can the same person be at once both prudent and incontinent.[1]
For we have shown that a prudent person must also / at the same   8
time be excellent in character, <and the incontinent / person is not>.[2]   10
{{ §2 However, a clever person may well be incontinent. Indeed, the
reason people sometimes seem to / be prudent but incontinent is that   11
<really they are only clever and> / cleverness differs from prudence in   12
the way / we described in our first discussion; though they are closely   13

14   / related in definition, they differ in <so far as prudence requires the correct> decision.³}}

8, 9   / Moreover, someone is not prudent simply by knowing; / he must also act on his knowledge. But the incontinent person does not.

14   [[§2 However ... decision.]]   §3 / He is not in the condition of
15   someone who knows and is attending, / but in the condition of one asleep or drunk.⁴

He acts willingly; for in a way he acts in knowledge both of what he is doing and of the end he is doing it for.⁵ But he is not base, since his decision is decent; hence he is half base. Nor is he unjust, since he is not a plotter. For one type of incontinent person does not abide by the result of his deliberation, while the volatile person is not even prone to deliberate at all.⁶

20   / In fact the incontinent person is like a city that votes for all the right decrees and has excellent laws, but does not apply them, as in Anaxandrides' taunt, 'The city willed it, that cares nothing for laws.'   §4 The base person, by contrast, is like a city that applies its laws, but applies bad ones.⁷

25   / Incontinence and continence are about what exceeds the state of most people; the continent person abides <by reason> more than most people are capable of doing, the incontinent person less.⁸

The type of incontinence that is found in volatile people is more easily cured than the type of incontinence found in those who deliberate but do not abide by it. And incontinents through habituation
30   are more easily cured than / the natural incontinents; for habit is easier than nature to change.⁹ Indeed the reason why habit is also difficult to change is that it is like nature, as Eunenus says, 'Habit, I say, is longtime training, my friend, and in the end training is nature for human beings.'¹⁰

35   §5 We have said, then, what continence and incontinence, / resistance and softness are, and how these states are related to each other.

[Pleasure]

11
[Disputed questions about pleasure]

1152b   [c12] / Pleasure and pain are proper subjects of study for the political philosopher, since he is the ruling craftsman of the end that we refer to in calling something bad or good without qualification.¹   §2 Further,

we must also examine them because we have / laid it down that virtue   5
and vice of character are about pains and pleasures, and because most
people think happiness involves pleasure—that is why they also call
the blessed person by that name (*makarios*) from enjoyment (*charein*).[2]

§3 Now it seems to some people that no pleasure is a good, either
in its own right or coincidentally, on the ground that the good is not
the same as pleasure.[3] / To others it seems that some pleasures are   10
good, but most are bad. A third view is that even if every pleasure is a
good, the best good still cannot be pleasure.

§4 The reasons for thinking it is not a good at all are these:[4] Every
pleasure is a perceived becoming towards <the fulfilment of something's> nature;[5] but no becoming is of the same kind as its end—for
instance, no <process of> building is of the / same kind as a house.   15
Further, the temperate person avoids pleasures. Further, the prudent
person pursues what is painless, not what is pleasant. Further, pleasures impede prudent thinking,[6] and the more we enjoy them, the
more they impede it; no one, for instance, can think about anything
during sexual intercourse. Further, every good is the product of a
craft, but there is no craft of pleasure. / Further, children and animals   20
pursue pleasure.

§5 To show that not all pleasures are excellent things, people say
that some are shameful and reproached, and that some are harmful,
since some pleasant things cause disease.

§6 To show that the best good is not pleasure, people say that pleasure is not an end, but a becoming.

These, then, are roughly the things said about it.

12
[Pleasure and good]

[c13] / These arguments, however, do not show that pleasure is not   25
a good, or even that it is not the best good.[1] This will be clear as
follows.

First of all, since what is good may be good in either of two ways,
as good without qualification or as good for some particular thing
or person, this will also be true of natures and states, and hence also
of processes and becomings.[2] And so, among the <processes and
becomings> that seem bad, some are bad without qualification but
for some person not bad, and for / this person actually choiceworthy.   30
Some are not choiceworthy for him either, except sometimes and for

a short time, not on each occasion.³ Some are not even pleasures, but appear to be; these are the <processes>, for instance, in sick people that involve pain and are means to medical treatment.⁴

§2 Further, since one sort of good is an activity and another sort is a state, the processes that restore us to our natural / state are pleasant coincidentally. Here the activity in the appetites belongs to the rest of our state and nature.⁵ For there are also pleasures / without pain and appetite, such as the pleasures of studying, those in which our nature lacks nothing.

A sign <that supports our distinction between pleasures> is the fact that we do not enjoy the same thing when our nature is being refilled as we enjoy when it is eventually fully restored.⁶ When it is fully restored, we enjoy things that are pleasant without qualification, but when it is being refilled, we enjoy even the contrary things. / For we even enjoy sharp or bitter things, though none of these is pleasant by nature or pleasant without qualification. Hence <these pleasures> are not pleasures <without qualification> either; for as pleasant things differ from one another, so the pleasures arising from them differ too.⁷

§3 Further, it is not necessary for something else to be better than pleasure, as the end, some say, is better than the becoming.⁸ For pleasures are not becomings, nor do they all / even involve a becoming. They are activities, and an end <in themselves>, and arise when we exercise <a capacity>, not when we are coming to be <in some state>.⁹ And not all pleasures have something else as their end, but only those in people who are being led towards the completion of their nature.

That is why it is also a mistake to call pleasure a perceived becoming.¹⁰ It should instead be called <an> activity of the natural state, and should be called not perceived, but unimpeded.¹¹ The reason it seems to some people to be a becoming is that / it is fully good <and hence an activity>; for they think activities are becomings, though in fact these are different things.

§4 To say that pleasures are bad because some pleasant things cause disease is the same as saying that some healthy things are bad for moneymaking.¹² To this extent both are bad; but / that is not enough to make them bad, since even study is sometimes harmful to health.

§5 Neither prudence nor any state is impeded by the pleasures arising from it, but only by alien pleasures.¹³ For the pleasures arising from study and learning will make us study and learn all the more.

§6 The fact that pleasure is not the product of a craft is quite / rea-   25
sonable; for a craft does not belong to any other activity either, but to
a capacity.[14] And yet, the crafts of perfumery and cooking do seem to
be crafts of pleasure.

§7 The claim that the temperate person avoids pleasure, that the
prudent person pursues the painless life, and that children and beasts
pursue pleasure—all these are solved by the same reply.[15] For we have
explained in what ways pleasures / are good, and in what ways not   30
all are good without qualification;[16] and it is these pleasures <that
are not good without qualification> that beasts and children pursue, whereas the prudent person pursues painlessness in relation to
these.[17] These are the pleasures that involve appetite and pain and
the bodily pleasures (since these involve appetite and pain) and their
excesses, whose pursuit makes the intemperate person intemperate.
That is why the temperate person avoids these pleasures / <but not   35
all pleasures>, since there are pleasures of the temperate person too.

13
[Pleasure and happiness]

[c14] / Moreover, it is also agreed[1] that pain is an evil, and is to   1153b
be avoided; for one kind of pain is bad without qualification, and
another is bad in a particular way, by impeding <activities>.[2] But
the contrary to what is to be avoided, insofar as it is bad and to be
avoided, is a good; hence pleasure must be a good. / For Speusippus'   5
solution—<that pleasure is opposite both to pain and to the good>
as the greater is contrary both to the lesser and to the equal—does
not succeed.[3] For he would not say that pleasure is essentially an
evil.[4]

§2 Besides, just as one science might well be the best good, even
though some sciences are bad, some pleasure might well be the best
good, even though most pleasures are bad.[5] Indeed, presumably, if
each state / has its unimpeded activities, and happiness is the activ-   10
ity—if the activity is unimpeded—of all states or of some one of them,
it follows that some unimpeded activity is most choiceworthy. But
pleasure is this, <namely, an unimpeded activity>;[6] and so some type
of pleasure might be the best good[7] even if most pleasures turn out to
be bad without qualification.

That is why all think the happy life is pleasant and weave / plea-   15
sure into happiness, quite reasonably. For no activity is complete if

it is impeded, and happiness is something complete. That is why the happy person needs to have goods of the body and external goods added <to good activities>, and needs fortune also, so that he will not be impeded in these ways.

§3 Some maintain, on the contrary, that we are happy when we are 20 broken on the wheel, or fall into terrible misfortunes, provided / that we are good.[8] Whether they mean to or not, these people are talking nonsense.[9]

§4 And because happiness needs fortune added, some believe good fortune is the same as happiness. But it is not. For when it is excessive, it actually impedes happiness; and then, presumably, it is no longer rightly called *good* fortune, since the limit <up to which it is good> is defined in relation to happiness.[10]

25 §5 / The fact that all, both beasts and human beings, pursue pleasure is some sign of its being in some way the best good: 'No rumour is altogether lost which many peoples <spread>. . . .'[11] §6 But since 30 the best nature and state neither / is nor seems to be the same for all, they also do not all pursue the same pleasure, though they all pursue pleasure. Presumably in fact they do pursue the same pleasure, and not the one they think or would say they pursue; for all things by nature have something divine <in them>.[12]

35 However, the bodily pleasures have taken over the name / because people most often aim at them, and all share in them; and so, since 1154a these are the only pleasures they know, people / suppose that they are the only pleasures.[13]

§7 It is also apparent that if pleasure is not a good and an activity,[14] it will not be true that the happy person lives pleasantly. For what will he need pleasure for if it is not a good?[15] Indeed, it will even be possi- 5 ble for him to live painfully; for / pain is neither an evil nor a good if pleasure is not, and why then would he avoid it? Nor indeed will the life of the excellent person be pleasanter if his activities are not also pleasanter.

14
[Bodily pleasures]

10 Those who maintain that some pleasures, such as the fine ones, / are highly choiceworthy, but the bodily pleasures that concern the intemperate person are not, should examine bodily pleasures.[1]

§2 If what they say is true, why are the pains contrary to these pleasures deplorable? For what is contrary to an evil is a good.

Then are the necessary <bodily pleasures> good only in the way that what is not bad is good? Or are they good up to a point? <Surely they are good up to a point.> For though some states and processes allow no excess of the better, and hence no excess of pleasure <in them> either, others do / allow excess of the better, and hence 15 also allow excess of the pleasure in them. Now the bodily goods allow excess. The base person is base because he pursues the excess, but not because he pursues the necessary pleasures; for all enjoy delicacies and wines and sexual relations in some way, though not all in the right way.

The contrary is true of pain. For the base person avoids pain / in 20 general, not <only> an excess of it. For not <all> pain is contrary to excess <of pleasure>, except to someone who pursues the excess <of pleasure>.

§3 [c15] We must, however, not only state the true view, but also explain the false view; for an explanation of that promotes confidence.[2] For when we have an apparently reasonable explanation / of why a 25 false view appears true, that makes us more confident of the true view. Hence we should say why bodily pleasures appear more choiceworthy.

§4 First, then, it is because bodily pleasure pushes out pain. Excesses of pain make people seek a cure in the pursuit of excessive pleasure and of bodily pleasure in general. And / these <pleasures 30 that are> cures <for pains> become intense—that is why they are pursued—because they appear next to their contraries.

Indeed these are the two reasons why pleasure seems to be no excellent thing, as we have said.[3] First, some pleasures are the actions of a base nature—either base from birth, as in a beast, or base because of habit, such as the actions of base human beings. Secondly, others are cures of something deficient, and it is better to be in a good state than / to be coming into it. In fact these[4] pleasures 1154b coincide with our restoration to complete health, and so are excellent coincidentally.

§5 Further, bodily pleasures are pursued because they are intense, by people who are incapable of enjoying other pleasures. Certainly, these people induce some kinds of thirst in themselves. What they do is not a matter for reproach, whenever <the pleasures> are / 5 harmless,[5] but it is base whenever they are harmful. These people do this because they enjoy nothing else, and many people's natural constitution makes the neutral condition painful to them.

For an animal is always suffering,[6] as the natural scientists also testify, since they maintain that seeing and hearing are painful. However, we are used <to seeing and hearing> by now, so they say, <and so feel no intense pain>. §6 Indeed, the / <process of> growth makes young people's condition similar to an intoxicated person's and <hence> youth is pleasant. Naturally volatile people, by contrast, are always requiring a cure, since their constitution causes their body continual turmoil, and they are always having intense desires. A pain is driven out by its contrary pleasure, indeed by any pleasure / at all that is strong enough; and this is why such people become intemperate and base.

§7 Pleasures without pains, however, have no excess.[7] These are pleasant by nature and not coincidentally. By coincidentally pleasant things I mean pleasant things that are curative; for the <process of> being cured coincides with some action of the part of us that remains healthy, and hence undergoing / a cure seems to be pleasant. Things are pleasant by nature, however, when they produce action of a healthy nature.

§8 The reason why no one thing is always pleasant is that our nature is not simple, but has more than one constituent, insofar as we are perishable; hence the action of one part is against nature for the other nature in us, and when they are equally balanced, the action seems neither pleasant nor / painful. For if something has a simple nature the same action will always be pleasantest.

That is why the god always enjoys one simple pleasure <without change>.[8] For activity belongs not only to change but also to unchangingness, and indeed there is pleasure in rest more than in change. 'Variation in everything is sweet'[9] / (as the poet says) because of some inferiority; for just as it is the inferior human being who is prone to variation, so also the nature that needs variation is inferior, since it is not simple or decent.

§9 So much, then, for continence and incontinence and for pleasure and pain,[10] what each of them is, and in what ways some <aspects> of them are good and others bad. It remains for us to discuss friendship as well.

Book VIII
[Friendship]

1
[Common beliefs and questions]

/ After that the next topic is friendship; for it is a virtue, or involves   1155a
virtue.

Further, it is most necessary for our life.[1] / For no one would   5
choose to live without friends even if he had all the other goods.[2]
Indeed rich people and holders of powerful positions, even more than
other people, seem to need friends. For how would one benefit from
such prosperity if one had no opportunity for beneficence, which is
most often displayed, and most highly praised, in relation / to friends?   10
And how would one guard and protect prosperity without friends,
when it is all the more precarious the greater it is?   §2 But in poverty also, and in the other types of misfortune, people think friends
are the only refuge.[3]

Moreover, the young need friends to keep them from error. The
old need friends to care for them and support the actions that fail
because of weakness. And those in their prime need friends to / do   15
fine actions; for 'when two go together . . . ',[4] they are more capable
of understanding and acting.

§3 Further, a parent would seem to have a natural friendship for
a child, and a child for a parent, not only among human beings but
also among birds and most kinds of animals. Members / of the same   20
species,[5] and human beings most of all, have a natural friendship for
each other; that is why we praise friends of humanity.[6] And in our
travels we can see how every human being is akin and beloved to a
human being.

§4 Moreover, friendship would seem to hold cities together, and
legislators would seem to be more concerned about it / than about   25
justice. For concord would seem to be similar to friendship, and they
aim at concord among all, while they try above all to expel civil conflict, which is enmity.[7] Further, if people are friends, they have no
need of justice, but if they are just they need friendship in addition;
and the justice that is most just seems to belong to friendship.[8]

§5 But friendship is not only necessary, but also fine.[9] / For we   30
praise lovers of friends, and having many friends seems to be a fine

141

thing. Moreover, people think that the same people are good and also friends.

§6 [c2] Still, there are quite a few disputed points about friendship.[10]
For some hold it is a sort of similarity and that similar people are
35   friends. Hence the saying 'Similar to similar', and / 'Birds of a feather',
and so on. On the other side, it is said that similar people are all like
the proverbial potters, quarreling with each other.[11]
1155b   / On these questions some people inquire at a higher level, more
proper to <the study of> nature.[12] Euripides says that when earth gets
dry it longs passionately for rain, and the holy heaven when filled with
5   rain longs passionately to fall into the earth;[13] / and Heracleitus says
that the opponent co-operates, the finest harmony arises from discor-
dant elements, and all things come to be in struggle.[14] Others, such as
Empedocles, oppose this view, and say that similar aims for similar.[15]

§7 Let us, then, leave aside the puzzles proper to natural science,
since they are not proper to the present examination, and let us exam-
10   ine the puzzles that concern human <nature>, / and bear on characters and feelings.[16] For instance, does friendship arise among all sorts
of people, or can people not be friends if they are vicious? And is there
one species of friendship, or are there more? Some people think there is
only one species because friendship allows more and less. But here their
15   confidence rests on an / inadequate sign; for things of different species
also allow more and less. We have spoken about these earlier.[17]

2
[The object of friendship]

Perhaps these questions will become clear once we find out what it
is that is lovable.[1] For, it seems, not everything is loved, but <only>
the lovable, and this is either good or pleasant or useful. However, it
20   seems that the useful / is the source of some good or some pleasure;
hence the good and the pleasant are lovable as ends.

§2 Now do people love the good, or the good for themselves? For
sometimes these conflict; and the same is true of the pleasant. Each
one, it seems, loves the good for himself; and while the good is lovable
25   without qualification, the / lovable for each one is the good for himself. In fact each one loves not what *is* good for him, but what *appears*
good for him; but this will not matter, since <what appears good for
him> will be what appears lovable.[2]

§3 There are these three causes, then, of love.[3] Now love for an inanimate thing is not called friendship, since there is no mutual loving, and no wishing of good to it. For it would presumably be ridiculous to wish good things / to wine; the most you wish is its preservation so that you can have it. To a friend, however, it is said, you must wish goods for his own sake.[4] If you wish good things in this way, but the same wish is not returned by the other, you would be said to have <only> goodwill for the other. For friendship is said to be *reciprocated* goodwill.

§4 Should we add that friends are aware of the / reciprocated goodwill? For many a one has goodwill to people / whom he has not seen but whom he supposes to be decent or useful, and one of these might have the same goodwill towards him. These people, then, apparently have goodwill to each other, but how could we call them friends, given that they are unaware of their attitude to each other? <If they are to be friends>, then, they must[5] have goodwill to each / other, wish goods, and be aware of it, because of one of the things mentioned above.[6]

3
[The three types of friendship]

[c3] But these <causes> differ from one another in species, so also, then, do the types of loving and types of friendship.[1] Hence friendship has three species, corresponding to the three objects of love. For to each object of love corresponds a type of mutual loving, combined with awareness of it.[2]

But those who love each other wish goods to each other in the respect in which they love each / other.[3] Those who love each other for utility love the other not in his own right, but insofar as they gain some good for themselves from him. The same is true of those who love for pleasure; for they like a witty person not because of his character, but because he is pleasant to themselves.

§2 Those who love for utility or pleasure, then, are fond of / a friend because of what is good or pleasant for themselves, not insofar as the beloved is who he is,[4] but insofar as he is useful or pleasant. Hence these friendships as well <as the friends> are coincidental, since the beloved is loved not insofar as he is who he is, but insofar as he provides some good or pleasure.

§3 And so these sorts of friendships are easily dissolved, when / the friends do not remain similar <to what they were>; for if someone is no longer pleasant or useful, the other stops loving him.

What is useful does not remain the same, but is different at different times.[5] Hence, when the cause of their being friends is removed, the friendship is dissolved too, on the assumption that the friendship aims at these <useful results>. §4 This sort of friendship seems to arise especially among older / people—since at that age they pursue the advantageous, not the pleasant—and also among those in their prime or youth who pursue the expedient.[6]

Nor do such people live together very much. For sometimes they do not even find each other pleasant. Hence they have no further need to meet in this way if they are not advantageous <to each other>; for each finds the other pleasant / <only> to the extent that he expects some good from him. The friendship of hosts and guests is taken to be of this type too.[7]

§5 The cause of friendship between young people seems to be pleasure. For their lives are guided by their feelings, and they pursue above all what is pleasant for themselves and what is at hand. But as they grow up <what they find> / pleasant changes too. Hence they are quick to become friends, and quick to stop; for their friendship shifts with <what they find> / pleasant, and the change in such pleasure is rapid. Young people are prone to erotic passion, since this mostly accords with feelings, and is caused by pleasure; that is why they love and quickly stop, often changing in a single day.

These people wish to spend their days together and to live / together; for this is how they gain <the good things> that correspond to their friendship.

§6 [c4] But complete friendship is the friendship of good people similar in virtue; for they wish goods in the same way to each other insofar as they are good, and they are good in their own right.[8] <Hence they wish goods to each other for each other's own sake.> / Now those who wish goods to their friend for the friend's own sake are friends most of all; for they have this attitude because of the friend himself, not coincidentally.[9] Hence these people's friendship lasts as long as they are good; and virtue is enduring.[10]

Each of them is both good without qualification and good for his friend, since good people are both good without qualification and advantageous for each other.[11] They are pleasant in the / same ways too, since good people are pleasant both without qualification and for each other.[12] <They are pleasant for each other> because each of them finds his own actions and actions of that kind pleasant, and the actions of good people are the same or similar.

§7 It is reasonable that this sort of friendship is enduring, since it embraces in itself all the features that friends ought to have. / For the cause of every friendship is good or pleasure, either unqualified or for the lover; and every friendship corresponds to some similarity. And all the features we have mentioned are found in this friendship because of <the nature of> the friends themselves. For they are similar in this way <i.e., in being good>.[13] Moreover, their friendship also has the other things—what is good without qualification and what is pleasant without qualification; and these are most lovable of all. Hence loving and friendship are found most of all and at their best in these friends.

§8 / These kinds of friendships are likely to be rare, since such people are few. Further, they also need time, to grow accustomed to each other;[14] for, as the proverb says, they cannot know each other before they have shared their salt as often as it says,[15] and they cannot accept each other or be friends until each appears lovable to the other and gains the other's confidence. / §9 Those who are quick to treat each other in friendly ways wish to be friends, but are not friends, unless they are also lovable, and know this. For though the wish for friendship comes quickly, friendship does not.

4
[Comparison between the types of friendship]

[c5] This sort of friendship, then, is complete both in time and in the other ways. In every way each friend gets the same / things and similar things from each, and this is what must / be true of friends. Friendship for pleasure bears some resemblance to this complete sort, since good people are also pleasant to each other. And friendship for utility also resembles it, since good people are also useful to each other.[1]

With these <incomplete friends> also, the friendships are most enduring whenever they get the same thing—pleasure, for instance— / from each other, and, moreover, get it from the same source, as witty people do, in contrast to the erotic lover and his beloved. For these do not take pleasure in the same things, but the lover takes pleasure in seeing his beloved, and the beloved takes pleasure in being courted by his lover.[2] When the beloved's bloom is fading,[3] sometimes the friendship fades too; for the lover no longer finds pleasure

10 in seeing his beloved, and the beloved is no longer / courted by the
lover. Many, however, remain friends if they have similar characters
and come to be fond of each other's characters from being accustomed to them.⁴ §2 Those who exchange utility rather than pleasure in their erotic relations are friends to a lesser extent and less
enduring friends.⁵

15 Those who are friends for utility dissolve the friendship / as soon as
the advantage is removed; for they were never friends of each other,
but of what was expedient for them.⁶

Now it is possible for bad people as well <as good> to be friends
to each other for pleasure or utility, for decent people to be friends
to base people, and for someone with neither character to be a friend
to someone with any character. Clearly, however, only good people
can be friends to each other because of the other person himself;⁷ for
20 bad people / find no enjoyment in one another if they get no benefit.

§3 Moreover, the friendship of good people is the only one that
is immune to slander. For it is not easy to trust anyone who speaks
against someone whom we ourselves have found reliable for a long
time; and among good people there is trust, the belief that he would
never do injustice, and all the other things expected in a true friend-
25 ship. But in the other / types of friendship <distrust> may easily arise.

§4 <Still, these are also types of friendship.> For people include
among friends <not only the best type, but> also those who are
friends for utility, as cities are—since alliances between cities seem
to aim at expediency—and those who are fond of each other, as children are, for pleasure. Hence we must presumably also say that such
30 people are friends, / but say that there are more species of friendship
than one,⁸ and that the friendship of good people insofar as they are
good is friendship primarily and fully, but the other friendships are
friendships by similarity.⁹ For insofar as there is something good, and
<hence> something similar to <what one finds in the best kind>,
<incomplete friends> are friends; for what is pleasant is good to lov-
ers of pleasure. §5 But these <incomplete> types of friendship are
not very regularly combined, and the same people do not become
35 friends for both / utility and pleasure. For things that <merely> coincide with each other are not very regularly combined.

1157b §6 [c6] / Friendship has been assigned, then, to these species.¹⁰
Base people will be friends for pleasure or utility, since they are

similar in that way. But good people will be friends because of themselves, since they are friends insofar as they are good. These, then, are
friends without qualification; the others / are friends coincidentally   5
and by being similar to these.[11]

5
[State and activity in friendship]

Just as, in the case of the virtues, some people are called good in
their state of character, others good in their activity, the same is
true of friendship.[1] For some people find enjoyment in each other
by living together, and provide each other with the <appropriate>
good things. Others, however, are asleep or separated by distance,
and so are not active in these ways, but are in the state that / would   10
result in the friendly activities; for distance does not dissolve the
friendship without qualification, but only its activity. But if the
absence is long, it also seems to cause the friendship to be forgotten; hence the saying 'Lack of conversation has dissolved many a
friendship'.[2]

§2 Older people and sour people do not appear to be prone / to   15
friendship. For there is little pleasure to be found in them, and no
one can spend his days with what is painful or not pleasant, since
nature appears to avoid above all what is painful and to aim at what
is pleasant.

§3 Those who welcome each other but do not live together would
seem to have goodwill rather than friendship.[3] For / nothing is as   20
proper to friends as living together; for those who lack something
desire benefit, but blessedly happy people <who lack nothing>, no
less than the others, desire to spend their days together—for a solitary
life fits them least of all.[4] But people cannot spend their time with
each other if they are not pleasant and do not enjoy the same things,
which they seem to do in the friendship of companions.

§4 [c7] / Now the friendship of good people is friendship most of   25
all, as we have often said. For what is lovable and choiceworthy seems
to be what is good or pleasant without qualification, and what is lovable and choiceworthy to a given person seems to be what is good or
pleasant to himself;[5] and both of these make one good person lovable
and choiceworthy to another good person.

30   §5 Loving would seem to be a feeling, but friendship a state. / For loving is directed no less towards inanimate things, but reciprocal loving requires decision, and the decision comes from a state; and <good people> wish the good things to the beloved for his own sake in accord with their state, not their feeling.[6]

35   Moreover, in loving their friend they love what is good for themselves; for when a good person becomes a friend / he becomes a good for his friend. Each of them, therefore, loves what is good for himself, and repays in equal measure the wish and the pleasantness of his
1158a   friend; for friendship is said to / be equality. And this is true above all in the friendship of good people.

6

[Characteristic activities in the different types of friendship]

Among sour people and older people, friendship is found less often, since they are worse-tempered and find less enjoyment in meeting
5   people, so that they lack the features that seem most typical and / most productive of friendship.[1] That is why young people become friends quickly, but older people do not, since they do not become friends with people in whom they find no enjoyment—nor do sour people. These people have goodwill to each other, since they wish goods and give help in time of need; but they scarcely count as friends, since they do not spend their days together or find enjoy-
10   ment in each / other, and these things seem to be above all typical of friendship.

      §2 No one can have complete friendship for many people, just as no one can have an erotic passion for many at the same time; for <complete friendship, like erotic passion,> is like an excess, and an excess is naturally directed at a single individual.[2] And just as it is difficult for many people to please the same person intensely at the same time, it is also difficult, presumably, for many to be good.   §3 But
15   one needs both / experience and familiarity, which is extremely difficult.[3] If, however, the friendship is for utility or pleasure, it is possible for many people to please;[4] for there are many people of the right sort, and the services take little time.[5]

      §4 Of these other two types of friendship, the friendship for pleasure is more like <real> friendship; for they get the same thing from
20   each other, and they find enjoyment in each other, / or <rather> in the same things. This is what friendships are like among young

people; for a generous <attitude> is found here more <than among older people>, whereas it is mercenary people who form friendships for utility.

Moreover, blessedly happy people have no need of anything useful, but do need sources of pleasure.[6] For they want to spend their lives with companions, and though what is painful is borne for a short time, no one could continuously endure even / the Good Itself if it 25 were painful to him.[7] That is why they seek friends who are pleasant. But, presumably, they must also seek friends who are also good, and good for them too; for then they will have everything that friends must have.

§5 Someone in a position of power appears to have separate groups of friends; for some are useful to him, others pleasant, / but 30 the same ones are not often both.[8] For he does not seek friends who are both pleasant and virtuous, or useful for fine actions, but seeks one group to be witty, when he pursues pleasure, and the other group to be clever in carrying out instructions; and the same person rarely has both features.[9]

§6 Though admittedly, as we have said, an excellent person is both pleasant and useful, he does not become a friend to a superior <in power and position> unless the superior is also / superior in virtue; 35 otherwise he does not reach <proportionate> equality by having a proportionate superior. This superiority both in power and in virtue is not often found.

§7 [c8] / The friendships we have mentioned involve equality, 1158b since both friends get the same and wish the same to each other, or exchange one thing for another—for instance, pleasure for benefit.[10] But, as we have said, they are friendships to a lesser extent, / and less 5 enduring. They seem both to be and not to be friendships, because of their similarity and dissimilarity to the same thing. For, on the one hand, insofar as they are similar to the friendship of virtue, they are apparently friendships; for that type of friendship includes both utility and pleasure, and one of these <inferior> types includes utility, the other pleasure. On the other hand, the friendship of virtue is enduring and immune / to slander, whereas these <inferior types> 10 change quickly, and differ from it in many other ways as well; to that extent they are apparently not friendships, because of their dissimilarity to that best type.

7

[Friendship between unequals]

A different species of friendship is the one that rests on superiority[1]—of a father towards his son, for instance (and in general of the elder towards the younger), of a husband towards his wife,[2] and of any sort of ruler towards the one he rules. These friendships also differ from

15 each other. For friendship / of parents to children is not the same as that of rulers to ruled; nor is friendship of father to son the same as that of son to father, or of husband to wife as that of wife to husband. For each of these friends has a different virtue and a different function, and there are different causes of love. Hence the ways of loving are different, and so are the friendships.

20 §2 / Now each does not get the same thing from the other, and must not seek it; but whenever children accord to their parents what they must accord to those who gave them birth, and parents accord what they must do to their children, their friendship is enduring and decent.

25 In all the friendships that rest on superiority, the loving / must also be proportional; for instance, the better person, and the more beneficial, and each of the others likewise, must be loved more than he loves; for when the loving accords with the comparative worth of the friends, equality is achieved in a way, and this seems to be proper to friendship.

30 §3 [c9] / Equality, however, does not appear to be the same in friendship as in justice.[3] For in justice equality is equality primarily in worth and secondarily in quantity; but in friendship it is equality primarily in quantity and secondarily in worth.

§4 This is clear if friends come to be separated by some wide gap
35 in virtue, vice, wealth, or something else; for then they / are friends no more, and do not even expect to be. This is most evident with gods,
1159a since they have the greatest superiority / in all goods. But it is also clear with kings, since far inferior people do not expect to be their friends; nor do worthless people expect to be friends to the best or wisest.

§5 Now in these cases there is no exact definition of how long people
5 are friends. For even if one of them loses a lot, the / friendship still endures; but if one is widely separated <from the other>, as a god is <from a human being>, it no longer endures.

§6 This raises a puzzle: Do friends really wish their friend to have the greatest good, to be a god, for instance?[4] For <if he becomes a god>, *he* will no longer have friends, and hence no longer have goods,[5] since friends are goods. If, then, it was right to say that one friend wishes / good things to the other for the sake of the other *him-* 10 *self*, the other must remain whatever sort of being he is. Hence it is to the other as a human being that a friend will wish the greatest goods—though presumably not all of them, since each person wishes goods most of all to himself.[6]

8
[Giving and receiving in friendship]

Because the many love honour they seem to prefer / being loved to 15 loving.[1] That is why they love flatterers. For the flatterer is a friend in an inferior position, or <rather> pretends to be one, and pretends to love more than he is loved; and being loved seems close to being hon-oured, which the many certainly pursue.[2]

§2 It would seem, however, that they choose honour coinciden-tally, not in its own right. For the many enjoy being honoured / by 20 powerful people because they expect to get whatever they need from them, and so enjoy the honour as a sign of this good treatment. Those who want honour from decent people with knowledge are seeking to confirm their own view of themselves, and so they are pleased because the judgment of those who say they are good makes them confident that they are good.[3] / Being loved, on the contrary, they enjoy in its 25 own right. That is why it seems to be better than being honoured, and friendship seems choiceworthy in its own right.[4]

§3 But friendship seems to consist more in loving than in being loved.[5] A sign of this is the enjoyment a mother finds in loving.[6] For sometimes she gives her child away to be brought / up, and loves him 30 as long as she knows about him; but she does not seek the child's love, if she cannot both <love and be loved>. She would seem to be satisfied if she sees the child doing well, and she loves the child even if ignorance prevents him from returning to her what is due to a mother.

§4 [c10] Friendship, then, consists more in loving; and people who / love their friends are praised; hence, it would seem, loving is the vir- 35 tue of friends.[7] And so friends whose love accords with / the worth 1159b of their friends are enduring friends and have an enduring friendship. §5 This above all is how unequals as well as equals can be friends, since this is how they can be equalized.[8]

Equality and similarity, and above all the similarity of those who are similar in being virtuous, is friendship.[9] For virtuous people are
5 enduringly <virtuous> in their own right, and enduring / <friends> to each other. They neither request nor provide assistance that requires base actions, but, one might say, even prevent it. For it is proper to good people to avoid error themselves and not to permit it in their friends.

Vicious people, by contrast, have no firmness, since they do not
10 even remain similar to what they were. They become / friends for a short time, enjoying each other's vice.[10] §6 Useful or pleasant friends, however, last longer, for as long as they supply each other with pleasures or benefits.[11]

The friendship that seems to arise most from contraries is friendship for utility, of poor to rich, for instance, or ignorant to knowledge-
15 able; for we aim at whatever we find we lack, and / give something else in return.[12] Here we might also include the erotic lover and his beloved, and the beautiful and the ugly. That is why an erotic lover sometimes also appears ridiculous, when he expects to be loved in the same way as he loves; that would presumably be a proper expectation if he were lovable in the same way, but it is ridiculous when he is not.[13]

20 §7 / Presumably, however, contrary seeks contrary coincidentally, not in its own right, and desire is for the intermediate.[14] For what is good for the dry, for instance, is to reach the intermediate, not to become wet, and the same is true for the hot, and so on. Let us, then, dismiss these questions, since they are rather extraneous[15] to our concern.

9

[Friendship in communities]

25 [c11] / As we said at the beginning,[1] friendship and justice would seem to be about the same things and to be found in the same people. For in every community there seems to be some sort of justice, and some type of friendship also. At any rate, fellow-voyagers and fellow-soldiers are called friends, and so are members of other commu-
30 nities. And to the extent / that they are in a community, to that extent there is their friendship, since to that extent also there is justice. And

the proverb 'What friends have is common' is correct, since friend-ship involves community.[2]   §2 But, whereas brothers and compan-ions have everything in common, what people have in common in other types of community is limited, more in some communities and less in others, since some friendships are also / closer than others, some less close.[3]

§3 / What is just is also different, since it is not the same for par-ents towards children as for one brother towards another, and not the same for companions as for fellow-citizens, and similarly with the other types of friendship. Similarly, what is unjust towards each of these is also different, and becomes more unjust as it is practised on closer friends.[4] It is more / shocking, for instance, to rob a companion of money than to rob a fellow-citizen, to fail to help a brother than a stranger, and to strike one's father than anyone else. Justice also nat-urally increases with friendship, since it involves the same people and extends over an equal area.

§4 All <these> communities, however, would seem to be parts of the political community.[5] For people / keep company for some advantage and to supply something contributing to their life. And the political community as well <as the others> seems both to have been originally formed and to endure for advantage;[6] for legislators also aim at advantage, and the common advantage is said to be just.[7]

§5 Now the other types of community aim at partial advantage.[8] / Sea-travellers, for instance, seek the advantage proper to a journey, in making money or something like that, while fellow-soldiers seek the advantage proper to war, desiring either money or victory or a city; and the same is true of fellow-members of a tribe or deme.[9] Some communities—religious / societies and dining clubs—seem to arise for pleasure, since these are, respectively, for religious sacrifices and for companionship.[10]

But all these communities would seem to be subordinate to the political community, since it aims not at some advantage close at hand, but at advantage for the whole of life.[11] <In religious festivals, for instance,> performing sacrifices and arranging gatherings for / them, people both accord honours to the gods and provide them-selves with pleasant relaxations.[12] For the long-established sacrifices and gatherings appear to take place after the harvesting of the crops, as a sort of first fruits, since this was the time when people used to be most at leisure.[13]

30   §6 All the types of community, then, appear to be parts of / the
political community, and these sorts of communities imply the appropriate sorts of friendships.

10
[Political systems]

[c12] There are three species of political system (*politeia*), and an
equal number of deviations, which are a sort of corruption of them.[1]
The first political system is kingship; the second aristocracy; and since
the third rests on property (*timêma*) it appears proper to call it a tim-
35   ocratic system, though / most people usually call it a polity.[2] §2 The
best of these is kingship and the worst timocracy.

1160b   / The deviation from kingship is tyranny. For, though both are mon-
archies, they show the widest difference, since the tyrant considers his
own advantage, but the king considers the advantage of his subjects.
5   For someone is a king only / if he is self-sufficient and superior in all
goods; and since such a person needs nothing more, he will consider
the subjects' benefit, not his own. For a king who is not like this would
be only some sort of titular king. Tyranny is contrary to this; for the
tyrant pursues his own good. It is more evident that <tyranny> is the
worst <deviation than that timocracy is the worst political system>;
but the worst is contrary to the best; <hence kingship is the best>.

10   §3 / The transition from kingship is to tyranny. For tyranny is the
degenerate condition of monarchy, and the vicious king becomes a
tyrant.

The transition from aristocracy <rule of the best people> is to oligarchy <rule of the few>, resulting from the badness of the rulers. They
distribute the city's goods contrary to people's worth, so that they dis-
15   tribute all or most of the goods / to themselves, and always assign ruling offices to the same people, counting wealth for most. Hence the
rulers are few, and they are vicious people instead of the most decent.

The transition from timocracy is to democracy <rule by the peo-
ple>, since these border on each other. For timocracy is also meant to
be rule by the majority, and all those with the property qualification
are equal; <and majority rule and equality are the marks of democ-
20   racy>. Democracy is the least / vicious <of the deviations>; for it
deviates only slightly from the form of a <genuine> political system.

These, then, are the most frequent transitions from one political
system to another, since they are the smallest and easiest.

§4 Resemblances to these—indeed, a sort of pattern of them—can also be found in households.[3] For the community of a / father and his   25
sons has the structure of kingship, since the father is concerned for his children. Indeed that is why Homer also calls Zeus father,[4] since kingship is meant to be paternal rule.

Among the Persians, however, the father's rule is tyrannical, since he treats his sons as slaves.[5] The rule of a master / over his slaves is   30
also tyrannical, since it is the master's advantage that is achieved in it. This, then, appears a correct form of rule, whereas the Persian form appears erroneous, since the different types of rule suit different subjects.

§5 The community of husband and wife appears aristocratic. For the husband's rule in the area where it is right accords with the worth <of each>, and / he commits[6] to the wife what is fitting for her.   35
If, however, the husband controls everything, he changes it into an oligarchy; for then his action does not accord / with the worth <of   1161a
each>, or with the respect in which <each> is better. Sometimes, indeed, wives rule because they are heiresses; these cases of rule do not accord with virtue, but result from wealth and power, as is true in oligarchies.

§6 The community of brothers is like a timocratic <system>, /   5
since they are equal except insofar as they differ in age. That is why, if they differ very much in age, the friendship is no longer brotherly.

Democracy is found most of all in dwellings without a master, since everyone there is on equal terms; and also in those where the ruler is weak and everyone is free <to do what he likes>.[7]

11

[Friendships in political systems]

[c13] / Friendship appears in each of the political systems, to the   10
extent that justice appears also.[1] A king's friendship to his subjects involves superior beneficence. For he benefits his subjects, since he is good and attends to them to ensure that they do well, as a shepherd attends to his sheep; hence Homer / also called Agamemnon shep-   15
herd of the peoples.[2]

§2 A father's friendship resembles this, but differs in conferring a greater benefit, since the father is the cause of his children's being, which seems to be the greatest benefit, and of their nurture and education. These benefits are also ascribed to ancestors; and by nature a father is ruler over sons, ancestors over descendants, and a king over subjects.

20   §3 / All these are friendships of superiority. That is why parents are also honoured. And justice is not the same in each of these friendships, but it accords with worth; for so does the friendship.

§4 The friendship of husband to wife is the same as in an aristoc-
25   racy. For it accords with virtue, in assigning more good / to the better, and assigning what is fitting to each. The same is true of justice in this case.

§5 The friendship of brothers is similar to that of companions, since they are equal and of an age, and such people usually have the same feelings and characters. Friendship in a timocracy is similar to this. For there the citizens are meant to be equal and decent, and
30   so rule in turn and on equal terms; / the same is true, then, of their friendship.

§6 In the deviations, however, justice is found only to a slight degree, and hence the same is true of friendship.[3] There is least of it in the worst deviation; for in a tyranny there is little or no friendship.

For where ruler and ruled have nothing in common, they have no
35   friendship, since they have no justice either.[4] This / is true for a crafts-
1161b   man in relation to his tool, and for the soul in relation to the body.[5] / For in all these cases the user benefits what he uses, but there is neither friendship nor justice towards inanimate things.[6] Nor is there any towards a horse or cow, or towards a slave, insofar as he is a slave. For master and slave have nothing in common, since a slave is a tool with
5   a soul and / a tool is a slave without a soul.[7]

§7 Insofar as he is a slave, then, there is no friendship with him. But there is friendship with him insofar as he is a human being.[8] For every human being seems to have some relation of justice with everyone who is capable of community in law and agreement;[9] hence also friendship, to the extent that he is a human being.[10]

§8 Hence there are friendships and justice to only a slight degree
10   in tyrannies also, but to a much larger degree in democracies; / for there people are equal, and so have much in common.

12

[Friendships in families]

[c14] As we have said, then, every friendship is found in a community. But we may set apart the friendship of families and that of

companions.¹ The friendship of citizens, tribesmen, voyagers, and
suchlike are more like friendships in a / community, since they appear   15
to reflect some sort of agreement.² Among these we may include the
friendship of host and guest.

§2 Friendship in families also seems to have many species, but
they all seem to depend on paternal friendship. For a parent is fond
of his children because he regards them as something of himself; and
children are fond of a parent because they regard themselves as being
from him.³

/ But a parent knows better what is from him than the children   20
know that they are from the parent; and the parent regards his children as his own more than the product regards the maker as its own.
For a person regards what comes from him as his own, as the owner
regards his tooth or hair or anything; but what is from him regards
its owner as its own not at all, or to a lesser degree.⁴ / The length of   25
time also matters. For a parent becomes fond of his children as soon
as they are born, but children become fond of the parent when time
has passed and they have acquired some comprehension or <at least>
perception. And this also makes it clear why mothers love their children more <than fathers do>.⁵

§3 Parents, then, love their children as they love themselves; for
those that are from themselves are other themselves of a sort, by being
separate.⁶ Children love parents because they regard themselves as
being from them. / Brothers love each other because they are from   30
the same <parents>. For the same relation to the parents makes the
same thing for both of them;⁷ hence we speak of the same blood, the
same stock, and so on. They are the same thing, then, in a way, even
though in separate people.

§4 Being brought up together and being of an age contributes
largely to friendship; / for 'two of an age'⁸ <get on well>, and those   35
with the same character are companions. That is why the friendship
of / brothers and that of companions are similar. Cousins and other   1162a
relatives are akin by being related to brothers, since that makes them
descendants of the same parents.⁹ Some are more akin, others less, by
the ancestor's being near to or far from them.

§5 The friendship of children to parents, like the friendship / of   5
human beings to gods, is friendship towards what is good and supe-
rior.¹⁰ For the parents conferred the greatest benefits on the children, since they cause their being and nurture and their education

once they have been born. §6 This sort of friendship also includes pleasure and utility, more than the friendship of unrelated people does, to the extent that <parents and children> have more of a life in common.[11]

10 / Friendship between brothers has the features of friendship between companions, especially when <the companions> are decent, or in general similar.[12] For brothers are that much more akin to each other <than ordinary companions>, and are fond of each other from birth; they are that much more similar in character, being from the same parents, nurtured together, and educated similarly, and the proof of their 15 reliability / over time is fullest and firmest. §7 Among other relatives too the features of friendship are proportional <to the relation>.

The friendship of husband and wife also seems to be natural. For human beings form couples more naturally than they form cities, to the extent that the household is prior to the city, and more necessary, and childbearing is shared more widely among the animals.[13] For 20 the / other animals, the community goes only as far as childbearing. Human beings, however, share a household not only for childbearing, but also for the benefits in their life.[14] For the difference between them implies that[15] their functions are divided, with different ones for the husband and the wife; hence each supplies the other's needs by contributing a special function to the common good. For this reason their friendship seems to include both utility and pleasure.

25 / And it may also be friendship for virtue, if they are decent. For each has a proper virtue, and this will be a source of enjoyment for them.[16] Children seem to be another bond, and that is why childless unions are more quickly dissolved; for children are a common good for both, and what is common holds them together.

30 §8 / How should a husband conduct his life towards his wife, or, in general, towards a friend? That appears to be the same as the question how they are to conduct their lives justly. For what is just is not the same for a friend towards a friend as towards a stranger, or the same towards a companion as towards a classmate.[17]

13
[Disputes in friendships between equals]

[c15] There are three types of friendship, as we said at the begin-35 ning, / and within each type some friendships rest on equality, while

others are in accord with superiority.[1] For equally good / people can
be friends, but also a better and a worse person; and the same is true
of friends for pleasure or utility, since they may be either equal or
unequal in their benefits. Hence equals must equalize in loving and
in the other things, because of their equality; and unequals must
make the return that is proportionate to the types of superiority.

§2 / Accusations and reproaches arise only or most often in friend- 5
ship for utility.[2] And this is reasonable. For friends for virtue are eager
to benefit each other, since this is proper to virtue and to friendship;
and if this is what they strain to achieve, there are no accusations or
fights.[3] For no one / objects if the other loves and benefits him, but if 10
he is gracious, he retaliates by benefiting the other. And if the superior gets what he aims at, he will not accuse his friend of anything,
since each of them desires what is good.

§3 Nor are there many accusations among friends for pleasure.
For both of them get what they want at the same time if they / enjoy 15
spending their time together; and someone who accused his friend of
not pleasing him would appear ridiculous, since he is free to spend his
days without the friend's company.

§4 Friendship for utility, however, is liable to accusations. For
these friends deal with each other in the expectation of gaining benefits. Hence they always require more, thinking they have got less than
is fitting; and they reproach the other because they get less than they
require and deserve. And those / who confer benefits cannot supply 20
as much as the recipients require.

§5 Now there are two ways of being just, one unwritten, and one
governed by rules of law. And similarly one type of friendship of utility would seem to depend on character, and the other on rules.[4] Accusations arise most readily if it is not the same sort of friendship when
they / dissolve it as it was when they formed it. 25

§6 Friendship dependent on rules is the type that is on explicit
conditions.[5] One type of this is entirely mercenary and requires immediate payment. The other is more generous and postpones the time
<of repayment>, but in accordance with an agreement <requiring>
one thing in return for another. In this sort of friendship it is clear and
unambiguous what is owed, but the postponement is a friendly aspect
of it. That is why some / cities do not allow legal actions in these cases, 30
but think that people who have formed an arrangement on the basis
of trust must put up with the outcome.

§7 Friendship <for utility> that depends on character is not on explicit conditions. Someone makes a present or whatever it is, as to a friend, but expects to get back as much or more, since he assumes that it is not a free gift, but a loan.

§8 If one party does not dissolve the friendship on the terms on which he formed it, he will accuse the other.[6] / This happens because all or most people wish for what is fine, but decide to do what is beneficial;[7] and while it is fine / to do someone a good turn without aiming to receive one in return, it is beneficial to receive a good turn.

§9 We should, if we can, make a return worthy of what we have received, <if the other has undertaken the friendship> willingly.[8] For we should never make a friend of someone who is unwilling, but must suppose that we were in error at the beginning, and received a benefit from the wrong person; for since it was not from a friend, and / this was not why he was doing it, we must dissolve the arrangement as though we had received a good turn on explicit conditions. And we will agree to repay if we can. If we cannot repay, the giver would not even expect it. Hence we should repay if we can. We should consider at the beginning who is doing us a good turn, and on what conditions, so that we can put up with it on these conditions, or else decline it.

§10 / It is disputable whether we must measure <the return> by the benefit accruing to the recipient, and make the return proportional to that, or instead by the good turn done by the benefactor. For a recipient says that what he got was a small matter for the benefactor, and that he could have got it from someone else instead, and so he belittles it. But the benefactor / says it was the biggest thing he had, that it could not be got from anyone else, and that he gave it when he was in danger or similar need.

§11 Since the friendship is for utility, surely the benefit to the recipient must be the measure <of the return>. For he was the one who required it, and the benefactor supplies him on the assumption that he will get an equal return. Hence the aid has / been as great as the benefit received, and the recipient should return as much as he gained, or still more, since that is finer.

But in friendships in accord with virtue, there are no accusations. Rather, the decision of the benefactor would seem to be the measure, since the controlling element in virtue and character lies in decision.[9]

14
[Disputes in friendships between unequals]

[c16] There are also disputes in friendships in accord with / superior- 25
ity, since each friend expects to have more than the other, but whenever this happens the friendship is dissolved.

For the better person thinks it is fitting for him to have more, on
the ground that more is fittingly allotted to the good person. And the
more beneficial person thinks the same. For it is wrong, they say, for
someone to have an equal share if he is useless; the result is a public
service, not a friendship, / if the benefits from the friendship do not 30
accord with the worth of the actions. <The superior party says this>
because he notices that in a financial community the larger contribu-
tors gain more, and he thinks the same thing is right in a friendship.[1]

But the needy person, the inferior party in the friendship, takes
the opposite view, saying it is proper to a virtuous friend to supply
his needy <friends>. For what use is it, as / they say, to be a friend of 35
an excellent or powerful person if you are not going to gain anything
by it?

§2 Well, it would seem that each of them is correct in what he / 1163b
expects, and that it is right for each of them to get more from the
friendship—but not more of the same thing. Rather, the superior person should get more honour, and the needy person more profit, since
honour is the reward of virtue and beneficence, but profit is what
supplies need.[2]

§3 / This also appears to be true in political systems. For some- 5
one who provides nothing for the community receives no honour,
since what is common is given to someone who benefits the community, and honour is something common. For it is impossible both to
make money off the community and to receive honour from it at the
same time; for no one / puts up with the smaller share of everything. 10
Hence someone who suffers a monetary loss <by holding office>
receives honour in return, but someone who accepts gifts <in office>
receives money <but not honour>; for distribution that accords with
worth equalizes and preserves the friendship, as has been said.[3]

This, then, is also how we should treat unequals. If we benefit from
them in money or virtue,[4] we should return honour, / and thereby 15
make what return we can. §4 For friendship seeks what is possible,
not what accords with worth, since that is impossible in some cases,
as it is with honour to gods and parents. For no one could ever make

161

a return in accord with their worth, but someone who attends to them as far as he is able seems to be a decent person.

20   That is why it might seem[5] that a son is not free to disown his / father, but a father is free to disown his son. For a debtor should return what he owes, and since, no matter what a son has done, he has not made a worthy return for what his father has done for him, he is always the debtor. But the creditor is free to remit the debt, and hence the father is free to remit.

At the same time, however, it presumably seems that no one would ever withdraw from a son, except from one who was far gone in vice.
25   For, quite apart from their natural friendship, it is / human not to repel aid. The son, however, if he is vicious, will want to avoid helping his father, or will not be keen on it. For the many wish to receive benefits, but they avoid doing them because they suppose it is unprofitable. So much, then, for these things.

Book IX
[Friendship]

1

[Friends with dissimilar aims]

In all friendships of friends with dissimilar aims proportion equalizes
35   and preserves the friendship, as has been / said. In political friendship, for instance, the cobbler receives a worthy exchange for his
1164a   shoes, and so do the weaver and the / others.[1] §2 Here money is supplied as a common measure; everything is related to this and measured by it.

In erotic friendships, however, sometimes the lover charges that
5   he loves the beloved deeply and is not loved in return; / and in fact perhaps he has nothing lovable in him. The beloved, however, often charges that previously the lover was promising him everything, and now fulfils none of his promises. §3 These sorts of charges arise whenever the lover loves his beloved for pleasure while the beloved loves his lover for utility, and they do not both provide these. For if
10   the friendship has these causes, it is dissolved whenever they / do not get what they were friends for; for each was not fond of the other himself, but only of what the other had, which was unstable.[2] That is why the friendships are also unstable.

Friendship of character, however, is friendship in itself,[3] and is stable, endures, as has been said.

§4 Friends quarrel when the results they get are different from those they want; for when someone does not get what he aims / at, it is like getting nothing. It is like the person who promised the lyre player a reward, and a greater reward the better he played. In the morning, when the player asked him to keep his promise, the other said he had paid pleasure in return for pleasure.[4] Now if this was what each of them had wished, it would be enough. But if one wished for delight and the other for profit, and one has got his delight / and the other has not made his profit, things are not right in their common dealings.[5] For each person sets his mind on what he finds he needs, and this will be his aim when he gives what he gives.

§5 But who should fix the worth <of a benefit>? The giver or the one who has already received it?[6] <Surely the latter.> For the giver would seem to entrust <the judgment> to the one who has received. This is what Protagoras is said to have done; / for whenever he taught anything at all, he used to tell the pupil to estimate how much the knowledge was worth, and that was the amount he used to collect.[7] In such cases, however, some prefer the rule 'Payment to a man . . . '.[8]

§6 But those who take the money first, and then do nothing that they said they would do, because their promises were / excessive, are reasonably accused, since they do not carry out what they agreed to.[9] §7 And presumably the sophists are compelled to make excessive promises, because no one would pay them money for the knowledge they really have. Therefore they take the payment, and then do not do what they were paid to do, and reasonably are accused.[10]

But where no agreement about services is made, friends / who give services because of the friend himself are not open to accusation, as we have said, since this what / the friendship that accords with virtue is like. And the return should accord with the decision <of the original giver>, since decision is proper to a friend and to virtue.[11]

And it would seem that the same sort of return should also be made to those who have shared philosophy in common with us. For its worth is not measured by money, and no / equivalent honour can be paid; but it is enough, presumably, to do what we can, as we also do towards gods and parents.[12]

§8 If the giving is not of this sort, but on some specified condition, presumably the repayment must be, ideally, what each of them

15

20

25

30

35

1164b

5

thinks accords with the worth of the gift. But if they do not agree on
this, it would seem not merely necessary, but also just, for the party
10   who benefits first to fix the repayment. / For if the other receives in
return as much benefit as the first received, or as much as he would
have paid for the pleasure, he will have got the worthy return from
him.

For this is also how it appears in buying and selling.   §9 And in
some cities there are actually laws that prohibit legal actions in voluntary bargains, on the assumption that if we have trusted someone we
15   must dissolve the community with / him on the same terms on which
we formed it. The law does this because it supposes that it is more
just for the recipient to fix repayment than for the giver to fix it. For
usually those who have something and those who want it do not put
the same price on it, since, to the giver, what he owns and what he is
giving appears to be worth a lot. But nonetheless the return is made
20   in the amount fixed by the / initial recipient. Presumably, however,
the price must be not what it appears to be worth when he has got it,
but the price he put on it before he got it.[13]

2

[Conflicts between different types of friendships]

[c2] Here are some other questions that raise a puzzle. Must you
accord <authority in> everything to your father, and obey him in
everything? Or must you trust the doctor when you are sick, and
25   should you vote for a military expert to be general?[1] / Similarly,
should you do a service for your friend rather than for an excellent
person, and return a favour to a benefactor rather than do a favour
for a companion, if you cannot do both?[2] §2 Surely it is not easy to
define all these matters exactly,[3] since they include many differences
30   of all sorts, in importance and unimportance, and in the fine and /
necessary.[4]

§3 Still, it is clear that not everything should be rendered to the
same person, and usually we should return favours rather than do
favours for our companions, just as we should return a loan to a creditor rather than give to a companion.[5]

§4 But presumably this is not always true either. If, for instance,
35   someone / has ransomed you from pirates, should you ransom him
1165a   in return, no matter who he is? Or if he does not need to / be ransomed, but asks for his money back, should you return it, or should

you ransom your father instead? For it seems that you should ransom
your father rather than even yourself.

§5 As has been said, then, we should, generally speaking, return
what we owe. But if making a gift <to B> outweighs <returning the
money to A> by being finer or more necessary, we should incline to
<making the gift to B> instead.[6] / For sometimes even a return of   5
a previous favour is not fair, whenever <the original giver> knows
he is benefiting an excellent person, but <the recipient> would be
returning the benefit to someone he thinks is vicious. For sometimes you should not even lend in return to someone who has lent
to you; for he expected repayment when he lent to a decent person,
whereas you have no hope of it / from a bad person. If that is really   10
so, then, the demand <for reciprocity> is not fair; and even if it is
not so, but you think it is so, your refusal of the demand seems not
at all strange.

§6 As has often been said, then, arguments about ways of being
affected and about actions are no more definite than their subject
matter. Clearly, then, we should not render the same things to everyone, / and we should not render everything to our fathers, just as   15
we do not make all our sacrifices to Zeus.[7] §7 And since different
things should be rendered to parents, brothers, companions, and
benefactors, we should accord to each what is proper and suitable.
This is what actually appears to be done; for instance, kinsfolk are the
people invited to weddings, since they / share the same family, and   20
hence share in actions that concern it; and for the same reason it is
thought that kinsfolk more than anyone ought to come to funerals.

§8 It seems that we ought to supply means of support to parents
more than anyone. For we suppose that we owe them this, and that it
is finer to supply those who are the causes of our being than to supply
ourselves in this way. And we should accord[8] honour to our parents,
just as we should to the gods, / but not every sort of honour; for we   25
should not accord the same honour to a father as to a mother, nor
accord to them the honour due to a wise person or a general.[9] We
should accord a father's honour to a father, and likewise a mother's
to a mother.

§9 <We should accord> to every older person the honour befitting age, by standing up, giving up seats, and so on. With companions
and brothers we should speak freely, and have / everything in com-   30
mon. To kinsfolk, fellow-tribesmen, fellow-citizens, and all the rest

we should always try to accord what is proper, and should compare what belongs to each, as befits closeness of relation, virtue, or usefulness. §10 Admittedly, the comparison[10] is easier with people of the same kind, and more difficult with people of different kinds. But the

35 difficulty is no reason / to give up the task; on the contrary, we should determine as far as we can.

3

[Dissolution of friendships]

1165b [c3] There is also a puzzle about dissolving or not dissolving / friendships with friends who do not remain the same. In the case of friends for utility or pleasure, perhaps there is nothing strange in dissolving the friendship whenever they are no longer pleasant or useful. For they were friends of pleasure or utility; and if these give out, it is reasonable not to love.

5 / We might, however, accuse a friend if he really liked us for utility or pleasure, and pretended to like us for our character. For, as we said at the beginning,[1] friends are most at odds when they are not friends in the way they think they are.

§2 And so, if we mistakenly suppose we are loved for our char-
10 acter, when our friend is doing nothing to suggest this, / we must hold ourselves responsible. But if we are deceived by his pretence, we are justified in accusing him—even more justified than in accusing debasers of the currency, to the extent that his evildoing debases something more precious.

§3 But if we accept a friend as a good person, and then he becomes bad, and seems so, should we still love him?[2] Surely we cannot, if not
15 everything, but only the good, / is lovable, and the bad is not lovable, and ought not to be loved. For we ought neither to love the bad nor to become similar to a base person, and we have said that similar is friend to similar.

Then should the friendship be dissolved at once <as soon as the friend becomes bad>? Surely not with every sort of person, but only with an incurably bad person. If someone can be set right, we should
20 try harder to rescue his character than / his property, insofar as character is both better and more proper to friendship. Still, the friend who dissolves the friendship seems to be doing nothing strange; for he was not the friend of a person of this sort, and hence if the friend has altered, and he cannot save him, he leaves him.

166

§4 But if one friend has stayed the same and the other has become more decent and far excelled his friend in virtue, should the better person still treat the other as a friend?[3] Surely he cannot. / This becomes clear in a wide separation, such as we find in friendships beginning in childhood. For if one friend still thinks as a child, while the other becomes a man of the best sort, how could they still be friends, if they neither approve of the same things nor find the same things enjoyable or painful? For they do not even find it so in their life / together, and without that they cannot be friends, since they cannot live together—we have discussed this.

§5 Then should the better person regard the other as though he had never become his friend? Surely he must keep some memory of the familiarity they had. Just as we think we must do kindnesses for friends more than for strangers, so also / we should accord something to past friends because of the former friendship, whenever it is not excessive badness that causes the dissolution.[4]

4
[Self-love and friendship]

[c4] / The defining features of friendship that are found in friendships to one's neighbours would seem to be derived from features of friendship towards oneself.[1] For a friend is taken to be someone who wishes and does goods or apparent goods to his friend for the friend's own sake; or one who wishes the friend to be and to live / for the friend's own sake—this is how mothers feel towards their children, and how friends who have been in conflict feel. Others take a friend to be one who spends his time with his friend and makes the same choices; or one who shares his friend's distress and enjoyment—and this also is especially true of mothers. And people define friendship by one of these features.[2]

§2 / Each of these features is found in the decent person's relation to himself, and in other people, insofar as they suppose they are decent. And it would seem, as has been said, that virtue and the excellent person are the standard in each case.[3]

§3 For the excellent person is of one mind with himself, and desires the same things in his whole soul.[4] / Hence he wishes goods and apparent goods to himself, and achieves them in his actions, since it is proper to the good person to reach the good by his efforts. He wishes and does them for his own sake, since he does them for

25

30

35

1166a

5

10

15

the sake of his thinking part, and that is what each person seems to be.[5] Moreover, he wishes himself to live and to be preserved. And he wishes this for his rational part[6] most of all.

20 §4 For being is a good for the good / person, and each person wishes for goods for himself. And no one chooses to become another person even if that other will have every good when he has come into being; for, as it is, the god has the good <but no one chooses to be replaced by a god>.[7] Rather <each of us chooses goods> on condition that he remains whatever he is; and each person would seem to be the understanding part, or that most of all. <Hence the good person wishes for goods for the understanding part.>

§5 Further, such a person finds it pleasant to spend time with
25 himself, and so wishes to do it. For his memories of / what he has done are agreeable, and his expectations for the future are good, and hence both are pleasant. And besides, his thought is well supplied with topics for study. Moreover, he shares his own distresses and pleasures, more than other people share theirs. For it is always the same thing that is painful or pleasant, not different things at different times. This is because he practically never regrets <what he has done>.[8]

30 / The decent person, then, has each of these features in relation to himself, and he is related to his friend as he is to himself, since the friend is another himself.[9] Hence friendship seems to be one of these features, and people with these features seem to be friends.

§6 But is there friendship towards oneself, or not? Let us dismiss
35 that question for the present. However, there / seems to be friendship insofar as someone is two or more parts. This seems to be true from
1166b what we have said, and / because an extreme degree of friendship resembles one's friendship to oneself.[10]

§7 The many, base though they are, also appear to have these features. But perhaps they share in them only insofar as they approve of
5 themselves and suppose they are decent. For / no one who is utterly base and unscrupulous either has these features or appears to have them.

§8 Indeed, even base people hardly have them.[11] For they are at odds with themselves, and have an appetite for one thing and a wish for another, as incontinent people do. For they do not choose things that seem to be good for them, but instead choose pleasant things
10 that are actually / harmful; and cowardice or laziness causes others to

shrink from doing what they think best for themselves.[12] And those who have done many terrible actions hate and flee from life[13] because of their vice, and destroy themselves.

§9 Besides, vicious people seek others to pass their days / with, and   15
flee from themselves. For when they are by themselves they remember many disagreeable actions, and anticipate others in the future;
but they manage to forget these in other people's company. These
people have nothing lovable about them, and so have no friendly feelings for themselves.

Hence such a person does not share his own enjoyments / and   20
distresses. For his soul is in conflict, and because he is vicious one
<part> is distressed at being restrained, and another is pleased <by
the intended action>; and so each <part> pulls in a different direction, as though they were tearing him apart.   §10 Even if he cannot
be distressed and pleased at the same time, still he is soon distressed
because he was pleased, and wishes these things had not become
pleasant / to him; for base people are full of regret.[14]   25

Hence the base person appears not to have a friendly attitude even
towards himself, because he has nothing lovable about him.

If this state is utterly miserable, everyone should earnestly flee
from vice and try to be decent; for that is how one will have a friendly
relation to oneself and will become a friend to another.

5
[Goodwill and friendship]

[c5] / Goodwill would seem to be a feature of friendship, but still it   30
is not friendship.[1] For it arises even towards people we do not know,
and without their noticing it, whereas friendship does not. This has
also been said before.

Nor is it loving, since it lacks intensity and desire, which follow
from loving.   §2 Moreover, loving requires / familiarity, but good-   35
will can also arise in a moment, as it does, / for instance, for contes-   1167a
tants.[2] For <the spectator> acquires goodwill for them, and wants
what they want, but would not co-operate with them in any action;
for, as we said, the goodwill arises in a moment and the fondness is
superficial.

§3 Goodwill, then, would seem to be a beginning of friendship,
just as pleasure coming through sight is a beginning of erotic passion.[3] / For no one has erotic passion for another without previous   5

pleasure in his appearance, but still one who finds enjoyment in
another's appearance does not thereby feel erotic passion for him, but
only if he also misses him in his absence and longs for[4] his presence.
Similarly, though people cannot be friends without previous goodwill, goodwill does not imply friendship; for when they have goodwill
people only wish goods to the other, and will not co-operate with him
in any / action, or go to any trouble for him.[5] Hence we might transfer
<the name 'friendship'>, and say that goodwill is inactive friendship,
and that when it lasts some time and they grow accustomed[6] to each
other, it becomes friendship.

It does not, however, become friendship for utility or pleasure; for
these aims do not produce goodwill either.[7] / For a recipient of a benefit returns goodwill for what he has received, thereby doing the just
thing. But those who wish for another's welfare because they hope to
enrich themselves through him would seem to have goodwill to themselves, rather than to him. Likewise, they would seem to be friends to
themselves rather than to him, if they attend to him because he is of
some use to them.[8] §4 And altogether goodwill results from some
sort of virtue and decency, whenever one person finds another to be
/ apparently fine or brave or something similar. As we said, this also
arises in the case of contestants.

6

[Friendship and concord]

[c6] Concord also appears to be a feature of friendship. That is why
it is not merely sharing a belief, since this might also happen among
people who do not know each other. Nor are people / said to be in
concord when they agree on just anything—on astronomical questions, for instance, since concord on these questions is not a feature
of friendship. Rather, a city is said to be in concord whenever <its cit-
izens> agree on what is advantageous, make the same decision, and
act on their common resolution.

§2 Hence concord concerns questions for action, and, more /
exactly, large questions where both or all can get what they want. A
city, for instance, is in concord whenever all the citizens resolve to
make offices elective, or to make an alliance with the Spartans, or to
make Pittacus ruler, when he himself was also willing.[1]

But whenever each person wants the same thing all to himself,
as the people in the *Phoenissae* do, they are in conflict.[2] For it is not

concord when each merely has the same thing in / mind, whatever it   35
is. Rather, each must also have the same thing in mind for the same
person; this is true, for instance, whenever both / the common people   1167b
and the decent party[3] want the best people to rule, since when that is
so both sides get what they seek.

Concord, then, is apparently political friendship, as indeed it is
said to be; for it is concerned with advantage and with what affects
life <as a whole>.[4]

§3 / Now this sort of concord is found in decent people. For they   5
are in concord with themselves and with each other, since they are
practically of the same mind;[5] for their wishes are stable, not flow-
ing back and forth like a tidal strait.[6] They wish for what is just and
advantageous, and also seek it in common.

/ Base people, however, cannot be in concord, except to a slight   10
degree, just as they can be friends only to a slight degree; for they seek
to overreach in benefits <to themselves>, and shirk labours and public services. And since each wishes this for himself, he interrogates
and obstructs his neighbour; for when people do not look out for the
common good, it is ruined. The result is / that they are in conflict,   15
trying to compel one another, but not wishing to do the just thing
themselves.

7

[Active benevolence and friendship]

[c7] Benefactors seem to love their beneficiaries more than the beneficiaries love them <in return>, and this is discussed as though it
were an unreasonable thing to happen. In most people's view, this
/ is because the beneficiaries are debtors and the benefactors are   20
creditors. For the debtor in a loan wishes the creditor did not exist,
whereas the creditor even attends to the safety of the debtor. In the
same way, then, a benefactor wants the beneficiary to exist because
he / expects gratitude in return, whereas the beneficiary is not atten-   25
tive about making the return.

Now Epicharmus might say that most people say this because
they 'take a bad person's point of view'.[1] Still, it would seem to be a
human point of view, since the many are indeed forgetful, and seek to
receive benefits more than to give them.

§2 However, it seems that the cause is more proper to <human>
nature, and the case of creditors is not even similar.[2] / For they do not   30

love their debtors, but in wishing for their safety simply seek repayment. Benefactors, however, love and like their beneficiaries even if they are of no present or future use to them.   §3 The same is true

35   of craftsmen; for each likes his own / product more than it would like

1168a   him if it acquired a soul.³ / Presumably this is true of poets most of all, since they dearly like their own poems, and are fond of them as though they were their children.

§4 The case of benefactors, then, resembles this; for the benefi-

5   ciary is their product, / and hence they like him more than the product likes the producer. The reason for this is that being is choiceworthy and lovable for all, and we are insofar as we are actual, since we are insofar as we live and act. Now the product is, in a way, the producer in his actuality; hence the producer is fond of the product, because he loves his own being.⁴ This is natural, since what he is potentially is what the product indicates in actuality.

10   §5 / At the same time, the benefactor's action is fine for him,⁵ so that he finds enjoyment in the one whom he acts on; but the one who is acted on finds nothing fine in the agent, but only, at most, some advantage, which is less pleasant and lovable.

§6 What is pleasant is actuality in the present, expectation for the

15   future, and memory of the past; but what is / pleasantest is the <action we do> insofar as we are actual, and this is also most lovable. For the benefactor, then, his product endures, since the fine is long-lasting; but for the person acted on, the useful passes away.

Besides, memory of fine things is pleasant, while memory of <receiving> useful things is not altogether pleasant, or is less pleasant—though the reverse would seem to be true for expectation.

20   Moreover, loving is like production, but / being loved is like being acted on; and <the benefactor's> love and friendliness are the result of his greater activity.

§7 Further, everyone is fond of whatever has taken effort to produce; for instance, people who have made money themselves are fonder of it than people who have inherited it. And while receiving a

25   benefit seems to take no effort, giving one is hard work. / This is also why mothers love their children more <than fathers do⁶ or more than children love mothers?>, since giving birth is more effort for them, and they know better that the children are theirs,⁷ and this also would seem to be proper to benefactors.

8
[Self-love and selfishness]

[c8] There is also a puzzle about whether one ought to love oneself most, or someone else; for those who like themselves / most are crit-   30
icized and denounced as self-lovers, as though this were something shameful.[1] Indeed, the base person seems to go to every length[2] for his own sake, and all the more the more vicious he is; hence he is accused, for instance, of doing nothing <for any end apart> from himself.[3] The decent person, on the contrary, acts for the fine, all the more the better he is, and for his friend's sake, / disregarding his own <interest>.   35

§2 / The facts, however, conflict with these claims, not unreason-   1168b
ably.[4] For it is said that we must love most the friend who is most a friend; and one is a friend to another most of all if he wishes goods to the other for the other's sake, even if no one will know about it. But these are features most of all of one's relation to oneself; and so too are all the other / defining features of a friend, since it has been said   5
that all the features of friendship extend from oneself to others.[5]

All the proverbs agree with this too, speaking, for instance, of 'one soul', 'what friends have is common', 'equality is friendship', and 'the knee is closer than the shin'.[6] For all these are true most of all in someone's relations with himself, since one is a friend to himself most of all. Hence he should also love / himself most of all.   10

There is a puzzle, then, not surprisingly, about which of these two views we ought to follow, since both inspire some confidence.   §3 Presumably, then, we must divide these sorts of arguments, and distin-
guish how far and in what ways those on each side are true. / If, then,   15
we grasp how those on each side understand self-love, perhaps it will become clear.

§4 Those who make self-love a matter for reproach ascribe it to those who award the biggest share in money, honours, and bodily pleasures to themselves. For the many desire and eagerly pursue these goods, assuming that they are best. That is why they are also contested.[7] Those who overreach for these goods gratify their appetites / and altogether their feelings and the non-rational part of the soul;   20
and this is the character of the many. That is why the application of the term <'self-love'> is also derived from the most frequent <kind of self-love>, which is base. This type of self-lover, then, is justifiably reproached.

§5 And plainly those who award themselves these goods are those

25 whom the many habitually call self-lovers. For if / someone were always eager above all to do[8] just or temperate actions or any other actions in accord with the virtues, and in general always gained the fine for himself, no one would call him a self-lover or blame him for it.

§6 This sort of person, however, more than the other sort, seems

30 to be a self-lover. At any rate he awards himself the finest / and best things all, and gratifies the most controlling <part> of himself, obeying it in everything. And just as the most controlling <part> seems above all others to be a city and every other composite system,[9] the same is true of a human being; hence someone loves himself most if he likes and gratifies this part.

35 Similarly, someone is called continent or incontinent because / his understanding is or is not the master, on the assumption that this is

1169a what each person is.[10] Moreover, / his own voluntary actions seem above all to be those that involve reason.[11] Clearly, then, this, or this above all, is what each person is, and the decent person likes this most of all.

That is why he most of all is a self-lover, but a different kind from

5 the one who is reproached. He is superior to him / by as much as the life guided by reason is superior to the life guided by feelings,[12] and as much as desire for the fine is superior to desire for what seems advantageous.[13]

§7 Those, then, who are unusually eager to do fine actions are welcomed and praised by everyone. And when everyone strains to

10 achieve the fine and concentrates on the finest / actions, everything that is right will be done for the common good, and each person individually will receive the greatest of goods, since that is the character of virtue.[14] And so the good person must be a self-lover, since he will both help himself and benefit others by doing fine actions. But the vicious person must not love himself, since he will harm both himself and his neighbours by following his base feelings.

15 §8 / For the vicious person, then, the right actions conflict with those he does. The decent person, however, does the right actions, since all understanding[15] chooses for itself what is best,[16] and the decent person obeys his understanding.

§9 It is quite true that, as they say, the excellent person labours

20 for his friends and for his native country, even if he ought to / die for them if he must; for he will sacrifice money, honours, and contested

goods altogether, achieving the fine for himself.[17] For he will choose intense pleasure for a short time over slight pleasure for a long time; a year of living finely over many years of undistinguished life; and a single fine / and great action over many small actions. This is presumably true of one who dies for others; he does indeed choose something great and fine for himself.

He is also ready to sacrifice money as long as his friends profit; for the friends gain money, while he gains the fine, and so he awards himself the greater good.   §10 He treats honours / and offices in the same way; for he will sacrifice them all for his friends, since this is fine and praiseworthy for himself. It is not surprising, then, that he seems to be excellent, since he chooses the fine at the cost of everything. It is also possible, however, to sacrifice actions to his friend, since it may be finer to be responsible for his friend's doing the action than to do it himself.[18]

§11 In everything praiseworthy, / then, the excellent person evidently awards himself more of the fine. / In this way, then, we ought to be self-lovers, as we have said. But in the way the many are, we ought not to be.[19]

9
[Why do we need friends?]

[c9] There is also a dispute about whether the happy person will need friends or not.[1] For it is said that blessedly happy and self-sufficient people have no need of friends. For they already have <all> the / goods, and hence, being self-sufficient, need nothing added. But one's friend, since he is another oneself, supplies what one's own efforts cannot supply. Hence it is said, 'When the god gives well, what need is there of friends?'[2]

§2 It would seem strange, however, to award the happy person all the goods, without giving him friends, which seems to be the greatest external good.[3] And if it is more proper to a friend to confer benefits than to receive them, and it is proper to the good person and to virtue to do good, and it is finer to benefit friends than to benefit strangers, the excellent person will need people to benefit.[4] Indeed, that is why there is a question about whether friends are needed more in good fortune than in ill fortune, / on the assumption that in ill fortune we need people to benefit us, and in good fortune we need others for us to benefit.

§3 And presumably it is also strange to make the blessed person solitary. For no one would choose to have all <other> goods and yet be alone, since a human being is a political <animal> that tends by nature to live together with others.[5] This will also be true, / then, of the happy person; for he has the natural goods, and clearly it is better to spend his days with decent friends than with strangers of any old character. Hence the happy person needs friends.

§4 Then what are those on the other side saying, and on what point are they correct? Perhaps <they say what they say> because[6] the many think that the useful people are friends.[7] Now certainly / the blessedly happy person will have no need of these, since he has <all> goods. Similarly, he will have no need, or very little, of friends for pleasure; for since his life is pleasant, it has no need of imported pleasure.[8] Since he does not need these sorts of friends, he seems not to need friends at all.

§5 This conclusion, however, is presumably not true. For we said at the beginning that happiness is a kind of / activity; and clearly activity comes into being, and does not belong <to someone all the time>, as a possession does. Now if being happy consists in living and being active; the activity of the good person is excellent, and <hence> pleasant in itself, as we said at the beginning; what is our own is also pleasant; and we are able to observe our neighbours more than ourselves, / and to observe their actions more than our own; it follows that a good person finds pleasure in the actions of excellent / people who are his friends, since these actions have both the naturally pleasant <features—they are good, and they are his own>. The blessed person, therefore, will need virtuous friends, given that he decides to observe virtuous actions that are his own, and the actions of a virtuous person who is his friend are of this sort.[9]

Further, it is thought that the happy person must live / pleasantly.[10] Now a solitary person's life is hard, since it is not easy for him to be continuously active all by himself; but in relation to others and in their company it is easier. §6 Hence his activity will be more continuous. It is also pleasant in itself, as it must be in the blessedly happy person's case. For the excellent person, insofar as he is excellent, enjoys actions in accord with virtue, and objects to actions / caused by vice, just as the musician enjoys fine melodies and is pained by bad ones.

§7 Further, good people's life together allows the cultivation of virtue, as Theognis says.[11]

If we examine the question more from the point of view of <human> nature,[12] an excellent friend would seem to be choiceworthy by nature for an excellent person. / For, as we have said, what is good by nature is good and pleasant in itself for an excellent person.   15

For animals, life is defined by the capacity for perception, but for human beings, it is defined by the capacity for perception or understanding; moreover, every capacity refers to an activity, and a thing is present fully in its activity; hence living fully would seem to be perceiving or understanding.[13]

/ Now life is good and pleasant in itself; for it has definite order,   20 which is proper to the nature of what is good.[14] What is good by nature is also good for the decent person; that is why life would seem to be pleasant for everyone.   §8 But we must not consider a life that is vicious and corrupted, or filled with pains; for such a life / lacks   25 definite order, just as its proper features do. (The truth about pain will be more evident in what follows.)[15]

§9 Life itself, then, is good and pleasant, as it would seem, at any rate, from the fact that everyone desires it, and decent and blessed people desire it more than others do—for their life is most choiceworthy for them, and their living is most blessed.

Now someone who sees perceives that he sees; one who / hears   30 perceives that he hears; one who walks perceives that he walks; and similarly in the other cases also there is some <part> that perceives that we are active; so that if we are perceiving, we perceive that we are perceiving, and if we are understanding, we perceive that we are understanding.[16] Now perceiving that we are perceiving or understanding is the same as perceiving that we are, since we saw that being is perceiving or understanding.

/ Perceiving that we are alive is pleasant in itself. For life is by   1170b nature a good, and it is pleasant to perceive that something good is present in us. Living is also choiceworthy, for a good person most of all, since being is good and pleasant for him; for he is / pleased to per-   5 ceive something good in itself together <with his own being>.

§10 The excellent person is related to his friend in the same way as he is related to himself, since a friend is another himself.[17] Therefore, just as his own being is choiceworthy for him, his friend's being is choiceworthy for him in the same or a similar way. We saw that

someone's own being is choiceworthy because he perceives that he
10   is good, and this sort of perception / is pleasant in itself. He ought,
then, to perceive his friend's being together <with his own>, and he
will do this when they live together, that is to say they share conversation and thought[18]—for in the case of human beings what seems to
count as living together is this sharing of conversation and thought,
not sharing the same pasture, as in the case of grazing animals.

15   / If, then, for the blessedly happy person, being is choiceworthy,
since it is naturally good and pleasant, and if the being of his friend is
closely similar to his own, his friend will also be choiceworthy.[19] What
is choiceworthy for him he ought to possess, since otherwise he will
in this respect lack something.[20] Anyone who is to be happy, then, will
need excellent friends.

10
[How many friends are needed?]

20   [c10] / Then should we make as many friends as possible?[1] Or is it
the same as with the friendship of host and guest, where it seems to
be good advice to 'have neither many nor none'?[2] Is this also good
advice in friendship, to have neither no friends nor excessively many?

25   §2 With friends for utility the advice seems very apt, since / it is
hard work to return many people's services, and one's life is insufficient[3] for it. Indeed, more friends <of this type> than are adequate
for one's own life are superfluous, and a hindrance to living finely;
hence we have no need of them. A few friends for pleasure are enough
also, just as a little seasoning on food is enough.

30   §3 Of excellent people, however, should we have as many / as possible as friends, or is there some proper measure of their number, as
of the number in a city? For a city could not be formed from ten people, but it would be a city no longer if it had a hundred thousand.[4]
Presumably, though, the right quantity is not just one number, but
1171a   anything between / certain defined limits. Hence there is also some
limit defining the number of friends. Presumably, this is the largest
number with whom one could live together, since we found that living together seems to be most characteristic of friendship.

§4 Now clearly one cannot live with many people and distribute
oneself among them.[5] Further these many people must also be friends
5   to one another, if they are / all to spend their days together; and this
is hard work for many people to manage.   §5 It also proves to be

178

difficult for many to share one another's enjoyments and distresses as their own,[6] since one is quite likely to find oneself sharing one friend's pleasure and another friend's grief at the same time.

Presumably, then, it is good not to seek as many friends as possible, and it is good to have no more than enough for living / together. 10 Indeed it even seems impossible to be an extremely close friend to many people. That is why it also seems impossible to be passionately in love with many people, since passionate erotic love tends to be an excess of friendship, and one has this for one person; hence also one has extremely close friendship for a few people.

§6 This would seem to be borne out in what people actually do. For the friendship of companions is not found in groups / of many people, 15 and the friendships celebrated in song are always between two people. By contrast, those who have many friends and treat everyone as close to them seem to be friends to no one, except in the way fellow-citizens are friends; indeed, these people are said to be ingratiating.[7] Certainly it is possible to have a fellow-citizen's friendship for many people, and still to be a truly decent person, not ingratiating; but it is impossible to be many people's friend / for their virtue and for themselves. We have 20 reason to be satisfied if we can find even a few such friends.

11
[Friends in good and ill fortune]

[c11] Do we need friends more in good fortune or in ill fortune?[1] For in fact we seek them in both; for in ill fortune we need assistance, and in good fortune we need friends to live with and to benefit, since then we wish to do good to them. Certainly it is more necessary to have friends in ill fortune; / that is why useful friends are needed here. 25 But it is finer to have them in good fortune. That is why we also seek decent friends; for it is more choiceworthy to do good to them and spend our time with them.

§2 The very presence of friends is also pleasant, in ill fortune as well as good fortune; for we have our pain lightened / when our 30 friends share our distress. Indeed, that is why one might be puzzled about whether they take a part of the pain from us, as though helping us to lift a weight, or, alternatively, their presence is pleasant and our awareness that they share our distress makes the pain smaller. Well, we need not discuss whether it is this or something else that lightens our pain; at any rate, what we have mentioned does appear to occur.

35   §3 / In fact, however, the presence of friends would seem to be
1171b a mixture / <of pleasure and pain>. For certainly the sight of our
friends in itself is pleasant, especially when we are in ill fortune, and
it gives us some assistance in removing our pain. For a friend consoles
us by the sight of him and by conversation, if he is dexterous, since he
knows our character and what gives us pleasure and pain.[2]

5   §4 Nonetheless, awareness / of his pain at our ill fortune is painful to us; for everyone tries to avoid causing pain to his friends. That
is why someone with a manly nature tries to prevent his friend from
sharing his pain.[3] Unless he is unusually immune to pain, he cannot
endure pain coming to his friends; and he does not allow others to
10   share his mourning at all, / since he is not prone to mourn himself
either. Females, however, and effeminate men enjoy having people to
wail with them; they love them as friends who share their distress. But
in everything we clearly must imitate the better person.

      §5 In good fortune, by contrast, the presence of friends makes it
pleasant to pass our time and to notice that they take pleasure in our
15   own goods. That is why / it seems that we must eagerly call our friends
to share our good fortune, since it is fine to do good. But we must
hesitate to call them to share our ill fortune, since we must share bad
things with them as little as possible; hence the saying 'My misfortune
20   is enough'. We should invite them / most of all whenever they will
benefit us greatly, with little trouble to themselves.[4]

      §6 Conversely, it is presumably appropriate to go eagerly, with-
out having to be called, to friends in misfortune. For it is proper to
a friend to benefit, especially to benefit a friend in need who has not
demanded it, since this is finer and pleasanter for both friends. In
good fortune one should come eagerly to help him, since friends are
needed for this also; but one should be slow to come to receive bene-
25   fits, / since eagerness to be benefitted is not fine. Presumably, though,
one should avoid getting a reputation for being a killjoy, as sometimes
happens, by refusing benefits.

      Hence the presence of friends is apparently choiceworthy in all
conditions.

12
[Shared activity in friendship]

30   [c12] What the erotic lover likes most is the sight of his beloved, /
and this is the sort of perception he chooses over the others, on the

assumption that this above all is what makes him fall in love and remain in love. In the same way, surely, what friends find most choice-worthy is living together. For friendship is community, and we are related to our friend as we are related to ourselves. Hence, since the perception of our own being is choiceworthy, so is the perception of our friend's being. / Perception is active when we live with him; hence, / not surprisingly, this is what we seek.[1]

§2 Whatever someone <regards as> his being, or the end for which he chooses to be alive, that is the activity he wishes to pursue in his friend's company. Hence some friends drink together, others play dice, while others do gymnastics / and go hunting, or do philosophy. They spend their days together on whichever pursuit in life they like most; for since they want to live with their friends, they share the actions in which they find their common life.

§3 Hence the friendship of base people turns out to be vicious. For they are unstable, and share base pursuits; and / by becoming similar to each other, they grow vicious. But the friendship of decent people is decent, and increases the more often they meet.[2] And they seem to become still better from their activities and their mutual correction. For each moulds the other in what they approve of, so that '<you will learn>[3] what is noble from noble people'.

§4 / So much, then, for friendship. The next task will be to discuss pleasure.[4]

Book X
[Pleasure]

1
[The right approach to pleasure]

/ The next task, presumably, is to discuss pleasure. For it seems to be especially proper to our <animal> kind; that is why, when we educate children, we steer them by pleasure and pain.[1] Besides, enjoying and hating the right things seems to be most important for virtue of char-acter. For pleasure and pain extend through the whole of our lives, and are of great importance / for virtue and the happy life, since peo-ple decide on pleasant things, and avoid painful things.

§2 And least of all, then, it seems, should these topics be neglected, especially given that they arouse much dispute. For some say plea-sure is the good, while others, on the contrary, say it is altogether

base.[2] Presumably, some <who say it is base> say so because they
30   are persuaded that it is so. Others, however, say it because / they
think it is better for the conduct of our lives to present pleasure as
base even if it is not. For, they say, the many lean towards pleasure
and are slaves to pleasures, and that is why we must lead them in
the contrary direction, because that is the way to reach the intermediate condition.[3]

§3 Surely, however, this is wrong. For arguments about feel-
35   ings and / actions are less credible than the facts; hence any con-
1172b flict between arguments and perceptible <facts> arouses / contempt
for the arguments, and moreover undermines the truth as well <as
the arguments>.[4] For if someone blames pleasure, but then has been
seen to seek it on *some* occasions, the reason for his lapse seems to be
that he regards *every* type of pleasure as something to seek; for the
many are not the sort to make distinctions.[5]

5   §4 / True arguments, then, would seem to be the most useful, not
only for knowledge but also for the conduct of life. For since they harmonize with the facts, they are credible; that is why they encourage
those who comprehend them to live by them.

Enough of this, then; let us now consider what has been said about
pleasure.

2

[Arguments about pleasure]

10   [c2] Eudoxus thought pleasure is the good,[1] because / he saw that all
<animals>, both rational and non-rational, seek it, and in everything,
he says, what is choiceworthy is good, and what is most choiceworthy
is supreme. The fact that all[2] are drawn to the same thing <i.e., plea-
15   sure>, indicates, in his view, that it is best / for all, since each <kind
of animal> finds its own good, just as it finds its own nourishment;
what is good for all, then,[3] what all aim at, is the good. These arguments of his were found credible because of his virtuous character,
rather than on their own <merits>. For since he seemed to be out-
standingly temperate, he did not seem to be saying this because he
was a friend of pleasure; rather, it seemed that what he said was how
it really was.

§2 He thought it was no less evident from consideration of the
contrary. For pain in its own right, he said, is something to be
20   avoided[4] for all, / so that, similarly, its contrary is choiceworthy for

all. Now what is most choiceworthy is what we choose not because of, or for the sake of, anything else; and it is agreed that this is the character of pleasure, since we never ask anyone what his end is in being pleased, because we assume that pleasure is choiceworthy in its own right.

Moreover, <he argued>, when pleasure is added to any other good, to just or temperate action, for instance, it makes that / good more   25 choiceworthy; and good is increased by the addition of itself.

§3 This <last> argument, at least, would seem to present pleasure as one good among others, no more a good than any other. For the addition of any other good makes a good more choiceworthy than it is all by itself. Indeed Plato uses this sort of argument to undermine the claim of pleasure to be the good.[5] For, he argues, / the pleasant life is   30 more choiceworthy when combined with prudence[6] than it is without it; and if the mixed <good> is better, pleasure is not the good, since nothing can be added to the good to make it more choiceworthy. Nor, clearly, could anything else be the good if it is made more choiceworthy by the addition of anything that is good / in itself.   §4 Then what   35 is the good that meets this condition, and that we share in also? That is what we are looking for.

But when some object that what everything aims at is not good, /   1173a surely there is nothing in what they say.[7] For if things seem <good> to all, we say they are <good>;[8] and if someone undermines confidence in these, what he says will hardly inspire more confidence in other things. For if <only animals> without understanding desired these things, there would be something in the objection;[9] but if prudent <animals>[10] also desire them, how can there be anything in it? And presumably even in / inferior <animals> there is some natural good,   5 superior to themselves, that seeks their own proper good.

§5 The argument <against Eudoxus> about the contrary would also seem to be incorrect.[11] For they argue that if pain is an evil, it does not follow that pleasure is a good, since evil is also opposed to evil, and both are opposed to the neutral condition <without pleasure or pain>. The objectors' general point here is right, but what they /   10 say in the case mentioned is false. For if both pleasure and pain were evils, we ought also to avoid both, and if both were neutral, we ought to avoid neither, or else avoid both equally. Evidently, however, we avoid pain as an evil and choose pleasure as a good; hence this must also be the type of opposition between them.

3

[Pleasure is a good, but not the good]

Again, if <as the objectors argue> pleasure is not a quality, it does not
follow <as they suppose> that it is not a good.[1] / For virtuous activities and happiness are not qualities either.[2]

§2 They say that the good is definite, whereas pleasure is indefinite
because it admits of more and less.[3] If their judgment rests on the
actual condition of being pleased, the same will also hold for justice
and the other virtues, where evidently we are said to have a certain
character more / and less, and to act more and less in accord with the
virtues;[4] for we may be more <and less> just or brave, and may do
just or temperate actions more and less. If, on the other hand, their
judgment rests on the <variety of> pleasures, then surely they fail to
state the reason <why pleasures admit of more and less>, namely that
some are unmixed <with pain> and others are mixed.[5]

§3 / Moreover, just as health admits of more and less, though it is
definite, why should pleasure not be the same? For not every <healthy
person> has the same proportion <of bodily elements>, nor does the
same person always have the same, but it may be relaxed and still
remain, up to a certain limit, and may differ in more and less. The
same is quite possible, then, for pleasure also.

§4 They hold that what is good is complete, whereas processes /
and becomings are incomplete, and they try to show that pleasure
is a process and a becoming. It would seem, however, that they are
wrong, and pleasure is not even a process.[6] For quickness or slowness
seems to be proper to every process—if not in itself (as, for instance,
with the universe), then in relation to something else. But neither of
these is true of pleasure. For though certainly it is possible to become
/ pleased quickly, as it is possible to become angry quickly, it is not
possible to be pleased quickly, even in relation to something else,
whereas this is possible for walking and growing and all such things
<i.e., for processes>. It is possible, then, to pass quickly or slowly
into pleasure, but not possible to be <quickly or slowly> in the corresponding activity, i.e., to be pleased quickly <or slowly>.[7]

§5 / And how could pleasure be a becoming? For one random
thing, it seems, does not come to be from any other; what something
comes to be from is what it is dissolved into. Hence whatever pleasure
is the becoming of, pain should be the perishing of it.

§6 They do indeed say that pain is the emptying of the natural <condition, and hence the perishing>, and that pleasure is its refilling, <and hence the becoming>.[8] Emptying and filling happen to the body; if, then, pleasure is the refilling of something / natural, what has the refilling will also have the pleasure. Hence it will be the body that has pleasure. This does not seem to be true, however. The refilling, then, is not pleasure, though someone might be pleased while a refilling is going on, and pained when he is becoming empty.[9]

This belief <that pleasure is refilling> seems to have arisen from pains and pleasures in connexion with food; for first / we are empty and suffer pain, and then we take pleasure in the refilling.   §7 The same is not true, however, of all pleasures; for pleasures in mathematics, and among pleasures in perception those through the sense of smell, and many sounds, sights, memories, and expectations as well, all arise without <previous> pain. In that case what will they be comings to be / of? For since no emptiness of anything has come to be, there is nothing whose refilling might come to be.

§8 To those who cite the disgraceful pleasures <to show that pleasure is not a good>, we might reply that these <sources of disgraceful pleasures> are not pleasant.[10] For if things are healthy or sweet or bitter to sick people, we should not suppose that they are also healthy, or sweet, or bitter, except to them, or that things appearing white to people with eye disease are white, except to them. Similarly, if things are pleasant to people in bad condition, we should not suppose that they are also pleasant, except to these people.[11]

§9 / Or else we might say that pleasures are choiceworthy, but not if they come from these sources, just as wealth is, but not if you have to betray someone to get it, and just as health is, but not if it requires you to eat anything and everything.[12]

§10 Or perhaps pleasures differ in species. For those from fine sources are different from those from shameful sources; / and we cannot have the just person's pleasure without being just, any more than we can have the musician's pleasure without being musicians, and similarly in the other cases.[13]

§11 Now the difference between a friend and a flatterer seems to indicate that pleasure is not good, or else that pleasures differ in species.[14] For in dealings with us the friend seems to aim at the good, but the flatterer at pleasure; / and the flatterer is reproached, whereas the friend is praised, on the assumption that in their dealings they have different aims.

§12 And no one would choose to live with a child's <level of> thought for his whole life, taking the greatest pleasure in the things that please children, or choose to enjoy himself while doing some utterly shameful action, even if he would never suffer pain for it.[15]

5   Moreover, there are many things that we would be eager / for even if they brought along no pleasure—for instance, seeing, remembering, knowing, having the virtues. Even if pleasures necessarily follow on them, that does not matter; for we would choose them even if no pleasure came about from them.[16]

10   §13 It would seem to be clear, then, that pleasure is not the / good, that not every pleasure is choiceworthy, and that some are choiceworthy in themselves, differing in species or in their sources <from those that are not>.[17]

Let this suffice, then, for discussion of the things said about pleasure and pain.[18]

4

[Pleasure is an activity]

[c3] What, then, or what kind of thing, is pleasure? This will become clearer if we take it up again from the beginning.[1] For seeing seems
15 to be complete / at any time, since it has no need for anything else to complete its form by coming to be at a later time. And pleasure is also like this, since it is some sort of whole, and no pleasure is to be found at any time that will have its form completed by coming to be for a longer time.[2]

§2 That is why pleasure is not a process either. For every process,
20 such as constructing a building,[3] takes time, / and aims at some end, and is complete when it produces the product it seeks, or, <in other words, is complete> in this whole time <that it takes>.[4] Moreover, each process is incomplete during the processes that are its parts, i.e., during the time it goes on; and it consists of processes that are different in form from the whole process and from one another.[5] For laying stones together and fluting a column are different processes; and both
25 are different from the <whole> production / of the temple. For the production of the temple is a complete production, since it needs nothing further <when it is finished> to achieve the proposed goal; but the production of the foundation or the triglyph is an incomplete production,

since <when it is finished> it is <the production> of a part.[6] Hence <processes that are parts of larger processes> differ in form; and we cannot find a process complete in form at any time <while it is going on>, but <only>, if at all, in the whole time <that it takes>.[7]

§3 The same is true of walking and the other <processes>. For / if 30 locomotion is a process from one place to another, it includes loco-motions differing in form—flying, walking, jumping, and so on. And besides these differences, there are differences in walking itself. For the place from which and the place to which are not the same in the whole racecourse as they are in a part of it, or the same in one part as in another; nor is traversing one line the same as traversing / another, 1174b since what we pass over is not just a line, but a line in a <particular> place, and this line and that line are in different places.[8]

Now we have discussed process exactly elsewhere.[9] But, at any rate, a process, it would seem, is not complete at every time; and the many <constituent> processes are incomplete, / and differ in form, 5 since the place from which and the place to which make the form of a process <and different processes begin and end in different places>.

§4 The form of pleasure, by contrast, is complete at any time. Clearly, then, it is different from a process, and is something whole and complete. This also seems true because a process must take time, but being pleased need not; for what is present in an instant is a whole.[10] / This also makes it clear that it is wrong to say that pleasure 10 is a process or a becoming.[11] For this is not said of everything, but only of what is divisible and not a whole; for seeing, or a point, or a unit, has no coming to be, and none of these is either a process or a becoming. Nor, then <is this said> of pleasure;[12] for it is a whole.

[c4] §5 Every perceptual capacity is active in relation to its / per- 15 ceptible object, and completely active when it is in good condition in relation to the finest of its perceptible objects.[13] For this above all seems to be the character of complete activity, whether it is ascribed to the capacity or to the subject that has it. Hence for each capacity the best activity is the activity of the subject in the best condition in relation to the best object of the capacity.

/ This activity will be the most complete and the pleasantest. For 20 every perceptual capacity and every sort of thought and study has its pleasure; the pleasantest activity is the most complete; and the most complete is the activity of the subject in good condition in relation to the most excellent object of the capacity. Pleasure completes the activity.

25 §6 But the way in which pleasure completes the activity is / not the way in which the perceptible object and the perceptual capacity complete it when they are both excellent—just as health and the doctor are not the cause of being healthy in the same way.[14]

§7 Clearly a pleasure arises that corresponds to each perceptual capacity, since we say that sights and sounds are pleasant; and clearly it arises most of all whenever the perceptual capacity is best, and is

30 active in relation / to the best sort of object. When this is the condition of the perceptible object and of the perceiving subject, there will always be pleasure, when the producer and the subject to be affected are both present.

§8 Pleasure completes the activity—not, however, as the state does, by being present <in the activity>, but as a sort of supervenient end, like the bloom on youths.[15] Hence as long as the objects of understanding or perception and the subject that judges or attends

1175a are in the right / condition, there will be pleasure in the activity. For as long as the subject affected and the productive <cause> remain similar and in the same relation to each other, the same thing naturally arises.

5 §9 Then how is it that no one is continuously pleased? Is it / not because we get tired? For nothing human is capable of continuous activity, and hence no continuous pleasure arises either, since pleasure is a consequence of the activity.[16] Some things delight us when they are new to us, but later delight us less, for the same reason. For at first our thought is stimulated and intensely active towards them, as our sense of sight is when we look closely at something; but later

10 the / activity becomes lax and careless, so that the pleasure fades also.

§10 Why does everyone desire pleasure? We might think it is because everyone also aims at being alive.[17] Living is a type of activity, and each of us is active towards the objects he likes most and in the ways he likes most. The musician, for instance, activates his hear-

15 ing in hearing melodies; the lover of learning activates his / thought in thinking about objects of study; and so on for each of the others. Pleasure completes their activities, and hence completes life, which they desire. It is reasonable, then, that they also aim at pleasure, since it completes each person's life for him, and life is choiceworthy.

[c5] §11 But do we choose life because of pleasure, or pleasure because of life? Let us set aside this question for now, since these / appear to be combined and to allow no separation; for pleasure never arises without activity, and pleasure completes every activity.[18]

5
[Pleasures differ in kind]

Hence pleasures also seem to differ in species.[1] For we suppose that things of different species are completed by different things. That is how it appears, both with natural things and with artifacts—for instance, with animals, trees, a painting, / a statue, a house, or an implement. Similarly, activities that differ in species are also completed by things that differ in species.   §2 Now activities of thought differ in species from activities of the capacities for perception, and the latter differ from each other in species; so also, then, do the pleasures that complete them.

This is also apparent from the fact that each pleasure is proper / to the activity that it completes.[2] For the proper pleasure increases the activity; for we judge each thing better and more exactly when our activity involves pleasure. If, for instance, we enjoy doing geometry, we become better geometers, and understand each question better; and similarly lovers of / music, building, and so on improve at their proper function when they enjoy it. Each pleasure increases the activity; what increases it is / proper to it; and since the activities are different in species, what is proper to them is also different in species.

§3 This is even more apparent from the fact that some activities are impeded by pleasures from other activities. For lovers of flutes, for instance, cannot pay attention to a conversation if they catch the sound of someone playing the flute, because they enjoy flute playing / more than their present activity; and so the pleasure proper to flute playing destroys the activity of conversation.

§4 The same is true in other cases also, whenever we are engaged in two activities at once. For the pleasanter activity pushes out the other one, all the more if it is much pleasanter, / so that we no longer even engage in the other activity. That is why, if we are enjoying one thing intensely, we do not do another very much. It is when we are only mildly pleased that we do something else; for instance, people who eat nuts in theatres do this most when the contestants[3] are bad.

15 §5 Since the proper pleasure makes an activity more / exact, longer, and better, but an alien pleasure damages it, clearly the two pleasures differ widely. For an alien pleasure does virtually what a proper pain does; for a proper pain destroys activity. If, for instance, writing or rational calculation has no pleasure and is in fact painful for us,

20 we do not write or calculate, since the activity / is painful. Hence the proper pleasures and pains have contrary effects on an activity; and the proper ones are those that arise from the activity in its own right. And as has been said, the effect of alien pleasures is similar to the effect of pain, since they ruin the activity, though not in the same way as pain.

25 §6 Since activities differ in degrees of decency and badness, / and some are choiceworthy, some to be avoided, some neither, the same is true of pleasures; for each activity has its own proper pleasure. Hence the pleasure proper to an excellent activity is decent, and the one that is proper to a base activity is vicious; for, similarly, appetites for fine things are praiseworthy, and appetites for shameful things are blame-

30 worthy. / And in fact the pleasure in an activity is more proper to it than the desire for it. For the desire is distinguished from it in time and in nature; but the pleasure is close to the activity, and so little distinguished from it that disputes arise about whether the activity is the same as the pleasure.

§7 Nonetheless, pleasure would seem to be neither thought nor

35 perception; / for that would be strange. Rather, it is because <pleasure and activity> are not separated that to some people they appear

1176a the same.[4] / Hence, just as activities differ, so do the pleasures. Sight differs from touch in purity, as hearing and smell do from taste; hence the pleasures also differ in the same way. So also do the pleasures of thought differ from these <pleasures of sense>; and both sorts have different kinds within them.

§8 Each <species of> animal seems to have its own proper pleasure, just as it has its own proper function; for the proper pleasure

5 will be the one that corresponds to its activity. / This is apparent if we also study each kind; for a horse, a dog, and a human being have different pleasures, and, as Heracleitus says, an ass would choose chaff over gold, since asses find food pleasanter than gold.[5] Hence animals that differ in species also have pleasures that differ in species; and it would be reasonable for animals of the same species to have the same pleasures also.

§9 / In fact, however, the pleasures differ quite a lot, in human   10
beings at any rate. For the same things delight some people, and
cause pain to others; and while some find them painful and hateful, others find them pleasant and lovable. The same is true of sweet
things. For the same things do not seem sweet to a feverish and to a
healthy person, or hot to an / enfeebled and to a vigorous person; and   15
the same is true of other things.

§10 But in all such cases it seems that what is really so is what
appears so to the excellent person. If this is right, as it seems to be,
and virtue, i.e., the good person insofar as he is good, is the measure
of each thing, then what appear pleasures to him will also really be
pleasures, and what is pleasant will be what he enjoys.[6]

/ And if what he finds objectionable appears pleasant to someone,   20
that is not at all surprising; for human beings suffer many sorts of
corruption and damage. It is not pleasant, however, except to these
people in these conditions.   §11 Clearly, then, we should say that
the pleasures agreed to be shameful are not pleasures at all, except to
corrupted people.[7]

But what about those pleasures that seem to be decent? / Of these,   25
what sort, or what particular pleasure, should we take to be the pleasure of a human being? Surely it will be clear from the activities, since
the pleasures are consequences of these. Hence the pleasures that complete the activities of the complete and blessedly happy man, whether
he has one activity or more than one, will be called the fully human
pleasures. The other pleasures will be human in secondary or even
more remote ways, corresponding to the character of the activities.

[Happiness: further discussion]

6
[Conditions for happiness]

[c6] / We have now finished our discussion of the types of virtue, of   30
friendship, and of pleasure.[1] It remains for us to discuss happiness in
outline, since we take this to be the end of human <aims>. Our discussion will be shorter if we first take up again what we said before.

§2 We said, then, that happiness is not a state. For if it were, someone might have it and yet be asleep for his whole life, / living the life   35
of a plant, or suffer the greatest misfortunes. / If we do not approve of   1176b
this, we count happiness as an activity rather than a state, as was said
in the previous <discussions>.[2]

Some activities are necessary, and, choiceworthy for some other end,[3] while others are choiceworthy in their own right. Clearly, then, we should count happiness as one of those / that are choiceworthy in their own right, not as one of those that are choiceworthy for some other end. For happiness lacks nothing, but is self-sufficient.[4] An activity is choiceworthy in its own right if nothing further apart from it is sought from it. This seems to be the character of actions that are in accord with virtue; for doing fine and excellent actions is choiceworthy for itself.

But pleasant amusements also <seem to be choiceworthy in their own right>.[5] For people choose them, not because of / other things— for they actually cause more harm than benefit, by causing neglect of our bodies and possessions. Moreover, most of those who are congratulated for their happiness resort to these sorts of pastimes. That is why people who are witty participants in them have a good reputation / with tyrants, since they offer themselves as pleasant <partners> in the tyrant's aims, and these are the sort of people the tyrant requires.[6] And so these amusements seem to have the character of happiness because people in supreme power spend their leisure in them.[7]

§4 Such people, however, are presumably no evidence. For virtue and understanding, the sources of excellent activities, do not depend on holding supreme power. Further, / these powerful people have had no taste of pure and civilized pleasure, and so they resort to bodily pleasures.[8] But that is no reason to think these pleasures are most choiceworthy, since boys also think that the things they honour are best. Hence, just as different things appear honourable to boys and to men, it is reasonable that in the same way different things appear honourable to base and to decent people.[9] §5 / As we have often said, then, what is honourable and pleasant is what is so to the excellent person.[10] To each type of person the activity that accords with his own proper state is most choiceworthy; hence the activity in accord with virtue is most choiceworthy to the excellent person.[11]

§6 Happiness, then, is not found in amusement; for it would be strange if the end were amusement, and our lifelong efforts / and sufferings aimed at amusing ourselves. For we choose practically everything for some other end—except for happiness, since it is the end; but serious work and toil aimed at amusement appears stupid and excessively childish. Rather, it seems correct to amuse ourselves so

that we can do something serious, as Anacharsis says;[12] for amusement would seem to be relaxation, and it is because we cannot /   35
toil continuously that we require relaxation. Relaxation, then, is not
<the> end; for we pursue it <to prepare> for / activity. But the happy   1177a
life seems to be a life in accord with virtue, which is a life involving
serious actions, and not consisting in amusement.

§7 Besides, we say that things to be taken seriously are better than
funny things that provide amusement, and that in / each case the   5
activity of the better part and the better person is more serious and
excellent; and the activity of what is better is superior, and thereby
has more the character of happiness.[13]

§8 Besides, anyone at all, even a slave, no less than the best person, might enjoy bodily pleasures; but no one would allow that a slave
shares in happiness, if one does not <also allow that the slave shares
in the sort of> life <that is needed for happiness>.[14] For happiness
is found not in these pastimes, but / in the activities in accord with   10
virtue, as we also said previously.

7

[Happiness and theoretical study]

[c7] If happiness is activity in accord with virtue, it is reasonable for
it to be in accord with the supreme virtue, which will be the virtue
of the best thing. The best is understanding, or whatever else seems
to be / the natural ruler and leader,[1] and to understand what is fine   15
and divine, by being itself either divine or the most divine element in
us. Hence complete happiness will be its activity in accord with the
proper virtue;[2] and it has been said that this activity is an activity of
study.[3]

§2 This seems to agree with what has been said before, and also
with the truth.[4] /   20

For this activity is supreme, since understanding is the supreme
element in us, and the objects of understanding are the supreme
objects of knowledge.

Further, it is the most continuous activity, since we are more capable of continuous study than any continuous action.[5]

§3 Besides, we think pleasure must be mixed into happiness; and
it is agreed that the activity in accord with wisdom[6] is the pleasantest
/ of the activities in accord with virtue. Certainly, philosophy seems   25
to have remarkably pure and firm pleasures, and it is reasonable that

those who have knowledge spend their lives more pleasantly than those who seek it.

§4 Moreover, the self-sufficiency that is spoken of[7] will be found in study most of all.[8] Admittedly the wise person, no less than the just person, and the other virtuous people, needs the good things that

30   are necessary for / life. Once these are adequately supplied, however, the just person still needs other people as partners and recipients of his just actions; and the same is true of the temperate person, the brave person, and each of the others. But the wise person is able, and more able the wiser he is, to study even by himself. Though, presum-

1177b   ably, he does / it better with colleagues, even so he is more self-suffi-cient than any other <virtuous person>.

§5 Besides, study would seem to be liked because of itself alone, since it has no result beyond having studied.[9] But from the virtues concerned with action we gain, to a greater or lesser extent, some-thing beyond the action itself.

5   §6 / Besides, happiness seems to be found in leisure; for we deny ourselves leisure so that we can be at leisure, and fight wars so that we can be at peace.[10] Now the virtues that are concerned with action have their activity in politics or war, and actions in these areas seem to deny us leisure. This seems completely true for actions in war, since no one

10   chooses to fight a war, and no one prepares it, for the / sake of fighting a war—for someone would have to be a complete murderer if he made his friends his enemies in order to have be battles and killings. But the actions of the politician also deny us leisure; apart from political activ-ities themselves, those actions seek positions of power and honours, or at any rate they seek happiness for the politician himself and for his

15   fellow-citizens, which / is something different from political science itself, and clearly is sought on the assumption that it is different.[11]

§7 Hence among actions in accord with the virtues those in pol-itics and war are preeminently fine and great; but they require trou-ble, aim at some <further> end, and are choiceworthy for something other than themselves.[12] But the activity of understanding, it seems,

20   is superior / in excellence because it is the activity of study, aims at no end apart from itself, and has its own proper pleasure, which increases the activity. Further, self-sufficiency, leisure, unwearied activity (as far as is possible for a human being), and any other fea-tures ascribed to the blessed person, are evidently in accord with[13]

25   this activity. / Hence a human being's complete happiness will be this

activity, if it receives a complete span of life, since nothing incomplete is proper to happiness.[14]

§8 Such a life would be superior to the human level. For someone will live it not insofar as he is a human being, but insofar as he has some divine element in him.[15] And the activity of this divine element is as much superior to the activity in accord with the rest of virtue as this element is superior to / the compound.[16] Hence if understand- 30 ing is something divine in comparison with a human being, so also will the life in accord with understanding be divine in comparison with human life. We ought not to follow those who exhort us to 'think human, since you are human', or 'think mortal, since you are mortal.'[17] Rather, as far as we can, we ought to be pro-immortal,[18] and go to all lengths to live a life in accord with / our supreme element; for 1178a however much this element may lack in bulk, by much more it sur- passes everything in power and value.

§9 Moreover, this <supreme element> seems to be the person, if the controlling and better element <is the person>.[19] It would be absurd, then, if he were to choose not his own life, but something else's. / And what we have said previously will also apply now. For 5 what is proper to each thing's nature is supremely best and pleasant- est for it; and hence for a human being the life in accord with under- standing will be supremely best and pleasantest, if understanding, most of all,[20] is the human being. This life, then, will also be happiest.

8

[Theoretical study and the other virtues]

[c8] But the life in accord with the other kind of virtue <i.e., the kind concerned with action> <is happiest> in a secondary way,[1] because / the activities in accord with this virtue are human.[2] For we do just 10 and brave actions, and the other actions in accord with the virtues, in relation to one another, by maintaining what is fitting for each person in contracts, services, all types of actions, and also in feelings; and all these appear to be human conditions.

§2 / Moreover, virtue of character in some aspects seems to arise 15 from the body, and in many <aspects> seems to be adapted to feelings.[3]

§3 Besides, prudence is inseparable from virtue of character, and virtue of character from prudence.[4] For the principles of prudence accord with the virtues of character; and correctness in virtues of

20   character accords with prudence. And since / these virtues are also connected to feelings, they are about the compound. Now the virtues of the compound are human virtues; hence the life and the happiness in accord with these virtues are also human.

The virtue of understanding, however, is separated <from the compound> for this much has been said[5] about it, since an exact account would be too large a task for our present project.

25   §4 Moreover, it seems to need external supplies very little, / or <at any rate> less than virtue of character needs them.[6] For let us grant that they both need necessary goods, and to the same extent; for there will be only a very small difference, even though the politician labours more about the body and suchlike. Still, there will be a large difference in <what is needed> for the <proper> activities <of each type of virtue>. For the generous person will need money for

30   generous actions; / and the just person will need it for paying debts, since wishes are not clear, and some people who are not just pretend to wish to do justice. Similarly, the brave person will need enough power, and the temperate person will need freedom <to do intemperate actions>, if they are to achieve anything that the virtue requires.[7] For how else will they, or any other virtuous people, make their virtue clear?

35   §5 / Moreover, it is disputed whether decision or action is more in
1178b   control of virtue, on the assumption that virtue <consists> in / both.[8] Well, certainly it is clear that the complete <good consists> in both;[9] but for actions many external goods are needed, and the greater and finer the actions the more numerous are the external goods needed.

§6 But someone who is studying needs none of these goods, for that activity at least; indeed, for study at least, we might say they

5   are even hindrances. / Insofar as he is a human being, however, and <hence> lives together with a number of other human beings, he chooses to do the actions that accord with virtue.[10] Hence he will need the sorts of external goods <that are needed for the virtues>, for living a human life.

§7 In another way also it appears that complete happiness is some

10   activity of study. For we traditionally suppose that the / gods more than anyone are blessed and happy; but what sorts of actions ought we to ascribe to them?[11] Just actions? Surely they will appear ridiculous making contracts, returning deposits and so on. Brave actions? Do they endure what <they find> frightening and endure dangers

because it is fine? Generous actions? Whom will they give to? And surely it would be strange if they actually had currency or anything like that. / And what would their temperate actions be? Surely it is vulgar praise <to say> that they do not have base appetites.[12] When we go through them, all the things that concern actions appear trivial and unworthy of the gods. Nonetheless, we all traditionally suppose that they are alive / and hence active, since surely not asleep like Endymion.[13] Then if someone is alive, and action is excluded, and production even more, what is left but study? Hence the god's activity, being superior in blessedness, will be an activity of study. And so the human activity that is most akin to this activity will, more than any others, have the character of happiness.[14]

§8 A sign of this is also the fact that other animals have no share / in happiness, being completely deprived of this activity of study. For the whole life of the gods is blessed, and human life is blessed to the extent that it has something resembling this sort of activity; but none of the other animals is happy, because none of them shares in study at all.[15] Hence happiness extends just as far as study extends, and the more someone / studies, the happier he is, not coincidentally but insofar as he studies, since study is valuable in itself. And so happiness will be some kind of study.[16]

[c9] §9 But we will need external prosperity also, since we are human beings; for our nature is not self-sufficient / for study, but we need a healthy body, and need to have food and the other services provided.[17] / Still, even though no one can be blessedly happy without external goods, we must not think that to be happy we will need many large goods. For self-sufficiency, discrimination, and action[18] do not depend on excess, §10 but we can do fine actions even if we do not rule earth and sea; for even from moderate resources / we can do the actions that accord with virtue.[19] This is evident to see, since private citizens seem to do decent actions no less than people in power do—even more, in fact. It is enough if moderate resources are provided; for the life of someone whose activity accords with virtue will be happy.

§11 / And Solon presumably described happy people well, when he said they had been moderately supplied with external goods, had done what he regarded as the finest actions, and had lived their lives temperately.[20] For it is possible to have moderate possessions and still to do the right actions. And Anaxagoras too would seem to have

supposed that the happy person was neither rich nor powerful, since
15   he said / he would not be surprised if the happy person appeared a
strange absurd sort of person to the many.²¹ For the many judge by
externals, since these are all they notice.   §12 Hence the beliefs of
the wise would seem to accord with our arguments.²²

These considerations too, then, produce some confidence. But the
20   truth in questions about action is judged from / what we do and
how we live, since these are what control <the answers to such ques-
tions>. Hence we ought to examine what has been said by applying
it to what we do and how we live;²³ and if it harmonizes with what we
do, we should accept it, but if it conflicts we should count it <mere>
words.

§13 The person whose activity accords with understanding and
who takes care of understanding and is in the best condition would
25   seem to be most loved by the gods.²⁴ For if the gods / pay some attention to human affairs, as they seem to, it would be reasonable for
them to take pleasure in what is best and most akin to them, namely
understanding; and reasonable for them to benefit in return those
who most of all like and honour understanding, on the assumption
that these people attend to what is beloved by the gods, and act cor-
30   rectly and finely. / Clearly, all these things are true of the wise person
more than anyone else; hence he is most loved by the gods. And it is
likely that this same person will be happiest; hence, by this argument
also, the wise person, more than anyone else, will be happy.

[From ethics to politics]

9

[Moral education]

[c10] We have now said enough in outlines about these things and
35   about the virtues, and about friendship and pleasure also.¹ Should /
1179b we, then, think that our decision <to study these> has achieved / its
end? On the contrary, the aim of studies about action, as we say, is
surely not to study and know about a given thing, but rather to act
on our knowledge.²   §2 Hence knowing about virtue is not enough,
but we must also try to possess and exercise virtue, or become good
in any other way.

5   §3 / Now if arguments were sufficient by themselves to make
people decent, the rewards they would command would justifiably
have been many and large, as Theognis says,³ and these ought to be

provided.[4] In fact, however, arguments seem to have enough influence to turn and inspire the civilized ones among the young people, and to make virtue take possession of a well-born character that truly loves what is / fine; but they seem unable to turn the many towards   10 being fine and good.

§4 For the many naturally obey fear, not shame; they avoid what is base because of the penalties, not because it is disgraceful. For since they live by their feelings, they pursue their proper pleasures and the sources of them, and avoid / the opposed pains, and have not even   15 a notion of what is fine and <hence> truly pleasant, since they have had no taste of it. §5 What argument, then, could reform people like these? For it is impossible, or not easy, to alter by argument what has long been absorbed as a result of people's characters.[5] But, presumably, we should be satisfied to achieve some share in virtue if we already have what we seem to need to become decent.[6]

§6 / Now some think it is nature that makes people good; some   20 think it is habit; some that it is teaching. The <contribution> of nature clearly is not up to us, but results from some divine causes in the truly fortunate ones.[7] Arguments and teaching surely do not prevail in everyone, / but the soul of the student needs to have been prepared   25 by habits for enjoying and hating finely, like ground that is to nourish seed.[8] §7 For someone who lives in accord with his feelings would not even listen to an argument turning him away, or comprehend it <if he did listen>; and in that state how could he be persuaded to change? And in general feelings seem to yield to force, not to argument. §8 /   30 Hence we must already in some way have a character suitable for virtue, fond of what is fine and objecting to what is shameful.

It is difficult, however, for someone to be trained correctly for virtue from his youth if he has not been brought up under correct laws; for the many, especially the young, do not find it pleasant to live in a temperate and resistant way.[9] That is why / laws must prescribe   35 their upbringing and practices; for they will not find these things painful when they get used to them.

§9 / Presumably, however, it is not enough if they get the correct   1180a upbringing and attention when they are young. Rather, they must continue the same practices and be habituated to them when they become men. Hence we need laws concerned with these things also, and in general with all of life. For the many / yield to compulsion   5 more than to argument, and to sanctions more than to the fine.[10]

§10 That is why legislators must, in some people's view, urge people towards virtue and exhort them to aim at the fine—on the assumption that anyone whose good habits have prepared him decently will listen to them—but must impose corrective treatments and penalties on anyone who disobeys or lacks / the right nature, and must completely expel an incurable. For the decent person, it is assumed, will attend to reason because his life aims at the fine, whereas the base person, since he desires pleasure, has to receive corrective treatment by pain, like a beast of burden. That is why it is said that the pains imposed must be those most contrary to the pleasures he likes.

§11 / As we have said, then, someone who is to be good must be finely brought up and habituated, and then must live in decent practices, doing base actions neither willingly nor unwillingly. And this will be true if his life follows some sort of understanding and correct order that prevails on him.

§12 Now a father's instructions lack this power to prevail and compel; / and so in general do the instructions of an individual man, unless he is a king or someone like that. Law, however, has the power that compels; and law is reason that proceeds from a sort of prudence and understanding.[11] Besides, people become hostile to an individual human being who opposes their impulses, even if he is correct in opposing them, whereas a law's prescription of what is decent is not burdensome.

§13 And yet, it is only in / Sparta, or in a few other cities as well, that the legislator seems to have attended to upbringing and practices. In most other cities they are neglected, and an individual lives as he wishes, 'laying down the rules for his children and wife', like a Cyclops.[12]

§14 It is best, then, if the community attends to upbringing, / and attends correctly. But if the community neglects it, it seems fitting for each individual to promote the virtue of his children and his friends— to be able to do it, or at least to decide to do it.[13] From what we have said, however, it seems he will be better able to do it if he acquires legislative science.[14] For, / clearly, attention by the community works through laws, and decent attention works through excellent laws; / and whether the laws are written or unwritten, for the education of one or of many, seems unimportant, as it is in music, gymnastics and other practices. For just as in a city the provisions of law and the types

of character <found in that city> have influence, / so also in a house- 5
hold a father's words and habits have influence, and all the more
because of kinship and because of the benefits he does; for his children are already fond of him and naturally ready to obey.[15]

§15 Further, education adapted to an individual is different from[16]
a common education for everyone, just as individualized medical
treatment is different. For though generally a feverish patient benefits from rest and starvation, presumably / some patient does not; 10
nor does the boxing instructor impose the same way of fighting on
everyone.[17] Hence it seems that treatment in particular cases is more
exactly right when each person gets special attention, since he then
more often gets the suitable treatment.

Nonetheless a doctor, a gymnastics trainer, and everyone else will
give the best individual attention if they also know / universally what 15
is good for all, or for these sorts. For sciences are said to be, and are,
of what is common <to many particular cases>.   §16 Admittedly
someone without scientific knowledge may well attend properly to a
single person, if his experience has allowed him to take exact note of
what happens in a given case, just as some people seem to be their
own best doctors, though / unable to help anyone else at all.[18] None- 20
theless, presumably, it seems that someone who wants to be an expert
in a craft and a branch of study should progress to the universal, and
come to know that, as far as possible; for that, as we have said, is what
the sciences are about.[19]

§17 Then perhaps also someone who wishes to make people better
by his attention, many people or few, should try to / acquire legislative 25
science, if laws are a means to make us good. For not just anyone can
improve the condition of just anyone, or the person presented to him;
but if someone can, it is the person with knowledge, just as in medical
science and the others that require attention and prudence.

§18 Next, then, should we examine whence and how someone / 30
might acquire legislative science? Just as in other cases <we go to the
practitioner>, should we go to the politicians, since, as we saw, legislative science seems to be a part of political science?[20] Or does the
case of political science appear different from the other sciences and
capacities? For evidently, in the other cases, the same people, such as
doctors or painters, who transmit the capacity to others actively practise it themselves. / By contrast, it is the sophists who advertise that 35
/ they teach politics but none of them practises it. Instead, those who 1181a

practise it are the political activists, and they seem to act on some sort
of capacity and experience rather than thought.[21]

5   For evidently they neither write nor speak on such questions,
though presumably it would be finer to do this than / to compose
speeches for the law courts or the Assembly; nor have they made politicians out of their own sons or any other friends of theirs.[22]   §19 But
it would be reasonable for them to do this if they were able; for there
is nothing better than the political capacity that they could leave to
their cities, and nothing better that they could decide to produce in
themselves, or, therefore, in their closest friends.

10   / Nonetheless, experience would seem to contribute quite a lot;
otherwise people would not have become better politicians by familiarity with politics.[23] That is why those who aim to know about political science would seem to need experience as well.

§20 By contrast, those of the sophists who advertise <that they
teach political science> appear to be a long way from teaching; for
they are altogether ignorant about the sort of thing political science

15   is, and the sorts of things it is about.[24] For if they had / known what it
is, they would not have taken it to be the same as rhetoric, or something inferior to it, or thought it an easy task to assemble the laws with
good reputations and then legislate. For they think they can select the
best laws, as though the selection itself did not require comprehension,[25] and as though correct judgment were not the most important
thing, as it is in music.

20   <They are wrong;> for those with experience in each area / judge
the products correctly and comprehend the ways and means of completing them, and what fits with what; for if we lack experience, we
must be satisfied with noticing that the product is well or badly made,

1181b   as with painting. Now laws would / seem to be the products of political science; how, then, could someone acquire legislative science, or
judge which laws are best, from laws alone?   §21 For neither do we
appear to become experts in medicine by reading textbooks.

And yet doctors not only try to describe the <recognized> treatments, but also distinguish different <bodily> states, and try to say

5   how each type of patient might be cured and / must be treated.[26] And
what they say seems to be useful to the experienced, though useless to the ignorant. Similarly, then, collections of laws and political
systems might also, presumably, be most useful if we are capable of
studying them and of judging what is done finely or in the contrary

way, and what sorts of <elements> fit with what. / Those who lack   10
the <proper> state <of experience> when they go through these collections will not manage to judge finely, unless they can do it all by
themselves <without training>, though they might come to comprehend them better by going through them.

§22 Since, then, our predecessors have left the area of legislation
uncharted, it is presumably better to examine it ourselves instead,
and indeed to examine political systems in general, / and so to com-   15
plete the philosophy of human affairs, as far as we are able.[27]

§23 First, then, let us try to review any sound remarks our predecessors have made on particular topics.[28] Then let us study the collected political systems, to see from them what sorts of things preserve and destroy cities, and political systems / of different types; and   20
what causes some cities to conduct politics well, and some badly.[29]
For when we have studied these questions, we will perhaps grasp better what sort of political system is best; how each political system
should be organized so as to be best; and what laws and habits it
should employ.[30]

Let us discuss this, then, having made a start.[31]

NOTES

Book I

1

1.§1–5. Lower and higher ends and goods.

(a) §1–2. Goods are found in the ends of different activities; some, but not all of these ends, are results distinct from the activities themselves.

1. **§1 1094a1–2 Every craft . . . some good:** CRAFTS are types of PRODUC-TION, aimed at some goal beyond their own exercise. DISCIPLINEs are theoretical, insofar as they do not produce a product such as a house. ACTION includes ACTIV-ITY that does not aim at any end beyond itself. In including action and decision as well as craft and inquiry among goal-directed pursuits, Aristotle makes it clear from the beginning that actions chosen for their own sakes are among the things chosen for the sake of some end, and hence (as he will go on to argue) for the sake of some ultimate end. The rest of the *Ethics* seeks to explain how this is possible, and why it matters. In 'seems to aim' Aristotle points out that he begins with an APPEARANCE.

If 'action and decision' refers to action on a decision, it does not follow that every single thing we do aims at some good; for some of the things we do are not ACTIONS on a DECISION (cf. 1111b9–15).

2. **1094a2–3 that is . . . right:** 'THAT IS WHY' refers, as usual, to a familiar fact that is explained by what has preceded. This parenthetical remark refers to the view of EUDOXUS; see 1172b9.

the good as what everything seeks: I.e., If A seeks x, A seeks x as good (i.e., taking x to be good).

[Less probably, Aristotle means to endorse Eudoxus' view that there is some one end that everything seeks, and this is the ultimate good.]

3. **§2 1094a3–5 But the ends . . . from the activities:** Cf. *Met.* 1050a21–b2. Here and in a16 the difference between ACTIVITIES with and without further products (see FUNCTION) corresponds to the later distinction between PRODUC-TION and ACTION. In a5 'action' has the sense noted in ACTION #2.

(b) §3–5. Disciplines and activities are subordinate to higher disciplines and higher ends. In these cases the higher ends are higher goods.

4. **1094a13 in the same way:** Read *ton auton de tropon*.

5. **§4 1094a9–14 But some of . . . further ones:** 'Sciences' is supplied except in 'sciences we have mentioned', a18. Aristotle refers to all the 'actions, crafts, and sciences' of a7. None of these disciplines meets his most stringent conditions for a SCIENCE.

6. **1094a14 In all such cases, then:** Read *en hapasais dê*.

2

2.§1–8. The highest good.

(a) §1–3. If there is a highest end, and therefore a highest good, this will be a goal to guide our life as a whole.

1. **§1 1094a18–22 If, then . . . best good:** This conditional says that if there is some x such that (1) x is an end, (2) we WISH for x for its own sake, (3) if there is any other good y that we wish for, we wish for y for the sake of x, then (4) x is the ultimate (highest, final) good.

So far Aristotle has shown that some goods satisfy (1), and that some ends, the ends of the ruling sciences, are higher than others. He now introduces (2), and mentions an end that is chosen 'because of itself', not only for the sake of some further end. (3) says that this is the good to which all other goods are subordinate. From this he infers (4). In 1097b1–6 he argues more directly for a highest end, and considers the possibility of several ends pursued for their own sakes. Cf. *EE* i 2.

(for if we do, . . . and futile): This parenthesis explains why we cannot choose everything for the sake of something else.

[Less probably, Aristotle intends this clause to be part of an argument for the existence of one ultimate good. (It would argue that if we must choose something (i.e., at least one thing) for its own sake, there must be some one thing (i.e., exactly one thing) that we choose for its own sake. The argument is fallacious; for, though all roads end somewhere, there may not be some one place where they all end.) The text, however, does not justify the attribution of this fallacious argument to Aristotle. He does not say that he has proved the existence of a highest good.]

2. **§2 1094a22–4 Then surely . . . right mark:** I.e., if we know about the highest good, we will have a target to aim at. Cf. *EE* 1214b6–15†; Plato, *Rep.* 519c2.

3. **1094a25–6 what the good . . . capacity:** Aristotle begins his answer to the first question in 4.1. He answers the second question first, in the next sentence.

(b) §4–8. The highest end is the concern of political science, which studies the overall good for the city and for the individual.

4. **§4 1094a26–7 the most controlling <science>—the highest ruling <science>:** No noun is provided with these adjectives. We might supply 'science' or 'science or capacity'. Aristotle has said in 1094a14–16 that the higher ends are the objects of the ruling sciences. He infers that the highest end is the concern of the highest ruling science.

5. **1094a27 political science:** Aristotle uses the adjective 'political' without a noun. He argues: (1) The highest good is the all-inclusive end. (2) The all-inclusive end is the end of political science. (3) Therefore the highest good is the end of political science.

6. **§7 1094b4 the other sciences concerned with action:** Retain *praktikais*.

7. **1094b5 will include . . . sciences:** The highest good is an ordered compound of non-instrumental goods; see 7.§1–5.

8. **§8 1094b7–9 For even if the good . . . and preserve:** §8 defends the conclusion reached in §7 about the scope of political science. Even if we are initially concerned about the good for an individual, this is also the foundation of the good society.

9. **1094b10 for a people and for cities:** 'People' (*ethnos*) is used to refer to (i) a nation, either the Greek people or (more often) a non-Greek nation (e.g., the Persians, the Scythians), or to (ii) a national group—for instance, Greeks living in several contiguous cities or villages sharing common traditions (e.g., the Arcadians). The Macedonians, Aristotle's own people (see Intro. §1), were an *ethnos* rather than a *polis*, whereas Athens (including the whole territory of Attica) was a *polis*, a CITY. Perhaps Aristotle uses the singular 'people' and plural 'cities' because he is thinking of the Greek people in the various Greek cities. In that case, he might refer to the ambitions of Philip and Alexander of Macedon.

10. **1094b10–11 And so . . . these things:** This sentence concludes the answer to the question asked in §3, about which science studies the highest good.

11. **1094b11 a sort of political science:** The discipline in the *Ethics* is sometimes called 'ETHICS' (*ēthika*). On political science, see vi 8.§1–2, *EE* 1218b12–16. It is 'a sort of political science' because it is concerned with basic political principles (cf. 1152b2). It seeks an account of the highest good for individuals and for communities (cf. *Pol.* vii 1–2), but it does not discuss constitutions, government, and other more narrowly political questions (which are taken up in the *Pol.*). Cf. 1181b12–23.

3

3.§1–8. The method of political science.

(a) §1–4. We must approach political science with realistic expectations, since its subject matter does not allow the highest degree of exactness.

1. **§1 1094b11–14 our discussion . . . different crafts:** Having introduced political science and set himself the task (1094a22, 'Then surely . . .') of saying what its end is, Aristotle explains how he will proceed, and how he expects his success to be judged. Hence he now describes the method of ETHICS, and the limitations of the method. On fitting the subject matter, cf. 1098a28, 1137b19.

2. **§2 1094b15–16 differ and vary so much:** Or 'involve so much difference and variation of opinion'.

3. **1094b16 convention . . . nature:** People see that what is JUST and FINE depends on circumstances; for instance, it is USUALLY but not always just to pay your debts (Plato, *Rep.* 331a). (Less probably, 'difference and variation' might be taken to refer to differences of opinion about what things are just and fine.) These people (see PROTAGORAS) infer that there is no objective truth about what is just and fine. They think that these rest on convention (lit. 'are by convention', *nomos*; see LAW), and not on NATURE.

4. **§3 1094b16–19 But . . . their bravery:** [Or 'And goods also very . . . ']. These facts about goods are Aristotle's answer to the argument from variation to convention. We find variations in goods, no less than in just and fine things, but we do not infer that goods are merely conventional. Aspirin, for instance, is not always good for relieving a headache, but it is not a matter of convention that it sometimes relieves headaches. Hence we should reject the argument from variation to convention in the case of just and fine things. See Plato, *Pr.* 334a–c, *Tht.* 172a, 177a–179b, and notes to iii 4.§4, v 7.§2–6.

5. **§4 1094b22–7 Each of our claims, . . . mathematician:** Aristotle turns from a comment on the method of ETHICS to a comment on the sort of education required to appreciate the difference between ethical argument and the sort of argument that might provide a demonstration (see SCIENCE).

Aristotle does not mean that all ethical principles are USUAL rather than universal, but he argues that many of those that give practical guidance are usual.

(b) §5–8. Since political science is inexact, we appreciate its conclusions properly only if we have the appropriate experience and maturity.

6. **§5 1095a2–6 This is why a youth . . . not knowledge:** Two reasons are given for excluding a YOUTH from these lectures ('student' lit. = 'hearer') on ethics:

1. **for he lacks . . . :** This is closely connected with the remarks about the EDUCATED person.

2. **Moreover . . . :** This relies more generally on the practical character of ETHICS #1, which has also been assumed in the restriction of ethics to USUAL truths. Upbringing: 1095b4, 1179b25.

7. **§8 1095a11–13 These are . . . propose to do:** This sentence summarizes c3 [less probably, c1–3] in reverse order.

4

4.§1–7. Ethical arguments must begin from common beliefs.

(a) §1–3. What is the highest good? Common beliefs agree that it is happiness, but disagree about what happiness is.

1. **§1 1095a14 Let us, then, begin again:** Aristotle returns to the question raised in c2, and asks what the good pursued by political science might be. As usual, we begin with APPEARANCES. Cf. *EE* i 6.

2. **1095a14 knowledge and decision:** The four items mentioned in 1094a1–2 are reduced to two.

3. **§2 1095a17–20 As far . . . being happy:** Everyone thinks the good is HAPPINESS, *eudaimonia*; Aristotle argues for this in 1097a34–b21. In identifying *eudaimonia* with 'living well' (or 'having a good life', *eu zēn*) and 'doing well' (or 'acting well' or 'faring well', *eu prattein*; see ACTION), he suggests that *eudaimonia* (a) involves one's life as a whole, and (b) consists in action. He examines both (a) and (b) further in i.9–10.

4. **1095a20–2 But they disagree . . . as the wise:** We need some clearer account (see REASON) and DEFINITION of happiness—of the types of states and activities it consists in; and we begin with a survey of some common views.

5. **§3 1095a26–8 Some, however . . . to be goods:** These are some of the wise, rather than the many. Aristotle refers to PLATO's Form of the Good, discussed in c6.

(b) §4–7. In examining these common beliefs we must begin from starting points that are familiar to us, and argue from these to ethical principles. To be familiar with the appropriate starting points, we need a good upbringing.

6. **§5 1095a30–2 We must . . . towards principles:** To justify beginning with appearances Aristotle adds a further remark on method. He distinguishes arguments from PRINCIPLES from arguments towards principles.

7. **1095a32–3 For Plato . . . towards them:** In 'used to ask' (the Greek imperfect tense) Aristotle indicates a recollection of what the historical PLATO said. See SOCRATES. Plato's question reminds us of *Rep.* 510bc, 533cd. The metaphor of the stadium suggests argument to and from a single set of principles.

8. **1095b1 far end:** Lit. 'limit'. In a Greek stadium the midpoint of the race is at the end farthest from the starting line.

9. **1095b2 For we should . . . two ways:** Having distinguished two directions of argument in relation to the same *archai*, Aristotle distinguishes two sorts of *archai*. One sort is 'known to us', one sort 'known WITHOUT QUALIFICATION' (see SCIENCE §5). Aristotle answers Plato's question: we are going from the *archai* known to us (the beginnings) on the way to *archai* known by nature (the theoretical principles).

10. **§7 1095b6–7 For the <belief> . . . is true> as well:** Lit. 'For the *archê* is the that, and if this appears adequately, he will not at all need in addition the because.' This *archê* is the beginning that is 'known to us'. We start from the 'that', accepted moral beliefs. These include (if we may judge from examples given in c5) not only particular beliefs such as 'I ought to keep this promise', but also general claims such as 'Honour is worth having only from the right people'. These beliefs are true or nearly true, but they need defence and justification from the 'why', a more theoretical principle that explains why they are true. We do not begin our inquiry with the 'why', because we reach it only after inquiry.

[Alternative paraphrase: 'In ethics, there is no because. Our only *archê* is the "that" and we do not look for any "why".' This is less probable, because it would be surprising if Aristotle had introduced his standard distinction between 'known to us' and 'known without qualification' without meaning to suggest, as he normally does, that we ought to be looking for principles that are known without qualification. Cf. 1098a33–b8.]

11. **1095b7–8 someone who . . . acquire them:** The 'beginnings' that we have or can easily acquire from good upbringing are (on the interpretation preferred so far) the starting points of our inquiry, not the theoretical principles we are seeking. See 1095a2, 1179b25, EDUCATION.

Aristotle has so far given two reasons why we need a good upbringing: (1) In 1095a2–11: we need to learn to control our feelings and impulses, so that we can benefit from instruction about morality. (2) In our present passage, he takes good upbringing to be necessary for the appropriate stock of moral beliefs that are necessary for moral inquiry.

12. **1095b9 Hesiod:** *Works and Days* 293, 295–7. 'Listens to one . . .' perhaps suggests what Aristotle has in mind in saying we can acquire the starting points.

5

5. §1–8. The 'three lives' embody common beliefs about the highest good.

1. **§1 1095b14 But let us begin . . . digressed:** Three traditional ways of life: *EE* 1214a31†, 1215a32–b14†. The criticisms of the three lives reflect Aristotle's criteria for the good: (1) The good involves distinctively human activities, not those of 'grazing animals', b20. (2) It must be our own, not heavily dependent on external conditions. (3) It must be complete ('However, this also . . .', §6). For defence of these criteria, see (1) 1097b33, 1118b1, 1170b12, 1174a1; (2) 1099b13; (3) 1097a28.

2. **§1–2 1095b14–19 For there are . . . of study:** Aristotle's sentences have been rearranged. Lit. 'For they would seem to conceive, not unreasonably, the good and happiness from the lives, the many and most vulgar as pleasure, whence they also like the life of gratification. For the most favoured lives are roughly three, the one just mentioned, the political life, and, third, the life of study. Now the many appear completely slavish . . .'

the lives: I.e., the three lives that are now described. These provide the patterns that people think of when they consider what the good is. [Or 'the lives <they lead>', i.e., people's practice determines their conception of the good.]

(a) §3. The life of gratification allows no scope for distinctively human activities.

3. **§3 1095b19–20 In this they appear . . . grazing animals:** The life of pleasure is dismissed as SLAVISH. Aristotle discusses it when he has examined pleasure, 1176b9–24.

4. **1095b22 Sardanapallus:** An Assyrian king (669–626) who lived in legendary luxury. Cf. Aristotle, *Protrepticus* fr. 16 (Ross). *EE* 1216a16–19†.

(b) §4–5. One form of the life of political activity aims at honour. Its conception of the good is superficial.

5. **§4 1095b23–4 This, however, . . . we are seeking:** The value of HONOUR: 1123b20, 1159a22. On the political life, cf. *EE* 1216a19–27†.

6. **1095b25–6 whereas we . . . from us:** What is 'our own' (or 'PROPER to us') must be some intrinsic feature of ourselves, not simply the product of other people's attitudes towards us. In saying that we 'intuitively believe' this (lit. 'divine'; cf. Plato, *Rep.* 505a1). Aristotle implies that we have not yet given a reason for our conviction; it is a 'that' without a 'why' (cf. 1095b6).

(c) §6. A superior form of the life of political activity aims at virtue. It overlooks the place of other goods in happiness.

7. **§6 1096a1–2 if this is the sort . . . philosopher's paradox:** The 'philosopher's paradox' (lit. 'thesis' or 'position', a term in DIALECTIC; *Top.* 104b18). Aristotle may allude to SOCRATES and the CYNICS. Cf. 1104b24, 1153b19–21. In Aristotle's view (i 10; cf. Plato, *Rep.* 361d), virtue makes us happier than we would be by living any other way, but virtue alone does not make us happy.

8. **1096a3 popular works:** Perhaps the *Protrepticus*, which may have been alluded to in §3; see POPULAR.

(d) §7. Consideration of the third life, the life of study, is postponed.

9. **§7 1096a4–5 The third . . . follows:** See x 6–8.

(e) §8. Footnote: The life of moneymaking is not parallel to the 'three lives'.

10. **§8 1096a5–6 The moneymaker's . . . forced . . . itself>:** If the supplement gives the right sense for 'forced', it is used in a broader sense than at 1110a1; cf. *EE* 1215a25–37†.

11. **1096a9–10 and many . . . against them:** Perhaps yet another reference to Aristotle's own POPULAR works. In a9 read *kai*.

6

6. §1–16. A philosophical conception of the good: the Platonic conception of the Form (Idea) of the Good.

1. **§1 1096a11–12 Presumably, though, . . . speaking of it:** Aristotle mentioned the Platonic belief in a universal and separated Form of the Good at 1095a26, and now proceeds to criticize it at length (cf. *EE* i 8, *MM* i 1). Much of the discussion is important for Aristotle's general criticism of Plato (cf. esp. *Met.* i 9), but less important for ethics. Aristotle is primarily concerned to argue against the view that goodness is a single property. If it were one, then knowledge of what is good for human beings would ultimately rest on knowledge of the single type of goodness found throughout the universe, such as is expressed in Plato's Form of the Good (*Rep.* 508–9, 517c, 534bc). The effect of Aristotle's claim that goods are HOMONYMOUS is to sever ethical argument from general cosmological theories about goodness (cf. 1155b1–10).

In §2–4 (a)–(c) Aristotle discusses the Form as a universal. In §5–7 (d)–(f) he discusses the separation of the Form. In §8–12 (g)–(h) he argues that the evident diversity of goods precludes any universal Form of the Good. In §13–16 (i)–(k) he argues that the Form is in any case irrelevant to ethics.

Aristotle states his objections briefly. A full understanding of this chapter (in contrast to the rest of the *Ethics*) requires a grasp of some of his major metaphysical doctrines.

2. **1096a13 friends:** Cf. 1164b2.

(a) §2. There is no universal for an ordered series.

3. **§2 1096a17–19 Those who . . . either:** Aristotle may argue: (1) The common property of being a member of some numerical series (i.e., one with relations of prior and posterior among its members) is the property of having some place within the series. (2) A Form for such a series would therefore have to be (i) the property of having a place within a series, and (ii) independent of, and hence prior to, the series. (3) But (i) and (ii) are inconsistent. (4) But the categories (see §3) form a numerical series. (5) Hence there cannot be any Form common to the categories.

4. **1096a19–20 But the good . . . relative:** SUBSTANCE ('what-it-is') and relative (e.g., double, half) are two of the categories, discussed more fully in the next argument.

(b) §3. There is no universal good across the categories.

5. **§3 1096a23–4 Further, good . . . spoken of:** Aristotle evaluates the Platonic claims in the light of his doctrine of the CATEGORIES. He relies on the claim that the categories reveal irreducibly different ways of being. Since being is not a single property, but is HOMONYMOUS, and since the goodness of any thing depends on the kind of thing it is, goodness is not a single property either (cf. *Top.* 107a3), contrary to the Platonist view.

6. **1096a24–5 in what-it-is . . . mind:** God and mind (or 'UNDERSTANDING', *nous*) are not merely examples of goods that are SUBSTANCES. They are what it is to be good in the category of substance.

(c) §4. There is no single Idea across different sciences.

7. **1096a32–3 And similarly . . . gymnastics:** From these cases in which there is no one science of goods even within a single category, Aristotle infers that there is no one science of the good across the categories, and hence no one Idea of good in all the categories.

(d) §5. It is useless for understanding goodness.

8. **§5 1096a34–5 One might be . . . So-and-So Itself:** Aristotle denies that separated Forms are both paradigms and instances of the properties to which they correspond. In the Platonic view, the Form of the Just is perfectly just and is separable from sensible just things. See *Met.* 987a32, 1078b9–1079a4, 1086a24–b13; Plato, *Phd.* 74.

9. **1096a35–b1 Man Itself and man:** The second 'man' here probably refers to the universal that is immanent in particulars. [Less probably, 'a man', i.e., a particular man.] Aristotle accuses Plato of pointlessly introducing separated, independent Forms. According to Aristotle, immanent universals (good, man, etc.) are all that we need for understanding the natures of things.

10. **1096b2–3 If that is so . . . is good:** Since Good Itself and good have the same account of good, it is no help to appeal to Good itself if one wants to understand the nature of good things as good; one should concentrate on the immanent good.

(e) §6. The eternity of the Form is irrelevant.

(f) §7 Even the Pythagorean view is more plausible.

11. **1096b5–7 But the Pythagoreans . . . followed them:** The PYTHAGOREANS and SPEUSIPPUS try to describe the natures of things in numerical terms.

(g) §8–11. There is no Form even for intrinsic goods.

12. **§9 1096b13–14 Clearly, then, . . . because of these:** At this stage Aristotle takes the defender of Forms to claim only that there is a single Form for all intrinsic goods (i.e., things that are good IN THEIR OWN RIGHT).

13. **§10 1096b17–18 for instance, prudence, . . . honours:** 'PRUDENCE' here may have the more general sense of 'rational awareness' (characteristic of, e.g., Plato's *Phil.*; cf. *EE* 1214a32†). On the different species of pleasure, see x 5.

14. **1096b19–20 Alternatively, . . . the Form will be futile:** The Form will be useless for its intended explanatory role, since it will not explain the goodness of anything else besides itself.

15. **§11 1096b21–2 then the same . . . all of them:** On the assumption that there is an Idea of good.

chalk: Lit. 'white lead', i.e., lead carbonate, produced from lead and used for whitening.

(h) §12. Goods are not homonymous by chance, but their connexions do not require the existence of a Form.

16. **§12 1096b26–7 But how . . . homonyms resulting from chance:** See HOMONYMOUS.

17. **1096b27–9 Is it spoken of from . . . other cases:** On the first suggestion ('all referring . . .'), cf. *Met.* 1003a27; *EE* 1236a14, b20. On analogy, cf. 1097b25, *Phys.* 191a8; *Met.* 1048a37. Reference to one thing is illustrated by instrumental goods and the goods to which they are means. Analogy is illustrated by intrinsic goods; sight is intrinsically good for the eye, and so on. Cases of analogy also support Aristotle's contention that goods differ 'in the respect in which they are goods'; seeing is the good of the eye because the eye's function is to see, cutting is the good of a knife because the knife's function is to cut, and so on.

(i) §13. The Form is irrelevant to action.

18. **§13 1096b30–1 Presumably, . . . <branch of> philosophy:** Aristotle tries to keep non-ethical discussions out of ethics. Cf. viii 1.§6. The discipline alluded to here is 'first philosophy', the subject matter of the *Metaphysics*, which studies 'being insofar as it is being' (see *Met.* iv 1). In that work Aristotle discusses homonymy (iv 2) and also criticizes Plato's theory of Ideas at length (e.g., in i 6, 9, vii 13–16, xiii 4–5).

19. **1096b32 some one good predicated in common:** Read *hen ti kai*.

(j) §14–15. The sciences do not appeal to the Form.

20. **§14 1097a1–3 for if we have . . . hit on them:** This whole 'for . . . ' clause is an argument offered by a believer in Forms.

(k) §16. The Form does not help the practice of the sciences.

21. **§16 1097a11–13 not even health, . . . at a time:** A doctor does not ask what promotes health universally, let alone what is good universally. On the role of UNIVERSAL and PARTICULAR in CRAFTS, cf. 1141b15, 1181a19; *Met.* 981a1–b20.

7

7.§1–8. A new approach to the good should avoid these objections to other views. We begin from plausible criteria for the good, and we find that happiness meets these criteria.

(a) §1. The good is the ultimate end.

1. **§1 1097a15–22 But let us return . . . other actions:** Aristotle begins from the diversity of goods that we must recognize if we reject the Platonic attempt to find unity in goods. The description of different goods recalls the reference to analogy in 1096b28. After these illustrations of diversity in goodness, Aristotle attends to (in 'but in every action and decision . . .') the unity in the different cases.

2. **1097a22–4 And so, . . . these ends:** The first part of this sentence repeats the conclusion drawn at the beginning of c2 above. The second part, allowing the possibility of many goods constituting the end, helps to explain why the beginning of c2 was a conditional claim. Aristotle now makes it clear that he has not proved that there is just one end of human action.

(b) **§2–5. The good is complete.**

3. **§2 1097a24 Our argument, . . . conclusion:** Aristotle reaches the conclusion he reached in 1094a18–26, by an argument that relies on the connexion between ends and goods (beginning from the points about analogy in c6). He has said nothing about the hierarchy of ends that he introduced in c1. So far he has not chosen between the two possibilities mentioned at the end of §1.

4. **1097a24–5 But we must . . . perspicuous:** More perspicuity is needed because c2 did not explain why we must recognize a single end. In §3–8 Aristotle argues that (1) the good satisfies some formal criteria (i 5.§1) and (2) happiness is the good (1095a17) because it satisfies these criteria. They are formal criteria because Aristotle thinks (cf. Plato, *Phil.* 20d, and x 2.§3) they are reasonable conditions for us to apply to the good even before we consider the claims of specific candidates claiming to be the good.

The formal criteria require the good to be (a) complete (§3–5), (b) self-sufficient (§6–7), and (c) most choiceworthy (§8), not counted as simply one good among many. Here (a) follows from our choosing the good only for its own sake and not also for the sake of something else; if there were some more complete end than the good, we would choose the good for the sake of that. The other two criteria explain completeness.

5. **§3 1097a25–8 Since there are . . . ends are complete:** See HAPPINESS #4; COMPLETE.

6. **1097a30 the most complete of these:** Cf. 1098a17, 1099a30, *EE* 1219a35. Alternatives: (1) Inclusive: we do pursue an unordered collection of ends, but the complete single end that is the whole formed by them. (2) Exclusive: we look for the single most complete end, excluding the other ends that are less complete.

Aristotle's previous remarks support (1), not (2). (2) may be held to support the view that Aristotle eventually (in x 6–8) identifies happiness with STUDY.

7. **§4 1097a33 always choiceworthy in its own right:** This probably means (a) 'both always choiceworthy, and also choiceworthy in its own right'. If it meant (b) 'choiceworthy in itself on those occasions when we choose it', this case would not be different (as Aristotle intends it to be) from the previous case ('and an end that is never . . .').

8. **§5 1097a34 Now happiness . . . qualification:** Aristotle has said (1095a18) that everyone agrees that the highest good is happiness. He now supports this agreed view. Our views about happiness, and especially about its relation to other

non-instrumental goods, suggest that it plays the role in practical thought that is appropriate for the highest good.

9. **1097b1 we choose always because of itself:** Probably this means (cf. §4) 'we always choose it, and always because of itself'.

10. **1097b2–5 Honour, pleasure, . . . shall be happy:** The highest good, chosen only for its own sake, is composed of the non-instrumental goods that are chosen both for their own sakes and for the sake of the highest good. Cf. 1174a4. To choose them for the sake of happiness is not to choose them purely as instrumental means, since the 'for the sake of' relation, as Aristotle understands it, includes the relation of part to whole. See DECISION #2. Aristotle develops the conception he introduced in 1094a27, when he described the end of political science as including the ends of other sciences concerned with actions.

[Or: Every good that is chosen both for itself and for the sake of the highest good is separate from (not a part of), and purely instrumental to, the highest good, even though it is also chosen for its own sake, and hence not for the sake of happiness. This interpretation might be defended from the discussion of happiness and theoretical study in x 6–8. But even if it fits Book x, it is not clearly intended in the present passage.]

(c) §6–7. The good is self-sufficient.

11. **§6 1097b6–7 The same conclusion:** That happiness is complete. See the last sentence of this paragraph.

12. **1097b7–8 For the complete . . . self-sufficient:** See HAPPINESS #4, 1177a27. The good is self-sufficient because it includes all choiceworthy non-instrumental goods.

[Or: It is self-sufficient because it includes everything needed for the single best non-instrumental good (happiness), even though it does not include other choiceworthy non-instrumental goods. This interpretation fits the view that happiness is eventually identified with study.]

13. **1097b8–11 What we count . . . political <animal>:** The social character of human beings and of human happiness: 1142a9, 1157b18, 1158a23, 1169b16, 1170b12, 1172a6, 1178b5; *Pol.* 1253a7†, 1280b33. In saying that the highest good must be sufficient for other people as well as the individual happy person, Aristotle implies that a person's good is social not only because (i) it requires some contribution by other people, but also because (ii) it includes the happiness of these other people. Aristotle defends (ii) in his account of friendship in *EN* viii–ix and in his account (in the *Pol.*) of the city (*polis*) as the community that fulfils human nature.

(d) §8. The good is most choiceworthy, not being counted as one good among many.

14. **§8 1097b17–18 <since> it is not counted . . . <If it were> counted . . . it <would be> more choiceworthy . . . <were> added:** Happiness is comprehensive (including all choiceworthy non-instrumental goods) because, if it were not comprehensive, we would face the absurd consequences that there could be a greater good

(i.e., the combination of happiness with some other non-instrumental good) than happiness itself. Cf. 1170b17, 1172b26, *MM* 1184a8–30†.

[Or '<if it is> not counted . . . <If it is> counted . . . it <is> more choiceworthy . . . <is> added.' Happiness does not embrace all choiceworthy non-instrumental goods, because we can identify a greater good than happiness (i.e., the combination of happiness with some other choiceworthy non-instrumental good). This interpretation might be held to anticipate the identification of happiness with STUDY.]

15. **1097b20–1 Happiness, then, . . . action:** This sentence shows that the previous argument about addition was intended to show that happiness is self-sufficient.

The demand for completeness does not demand the maximum quantity of each non-instrumental good; 1100b22–8, 1101b1–9.

7. §9–16. *The good is the excellent fulfilment of the human function, and hence it is activity of the soul in accord with complete virtue in a complete life.*

(a) §9–10. The good of F depends on the function of F.

16. **§9 1097b22–4 But presumably . . . best good is:** Aristotle now begins an account of the good, conforming to the formal criteria just presented. So far the statement of the formal criteria has not made it clear what sort of life satisfies them (though Aristotle has implied that the 'three lives' of c5 do not satisfy them).

17. **§10 1097b26–7 seems to depend on its function:** Lit. 'seems to be in its function'. 'In' (sometimes 'consists in', but sometimes 'depends on'): *Phys.* 210a14–24.

The examples from crafts suggest that the FUNCTION of F things is the goal-directed activity that is essential to F; a sculptor, e.g., essentially aims at sculpting the relevant material into a specific shape.

Aristotle appeals to the function of F to identify what is good for F. (Contrast *EE* 1218b37–1219a6, Plato, *Rep.* 352d–353b, which explain the virtue, i.e., the goodness, of F by reference to the function of F.) What is good for Pheidias, insofar as he is a sculptor, is the sculpting activity.

(b) §11–13. The distinctive human function.

18. **§11 1097b28–30 Then do . . . no function:** Aristotle intends this to be a genuine question, which he answers in 12–13 by reference to different types of SOUL.

[Or: This is a rhetorical question that marks an inductive argument: since these human beings have functions, a human being, as such, has a FUNCTION. This is a feeble argument.]

19. **1097b30 idle, without any function:** Just one Greek word, *argon* (i.e., 'without *ergon*').

20. **Or, just as . . . of these:** The previous question is repeated with different examples.

[Or: A rhetorical question that marks an implicit argument: since the parts of a human being have functions, the whole must have a function too.]

21. **§12 1097b1098a1 What, then, . . . and growth:** Aristotle assumes that (i) a human being is essentially a living being, and (ii) a living being is essentially organized for goal-directed activities. Because of (ii), living beings have functions, according to the conception of function applied to craftsmen and organs in §10–11. The examples in §11 show that Aristotle does not take intention to be necessary for the goal-directed activity that he identifies with a function.

The different kinds of life that Aristotle describes here correspond to the different kinds of SOUL distinguished in *DA* ii 1–3. Soul, as Aristotle conceives it, is relevant here because a creature's soul is its essence.

22. **1098a1–3 The life . . . every animal:** In attributing a life of sense PERCEP-TION to non-rational animals, Aristotle does not deny that they are also essentially living creatures that engage in nutrition and growth. He means that the activities in their life—including those relevant to nutrition and growth—are controlled by their sensory states, and therefore by their desire (see *DA* 414b1–6†, 433b31–434a10†).

23. **§13 1098a3 life of action:** This life of ACTION includes other activities besides reasoning (just as a non-rational animal's life includes more than just percep-tion). But it is essentially guided by reasoning, as a dog's activities are guided by per-ception. When Aristotle looks for the 'special' human function, he does not look for one specific activity that is peculiar to human beings. (If that were his aim, why pick on reasoning? Why not mention the use of cosmetics, the building of skyscrapers, the use of weapons of mass destruction?) He looks for the type of activity that is essential to human beings, as distinct from other living creatures. Cf. 1166a16–17.

'Life of action' might include (1) a life of rational action, as opposed to the goal-directed movements of non-rational animals; (2) a life including rational action that is its own end (according to Aristotle's narrow use of 'action'), in contrast to STUDY; and (3) a life of goal-directed activity that is its own end, in a broad sense of 'activity' that may include study (cf. *Pol.* 1325b16–30†). Aristotle may intend all of these.

24. **1098a3 the <part of the soul> that has reason:** Lit. 'what has reason'. This anticipates the division of the soul into parts (hence 'of it' in the next sentence). See 1102b13–1103a10.

25. **1098a4–5 One <part> . . . and thinking:** The part that obeys reason is non-rational DESIRE (1102b25–8). This is different in human beings from non-rational desire in non-rational animals, because it is capable of agreeing with practical reason. Aristotle anticipates the account of VIRTUE of character that he begins in i 13.

26. **1098a5–7 Moreover, life . . . fully:** Since the human function requires activ-ity, not merely a STATE, which is a sort of CAPACITY, we are not subject to the objection that ruled out identification of happiness with virtue (1095b31–1096a2).

27. **in accord . . . requiring reason:** The first relation to reason belongs to the part of the soul that is inherently rational. The second relation belongs to the part that obeys reason.

(c) §14–17. Function, virtue, and the human good.

28. **§14 1098a10–12 And the same . . . play it well:** Here (as in §10, '<doing> well') 'well' includes more than competent or skillful performance. Playing well is achieving one's good as a harpist, i.e., one's good insofar as one is considered simply

as a harpist. Similarly, the virtue that makes someone do well as a human being is the virtue that makes one achieve one's own good as a human being; this matters more than one's good as a harpist, since our essential function is to be human beings, not to be harpists. Aristotle needs this connexion between virtue, doing well, and achieving one's own good, if he is to argue legitimately from the actions of a good and virtuous human being to the good of a human being.

29. **§15 1098a16–17 And so . . . with virtue:** Our good requires us to perform the function of a human being. But simply performing the function will not ensure our good; many people may live human lives, and in doing so perform human functions to some extent, and still may be badly off in their lives (*EE* 1215b27–31†). In that case 'performing one's function' cannot be a sufficient account of a person's good. In such cases people do not perform the human function well. To achieve our good we must perform the human function well. To perform it well is to perform it according to virtue. In i 13 Aristotle begins the task of identifying the relevant virtues.

30. **1098a17–18 and indeed . . . more virtues than one:** See §3 above. Here again we must explain why Aristotle says 'most complete' rather than 'all'. An exclusive or an inclusive answer might be given.

31. **§16 1098a18 complete life:** This is the last clause of the definition. [Less probably, a note added to the definition.] See 1101a6, 1177b25; *EE* 1219b5; *MM* 1185a5. Complete virtue needs a complete life (which need not, however, be a whole lifetime; see 1101a6–13) because virtuous activities need time to develop and to express themselves fully. This is especially clear with friendship, 1157a10, 1158a14, and with prudence, 1143b7. The fact that virtue is enduring contributes to the completeness of a life; see 1100b12–17, 1140b28–30, 1156b11–12.

7. §17–23. Attention to the proper method of ethics prevents us from asking inappropriate questions about this account of the good.

32. **§17 1098a20–2 Let this, then, . . . later:** One might take either x 6–8 (which refers back to i 7) or, more generally, the rest of the *EN* to fill in some details of this sketch.

33. **1098a22 to be everyone's task:** I.e., everyone ought to take on this task. [Or everyone can, i.e., it is easy for everyone.] Lit. 'to belong to everyone'. The same question arises in the next sentence.

34. **§18 1098a26–9 But we ought . . . of discipline:** The comment on filling in details prompts Aristotle to add a word about the degree to which we can reasonably expect details to be filled in. This is a third discussion of method (cf. 1094b11, 1095a28). First, he applies his remarks in c3 about exactness to the discussion of the highest good.

35. **§19 1098a31 what, or what sort:** See DEFINITION #3.

36. **1098a32–3 We must . . . other areas too:** I.e., we must seek the appropriate degree of exactness. Irrelevant digressions would result from seeking inappropriate exactness.

37. **§20 1098a33–b3 Nor should . . . the principle:** This passage on *archai* is concerned with theoretical principles known without qualification (in this case, the account of happiness), and not (as in 1095b6) with the starting points in our inquiry.

Starting points are beliefs that need some further explanation. Theoretical principles provide the necessary explanation, and so a further explanation cannot be given for them.

[Or one might take this passage to restate 1095b1 8 (second interpretation).]

38. §21 1098b3–4 **Now among principles . . . other means:** This translation assumes that Aristotle is still considering theoretical principles. Habituation (see EDUCATION) is discussed further in the following books. In 'some sort of habituation', he may mean to indicate that he does not have in mind habituation, as we might ordinarily conceive it. See EDUCATION #5.

[Or one might suppose that he is considering *archai* more generally (including both starting points and theoretical principles).]

39. §23 1098b5–6 **For they carry great weight:** Aristotle recalls his claim about knowledge of the highest good, 1094a23.

40. 1098b7 **for the principle . . . whole:** A Greek proverb: 'well begun is more than half done'.

8

8. §1–17. *This account of the good accords with the relevant common beliefs.*

(a) §1. The relevance of common beliefs.

1. **§1 1098b9–11 We should . . . about it:** This further remark on method tests the claim to have found a principle. 'From the conclusion and premises' refers to deductive INFERENCE, which has been used in arguing from general formal features of the good and from the human function. Following the method of considering APPEARANCES (see ETHICS #7), we appeal to common beliefs to confirm our claims about happiness.

(b) §2. Our account matches a common division of goods.

2. **§2 1098b12–14 Goods are divided, . . . body:** Goods of the soul are those that depend on the condition of the soul, rather than on the body or on conditions outside the agent. Cf. 1099b11–25. See GOODS #6.

(c) §3–4. Our account fits common views about the end and about happiness.

(d) §5–7. Our account explains the variety of conceptions of happiness.

3. **§5 1098b22–3 Further, all . . . described:** Common views about happiness: *Rhet.* i 5.

4. **§6 1098b24 to others prudence:** 'Prudence' (phronesis) may have a more general range than it usually has in *EN*. Cf. 1096a17; *EE* 1214a32†.

5. **1098b25 including pleasure or requiring it:** Lit. 'with pleasure or not without pleasure'. Activities that include pleasure are sources of pleasure in themselves. Those

that require pleasure are not in themselves sources of pleasure, but have sources of pleasure added to them. Cf. 1099a15.

(d) §8–9. Happiness requires more than virtue.

6. **§9 1098b31–3 Presumably, . . . its activity>:** Cf. 1095b31–1096a2. Happiness requires not only virtue but also activities that actualize the virtue in the circumstances that are discussed in c10.

7. **1099a6 act correctly:** I.e., act successfully (as in 'getting the correct answer' in an arithmetic test).

(e) §10–13. Happiness requires more than pleasure.

8. **§10 1099a7 Moreover, . . . pleasant in itself:** On PLEASURE, cf. 1104b3, 1175a21–6.

9. **§11 1099a11–12 Now the things . . . conflict:** The sources of pleasure conflict with one another. If I have an excessive desire for food, I may make myself ill by overeating, and so interfere with my other pleasures. On 'pleasant by nature', cf. 1153a5, 1176a19.

10. **§12 1099a15–16 Hence these people's life . . . pleasure within itself:** Cf. 1169b26.

(f) §14. Our account shows how happiness satisfies the traditional ideals.

11. **§14 1099a24–8 'What is . . . heart's desire':** The inscription at the temple of Delos: *EE* 1214b1–8†; Theognis 225.

12. **1099a29–31 and we say happiness . . . the best one:** The best activity v. all these activities, cf. 1098a16–18.

(g) §15–17. Happiness requires external goods as well as virtue and pleasure.

13. **§15 1099a31–2 Nonetheless, . . . resources:** Happiness does not depend entirely on us. Our choices and actions are decisive for our happiness, but the activities required by happiness also depend on external GOODS #6 as resources. 'For first of all' and 'Further' introduce two roles of external goods that are discussed in c9–10.

14. **§16 1099b3 character of happiness:** Hence such people are not good candidates for happiness. Cf. 1176b16, 1177a6, 1178b23.

9

9.§1–11. Happiness consists in our activities, not in good luck, but it depends on luck and external circumstances.

(a) §1–6. We achieve happiness by our own action, not by luck.

1. **§1 1099b9–11 This also . . . fortune:** Cf. Plato, *Meno* 71a1–4, 100b2–4.

2. **§6 1099b24–5 and it would . . . fortune:** Cf. 1095b23–6. Happiness is something of our own, not something we passively receive from other people or from external circumstances. It depends largely on our own actions; we are not at the mercy of FORTUNE for the major components of our happiness. Happiness partly consists in virtuous actions; and being virtuous is up to us, not entirely dependent on fortune (cf. iii 5).

(b) §7–11. Since happiness requires complete virtue in a complete life, it is not entirely independent of good and bad luck.

3. **§7 1099b26 a certain sort . . . with virtue:** Hence not a result of fortune.

4. **§8 1099b28–32 Further, this . . . fine actions:** Since political science aims at the best good, and seeks to secure it through education of character, it presupposes that happiness consists primarily in character and action, not in fortune.

5. **§9 1099b32–1100a5 It is not surprising . . . complete life:** Children, animals, and happiness: 1178b25–8; *Phys.* 197b6; *EE* 1219b5.

6. **§11 1100a7–8 the Trojan . . . Priam:** Aristotle refers not only to Homer, but to other stories about the Trojan War. As king of Troy, Priam was rich, prosperous, and successful, amply meeting the normal standards for happiness, until the Greeks came, destroyed Troy, and killed Priam himself. See Homer, *Iliad* xxii 44–76. Like Croesus in Herodotus, he provides a clear example of someone whose life was apparently ruined by the way it ended.

10

10.§1–16. Happiness is not completely stable, but it is stable enough to justify us in calling people happy during their lifetime.

(a) §1–2. Solon's advice to call no one happy until he is dead does not mean that we can be happy when we are dead.

1. **§1 1100a10–11 Then should . . . end:** In Herodotus i 30–2, Solon advises the prosperous and overconfident Croesus not to judge people's happiness (especially Croesus' own) during their lifetime, but to wait until they are dead, to see how their lives end. This advice applies especially to Priam, whose life went well until near its end.

(b) §3–5. It is not clear that someone's past happiness is fixed, even after his death.

2. **§3 1100a14–17 We do not . . . and misfortunes:** Solon thinks happiness is complete success, and that (e.g.) Croesus lacks complete success if his success does not last his entire lifetime. Since external conditions beyond Croesus' control may interfere with success, we are wise to wait until the end of his life, when we can be sure that they have or have not interfered, before we decide whether he was happy.

3. **1100a17–21 But this claim . . . suffer misfortune:** Even the end of a person's life may be too soon to tell if he was or was not really successful in his aims. If someone is happy, he succeeds in fulfiling his aims. If, then, he aims at the welfare of

his children, his success, and hence his happiness, depends on what happens after his death, when his children succeed or fail.

4. **§4 1100a27–9 Surely, then, . . . to have been miserable:** Queen Victoria died in 1901; her descendant Czar Nicholas was deposed in 1917. The absurdity that Aristotle considers here is not (a) 'Victoria has now become unhappy' (said in 1917); see a14–15, 'we do not say . . .'. He considers the different absurdity (b) 'It has now (in 1917) become true that Victoria was (before 1901) unhappy'. What was true of her in her lifetime cannot be affected by every fluctuation of fortune after her death (but it can be altered by some fluctuations; see previous note).

(c) §6–8. It is possible to be happy during one's lifetime.

5. **§7 1100a34–5 Would it . . . happiness he has:** Aristotle rejects the attitude that refuses to ascribe happiness until after someone's death.

6. **1100b2–4 for we suppose . . . to and fro:** The attitude Aristotle has rejected would be reasonable, if happiness consisted primarily in good fortune; for in that case happiness would be as unstable as fortune. If someone can be happy in his lifetime, happiness does not consist primarily in good fortune.

(d) §9–11. The life of virtuous activity meets the legitimate demand for happiness to be stable.

7. **§9 1100b8 For his . . . does not rest on them:** [Or 'does not consist in them'. The Greek has simply 'in'; cf. iii 1.§15, note.] In Aristotle's view, Solon is mostly, but not entirely, wrong. A virtuous person's main aim is the exercise of his virtues in his life. He can succeed in this, and hence achieve the main component of his happiness, independently of fortune. Since, however, some conditions and elements of happiness depend on fortune, happiness is not entirely stable.

8. **§10 1100b12–14 For no human . . . the sciences:** The stability of virtue: 1105a33, 1140b29, 1156b12, 1159b2, 1164a12, 1172b9. The virtues deal with one's life as a whole, and so one has reason to exercise them in all one's dealings. FRIENDSHIP supports this constant exercise: 1170a7 (cf. 1154b20, 1175a3, 1177a21), 1172a1–8.

9. **§11 1100b21–2 'good, foursquare, and blameless':** Simonides fr. 379 (Page). Cf. Plato, *Pr.* 339b.

(e) §12–14. The happiness of virtuous people is not entirely stable, because it is not immune to external circumstances. But even bad luck cannot make them miserable.

10. **§12 1100b25–8 But many major . . . fine and excellent:** External goods 'add adornment': 1123a7, 1124a1.

11. **1100b30–3 And yet, . . . and magnanimous:** See 1123b29. Because virtuous people do not overestimate external goods, they are not be crushed by misfortune. See 1166a29. Making the best of available resources: *Pol.* 1332a19.

12. **§13 1100b35–1101a1 For a . . . prudent person:** 'PRUDENT', usually translates *phronimos*, but here translates the cognate *emphrôn*.

13. **§14 1101a6–8 If this . . . Priam's:** The happy person does not become miserable even in misfortune; he is happy nor unhappy (miserable), but simply not happy. Here Aristotle uses 'blessed' (*makarios*) as well as 'happy' (*eudaimôn*). In some places (see *EE* 1215a10†, 1215b1–14|) being *makarios* seems to indicate a higher degree of well-being (more suitable to gods than to human beings) than the merely *eudaimôn* person possesses. But this chapter draws no distinction between *makarios* and *eudaimôn*.

14. **1101a10 nor shaken . . . misfortunes:** Read *outh'hupo*.

(f) §15–16. Hence a virtuous person can be called happy in his lifetime, even though he is not assured of happiness throughout his life.

15. **§15–16 1101a16–21 Or should we . . . human being is:** Aristotle decides, in the light of §14, that we can call a person happy while he is alive, keeping in mind that we are speaking of human happiness, which is subject to the fluctuations of fortune.

[Or, with a different punctuation: 'Or should we add . . . appropriate end? Since the future . . ., we shall say . . . human being is.' We cannot call a person happy while he is alive.]

11

11.§1–6. Solon is partly right. What happens after one's death can affect one's happiness slightly.

(a) §1–4. Postmortem misfortunes differ in degree and in their impact on one's past happiness.

1. **§4 1101a30–1 much more . . . course of it:** In Aeschylus' *Agamemnon*, for instance, the crimes of Agamemnon (who sacrificed his daughter) and of Atreus (who killed the sons of his brother Thyestes, and served them up for Thyestes to eat) are mentioned, but they affect us less than the murder of Agamemnon, which happens during the play.

(b) §5–6. But in any case their impact is slight.

12

12.§1–8. The difference between praise and honour suggests that virtue (an object of praise) is inferior to happiness (an object of honour).

1. **§1 1101b12 for . . . capacity:** A simple CAPACITY, or ability, is neither praiseworthy nor honourable. See 1106a6–10; *MM* 1183b30–5.†

(a) §2–3. Objects of praise.

2. **§2 1101b12–14 Whatever . . . to something:** On praise, cf. *MM* 1183b20–38†. Praise is accorded to what is FINE #3 because it is the agent's own achievement, resulting from his own voluntary effort under human conditions (hence it is inappropriate to the gods; 1178b16). Congratulation, however, belongs to success in action; this is what distinguishes happiness from virtuous action, which is not sufficient by itself for the complete success required in happiness (cf. 1177b18).

(b) §4–7. The best good is above praise.

3. §4 1101b24–5 **godlike:** Or 'divine'. Cf. 1145a18–27.

4. §5 1101b27–8 **Indeed, Eudoxus . . . of pleasure:** See 1094a2, 1172b9. Aristotle endorses EUDOXUS' claim that some goods are too good to be praised. He does not endorse the argument for hedonism that Eudoxus derives from this claim.

(c) §8. Happiness is above praise because it is the principle.

5. §8 1102a2–3 **for <the . . . other actions:** Lit. 'for the sake of this we do all the other things'. 'This' probably refers to 'principle' (*archê*). Aristotle assumes that we do all our actions for the sake of happiness. It is the PRINCIPLE because our deliberation (see DECISION) begins from our conception of happiness as the highest good; and we aim at it as the END, since we try to find the action that will best realize our conception of happiness.

13

13.§1–19. The soul and the virtues.

(a) §1–4. A discussion of happiness requires a discussion of virtue.

1. §1 1102a5–7 **Since happiness . . . happiness better:** This is a better place to begin Book ii than the place where our mss. divide the books. Aristotle summarizes what he has said, and anticipates what comes next.

He refers back to his definition of happiness in 1098a16–18. In 'a certain sort' (*tis*) he may allude to the parts of the definition that he leaves out here: (a) the demand for the best and most complete virtue, and (b) the demand for a complete life. He has discussed (b) in c9–11. It is reasonable to consider (a) when we have examined the specific virtues, and seen that there are a number of them (as 1098a17 suggested). Hence the next task is to discuss virtue.

In his account of happiness Aristotle has not yet said what the virtues are, and whether happiness requires justice or injustice, kindness or cruelty, bravery or cowardice. Aristotle begins his answer to that question. Following the suggestion in 1098a3, he considers the rational and non-rational parts (see DESIRE) of the human SOUL. The condition that promotes happiness will be the proper relation between the rational and the non-rational parts.

2. §2 1102a8 **the true politician:** Aristotle recognizes that his conception of political science and of the politician does not entirely fit the common conception of what politicians do. Cf. *EE* 1216a23–7†.

3. §3 1102a10–11 **Spartan and Cretan legislators:** Aristotle commends their systematic supervision of moral education. See SPARTA.

4. §4 1102a12–13 **Since, then, . . . beginning:** This was the decision announced in c2, to pursue political science.

(b) §5–8. A discussion of virtue requires a discussion of the soul.

5. §7 1102a18–20 **If this . . . body as well:** Cf. Plato, *La.* 189e–190c (adapted by Aristotle).

6. **1102a23 Hence . . . <as the student of nature> . . . soul:** The account of the SOUL in the *De Anima* belongs to Aristotle's natural philosophy.

7. **§8 1102a25–6 for a more exact . . . requires:** Cf. 1094b11–27. On the present question EXACTNESS is not impossible, but irrelevant.

(c) *§9–10.* The soul is divided into rational and non-rational parts.

8. **§9 1102a26–7 <We> have . . . less popular>:** [Or ' . . . even in the POPULAR works'].

9. **§10 1102a28–32 But are these . . . present purposes:** Parts: *DA* 413b13–32†, 432a15–b8, 433a31–b13†. By 'two <only> in definition' (*logos*) Aristotle means what he means when he speaks of things that are 'the same, but their being is not the same'; cf. 1130a12–13.

(d) §11–14. One sort of non-rational part operates without our awareness, and is therefore irrelevant to ethics.

10. **§11 1102a32–b2 Consider the non-rational . . . capacity to them:** In this section it is useful to remember that Aristotle ascribes SOULS to plants as well as to animals. 'Full-grown' translates *teleion*, also translated 'COMPLETE'.

(e) §15–19. Another sort of non-rational part includes non-rational desires; it is capable of agreeing or disagreeing with the rational part.

11. **§15 1102b18–19 uncontrolled:** Literally 'loosed', i.e., moving independently, not under one's control.

12. **§17 1102b26–8 At any rate, . . . reason in everything:** Continence and virtue: 1111b14, 1115b10, 1119a11, 1151b34.

13. **§18 1102b30 the <part> . . . in general desires:** Aristotle does not mean that the non-rational part is the only part that has DESIRES; for the rational part has the type of rational desire that Aristotle calls 'wish' (*boulêsis*). He means that the desires of the non-rational part are simply desires, i.e., they lack the rational element that is essential to desire for the good.

14. **1102b31–3 This is . . . in mathematics:** [Or ' . . . in the way in which we 'take account' (lit. 'have *logos* [reason, account]') of father or friend, not in the way in which we <give an account> . . . '.]

15. **§19 1103a1–3 If, then, . . . a father:** Aristotle has now explained the two ways of acting 'in accord with reason' that he introduced in 1098a3–5. The non-rational part that includes desires is not inherently rational, but is capable of following the reason in the inherently rational part.

(f) §19. Different types of virtue are required for the non-rational part (capable of agreeing with the rational part) and for the rational part.

16. **1103a3–4 The division . . . virtues of character:** The virtues of character do not involve only the non-rational part. They all require PRUDENCE, which belongs to the rational part. Some of the virtues of thought—prudence, good deliberation, understanding and consideration—require the right training of the non-rational part; see vi 9, 11.

Book II

1

1.§1–8. Virtues of character do not belong to us by nature, but are acquired by habituation.

1. **§1 1103a14 Virtue, then . . . character:** This continues from i 13. As we saw (1102a5–7), a new book really begins with i 13, and not here.

2. **1103a17–18 Virtue of . . . 'ethos':** Aristotle plays on the similarity between *êthos* (character) and *ethos* (habit). On habit, see EDUCATION #1. Etymological speculations: 1112a16, 1132a30, 1140b11, 1152b7; they are part of the appeal to ordinary language, which in turn is part of Aristotle's appeal to APPEARANCES.

(a) §2–4. Virtue of character is not a natural condition, since a natural condition is not changed by habituation.

3. **§3 1103a25–6 Rather, we are . . . habit:** NATURE is not neutral, equally suited for virtue or vice, but appropriately completed by virtue. See COMPLETE.

(b) §4. We acquire crafts and virtues by practice, but we do not acquire natural conditions in that way.

4. **§4 1103a34–b2 we become just . . . actions:** We do not exercise the virtues before we possess them. We do the virtuous actions before we possess the virtues. See ii 4.

(c) §5. Legislators are concerned with virtue, and hence with habituation.

5. **§5 1103b3–5 For the legislator . . . his goal:** The proper role of the legislator, see LAW.

(d) §6–8. We acquire virtues by learning to do the actions that are required by the virtues.

6. **§7 1103b21–2 To sum it up . . . similar activities:** 'Similar': I.e., 'similar to each other'. Habituation involves the repetition of the same sort of activity in the same conditions. [Or 'similar' might mean 'similar to the state resulting from them', assuming that, e.g., brave actions are similar to bravery.]

7. **§8 1103b22–3 That is . . . in the states:** The account of moral training strongly stresses habituation. The actions required by the virtues (e.g., a brave action such as standing firm) must be practiced, if we are to acquire the right STATE of character. Habituation is needed because we need more than mere instruction, 1103a15; non-rational desires must also be trained. While we are being trained, our virtuous actions are not caused by the virtue. See EDUCATION #2–3.

2

2.§1–9. The right method of habituation.

(a) §1. The aim of ethical theory is practical.

1. **§1 1103b26–9 Our present . . . benefit to us:** Practical results: ETHICS #1. Aristotle says that finding true theories is not our end; he does not deny, but assumes, that they are a means to our end. True theories are all the more important when the practical purpose of ethics is considered; see note to x 1 §3.

(b) §2. Virtuous actions must accord with the correct reason. This general formula needs to be explained in more detail if it is to be practically helpful.

2. **§2 1103b31–2 First, then, . . . correct reason:** Aristotle begins with an APPEARANCE, a common belief about virtue, which he gradually explains and defends; see 1107a1, 1138b18, 1144b21. Correct reason: REASON #3.
   3. **1103b32 a common <belief>:** [Or 'common <to all the virtues>'].

(c) §3–5. Ethics is inexact both at the universal and at the particular level, but we must give as much practical help as we can.

4. **§3 1104a1 actions we should do:** Read *prakteôn*.
   5. **1104a2–5 As we also . . . fixed answers:** Aristotle refers back to the discussion of inexactness in i 3.§1–4. The lack of fixed answers reflects the fact that ethics requires us to rely on usual principles.
   6. **§4 1104a5–10 While this . . . navigators do:** This is a new source of inexactness in addition to the source mentioned in §3. Not only are some ethical principles merely usual, but they are also impossible to apply in practice by any systematic craft.
   7. **§5 1104a10–11 The account . . . offer help:** Aristotle suggests that this treatise will offer help in dealing with practical questions. See ii 9; 1126a32–b10; 1164b27–1165a14.

(d) §6–7. Habituation must avoid excess and deficiency and must aim at a mean in the actions that promote a virtue.

8. **§6 1104a13–14 (for we must . . . not evident):** For this maxim, cf. *MM* 1185b15; Anaxagoras, DK 59 B 21a.
   9. **§7 1104a22–7 Similarly, if he gratifies . . . by the mean:** The doctrine expounded in ii 6 is anticipated here. So far, however, Aristotle only argues that virtue is acquired by a mean—neither total repression ('insensibility': 1107b4–8) nor total indulgence of a natural desire or FEELING. He later argues that virtue also consists in an intermediate condition.

(d) §8–9. We must also aim at a mean in the actions that actualize the virtue.

10. **§8 1104a27–9 But these actions . . . same actions:** In §6–7 Aristotle has been concerned with finding the mean in the actions through which we acquire a virtue. He now extends his claim about the mean to the actions that we perform after we have acquired the virtue.

3

3. §1–11. The importance of pleasure and pain in moral training.

(a) §1. Virtue is about pleasure and pain.

1. **§1 1104b3–5 But we must take . . . state:** In 'But . . .' Aristotle corrects a possible misunderstanding of his emphasis on actions in c2. Virtue does not consist simply in the correct actions, but also requires the appropriate attitudes. The right kind of pleasure (1099a7) must also supervene (cf. 1174b33). Virtuous persons do not simply get pleasure from virtuous action, but they also take pleasure in the very fact that the actions are virtuous—hence 'enjoys this <abstinence> itself'. See 1175a18–31.

2. **1104b6–7 if he is grieved . . . intemperate:** The person who is grieved at being denied the intemperate satisfaction of bodily appetites is intemperate, not continent (see 1102b27, INCONTINENT). The intemperate person may find that he has to refrain from an improper pleasure (e.g., if he sees that he cannot avoid detection if he commits adultery), and will be grieved and resentful if he has to deny himself such pleasures. The continent person, however, has been trained to have some of the virtuous person's desires, and hence he does not resent abstinence from improper pleasures. He is continent rather than virtuous because he also has strong appetites for these pleasures.

3. **1104b8–9 For virtue . . . and pains:** This is the general thesis of this chapter. It is defended by the series of points that follow in the rest of the chapter. §6 and §11 repeat the thesis.

(b) §1–2. Pleasure and pain turn us in the right or wrong direction.

4. **§2 1104b11–12 as Plato says:** Plato, *Rep.* 401e; *Laws* 653e.

(c) §3–4. Feelings imply pleasure and pain.

5. **§3 1104b14–15 but every feeling . . . pain:** FEELINGS: 1105b21–3.

(d) §5–6. Pleasure and pain lead us into error.

6. **§5 1104b24–5 These <bad . . . pleasures and pains>:** This may refer to the views of SPEUSIPPUS (cf. Plato, *Phil.* 42e–51a; 1153a31) or the CYNICS.

(e) §7. Pleasure is involved in every sort of choice.

7. **§7 1104b30–2 For there are three . . . and painful:** On these three possible objects of choice, cf. 1126b29, 1155b18, FINE. These are three types of goods. The fine and the pleasant are goods that are chosen for their own sakes.

(f) §8–9. Pleasure is our earliest motive.

(g) §10. It is difficult to resist pleasure.

8. **§10 1105a8 Heracleitus . . . spirit>:** Probably Aristotle alludes to a remark by Heracleitus on resisting spirit (see DESIRE). See DK 22 B 85.

4

4.§1–6. Our account of habituation requires us to distinguish doing the virtuous actions from having the virtuous character.

(a) §1. Puzzle: How can we do the right actions without being in the right state? Examples from the crafts.

1. **§1 1105a17–19 Someone might be . . . temperate actions:** The puzzle arises because 1104a26–b3 emphasized the similarity between the actions that we learn to do when we are being habituated and the actions that we do when we are virtuous. We might suppose that if the actions are the same, their motive must be the same too, so that we can learn to be virtuous only if we already have the motive of the virtuous person. This is a practical analogue of the puzzle about learning that Meno raises at Plato, *Meno* 80a–e, discussed by Aristotle in *APo* 71a20–b8. Aristotle replies that the objector's argument (1) rests on an alleged feature of the crafts, and hence (2) assumes that virtues are analogous to crafts in the relevant ways.

(b) §2. A parallel between virtues and crafts.

2. **§2 1105a21–2 Or are . . . crafts as well:** Aristotle's first reply challenges (1), and argues that the crafts do not support the objection.

(c) §3–5. A contrast between virtues and crafts.

3. **§3 1105a26–7 Moreover, . . . virtues:** The second reply is independent of the first, and challenges (2), insisting on an important difference between virtues and crafts. It contrasts the value of acting from craft knowledge—purely instrumental value, simply a means to the right product—with the value of acting from virtue.

4. **1105a27–8 For the products . . . have been produced:** Lit. 'the things coming to be by crafts have the well in themselves . . .'. Aristotle is not taking back the point he has made in the first reply, that someone might produce a good product accidentally. He means that the goodness and badness of production is determined by its usefulness for producing the product; a better method of production is better because it is better at producing the right sort of product.

5. **1105a28–30 But for actions . . . right qualities:** The value of acting virtuously, as opposed to a craftsman's production (the process), is not simply determined by its efficiency in producing a product; it also has its characteristic motive. The value of virtue is intrinsic; acting virtuously is not valuable simply as a means to some further result (e.g., acting kindly is not simply a means to making someone feel better). The intrinsic value of virtue reflects the virtuous person's motive, shown by the second condition in a32. The demand for a specific motive differentiates virtue from craft, and hence differentiates the training required for each of them; this is Aristotle's answer to the puzzle raised in the chapter. On virtuous action v. production, see 1106b14–16; ACTION #3.

6. **1105a31 <that he is doing them>:** I.e., that he is doing virtuous actions. [Or he must know what he is doing, and not be acting because of ignorance. See 1111a22–4.]

7. **§5 1105a33–b2 As conditions . . . knowing:** Aristotle passes from (a), the contrast between products produced well and actions done well, to (b), the contrast between good craftsmen and virtuous agents. The two contrasts are connected, because an action is done well only if it a good agent does it from the right state (whereas a product can be produced well even if a good craftsman does not produce it).

(d) §6. The importance of habituation.

8. **§6 1105b14–18 They are like a sick . . . philosophy:** Aristotle sometimes cites MEDICINE to illustrate people's lazy and unrealistic attitude to moral theory and instruction. Cf. 1114a15–16.

5

5.§1–6. *The genus of virtue of character: it is a state.*

(a) §1–2. The difference between feelings, capacities, and states.

1. **§1 1105b19–21 Next . . . one of these:** Aristotle sets out to define virtue by elimination. The three 'conditions' are the different conditions of soul concerned with action. Neither FEELINGS nor CAPACITIES are the same as virtues, because they are the raw material of virtue; they require training and organization, as 1104a20 implied. In this chapter Aristotle gives the genus of virtue; in c6 he gives the differentia (see DEFINE).

2. **§2 1105b25–6 By states I mean . . . to feelings:** 'STATE', *hexis* (lit. 'having'), is formed from *echein*, 'to have'. 'Well (badly) off' translates *echein* with the adverb, lit. 'have well (badly)'. (Greek says 'How do you have?' for the English 'How do you do?' or 'How are you?'.) Aristotle argues that a state is not *merely* a capacity. He does not deny, but indeed believes, that a state is a *type* of capacity; see, e.g., 'able to' in 1104a32–b3, indicating the type of capacity that is included in the state of character.

(b) §3–4. Virtues are not simply feelings.

3. **§3 1105b28–9 First, then, . . . are feelings:** Aristotle offers four arguments for this claim: (1) 'For we are . . . have feelings.' (2) 'Further, we are neither . . . have virtues or vices.' (3) 'Further, we are angry . . . require decision.' (4) 'Besides, insofar . . . rather than moved.'

4. **§3 1105b31–1106a3 Further, we are . . . have virtues or vices:** Praise and blame are proper to VOLUNTARY actions; here Aristotle introduces a question that he discusses further in iii 1. In iii 5 he considers whether praising virtue and blaming vice is ever justified.

The contrast between being 'simply (*haplôs*; see UNQUALIFIED) angry' and being 'angry in a particular way' is also connected to issues about voluntariness. Aristotle assumes that it is up to us to modify our feelings so that they are appropriate; that is why we are praised for being angry appropriately.

5. **§4 1106a3–4 but the virtues . . . require decision:** After introducing praise and blame, and hence questions about the VOLUNTARY, Aristotle mentions DECISION, already introduced in 1105a31, and discussed in iii 2–4.

(c) §5. Virtues are not capacities.

6. **§5 1106a10 we have discussed this before:** See 1103a17–b2.

(d) §6. Hence they are states.

6

6.§1–20. The differentia of virtue of character: it is an intermediate state.

(a) §1–3. Human virtue realizes the human function.

1. **§1 1106a14–15 But we must . . . what sort of state it is:** 'What' often marks the genus, and 'what sort' the differentia; DEFINITION #3.

2. **§2 1106a15–17 It should be . . . functions well:** The connexion between virtue and FUNCTION was urged in 1098a7; cf. 1139a16; Plato, *Rep.* 352d. As i 13 argued, a virtue requires the right relation among different parts of the soul, so that someone's actions are guided by reason. Here Aristotle expands his earlier suggestion (in 1104a26) that guidance by reason requires neither total repression nor total indulgence of non-rational desires. Hence the connexion between virtue and function leads directly into the doctrine of the mean.

(b) §4–8. The numerical mean must be distinguished from the mean relative to us, which is the aim of the expert in athletic training.

3. **§4 1106a24–6 We have . . . virtue has:** Aristotle does not intend his appeal to the MEAN and to the EQUAL to offer a precise, quantitative test for virtuous action that we can readily apply to particular cases—as though, e.g., we could decide that there is a proper, moderate degree of anger to be displayed in all conditions, or in all conditions of a certain precisely described type. The point of the doctrine, and of Aristotle's insistence on the 'intermediate relative to us', is that no such precise quantitative test can be found. It cannot be found because virtue accords with correct reason, as its relation to the FUNCTION of a human being requires; correct reason may require extreme anger at extreme injuries and slight anger at trivial offences; in both cases moderate anger would be wrong. To find the mean relative to us is to find the state of character that correct reason requires, neither suppressing nor totally indulging non-rational desires. This mean state cannot be identified in purely quantitative terms, however. The conditions that define it are ineliminably normative.

4. **§5 1106a31–3 the same for all . . . not the same for all:** The mean 'relative to us', is not relative to different people, but relative to human beings (as opposed to other sorts of things), i.e., appropriate for human nature. This aspect of the doctrine of the mean spells out Aristotle's claims about the human function.

[Or we might take 'the same for all' as 'the same for everyone'. The Greek 'all' might be masculine or neuter.]

(c) §9–14. The virtuous person, like the expert in a craft, aims at the mean. The special concern of virtue is the mean in feelings and actions.

5. **§9 1106b8–9 This, then, . . . product conform to that:** 'Product' translates *ergon,* translated 'FUNCTION' in 16–24. Here Aristotle argues, as he often does, from crafts to virtues—from the way in which a craft achieves its *ergon,* product, to the way in which virtue achieves its *ergon,* function.

6. **1106b14–16 And since virtue, . . . intermediate:** Nature and craft: *PA* 639b19; *Phys.* 194a21. Though in certain respects virtue is less EXACT than some crafts (cf. 1104a7–10), it differs from craft insofar as a craft is a CAPACITY that can be used well or badly, whereas virtue is the direction of a capacity to the right use (1105a25–6). Hence we may expect virtue to aim more precisely on the right end, and therefore (since this aim requires aiming at the mean) to aim at the mean.

7. **§12 1106b25–6 deficiency is blamed:** Read *hê elleipsis psegetai.*

8. **1106b35 'for we are noble . . . sorts of ways':** Author unknown.

(d) §15–17. The definition of virtue: it is a mean, guided by prudence.

9. **§15 1106b36–1107a2 Virtue, . . . define it:** Parts of this definition have been anticipated at 1105a31, 1103b21. The reference to the PRUDENT person might be derived from 1106b8–16, by taking the prudent person to correspond to the craftsman finding the mean. But the defence of the definition mostly comes later. See 1111b5, 1138b18, 1144b21.

(e) §18–20. Clarification of the definition; some descriptions of actions imply vice, and therefore preclude any mean.

10. **§18 1107a8–9 Now not every . . . the mean:** §17, indicating that we need to be careful about the sense in which virtue is a mean and an extremity, prompts this clarification. (In §20, 'since the intermediate is a sort of extreme', Aristotle repeats the point of §17.) We cannot find a virtue by taking just any description of a type of action or feeling, and claiming that there is a virtue in finding the mean in that; for the action or feeling may be a vicious one. Aristotelian virtues include mean conditions of natural desires and tendencies. They also include mean conditions of desires and tendencies (e.g., love of honour) that develop in normal forms of social life. In these cases we can find a mean only in the case of desires that do not inherently involve an excessive or deficient cultivation of feelings and desires. To decide whether they are excessive or deficient we need to know whether they do or do not conform to what we ought to do, when we ought to do it, and so on. The various conditions that determine what is RIGHT are not defined by reference to the mean, but, on the contrary, the mean is determined by these different aspects of the right.

11. **1107a9–12 For the names . . . among actions:** Aristotle asserts that some types of action, in any circumstances, are always wrong. What does he mean by this? We might say that we would not *call* anything theft or murder unless we thought it wrong. Aristotle might say the same of adultery (it is the unjust use of a wife who justly belongs to another man). Cf. 1135b27–1136a1.

7

7.§1–16. The definition of virtue as a mean applies to the specific virtues of character.

1. **§1 1107a28–32 However, . . . accord with these:** See PARTICULAR. Aristotle looks for accounts of virtues that are more 'particular' in the sense of describing specific virtues; these virtues are not themselves token actions (Leonidas' last stand at Thermopylae) or states (Leonidas' bravery). But when Aristotle adds 'since actions are about particular cases', he seems to refer to token actions. He intends his account of specific virtues to be helpful in practical questions, as he promised in 1104a10–11.

2. **1107a32–3 Let us, . . . chart:** Aristotle probably has a table of the different means and extremes on a chart in his classroom. Cf. *EE* 1220b37, *DI* 22a22. This chapter anticipates the detailed argument of iii 6–v, and in some ways makes its aim clearer: (1) The virtues are classified into groups. (2) Aristotle seeks to show that for every genuine virtue of character the doctrine of the mean explains why it is a virtue. (3) In some cases this is fairly easy, where (as with bravery) Aristotle can find a trio of mean, excess, and deficiency already recognized in ordinary beliefs. But sometimes it is hard, where we do not naturally think of a trio, and have no names for some of the alleged members. This is why Aristotle's remarks on the 'nameless' virtues are important (see 1107b2, VIRTUE). He wants to show that his doctrine applies here too, and hence that the trio is recognizable even where common beliefs have not yet recognized it.

(a) §2–3. Virtues concerned with feelings.

(b) §4–9. Virtues concerned with external goods.

3. **§8 1107b31–1108a1 This is why . . . indifferent to honour:** This comment explains why Aristotle thinks it important to identify virtues that have no name to distinguish them clearly from the extremes. The absence of a clear way to distinguish them from the extremes leads to two mistakes: (1) The person at the extreme claims to have the virtue. When Aristotle says the extreme people lay claim to the intermediate area, he means not (a) they agree that virtue is a mean and claim, 'We have the mean state', but (b) they claim that the virtue (which Aristotle takes to be a mean state) is the state (in fact extreme) they have. (2) We (not the extreme people) refer to the intermediate person by the name of one of the extremes. In case (1) the speaker does not correctly identify the genuinely virtuous state. In case (2) we correctly identify it, but we use a misleading name. Cf. 1126a17–18.

(c) §10–13. Virtues concerned with social life.

(d) §14–16. Mean states that are not virtues.

4. **§15 1107b35–1108a6 Proper indignation . . . <other people's misfortunes>:** These mean states are not discussed further in the *EN*. Cf. *EE* iii 7; *Rhet.* ii 6, 9–10.

(e) §16. Justice.

5. **§16 1108b6–7 There will . . . elsewhere . . . these:** 'These' might be the states mentioned in §15 (in which case Aristotle might refer to *Rhet.* ii) or all the virtues of character mentioned (looking forward to Books iii–iv).

8

8. §1–8. Different virtues involve different relations between the mean state and the extremes.

(a) §1–3. The mean state is opposed to each extreme.

1. **§2 1108b19–23 For the brave . . . wasteful person:** The doctrine of the mean explains disputes and errors about the virtues, as a good theory should (1154a22). Those who do not fully understand the requirements of the virtue identify it with one extreme, which is legitimately criticized by the other extreme; cf. 1125b4–18; *Rhet.* 1367a32–b7.

(b) §4–5. Each extreme is more opposed to the other extreme than to the mean state.

(c) §6–8. In some cases one extreme is more opposed than the other is to the mean state.

2. **§7 1109a7–8 Since sometimes one extreme . . . intermediate condition:** How is one extreme nearer to the mean? Perhaps, e.g., the rash person has the same sort of attitude to fears that the brave person has, but goes too far with it, whereas the coward has not developed the right sort of attitude at all. Cf. 1121a20, 1122a13, 1125a32, 1127b31.

9

9. §1–9. Since it is difficult to reach the mean, we must try to give practical advice, even though it is imprecise.

1. **§2 1109a28–9 is no longer . . . do it:** The difficulty of acting virtuously: 1137a4–26.

(a) §3–4. We must avoid the extreme that is more opposed to the mean.

2. **§3 1109a30–2 That is why . . . spray and surge.':** Aristotle offers practical advice, as he promised (1104a10), stressing that his doctrine does not offer precise answers to particular questions. See ETHICS #9, PERCEPTION. He quotes Homer, *Od.* xii 219, inaccurately (Circe's advice, not Calypso's).

3. **§4 1109a34 extremely accurately:** (*akrôs*). A pun on *akrôs* = 'extremely' and *akron* = 'extreme' (as opposed to intermediate); cf. 1107a8, 23 (the mean is, in one sense, an extremity).

(b) §4–5. We must avoid the extreme that we drift into more easily.

(c) §6. We must be especially careful with pleasures.

4. **§6 1109b9–12 Hence we must react . . . less in error:** In Homer (*Il.* iii 156) the Trojan elders comment on Helen's beauty: 'Her face is uncannily like the faces of the immortal goddesses. But, beautiful though she is, let her depart in the ships; may she not be left behind to cause grief to us and our children' (158 60).

(d) §7–9. This advice is necessarily inexact; in particular cases we must rely on perception.

5. **§8 1109b22–3 Such things . . . perception:** Lit. 'Such things are in particulars and the judgment (or 'discrimination') is in perception.' 'Such' might refer back to 'nothing else perceptible' just mentioned, or it might include the circumstances and degrees mentioned just before that. See PERCEPTION.

Book III

1

1.§1–3. Introduction to the discussion of responsibility

(a) §1–2. The relevance of voluntary action; it is required for praise and blame, and hence for virtue.

1. **§1 1109b30–2 Virtue, then, . . . they are involuntary:** The chapters on voluntary action and responsibility (iii 1–5) continue the discussion of virtues of character. Aristotle has said that virtue is praiseworthy (1101b14, 1106a2), and now argues that praise is appropriate. In 1107a1 he made DECISION essential to virtue, and in iii 2–3 he discusses its nature and its relation to the voluntary. He has assumed that if happiness consists in virtuous activity, it will, to this extent, be up to us, not dependent on FORTUNE, 1099b13–25. He needs to show that virtue is up to us; he turns to this task in iii 5.

2. **§2 1109b33–5 This is also . . . corrective treatments:** This reference to legislators reflects the close relation between legislation (see LAW) and moral EDUCATION.

(b) §3. Initial account of involuntary action; it results from force or ignorance.

3. **§3 1109b35–1110a1 It seems . . . involuntary:** We begin with APPEARANCES, the two conditions that 'seem' to make action involuntary. Aristotle argues (§21–7) that these are two types of involuntary action, and that the conditions discussed in 1110a4–1111a2, 1111a24–b3 do not make an action involuntary.

1.§3–12. Clarification of the conditions for force.

(a) §3. Initial statement; forced action requires (i) an external principle, and (ii) no contribution by the agent.

4. **1110a2–3 or <rather> the victim:** Lit. 'the one affected', *ho paschôn*; see FEELING. If I break a window because the wind blows me into it, I am a passive victim rather than an agent.

[Or 'or the one having the feeling' (cf. 'feelings and actions', 1109b30).]

5. **1109a2 contributes nothing:** Do I contribute nothing if you force me to do something I already want to do? We might say (a) yes, since my wanting makes no difference to what actually happens; (b) no, since my wanting is a contribution, though it is not used in this case. Aristotle probably intends (b); cf. 1110b11–13, 18–24, 1111a32; *EE* 1224b8. 'Force' is not always used in the narrow sense defined here; cf. 1096a6, 1119a30–1.

(b) §4–5. Actions under duress sometimes seem forced, but sometimes do not.

6. **§4 1110a4–5 But what about actions . . . something fine:** In §4–12 Aristotle rejects two possible claims about these disputed actions: (1) They are forced, and hence involuntary. (2) They are not forced but they are involuntary, so that Aristotle's initial two conditions for involuntariness are not exhaustive. In §10 Aristotle answers (1). He answers (2) by arguing that these disputed actions are voluntary.

7. **1110a5–7 Suppose, for instance, a tyrant . . . will die:** Actions done under duress in response to such threats are 'against one's will', and so are offered as apparent cases of involuntary actions.

8. **§5 1110a8–9 However, the same . . . storms:** To show that actions responding to threats are not forced, Aristotle cites the abandoning of cargo in a storm. (See OCD, s.v. 'Maritime loans'.) Aristotle takes this to be a voluntary action, since we clearly have a choice about whether to do it, and a sensible person would choose to do it.

9. **1110a9–10 For no one . . . without qualification:** To do F willingly 'WITHOUT QUALIFICATION' is to find F itself desirable. Aristotle contrasts this with doing F willingly only in certain circumstances, such as those he describes. He marks the same contrast when he speaks of choosing to do F 'in itself', *kath'hauto* (a19, b3). Cf. 1151b2.

(c) §6. Actions under duress are mixed, since they have some voluntary and some involuntary aspects. But, taken as a whole, they are voluntary, since their principle is in the agent.

10. **§6 1110a11–12 These sorts . . . are mixed:** Aristotle treats actions under duress as a mixture of voluntary and involuntary. In an action such as abandoning cargo in a storm we can distinguish an involuntary element (abandoning the cargo) and a voluntary element (abandoning it in a storm to save one's life). One aspect of a mixed action is repugnant (not merely unwelcome) even though I recognize that I have to do it. The circumstances in which I choose it are extreme circumstances that I would prefer to avoid; whichever option I choose, I will be worse off than I was before I made the choice.

11. **1110a15–18 Now in fact . . . or not to do them:** Since the PRINCIPLE (i.e., the causal source) is in the agent, the actions are really voluntary and 'up to' the agent. The agent's state of mind is the principle of the action not only because it is its temporal origin, but also because it explains its character. If I am forced (in Aristotle's narrow sense) to strike you a hard blow, because someone else hits your nose with my

fist, the strength of the blow does not reflect my view that it would be best to strike you hard; but if I perform a mixed action, the character of my action reflects my view of what is best in these bad circumstances.

> (d) §7–9. These mixed actions are praised and blamed. Sometimes they are pardoned; but even then we recognize that duress does not always remove blame. This treatment of mixed actions presupposes that they are voluntary.

12. **§7 1110a23–6 But in some . . . would endure:** On overstraining, cf. 1115b8, 1116b16, 1121b26. 'Compel' translates *anankazein* (or 'necessitate'). Such compulsion must be distinguished from force (*bia*). Cf. 1180a4–5. I am not forced to do these mixed actions that I am compelled to do, because it is my choice that makes me do them; if I say 'I had no choice', I mean that there was no reasonable alternative, not that my choice made no difference or that I was psychologically incapable of refraining from making the choice I made.

13. **§8 1110a26–9 But presumably . . . appear ridiculous:** Aristotle counters a false inference that someone might make from his previous remark about pardon and overstraining. He insists that we cannot always accept the agent's claim 'I had no choice' or 'I couldn't avoid it'. Amphiaraus, the father of Alcmaeon, had been compelled against his will by his wife Eriphyle to join the expedition of the Seven against Thebes. Foreseeing his death in the expedition, he ordered Alcmaeon to kill Eriphyle, and threatened him with his curse if he failed to carry out the order. Alcmaeon's situation is, therefore, similar to that of Orestes (see Aeschylus' *Choephori*), who had to choose between killing his mother and disobeying his father. In Aristotle's view, even though Alcmaeon faced serious consequences if he failed to kill his mother, and even though those consequences would often justify the claim that he had no choice, they do not justify such a claim when the alternative is killing his mother.

Aristotle refers to Euripides' lost play the *Alcmaeon* (see TGF fr. 69). The quotation in 1136a13–14 suggests that it discussed Alcmaeon's plea of involuntariness.

> (e) §10. Mixed actions, therefore, are not forced, and they do not raise any difficulty for our account of force.

14. **§10 1110b5 These are involuntary . . . voluntary:** As §6 said, the principle of this particular action is the choice based on the belief that (for instance) it is better to refuse to kill this innocent person than to save ten other people by killing him. Since my belief and my choice explain this particular action, the action is voluntary.

> (f) §11–12. The pleasant and the fine do not force us, and therefore actions aiming at the pleasant or the fine are not involuntary.

15. **§11 1110b13–14 it is ridiculous . . . snared by such things:** This explains why Aristotle believes it is unreasonable to suppose we are forced by pleasant and fine things. It is up to us to choose whether to act on our judgment that something is pleasant or fine, and hence our beliefs and our choices are the principle of the action.

1.§13–19. Clarification of the type of ignorance that makes an action involuntary.

(a) §13. Actions done because of ignorance but without regret are non-voluntary, but not involuntary.

16. **§13 1110b19–22 For if someone's . . . no pain:** The distinction between the non-voluntary and the involuntary is irrelevant to whether the agent is responsible for the action. But it is relevant to his character. If he is pleased at something he has done because of ignorance, he shows what sorts of actions he is willing and prepared to do, and is rightly blamed or praised for his attitude to these actions. Cf. note to §3 above.

(b) §14–15. Actions done in ignorance but not because of ignorance are not involuntary.

17. **§15 1110b33 <This> ignorance . . . cause for blame:** The translation and supplements assume: (1) 'ignorance of what is beneficial', 'ignorance in the decision', and 'ignorance of the universal' all refer to the same thing; (2) this is the type of ignorance ascribed to the drunken and angry people described here. Aristotle is thinking of someone whose anger makes him think it is all right to shoot the offender (cf. 1149a25), not of someone whose anger makes him unaware of the fact that he is shooting, or that he is shooting this person.

In these cases the cause of the wrong action is the fault in the agent's character, not the agent's ignorance. Hence it is not action because of ignorance of the sort that removes us from blame (see further 1113b30 on ignorance of fact).

18. **1110b33–1111a1 which the action consists in and is concerned with:** [Or 'which the action depends on . . . '.] Lit. 'which the action is in and about' (cf. 1109a22).

(c) §16–19. Actions done because of ignorance of particulars are involuntary.

19. **§17 1111a11–12 Again, . . . as Merope did:** This alludes to Euripides' lost play *Cresphontes*. Cf. *Poet.* 1454a5.

20. **§18 1111a18 what he is . . . does it:** Read <*ho*> *kai hou heneka*. Here '*hou heneka*' probably refers to the actual, rather than the intended, result.

21. **§19 1111a19–21 Hence the agent . . . regret for his action:** This section ends the explanation of 'because of ignorance' that Aristotle began in §13.

1.§20–7. Definition of the voluntary.

(a) §20. Action done with knowledge of the particulars is voluntary.

22. **§20 1111a23–4 what has its principle . . . constitute the action:** The reference to an internal principle recalls §6, 10, and implies the absence of force. Though Aristotle has not described the nature of this principle fully, he implies that it includes an agent's desires and choices. The principle is in the agent only if he knows the particulars. Cf. 1135a23–31.

(b) §21–7. Reply to an alleged counterexample to the definition: to act on a non-rational desire is not to act involuntarily.

23. **§21 1111a24–5 For, presumably, . . . is involuntary:** An opponent argues that Aristotle has not given a sufficient condition for voluntary action, because we can act on an internal principle and with knowledge, but still involuntarily, if we act on a non-rational DESIRE.

Aristotle gives six arguments in reply: (1) 'For, first of all, . . . ; (2) Next, among . . . ; (3) And presumably . . . ; (4) Again, what is . . . ; (5) Moreover, how . . . ; and (6) Besides, non-rational . . . '.

24. **§22 1111a25–6 For, first . . . children:** In this reply Aristotle assumes that non-rational animals and children are voluntary agents.

25. **§24 1111a30 ought to desire:** Aristotle endorses the principle 'ought implies can'. On 'ought' (*dei*), see RIGHT.

2

2.1–17. *Voluntary action and decision*

(a) §1–2. Virtue requires not only voluntary action, but action on decision.

1. **§1 1111b5–6 for decision . . . actions do:** Non-rational desire is an internal principle that makes an action voluntary, but it is not enough for virtue (cf. 1107a1). Rational wish, deliberation, and decision are needed for someone to act on a correct conception of what makes virtuous action FINE and good in itself.

2. **§2 1111b9–10 and the actions we do on the spur of the moment . . . decision:** These actions need to be carefully distinguished from spontaneous actions that result from a decision; cf. 1117a17–22.

(b) §3–6. Decision is not appetite or spirit.

3. **§4 1111b13–14 Again, the incontinent . . . not on decision:** Decision requires (as we are about to learn) both wish for the end and deliberation about the means. An incontinent may act on deliberation (1142b18–20), but he does not act on a decision, because he acts on appetite, and not on a wish, i.e., a rational desire. Cf. 1111b19–20, 1113a11–12.

4. **§5 1111b16–18 Besides, the object of appetite . . . object of decision:** We consider pleasure and pain when we make a decision, but insofar as they contribute to good and bad.

(c) §7–9. It is not wish.

5. **§7 1111b19–20 But further . . . close to it:** Decision is not wish, for the three reasons given in §7, 8, 9. But it is based on a wish, not on the non-rational DESIRES, spirit and appetite (1113a11–12, a20, b3–5).

6. **1111b20–2 For we do not decide on impossible . . . a fool:** 'Anyone claiming . . . ' shows that Aristotle means that we do not decide to do what we *think* is impossible; cf. 'what is up to us', b30.

7. **1111b23–4 achievable through our own agency:** Lit. 'through us'. Agency, however, is clearly intended. If you force me to stand between you and someone firing shots at you, you are not protected 'through me' in the sense that concerns Aristotle here.

8. **1111b24 victory . . . athlete, for instance:** Prizes were awarded to the best actors in the Athenian dramatic festivals. Cf. 1166b35.

9. **§9 1111b26–7 Again, . . . means to the end:** See MEANS.

(d) §10–15. It is not belief.

10. **§10 1111b30–1 Nor is it belief:** §10–14 give five arguments for this claim.

11. **§13 Further, decision . . . believing truly:** Correctness of belief and desire: 1139a21–31.

12. **1112a7–8 Moreover, we decide . . . good:** I.e., we decide on something after inquiry and deliberation (see iii 3), and so we come as close as we can to knowing that the action we decide on is good.

[Or knowledge is a necessary condition for decision, but not for belief. Or knowledge does not exclude decision, but it excludes mere belief.]

(e) §16–17. Decision requires deliberation.

13. **§17 1112a16–17 and even the name . . . other things:** 'Before' might indicate (1) temporal priority—choosing before something else (i.e., action); or (2) preferential priority—choosing one action in preference to another. The previous remark on prior deliberation suggests that Aristotle has (a) in mind here. Cf. *EE* 1226a6–9; *MM* 1189a12–16.

3

3.§1–20. Deliberation and decision.

(a) §1–2. The scope of deliberation is confined to what a sensible person would deliberate about.

(b) §3–7 We deliberate only about things that are up to us.

1. **§6 1112a28–9 But we do not . . . best political system:** The transposition of this passage from its place in the mss. gives a better sequence of thought. This is an example of something that comes about through human effort but is not an appropriate object of deliberation for every group of human beings.

(c) §8–10. We deliberate only in cases that raise a question about what do to.

2. **§9 1112b6–7 about beliefs more than about sciences:** Read *peri tas doxas*. [OCT: 'about crafts'.]

(d) §11–16. We deliberate about means to ends, not about ends.

3. **§11 1112b11–12 We deliberate . . . to ends:** Aristotle has been saying what deliberation is not about; he now turns to a more positive description. On this

restriction to MEANS, see 1111b27; *Rhet.* 1355b10. To deliberate about action we must begin with some conception of an end, but the means to it may be constituents of it—actions that are FINE and good in themselves, and hence ends in themselves. This is how the PRUDENT person deliberates.

4. **1112b15 ways and means:** Lit. 'how and through what things it will be'.

5. **1112b17 most easily and most finely:** Considerations of efficiency are not the only ones that matter. The virtuous and PRUDENT person aims at what is FINE. Cf. 1140a24–8.

6. **§11–12 1112b20–4 For a deliberator . . . comes into being:** The geometer considers how to construct a complex figure by analysing it into simpler figures, until he finds the first one that he should draw.

7. **§13 1112b26–7 but if the action . . . undertake it:** The decision is the last mental event preceding the action; once we find that an action is possible, we undertake it (lit. 'put their hand to acting'). Hence the beliefs and desires described in 1147a25–31 should be part of the deliberation.

(e) §17–20. Decision results from wish and decision, and hence it is also about what promotes an end.

8. **§18 1113a7–9 This is also . . . to the people:** This Homeric reference (cf. *Il.* ii 48–141; *Od.* xxiv 412–71) implies that the deciding part of an agent is also the guiding (or 'leading') part—the one that guides our actions. Once the Homeric king decided, the people normally endorsed it without further debate. (They did not always endorse it, just as we do not always act on our decisions.)

9. **§19 1113a12 we desire . . . wish:** Read *boulêsin.* Cf. 1113b3–5. Decision requires wish, as opposed to non-rational DESIRE.

4

4.§1–6. Wish: rational desire for the end.

(a) *§1–3. According to one view, wish is for the good; according to another view, it is for the apparent good.*

1. **§2 1113a17 object of wish:** This tries to capture the broad range of *boulêton,* which might refer to what can be wished, to what is wished, or to the proper object of wish. (See CHOICEWORTHY.) Aristotle tries to clarify the different uses of *boulêton* in this chapter.

2. **§3 1113a20–2 But for those who say . . . appear good to different people:** The exact point of §2–3 is obscured by the obscurity in 'object of wish'. Two points might be relevant here. (1) When I wish for health (for instance), I wish for it 'as good', i.e., I want it because I believe it is good, not because I believe it appears good. (2) The proper object of wish—i.e., the suitable object for the well-informed person—is the good, but each person thinks that what appears good to him is the proper object of wish. Similarly what is known by nature (1095b3) is what the fully informed person thinks he knows. Probably Aristotle's main point here is (2). Cf. 1155b21–7; *EE* 1235b25–9.

(b) §4–6. Solution: the good person is the appropriate measure of the proper object of wish.

3. **§4 1113a28–9 Similarly in the case of . . . hot, heavy and so on:** In 'healthy to . . .' the Greek dative is translated by 'to', though it was previously translated 'for'. It is not clear whether Aristotle means (i) broccoli is really healthy for healthy people, and antibiotics are really unhealthy for them, but antibiotics are really healthy for sick people and broccoli is really unhealthy for them; or (ii) healthy people judge correctly that broccoli is healthy for them, but sick people judge incorrectly that drinking a lot is healthy for them, though in fact it is not. Probably Aristotle means (ii). Cf. 1173b205, 1176a15–22.

4. **§5 1113a31–3 Presumably, . . . standard and measure:** The excellent person as standard; 1166a12, 1170a21, 1176a15–16. Aristotle replies to PRO-TAGORAS' principle, Plato, *Tht.* 152a (cf. 1094b15). We might take his reply in two ways: (a) Ontological: the good person's approval constitutes something as good, and it is not good independently of being chosen. (b) Epistemological: things are good independently of being chosen, and the good person is the one who can be relied on to approve of the things that are genuinely good. The end of §4 suggests (b).

5

5. §1–20. Virtue and vice are in our power.

(a) *§1–6.* The actions that proceed from virtue and vice are in our power.

1. **§1 1113b3 We have found:** Read *ontos de.*

2. **1113b5–6 The activities of the virtues . . . the end>:** These activities are probably those that result from having a virtue; they are not simply the brave actions (e.g.) that a non-brave person might also do (cf. 1105a28–b9). Aristotle turns to one major task of his discussion of voluntary action—to show that being virtuous is up to us, something that we can determine by our own voluntary action and decision. He argues first that since 'the activities of the virtues' are up to us, being virtuous is also up to us.

3. **§3 1113b111–4 But if doing, . . . decent or base is up to us:** Aristotle argues: (1) It is up to us to do fine or shameful actions. (2) Doing fine or shameful actions = being virtuous or vicious. (3) Hence it is up to us to be virtuous or vicious.

(2) is true only if 'doing fine or shameful actions' refers to doing them for the virtuous person's reasons (as in 'the activities of the virtues' above). To show that this is up to us, Aristotle needs to show that the mental states—wish and decision—that make us act for the virtuous person's reasons are up to us. He tries to show this in 1113b21–1114a3.

4. **§4 1113b14–15 'no one . . . unwillingly blessed':** Quoted from Epicharmus (fifth-century comic poet): DK 23 B 7.

5. **§6 1113b19–20 and we cannot refer . . . up to us:** In b20 read *tas eph'hêmin.* The previous sentence shows that Aristotle takes 'we are the principles of our actions'

and 'the principles of our actions are in us' to be equivalent. Here, as in 1110a17–18, b4, Aristotle takes x's having its principle in me to imply that x is up to me and that I do x voluntarily.

What does he mean by saying that we cannot find principles apart from those up to us? We might take him to deny determinism (the doctrine that every event has sufficient causal conditions in some previous event); for if my internal principle itself had some cause, would this not provide a principle apart from the principle in me? We need not accept this indeterminist interpretation, however. If Aristotle takes a principle to be explanatory as well as causal, he may mean that only my internal principle really explains the character of my action; if my internal principle itself has some cause determining it, that determining cause does not explain the character of my action. If this is Aristotle's position, his claim about internal principles does not commit him to indeterminism. (See Intro. §10.)

(b) §7–9. Our practices of reward and punishment presuppose that virtue and vice are in our power.

6. **§7 1113b24–5 caused by ignorance . . . not responsible for:** On 'responsible', see CAUSE. In 1114a1 below, 'caused by' translates *dia*.

7. **§8 1113b30–1 Indeed, legislators . . . responsible for the ignorance:** Aristotle supplements, but does not reject, the treatment of ignorance of fact at 1110b18–1111a2. We are responsible not for the action caused by ignorance, but for the ignorance that caused the action.

8. **1130b31–3 A drunk, . . . causes his ignorance:** This law was apparently not common in Greek states, but (according to *Pol.* 1274b18–23) peculiar to Pittacus (c. 650–570 BC, ruler of Mytilene; cf. 1157a32). It might be taken to suggest that the drunk person is responsible both for being drunk and for what he does when he is drunk (since he is punished for both). Aristotle need not endorse this view; the double punishment might be taken as a warning to avoid getting drunk (as the comment in the *Politics* suggests).

(c) §10–16. Virtue and vice, no less than health and sickness, are in our power.

9. **§10 1114a3–4 But presumably . . . inattentive:** Aristotle has argued that legal practices show we are held responsible for our mental state. An objector now argues: 'These legal practices are unjustified. For (a) our mental states are simply the effects of the characters we have, and hence (b) we are not responsible for them.' Aristotle accepts (a), but denies that (b) follows from (a).

10. **1114a4–7 Still, he is himself . . . corresponding sort of person:** Here Aristotle replies to the objector as follows: (1) We were in control of forming our characters. (2) Hence we are responsible for the characters we have. (3) Hence we are responsible for the mental states formed by these characters. If he believes (1), Aristotle must assume that childhood training does not form our character to an extent that puts it beyond our control.

11. §13 1114a12–13 **<Hence> if . . . willingly unjust:** In the mss. (and OCT) this sentence follows 'not to wish to be intemperate' in §13. The transposition gives a clearer sequence of thought. In this sentence Aristotle argues that it is reasonable to hold people (other than the totally insensible) responsible for their bad character, since they form it knowingly.

12. **1114a11–12 Further, it is unreasonable . . . wish to be intemperate:** Aristotle answers the objection that people who do injustice do not always wish (*boulesthai*) to be unjust, and therefore (the objector assumes) are not responsible for being unjust or for doing injustice. Aristotle answers that their attitude is unreasonable, and no excuse for their behaviour.

[Or 'Moreover it is unreasonable <to expect> someone doing injustice not to wish to be unjust . . .' (which would imply, implausibly, that everyone who does injustice wishes to be unjust).]

13. §14 1114a13–14 **This does not . . . will be just:** According to the analysis of wish in iii 2, my wishing I were healthier or less lazy does not ensure that I seriously intend to do anything about it. Similarly, merely wishing I were just does not ensure that I will become just. Aristotle does not say that an unjust person cannot form a serious intention and decision to become just, or that such an intention and decision is never effective. Hence he does not say, in this passage, that (iii) there is no hope for a vicious person.

14. **1114a15–16 And if, . . . doctors:** MEDICINE serves as an example of people's readiness to shift responsibility from themselves; cf. 1105b14–16.

15. **1114a19 the principle was up to him:** In a19 read *hê gar archê ep' autô(i)*.

16. **1114a20–1 though once . . . have it <now>:** If I have thrown a stone and broken a window, I cannot now make it true that I have not thrown the stone or that I have not broken the window, but I can retrieve the stone and I can repair the window. Similarly, if I have become vicious, I cannot make this not have happened; hence, I must reckon with the fact that I have become vicious, if I am considering how to improve. The effects of vice do not necessarily make the vicious person's condition hopeless. (Cf. 1150a21–2.)

[Or the vicious person cannot improve his condition once he has become vicious. This claim is not justified by the analogy with the stone.]

(d) §17. Our conception of the end is up to us.

17. **§17 1114a31–b1 But someone may say . . . the end appears to him:** Aristotle considers this argument: (i) The character we form depends on our appearance of the good. (ii) But our appearance of the good depends on the character we already have. (iii) Hence we are not in control of the appearance. (iv) Hence we are not in control of the character we form. (v) Hence we are not responsible for the formation of our characters. Aristotle denies that (iii) follows from (ii).

18. **1114b1–3 <We reply . . . how <the end> appears:** This is the first reply to the argument just presented. Aristotle insists that the character forming our appearances is itself malleable and hence the appearance is in our control. In 'if each person . . .', Aristotle accepts the antecedent of the conditional.

(e) §17. If we are not responsible for acting badly, vice and virtue are equally beyond our control.

19. **1114b3 Suppose, on the other hand, that no one:** Read *ei de mêdeis* (OCT: 'Otherwise, no one…'). Aristotle's second reply to the opponent's argument in §17 points out the unacceptable consequences of denying responsibility for evildoing altogether.

20. **1114b9–12 for <according . . . good nature:** This all explains the previous claim that someone who has this sense has a *good* nature. 'Given that . . .' explains the claim that this gift is greatest and finest. In b9 read *ei par.*

21. **1114b12–13 If all . . . than vice:** If no one is responsible for acting badly, all actions, good or bad, are the inevitable results of natural conditions that are beyond our control.

(f) §18–20. If the end or the means are in our control, virtue and vice are in our control.

22. **§19 1114b16–17 Let us . . . depends on him:** Aristotle repeats the first reply he offered in §17. Since our conception of the end depends on us, so does our character.

23. **1114b17–18 Alternatively, . . . other things voluntarily:** Even if we are not responsible for the appearance of the end (i.e., if Aristotle's first reply is rejected), we still need not embrace the position whose consequences are expounded at the end of §17. Even if the virtuous and the vicious person share the same conception of the end, for which neither is responsible, they differ in their conception of 'the other things', i.e., presumably, the means to the end. Given the wide scope of MEANS, differences about these make the difference between virtue and vice. Aristotle assumes that the 'fixed' conception of the end will be rather schematic (with its specific content to be filled in by deliberation), and not as determinate as it is taken to be at the end of §17.

24. **1114b20–1 for the bad . . . the end <appears>:** Lit. 'for similarly to the bad person also belongs the because of (*dia*) himself in the actions, even if not in the end'.

25. **§20 1114b21–4 Now the virtues, . . . end we lay down:** Lit. 'If, then, the virtues . . .'. Aristotle reasserts his first reply (in b1–3). In saying that we are jointly responsible, Aristotle acknowledges that we are not the sole causes of our states since nature and upbringing contribute also. Cf. vii 5, 1149b27–1150a8.

5. *§21–3. Summary of the account of virtue of character.*

26. **§21 1114b26–30 We have now discussed . . . prescribes:** This passage summarizes the whole of ii 1–iii 5, showing again that iii 1–5 is part of the discussion of virtue of character in general.

27. **§22 1114b30–1115a3 But actions and states . . . states are voluntary:** If §22 is in the right place, it is a parenthetical comment that interrupts the connexion between §21 and §23. It returns to questions that were discussed in §10–13.

28. **§23 1115a4–5 Let us now . . . how many of them there are:** In iii 1–5 Aristotle concluded his general account of virtue, begun in i 13. He now begins his discussion of the individual virtues.

6

6. §1–6. The scope of bravery.

1. **§1 1115a6–7 First let us . . . fear and confidence:** BRAVERY and temperance are the first two virtues to be discussed because they are the two primary virtues concerned with FEELINGS (1117a24). See Plato, *La.*, *Ch.*, *Rep.* iv, *St.* 306e–end. The structure of bravery is more complex than that of some virtues (for generosity cf. 1121a16, b17), since it involves the correct training of two feelings, not (as with temperance) of just one. Someone could train himself not to be excessively afraid, and still have no positive confidence or enthusiasm for facing dangers in a good cause. Since confidence also affects someone's readiness to face danger, it must also be trained if someone is to acquire the right attitude towards danger.

2. **§2 1115a8 frightening:** Or 'fearful' (*phoberon*). This term covers actual, possible, and appropriate objects of fear. Cf. iii 4 on *boulêton*, and CHOICEWORTHY.

3. **1115a9 hence people define . . . bad:** See Plato, *Pr.* 358d.

(a) §3–5. Bravery is not about every sort of fear and danger.

4. **§4 1115a20–2 for some people . . . losing money:** In saying that cowards can be generous, Aristotle seems to challenge his belief in the inseparability of the virtues; see 1144b32, VIRTUE.

5. **§5 1115a22 on children or women:** Read *gunaikas* (OCT: 'is afraid of one's wife or children suffering wanton aggression').

(b) §6–12. Bravery is concerned with the fear of death, and primarily with the fear of death in war.

6. **§8 1115a29–31 Surely in the finest . . . finest danger:** In his historical circumstances, in which citizens were regularly required to fight in defence of their city, Aristotle regards death in war as the FINEST way to die. The reason he gives is that here (as opposed to death in a shipwreck) someone has a chance to display his abilities in action; he does not just keep a stiff upper lip. Aristotle also assumes that the conditions are fine, because it is fine to defend one's city and its common good. Contrast the attitude of mercenaries, 1116b5.

Shipwrecks were not unusual in the Greek and Roman world. St Paul was shipwrecked three times; see 2 Corinthians 11:25. Cf. Aulus Gellius, *Noctes Atticae* xix 1 (even Stoics go pale in storms at sea).

7

7. §1–13. Bravery and the corresponding vices.

(a) *§1. The brave person is not completely free of fear.*

1. **§1 1115b8 too frightening for a human being to resist:** Lit. 'beyond a human being'. They involve 'overstraining'; see 1110a25, 1116b16.

(b) §2–5. But he faces dangers with the appropriate confidence on the right occasions.

2. **§2 1115b10–13 The brave person . . . aimed at by virtue:** The brave person is not expected to be fearless; he will not fear the danger less than it warrants. Nor does he force himself to act despite a strong desire to run away (this would make him analogous to the continent person; see INCONTINENT). The appropriate degree of fear does not overcome or paralyse him.

(c) §6. He aims at the fine.

3. **§6 1115b21–2 Now to the brave person . . . by its end:** The brave person's judgment is correct, given the principle in 1113a29, 1166a12, 1176a15. If a virtue is FINE, the end that defines it (actions in accord with its state of character) is also fine.

(d) §7–9. The vice of excessive confidence and deficient fear: fearlessness.

4. **§7 1115b24–6 Among those who go . . . have no names:** See 1107a34, VIRTUE.

5. **1115b26–8 He would be . . . about the Celts:** See OCD, s.v. 'Celts'. In Aristotle's time they lived north of the Mediterranean, from Galicia (Ukraine) to Galatia (southern Turkey). In 390 they sacked Rome. For this story about them, cf. Strabo, *Geography* vii 2. For this view about the northern peoples, cf. *Pol.* 1327b23–7; Plato, *Rep.* 435e.

6. **§8 1115b29–30 The rash person . . . pretender to bravery:** On boasters, see 1127a20.

7. **§12 1116a7–9 Moreover, rash . . . until then:** This passage may be out of place. It would fit better after §9.

(e) §10–12. The vice of excessive fear and deficient confidence: cowardice.

(f) §13. The brave person's concern with the fine is a crucial differentiating feature.

8. **§13 1116a14 For shirking burdens is softness . . . is fine:** Softness (*malakia*): 1145a35, 1150b1.

8

8. §1–17. Other conditions are sometimes called bravery, but must be distinguished from genuine bravery.

1. **§1 1116a15–17 Bravery, then, . . . also called bravery:** Aristotle has explained that bravery demands both the proper training of the feelings and the right motive ('for the sake of the fine'). He explains the APPEARANCES (ETHICS #7): some commonly accepted types of bravery are not genuine bravery.

(a) §1–5. The bravery of citizens.

2. **§2 1116a21–6 That is how Homer '. . . fled from me':** Homer, *Il.* xxii 100 (Hector on Polydamas); viii 148–9 (Diomede on Hector).

3. **§3 1116a27–9 for it is caused . . . honour:** On SHAME, see also iv 9. These citizen soldiers aim at honour, which is FINE. But they do not aim at the fine, as the virtuous person does. If they aimed at the fine, they would recognize that the action itself is fine whether or not it receives honour. On the inadequacy of HONOUR, see 1095b23, 1159a22.

4. **§4 1116a33–5 as Hector '. . . dogs':** Aristotle inaccurately recalls Homer, *Il.* xv 348–51, combining it with ii.391–3.

5. **§5 1116a36–b2 Commanders who strike . . . compel them:** 'Strike . . .' may refer to the use of whips by Persian commanders at Thermopylae (Herodotus vii 223); Greeks often thought of barbarians as lacking true bravery. The second example, however, may refer to the tactics of Spartan commanders (Anon., *in EN* = CAG xx 165.1–3). Since Spartans were regarded by many (though not by Plato and Aristotle) as models of bravery, the suggestion that, in this instance, they are no better than barbarians might surprise Aristotle's readers.

(b) §6–9. Experience and expertise.

6. **§6 1116b3–5 Experience about . . . bravery is scientific knowledge:** Aristotle mentions the fact about experience as an explanation of SOCRATES' mistaken conception of bravery. He does not accuse Socrates of identifying bravery with experience. See Plato, *La.* 192e–196d; *Pr.* 349e–351b.

7. **1116b6–7 In wartime <professional> soldiers . . . familiar with these:** These are mercenaries. These are not paid volunteers defending their own city for pay, but foreigners hired by a city, and with no further attachment or loyalty to it. Cf. Machiavelli, *Prince*, ch. 12.

8. **§9 1116b15–16 <Professional . . . danger overstrains them:** Overstraining: 1115b8, 1110a25.

9. **1116b17–19 For they are the first . . . temple of Hermes:** At Coronea in Boeotia, in 353 the mercenaries deserted the Coronean citizens.

(c) §10–12. How spirited people differ from brave people.

10. **§10 1116b23–6 Spirit is also . . . full of spirit:** On spirit (*thumos*), see DESIRE. *Thumos* is the source of spirited, self-assertive, and impulsive feelings and actions. Cf. 1111b18, 1149a25.

11. **1116b27–9 hence Homer's '. . . blood boiled':** See Homer, *Il.* xi 11, xiv 151, xvi 529, v 470, xv 232, 594; *Od.* xxiv 318–9. The last phrase is not Homeric, but may belong to a lost epic (cf. [Theocritus] xx 15).

12. **§11 1116b35–1117a1 hungry asses . . . beaten:** Homer, *Il.* xi 558–62. The following remark on adulterers suggests that Aristotle would not count Mozart's Don Giovanni as brave, even though he faces dangers in his pursuit of women.

13. **1117a4–5 The <bravery> . . . the goal:** This sentence goes better at the end of §12. The natural basis of a virtue is contrasted with the complete virtue in vi 13. §1–2. Cf. *EE* 1234a28–30.

(d) §13–15. How hopeful people differ from brave people.

14. **§15 1117a17–20 Indeed, that is . . . less from preparation:** Aristotle assumes that 'emergencies' (lit. 'sudden things', or 'things done on the spur of the moment'; cf. 1111b9–10) are matters for decision. Someone's decision to meet danger forms his STATE of character, so that when a danger arises suddenly he does not need still further deliberation to cause him to act.

15. **1117a20–2 For if . . . <we must decide> in accord with our state of character:** The virtuous person's action sometimes results from his decision even if deliberation and decision do not immediately precede it; see 1142b2, 1144b26, 1150b19, DECISION #4.

(e) §16–17. Why ignorance may be mistaken for bravery.

16. **§16 1117a26–7 That was what happened . . . Sicyonians:** The Spartans were wearing shields taken from their fleeing Sicyonian allies. When the Argives (together with the mercenaries fighting on their side) realized they were dealing with the more formidable Spartans, they ran (Xenophon, *Hellenica* iv 4.10, dated 392).

9

9.§1–7. Since the brave person values life, brave action involves pain and loss, though it also involves the pleasure proper to the virtue.

1. **§4 1117b7–9 And so, if the same . . . failure is shameful:** Aristotle does not mean that the end pursued in bravery really is small, or that the brave person does not take pleasure in it. He means that the end is surrounded by evils that the brave person regrets, and that might lead someone who is not a brave person to overlook the pleasure to be found in brave action. Pleasure and virtue: 1104b3–8, 1121a1–4.

2. **§6 1117b17–18 But presumably . . . soldiers:** This section continues the argument of §4. Soldiers: 1116b6. The brave person is not wholly unafraid, but he is not paralysed by fear if he sees that it is fine to face dangers, because some worthwhile cause is at stake. Cf. 1124b6.

10

10.§1–11. The pleasures that are relevant to temperance.

1. **§1 1117b23–4 for bravery . . . non-rational parts:** A reader of *Republic* iv might take this view.

(a) §2. Non-bodily pleasures are not relevant.

(b) §3–7. Not all the pleasures of the senses are relevant.

2. **§5 1118a9–10 Nor is this . . . except coincidentally:** See *EE* 1231a6.

3. **§5 1118a12–13 perfumes . . . his appetite:** The intemperate person finds the smell of some perfumes pleasant if he associates them with sexual pleasure. Similarly, the smell of roasting meat is pleasant for him if he associates it with eating. In contrast to the previous cases, he would not necessarily find these smells pleasant apart from their associations.

4. §6 1118a13–15 **And we can see . . . if they are hungry:** The intemperate person enjoys these things even if he is not hungry.

5. §7 1118a22–3 **'a deer . . . goat':** Homer, *Il.* iii 24.

(c) §8–11. Only the pleasures of taste and touch—especially those of touch—are relevant.

6. §8 1118a23–5 **The pleasures . . . and bestial:** These desires develop in relative independence of those he excludes from temperance. We have them as part of the nature we share with other animals (1118b1), apart from our particular social environment or our individual choices and rational preferences. Since there is no common explanation of overindulgence of desires as a whole, overindulgence is not a single vice. Different forms of overindulgence associated with different desires need separate training; a reduction in someone's desire to listen to music will not necessarily reduce his excessive liking for whiskey. Cf. vii 4, 1151a29–b3.

7. 1118a26 **These pleasures are touch and taste:** Aristotle identifies pleasure with the activity enjoyed (as when we say, 'Listening to music is one of my chief pleasures in life'). Pleasure and its object: 1153a2–7, 1175b32–6.

8. §10 1118a32–b1 **That is why a glutton . . . touching:** Philoxenus (*EE* 1231a17; *[Probl.]* 950a3; cf. Aristophanes, *Frogs* 934).

11

11.§1–8. The extreme states and the mean.

(a) §1–2. Common v. distinctive appetites.

1. §1 1118b10–11 **as Homer says, . . . for sex:** Homer, *Il.* xxiv 130–1.

(b) §3–5. Errors in relation to different appetites.

2. §3 1118b19–20 **That is why . . . what is right:** The word rendered 'gluttons' might also be rendered 'ravenous about their bellies'.

(c) §6. The excess: intemperance.

(d) §7. The deficiency; insensibility.

(e) §8. Temperance is the mean state in relation to these appetites and pleasures.

3. §8 1119a12–15 **For he finds . . . of that sort:** Cf. 1115b12. The temperate person does not have to restrain or overcome intense, wayward appetites; that is what the CONTINENT person does. His appetites agree with his rational decision about the right extent of indulgence; see 1102b27, 1152a1.

12

12.§1–10. Two further notes on intemperance.

(a) §1–4. Intemperance compared with cowardice; aspects of voluntariness and involuntariness in each of these vices.

1. **§1 1119a21–3 Intemperance is more . . . to be avoided:** The different degrees of resemblance to involuntary actions and conditions depend on the extent of pleasure and pain (cf. 1110b11, 1111a32). Cowardice seems more voluntary than cowardly actions because it is less painful; cowardice is a source of pain in particular circumstances. Intemperance, however, is a source of pleasure in particular circumstances, so that particular intemperate actions seem more voluntary than the state of being intemperate.

2. **§3 1119a30–1 That is why . . . seem to be forced . . . involuntary>:** Here 'seem' reports a common belief that conflicts with Aristotle's account of force in 1110a1–2.

(b) §5–9. Different, but related, uses of 'intemperance'.

3. **§5 1119a33–b1 We also apply the name . . . some similarity:** Aristotle appeals to the relation between 'intemperate' (or 'unrestrained', *akolastos*) and 'temper' (or 'check', *kolazein*; see CORRECTIVE TREATMENT and TEMPERANCE) to make his point about CHILDREN.

4. **§8 1119b13–15 And just as the child's . . . follow reason:** The 'guide' (*paidagôgos*) was the slave who took a child to school and elsewhere. Cf. 1121b11, St Paul, Galatians 3:24.

Book IV

1

1.§1–11. The scope of generosity.

(a) §1–2. It is concerned with wealth.

1. **§1 1119b25–6 but in the giving and taking . . . giving:** 'Take' and 'acquire' translate *lambanein* and cognates.

(b) §3–5. The vices opposed to generosity involve the misuse of wealth.

2. **§4 1119b32–4 That is why . . . not properly called wasteful:** As often (cf. 1118a23–6), Aristotle wants to distinguish virtues and vices more sharply than they are commonly distinguished; see VIRTUE #7.

(c) §6–11. Generosity involves the correct use of wealth, especially in giving rather than in taking.

3. **§6 1120a4–8 Whatever has a use . . . generous person:** Generosity is the first of the virtues concerned with external goods (cf. v 1.§9). These goods must be used

well if they are to benefit the person who has them; and the different virtues dealing with external goods are the states of character that use them well. The generous person is the one who takes and gives money correctly. Aristotle does not say much about where he takes it from and to whom he gives it; but cf. 1120a5, b3; 1121b5; 1122a10. The answer will come partly from the requirements of justice (1120a20), but even more from the requirements of friendship (cf. ix 2). The FINE goal pursued by the generous person will reflect his desire to benefit friends and fellow-citizens. He is not indiscriminately open-handed or charitable.

4. §7 **1120a9–11 That is why . . . wrong sources:** The next paragraph (§7–11) gives reasons: (1) 'For it is more proper . . . not to (§8) do shameful ones.' (2) 'Moreover, thanks go . . . <to the giver>.' (3) §9 'Besides, not taking . . . is another's.' (4) §10 'Further, . . . praised at all.' (5) §11 'Besides, generous . . . their giving.'

5. **1120a11–13 For it is more proper . . . shameful ones:** Aristotle does not explain here why a virtue has this active aspect. But see ix 7. The connexion that he assumes between RIGHT action (in the previous sentence) and FINE action in this one suggests that we achieve the MEAN (and hence what is right) by finding actions that are fine (and hence promote a common good). Cf. 1122b6–7.

1.§12–23. The outlook of the generous person.

(a) §12–14. In his giving he aims at the fine, and takes pleasure in the action.

6. **§12 1120a25 give correctly:** Probably this is meant to support the claim that the generous person's actions are FINE.

[Or we might put a full stop before this phrase, and translate 'He will also give . . . ', marking a further feature in addition to doing fine actions for the sake of the fine.]

7. **§13 1120a26 Moreover . . . with pleasure:** Cf. 1104b3–8, 1117b7–9, 1121a1–4.

(b) §15–17. His attitude to acquisition is neither grasping nor wasteful.

8. **§16 1120a33–4 since he . . . not for him:** Cf. 1124b9–12.

(c) §18–20. He is unstinting in his giving.

9. **§19 1120b9–11 Hence one . . . less to give:** The widow giving her mite is more generous than rich people whose large gifts are not costly to them (Luke 21:1–4).

10. **§20 1120b11–14 Those who have not acquired . . . poets do:** Cf. Plato, *Rep.* 330bc; 1161b18, 1167b34.

(d) §20–3. He is neither anxious to be wealthy nor indiscriminate in his giving.

(e) §24–8. He achieves the mean in the appropriate pleasures and pains.

11. **§25 1121a1–4 If the generous . . . right way:** Probably Aristotle is not thinking of lapses by the generous person, in which he knowingly refuses to give to a worthy

cause. He refers to cases in which the generous person's reasonable and praiseworthy giving has an inappropriate result (if, for instance, he gives money to someone who—contrary to reasonable expectation—misuses it). External success in virtuous actions that reach their intended result is part of HAPPINESS.

12. **§27 1121a5–7 and is more grieved . . . Simonides:** This seems to refer not to any surviving poem of Simonides, but to the poet's reputation for avarice. Cf. *Rhet.* 1391a6–12, 1405b23–8.

1.§29–36.*Wastefulness: the vice of excess.*

(a) §30–2.Wastefulness without ungenerosity.

13. **§31 1121a19–21 However, such . . . the intermediate condition:** One extreme is 'more contrary' to the mean than the other, for the two reasons given in ii 8. This wasteful person has the desirable trait and motive, which need not be cultivated further to produce generosity, while the ungenerous person does not have it at all. Hence (a25) Aristotle notes that this wasteful person does not even seem to be base. This view rests on the degree of benefit or harm done to other people by the vices; see 1121a29, 1123a32.

14. **§32 1121a29–30 the ungenerous . . . even himself:** Aristotle assumes that virtue benefits other people. See v 1 on general justice; FINE.

(b) §33–6.Wastefulness combined with ungenerosity.

15. **§33 1121a30–2 Most wasteful people, . . . are ungenerous:** Someone who is prone to intemperance is also prone to wastefulness and susceptible to flatterers (1127a7). Though Aristotle wanted to distinguish wastefulness from intemperance and from vice in general (1119b31), he also marks connexions between different vices.

16. **§34 1121b2 for they have an urge to give:** 'Urge' translates *epithumia*, usually rendered 'appetite' (see DESIRE). Aristotle implies that it is an irrational and indiscriminate desire.

17. **§36 1121b10–11 If, then, the wasteful . . . changes into this:** On being 'without a guide' (*apaidagôgêtos*), cf. 1119b13–15.

1.§37–45. *Ungenerosity: the vice of deficiency.*

18. **§37 1121b12–13 Ungenerosity, . . . incurable:** Is VICE incurable? Cf. 1114a20–1, 1150a22.

19. **1121b13–14 since old age . . . ungenerous:** On the effects of old age, see YOUTH.

(a) §39. Ungenerosity in giving too little.

20. **§39 1121b21–2 For the people . . . skinflints:** Contemporary Greek seems to have had many terms for ungenerous people. Cf. *EE* 1233a12; *MM*1192a8–10.

21. **1121b25–6 For some . . . anything shameful:** This sort of compulsion is present in some voluntary action: 1110a32–b1.

22. **1121b28–9 Others keep their hands . . . afraid:** On this sort of fear cf. 1115a20. Virtue requires some confidence in one's own ability and in FORTUNE (1178a28). This sort of confidence belongs to magnanimity.

23. **1121b30 hence, they say, they are content:** Read *areskein*.

(b) §40–3. Ungenerosity in taking too much, or taking from the wrong sources.

24. **§40 1121b32–3 those, . . . degrading occupations:** 'Degrading' renders *aneleutheron*, also translated by 'ungenerous'; see GENEROUS.

25. **§43 1122a7–8 the gambler and the robber:** Delete *kai ho lêstês*.

(c) §44. Ungenerosity is worse than wastefulness.

2

2.§1–10. Magnificence compared to generosity.

(a) §1–3. Magnificence must be on a large scale.

1. **§2 1122a24–5 But large scale . . . not the same:** These tasks face someone who has to provide for the expenses of the warship or delegation. In Athens *leitourgiai*, 'public services' (1163a29, 1167b12; see OCD, s.v. 'liturgy, Greek') were imposed on wealthy citizens at their own expense (cf. 1122b22, three services). A public-spirited citizen would be keen to overfulfil his task in a way that would benefit the community (e.g., he might fit out a warship to sail and fight better than the average), and this would be a legitimate source of honour. For someone else, overfulfilment in a pointlessly extravagant way would be an opportunity to display his wealth; he might decorate his ship expensively without making it a better warship (1123a19–27).

2. **§3 1122a27 'gave . . . wanderer':** Homer, *Od.* xvii 420.

3. **1122a28–9 for the . . . does not imply magnificence:** Why is generosity different from magnificence? It is not simply because not some generous people are not wealthy enough for large benefactions. If a generous person came into money, his generous desires would not be enough to make him magnificent; for without further practice and habituation he would lack the judgment and tact that are needed for suitable large benefactions. On the connexions between the virtues, see 1144b32–1145a2.

(b) §4. The vices of deficiency and excess.

4. **§4 1122a32–3 not because . . . and in the wrong way:** Aristotle does not intend the doctrine of the mean to refer to some quantitative measure. In this case it is the fact that the intended objects are inappropriate that makes the excess and the deficiency vicious.

(c) §5–9. Magnificence achieves the mean and aims at the fine.

5. **§6 1122b2 now . . . expenditures:** Read *hai de*.

6. **§7 1122b6–7 In this . . . feature of the virtues:** Because of this connexion between virtuous action and the FINE (see 1120a11–13), fine action is necessary for reaching the MEAN proper to the virtues.

(d) §10. Magnificence requires generosity.

7. **§10 1122b14–17 For a possession . . . admirable to behold:** 'Result' translates *ergon* (see FUNCTION). 'Excellence' translates *aretê*, usually translated 'virtue'. The magnificent person has the judgment that produces FINE results on a grand scale.

8. **1122b18 and the excellence . . . large scale:** In b18 delete *megaloprepeia*.

2.*§11–20. The proper sphere of magnificence: honourable expenditure.*

(a) §11–15. The primary sphere: public expenditure.

9. **§11 1122b21–2 provoke . . . common <good>:** These expenses that 'provoke a good competition for honour' (*euphilotimêta*) give a proper focus for one's pursuit of HONOUR. Aristotle recognizes that this is a reasonable motive when it has the right object; cf. 1169a8. On *philotimia*, 'love of honour', see iv 4.

(b) §15–20. The secondary sphere: private expenditure.

10. **§16 1123a7 adornment:** Cf. 1100b26, 1124a1.

11. **§17 1123a11–13 the most magnificent . . . particular kind of object:** Retain the mss. text in a12.

12. **§18 1123a16 paltry:** *Aneleutheron*, usually rendered 'ungenerous'.

2.*§20–2. The vices opposed to magnificence.*

(a) §20. Vulgarity.

13. **§20 1123a22 He gives his club . . . wedding banquet:** This is a private dining club in which each member takes his turn in providing dinner for the club. Lavish spending by one member might provoke a pointless competition among the richer members, and would embarrass the poorer members who could not keep up with the Joneses' dinner parties.

14. **1123a23–4 and when he supplies . . . Megara:** In the ancient world purple was an expensive dye. To pay for purple costumes for a chorus would be a pointless display (like bringing them on in mink coats) that would not improve the choral performance.

15. **1123a26–7 Where a large . . . small expense is right:** Sometimes a large expense may be appropriate but inconspicuous, and here the vulgar person will stint. A warship might look seaworthy, but be unsafe if it meets bad weather. A vulgar person will gamble on the chance of good weather (since people will not notice how much he has spent if they simply look at the outside of the ship), whereas the magnificent person will equip the ship for bad weather.

(b) §21. Stinginess.

(c) §22. Conclusion

16. **§22 1123a32–3 they do no harm to one's neighbours:** Cf. §20 above. Aristotle seems entitled to say, at most, that these vices do not involve a positive intent to harm one's neighbours.

3

3.§1–16. The essential characteristics of magnanimity.

1. **§1 1123a34–5 Magnanimity . . . great things:** 'Magnanimity' is the traditional Latinized form of *megalopsuchia* (lit. 'having a great soul'), and captures some aspects of it fairly well. The *megalopsuchos* will not be calculating, suspicious, ungenerous, or prone to nurse petty grievances, 1125a3. *Megalopsuchia* is concerned with HONOUR in its different aspects: (a) how and for what a person honours and esteems himself; (b) what he expects others to honour him for; (c) which other people he honours and for what; (d) which other people he wants to honour him.

The magnanimous person takes the right attitude to honour. Aristotle rejects the view of life that aims exclusively and indiscriminately at honour from other people's good opinion (cf. 1095b23, 1159a22–5). But he does not want the virtuous person to ignore honour altogether. It is a genuine good, 1123b20; the virtuous person demands it for himself for his virtue, accords it to others for their virtue, and listens to others when they are qualified to honour him. He does not isolate himself from other people's opinions; nor does he try to make himself agreeable by taking their opinions of him more seriously than they deserve, or by honouring them more than they deserve. Here magnanimity is closely connected with truthfulness; cf. 1124b30 with iv 7.

Aristotle's virtue of magnanimity is sometimes thought to be opposed to the Christian virtue of humility. (Mill, for instance, in *On Liberty*, ch. 3, contrasts 'pagan self-assertion' with 'Christian self-denial'.) But one may doubt whether the two virtues are really opposed. Aristotle believes one ought not to lie about one's own merits or other people's, if lying results from a desire to ingratiate oneself with others (see 1127a6–10). But a genuine virtue of humility does not require the actions and attitudes that Aristotle condemns. See especially Aquinas, *Summa Theologiae* 2–2 q129 a3 ad 4.

    (a) §3–13. The virtue and the opposed vices.

2. **§3 1123b1–2 The magnanimous person, then, seems:** In this chapter in particular, Aristotle uses 'seem' (*dokein*) to refer to commonly held beliefs (or APPEARANCES) about the magnanimous person. He does not assume that all these common beliefs identify essential, or even genuine, features of the virtuous person (see note to §34 below). But his account of the virtue tries to explain the various common beliefs. Even if he thinks they are false beliefs, he tries to show how, given his account of the virtue, it is intelligible that people hold them (following the principle stated in 1154a22–5).

3. **1123b2 worthy:** *Axios*. Here 'worthy' is better than 'deserving', since Aristotle is concerned with an objectively valuable quality rather than with the basis of an entitlement. I may deserve and be entitled to unemployment pay because I am out of work, but being out of work is hardly part of my WORTH.

4. **§5 1123b6–8 just as beauty . . . not beautiful:** On this aesthetic shortcoming of small people, cf. *Poet.* 1450b35.

5. **§7 1123b9–10 Someone . . . pusillanimous:** 'Pusillanimous' captures the opposition to 'magnanimous' suggested by the Greek. It involves some misuse of the word, given its current English sense, which covers only part of what is conveyed by the Greek *mikropsuchia* (lit. 'little-souledness').

6. **§12–13 1123b24–6 The pusillanimous . . . for the magnanimous person:** These two sections fit better after §8 than after §11, where they appear in the mss.

7. **§11 1123b22–4 And even without argument . . . their worth:** Read *hoi megaloi.* Aristotle appeals to common beliefs about greatness. These beliefs suggest that greatness involves honour, even without the argument just given to connect worth and honour.

(b) §1416. Magnanimity requires outstanding virtue.

8. **§14 1123b28–9 For in every case . . . must be good:** The magnanimous person demands honour for himself for the right reasons; but what is most worthy of honour is virtue; hence the magnanimous person must be virtuous. Magnanimity will make the virtues greater (1124a2) because his self-esteem and true perception of its proper basis will make him want to deserve it. Since the magnanimous person values virtue above all, he is not attracted by the rewards of cowardice or injustice, 1123b31; nor will he be shattered by strokes of adverse FORTUNE, 1100b32, 1124a12–20.

9. **1123b29–30 Greatness in each . . . magnanimous person:** The first part of §14 argues from the fact that the magnanimous person deserves the greatest things to the conclusion that he has great virtue. The end of §14 and §15 argues for the same conclusion, but from common beliefs (see note to §3 above) about the magnanimous person.

10. **§15 1123b31 Surely:** Read *oudamôs g'.*

11. **§16 1124a1 adornment:** Cf. 1100b26, 1123a7.

3.*§17–34. Further characteristics of the magnanimous person.*

(a) §17. He has a discriminating attitude to honour.

12. **§17 1124a4–5 The magnanimous . . . dishonours:** This section (§§17–34) deals with commonly recognized features of the magnanimous person that Aristotle takes to be explained by the primary features that he has already discussed.

13. **1124a10–11 make light:** I.e., count it as unimportant (lit. 'count it a small matter').

(b) §18–22. His discriminating attitude to external goods distinguishes him from pretenders to magnanimity.

14. **§18 1124a20 that is why he seems arrogant:** Here Aristotle does not endorse what seems to people.

15. **§19 1124a23–4 That is why these . . . for these goods:** Nor does he endorse the common view that wealth by itself deserves honour. But he agrees that when wealth is honoured, the honour makes magnanimous people more magnanimous,

since it stimulates them to do more to deserve honour and to show that they deserve it; see §14 above. Cf. 1100b24–6.

16. **§21 1124a29–30 They become . . . other goods:** Read *hubristai ta toiauta*.

17. **§22 1124b5–6 For the magnanimous person is justified when he thinks less . . . no good reason:** 'Think less' renders *kataphronein*, which may mean 'look down', 'disdain', 'despise'. But it may simply connote (i) a recognition of comparative merit, without (ii) contempt for others. Non-magnanimous people display (ii), but the magnanimous person displays only (i). For (i), cf. Thucydides ii 62.3–4.

(c) §23. He is discriminating, but fearless in his attitude to danger.

18. **§23 1124b6–7 He does not face . . . lover of danger:** Read *mikrokindunos oude puknokindunos, dia to oliga timan, oude philokindunos*. This attitude to danger is evidence of bravery. The magnanimous person would not be braver if he faced all dangers indiscriminately; see 1117b17, 1169a22.

(d) §24–6. He prefers the active to the passive aspects of friendship.

19. **§24 1124b9–10 He is the sort . . . to the inferior:** He is the benefactor in unequal FRIENDSHIPS; see 1163b1–5. For the explanation of his attitude, see 1168a10.

(e) §26–34. His outlook is reflected in his everyday dealings with other people.

These various expressions of magnanimity are explained by the importance that the magnanimous person attaches to virtuous action.

20. **§25 1124b15–16 Thetis . . . done him:** Homer, *Il.* i 504–10.

21. **1124b16–17 and the Spartans . . . from them:** According to Anon., in *EN* = CAG xx 189.12–18, this follows the account by Callisthenes, a historian and Aristotle's nephew. In 369 the Spartans asked for Athenian help against Thebes.

22. **§26 1124b19 displays his greatness:** Lit. 'is great'.

23. **1124b20 ordinary people:** Lit. 'intermediate'.

24. **§27 1124b23–6 He stays away . . . great and renowned:** He seeks honour, for the appropriate sorts of actions, but he does not compete for honour with others. Cf. 1168b25–1169b2.

25. **§28 1124b26–7 Moreover, he must be open . . . frightened person:** He is not ready to sacrifice virtue to curry favour with others for his security or profit; nor does he think so much of the penalties of honesty that he is afraid of them.

26. **1124b27 He is concerned for the truth:** Read *melein*.

27. **1124b30–1 And he speaks the truth . . . self-deprecating:** He avoids displaying his own greatness in a way that would humiliate inferior people, b19. He is not moved by the self-deprecating person's reason, though their behaviour may be similar; see 1127b22.

[Or 'except for the things he says because of self-deprecation to the many', implying that the magnanimous person sometimes speaks in a self-deprecating way.]

28. **§29 1124b31–1125a2 He cannot let . . . flatterers:** Lit. 'he cannot live in relation to another . . .'. Cf. *EE* 1233b36; *Pol.* 1254a8–17, b21; *Met.* 982b25. Having our own ends determined not by our own choices and values, but by the use someone else can make of us, is repugnant to the magnanimous person; it is an aspect of SLAVERY that Aristotle also sees in flattery (see iv 6). The magnanimous person makes an exception for his friend because the best kind of friendship allows virtuous people to share their ends; see 1156b7–24.

29. **§31 1125a8–9 except . . . aggression:** Lit. 'except because of wanton aggression'. He will respond to WANTON AGGRESSION (cf. 1126a7), but he has no reason to suppose he will commit it himself; it is for those who counterfeit magnanimity, 1124a29.

[Or 'except to commit wanton aggression on others'.]

30. **§34 1125a12–16 The magnanimous . . . hasty movements:** 'Seems' (see §3 above, and APPEARANCE) suggests a popular stereotype. Aristotle does not necessarily endorse it, but his account explains why this stereotype is associated with magnanimity.

3.§35–8. The vices opposed to magnanimity.

(a) §35. Pusillanimity.

(b) §36–7. Vanity.

31. **§37 1125a32–4 Pusillanimity is more opposed . . . worse:** On different degrees of opposition to the mean, cf. 1109a5, 1121a19–30.

(c) §38. Conclusion.

32. **§38 1125a34–5 Magnanimity, . . . great honour:** The emphasis falls on 'great'. This conclusion of the treatment of magnanimity prepares for the immediately following discussion of the virtue concerned with small honours.

4

4.§1–6. The virtue concerned with small honours.

(a) §1. It must be distinguished from magnanimity.

1. **§1 1125a36–b4 But, as we said in the first discussion, . . . magnificence:** Cf. 1107b25.

(b) §2–4. The excess and the deficiency.

2. **§2 1125b6–8 Just as the taking . . . right way:** Recognition of a nameless virtue (see 1107a34) confirms the doctrine of the mean. If we see only a choice between love of honour and indifference to honour, we find ourselves praising both on different occasions. Hence the state that we ought to cultivate cannot be either of them; the reasonable state must be intermediate between them.

3. **§4 1125b14–15 Clearly, since . . . every case:** Cf. 1118b22.

4. **1125b17–18 Since the mean . . . to themselves:** This illustrates the importance of identifying mean states that have no established names (see 1107b29–1108a1, 1127b6–7). In this case the extremes seem to have the field to themselves, because we readily think the only contenders for the virtue are love of honour and indifference to honour, even though, in different contexts, we recognize the errors of each. We do not recognize, until Aristotle points it out, that these two extreme attitudes are not the only options.

(c) §5–6. The mean state in relation to honour.

5

5.§1–15. Calmness.

(a) §1–4. The mean state concerned with anger.

1. **§1 1125b26–9 Calmness is the mean . . . nameless:** Calmness is another virtue concerned with FEELINGS, as bravery and temperance were. Like bravery (1116b23), it is concerned with spirit, *thumos* (see DESIRE), especially as displayed in ANGER. But it is discussed at this stage, with the next three virtues, because they all concern ways of getting on with other people. (Contrast the order in *EE* iii 3; *MM* i 22.) Aristotle is concerned with anger especially insofar as it tends to offend and antagonize others, and with lack of anger insofar as it reflects an unreasonable (and, in a wider sense than Aristotle allows, cowardly) fear of offending others.

2. **§3 1125b33 if calmness is praised:** If we are to use 'calm' in a favourable sense, we must take it to indicate the state he describes, not the extreme state of deficient anger.
[Or 'Since calmness . . . '.]

(b) §5–6. The vice of deficiency.

3. **§6 1126a7–8 Such willingness . . . slavish:** On accepting insults, cf. 1125a8–9. On slavishness, cf. 1132b34–1133a1, SLAVE #3.

(c) §7–12. The vice of excess and its different forms.

4. **§11 1126a28 penalty and corrective treatment:** Read *timôrias kai*.
5. **§12 1126a30 comes more naturally to human beings:** Lit. 'is more human'.

(d) §13–15. It is difficult to find the mean in relation to anger.

6. **§13 1126a36–b2 but sometimes . . . ruling others:** Manliness: MAN. We incline to think that someone who complains about ill treatment is a properly self-respecting and self-assertive person who will be able to dominate others.
7. **§13 1126b4 and <we make it> by perception:** Read *kai tê(i) aisthêsei*, lit. 'the judgment is in particulars and by perception'. Aristotle refers back to the role that he gave to perception in 1109b22–3.

6

6. §1–9. Friendliness in social intercourse.

(a) §1–2. The vices of excess and deficiency.

1. **§1 1126b11–14 In meeting people, . . . they meet:** The vices opposed to friendliness and those opposed to calmness have similar sources. The ingratiating person (lit. 'pleaser') cares too much, and the cantankerous person too little, about other people's opinions. These attitudes in turn may result from the wrong attitude to honour—the attitude that the magnanimous person avoids. The attitude of irascible and ill-tempered people is a source of indifference to honour (not mentioned in iv 3–4).

(b) §3–9. The mean state. The friendly person takes the right attitude to causing pleasure and pain in others.

2. **§5 1126b22–3 not including any <specific> feeling:** See FRIENDSHIP #6.

3. **1126b27 for the proper . . . strangers:** We do not owe to strangers either the degree of delicacy in sparing feelings, or the degree of frankness in pointing out defects, that would be appropriate between friends. A less probable translation: 'For it is not equally proper to spare the feelings of familiar companions and of strangers, nor equally proper to cause them pain' (i.e., it is more proper to spare the feelings of friends, and less proper to cause pain to friends).

4. **§6 1126b29 the fine and the beneficial:** Consideration of what is fine and what is beneficial is prior to consideration of pleasure, and even to consideration of future pleasure against present pleasure, 1127a5. For the three aims of action, see 1104b30–5, 1155b18–21; *Top.* 104b30.

5. **§8 1127a2–3 What he will . . . causing pain:** 'IN ITSELF' marks the contrast between the action considered without reference to its longer-term consequences and the action with the consequences considered (see next sentence). Cf. the example of throwing cargo overboard, 1110a9–11, 18, b3. 'Without qualification' (see UNQUALIFIED) sometimes marks the contrast that is marked here by 'in itself').

6. **1127a4–5 But he will . . . expedient:** Aristotle suggests how the virtuous person will consider PARTICULAR cases (see 1165a2–4). If he considers the fine and the expedient in general, he takes the point of view of each virtue, supporting the claim in 1144b32.

(c) §9. The vices of excess and deficiency show the wrong attitudes to causing pleasure and pain.

7. **§9 1127a8 with no ulterior purpose:** Lit. 'not because of something else'. Cf. 1127a26 (lit. 'not for the sake of something'). It does not follow that the ingratiating person is unselfish. He may still be currying favour with you, but he is not out for your money or political influence, as the flatterer is, but only for your favour. Cf. 1171a15–17.

8. **1127a11–12 However, the extremes . . . has no name:** Cf. 1125b23–5. Once again, because the mean condition lacks its own name, people tend not to notice that the virtue is a mean.

7

7.§1–17. Truthfulness in social relations.

(a) §1–6. In this case also there is a mean state, though it is nameless.

1. **§1 1127a15–17 and if we survey . . . are means:** We see that they are means, because the virtuous attitude to these cases cannot be described non-evaluatively, but has to incorporate 'right way', etc. Cf. 1106a24–6.

2. **§2 1127a21 boaster:** Cf. 1115b29.

3. **§4 1127a23–6 The intermediate . . . belittling:** This sort of truthfulness is not honesty in general, but honesty about oneself. The motives for deviating from it are similar to the motives that cause the extremes about honour, and are related to the sources of the vices in iv 5–6. Hence truthfulness is characteristic of the magnanimous person, 1124b27.

(b) §7–9. The mean state: the right attitude towards telling the truth about oneself.

(c) §10–13. The vice of excess: boastfulness.

4. **§10 1127b11 pointlessly foolish:** Lit. 'vain' (*mataios*, also 'futile' in 1094a27).

5. **§11 1127b12 as a boaster:** Read *hôs alazôn*.

6. **§12 112714–16 It is not a person's capacity, . . . liar:** These different people have the same capacity for exaggeration, but different states of character because they decide to use their capacities in different ways. Cf. 1106a2–10, 1117a4, 1152a13–14, *Met.* 1004b24; *Top.* 165a30; *Rhet.* 1355b17.

7. **§13 1127b20 a wise diviner or doctor:** Read *sophon <ê> iatron.* Cf. MEDICINE.

(d) §14–17. The vice of deficiency: self-deprecation.

8. **§14 1127b25–6 The qualities . . . Socrates also used to do:** This refers to SOCRATES' frequent disavowal of knowledge about the virtues, which was often regarded as self-deprecation (*eirôneia*; hence 'Socratic irony', Plato, *Rep.* 337a). Aristotle does not say that Socrates had the vice of self-deprecation. If Socrates' disavowals of knowledge were sincere and truthful, no self-deprecation was expressed.

9. **§15 1127b27–8 Sometimes, indeed, this even . . . is boastful:** The Spartans were ostentatiously austere in their dress, because they wanted to display their indifference to mere comfort.

8

8.§1–12. Wit.

(a) §1–3. There is a mean in relaxation and amusements.

1. **§2 1128a3–4 And, clearly, . . . be deficient:** When we study the virtues, we see that wit is also a mean, because it cannot be identified with simply raising a laugh.

2. **§3 1128a4–5 Those who go to excess . . . buffoons:** The term rendered by 'buffoon' (*bômolochos*) originally signifies someone who 'hangs around altars (*bômoi*)' to steal bits of sacrificial meat. Hence the term applies to someone who plays tricks and tells jokes to ingratiate himself with another. His motives are similar to those of the flatterer or ingratiating person. Similarly, the 'boorish' (lit. 'rustic', as opposed to urbane) people (cf. 1156b13) show the crusty indifference of the ill-tempered people in iv 6. The proper sort of wit is an Aristotelian virtue because it reflects the right attitude to pleasing others; this in turn reflects the right valuation of other people's good opinion of us. See 1156a13, 1158a31, 1176b14.

(b) §4–10. Characteristics of the mean state and of the witty person.

3. **§5 1128a17 Dexterity:** This trait has a wider scope than wit; cf. 1171b3.

4. **§6 1128a22–5 This can also . . . more seemly:** The 'shameful abuse' (Aristotle perhaps means that one ought to be ashamed of abusing someone in such terms), *aischrologia*, characteristic of old comedy (e.g., Aristophanes) is shameful because it is expressed in obscene language and because it expresses vulgar personal insults. Cf. *Pol.* 1336b3–6. The New Comedy of Menander reflects the difference Aristotle describes (though he probably does not use 'new comedy' in any technical sense). See OCD, s.v. 'Comedy, Greek, Old' and 'Comedy, Greek, New'.

5. **§7 1128a25–8 Then should . . . hateful or pleasant:** The second definition, referring to what gives pleasure or pain to the hearer, seems more precise than the first. But Aristotle raises a doubt about it in 'Perhaps, though . . .'; he implies that the witty person's jokes may displease some people—either humourless boors or those who prefer buffoons. The first definition is more suitable, since it limits the sorts of people whose reactions are to be considered.

6. **§8 1128a29 he is prepared to make himself:** Read *kan poiein*.

7. **§10 1128a22 a sort of law to himself:** This phrase is used in later moral philosophy to express the essential character of moral agency (see St Paul, Romans 2:16; Butler, *Sermons*, ii). Though Aristotle uses it casually and without theoretical emphasis, it conveys an important aspect of the virtuous character. Virtuous people do not need the instructions of external laws, because their own understanding guides their actions correctly.

8. **1128a32–3 the intermediate . . . or witty:** Neither of these terms is wholly suitable for the relevant virtue, since neither captures the basis for the restraint on telling jokes. This is another mean that lacks a completely suitable name.

(c) §10–12. The vices of excess and deficiency.

9

9. §1–8. Shame.

(a) §1–3. Shame is not a virtue, but a feeling appropriate for some people.

1. **§1 1128b10–11 It is not appropriate . . . character>:** In this chapter 'shame' translates *aidôs*, and 'disgrace' indicates *aischunê* or a cognate; Aristotle's argument, however, seems to depend on the identification of *aidôs* with *aischunê*. See SHAME.

2. §3 **1128b17–18 since they live by their feelings:** YOUTH and living by feelings; 1095b2–11, 1119a33–b7, 1169a4–6.

(b) §4–8. Shame is not appropriate for the virtuous person.

3. §7 **1128b29–31 Shame might, . . . to the virtues:** The assumed situation that would warrant shame is so far from anything that the virtuous person would do that it is pointless for him to acquire a tendency to be ashamed in that situation. Line 1124b10 is not an exception to Aristotle's claim here, since it is not concerned with base actions.

Aristotle is concerned here with retrospective shame at actions we have done. He denies it to the virtuous person. He does not consider the anticipatory shame of 1115a16, where I am properly ashamed when I even think of the possibility of doing a wrong action. He need not be rejecting that type of shame here, since it will apparently be a motive for the virtuous person (though not one of his virtues).

Cf. the treatment of shame in *MM* i 29 (apparently treating it as a virtue, though cf. 1193a36) and *EE* 1233b26–9 (a mean that is not a virtue).

4. **1128b33–5 Continence . . . say later:** Continence is discussed in Book vii, one of the books that are common to *EN* and *EE*. See Intro. §3.

Book V

1

1. §1–11. The two types of justice.

(a) §1–6. Justice is a state of character, and hence may be studied by reference to its contrary.

1. §1 **1129a6 the same discipline:** Aristotle has told us (i 2) that the relevant DISCIPLINE is political science.
[Or 'the same line of inquiry', i.e., dialectic, which Aristotle goes on to illustrate.]

2. §3 **1129a6–9 We see . . . wish what is just:** On Books v–vii and their relation to the *EN* and *EE*, see Intro. §3. We begin with some standard dialectical (see ETHICS #5) forms of argument. See *Top.* 106a9, 145b34, 147a17. 'Makes us just agents' (lit. 'from which people are doers (*praktikoi*) of just things') probably includes the two components distinguished as DOING JUSTICE and wishing what is just.

3. **1129a11 we also:** I.e., we as well as people in general. We should take these common beliefs as our starting point. Cf. i 4; *EE* i 3, 6.

4. §4 **1129a13–14 capacity . . . contrary activities:** This is a rational capacity. See CAPACITY #3.

5. §5 **1129a18 from the other contrary:** See *Topics* 113b27–114a7.

(b) §7–11. The two types of justice—general and special justice—are clear from their contraries.

6. §7 **1129a26–31 Now it would . . . keys homonymously):** The two types of justice are not HOMONYMS by chance (as a bank of a river and a bank for savings

are homonymously banks; Aristotle uses the Greek 'key', which is used both for keys that open locks and for an animal's collar bone). Aristotle goes on to explain how the definitions of general and special justice are connected (because special justice is an aspect of general justice).

7. **§8 1129a32–3 overreaching and unfair:** On fairness (*ison, isotês*), see EQUAL.

8. **§9 1129b2–4 goods—not with . . . not always good:** These external depend on FORTUNE; see 1098b12, 1099a31, 1153b24; *EE* 1248b38. In 'without qualification' (*haplôs*; see UNQUALIFIED) Aristotle means that it is true to say 'wealth is good for a human being', without qualification, because human beings can use wealth well, and if they use it well, it promotes their his happiness. But it may still be bad for this or that particular vicious human being (we now no longer speak without qualification) who uses his wealth to make himself more intemperate and less happy. Only the good person will use these goods of fortune so that they are reliably good for him.

Many goods of fortune are in limited supply, and therefore matters of competition (1168b19; *EE* 1248b28). Often one person gets more of them by depriving someone else of them. Hence the person who overreaches is unfair because he profits by another's inappropriate and undeserved loss. See 1167b4–16.

1.§12–20. General justice.

(a) §12–14. It is concerned with the observance of law, which prescribes actions appropriate to all the virtues.

9. **§12 1129b11–14 Since, as we saw, . . . each of them is just:** Aristotle does not say here that every system of positive law is just. In this context the *nomimon* is the lawful rather than the merely legal (cf. CHOICEWORTHY). In 'legislative <science>' Aristotle refers to the correct laws. Cf. 1130b22.

10. **§13 1129b14–15 Now in every . . . the laws aim:** Aristotle refers to his division between correct and deviant political systems, described further in viii 10. 'Some other such basis' refers to the different bases on which different ruling groups rest their position.

[Or 'Now the laws speak about every matter, aiming . . .'.]

11. **1129b16 either at . . . virtue:** Read *pasin ê tois kuriois ê kat'aretên ê*.

12. **1129b17–19 And so in one way . . . political community:** Parts of happiness cf. *EE* 1214b27†; *Rhet.* 1360b19†; *MM* 1184a26†. For this account of justice, cf. *Pol.* 1283a38.

(b) §15–20. And so general justice requires complete virtue of character.

13. **§15 1129b25–7 This type of justice, . . . to another:** General justice is not an additional virtue beyond the other virtues of character. Because virtue as a whole aims at the good of another, and this is the aim of general justice, general justice is virtue as a whole in its other-directed aspect; see §20.

Why does Aristotle assume that virtue as a whole aims at the good of others? See FINE.

14. **1129b27–30 And that is why . . . summed up:** Here and in §16–17 'THAT IS WHY' cites a common belief Aristotle has now explained. He quotes Euripides'

lost play *Melanippe* (TGF fr. 486) and Theognis 147 (which continues 'and every man, being just, is good').

15. **1129b31 complete exercise of complete virtue:** Read *tês teleias aretês teleia chrêsis estin.*

16. **§16 1130a1–2 That is why Bias . . . a community:** Bias (sixth century) was one of the Seven Sages (on whom, see DK 10; OCD, s.v.). This remark is not attributed to Bias elsewhere.

17. **§17 1130a3–5 That is also why . . . of the community:** Thrasymachus claims that justice is good for other people, but harmful to the just person himself (Plato, *Rep.* 343c; cf. 1134b5). Aristotle accepts the first part of Thrasymachus' claim, but not the second part.

18. **§18 1130a5–7 The worst . . . towards others>:** Cf. 1160a5.

19. **1130a7–8 And the best . . . difficult task:** On virtue and difficulty, cf. 1102b32. In a7 read *all' ho.*

20. **§20 1130a12 For virtue . . . to be justice:** This is a standard way (cf. 1102a30, 1141b24, *DA* 427a2) of indicating that two distinct definitions are satisfied by one thing because of its different properties. Because virtue as a whole benefits others in the ways described it can properly be called justice. See DEFINITION.

2

2.§1–13. Special justice contrasted with general.

(a) §1–6. Special injustice is a specific vice, not vice in general.

1. **§2 1130a16 A sign . . . :** In §2–3, 4, and 5 Aristotle gives three arguments for the distinctness of special justice.

2. **1130a19–22 But when someone . . . with injustice:** 'Gain' is too brief a description of the motive for special injustice. The unjust person wants gain that is unfair, at the expense of what is justly due to another.

3. **§6 1130a33 synonymous:** See HOMONYMOUS. Aristotle means that they are partly synonymous, because their account is partly the same. Cf. our use of 'animal' both for the genus that including human beings and for non-human animals. Cf. 1147b35.

4. **1130b1–5 For both . . . excellent person:** The order is chiastic. Aristotle claims (a) special injustice is distinct from general, but (b) the two types of injustice have definitions in the same genus. In his support he mentions (b) the definition that refers to another, and (a) the different concerns of each type of injustice. In describing the concerns of special injustice, Aristotle gives examples, and adds '(or whatever single name . . .)'. The name he suggests later is 'profit' (or 'gain', *kerdos*); see 1132a10–19.

(b) §7–9. Special justice, as opposed to general, is especially concerned with fairness.

5. **§7 1130b7 what, and what sort of thing:** Aristotle's usual way of referring to genus (what) and differentia (what sort). See DEFINITION #3.

6. **§8 1130b8–9 The unjust . . . the fair:** Aristotle reintroduces his earlier distinction between lawfulness and fairness, to explain the differences between different types of injustice. He argues from contraries, in the way described in 1129a17: (1) 1129a26–b11: Justice and injustice are homonymous because one type of each is connected with lawfulness, and the other type with fairness. (2) 1129b11–1130a13: The type connected with lawfulness is the whole of virtue. (3) 1130a14–32: The type of injustice connected with overreaching is a proper part of vice. (4) 1130a32–b7: Hence the special justice that avoids overreaching is a proper part of virtue.

(c) §10–11. We need not discuss general justice in detail.

7. **§10 1130b18–20 Let us, then, set aside . . . to another:** The subdivisions of general justice are the particular virtues described in Books iii–iv.

8. **1130b20–22 And it is evident . . . this type of justice and injustice:** The general justice prescribed by law is virtue and vice as a whole. for two reasons: (a) 'For most lawful . . . each vice'; the laws prescribe actions that are the characteristic expressions of virtues. (b) 'Moreover, the actions . . . common good'; the laws prescribe actions that characteristically produce the virtues.

9. **1130b22–3 For most . . . virtue as a whole:** Read *prattomena*. The lawful: 1129b12. Since Aristotle thinks positive law is fallible in its moral prescriptions, he emphasizes that not every good citizen (i.e., a citizen matching the ideal of a given system of positive law) is a genuinely good man.

10. **1130b23–4 for the law . . . each vice:** The broad scope of 'in accord with' (*kata*) makes it hard to say whether, in Aristotle's view, laws prescribe being virtuous or simply action in conformity to virtue.

11. **§11 1130b26–9 We must wait . . . good citizen:** This sentence is a parenthetical promissory note, prompted by the mention of moral education. The question about EDUCATION is considered again in x 9 (but not in the surviving parts of the *EE*; see Intro. §3) and in *Pol.* vii. On the virtues of a man and of a citizen, see *Pol.* iii 4.

(d) §12–13. But we need a detailed description of special justice.

3

3.§1–17. Justice in distribution.

(a) §1–5. Justice requires equality.

1. **§1 1131a10–11 Since the unjust . . . unfair <extremes>:** Aristotle's word *ison* is translated by 'fair', 'EQUAL', or 'fair and equal'. Here he moves from fairness, which is characteristic of all types of special justice, to the different types of equality that embody that fairness in different types of special justice. On the *ison*, cf. 1106a24–6.

(b) §6–7. Equality involves treatment proportionate to worth.

2. **§7 1131a25–9 For all agree . . . virtue:** Different political systems agree that just distribution should be equal to WORTH (cf. 1123b2). But they differ on what

counts as the sort of worth relevant in just distributions of powers and offices. (Greek cities normally regard public offices as rewards and advantages; they are sources of honour, and usually also of profit without any necessary dishonesty.) Cf. *Pol.* iii 9.

(c) §8–17. Hence justice requires proportionate treatment.

3. **§8 1131a30 For proportion . . . units:** Aristotle contrasts (a) 'The number 3 is the successor of 2' with (b) 'there is a large number of people in the room'. In (b) the number consists of people, not of abstract units as in (a). Cf. *Phys.* 219b5, 224a2.

4. **§9 1131b1–3 If, for instance, . . . will be four:** If line A is 3 inches, line B 6 inches and line C 12 inches, the proportion of A to B is the same as that of B to C.

4

4.§1–14. Justice in rectification.

(a) §1–3. It is different from justice in distribution, since it involves numerical equality.

(b) §4–7. Judges seek to rectify by reaching a mean between gain and loss.

1. **§4 1132a6–7 And so the judge . . . unequal:** In Athens, and in some other Greek cities, the 'judges' are the members of large popular juries, whose president is not a trained or authoritative legal official. Here Aristotle is not discussing their punitive function, but only one sort of injustice that they have to correct. See OCD, s.v. 'Law and procedure, Athenian'.

2. **1132a9–10 and the judge . . . profit:** Rectification and adjustment are appropriate even in cases where no definite sum of profit and loss can be identified, as it can be in financial transactions. Aristotle explains and defends the broad use of 'profit' in §13–14.

[Or 'tries to restore equality by inflicting a loss . . . profit'.]

3. **§7 1132a31–2 a sort of . . . just:** Lit. 'a just ensouled'.

(c) §8–12. How numerical equality is restored.

4. **§8 1132a24–7 The judge restores . . . smaller part <CB>:** Aristotle is thinking of a single line like this:

```
A           E        D        C              B
_____
```

On this line AD = DB and ED = DC. In a32, 'For when . . . to the other', Aristotle assumes that the offender begins with AD, the victim with BD, and the offender takes DC off the victim, adding DC to AD (AD = BD); then 'the one part (AC) exceeds the other (CB) by the two parts (ED and DC)'. Restoration of equality requires us not only to take DC from the offender (who then still exceeds the victim by ED; 'for if a part . . . by just one part'), but also to restore DC to the victim (who would otherwise fall short of BD by DC; 'Hence the larger . . . one part').

5. **§12 1132b6–9 Let lines AA′, . . . exceeds BB′ by CD:** This illustration involves these lines:

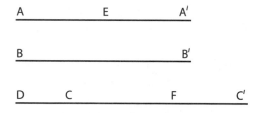

Here CF = AE. This differs from the previous illustration in that we need not assume that DC = CF (and hence DC = AE), i.e., we need not assume that the offender gains exactly what the victim loses.

At the end of §12 the mss. add a sentence that also occurs at 1133a14–16. OCT deletes it here.

(d) §13–14. A note on 'profit' and 'loss'.

6. **§13–14 1132b11–20 These names 'loss' . . . <the transaction>:** This general use of 'loss' and 'profit' was introduced in §5–6.

5

5.§1–16. *Justice in exchange.*

(a) §1–9. It requires proportionate, not simple, reciprocity.

1. **§3 1132b25–7 though people '. . . be done':** Rhadamanthys judged people in Hades after their death; cf. Plato, *Gorg.* 523e. Aristotle quotes Hesiod (fr. 286; the previous line is 'If someone sows bad things, he will reap bad gains').

2. **§6 1132b34–1133a1 since otherwise . . . slavery:** Failure to retaliate shows lack of concern (thought to be characteristic of a SLAVE) for one's own status and worth; cf. 1126a3–8.

3. **§7 1133a3–5 Indeed, that is why . . . gracious again:** See THAT IS WHY. 'Grace' (*charis*) includes grace, gratitude, thanks and favour; see CULTIVATED.

4. **§9 1133a16–18 For no community . . . equalized:** A COMMUNITY requires members whose dissimilarity makes it possible for them to gain from association and exchange, *Pol.* 1261b22–34.

(b) §10–16. Money secures proportionate reciprocity in exchange.

5. **§10 1133a23–4 equal to a house:** Delete *ê trophên.*

6. **§11 1133a26–8 In reality, . . . same exchange:** Cf. Plato, *Rep.* 369b–d. Currency (see LAW) is a 'pledge' of need to the extent that my need for a bed is a reason to pay you money for it. Aristotle does not go into much detail about the correlation between need and the monetary price. But the sort of proportion described in

1133a32 suggests that A and B achieve equality when the price that A pays for the shoes corresponds to A's need for them. Need is not the same as demand; A's need for B's shoes does not change even though B may increase demand for B's shoes by restricting production or buying out his competitors. On exchange cf. 1163b32.

7. **1133a30–1 And currency . . . to make it useless:** Aristotle alludes to the connexion between *nomisma* (currency) and *nomos* (convention). See LAW #1.

8. **§12 1133a31–b4 However, they must . . . produced in them:** On the right way to fix price and value, cf. 1164b20.

5.§17–19. The connexion between justice and the doctrine of the mean.

9. **§17 1133b29–32 We have now . . . having too little:** Aristotle summarizes his account of justice, and connects it with the doctrine of the mean. Here and in the next several sections, the connexion of thought is not completely clear, and some editors have proposed transpositions of the text. Some suggest that 5.§17–19 and 6.§1–2 should be placed after 6.§5, at the end of the discussion of political justice.

10. **1133b32–3 Justice is a mean, . . . intermediate condition:** Justice 'is about (lit. 'is of') an intermediate condition', because the intermediate condition relevant to justice is determined by the way in which just actions and states of affairs are intermediate and EQUAL—between suffering undue harm for another's benefit and gaining undue benefit by another's harm. In the case of the other virtues, the property of being intermediate belongs to the state of the virtuous person, not to the corresponding ACTIVITIES. In the case of justice, this property belongs to the activities. In pointing out this difference Aristotle does not deny that the state of character which is justice is a mean in the ordinary sense, between grabbing benefits at other people's expense (DOING INJUSTICE) and acquiescence in suffering harm from reluctance to assert one's claim against another (suffering injustice); cf. 1138a28.

11. **1134a1 injustice is about the extremes:** Both the excess and the deficiency involve injustice, in contrast to the other vices, where the excess (e.g., intemperance) and the deficiency (e.g., insensibility) are different vices.

6

6.§1–2. Unjust action must be distinguished from unjust character.

1. **§1 1134a17–19 Since it is possible . . . or brigand, for instance:** This passage introduces the question about unjust actions and being unjust (cf. ii 5) that is discussed more fully in c8. Cf. 1136a2.

6.§3–9. Political justice.

(a) §3–4. Conditions for political justice: freedom and equality.

2. **§3 1134a23–4 Now we have . . . to the just:** This discussion of political justice does not seem to be closely connected with either of the previous two sections (5.§17–19 and 6.§1–2).

3. **§4 1134a25–6 both the just . . . politically just:** §8 below suggests that these are two names for the same thing.

4. **1134a26–8 The latter belongs . . . numerically equal:** At the beginning of his general remarks on justice in political society (in a *polis*; see POLITICAL), Aristotle distinguishes this type of justice from the types found in other COMMUNITIES (cf. viii 9–11). For the account of the *polis*, see *Pol.* 1252b27|, 1278b15, 1280b40.

5. **1134a32–3 Where there is . . . injustice:** The distinction between doing injustice and injustice itself (i.e., being unjust) has been drawn in ii 4 and in §1–2 above. It is explained more fully in c8 below.

6. **1134a34 things that . . . are bad:** I.e., the goods mentioned in v 1.

> (b) §5–7. Political justice requires the rule of law, to prevent injustice by rulers.

7. **§5 1134a35 That is why . . . ruler:** The characteristics of injustice explain the common practice (see THAT IS WHY) of distrusting unchecked political power vested in a single ruler. Aristotle connects the rule of LAW with the impersonal and impartial rule of reason (which will be correct reason when the law is correct); cf. *Pol.* 1287a18–32.

8. **1134b1–2 guardian . . . the equal:** Hence he must not award himself too many goods.

9. **§6 1134b3–4 For since . . . good without qualification:** I.e., the goods mentioned in §4.

10. **1134b5–6 That is why . . . another person's good:** On this common belief, cf. 1130a3.

11. **§7 1134b7–8 The people . . . tyrants:** On tyrants, see 1160a36–b12, *Pol.* 1266b38–1267a17.

> (c) §8–9. Relations within a family do not raise questions of political justice, but they raise analogous questions.

12. **§8 1134b9–11 For there is no unqualified injustice . . . part of oneself:** These cases allow only a derivative sort of injustice, partially resembling the injustice that is properly so called. On parts of oneself, cf. 1161b18.

13. **§9 1134b13 Hence there is no injustice in relation to them:** Read *auta.* [Or, reading *hauton*, 'to himself'.]

14. **1134b14–15 For we found . . . equality in ruling and being ruled:** This equality includes an equal right to rule and be ruled. Aristotle takes this to be characteristic of free citizens; *Pol.* 1283b14.

15. **1134b15–17 <Approximation . . . relations with a wife . . . as just:** On justice between husband and wife, cf. 1162a16, WOMAN.

7

7.§1–5. Justice by nature and by law.

> (a) §1–2. The diversity of laws persuades some people that there is no such thing as natural justice.

1. **§1 1134b23–4 (for instance, . . . Brasidas):** The Spartan general Brasidas (Thucydides v 11) after his death received sacrifices in Amphipolis as a liberator; his

cult is introduced as an example of a strictly local observance initiated by DECREE. (See OCD, s.v. 'Hero-cult'.) Amphipolis was close to Stagira, Aristotle's birthplace.

(b) §3–5. Natural justice, however, allows some variation in different circumstances; hence the existence of variation does not count against the existence of natural justice.

2. §3 1134b28–9 **though . . . the gods:** What is natural for them is also invariable.

3. §4 1134b31 **admit of being otherwise:** They are not NECESSARY, but subject to change.

4. 1134b32–3 **It is clear . . . will apply:** This is the distinction between the natural and the unchangeable, which shows us that even in things that are subject to variation something may be natural.

Read *homoiôs? dêlon de kai epi tôn allôn kai ho.*

5. 1134b34–5 **for the right hand . . . become ambidextrous:** Aristotle returns to the question about LAW and NATURE that was raised at 1094b16 (cf. *Top.* 173a7, PROTAGORAS). Natural facts about a human being make it easier and more beneficial, Aristotle thinks, to use the right hand more than the left, though it is possible to disregard this natural advantage and to use both hands equally (cf. *PA* 666b35, 671b28, 672a24, 684a25; *MM* 1194b30). Analogously, human communities can survive under many sorts of laws and conceptions of justice, but it remains true that human nature and the human good make one conception of justice the correct one.

6. §5 1135a3–5 **Similarly, . . . since political systems also differ:** 'Since' implies that the content of law both should and characteristically does reflect the character of the political system; *Pol.* 1289a11–25.

7. 1135a5 **Still, only one . . . best everywhere:** In *Pol.* vii Aristotle describes the best political system. In saying that it is the best everywhere, he does not mean that every city should try to achieve it.

7. §6–7. *Just actions may be understood as universals and as particulars.*

8. §6 1135a5–8 **Each <type . . . is universal:** §6–7 are a note that does not seem to be connected with the preceding discussion of political justice, but introduces the discussion of voluntary and involuntary that follows in c8. Aristotle contrasts action types ('universals', such as killing an innocent victim) and determinate action tokens ('particulars', such as Smith's killing the innocent victim Jones yesterday at 9:15 a.m.). What is voluntary or involuntary is a determinate action token; cf. 1110a14–15.

9. §7 1135a10–11 **when this has . . . of injustice:** What has been done is a particular action token, which can be considered as voluntary or involuntary. 'Before it is done', the properties of the universal action type define a possible act of injustice.

8

8. §1–5. *Just actions, justice, and the voluntary.*

(a) §1–2. Acts of injustice must be voluntary.

1. **§1 1135a15–19 Given this account . . . just or unjust:** This chapter repeats some of the distinctions drawn in iii 1, now in a specifically juridical context (cf. 1109b34). Cf. also *EE* ii 6–10, esp. 9.

(b) §3. Voluntary action must be up to the agent and must rest on the appropriate knowledge.

2. **§3 1135a23–5 As I said . . . for what goal):** Lit. 'I call voluntary, as had also been said before, whatever among the things up to him someone does knowing and not being ignorant either of whom or by what or for the sake of what (e.g., . . .).' 'Up to the agent' does not occur in the account of the voluntary in 1111a22–4. Cf. *EE* 1225b7–11.

3. **1135a25–6 and <does> . . . force:** On doing something coincidentally, see 1135b2–8.

[Or 'and <knows> . . .'. Cf. b28–31; EE 1225b5–6.]

4. **1135a28–30 But . . . know he is your father:** 'But . . .' (*de*, answering *men* in a23) points out that the list in a25 is not discriminating enough. For I could know one thing about my victim and be ignorant of something else; what I have done voluntarily to him depends on what I knew about him.

5. **1135a33–b1 For we also . . . or involuntary:** This sentence explains why 'up to the agent' is needed in the definition of voluntary. These natural processes that are neither voluntary nor involuntary were not explicitly considered in iii 1. But they are not necessarily counterexamples to the account in iii 1. If beliefs and desires are the PRINCIPLE of voluntary action, these natural processes are not voluntary. See 1111a22–4.

(c) §4. Coincidentally just and unjust actions.

6. **§4 1135b2–6 Both unjust . . . except coincidentally:** I do an unjust action COINCIDENTALLY if (i) the action is in fact unjust, and (ii) its being unjust is no part of my reason for doing it (cf. 1138b3; *Met.* 1025a25, 1027a1). If I do an unjust action because of ignorance (I break my promise without realizing I am doing it), it is easy to see why Aristotle thinks it is only doing injustice coincidentally. But suppose I know it is unjust and either (a) I don't care but I do it for some other reason, or (b) I do care but still do it because of fear. Aristotle seems to think that (b) counts as doing injustice coincidentally; but what about (a)? And is the account of (b) consistent with 1110a4–b9? Cf. *EE* 1225a3–33†. For coincidences, cf. 1154b17, 1157a35.

(d) §5. Voluntary action v. action on decision.

7. **1135b10–11 We act on . . . deliberation:** Aristotle omits wish, the other necessary condition for a decision. See 1113a11–12, 1113b3–5.

8. §6–12. Different ways of violating justice.

(a) §6–7. Errors result in involuntary actions.

8. **§7 1135b18–19 If, then, the infliction . . . it is outside:** Misfortunes and errors are two subclasses of the class of errors introduced in §6. §7 uses 'error' for a species rather than for the genus.

(b) §8–12. Only the wrong decision makes an agent unjust. This distinction explains why we pardon some unjust actions, but not others.

9. **§8 1135b25 But whenever . . . unjust and vicious:** This is the third of the three types of harm mentioned in §6.

10. **§9 1135b25–7 That is why . . . to anger:** The distinction between doing injustice and being unjust (i.e., having an unjust decision) explains the common practice of treating actions resulting from spirit (see DESIRE; here Aristotle has anger especially in mind) differently from those resulting from forethought. Cf. *EE* 1226b36–1227a2; *MM* 1189b3–6.

11. **§10 1135b31–3 Rather <in cases . . . is unjust>:** Aristotle is contrasting disputes involving acts of injustice and anger with disputes involving unjust DECISION and character. To illustrate the second kind of case he mentions deliberate and premeditated fraudulent transactions.

12. **§11 1136a1–2 and this . . . agent unjust:** This answers the question in 6.§1.

13. **§12 1136a6–9 For if someone's error . . . not to be pardoned:** For 'in ignorance' and 'caused by ignorance', cf. 1110b25–1111a2. Here Aristotle distinguishes actions done in ignorance from those that are caused by a vice or a human feeling from those caused by a feeling that is neither natural nor human; cf. 1148b15–1149a10, 1149b4, 1149b27–1150a1. People are not blamed for such states (cf. 1113b21–1114a3). Why should they not be pardoned for acting on them? Perhaps Aristotle means that an agent moved by these states will not respond suitably to pardon as an ordinary rational agent would.

9

9.§1–17. Puzzles about justice and injustice.

(a) §1–3. Can someone suffer injustice voluntarily?

1. **§1 1136a11–14 First of all, . . . both unwilling:** Aristotle quotes from Euripides' *Alcmaeon* (TGF fr. 68), cited at 1110a27–9. He quotes an exchange between two speakers, the first of whom is Alcmaeon.

(b) §4–8. The incontinent person may seem to suffer injustice voluntarily, but in fact he does not.

2. **§6 1136b5–9 If so, someone is harmed . . . excellent> to do:** According to Aristotle, the incontinent suffers harm (e.g., if he ruins his health by overindulgence, knowing he should not) against his wish (his rational DESIRE); hence he seems to suffer injustice. Aristotle replies that the incontinent person does not wish to suffer injustice. This reply seems inadequate, since wishing is not necessary for voluntariness (though cf. 1169a1).

3. **§7 1136b9–11 as Homer . . . cows' worth:** Homer, *Il.* vi 236.

(c) §8–13. Is it possible to do injustice to oneself?

4. **§9 1136b21–2 he overreaches . . . good:** Speaking of OVERREACHING for what is fine without qualification (see UNQUALIFIED) is an oxymoron. It does not match Aristotle's account of overreaching, since this kind of 'overreaching' is not vicious; cf. 1168b19–30. 'Overreach' (*pleonektein*) is closely related to 'having more' (*pleon echein*); cf. Plato, *Rep.* 349b.

(d) §14–16. Being just requires more than simply doing just actions.

5. **§14 1137a4–9 People think . . . and not up to us:** This section is not connected with what has preceded. It returns to the distinction between doing justice and being just that was set out in c8 and in ii 4. In saying that it is not up to us to be in a certain state when we act, Aristotle means that we cannot choose to act, here and now, from a state of character that we have not yet formed in ourselves. Aristotle does not deny that it is up to us to form a state of character. Cf. 1114a11–21.

Two features distinguish the virtuous person from someone who simply does virtuous actions: (1) He responds flexibly to particular situations, more accurately than someone who just has true beliefs about actions that are virtuous. (2) He does the right actions from the right STATE and motive. (2) explains (1) because the right state includes PRUDENCE, which responds flexibly and correctly to particular situations; cf. 1114b14, 1180b20.

6. **§16 1137a17–19 For the same . . . each of the actions:** This puzzle concerns the difference between craft (a capacity) and virtue (a state). Cf. 1140b21–4.

(e) §17. The scope of justice explains some of the difficulties and disputes.

7. **§17 1137a26–7 Just things . . . deficiency of them:** This section is not connected with its surroundings. To understand disputes about justice, we should remember that it involves external goods. Since they can be misused, some judgment is needed about their proper use and appropriate distribution; and this is why disputes arise.

8. **1137a30 and this . . . human:** Justice is suitable for normal human beings, not for gods.

10

10.§1–8. Puzzles about decency and justice.

(a) §1. Decency appears to conflict with justice.

1. **§1 1137a31–3 The next task . . . to the just:** This discussion of DECENCY may be out of place; c11 resumes the topics of 9.–13. The present chapter interrupts that sequence. It is more relevant to 9.§14–16; for decency about particular cases will be part of the just person's character, and sensitivity to the relevant considerations will be expected of the just person.

2. **1137b1–2 we transfer . . . instead of 'good':** See HOMONYMY. It is common to use 'decent' to refer, by meiosis, to goodness in general. The *EN* often follows this common usage.

3. **1137b4–5 what is decent is not excellent:** Delete *ou dikaion*. [Or, without the deletion, 'or what is decent is not just'.]

> (b) §2–7. Decency does not conflict with justice, correctly understood.

4. **§4 1137b19 since that . . . bound to be like:** On the subject matter of ethics, cf. 1094b12, 1098a28.

5. **§6 1137b25 the just without qualification:** I.e., it needs no qualification. See UNQUALIFIED #3.

6. **1137b26–7 rectification . . . deficient:** Aristotle tries to resolve the puzzles raised by common views of decency, and to show why the beliefs causing the puzzles are true up to a point (see ETHICS #7), and how his account explains them (marked by 'That is why . . .'). If we confine justice to law observance (cf. 1129b11), justice and decency appear to conflict, to the disadvantage of justice. Aristotle however argues (1129b17) that the law aims at, but may not achieve, justice, so that justice and decency do not conflict.

7. **§7 1137b31–2 as the lead . . . the stone:** Probably this is a flexible lead ruler that could be made to fit the shape of an irregular stone, and hence could be used to find a second stone to fit next to the first in a dry stone wall. For this purpose, having a rigid ruler would be useless. The rule or standard should be adaptable to the circumstances.

> (c) §8. Definition of decency.

11

11. §1–6. Puzzles about injustice to oneself.

> (a) §1–3. General injustice.

1. **§1 1138a4–5 Whether it is possible . . . been said:** Here we return to the questions discussed in 9.1–13.

2. **1138a 6–7 we are legally . . . kill ourselves:** Read *ouk ea(i)*. [Or, with OCT: *ou keleuei*, 'does not command'.] Delete *ha de mê keleuei, apagoreuei*. [Or, with OCT: 'and what it does not command, it forbids'.]

3. **§3 1138a12–14 That is why . . . does injustice to the city:** The specific form of 'dishonour' (*atimia*) that Aristotle has in mind is the loss of the status of a free citizen (see Aeschines, *in Ctesiphontem* 244), and hence the withdrawal of civil rights. See OCD sv 'atimia'.

> (b) §4–6. Special injustice.

4. **§5 1138a20–1 and results from a decision:** To make this consistent with c8, we need to take 'and' as equivalent to 'or' (i.e., some instances are merely voluntary; others result from decision).

11.§7–8. Is it worse to do injustice or to suffer it?

5. **§7 1138a28–31 It is also evident . . . intermediate amount are bad>:** The account of doing and suffering injustice applies the doctrine of the mean. Cf. 1133b33.

6. **1138a31–3 But doing injustice . . . state of> injustice):** Aristotle reverts to the distinction drawn in c8.

11.§9. Can there be justice and injustice within a single person?

7. **§9 1138b8–13 For in these discussions . . . for ruler and ruled:** Cf. 1166b19; Plato, *Rep.* 442d–444e. In contrast to Plato, Aristotle maintains that there can only be a qualified sort of justice within a person (for this contrast, cf. 1134b18). In b11, 'against one's own desires', read *heautou*. [Or, with OCT: *heautôn*; 'their own desires'.]

8. **§10 1138b13–14 So much, . . . character:** This concluding sentence prepares for the transition to virtues of thought in Book vi.

Book VI

1

1.§1–7. A full account of virtue of character requires an account of the virtues of thought.

(a) §1–3. To explain the definition of virtue as a mean involving the correct reason, we must give an account of the correct reason.

1. **§11138b18–20 Since we have . . . determine what it says:** The general formula in the account of the virtues needs to be made more precise; cf. 1103b21, *EE* 1220a13–29, 1222b5–9, 1249a22–b7. 1107a1 implied that reference to PRUDENCE is needed to explain what the correct reason (see REASON #3) is and what it aims at. The search for an account of the correct reason leads naturally into a discussion of the virtues of thought (1103a3), which includes prudence.

2. **§2 1138b26 true, but it is not at all clear:** Cf. *EE* 1216b32†, 1220a16.

3. **§3 1138b34 that is to say:** Lit. 'and'.

4. **1138b34 definition:** [Or 'distinguishing mark'.]

(b) §4–7. An account of the correct reason requires an account of the virtues of the rational parts of the soul.

5. **§5 1139a3–5 Previously, . . . one non-rational:** The division of the soul: i 7 and i 13.

6. **1139a6–8 Now we should . . . being otherwise:** The part of the soul concerned with SCIENCE is contrasted with the part concerned with non-scientific rational calculation about non-NECESSARY states of affairs. In fact not all of these states of affairs are matters of rational calculation and deliberation, as 1112a26–b9 makes clear. In 1139a8 read *hen de hôn endechontai*. [OCT, 'beings that admit of being otherwise'.]

7. §7 1139a16 **the best state:** Cf. *EE* 1218b38.

8. 1139a16–17 **Now a thing's virtue ... function of each part>:** Aristotle refers to the human FUNCTION (i 7; *EE* ii 1), and to the connexion between virtue and FUNCTION; cf. 1106a15. The supplement tries to make it clear that this sentence introduces the argument of c2.

2

2.§1–6. Virtue of character requires correct decision, and therefore requires both correct thought and correct desire.

(a) §1–3. The role of thought in action.

1. §1 1139a18 **sense perception, understanding, desire:** This chapter does distinguish UNDERSTANDING from THOUGHT and REASON. Contrast c6, 1143a35–b5.

2. §2 1139a18–20 **Of these ... no share in action:** Here and in the rest of the chapter, 'action' refers to rational action on a DECISION. See *EE* 1222b18–20†; ACTION #2.

3. §3 1139a29–30 **for truth ... correct desire:** Aristotle explains why practical thought must be concerned with truth.

(b) §4–5. The relation of thought and desire in a correct decision.

4. §4 1139a31 **Now the principle:** In this chapter 'PRINCIPLE' refers to the causal origin, as in 1113a6.

5. 1139a31–2 **the source of motion, not the goal:** Lit. 'that from which the motion <is> but not that for the sake of which (*hou heneka*) <the motion is>'. Aristotle refers to the efficient and final CAUSES. 'Goal' translates both *telos* and *hou heneka*.

6. 1139a32–3 **But the principle ... reason:** We need virtue of thought to find the true reasoning, and we need the right sort of character if we are to follow true reasoning in our actions. Our character must agree with true reasoning if we are to have a genuine virtue of character. The rest of Book vi looks for the true reasoning that is needed.

Aristotle does not make it clear whether (a) desire is prior to all reasoning, and goal-directed reasoning is subordinate to this desire, or (b) goal-directed reasoning may itself produce the relevant desire. See §5. The DESIRE that underlies decision is not non-rational desire, but rational wish (*boulêsis*) aiming at the good (cf. 1113a9–12). 'Goal-directed reason' might refer to the reasoning on the basis of which we come to believe that x is good for its own sake and hence form a wish for x.

7. 1139a33–4 **That is why ... and character:** The explanation 'for acting ... ' suggests that 'decision' in the previous clause refers to correct decision. 'Acting well' (*eupraxia*; see ACTION) might also be rendered 'doing well', i.e., faring well. It is cognate with *eu prattein* ('do well', 1095a19).

8. §5 1139a35–6 **Thought by itself ... with action <moves us>:** 'ACTION' refers only to action done for its own sake. See ACTION #3. Thought moves us to action only when it is for the sake of some end. Aristotle might mean: (a) Thought moves us when it is directed towards some end that we already desire. (b) Thought

moves us when it is directed towards some end that we recognize as worthy of desire. If he intends (a), he implies that thought moves us only if we already desire an end. If he intends (b), he allows thought to move us even in the absence of a prior desire. See §4.

Aristotle does not say that thought moves us to action only if it depends on a desire that is independent of thought; for wish is not necessarily independent of thought. Contrast Hume, *Treatise* ii 3.3.

9. **1139b1–2 For this thought . . . <further> goal:** Aristotle anticipates (as he did in i 1) the division between PRODUCTION and ACTION, which he explains in vi 4–5. Production aims at some product that is itself subordinate to some end pursued for its own sake, which is the end of action.

10. **1139b4 and desire is for the goal. That is why . . . :** A different punctuation: 'Now desire is for the goal. That is why . . .'.

11. **1139b4–5 either understanding . . . thought:** Lit. 'either desiderative understanding or thinking desire.'

(c) §6. The virtues of thought that are relevant to correct decision.

12. **§6 1139b9–11 That is why Agathon . . . never happened:** Agathon (TGF fr. 5) was an Athenian tragic poet (end of fifth century). He is a character in Plato's *Symposium*.

13. **1139b12–13 The function . . . towards the truth:** Since practical thought is concerned with action and decision, it must be concerned with deliberation, and hence must belong to the rationally calculating part. Aristotle returns to the division into two rational parts at 1139a6–16.

3

3.§1. The virtues of thought.

1. **§1 1139b14 Then let us . . . soul:** This section introduces the discussion of the particular virtues of thought. 'Begin again' alludes to the discussion of the particular virtues of character.

3.§2–4. Scientific knowledge.

(a) §2. It is about necessary facts.

2. **§2 1139b18–19 What science is . . . similarities:** In the strictest sense of 'science', practical disciplines are not sciences. See SCIENCE #2.

(b) §3. Its principles cannot be scientifically known.

3. **§3 1139b26–7 But all teaching . . . already known:** See *APo* i 1. In 'already known' *prognôskomenôn*, 'know', *gignôskein*, has a wider scope than *epistasthai*, the verb corresponding to *epistêmê*, 'scientific knowledge'. We can *gignôskein* (i.e., grasp, be acquainted with) something without scientific knowledge of it.

4. **1139b27 analytics:** Aristotle may be using this simply as a description of a work, not as its title.

5. **1139b28–9 Induction <leads to> the principle, i.e., the universal:** In b28 read *tês arches*. [Or with OCT: 'is the beginning'.] This may allude to the literal sense of 'INDUCTION', i.e., 'leading on'.

(c) §4. It requires demonstration from indemonstrable principles.

6. **§4 1139b32–3 analytics:** See *APo* i 3.

7. **1139b35 scientific . . . coincidentally:** We know something that is in fact a matter of scientific knowledge, but we do not grasp it as a matter of scientific knowledge. The propositions we know belong to an episteme (body of knowledge), but we lack the appropriate cognitive state. See COINCIDENT.

4

§1–6. Craft.

(a) §1–2. The difference between production and action.

1. **§1 1140a1–2 What admits . . . action:** Aristotle begins to draw the important distinction between ACTION and PRODUCTION by describing production and the CRAFT that is concerned with it. For the distinction that he attributes to his POPULAR works, see *MM* 1197a3; Plato, *Ch.* 163b. Aristotle rejects SOCRATES' identification of virtue with craft knowledge. See 1140b21–5.

2. **§2 1140a5 Nor . . . in the other:** Read *kai oude*.

(b) §3–6. Craft is concerned with production.

3. **§4 1140a11 and the exercise . . . study:** Read *technazein theôrein*.

4. **1140a15–16 nor with things . . . in themselves:** On natural things, see CRAFT, NATURE.

5. **§5 1140a20–1 as Agathon . . . of craft:** Agathon, TGF fr. 6.

5

5.§1–4. Prudence.

(a) §1–2. It requires deliberation about living well.

1. **§1 1140a24–5 To grasp . . . call prudent:** Aristotle sometimes uses *phronêsis* with a wide scope, including both theoretical and practical wisdom. He suggests that attention to a common use of *phronimos* helps us identify a virtue of practical reason. See PRUDENCE #1–2.

2. **1140a26 deliberate finely:** 'Finely' (*kalôs*) is often used more or less equivalently to 'well'. In its narrower sense, however, it is the characteristic aim of the virtues of character (see FINE), and Aristotle may intend this narrower sense here, as in the account of deliberation at 1112b17.

3. **1140a27 some restricted area:** Or 'partial' (*kata meros*).

4. **1140a28 what sorts of things are means to living well altogether:** On MEANS, see 1111b27, DECISION #2. 'Living well' is equivalent to 'happiness'; see 1095a19. On the general scope of prudence, see 1094b6 (for the connexion with

POLITICAL SCIENCE, see 1141b23), 1160a21; Plato, *Pr.* 318e. The prudent person does not simply find means to ends that are taken for granted. He begins with the very indefinite conception of the end as 'living well', and his deliberation shows him the FINE actions and states that living well consists in.

5. **§2 1140a28–30 A sign . . . no craft:** Cf. 1112a34, *Rhet.* 1357a1. The common use of 'prudent' for deliberation outside the area of a craft is justified; for since prudence is concerned with living well in general, it must be concerned with ACTION #3, not with production; hence it cannot be a craft.

(b) §3. It is neither scientific knowledge nor craft.

(c) §4–5. It is concerned with action, not production.

6. **§4 1140b6–7 For production . . . acting well itself:** This sentence explains why prudence is concerned with ACTION (in the narrow sense) and not with production. If it is concerned with living well in general, it must also be concerned with the unqualified end, which is action, the end of production (1139b1–4). Hence it is concerned with acting well (*eupraxia*; see 1139a34).

Serious difficulties arise unless Aristotle allows the same event to be both an action (insofar as it is done for its own sake) and a production (insofar as it is done for the sake of some end external to it). Many events that are virtuous actions, and as such decided on for themselves, are also productions; consider, for instance, a magnificent person's effort to have a suitable warship equipped. Similar questions arise about the relation between MOVEMENTS and ACTIVITIES. Cf. 1177b16–18.

5.§5–8. Defence of the account of prudence.

(a) §5. It fits the character of people who are recognized as prudent.

7. **§5 1140b7–10 That is why Pericles . . . such people:** Aristotle appeals to APPEARANCES (see ETHICS #7) to confirm his account. The account in turn vindicates the appearances, showing that they are reasonable if they rest on something like Aristotle's conception of prudence. Aristotle is not committed to endorsing all the appearances (he rejects some appearances about prudence at 1141b28). Here he appeals to recognized examples of prudent people. Pericles' prudent judgment on political and strategic questions is often emphasized by Thucydides (see esp. i 139.4; ii 65; perhaps ii 65.8 on Pericles' incorruptibility explains Aristotle's claim that such people know what is good for themselves). Aristotle is not necessarily endorsing Pericles' political outlook. He simply mentions him as a figure from the past to whom many would attribute this sort of good judgment. Cf. *Ath. Pol.* 27.1–28.2.

(b) §5–6. It fits the recognized connexion between prudence and temperance.

8. **1140b11–12 This is also . . . phronêsin):** Aristotle's fanciful etymology (cf. Plato, *Cra.* 411e) indicates the special connexion of prudence, as opposed to some other virtues of thought, to character. The special connexion results from the fact that prudence is about action, and hence about actions to be chosen for their own sakes.

Prudence requires knowledge of non-instrumental goods; but any conviction about non-instrumental goods must compete with conceptions of good that we form from our uneducated desire for PLEASURE; cf. 1113a33. In a badly educated person, the pleasure-based conceptions of good prevent the formation of the convictions required for prudence.

Repeated mistaken indulgence in the wrong pleasures will result in our losing our belief in their wrongness; cf. 1144a31. Repeated INCONTINENCE degenerates into intemperance; cf. 1114a15.

9. **§6 1140b16–17 For the principles . . . <we act>:** The end we want to achieve (the object of WISH) is the PRINCIPLE (i.e., starting point) of deliberation and hence of action. If we wish for the wrong end, our action will be misdirected.

10. **1140b17–18 can appear . . . cannot appear:** 'Can' and 'cannot' render *euthus*, 'immediately' (i.e., 'it follows that').

11. **1140b19–20 corrupts the principle:** Aristotle begins with 'PRINCIPLES' in the plural, but he seems to have in mind just one principle, which is the goal, i.e., the ultimate end. He seems to be referring to an agent's conception of the final good, i.e., of happiness. Cf. 1144a31–6, 1151a25–6.

12. **1140b20–1 And so prudence . . . human goods:** Since (1) temperance preserves prudence, and (2) what temperance preserves is true supposition about action, and especially about non-instrumental goods achievable in action, it follows that (3) this is the sort of supposition that prudence must be.

(c) §7–8. It fits the common belief that prudence cannot be misused or forgotten.

13. **§7 1140b21–5 Moreover, there is virtue . . . not a craft:** Aristotle rejects the attempt to identify prudence with a craft. He attributes the position he rejects to Socrates in Plato's early dialogues. See 1137a19; *MM* 1197a18; *Rhet.* 1355b2; *Met.* 1025a6; Plato, *HMi.* 375d–376c, *Rep.* 333e. The same point of disagreement with Socrates is expressed in Aristotle's distinction between CAPACITIES and STATES.

14. **§8 1140b28–30 A sign . . . prudence cannot:** Forgetting: 1100b11. Since prudence is about human goods, we do not find ourselves with no occasion to use it, so that we might come to forget it. Aristotle probably also refers to the close connexion of prudence with character and habit, and hence with the virtuous person's immediate response to situations. I may need to make an effort to recall how to open a coconut, but I do not need to make an effort to recall that I ought to be angry about injustice.

6

6. §1–2. Understanding.

(a) §1. There must be a virtue of thought concerned with principles.

1. **§1 1141a1–2 Nor is wisdom <exclusively> about principles:** The supplement seems to be required by 7.§3 (see note), which implies that wisdom includes understanding.

(b) §2. This virtue must be understanding.

2. **§2 1141a7–8 The remaining . . . understanding about principles:** Here 'UNDERSTANDING' has its strictest use (#3a). When SCIENTIFIC KNOWLEDGE is also spoken of in the strictest way, so that it requires demonstration, understanding a truth excludes having scientific knowledge of it, since no further account or REASON (1140b33) can be given of the PRINCIPLES of which we have understanding. See also 1142a25, 1143a35.

7

7. §1–5. Wisdom.

(a) §1–3. It embraces scientific knowledge and understanding.

1. **§1 1141a9–10 We ascribe wisdom . . . exact expertise in the crafts:** Here EXACTNESS implies that a piece of work is complete and finished in detail.

2. **1141a10 Pheidias . . . Polycleitus:** Aristotle mentions famous sculptors of the fifth century (just as 1140b8 mentioned Pericles, a famous politician of the fifth century).

3. **§2 1141a14–16 (as Homer . . . anything else'):** Aristotle, like other ancient readers, ascribes the comic epic *Margites* to Homer (here he quotes fr. 2).

4. **§3 1141a18–20 Therefore wisdom . . . coping stone:** Aristotle implies that wisdom includes understanding (cf. 1141a5–8). He defends the narrow use that confines 'wisdom' to scientific knowledge and understanding, and thereby to necessary truths. These are also the subject matter of theoretical STUDY. The common use of 'wisdom' applies it to many more areas. But common sense also agrees that wisdom requires exact knowledge; since Aristotle thinks exact knowledge is confined to scientific knowledge and understanding, he claims that common sense implicitly supports his restricted use of 'wisdom'.

(b) §3–5. In contrast to prudence, wisdom is concerned with the highest realities.

5. **1141a20–1 For it would . . . most excellent science:** 'Science' is supplied from here to the end of 8.§3 (the Greek has only feminine adjectives without nouns). (But in §5 below 'scientific knowledge' = *epistêmê*.) Aristotle often speaks of, e.g., political science and MEDICAL science, but these disciplines do not meet Aristotle's strictest criteria for a SCIENCE.

6. **§4 1141a22 Moreover:** Read *ei d'*.

7. **1141a24–5 the content of wisdom . . . the content of prudence:** Lit. 'the wise', 'the prudent' (and 'what is white' = lit. 'the white').

8. **1141a26 would call . . . such questions:** Read *phaien an* and *epitrepseian an*.

9. **1141a26–8 That is why . . . their own life:** Animal prudence: *Met.* 980b21; *GA* 753a7–17.

10. **1141a28–9 It is also . . . political science:** Unlike Plato, Aristotle sharply distinguishes the subject matter of wisdom and of prudence. Wisdom not only has no immediate practical end; it does not even study the same things, because the things

studied by prudence are not necessary states of affairs. The objects of demonstrative science are the most honourable (or 'valuable', *timion*). They deserve most HONOUR because (a) they are the necessary and unchanging principles of the universe, and necessity and unchangingness are the marks of divine realities (see GOD #6); and (b) they are thoroughly intelligible to reason because the truths about them are necessary and exceptionless, not exposing reason to ignorance or mistake (cf. 1139b21 on the non-necessary). Hence demonstrative scientific knowledge of necessary truths is the fullest expression of a human being's capacity for rational thought, hence the best ACTIVITY, and hence the highest VIRTUE of thought; in demonstration rational inference by itself can reach justified true conclusions starting from necessary premises, with no exceptions or qualifications.

11. **1141a31–2 there is no one . . . specific good:** Hence, if we identify wisdom with prudence, we will have to recognize many types of wisdom (since the good is different for each type of animal). This result is unacceptable because it conflicts with our assumption that wisdom is a single science with a unified content.

12. **1141a33–b2 It does not matter if human beings . . . the universe:** One might reply to the previous objection: 'It is all right to identify wisdom with prudence, and say that wisdom is the science of the best things, because human beings are the best animals.' Aristotle answers that 'because . . . ' is not a good enough reason for identification, since human beings are not the best things in the universe, and therefore do not provide a suitable subject matter for wisdom.

13. **§5 1141b6–7 Anaxagoras or Thales:** These are NATURALISTS, whom Aristotle takes (*Met.* i 1–4) to have been implicitly seeking wisdom, as he understands it. See 1155b8–9, 1179a15; *EE* 1216a11†; *Pol.* 1259a6; Plato, *Tht.* 174a. Just as Aristotle appealed to common views about the sorts of people who are called *phronimoi* (1140a25), he appeals to common views about *sophoi* who meet the conditions laid down earlier in the chapter.

7.§6–7. Prudence contrasted with wisdom.

(a) §6. It is concerned with action.

14. **§6 1141b8–12 Prudence, . . . achievable in action:** From here until the end of c8 divisions into chapters and sections are not clear, and the connexion of thought is not obvious. Aristotle now returns to the discussion of prudence, interrupted at the end of c5. He emphasizes the differences between wisdom and prudence, by expanding his description of prudence.

more than anyone else: Or 'more than anything else' (*malista*).

15. **1141b12–13 The unqualifiedly good . . . human being:** Good deliberation: see c9.

(b) §7. Hence it must consider particulars.

16. **§7 1141b14–16 Nor is prudence . . . is about particulars:** On prudence and PARTICULARS, see 1142a20–30, 1143a28–b14.

In this passage, 'particulars' seems to refer to relatively determinate types (e.g., 'bird meat' as opposed to 'light meat') rather than to particular instances (individuals, e.g., this piece of chicken). The prudent person also needs to be familiar with particular instances; cf. 1143b3.

How is this concern with particulars related to the claim that prudence is a deliberative virtue? If particulars are determinate types, identification of particulars is part of good deliberation. If they are particular instances, they are not discovered by deliberation, but perception of them is needed for successful deliberation; see 1112b34–1113a2.

17. §7 1141b18–19 **For someone . . . <hence> healthy:** This person knows why light meat is healthy. The grasp of the CAUSE is characteristic of CRAFT and SCIENCE. By contrast, the one who knows only that chicken is light and healthy does not know why it is healthy, but can identify healthy meat.

18. 1141b20 **bird . . . healthy:** Retain *koupha kai.*

19. 1141b22 **Here too, however, . . . <science>:** Perhaps this sentence should begin c8.

Aristotle corrects a false impression that might arise from his previous remarks; he does not mean that general principles are unimportant for the prudent person. Prudence must include a ruling science (cf. 1094a27, 1152b2). Cf. 1180b11–28.

8

8.§1–9. The range of prudence: universals and particulars.

    (a) §1–3. Different applications of prudence, to the individual and to the community.

1. §1 1141b24 **their being . . . same:** See 1130a12. Aristotle continues the thought of the last sentence of c7, which counterbalanced his remarks about prudence and particulars by emphasizing the universal, comprehensive scope of prudence; this was the scope he claimed for POLITICAL SCIENCE in 1094a26 (cf. *EE* 1218b12).

2. §2 1141b26 **particulars:** Read *hôs kath'hekasta.*

3. 1141b26 **<to both types>:** Aristotle rejects a common view that (a) confines prudence to concern for my own good and no one else's, and (b) confines political science to the political and legislative process. In (a) we neglect the connexion between the agent's good and other people's (1097b9) that makes ethics inseparable from political science. In (b) we neglect the principles that should guide political action.

4. 1141b27 **decree:** DECREES are about what to do in particular cases, in contrast to LAWS, which belong to the legislative form of prudence.

5. 1141b28–9 **That is why only . . . into practice:** On politically active people (*politeuomenoi*), cf. 1181a1.

    (b) §4. Prudence considers an individual's good with reference to a community.

6. §4 1141b34 **one species <of prudence>:** Delete *gnôseôs.* Aristotle emphasizes the universal scope of prudence, and argues against the assumptions that underlie a common restrictive view.

7. **1141a34 But there is . . . about it:** Or 'It is very different <from the other species>'.

8. **1142a2 too active:** Or 'busybodies' (*polupragmones*), a standard pejorative term for excessive involvement in politics (especially on the side disapproved of by the speaker). Cf. Plato, *Gorg.* 485e–486d. Aristotle neither endorses the ordinary political life (cf. 1095b22, 1179a1; *EE* 1215a23–7†; *Pol.* vii 3†–4) nor recommends withdrawal from political concerns.

9. **1142a2–6 Hence Euripides . . . too active . . . :** Odysseus says this in Euripides' lost play *Philoctetes* (TGF fr. 787–8), before he engaged in the morally dubious tricks involved in stealing Philoctetes' bow (if the plot resembled that of Sophocles' *Philoctetes* on this point). Odysseus regrets having abandoned the quiet life of an ordinary soldier. Cf. 1146a19–20, 1151b17–21.

10. **1142a7 For people seek . . . prudent people:** The common view about prudent people is understandable, because it rests on a common, though false, belief about the human good. See ETHICS #8.

(c) §5–7. Since prudence must take account of these various considerations, it is difficult to acquire and depends on experience.

11. **§5 1142a5–7 A sign . . . to be found:** The reference of 'what has been said' is not clear. In explaining the different views about prudence Aristotle mentions the difficulty of its subject matter. Part of the difficulty is the need for EXPERIENCE of particulars, which leads us back to the topic of 7.§7.

12. **§6 1142a16–18 Indeed we might . . . natural science:** This is connected to §5 because it offers a further illustration of the importance of experience.

13. **1142a18 reached through abstraction:** Abstraction (*aphairesis*, removal) involves the removal in thought, i.e., ignoring, of all the features of an object except those relevant to the particular question—for instance, the non-geometrical properties of physical objects—are abstracted when we study them geometrically (i.e., insofar as they are geometrical objects); see *Phys.* 193b31–4; *Met.* 1077b17–1078a31. Since these disciplines attend to fewer properties of physical objects, they demand less detailed empirical familiarity with the objects, and especially demand less than is demanded by natural science.

14. **1142a19 principles:** Or 'beginnings' (*archai*). The translation and supplement assume that Aristotle is referring to the theoretical principles of the science, not to the starting points in perception.

15. **1142a19–20 Young people, . . . the words:** They lack relevant experience. Cf. 1147a21–2.

16. **§7 1142a20–2 Further, the particular:** The fact that prudence deals with particulars, and hence requires experience, supports the claim in §4 about the difficulty of the questions that concern prudence.

In this sentence the PARTICULARS are particular instances (e.g., this water here, as in the next sentence), rather than determinate types (cf. 1141b15).

(d) §8–9. Since prudence considers particulars, it is neither scientific knowledge nor understanding.

17. **§8 1142a23–5 It is apparent . . . achievable in action:** The reference of 'as we said' is not clear. Since Aristotle has just remarked in §7 that prudence is concerned with particulars, he returns to the topic of 7.§7, which also leads him back to the discussion of UNDERSTANDING in c6. The 'last thing' that concerns prudence is last as one proceeds from the more general to the more particular (cf. 1143a32–5, 1146a9).

18. **§9 1142a25 Hence . . . understanding:** Or perhaps 'Hence it corresponds to understanding' (in that both are concerned with things that cannot be further defined—though for quite different reasons).

19. **1142a25–6 For understanding . . . <first> terms:** Understanding grasps the primary terms in a demonstrative SCIENCE. ('Terms' [*horoi*] might refer to the things defined or to the DEFINITIONS.) These come first in a demonstrative science (not in a practical science) because they are the most universal. Prudence is concerned with terms that come last in a practical science (not in a demonstrative science) because they are the most particular. Aristotle does not deny his normal claim that prudence also grasps the first principles in practical affairs; for this claim, cf. 1140b18, 1142b33. He omits his normal claim about prudence grasping general principles, because he attends to a point of contrast between prudence and theoretical understanding.

20. **1142a27 This is not . . . special objects:** Having said that prudence is concerned with particulars, Aristotle argues that it must include some sort of PERCEPTION, since this is how we become aware of particulars. To specify the sort of perception he has in mind, he contrasts it with the ordinary perception of 'special objects' ('objects' supplied in this paragraph), i.e., colour, sound, etc., which are 'proper sensibles', the objects proprietary to sight, hearing, etc. See *DA* ii 6.

21. **1142a28 mathematical objects:** Retain *en tois mathêmatikois*.

22. **1142a29 stop there too:** We have to recognize, without being given any further reason, that the triangle is the last, i.e., the simplest, mathematical figure. In 'stop there too' Aristotle means that unless we can recognize something without being given a further argument, we will face an infinite regress. He made this point about deliberation and perception in 1112b34–1113a2.

23. **1142a29–30 This is another . . . prudence is:** Lit. 'But this is more (or 'rather') perception than prudence, but another species of it'. Read *ê <hê> phronêsis*.

By 'another species' Aristotle probably means 'another species besides perception of proper sensibles (colours, sounds, etc.)'. He contrasts (a) the perception of a triangle as the last figure with both (b) perception of proper sensibles, and (c) the perception proper to prudence. He recognizes that (c) is less like (a) than (b) is. He may have in mind the fact that the perception proper to prudence requires grasp of a more elaborate range of theoretical judgments (those that figure in ethical deliberation) than we need for either (a) or (b).

9

9.§1–8. *Good deliberation.*

(a) §1–3. Since it includes inquiry, it must be distinguished from the intellectual states that result from completed inquiry.

1. **§1 1142a32–3 We . . . good deliberation is:** Aristotle returns to the description of the 'unqualifiedly good deliberator' who was introduced in 1141b12–14, and proceeds to explain it. He does not refer to anything in 1141b14–1142a30.

2. **§2 1142a34–b1 not scientific knowledge . . . already know:** See Plato, *Meno* 71b, 80de. Aristotle assumes that SCIENCE (scientific knowledge) is a type of knowledge (*eidenai*).

3. **1142b2–5 For good guessing . . . deliberate slowly:** Deliberation, and hence DECISION, requires a process that takes time and precedes the action. Cf. 1117a20.

4. **§3 1142b10 no correctness . . . knowledge:** There is no proper subset of scientific knowledge that is correct, since all scientific knowledge must be correct.

5. **1142b11 and correctness . . . truth:** Correctness in deliberation, however, does not consist in truth; see 1112a5.

6. **1142b11–12 Further, . . . determined:** We deliberate about something because it is not yet determined what it is best to do.

7. **1142b13 For thought . . . assertion:** Hence, it is not belief either, since belief requires asserting (i.e., assenting to) what one believes.

(b) §4–7. Correctness in deliberation requires the correct conclusion and the correct process, aiming at the correct end.

8. **§4 1142b16–17 what <this . . . <correctness> about:** Delete *hê boulê*.

9. **1142b17–18 Since there are . . . every type:** The CORRECTNESS of the prudent person's deliberation must be distinguished from the other types. Good deliberation is not simply the discovery of the most effective means to ends that are taken for granted.

10. **1142b19 what he proposes to see:** I.e., the result he aims at.

11. **1142b19–20 and so . . . correctly:** If all it takes to deliberate correctly is to find the means to one's end, the incontinent deliberates correctly, Aristotle denies the antecedent of this conditional.

12. **1142b20 but . . . great evil:** One may act incontinently as a result of deliberation about the satisfaction of one's bad appetite. But the incontinent does not act on a DECISION (1111b13–14). The DESIRE that originates the incontinent's deliberation is a non-rational appetite, not the rational wish that is required for decision.

In contrast to the incontinent person, the vicious person acts on a decision, and hence on a wish (1151a6–7). Simply acting on some sort of decision and wish is not sufficient for good deliberation.

13. **1142b21–2 for the sort of correctness . . . reaches a good:** A vicious person might deliberate correctly about ways to make money dishonestly. In one respect he reaches a good, since wealth is a good. In another respect, however, he fails to reach a good, since wealth is not a good for him, given that he is vicious (1129b1–6). This second respect is the one Aristotle has in mind here.

14. **§5 1142b22–4 However, we can reach . . . term is false:** The good deliberator, and therefore the prudent and virtuous person, must reach the correct conclusion by the right route. If my deliberation tells me correctly that I ought not to steal now, but does not tell me this for the right reasons (if, for instance, it tells me I ought not to steal simply because I am likely to be found out, or because my victim is a friend of mine), it is not good deliberation.

15. §7 1142b27–8 **Further, our . . . <limited> end:** Lit. 'Further, it is possible to have deliberated well both without qualification and towards some end'.

16. **1142b29–31 Hence unqualifiedly good . . . <limited> end:** The unqualified end is the end for a human being. It is not merely the end in relation to some limited aim or imperfection of a particular human being; cf. 1139b2.

17. §7 **1142b32–3 what is . . . supposition:** Aristotle affirms that prudence is correct supposition about the unqualified end. Cf. 1140b12–13. His saying this has been taken to conflict with his claim that prudence is concerned only with deliberation about what promotes the end (1140a25–8). We need not believe there is any conflict, however, if we bear in mind the broad scope of MEANS (*ta pros to telos*; see DECISION), and hence of deliberation. As a result of deliberating about what promotes happiness, we discover its constituents, and so we have a more precise conception of happiness. This precise conception is probably what Aristotle has in mind when he says that prudence is true supposition about the end. Deliberation both precedes this true conception of the end and follows it (since a fairly precise conception of happiness is the basis for further deliberation about what to do). This passage does not make it clear whether Aristotle is thinking about the deliberation that forms the correct supposition about the end, or about the deliberation that follows it; he may well have both in mind. Cf. 1144a8, 31.

[Or 'about which (sc. what is expedient as a means) prudence is . . . '.]

10

10.§1–4. Comprehension.

(a) §1. It has the same subject matter as prudence.

1. §1 **1142b34–1143a1 Comprehension, . . . comprehend well:** As 11.§2 shows, this chapter fits at the end of c8, as part of the survey of intellectual virtues that leads up to the discussion of particulars in c11. It does not fit so naturally at the end of c9 (though deliberation is mentioned in 1143a6), which did not fit naturally at the end of c8 (see 1142a31).

(b) §2–4. In contrast to prudence, it is not prescriptive.

2. §2 **1143a8–10 For prudence is prescriptive . . . judges:** Cf. *EE* 1220a9, b6. Comprehension recognizes that the phronimos has found the correct steps to achieve the end he had in view, but it does not necessarily conclude that something ought to be done. Comprehension says, 'If you apologize to him, he will be less resentful'. Prudence says, 'Since you must remove his resentment, you must apologize to him'.

3. **1143a10 for, . . . with comprehension:** Read *kai gar sunetoi*.

4. §4 **1143a16–18 It is derived . . . comprehending:** The Greek *manthanein* used here is applied both to the process of learning and to the grasp of the subject that we have learnt; this grasp is identified with comprehension.

11

11.§1. Consideration and considerateness.

1. **§1 1143a19–20 The <state> . . . decent person:** Aristotle describes the connexion between 'consideration' (*gnômê*; or 'good judgment') and 'considerateness' (*sungnômê*; see PARDON) and their relation to the decency that is described in v 10.

11.§2–7. The application of practical thought to particulars.

(a) §2–3. Different virtues are needed to grasp particulars.

2. **§2 1143a25 It is reasonable . . . direction:** Aristotle sums up some of his remarks on the intellectual virtues, and draws some conclusions. He does not refer back to c9 (on good deliberation), which, fits better after 7.§6 than after c8.

3. **1143a29 i.e.:** Lit. 'and'. Cf. 1142a23–5.

4. **§3 1143a32–5 Now all . . . last things:** This explains why all the states that have been mentioned are concerned with particulars.

(b) §4–6. The role of understanding in grasping particulars.

5. **§4 1143a35–6 Understanding . . . directions:** 'In both directions' indicates that here 'last' indicates both the last things as you go towards the more universal (hence in a36 they are the 'first terms') and the last things as you go from universal to particular (hence 'last' in a 36). As in 8.§9, Aristotle contrasts (a) understanding in demonstrative science with (b) the way in which prudence is aware of particulars. In 1142a25 he called (b) a type of perception that he opposed to understanding. Here he calls (b) a type of understanding. He calls it understanding because it is analogous to (a), insofar as no further account or reason can be given for our grasp of the particular, just as none can be given for our grasp of a first principle of demonstration. Though the terms used here are different from those in 1142a25, the same basic contrast is drawn between prudence and understanding.

[Or: Instead of the contrast between (a) and (b) above, Aristotle might mean that practical nous is concerned with both with general principles and with particular actions.]

6. **1143a36 both about . . . last:** 'First' and 'last' mark the contrast that was just marked by using 'last in both directions'.

7. **1143b3 In <premisses> . . . minor premiss:** Lit. 'of the last and the admitting and of the other premiss (*protasis*)'. 'Minor premiss' presupposes the account of practical INFERENCE at 1147a25–31; cf. 1144a31. Understanding finds the relevant features of particular situations, so that general principles can be applied to them. If, for instance (cf. 1122a22–6), a general principle says, 'Excessive display in equipping warships should be avoided', some grasp of what would be excessive in this particular case, in fitting out this warship, is needed.

8. **1143b4–5 For these . . . particulars:** Lit. 'for these are the *archai* of that for the sake of which; for universals are from (or 'out of', *ek*) particulars.' We might translate *archai* by 'principles' rather than 'beginnings'. But the following clause suggests that Aristotle is thinking of the process of acquiring universals, not of the PRINCIPLES that are our basic premisses. If we use understanding of particulars to identify the appropriate features of particular situations, we form more useful and determinate rules; see 1141b14–16. This process is induction; see INFERENCE.

9. **§5 1143b5 We must ... understanding:** 'Understanding' refers to the state called 'perception' (as opposed to understanding) in 1142a25–30. In the earlier passage, Aristotle said he was not referring to ordinary perception. In the present passage the difference from ordinary perception is marked by 'understanding'.

10. **§6 1143b9–10 That is why ... about them:** In practical (as opposed to theoretical) reasoning we begin from understanding exercised in particular situations, and we form generalizations that will be applicable to particular situations. This interpretation requires us to take 'demonstrations' rather loosely, since Aristotle normally contrasts demonstrative science with ethical reasoning (as in §4).

In the mss. this sentence comes in §6, after 'as though nature were the cause'.

(c) §5–7. These virtues of thought concerned with particulars develop through experience.

11. **§5 1143b6 That is why ... naturally:** The fact that EXPERIENCE is needed for prudence (cf. 1142a14–16) explains (see THAT IS WHY) the mistaken view that prudence grows naturally.

12. **1143b6–7 no one ... wisdom:** Wisdom requires demonstration, which requires teaching (1139b25).

13. **§7 1143b14–17 We have said, ... the soul:** The reference to the two parts of the soul recalls 1139b12–13. The discussion in c8–11 has clarified the contrast between wisdom and prudence.

12

12. §1–3. Puzzles about prudence and wisdom.

(a) §1. How do they contribute to being virtuous? Puzzle 1: What use is wisdom?

1. **§1 1143b18 One might, ... use they are:** The discussion of these puzzles takes up all of c1213.

(b) Puzzle 2: What use is prudence for being virtuous?

2. **1143b21–8 For knowledge ... are states:** The translation departs from the structure of the Greek. Lit. 'What do we need it for, if prudence is that about the just things and fine things and good things for a human being, and these are the things it belongs to the good man to do, but we are no more prone to act by knowing them, if the virtues are states, just as neither the healthy things nor the fit things (as many as are spoken of not by producing but by being from the state)—for we are no more prone to act by having the medical and gymnastic?'

This puzzle rests on the assumption that just as (1): (a) I can do what is healthy and hence (b) be healthy, without (c) knowing medicine, so also (2): (a) I can do what is virtuous and hence (b) be virtuous, without (c) having prudence. Aristotle challenges the alleged parallel between (1) and (2). He denies that (2b) follows from (2a), if (2a) is understood so as not to require prudence; see 1144a11.

Since virtues are STATES of character, they are put into practice in virtuous actions. They are not merely theoretical disciplines.

(c) §2. Puzzle 3: how does prudence help us to become virtuous?

3. **§2 1143b28 useful:** Read *chrēsimon*.

4. **1143b29–30 should we . . . already excellent:** This puzzle assumes that prudence is analogous to a specialized CRAFT whose products are useful to me, but whose practice I can leave to someone else; though I value the product of MEDICINE, I need not be a doctor myself. This objection reflects failure to distinguish prudence and virtue from craft (cf. 1105a26–b5).

5. **1143b30 Nor, however, . . . matter to them:** Read *mê ousi* and *autois echein*.

(c) §3. Puzzle 4: does prudence control wisdom?

6. **§3 1143b35 for the science . . . each thing:** This clause argues that prudence should control wisdom. Aristotle examines this argument in 1145a6–11.

12. §3–9. Wisdom, prudence, and virtue of character.

(a) §3–6. Answer to Puzzle 1: the value of wisdom and prudence.

7. **§4 1144a1–2 First of all, . . . <of the soul>:** In reply to the first puzzle (in §1), Aristotle maintains the non-instrumental value of wisdom and prudence. These are part of the formal CAUSE of happiness. We say, 'He is healthy because his body is in a healthy condition which is . . . (giving details)'; we thereby say what health consists in. Similarly we say, 'He is happy because he is wise and . . . (adding the other components)'; we thereby say what happiness consists in.

8. **§5 1144a4 health produces <health>:** Or 'health produces <happiness>'.

9. **§6 1144a6–7 Further, we fulfil our function:** Virtue and FUNCTION: 1139a16–17, b12.

10. **1144a7–8 for virtue . . . <correct>:** For this division of labour between virtue and prudence, cf. 1144a20, 1145a4, 1178a16. We might take it to imply that (a) prudence finds the means to an end, and (b) this end has already been fixed by virtue, independently of prudence. Claim (a) is correct, if we take account of the wide scope of 'means'. But then (b) is open to question. For if deliberation about happiness produces a correct conception of the nature (components) of happiness, it produces the virtuous person's correct conception of the end (see 1142b33). In that case, contrary to (b) above, prudence itself helps to fix the goal that virtue aims at, so that virtue of character does not makes the end correct independently of prudence. On this question about virtue, cf. *MM* 1190a8–33; *EE* ii 11 (it is not anticipated so explicitly in the earlier books of the *EN*).

11. **1144a10 no such virtue:** No virtue that corresponds to the human FUNCTION belongs to the purely nutritive part of the soul.

(b) §7. Virtue of character requires the correct decision.

12. **§7 1144a11 To answer . . . :** The answer seems to come first in §10, where Aristotle says that prudence requires cleverness. A fuller answer comes in 13.§2.

13. **1144a11 better at achieving:** Or 'more prone to do'. (*praktikôteroi*). To answer the puzzle, Aristotle goes back to his claim that virtue of character involves the correct decision, which causes one to choose the virtuous actions for their own sakes.

14. **1144a14–17 we say . . . either unwillingly, . . . ought to do:** 'Unwillingly' might refer to force, or to the conditions mentioned in 1135b4–8.

15. **1144a17–20 Equally, . . . actions themselves:** See 1105a32 (cf. 1134a20, 1135b35). A decision, and hence deliberation about what promotes an end, is necessary for choosing the correct actions for their own sakes (i.e., as part of the conception of happiness that one has reached by deliberation).

(c) §8–10. Prudence requires both cleverness and virtue of character.

16. **§8 1144a20 Virtue . . . correct:** We might take this in either of two ways: (1) When Aristotle says that virtue makes the decision correct, he includes the roles that he ascribed to virtue and to prudence in §6, since both of these are required for a correct decision. The role he attributes to cleverness is not the deliberative task of finding what promotes an end. (2) He repeats what he said in §6 when he said that virtue makes the goal right; hence he means, strictly speaking, that virtue makes our decision aim at the right goal. In that case, the role he attributes to cleverness is the same as the role he attributed to prudence in §6; finding what promotes the end. Prudence differs from cleverness only because our deliberative ability is called 'prudence' only if it serves the correct end.

17. **1144a21–2 But the actions . . . capacity:** Cf. *EE* 1227b40†. In 'the actions . . . fulfil the decision', Aristotle does not speak of the means that prudence finds by deliberation, in advance of a decision. He refers to non-deliberative facility and resourcefulness in finding ways to carry out a decision once it has been made. He never says that cleverness involves deliberation.

18. **§9 1144a24–5 to be able to do . . . goal is assumed:** Here Aristotle speaks of means to a goal, after speaking of ways to carry out a decision. He is referring to the same actions in different ways. Once again, he takes the mark of cleverness to be resourcefulness in action, not in deliberation.

19. **1144a25–6 and to attain them:** Or 'to hit on them' (i.e., to discover or identify them). Read *tunchanein autôn*. Cf. *EE* 1227b40†. If the role of cleverness is non-deliberative, Aristotle perhaps makes room for it in 1112b34–1113a2, where he recognizes the limits of deliberation. In that case, he returns here to the concern of prudence with particulars, which he discussed in c11.

20. **1144a28 both prudent . . . clever:** Read *kai tous panourgous*.

21. **§10 1144a28–9 Now prudence is not cleverness:** Read *ouch hê deinotês*.

22. **1144a29–30 But <prudence> . . . with virtue:** Lit. 'The state comes to be for this eye of the soul not without virtue.' Aristotle relies on his standard contrast between CAPACITY and STATE (cf. 1106a6–9) to make it clear that prudence requires our capacities to be turned in the right direction. Until someone is virtuous he has only an aptitude (a capacity) for prudence, not prudence itself. Cleverness in action is not sufficient for prudence, which also requires the right ends that belong to virtue, and hence requires the correct decision (1152a10). Aristotle does not mean, however, that the prudent person is simply a clever person who has also

been well brought up. He has the right end because he has deliberated 'well' in the way explained in c9.

23. **1144a31–3 For inferences . . . sake of argument):** Cf. 1143a35–b5. Here Aristotle considers the major premiss. Only the good person has the correct conception of what the highest good consists in. He reaches this conception by good deliberation; cf. 1142b32. The stringent conditions for good deliberation (see esp. 1142b22–6) explain why even continent and incontinent people cannot have the right conception of the good, even though their decision is in some way correct (cf. 1151a20–6). On the bad effects of vice, see 1140b11.

13

13.§1–8. The connexion between virtue of character and prudence.

(a) §1–2. Full virtue, as opposed to natural virtue, requires prudence.

1. **§1 1144b1 We must, . . . again:** Having argued that prudence requires virtue, Aristotle now argues that virtue requires prudence.

2. **1144b1–4 For virtue . . . natural virtue . . . full virtue:** Cf. 1117a4, 1127b14, 1151a18, 1179b21–6; NATURE #1. Aristotle refers to natural aptitudes, not to genuine virtues (cf. 1103a23).

3. **1144b6–9 But still we look . . . evidently harmful:** Those who lack prudence lack full (see CONTROLLING) virtue, because they lack the appropriate discernment and flexibility in less familiar situations (cf. 1137a9, 1180b20).

4. **1144b12 so it is with virtue:** I.e., naturally well-endowed people who lack understanding will harm themselves.

5. **§2 1144b14–17 And so, . . . acquired without prudence:** The condition that Aristotle contrasts with mere natural aptitude is full virtue of character, which includes prudence. (He also calls this 'habituated virtue', 1151a18–19.) Virtue of character is not simply the result of good upbringing without prudence (cf. 1095b4–9). Since virtue of character includes prudence, habituation' is complete only when the person being habituated has acquired prudence.

(b) §3–7. Virtue of character and prudence require each other.

6. **§3 1144b18–19 Socrates used to undertake:** 'Used to' signals a reference to the historical SOCRATES; cf. 1095a32. Socrates examines and (many readers believe, in agreement with Aristotle) defends the identification of every virtue with knowledge of good and evil in the *La.* and *Pr.* Plato rejects this doctrine in *Rep.* iv.

7. **1144b18 <cases of> prudence:** Lit. 'prudences'. Perhaps '<forms of> prudence'. The same question arises where '<cases of>' is supplied in §5.

8. **§4 1144b21–3 Whenever people now . . . the correct reason:** Aristotle now answers the question about the correct reason that he raised in c1 (cf. 1103b32). The correct reason is specified by prudence (1107a1); the description of prudence has explained more fully what the content of the correct reason will be.

9. **§5 1144b26 in accord with (*kata*) the correct reason:** I.e., behavioural conformity, doing the actions that correct reason prescribes.

10. **1144b27 involving (*meta*) the correct reason:** I.e., actions that are guided by the agent's own correct reason. These actions rest on the correct DECISION. See ii 4, 1144a13–20; *MM* 1198a14–21†.

11. **§6 1144b32–4 And in this way . . . one another:** Though Aristotle rejects the Socratic belief in the unity and identity of all the virtues, he thinks (a) each virtue is inseparable from prudence (1107a1, 1138b18–34, 1178a16–19), and (b) prudence is inseparable from all the virtues. It follows that (c) each virtue is inseparable from all the other virtues. We have seen why he believes (a); but (b) and (c) seem to neglect the role of external conditions in some of the virtues (magnificence and magnanimity, for instance); cf. 1122a28, 1123b5, 1125b4 (and for a different sort of exception, see 1115a20). To cope with these cases (b) and (c) seem to need revision (as Aquinas suggests in *ST* 1–2 q65 a1 ad 1). Cf. *MM* 1199b36–1200a11†.

12. **1145a1–2 for one has . . . single state:** Read *mia(i) ousê(i) huparchousê(i)*. Lit. 'for at the same time as prudence, being one, being present, all will be present'.

13. **§7 1145a2–4 And it is clear . . . soul>:** We return to the first puzzle (12.§1). Though Aristotle has officially been answering the second and third puzzles until now, he has also made his answer to the first more convincing by suggesting how prudence is the virtue of a rational part of the soul.

14. **1145a4–5 and because . . . without virtue:** This is a second reason why we would need prudence even if it did not affect our action. We would need it in order to have the right decision, and hence the right character.

15. **1145a5–6 for <virtue> . . . means to the end:** This clause takes up the previous 'without prudence or without virtue', in chiastic order. By 'achieve the end', Aristotle probably means 'achieve the right grasp of the end' (which he previously expressed by saying that virtue makes the end correct), rather than 'attain the end we were aiming at'. The questions raised above about the relation between virtue and prudence arise again here (cf. 1144a20–b1). Aristotle probably does not mean that virtue, independently of prudence, fixes the right end, and then prudence finds what promotes it. For he has just insisted that virtue (which makes the end correct) requires prudence (which makes the things promoting the end correct); hence, it seems, we cannot make the end correct without making the things promoting the end correct. This conclusion is reasonable if prudent deliberation about what promotes the ultimate end (i.e., what constitutes happiness, fixing our conception of happiness) results in a correct conception of the end (i.e., of what constitutes happiness). On virtue and prudence, cf. 1178a16.

(c) §8. The relation of prudence to wisdom.

16. **§8 1145a6–8 Moreover, prudence . . . control health:** Wisdom has its place in a life organized and planned by prudence, but it is not thereby of less value than prudence. The place of wisdom in happiness is explained in x 6–8. Cf. *MM* 1198b9–20.

Book VII

1

1.§1–5. Introduction to the discussion of incontinence.

(a) §1–3. Conditions superior to virtue and inferior to vice.

1. **§1 1145a20–2 Thus Homer . . . a god:** Homer, *Il.* xxiv 258–9.

2. **§2 1145a22–7 If therefore, . . . than vice:** On the gods, cf. 1178b10. On becoming gods, cf. 1159a5, 1166a19.

3. **§3 1145a29 divine man:** Aristotle uses a Doric (Spartan) dialect form ('*seios*' for '*theios*') to show that he is quoting a Spartan expression.

(b) §4. Conditions between virtue and vice: continence and incontinence.

(c) §5. The method of inquiry.

4. **§5 1145b2–3 As in . . . appearances:** These appearances (*phainomena*) are the 'common beliefs' that Aristotle goes on to mention. Aristotle's method: ETHICS #5. The rest of the discussion of incontinence is clearly organized around the puzzles (*aporiai*; see ETHICS #6) that Aristotle proceeds to raise.

5. **1145b5 ways of being affected:** *Pathê*, usually rendered by 'FEELINGS'. Here Aristotle refers broadly to the conditions he has just mentioned, which are not simply feelings.

6. **1145b4–6 ideally, . . . most important:** Aristotle takes the common beliefs seriously, but he does not promise to defend them all. In the case of incontinence he does not defend them all. One might ask how Aristotle decides how a specific belief is one of the 'most important' (or 'CONTROLLING', *kurion*) beliefs that need to be preserved.

1.§6–7. Common beliefs about incontinence.

7. **§6 1145b8–9 Continence and . . . conditions:** Aristotle turns to a survey of the relevant common beliefs, before he asks how far they should be accepted.

2

2.§1–11. Puzzles arising from the common beliefs about incontinence.

(a) §1–5. In what sense does the incontinent person correctly grasp what he ought to do?

1. **§1 1145b21–2 We might . . . acts incontinently:** §1–5 discuss the various ways in which the incontinent person might have a correct supposition. 'SUPPOSITION' is the generic term for a cognitive state. Aristotle thinks it important to decide exactly what sort of cognitive state, and about what, the incontinent is in. 'Knowledge' in this discussion renders *epistêmê*.

[Or 'how, when someone has a correct supposition, he acts incontinently'.]

2. **1145b23 Socrates used to think:** As in 1144b18–21, Aristotle uses the Greek imperfect tense to refer to the historical SOCRATES.

3. **1145b24 dragged around like a slave:** See Plato, *Pr.* 352bc. Aristotle takes this Platonic dialogue to reflect the views of the historical Socrates.

4. **1145b26–7 For no one . . . the conflict>:** Socrates argues (*Pr.* 353c–357e) that the presence of knowledge ensures I will not act against what I know to be best, because knowledge is firm and not liable to change (but cf. *Pr.* 358b). If at time t1 I have true belief that x is better than y, and at later time t2 I do y rather than x, then, in Socrates' view, I must have changed my mind so that at t2 I believe that y is better than x.

5. **§2 1145b28 contradicts things that appear manifestly:** I.e., they seem obviously true. [Or 'manifestly contradicts'.]

6. **1145b29–31 if ignorance . . . eventually does>:** In 'For . . . ' Aristotle explains why the Socratic position conflicts with obvious appearances. The incontinent person grasps the right thing to do before he does the wrong thing. But though the Socratic position is wrong, reference to other some type of ignorance may explain incontinence. On 'affected', see FEELING.

7. **§5 1146a7–9 For on this view . . . other virtues:** Aristotle summarizes some of his claims about PRUDENCE in Book vi. Since prudence requires right action and virtue, it excludes incontinence; 1144a29, 1152a6.

(b) §6. Must the incontinent person have bad desires?

8. **§6 1146a9 Further:** 'Further' (*eti*) marks a shift from the puzzles about right supposition in §1–5 to a more varied set of puzzles, marked by repeated use of 'further' in §6–11.

(c) §7–9. Is incontinence sometimes desirable?

9. **§7 1146a19–20 Take, . . . Philoctetes:** Sophocles, *Philoctetes* 895–916. Cf. 1151b17–21, 1142a3–6. Odysseus had persuaded Neoptolemus to win Philoctetes' confidence, and then betray him by stealing his bow. Neoptolemus cannot bring himself to betray Philoctetes, but breaks his promise to Odysseus instead.

10. **§8 1146a21–3 Further, the sophistical . . . paradoxical results:** An argument put forward by a SOPHIST (cf. Plato's *Euthydemus*) aims to confuse the opponent, not to explore any genuine puzzle. Nonetheless, it may raise a genuine puzzle.

11. **1146a23 in encounters:** Read *entuchōsin*.

12. **1146a24–7 for thought is tied up . . . solve the argument:** On this effect of puzzles, cf. *Met.* 995a28.

(d) §10. Is incontinence worse than intemperance?

13. **§10 1146a30–2 Further, if someone . . . persuaded and decides to do:** This is the intemperate person. DECISION #1 requires wish, not only deliberation; cf. 1146b22.

(e) §11. What is the range of incontinence?

14. **§11 1146b2 If so, . . . simply incontinent:** He is said to be incontinent 'simply' (or 'without qualification'; see UNQUALIFIED), without mention of any specific area of incontinence.

2.§12–3.§1. The right approach to the puzzles.

15. **§12 1146b6 These, . . . that arise:** 2.§12 and 3.§1, finish the discussion of the puzzles and list the next questions.

16. **1146b7 solution:** Lit. 'loosing'. The metaphor of binding is continued from 1146a24. Cf. *EE* 1215a7†.

3

3.§2. The difference between incontinence and intemperance.

1. **§2 1146b14 We begin:** The first puzzle to be discussed is the last one just mentioned.

2. **1146b17 by their attitudes:** Lit. 'by how'. Read *pôs*.

3. **1146b19–20 For the simply incontinent . . . intemperate person:** The present sentence has two functions: (1) It answers the previous question. (2) It rules out the second of the three possibilities mentioned above; Aristotle argues that the distinctive feature of the incontinent cannot be simply his attitude (since one can take the same attitude in actions that do not manifest simple incontinence).

4. **1146b20–1 Nor is he . . . as intemperance:** This argues against the first of the three possibilities mentioned; incontinence cannot be distinguished purely by the range of incontinent actions, which is also the range of intemperance.

5. **1146b22–4 For the intemperate . . . pursues it:** The DECISION of the vicious person is different from that of the incontinent person. The incontinent person in some way makes the correct decision (only in some way; cf. 1144a31–6).

3.§3–14. In what sense does the incontinent person have or lack the appropriate knowledge?

(a) §3–4. The difference between knowledge and belief is irrelevant to this question.

6. **§3 1146b24–5 Now . . . with knowledge:** We now turn to the first of the questions announced in §1.

7. **§4 1146b30–1 as Heracleitus makes clear:** Probably Aristotle refers to the dogmatic and oracular style of Heracleitus' short and paradoxical remarks, which are unsupported by any argument that might warrant a claim to knowledge. Cf. *MM* 1201b5–9. [Or Aristotle might refer to some lost remark of Heracleitus.]

(b) §5–6. To understand incontinence we must grasp the various ways in which knowledge may be merely potential.

8. **§5 1146b31–3 But we speak . . . using it:** Aristotle examines various ways of knowing and not knowing. In §5–8 he discusses different cases that do not completely

fit incontinents, but eventually help us to understand some aspects of the incontinent's state of mind. §5–8 show how someone can fail to draw the right conclusion about a particular case. The incontinent is different from these cases because he makes the right DECISION (1148a9, 1150b30, 1151a25, 1152a17), and therefore at some stage draws the right conclusion. These cases are nonetheless relevant to the incontinent's condition when he acts; see 1147b10–12.

9. **1146b33 attending:** See STUDY.

10. **§6 1147a3 particular premiss:** Lit. 'partial' (*kata meros*), mentioning particulars (*kath'hekasta*).

11. **1147a3–4 For it is particulars . . . in action:** The particular premiss specifies the relevant particulars; hence we fail to act if we lack this premiss.

12. **1147a4 There are also . . . universal:** These are not universal premisses, but universal terms or concepts (e.g., 'healthy' or 'dry') that may appear in either the universal or the particular premisses that have just been mentioned.

13. **1147a9–10 astounding . . . other sort:** Someone who knows that dry food is healthy for a human being, that he is a human being, and that chicken is dry, but does not know that this piece is chicken, may fail to choose this piece of chicken. It is astounding, however, if he has all this knowledge and still fails to choose it. Aristotle's eventual solution implies that the incontinent, at the time of acting, lacks some of this knowledge in some way; see 1147b15–17.

(c) §7–8. One type of potential knowledge is especially relevant to incontinence.

14. **§7 1147a10–12 For we see . . . do not have it:** Someone may know French but, because of his present condition, have no access to his knowledge; he does not apply the knowledge in the normal way.

15. **1147a15 those affected by strong feelings:** Lit. 'those in affections' (*pathê*); see FEELING.

16. **1147a16 disturb the body:** These processes are studied by NATURALISTS. See 1147b8–9.

17. **§8 1147a18–9 saying the words . . . having it>:** Having suggested that incontinents are analogous to the people just mentioned, Aristotle considers an objection: 'The cases are not analogous. For if I'm asleep, my knowledge is unavailable to me because I don't draw any conclusions at all. But the incontinent draws the right conclusions from his knowledge.' In reply Aristotle observes that simply saying the right words is not proof of really *drawing* the right conclusion.

Here Aristotle is describing the state the incontinent is in when he is overcome by his incontinent desire, not the state he is in before he is overcome (see 1145b28–31 on the importance of this distinction). In §9 he reverts to the time before the incontinent is overcome.

18. **1147a21–2 And those . . . takes time:** On learners, cf. 1142a19–20. This is another case in which we do not attach the normal significance to their utterances, because we do not assume that they really understand or believe what they are saying.

19. **1147a22–4 We must . . . actors do:** Here as at the end of §7, Aristotle says which of the examples he has just given is most relevant to incontinence.

(d) §9–11. When someone acts incontinently, the normal connexion between universal and particular beliefs is disrupted by appetite.

20. **§9 1147a24–5 Further, we may . . . nature:** The following discussion from a natural (i.e., psychological; see NATURE) point of view refers to the structure of practical INFERENCE; cf. *DA* 431a15; *MA* 7; *Rhet.* 1392b19. At least three interpretations of the following remarks are worth considering:

1. The incontinent never grasps the minor premiss of the good syllogism, and therefore never completes the good syllogism.

2. He draws the conclusion of the good syllogism, but only in a non-standard way (as the learner does), so that he does not act on it.

3. He draws the conclusion of the good syllogism, but then loses it, because he loses the connexion between the good major and the good minor premiss.

The following notes defend (3).

21. **1147a26–7 result in one <belief>:** This one belief affirms the conclusion of the practical inference (e.g., 'this must be tasted'). This is referred to in 'what has been concluded'.

22. **1147a27–8 it is necessary, . . . has been concluded:** Lit. (following the Greek word order) 'it is necessary that the thing that has been concluded, in the one case the soul affirms, and in productive does at once.' In 'in the one case' Aristotle probably refers to purely theoretical beliefs that have no immediate bearing on action; in these cases one stops short at affirming the conclusion. After 'productive', the most likely supplement is 'beliefs'; a less likely one would be 'premisses'. It is puzzling that Aristotle uses 'PRODUCTIVE' here, referring to instrumental reason, where we might expect a more general reference to ACTION; perhaps he is influenced by his choice of example.

'The thing that has been concluded' is the object both of 'affirms' and 'does'. Practical inferences require the mental drawing of a conclusion in a belief (cf. 'result in one belief' above).

23. **1147a30–1 it is necessary . . . at the same time:** Probably 'unhindered' refers to external hindrances as in *Met.* 1048a10–24; *DA* 417a27. In that case, an incontinent desire does not prevent someone from acting 'unhindered'; hence Aristotle seems to imply that the incontinent acts 'at once' on the conclusion of correct practical inference. How, then, can his conclusion fail to have its usual effect on action? This is the question Aristotle tries to answer in his account of how incontinence happens.

24. **§10 1147a31–2 the universal <belief> hindering him from tasting:** We may call this belief 'the good major premiss'. It corresponds to 'Everything sweet must be tasted' in the previous example. Aristotle does not say what the universal belief says. Most probably it is 'Nothing pleasant must be tasted' (i.e., one must not taste anything pleasant); this is probably not meant to be realistic, but just to bring out the main point about incontinence (since the incontinent has misguided appetites that need to be restrained).

[Or the universal belief might be 'Nothing sweet must be tasted.']

25. **1147a32–3 he has the second <belief>, that everything sweet is pleasant and this is sweet:** This is the 'good minor premiss' attached to the good major premiss just stated.

[Or (i) 'everything sweet is pleasant' and (ii) 'this is sweet' might be taken as two distinct beliefs. In that case (i) might be the 'bad major premiss' of a rival inference; this leads to further differences of interpretation at later stages of the account.]

26. **1147a33 this <belief> is active:** Probably this refers to the whole good minor premiss. Aristotle explains that the first three cases of actual and potential knowledge (1146b31–1147a10) do not apply to the incontinent at this stage.

[Or, if we accept the alternative mentioned in the previous note, this clause refers only to (ii).]

27. **1147a33–4 but it turns out that appetite is present in him:** He has an appetite (i.e., a non-rational DESIRE; for its role in incontinence, cf. 1102b13–25, 1111b13–15) for the pleasant. Hence the belief that is his good minor premiss focuses both his good major premiss (expressing his rational desire) and his appetite on this particular thing (e.g., a sweet cake).

28. **1147a34 The <belief>, then, . . . tells him to avoid this:** The supplement implies that this belief is belief in the good conclusion formed from the good major and good minor premisses. The incontinent person draws and believes the good conclusion. Hence, he has formed the correct decision (cf. 1112b24–7). Further, given the end of §9, he must immediately act. Probably Aristotle means that his acting consists in his trying to avoid tasting this sweet thing.

[Or 'the belief' might refer to the belief in the good major premiss only. But how could the good major premiss tell the agent to avoid this particular thing?]

29. **1147a34–5 for each . . . initiating motion:** The 'for' explains why it is not surprising that appetite moves us. We have learnt in i 13 that the DESIRES in each part of the SOUL may conflict. Though the incontinent has drawn the good conclusion, his appetite moves him to taste the sweet thing, since his belief in the good minor premiss has made him aware of the opportunity for pleasure.

[Or 'for <appetite> is capable of moving each of the <bodily> parts'.]

30. **1147b1–2 The <second> belief . . . own right:** Aristotle refers to the incontinent's belief in the good minor premiss. This causes his incontinent action (since without it his appetite for pleasure would not be aware of this present opportunity for pleasure), but simply holding this belief is not opposed to the correct reason (indeed, it is a premiss leading to the good conclusion).

31. **§11 1147b3–5 That is also why beasts . . . particulars:** Non-rational ANIMALS cannot form universal beliefs of the sort exemplified in the good major premiss.

(e) §12–14. Hence the incontinent person lacks a certain kind of knowledge.

32. **§12 1147b6–7 How is the ignorance . . . knowledge:** So far Aristotle has said nothing to explain or defend the claim that the incontinent is ignorant. His explanation and defence comes in §13–14.

33. **1147b8–9 We must hear it from the naturalists:** Here Aristotle uses 'NATURALISTS' not for those who offer general theories of NATURE, but for those who provide the sorts of material details of physical processes that he has mentioned in 1147a16.

34. **§13 1147b9–10 Since the last . . . perceptible:** The last premiss (*protasis*) is probably the whole good minor premiss, i.e., 'everything sweet is pleasant, and this is sweet'. See note to §10 above for other possible views.

[Or 'Since the last proposition . . . ', referring to the good conclusion.]

35. **1147b9–10 this is what . . . affected:** Aristotle assumes that if the agent had the good minor premiss when he was being affected by the appetite that causes him to act incontinently, he would not act incontinently. He assumes this because he also assumes that (i) if he had the good minor premiss, he would also have the good conclusion, and (ii) if he had the good conclusion, he would act on it (see end of §9).

We might object that Aristotle's claim conflicts with two other admitted facts: (a) The incontinent must have had the good minor premiss in order to reach the good conclusion, which 'tells him to avoid this' (see §10). (b) He must still believe the good minor premiss in order to act incontinently, since it shows him that this particular thing is pleasant.

Aristotle replies to (a) that the incontinent had the good minor premiss, but no longer has it when he is being affected. In reply to (b), he distinguishes believing a proposition, from believing it as part of an inference. Only in the latter case do we have a major or minor premiss. I make an inference only if I 'combine' (*sumtheôrein*) two beliefs properly (§9 above: 'these two beliefs result in one belief'; cf. *APr* 67a37). If I do not combine them, I do not have them as premisses, even though I still believe them. In the incontinent, then, the belief that initially constituted the good minor premiss becomes disconnected from the good major premiss, and no longer constitutes the good minor premiss. It is now connected with an appetite for pleasure, not with a rational desire.

36. **1147b11–12 Or <rather> the way . . . words:** An objector points out that the incontinent says all the words of the good minor premiss and the good conclusion. Aristotle replies that the incontinent no longer genuinely infers the good conclusion, but simply says its words without believing them, as actors do (cf. 1147a22–4).

37. **1147b12 as the drunk . . . Empedocles:** See §7–8 above.

38. **1147b13–14 And since the last term . . . universal term:** The 'last term' (for 'term', cf. 1142a26) is probably what 1147b9 has called the 'last premiss', i.e., the good minor premiss. [Or perhaps he again refers to the conclusion.] Similarly, the 'universal term' is probably the good major premiss.

39. **§14 1147b15–17 is not the sort . . . perceptual knowledge:** 'Fully knowledge' probably refers to the good conclusion, expressing the agent's knowledge that he ought not to taste this sweet thing. This knowledge is not dragged about (from rational desire to appetite) in the incontinent; for he does not connect it with his appetite, but simply loses it. Socrates is, therefore, correct in thinking that some kind of ignorance is needed to explain incontinence.

4

4.§1–6. Simple incontinence v. qualified incontinence.

(a) §2. Different types of pleasure.

1. **§2 1147b23–5 Some sources . . . choiceworthy in their own right, . . . excess:** Cf. 1110b3, 1129b1; see UNQUALIFIED. Continence and incontinence have a limited range for the same reason that temperance has; see 1119b11–20.

(b) §2. Qualified forms of incontinence.

2. **1147b35 Olympic victor named Human:** The winning boxer in the Olympics of 456 was called Anthropos (see HUMAN BEING). Aristotle and his school compiled a list of victors in the Olympic games (for chronological purposes); see Diogenes Laertius v 21.

3. **1148a3 either unqualified or partial:** Less plausibly, this might be attached to 'incontinence', to mark two types of simple incontinence.

(c) §3–4. Simple incontinence and intemperance are about the same types of pleasures and pains.

4. **§4 1148a17 the intemperate person decides . . . does not:** Cf. 1119a1; 1146b22; 1150a19–23, b29; 1151a7, 22; 1152a4, 15–24. The intemperate person has a settled DECISION and policy of pursuing the bodily pleasures before him; this is what he mistakenly regards as the good to be pursued, 1113a28. Hence he does not suffer the conflicts of the incontinent; but cf. 1166b5–29. Since the incontinent has a correct decision, and violates it by his incontinent action, he suffers conflicts.

(d) §5–6. Some forms of qualified incontinence are not blameworthy.

5. **§5 1148b2 vice:** Here 'VICE' translates *mochthêria*, but in 1148a3, b10, it renders *kakia*. No distinction seems to be intended.

6. **§6 1148b6 but also blameworthy:** Aristotle assumes that none of the conditions he has just mentioned is blameworthy.

5

5. §1–9. Simple incontinence contrasted with bestial and diseased states.

(a) §2. Bestiality.

1. **§2 1148b20 the female human being:** This use of *anthrôpos* seems to indicate disapproval; cf. *MM* 1188b33. Aristotle perhaps relies on collections of Greek stories about foreigners, such as one finds in, e.g., Herodotus ii (on the Egyptians), iv (on the Scythians).

2. **1148b24 what is said about Phalaris:** Phalaris was TYRANT of Acragas in Sicily (570–49 BC). He is supposed to have roasted his enemies alive in a bronze bull (the previous example and §7 below may suggest that they were also eaten). 'Is said' might indicate doubts about the story.

(b) §3. Disease.

(c) §4–7. These conditions allow only qualified vice, and hence qualified incontinence.

3. **§4 1148b32–3 If nature . . . mounting:** Aristotle relies on the association between 'incontinence' (*akrasia*) and being overcome or failure to control (*kratein*). He means that WOMEN are by nature the passive partners in sexual intercourse.

4. **§6 1149a9–10 naturally lack . . . sense perception:** See ANIMALS.

(d) §8–9. Simple vice and simple incontinence.

5. **§9 1149a23 transference:** See HOMONYMY.

6

6.§1–5. Simple incontinence contrasted with incontinence about spirit.

(a) §1. Simple incontinence is less closely related to reason.

1. **§1 1149a33–4 as though . . . at once:** When we act on spirit (*thumos*; evidently Aristotle has ANGER especially in mind here) we have some beliefs about the RIGHTNESS of what we are doing, and we are not simply moved by pleasure or pain. Cf. 1146b23, 1151a23, 1152a6. 'As though' indicates that this is not a genuine DECISION; see 1111b18.

This description of spirit recalls Plato's remarks about it in *Rep.* iv (e.g., 440b–441c).

2. **1149a34–b1 Appetite, . . . gratification:** Appetite does not go through the quasi-inference that Aristotle has just attributed to spirit. It is immediately moved by the prospect of pleasure.

(b) §2. It is less natural, and hence less pardonable.

3. **§2 1149b4–6 Further, it is more pardonable . . . are common:** The actions considered here are pardonable not because they are involuntary, but because they reflect pardonable lapses in human nature (1110a23), expressing tendencies that are appropriate for a human being (1115b8), though they have misled someone on this occasion. No such excuse can be given for the excessive appetites of the incontinent person. (1136a5, by contrast, refers to involuntary but unpardoned actions.)

4. **1149b8–11 It is just as the son . . . our family:** The last scene of Aristophanes' *Clouds* (from 1321) illustrates the conflicts between fathers and sons mentioned here and in the next example.

(c) §3. It involves more plotting.

5. **§3 1149b14–15 Now the spirited . . . is open:** This is true of someone who lashes out on an angry impulse. Aristotle does not discuss those whose anger causes them to hold a grudge and to plot revenge; these people are not incontinent in relation to anger.

6. **1149b16 trick weaving Cypris:** Author unknown.

7. **1149b17–18 'Blandishment . . . prudent':** See Homer, *Il.* xiv 214, 217 (from the episode in which Hera seduces Zeus, and distracts him from the course of the fighting around Troy).

(d) §4–5. It more justly provokes anger.

6. §6–7. The range of pleasures proper to intemperance, and hence to incontinence.

8. **§6 1149b26–7 Now we must grasp . . . and pleasures:** §6–7 begin a comparison between intemperance and incontinence that extends into c7.

9. **1149b34 For beasts . . . human beings are:** Decision and RATIONAL CALCULATION are necessary for virtue, vice, and incontinence.

10. **§7 1150a1–3 Bestiality . . . absent altogether:** Cf. *Pol.* 1253a31†.

11. **1150a4–5 For in each . . . principle:** Lit. 'for always the badness of what lacks a principle is less destructive, and understanding is a principle.' Even inanimate things, if they are natural, have an internal PRINCIPLE of some of their movements (see NATURE); and so do beasts. But only rational agents have an internal principle that is subject to choice and decision, and therefore makes them good or bad.

7

7. §1–8. Incontinence and the vices corresponding to it.

(a) §1–2. Intemperance and softness.

1. **§1 1150a11–13 Now it is possible . . . most people:** See ETHICS #4, 1118b23, 1125b14, 1150b12, 1151a5, 1152a7. Deviations from the average or most frequent are underlie judgments about whether someone is incontinent. But the average is not the proper norm for complete virtue.

2. **§2 1150a19–20 because they . . . on it:** Read *hê(i) kath'huperbolas kai dia prohairesin*.

3. **1150a21–2 He is intemperate; for . . . incurable:** 'For' explains why 'intemperate', *akolastos*, is the right name. The *akolastos* lacks *kolazein* (CORRECTIVE TREATMENT; see also TEMPERANCE). Aristotle means, 'He is also *akolasto* because he is incurable and hence incorrigible'. He has 'no regrets', because he acts on his firm and settled DECISION. See 1105a33, 1110b19, 1148a17; but cf. 1166a29, b6–25.

(b) §3. Intemperance is worse than incontinence.

4. **§3 1150a25–7 One of those . . . differ from each other:** The sequence of thought in the next few paragraphs is not easy to follow. (The ms. text may be disordered.) Here Aristotle shifts from the two vices—intemperance (resulting from the decision to pursue pleasure) and its negative counterpart (resulting from the decision to avoid pain)—to incontinence and its negative counterpart, which do not include a mistaken decision.

5. **1150a27–30 Now it would seem . . . anger:** This contrast seems to oppose incontinence (and similar states) to vice (a state involving decision). It does not seem to be about the two states (not involving decision) just mentioned.

6. **1150a31–2 One of . . . intemperate:** These two states are the negative counterparts of intemperance and intemperance itself (mentioned at the end of §2). Aristotle calls the negative counterpart 'more a species of softness', to indicate that 'softness' is not really the correct name for it. 'Softness' refers to the negative counterpart of incontinence (mentioned at the beginning of §3).

(c) §4–7. Incontinence contrasted with softness.

7. **§4 1150a32–3 The continent . . . soft:** These are the two states mentioned at the beginning of §3. 'Softness' is softness properly so called (as opposed to the 'species of softness' that is the negative counterpart of intemperance, mentioned at the end of §3). On softness, see 1116a14, 1145a35, 1148a11, 1179b33; *Rhet.* 1384a2. It implies inability, reluctance or refusal to undertake necessary pains and burdens; it often includes a suggestion of effeminacy (cf. 1150b15).

8. **§5 1150b2 self-indulgent:** The term used, *trupheros*, is cognate with *truphê*, 'luxury'; cf. 1145a35; *Pol.* 1295b17, 1310a23.

9. **1150b3–4 This person . . . lifting it:** He trails his cloak because it is too much bother to lift it. Aristotle seems to be making fun of this affectation, as he made fun of the son attacking his father. It was a sign of status and nonchalance. Cf. *Rhet.* 1383b38; [Plato], *Alc.*122b; Demosthenes, *FL* 361.

10. **§6 1150b9–10 Theodectes' . . . Carcinus' . . . Xenophantus:** See TGF p. 803 (Theodectes), p. 797 (Carcinus); these are two fourth-century dramatists. Aristotle may refer to the Xenophantus who was a musician in the court of Alexander.

(c) §8. Two types of incontinence: impetuosity and weakness.

11. **§8 1150b19–22 One type . . . not deliberated:** Cf. 1151a1–3, 1152a17. Does the impetuous incontinent fit the account given in 1147a31–5? See 1117a20, DECISION #5. He can make the right decision because of his previous deliberation even if he does not deliberate afresh on this occasion.

12. **1150b22–5 For some . . . or painful:** If A tickles B, A will expect B to tickle A back, and if A expects this, A will not find it so ticklish. Cf. *[Probl.]* 965a11. 'Notice something in advance' marks the point of comparison with impetuous people.

13. **1150b25–8 Quick-tempered . . . appearance:** In Aristotle's physiological theory (see *[Probl.]* 30; *PN* 453a19) excessively hot black bile (*melaina cholê*) makes someone easily excitable and prone to strong feelings when he is excited. This is the 'volatile' (*melancholikos*) person; cf. 1154b11. 'Melancholy', in its contemporary English sense, would be a misleading translation. Ajax (in Sophocles' play) is an example of a volatile person, liable to abrupt and violent changes of feelings.

On appearance v. reason, cf. *EE* 1235b26–8.

How are these two types of incontinence connected to the account that Aristotle offered in c3, which does not seem to recognize their different relation to deliberation?

8

8.§1–5. Why intemperance is worse than incontinence.

(a) §1–3. Intemperance, unlike incontinence, is incurable.

1. **§1 1150b31–2 That is why . . . curable:** Aristotle answers the puzzle he raised in 2.§10. On incurability, cf. 1114a16, 1121a20, 1121b33, 1165b18, 1180a9. Aristotle seems to think that if the incontinent deliberates better (or, in the case of the impetuous person, if he deliberates at all on these occasions, 1152a27), he will see

that it is not worthwhile to abandon his decision and to pursue the pleasure offered by incontinent action. This conclusion is supposed to cure the incontinence.

2. **1151a4–5 For the incontinent . . . for most people:** The mss. have this sentence at the end of §2.

3. **§2 1151a1–2 those who abandon . . . do not abide by it:** Aristotle contrasts impetuous and weak incontinence, described in 1150b19–28.

4. **§3 1151a8–10 As Demodocus . . . would do:** Demodocus (sixth century) fr. 1 (West).

(b) §4–5. Intemperance, unlike incontinence, destroys principles.

5. **§4 1151a16–17 in actions the end . . . in mathematics:** The assumptions in a demonstrative science are the basic PRINCIPLES grasped by UNDERSTANDING (see 1141a3–8, 1143a35–b3; *EE* 1227a5–13; *APo* 72a14–24).

6. **1151a17–19 Reason does not teach . . . principle:** Cf. the role of prudence in 1144a8, 1144b3, 1145a4. Virtue, including prudence, requires more than purely cognitive training. But habituated virtue itself requires prudence (see 1144b15–17).

7. **§5 1151a25–6 since the best . . . in him:** The incontinent has the right principle because he has the right wish and makes the right DECISION. He reaches the right conclusion, before he is affected by the feelings that result in incontinence. Repeated incontinence would expose him to the corrupting effects of pleasure; cf. 1140b15–20.

Is this claim that the incontinent has the right principle consistent with the claim at 1144a34–6 that only the virtuous person grasps the right principle? Perhaps the incontinent reaches the right conclusion in his decision, but does not reach it by exactly the right deliberation, and therefore has an incomplete conception of the ultimate end. See vi 9 on good deliberation.

9

9. §1–6. Continence.

(a) §1. Continence requires the correct decision.

1. **§1 1151a29–30 Then is someone continent . . . correct decision:** Cf. 1146a16–31.

2. **1151a33–5 Perhaps in fact . . . decision in itself:** Aristotle seems to mean this: 'The incontinent and the continent differ in their tendency to abide by their decision; hence this difference distinguishes them COINCIDENTALLY. But it is not the real basis of the distinction between them, and hence it is not how they differ IN THEIR OWN RIGHT. The continent person, as such, abides by the correct decision, and the incontinent, as such, fails to abide by it; hence the real distinction requires reference to the correct decision.' On choosing coincidentally, cf. 1110a8–11, 18–19, b3–5. If I do not choose F in itself, then I do not choose F without qualification (see UNQUALIFIED), but only with the qualification that F is a means to G. Here what the continent person abides by in its own right and for its own sake is his correct decision; he abides by it because it is true. Since his correct decision is his decision,

he abides coincidentally by his decision, but abides by it because it is correct, not because it is his decision.

Why does Aristotle insist on this basis for distinguishing the incontinent and the continent? Why not say that the person who abides by the right principles and the person who abides by the wrong principles are continent in just the same way? The claims about pleasure and good, and about the corrupting effects of pleasure, do not apply in the same way to a 'continent' or 'incontinent' about bad principles. If I do not always follow my intemperate desire, it will not be because the pleasure at hand is too attractive (for the pleasure is what the intemperate decision decides on); nor will repeated failure to follow the intemperate decision make me more prone to intemperance. Since different psychological explanations and treatments are required, these are different conditions.

(b) §2–3. Hence continence differs from undesirable stubbornness.

3. §2 1151b4–5 Now there are ... their belief: These people might also be confused with continent people, if we do not bear in mind the real basis for the genuinely continent person's sticking to his views.

4. §3 1151b15–16 if their ... decrees: Aristotle refers to the decrees (i.e., resolutions) that were voted on by the Athenian popular Assembly. See 1134b24, 1141b27.

(c) §4. Similarly, incontinence must be distinguished from desirable conditions that are easily confused with it.

5. §4 1151b17–18 There are also ... Philoctetes: To reinforce his claims about the correct basis for distinguishing incontinence from continence, Aristotle returns to the example of Neoptolemus, mentioned in 1146a20.

6. 1151b20 for telling ... pleasant to him: Read hêdu. [OCT: 'was fine to him'.]

7. 1151b21–2 for not everyone ... shameful pleasure: Aristotle denies that Neoptolemus displayed a desirable form of incontinence. Hence he implicitly rejects the parallel conclusion that some people have drawn from Huckleberry Finn's protection of a slave despite telling himself he was acting wrongly, or from a Nazi soldier moved by pity to fail in his duty, as he conceived it, to kill Jews. Neoptolemus' motives show that he did not act incontinently.

(d) §5. The vice of deficiency corresponding to continence.

8. §5 1151b23–5 There is also ... incontinent: This section helps to distinguish continence from states that might be confused with it. Someone who irrationally refrains from the right bodily pleasures is similar to the continent person in avoiding the excessive pleasures that the incontinent pursues. He is not continent, however, because he does not act from the continent person's reasons and motives.

(e) §6. The difference between continence and temperance.

9. §6 1151b32–4 Now many ... similarity: Aristotle takes up the common beliefs, mentioned in 1145b14–17, that reflect some uncertainty about the difference

between temperance and continence. To distinguish continence from temperance, we need to recognize the different mental conditions involved.

10. **1152a3 The temperate . . . led by them:** See 1119b12–15.

10

10.§1–4. Incontinence and prudence.

(a) §1–3. Incontinent people are not prudent.

1. **§1 1152a6–7 Nor can . . . incontinent:** Aristotle turns to the common belief mentioned in 1145b17–20, just after the belief that he has discussed in 9.§6. This chapter is a series of loosely connected remarks on incontinence.

2. **1152a7–8 For we have . . . is not>:** In 1144a23–b17 Aristotle has examined the relation between cleverness and prudence.

3. **§2 1152a10–14 However, a clever . . . correct> decision:** This passage is transposed from its place in the mss. and OCT (following 'But the incontinent person does not' in the next paragraph). The transposition makes a better connexion both with §1 and with §3. 'Account' (*logos*) might be replaced by 'reason'. On difference in decision, see 1127b14.

(b) §3–4. Nor are they vicious.

4. **§3 1152a14–15 He is not in . . . or drunk:** See the description of incontinence in 1147b6–9. If the incontinent were prudent, he would have to attend to his knowledge, but he does not.

5. **1152a15–16 He acts willingly . . . doing it for:** The voluntary character of action on knowledge is explored in 1111a2–6, 1135a23–31. Aristotle qualifies the claim that the incontinent acts on knowledge with 'in a way'. He may allude to the incontinent's loss of the good minor premiss when he is under the influence of his misguided feelings, 1147b9–12.

6. **1152a18–19 For one type . . . deliberate at all:** Aristotle returns to the division between impetuous and weak incontinence, in 1150b19–28.

7. **§3–4 1152a19–24 In fact the incontinent . . . bad ones:** §3–4 interrupt the contrast between the two types of incontinence. §3 amplifies the difference between the incontinent and the intemperate. See Anaxandrides (a fourth-century comic dramatist) fr. 67 (Kock).

10.§4–5. Different types of incontinence.

8. **§4 1152a25–7 Incontinence and . . . incontinent person less:** This remark (cf. 1150a9–16) interrupts the discussion of impetuous and weak incontinence.

9. **1152a27–30 The type of . . . to change:** Aristotle strengthens the suggestion in §3 that the impetuous incontinent is less bad because he is less of a 'plotter', since he does not deliberate. Incontinence caused by nature and by habit have not been distinguished earlier.

10. **1152a30–3 Indeed the reason . . . human beings:** This note on habit helps to explain the importance of habituation. Cf. ii 1, iii 5, x 9. Aristotle quotes Euenus (fifth-century SOPHIST) fr. 9 (West).

11

11.§1–6. Questions about pleasure and good.

(a) §1–2. The importance of pleasure.

1. **§1 1152a1–3 Pleasure and . . . without qualification:** The discussion of pleasure follows naturally on the account of the virtues, to which the account of incontinence was an appropriate supplement. However, Aristotle discusses pleasure again in x 1–5 with no reference to the treatment in vii. This is one reason for thinking that the three books including the treatment of pleasure were originally written for the *EE*; see Intro. §3. But Aristotle may have meant them to be part of the *EN*. Though the two discussions overlap in places, the discussion and rejection of arguments against the goodness of pleasure in Book vii include details that are not repeated in Book x. Aristotle may have thought this discussion worth keeping, even when he had written Book x. See 1153b7–14, 1175b34–6, 1176a30–2.

2. **§2 1152b4–8 Further, we must . . . (*chairein*):** On the virtues, see 1104b3, 1172a21; *EE* 1220a37, 1221b32. On happiness, see 1098b25.

(b) §3. Objections to pleasure.

3. **§3 1152b8–10 Now it seems . . . same as pleasure:** After noticing the general tendency (attributed to 'most people' in §2) to connect happiness with pleasure and enjoyment, Aristotle notices a contrary tendency in the views of 'some people'. In this book Aristotle especially attacks the arguments to show that pleasure is not a good.

(c) §4. Arguments to show that pleasure is not a good.

4. **§4 1152b12–13 The reasons . . . these:** §4–6 present these objections: (1a) Pleasure as becoming. (1b) Temperance and pleasure. (1c) Prudence and pleasure. (1d) Pleasure as impediment. (1e) Pleasure and craft. (1f) Animals and children. (2a) Shameful pleasures. (2b) Harmful pleasures. (3) Pleasure not an end. He answers these objections in the following discussion.

5. **1152b13 Every pleasure . . . nature:** Something's nature is not necessarily its original state. Here it is the complete and perfect state that something grows and develops into. See NATURE #2.

6. **1152b15 Further . . . prudent thinking:** Or 'intelligent thinking'. (*Phronein* may have a general sense here. See PRUDENCE.)

(d) §5. Arguments to show that not all pleasures are good.

(e) §6. Argument to show that pleasure is not the best good.

12

12. §1–7. Pleasure and good: replies to objections.

(a) §1–2. Unqualified v. coincidental pleasures.

1. **§1 1152b25–6 These arguments, . . . best good:** Aristotle does not argue that pleasure is the final good. He argues that these objections do not show that it is not the final good. A better objection: 1172b26–35.

2. **1152b26–8 First of all, . . . and becomings:** Aristotle applies his distinction between types of goods to types of pleasures; see UNQUALIFIED. The difference between processes and becomings (see MOVEMENT) is not exploited in vii; see x 4.

3. **1152b31 not on each occasion:** Read *aei d'ou*. [OCT: 'not without qualification'.]

4. **1152b31–2 Some are not . . . treatment:** Aristotle often distinguishes real from apparent goods. He suggests an analogous distinction in pleasures. Cf. 1113a31, 1173b20, 1176a22.

5. **§2 1152b33–5 Further, since . . . nature:** The pleasure that we feel in recovery is not the process of recovery. In recovery it is the ACTIVITY of the healthy part (the rest of our nature, i.e., the part undisturbed by the illness) that is the source of pleasure. The pleasure itself neither is nor requires any process of recovery.

6. **1153a2–3 we do not enjoy the same thing . . . eventually fully restored:** Delete *hêdei*. Read *kai <êdê>*.

7. **1153a6–7 for as pleasant . . . differ too:** Aristotle distinguishes the activity in which pleasure is taken from the pleasure that is taken in it. See 1175b34–6.

(b) §3. Pleasures are not becomings.

8. **§3 1153a7–9 Further, it is not . . . becoming:** An answer to objection (3) (see 1152b12–24).

9. **1153a10–11 They are activities, . . . some state>:** This is Aristotle's alternative to his opponents' view of pleasure as a becoming or process (cf. 1173a31–b7, x 4).

10. **1153a12–13 That is why . . . becoming:** An answer to objection (1a).

11. **1153a14–15 <an> activity . . . unimpeded:** [Or '<the> activity . . .'.] Since §2 has distinguished the activity enjoyed from the pleasure taken in it (see previous note), Aristotle probably does not identify pleasure with unimpeded activity as a whole. Probably he means not that the pleasure taken in running is the unimpeded activity of running, but that the pleasure is an unimpeded activity additional to the running. Cf. 1153b9–19, 1175a3–10.

(c) §4. Pleasures may still be good even if they have bad results.

12. **§4 1153a17–18 To say that pleasures . . . moneymaking:** Answer to objection (2b).

(d) §5. The pleasure proper to an activity does not impede it.

13. **§5 1153a20–2 Neither prudence . . . alien pleasures:** Answer to (1d).

(e) §6. Pleasure and craft.

14. **§6 1153a23–5 The fact that pleasure . . . capacity:** Answer to (1e). On pleasure and craft, see *MM* 1206a26–31; Plato, *Gorg.* 462b–466a.

(f) §7. The virtuous person does not avoid all pleasures, but only inappropriate ones.

15. **§7 1153a27–9 The claim . . . same reply:** Answer to (1b), (1c), and (1f).

16. **1153a29–30 in what ways pleasures . . . without qualification:** Read *pôs agathai kai pôs ouk agathai <haplôs>* [Or with OCT 'in what ways pleasures are good without qualification, and in what ways they are not good'.]

17. **1153a31–2 the prudent person . . . these:** The prudent person discriminates, and does not reject pleasure altogether, contrary to the exaggerated view (perhaps held by SPEUSIPPUS) rejected in 1104b24; cf. 1119a11–20.

13

13.§1–7. Pleasure and happiness.

(a) §1. The badness of pain supports the view that pleasure is good.

1. **1153b1 Moreover, it is also agreed . . . :** Answer to objection (1). Aristotle now begins to argue more positively.

2. **§1 1153b2 bad . . . impeding <activities>:** Read *pê(i), tô(i)*.

3. **1153b4–5 For Speusippus' . . . succeed:** Aristotle replies to an objection to his previous claim that the contrary to what is bad is good. Speusippus applies a doctrine of the mean to pleasure and pain, taking pleasure and pain to be the extremes, and the good to be intermediate between them.

4. **1153b6–7 For he . . . an evil:** If Speusippus were right, pleasure and pain would both have to be essentially bad, as the excess and the deficiency are. But pleasure is not essentially bad. Hence pleasure and pain are not extremes to which the doctrine of the mean applies. Hence the good is not to an intermediate state between them.

(b) §2. The account of happiness as unimpeded activity leaves open the possibility that some pleasure is the best good.

5. **§2 1153b7–9 Besides, just as . . . pleasures are bad:** Further reply to objection (3).

6. **1153b9–12 Indeed, presumably, . . . an unimpeded activity>:** Lit. 'Presumably it is also necessary, if there are unimpeded activities of each state, whether the activity of all of them is happiness, or of some one of them, if it is unimpeded, for it to be most choiceworthy; and pleasure is this.' Aristotle argues that, for all the objections have shown, pleasure might still be the highest good; cf. 1173b31–1174a1. Pleasure meets one necessary condition for happiness, since it is an unimpeded activity; and the possibility remains open that the right sort of pleasure might be the activity that is happiness. Aristotle's view on this question is explained only when he explains more fully the relation between the activity that is pleasure and the activity in which the pleasure is taken. See 1175a19.

[Or 'this' might refer to be 'most choiceworthy' rather than 'an unimpeded activity'.]

[Or 'this' might refer to 'unimpeded activity' rather than 'an unimpeded activity'. Then the argument would be: (a) Happiness is a type of unimpeded activity. (b) Pleasure is identical to unimpeded activity. (c) Therefore happiness is a type of pleasure.]

7. **1153b12–13 and so . . . might be the best good:** [Or 'would be . . . '].

(c) **§3–4. Happiness requires pleasure and good fortune in addition to virtue.**

8. **§3 1153b19–20 Some maintain, . . . are good:** Aristotle rejects the identification of happiness with virtue; cf. 1095b31–1096a1. (*EE* has no parallel.) The virtuous person who is tortured can be brave, but he is hindered from activating his other capacities; hence his activity cannot be complete. On FORTUNE, see 1099a31; *EE* viii 2; *Phys.* 197b25.

9. **1153b20–1 Whether they . . . nonsense:** Lit. 'Willingly (see VOLUNTARY) or unwillingly, they are saying nothing.'

10. **§4 1153b23–5 For when it . . . to happiness:** Good fortune is subject to the limits that apply to the goods described in 1129b1–6.

(d) **§5–6. The universal pursuit of pleasure supports the view that some pleasure is the good.**

11. **§5 1153b27–8 'No rumour . . . <spread> . . .':** Hesiod, *Works and Days* 763–4. Hesiod continues: 'She (sc. rumour) also is a goddess' (or 'a sort of goddess').

12. **§6 1153b32 for all things . . . divine <in them>:** See GOD #4.

13. **1153b33–1154a1 However, the bodily . . . only pleasures:** This answers an objection to the argument just given. A one-sided choice of examples of pleasures may mislead us.

(e) **§7. The importance of pleasure in happiness implies that it is a good.**

14. **§7 1154a1–2 It is also . . . activity:** Read *mê <hê>* and *kai energeia*.

15. **1154a2–4 it will not be true . . . not a good:** Aristotle returns to objection (1), and so passes from considering whether pleasure is the good to considering whether it is a good. He assumes that happiness is the highest good including all goods (HAPPINESS #2). Hence, if pleasure is not a good, we ought not to expect happiness to include pleasure. In that case, our view will conflict with the common belief that happiness must include pleasure and exclude pain (1099a7–31).

14

14. §1–8. Bodily pleasures, and their degree of goodness.

(a) **§1–2. They are good, within the proper limits.**

1. **§1 1154a8–10 Those who maintain . . . examine bodily pleasures:** The discussion of bodily pleasures in this chapter is a further reply to objection (2).

(b) §3–4. It is easy to pursue bodily pleasures to excess; that is why people mistakenly regard pleasure as bad in itself.

2. **§3 1154a22–3 We must, . . . promotes confidence:** See ETHICS #8. Since the discussion is organized around the common beliefs about pleasure that were introduced in c11, it is reasonable for Aristotle to show that his theory can account for the beliefs that he rejects.

3. **§4 1154a31–2 Indeed these . . . have said:** This paragraph is a parenthetical remark. The features that make bodily pleasures desirable to some people also lead some theorists—who generalize mistakenly from bodily pleasures to all pleasures (see 1153b33–1154a1)—to infer that no pleasures are good.

4. **1154b1 In fact these:** Read *hai dê*.

(c) §5–7. Bodily pleasures are intense, because of our natural imperfections.

5. **§5 1154b4 whenever <the pleasures> are harmless:** Or 'whenever <the thirsts> . . .'.

6. **1154b7 For an animal is always suffering:** Perhaps Aristotle quotes or paraphrases the NATURALIST Anaxagoras. This paragraph (to the end of §6) explains the claim that some people's natural constitution makes them so restless that they cannot bear a neutral condition without pain or pleasure. Aristotle mentions three cases: (a) Normal people are used to the pains involved in natural processes and exertions. (b) Young people find these natural processes pleasant because they happen so quickly. (Cf. *[Probl.]* 955a1–17.) (c) Volatile people (see 1150b25–8) find the natural processes painful.

7. **§7 1154b15–16 Pleasures . . . no excess:** The discussion of pleasures that involve pain and restoration leads Aristotle to contrast such pleasures with ones that do not involve these conditions.

(d) §8. These natural imperfections explain our pursuit of variety in pleasures.

8. **§8 1154b26 That is why the god . . . <without change>:** The GOD is better than we are because he can attain all at once what we can obtain only to some degree over time. COMPLETE human happiness must include various activities if we are to approximate to the divine happiness that is complete all at once. Cf. *Met.* 1072b14–20.

9. **1154b28–9 Variation . . . sweet:** Euripides, *Orestes* 234.

(e) §9. Conclusion on incontinence and pleasure.

10. **§9 1154b32–3 So much . . . and pain:** This is the only passage that shows that incontinence and pleasure were meant to be treated in the same discussion.

Book VIII

1

1. §1–5. Common beliefs about friendship.

(a) §1–4. Friendship is necessary in a wide range of circumstances.

1. **§1 1155a4–5 Further, . . . necessary . . . life:** 'Necessary' does not refer only to the instrumental value of friendship. Many of the examples illustrate the non-instrumental value we attach to friendship. Friendship is a necessary part of any desirable human life. The ways in which friendship is necessary are discussed in §1–4; §5 turns to the ways in which it is a virtue or involves virtue, by considering how it is fine.

2. **1155a5–6 For no one . . . all the other goods:** Hence friendship is not merely instrumental. See ix 9.

3. **§2 1155a11–12 But in poverty . . . only refuge:** Friendship is not merely appealing when everything else is going well. It is also necessary in other material circumstances, and at different stages of life.

4. **1155a15 'when two go together . . .':** Homer, *Il.* x 224 (Homer continues: one person alone has inferior wits).

5. **§3 1155a19 Members of the same species:** Lit. 'members of the same race'. But the rest of the paragraph shows that Aristotle has species in mind (i.e., friendship among dogs or human beings, rather than friendship among greyhounds or Greeks).

6. **1155a20–1 that is . . . humanity:** The rest of viii–ix does not discuss friendship directed towards other people in general, or to people one does not know. Such an attitude are not prominent explicit in Aristotle's ethical theory. But he takes its praise-worthiness for granted.

7. **§4 1155a22–6 Moreover, friendship . . . enmity:** On friendship and justice, see c9–11. On concord, see ix 6.

8. **1155a28 and the justice . . . friendship:** Perhaps this refers to decency, discussed in v 10. At any rate, decency illustrates what Aristotle has in mind.

(b) §5. It is fine as well as necessary.

9. **§5 1155a28–9 But friendship . . . fine:** 'Fine' repeats the claim in 'a virtue or involves virtue' in 1155a4. Friendship might be necessary for a good life, as FORTUNE and pleasure are, without being admirable and praiseworthy (cf. 1101b11, 1109b31), as a person's own achievement; hence Aristotle is careful to insist that friendship is also praiseworthy. See 1159a23, 1169a8, 35.

1. §6–7. Puzzles about friendship.

(a) §6. Is it based on similarity or on difference?

10. **§6 1155a32 Still, . . . about friendship:** Following his normal practice (cf. the discussions of incontinence and of pleasure), Aristotle, having set out the common beliefs, turns to the puzzles (see ETHICS #6).

11. **1155a34–5 similar to . . . each other:** See Homer, *Od.* xvii 218; Hesiod, *Works and Days* 225. (No known source for 'Birds of a feather'.)

12. **1155b1–2 more proper to . . . nature:** These are views of NATURALISTS. Aristotle largely ignores these disputes, but he alludes to them in 1159b21–4. Cf. *EE* 1235a4–29; *MM* 1208b7–20; Plato, *Lys.* 214a.
13. **1155b2–4 Euripides . . . earth:** Euripides, TGF fr. 898.
14. **1155b4–6 Heracleitus . . . struggle:** DK 22 B 80.
15. **1155b6–8 Others, . . . Empedocles, . . . similar:** DK 31 B 22, 62, 90.

(b) §7. Puzzles relevant to ethical discussion.

16. **§7 1155b8–10 Let us, then, leave . . . characters and feelings:** Aristotle prefers to avoid digressions from ethics into cosmology or other non-ethical areas. Cf. 1096b31, 1159b23; *GC* 316a11–14; *EE* 1217a3†, 1218b33.
17. **1155b15–16 We have . . . earlier:** This sentence might refer to ii 8, or to *Catg.* 6b10–7.

2

2. §1–4. Conditions for friendship.

(a) §1–2. The object of friendship: the lovable.

1. **§1 1155b17–18 Perhaps these . . . lovable:** 'Lovable' renders *philêton*, which might be rendered 'what is loved', 'what can be loved', 'proper object of love', 'what deserves to be loved'. On this ambiguity, see CHOICEWORTHY. For the three objects of love, see 1104b30.
2. **§2 1155b21–6 Now do people love . . . will be what appears lovable:** Aristotle distinguishes (a) what is lovable without qualification, (b) what is lovable for (or to; cf. 1113a12–21, 1173b20–5) each person, and (c) what appears lovable to each person. This division needs to be compared with iii 4. See also UNQUALIFIED, 1156b13.

(b) §3. Friendship requires reciprocal goodwill.

3. **§3 1155b27 There are these three causes, then, of love:** Lit. 'There being three things because of (*dia*) which they love'. The different types of friendship are 'for' (*dia*) character, utility, and pleasure. Here '*dia*' might refer either to the final or to the efficient CAUSE of the friendship. (Cf. 'They're hanging men and women for the wearing of the green', clearly with an efficient-causal rather than a final-causal sense.) Most probably it refers to both; since the remark that these are the causes of love summarizes the account of how they are the objects of love, 'causes' ought to include the aim of the friendship as well as the origin. 1156a31, 1172b21 associate '*dia*' clearly with the final cause.
4. **1155b29–31 For it would presumably . . . own sake:** The contrast with wine seems to make two points: (1) We cannot really wish good to it; that is, we cannot wish for its welfare. It has no choices, desires, or aims of its own. Its good consists simply in its being preserved for our use. (2) Since it has no choices, etc., of its own, we cannot wish goods to it for its own sake. We wish goods to our friend for his own sake, insofar as we regard a friend's having certain aims and desires as a good reason

(under certain conditions) for us to satisfy them. This is the same attitude that we take to our own aims and desires.

When Aristotle says that 'it is said' we must wish goods to our friend for his own sake, he does not thereby endorse this common belief. The different kinds of friendship may meet this condition to different extents. See next note.

(c) §4. It also requires mutual knowledge of reciprocal goodwill.

5. **§4 1156a3–4 <If they are to be friends>, then, they must:** 'They' are the people (just mentioned) who have mutual goodwill. Mutual knowledge needs to be added to mutual goodwill to create friendship.

[Or: 'They' are friends in general, and wishing good to the friend for his own sake is a necessary condition for friendship.]

6. **1156a5 because of one of the things mentioned above:** I.e., (1) any of the three causes mentioned is a basis for goodwill; or (2) One (and perhaps only one) is a basis for goodwill.

3

3.§1–5. Incomplete types of friendship.

(a) §1–3. Friendships for utility and pleasure are coincidental.

1. **§1 1156a6–7 But these <causes> . . . of friendship:** The connexion of thought would be clearer if these three sentences formed the end of c2, and c3 began with the next paragraph.

2. **1156a9–10 For to each object . . . awareness of it:** Aristotle justifies the threefold division of friendship from the description of friendship in c2, except that he does not mention goodwill here (see next note).

3. **1156a10–12 But those . . . each other:** This begins a new topic: to what extent are all three types of friendship genuine friendships. In pointing out that different types of friends wish good to the other in different ways, Aristotle suggests that in the incomplete friendships (those for utility and pleasure) goodwill is only partial. In these friendships A wishes good to B only insofar as B is useful or pleasant to A, not for B's own sake. 1167a10–21 seems to exclude UNQUALIFIED goodwill from the incomplete friendships; cf. 1156b8; 1157a15, 18; 1164a10.

The three types of friendship are literally 'because of (*dia*; see 1155b27) the pleasant', 'because of the useful', and 'because of being such' (*poios*, i.e., a certain sort of person).

4. **§2 1156a16 not insofar as the beloved is who he is:** Read *ouch hê(i) ho philoumenos estin hosper estin*, as in the next sentence. Aristotle takes (1) A loves B for who B is, (2) A loves B in B's own right, not coincidentally, and (3) A loves B for B's own sake, to imply one another. The implication between (3) and (1)–(2) is less obvious; but see previous note.

(b) §3–4. Friendship for utility.

5. **§3 1156a21–2 What is useful . . . different times:** In the rest of §3 and in §4, Aristotle defends the claim in the first sentence of §3, as it applies to friendship for utility. In §5 he defends the claim as it applies to friendship for pleasure.

6. **§4 1156a24–6 This sort . . . older people . . . expedient:** See YOUTH.

7. **1156a31–2 The friendship of hosts . . . this type too:** If A is an Athenian and B is a Spartan, each is the *xenos* of the other if A provides B with hospitality in Athens and B does the same for A in Sparta, and they provide each other with other sorts of reciprocal mutual aid. Hence *xenos* may be translated both 'host' and 'guest'. See OCD, s.v. 'Friendship, ritualized'.

(c) §5. Friendship for pleasure.

3. §6–9. Complete friendship.

(a) §6. Friendship for virtue is non-coincidental.

8. **§6 1156b7–9 But complete . . . good in their own right:** Aristotle applies the general claim in 3.§1 (see note) that 'those who love each other wish goods to each other <only> insofar as they love each other' to the case of friendship for virtue.

9. **1156b9–11 <Hence they . . . not coincidentally:** The supplement indicates what is taken for granted in the claim that friends for virtue love each other for their own sake. This feature of friendship has not been mentioned since 1155b31. Aristotle now concludes that in the best kind of friendship three conditions coincide: (1) A loves B for B's own sake. (2) A loves B for what B really is. (3) A loves B because B has a virtuous character. He suggests again (see 1156a14–19) that each of these conditions implies the other two.

He defends the connexion between (2) and (3) in 'they are good in their own right' (i.e., their good character is an essential property of them). To connect (1) and (2) he seems to assume that A would not find B worth loving for B's own sake if he did not love B for himself, for what B essentially is, and A would not love B for what B essentially is if B were not essentially good (cf. 1157a18).

10. **1156b11–12 Hence these people's . . . virtue is enduring:** See 1100b11. Complete stability is not guaranteed; see 1165b23.

11. **1156b12–14 Each of them is both . . . advantageous for each other:** Cf. 1155b21–5.

12. **1156b14–16 They are pleasant . . . each other:** On pleasure, see 1099a7, 1176a10.

(b) §7. It is stable.

13. **§7 1156b22 For they are . . . good>:** Read *homoioi*.

(c) §8–9. It is rare.

14. **§8 1156b25–6 Further, they need . . . each other:** Lit. 'time and accustoming are needed'; cf. 1157a11, 1158a15, 1167a11.

15. **1156b26–8 for, as the proverb says, . . . it says:** Lit. 'before they have poured out together the salts spoken of'. Greeks spoke of table companions as sharing 'salt and table'; hence the proverb means that people must share many meals before they can know each other (a peck of salt; *EE* 1238a2).

4

4. §1–6. Similarities between complete and incomplete friendship.

(a) §1–2. The stability of incomplete friendships rests on their similarity to complete friendship.

1. **§1 1156b33–1157a3 This sort of friendship . . . useful to each other:** The account of complete friendship between virtuous people has two roles: (1) It explains how the inferior forms of friendship are not fully friendships, since they lack the essential element of goodwill. (2) It explains why they are nonetheless appropriately called friendships, since each of them has some of the central features of complete friendship. Here Aristotle turns to (2).

2. **1157a6–8 For these . . . by his lover:** Aristotle explains parenthetically the contrast between witty people, who take pleasure in the same thing, and the erotic lover and beloved, who take pleasure in different things.

3. **1157a8 When the beloved's bloom is fading:** 'Bloom' refers to the time in which an adolescent boy was thought to be especially desirable to an older man. Cf. 1175a33; OCD, s.v. 'Homosexuality'.

4. **1157a10–12 Many, however, . . . accustomed to them:** It is not clear whether Aristotle takes this fondness for character to indicate (a) friendship for pleasure (as in the witty people he has mentioned), or (b) transformation of friendship for pleasure into complete friendship.

5. **§2 1157a12–14 Those who exchange . . . less enduring friends:** Aristotle adds another type of erotic friendship to those based on pleasure.

6. **1157a14–16 Those who are friends for utility . . . expedient for them:** This follows awkwardly on the previous sentence. The connexion of thought is clearer if we connect this sentence with the paragraph beginning 'With these <incomplete friends> also, . . .' (1157a3), and treat the intervening two paragraphs as a parenthesis.

(b) §2–3. Moreover, the instability of complete friendships results from their difference from complete friendship.

7. **1157a18–19 Clearly, however, . . . other person himself:** The connexion between complete friendship and concern for the other for his own sake is reaffirmed; cf. 1156b7–11. Bad people can find some pleasure in features of each other (cf. 1159b10, 1166b13), but a bad person, Aristotle assumes, cannot find pleasure in the other person himself, but only in some non-essential property of him.

(c) §4–6. The degrees of similarity to complete friendship explain why other types of friendship count as friendship.

8. §4 1157a29–30 **Hence we must . . . than one:** Aristotle does not say that the friendships are HOMONYMOUS. But his reasons for recognizing different species of friendship are similar to his reasons for recognizing homonymy; he wants to explain the common beliefs and to justify them as far as possible. His view here seems to be that there is one DEFINITION of friendship, which is fully satisfied only by complete friendship, and is only partly satisfied by friendships for pleasure and utility; see 1158b1–11. Cf. the relation suggested in *EE* 1236a7–32, b17–27; *MM* 1209a19–36.

9. **1157a30–2 and that the friendship . . . by similarity:** The rest of the paragraph defends this claim. First, the sentence 'For insofar as there is something good . . .' urges that the incomplete friendships really have something in common with complete friendship, and therefore should be counted as friendships. By contrast, the two sentences of §5 'But these <incomplete> types of friendship . . . very regularly combined' point out the differences from complete friendship, and show why the other types are friendships merely by similarity.

10. §6 **1157b1 Friendship has . . . species:** Summary of c3–4.

11. **1157b4–5 These, then, are friends . . . similar to these:** When A and B are 'friends coincidentally', A is not a friend of B himself, but of the pleasant or useful features that coincidentally (non-essentially) belong to B.

5

5.§1–5. *The characteristics of friendship are fully present only in complete friendship.*

(a) §1. Friendship requires both states and activities.

1. §1 **1157b5–7 Just as, . . . of friendship:** The relevance of this discussion of STATES and their corresponding ACTIVITIES becomes clear only in §4; Aristotle is considering further recognized aspects of friendship that are fully present only in complete friendship.

2. **1157b13 'Lack of conversation has dissolved many a friendship':** Unknown poet: see Athenaeus v 187.

(b) §2–3. The appropriate activities imply pleasure in living together.

3. §3 **1157b18–19 goodwill rather than friendship:** On goodwill, cf. 1155b32–11156a5, ix 4.

4. **1157b19–22 For nothing is as proper . . . solitary life fits them least of all:** On the solitary life, cf. 1097b8–11. Aristotle is not thinking of people living in the same house (which was not a very important center of a well-off Athenian man's life), but of shared activities; hence they 'spend their days' in the ways described in ix 12. Aristotle returns to this aspect of happiness in 1169b3–22.

(c) §4–5. Only complete friendship includes the right activities and attitudes.

5. §4 **1157b26–7 choiceworthy to . . . good or pleasant to himself:** Instead of 'to' we might prefer 'for'. Cf. 1113a12–21, 1155b21–6, 1173b20–5.

6. **§5 1157b29–32 For loving . . . not their feeling:** The argument implies that a good person wishes good because of his DECISION #6. Like the virtues, friendship is associated with the appropriate state and decision.

6

6. §1–7. *The characteristics of friendship in the incomplete friendships.*

(a) §1. They are more typical of friendship for pleasure.

1. **§1 1158a1–4 Among sour . . . productive of friendship:** There is no good reason to begin a new chapter here. Aristotle continues his contrast between the actions and attitudes characteristic of complete friendship and those of incomplete friendships. See YOUTH.

(b) §2–3. Both types of incomplete friendship are superficial in comparison with complete friendship.

2. **§2 1158a11–13 for <complete . . . single individual:** The supplement assumes that the comparison with excess applies both to complete friendship and to erotic passion. Alternatively, one might take it to apply only to erotic passion; in that case, 'for . . .' would be a parenthesis.

On the right number of friends, see 1171a6.

3. **§3 1158a14–15 <But one needs . . . difficult:** This helps to explain the rarity of complete friendship. Since a person's goodness does not become clear at once, we need both experience (over some length of time) and familiarity (in many situations). Since it is difficult to have the right experience and familiarity with many people, the relevant kind of friendship cannot extend to many people.

4. **1158a16 for many people to please:** Read *pollous areskein*.

5. **1158a17–18 and the services take little time:** This marks a contrast with the time and experience needed to form complete friendships.

(c) §4. Friendship for pleasure comes closer to complete friendship.

6. **§4 1158a22 Moreover, blessedly . . . sources of pleasure:** A BLESSEDLY HAPPY person requires friendship as part of his life; see ix 9.

7. **1158a24–5 no one . . . Good Itself . . . painful to him:** This alludes to the Platonic Idea (see i 6).

(d) §5–6. Friendships for pleasure and for utility do not often coincide.

8. **§5 1158a27–30 Someone in a position . . . not often both:** This separation of pleasure from usefulness indicates that the friendships are different both from each other and from complete friendship.

9. **1158a30–3 For he does not seek . . . has both features:** Wit: 1128a4, 1176b14. Favourites who try to amuse tyrants cannot be expected to have the virtue of wit.

(e) §7. Conclusion on complete and incomplete friendships.

10. **§7 1158b1–3 The friendships we have mentioned . . . pleasure for benefit:** This section summarizes c5–6 (following the summary at the end of c4). In recalling the earlier reference to equality in exchange (in 4.§1) it also prepares us for the discussion of friendship between unequals in the following chapters.

Aristotle does not say that the inferior friendships resemble complete friendship by including goodwill.

7

7.§1–6. Friendship between unequals.

(a) §1–2. Different types of friendship correspond to different roles and relations.

1. **§1 1158b12 rests on superiority:** Lit. 'in accord with (*kata*) superiority'. The threefold division of friendships between equals is meant to apply to unequals too. Aristotle does not say so here, but see 1162a34–b4.

2. **1158b13 husband towards his wife:** or 'man to WOMAN' (and in the next sentence).

(b) §3–4. The equality and proportion that are proper to friendship.

3. **§3 1158b29–30 Equality, however, . . . justice:** The remark on equality in the previous sentence prompts Aristotle to guard against any misunderstanding. The type of EQUALITY relevant in friendship is not the proportional equality of 1131a11, but numerical equality; the friendship is in danger if this is violated too seriously. Cf. 1163b11.

(c) §5–6. The stability of friendship between unequals depends on the appropriate proportion.

4. **§6 1159a5–7 This raises a puzzle . . . god, for instance:** The puzzle is this: (1) The greatest good is to be a god. (2) If you are a god you have no friends. (3) If I am your friend, I don't wish you to have no friends. (4) Hence I do not wish you to be a god. (5) Hence I do not wish the greatest good to you. Though (2) and (3) are not explicit in the text, they seem to be needed.

Aristotle's reply assumes a distinction between (1) and the claim: (1a) The greatest good for you is to become a god. Though (1) is true, (1a) is false, because you cannot both remain in existence and become a god. Becoming a god is the replacement of you by a god, not a further state of you. Since the only way for you to be a god would be to remain in existence and to become a god, and this is impossible, being a god is not a possible good for you; it could only be a good for the god who replaces you. Hence (5) does not follow from (4). Cf. 1166a20.

5. **1159b7–8 For . . . he will . . . no longer have goods:** Or 'For he will no longer be our friend, and hence will not be a good for us . . .'.

6. **1159a12 since each person . . . to himself:** Self-love: ix 4, 8.

8

8.§1–7. Giving and receiving in friendship.

(a) §1–2. In many cases, people choose being loved for its own sake.

1. **§1 1159a12–14 Because the many . . . to loving:** This section seems to continue the discussion of proportion and equality in friendship. Here Aristotle considers the suggestion that people value their friends simply as a source of honour. The connexion with friendship between unequals becomes clear only in §4–5.

2. **1159a14–17 For the flatterer . . . certainly pursue:** Susceptibility to flattery is a sign that people value having friends (i.e., people who are friendly to them) as a source of honour. Love of HONOUR (see iv 4) makes someone susceptible to the attention of flatterers (see iv 6). In the right conditions one person's vices encourage further vices in others. This point is relevant to the other Aristotelian virtues and vices as well (cf. 1121b3–12).

3. **§2 1159a22–4 Those who want honour . . . they are good:** Aristotle answers the claim in §1 by arguing, first of all, that honour, taken without qualification, cannot be the end for which people want to have friends. For people want honour only with certain qualifications. Honour as a confirmation of virtue: 1095b24–30.

4. **1159a25–7 Being loved, . . . its own right:** This is Aristotle's second argument against the claim in §1. Not only is honour the wrong end to explain people's liking for having friends; we do not need to refer to any ulterior end. Though having friends is sometimes a source of honour, people actually value this passive aspect of friendship (i.e., having people who are friendly to oneself) for its own sake.

(b) §3–5. But loving is especially characteristic of friendship.

5. **§3 1159a27–8 But friendship . . . than in being loved:** Aristotle now turns from the passive to the active side of friendship (from being loved to loving). While he has shown in §2 that people value the passive side of friendship for its own sake, he now argues that this is not enough to make them genuine friends, since a friendship requires the active side too.

6. **1159a28 A sign . . . finds in loving:** Maternal love: 1161b26, 1166a5, 1168a25.

7. **§4 1159a33–5 Friendship, then, consists . . . virtue of friends:** On those who love their friends (*philophiloi*), see the common belief reported in 1155a29–30. We now explain why friendship is a virtue and praiseworthy; its active aspect is a praiseworthy ACTIVITY.

8. **§4–5 1159a35–b2 And so friends . . . can be equalized:** Aristotle now applies his discussion of the passive and active sides of friendship to the topic of friendship between unequals. A genuine friendship between unequals can be formed only to the extent that the friends value the active as well as the passive side of their friendship.

(c) §5–6. The primacy of loving explains why virtuous friendship is stable.

9. **§5 1159b2–3 Equality and . . . is friendship:** This (rather than the previous sentence) is probably the right place to begin a new section. Aristotle has just set out

a general condition for genuine friendship between unequals. He now argues that—here as in friendship between equals—virtuous people best fit the general condition.

10. **1159b7–10 Vicious people, . . . each other's vice:** For this contrast between virtuous and vicious people, cf. 1156b12, 1157a18. On the vicious, see 1166b6–29, 1172a9; *EE* 1239b11. For the vicious person's instability, cf. 1148a17, 1150a21, 1150b29. The vicious person has no reason to value his vicious friend's vice for its own sake as a good. He may find it pleasant because of the similarity to his own character. But this will be only one of the many pleasures the vicious person pursues because of his decision; his friend cannot rely on him when something pleasanter comes along. The virtuous person, by contrast, values virtuous actions as good in themselves.

11. **§6 1159b10–12 Useful or pleasant . . . pleasures or benefits:** Lit. 'Useful and pleasant . . .'. Probably this remark includes people who are not virtuous (and so do not love others for their character), but who are not vicious either (and so are not unreliable in the ways Aristotle has mentioned). (Virtuous people may also be included coincidentally, insofar as they form friendships for utility and for pleasure.)

[Less probably, the remark refers to vicious people who are both useful and pleasant, not just one of the two.]

(d) §6–7. This makes it clear that friendship involves contraries only to a limited degree.

12. **1159b12–15 The friendship that seems . . . in return:** This (rather than the previous sentence) is probably the right place to begin a new section. Aristotle's remarks about the active and passive aspects of friendship, and about pleasure and utility, prompt him to add a note on the dispute about whether friendship involves contraries (1155a35–b6).

13. **1159b15–19 Here we might . . . when he is not:** This is a parenthetical comment on erotic lovers, who seem to provide a good example of love between contraries. The main argument resumes in §7.

14. **§7 1159b19–21 Presumably, . . . the intermediate:** Aristotle has two answers to the suggestion that friendship is between contraries: (a) It is not strictly the contrary that is sought, but the 'intermediate'; we do not seek to go to the contrary extreme, but to fulfil some need or lack. (b) But even this model does not work for friendship in general; it works only for friendship for utility.

15. **1159b24 extraneous:** The speculations of NATURALISTS are irrelevant to ethics; 1155b8–9.

9

9. §1–6. Community and friendship.

(a) §1. Both justice and friendship involve community.

1. **§1 1159b25 As we said at the beginning:** See 1155a22. Cf. 1162a29.

2. **1159b31–2 The proverb . . . involves community:** This proverb is attributed to the PYTHAGOREANS. It is often quoted by Plato (e.g., *Lys.* 207e, *Rep.* 424a).

3. **§2 1159b32–4 But, whereas brothers and companions . . . some less close:** 'Companion' must indicate a relatively close and long-lasting relationship of

habitual companions rather than, for instance, 'travelling companions' making just one journey together.

> (b) §2–3. Different communities require different types of justice and friendship.

4. **§3 1160a2–4 Similarly, what is unjust ... closer friends:** Cf. 1130a5. Justice is concerned with the COMMON good of a community (1129b17), and the growth of friendship will increase the desire to treat other people justly. We might be inclined to see possible conflicts between the demands of friendship and the good of a community (suppose the good of the community requires the sacrifice of my friend's interests). Here Aristotle will see conflicts between two types of friendships. It is only in the best community that such conflicts will not happen; elsewhere the states of character required by the community will not be the same as those of the virtuous person (cf. 1130b29; *Pol.* iii 4).

> (c) §4–5. But all these communities are subordinate to the political community and to its proper good.

5. **§4 1160a8–9 All the communities ... political community:** §4–6 mark a continuation of the argument of §1–3, and also a contrast with it. The emphasis of §1–3 has fallen on the difference between the communities characteristic of different types of friendship; this difference might lead us to think that we can say nothing general about the kind of community that is required for friendship. §4 corrects this impression by insisting that the political community has some superordinate place in relation to the other communities; this is a particular example of the role of the political community that he has mentioned at 1094a27–b10, 1141b23–33.

6. **1160a11–12 And the political ... advantage:** The comparison between the city and other communities begins with what they have in common: aiming at advantage.

7. **1160a12–14 for legislators ... to be just:** In mentioning the common advantage, Aristotle anticipates the contrast he will draw between the CITY and other communities. Cf. 1129b14–19. He does not say that the city aims only at advantage; hence he leaves room for the important further aim mentioned in *Pol.* 1280a25–1281a4.

8. **§5 1160a14–15 Now the other ... partial advantage:** This begins the contrast with the city.

9. **1160a18 tribe or deme:** These were electoral districts in Athens; they also had governmental and religious functions. See OCD, s.v. 'Demes', 'Phylai'.

10. **1160a19–20 Some communities ... companionship:** This sentence is a footnote to the list of communities aiming at advantage. Aristotle takes the opportunity to mention that communities aiming at pleasure are also subordinate to the city, as he explains in the following passage. Religious societies and dining clubs are mentioned together because the religious sacrifice of animals would be an occasion for a common meal.

11. **1160a21–3 But all ... whole of life:** The other communities are parts of the political community because each is affected by its relation to other social institutions; the city regulates them for the common good. The comprehensive character of

POLITICAL SCIENCE corresponds to the comprehensive character of the political community; cf. *Pol.* 1252b27–31†, 1278b15–30, 1280b23–1281a4. Partly, Aristotle is describing the activities of states he knows. But he also thinks these activities are essential for happiness, and hence wants them extended beyond their present scope; cf. 1180a24–9.

12. **1160a23–5 <In religious . . . relaxations:** Something may have been lost from the text here. The supplement suggests a possible connexion of thought. The comprehensive concern of the city is shown by its regulation of religious festivals for advantage (by honouring the gods) and pleasure. By establishing religious holidays, the city fits the smaller communities into its comprehensive concerns.

13. **1160a25–7 For the long-established . . . leisure:** People would gather for religious observances and for enjoyment anyhow, but the city establishes these holidays at harvest time because this is the best time to relax, from the point of view of the larger community.

10

10.§1–6. Political systems and the corresponding communities.

    (a) §1–3. Different types of political systems and the characteristic deviations from them.

1. **§1 1160a31–2 There are three . . . corruption of them:** The relevance of c10 becomes clear only in c11. After having shown that the city regulates and organizes smaller communities within it, Aristotle argues that the different types of constitutions encourage different sorts of organization and different types of friendships. The particular effect of a city on the smaller communities within it depends on its constitution. Aristotle discusses these political systems and their changes in *Pol.* iii 7–8, 14–17; iv–vi. See also OCD, s.v. 'Democracy', 'Oligarchy'.

2. **1160a33–5 and since the third . . . polity:** Aristotle uses *politeia* both for a political system or constitution in general and for what he calls the timocracy; see *Pol.* 1279a37.

    (b) §4–6. The structure of these different systems can also be found in non-political communities.

3. **§4 1160b22–4 Resemblances . . . households:** This section introduces a secondary purpose of the discussion of political systems. The social relations characteristic of the different systems can also be found in different households; hence, our understanding of these relations on the one level may help us to understand them on the other.

4. **1160b26 Homer . . . father:** Frequent in Homer, e.g., *Il.* i 603.

5. **1160b27–9 Among the Persians, . . . slaves:** The basis of this claim about the Persians is not clear (cf. Herodotus i 136). On rule over SLAVES, see 1161b3; *Pol.* i 4, 1254b2–24, 1255b16–22.

6. **§5 1160b35 commits:** Or 'assigns' (lit. 'duly gives', *apodidonai*). Cf. 1164b30.

7. **§6 1161a6–8 Democracy . . . dwellings without a master, . . . free <to do what he likes>:** A mere 'dwelling' (*oikêsis*) differs from a proper 'household' (*oikia*)

in having no definite structure (which, in Aristotle's view, requires a head); a 'rooming house' might be an example. On FREEDOM—in Aristotle's view, a regrettable feature of democracy—see *Pol.* 1310a31 (associated with *eleutheria*; see GENEROUS). This vice is not confined to democracy; cf. 1180a26.

11

11.§1–8. Friendships in different political systems and in the corresponding non-political communities.

(a) §1–5. Different systems and communities result in different types of friendship.

1. **§1 1161a10–11 Friendship appears . . . justice appears also:** Aristotle suggests that a specific form of friendship is possible only to the extent that people are related in ways that would make the transactions characteristic of such a friendship just. If, for instance, a king is not superior to his subjects in the way that genuine kingship requires, an attempt to represent his attitude to a subject as 'kingly' friendship is a fraud.

2. **1161a14–15 Homer . . . peoples:** Homer, *Il.* ii 243 (and often).

(b) §6–8. Deviant systems undermine community and so undermine friendship.

3. **§6 1161a30–2 In the deviations, . . . of friendship:** In deviant systems, the beliefs that, if true, would support genuine friendship are false. The tyrant is not superior to his subjects in the way that a king ought to be, and so he is not entitled to expect the attitudes that would be properly directed towards a king. If the subjects have these attitudes towards him, they must be deceived; since the deception may be recognized, their attitude is unstable.

4. **1161a32–4 For where . . . no justice either:** The mention of tyranny leads Aristotle into a further discussion of other relations where ruled and ruler have nothing in common. He comes back to the main point about constitutions in §8.

5. **1161a34–5 This is true for a craftsman . . . soul . . . body:** The SOUL uses the body as its instrument. See *DA* 412b10–413a3†; *PA* 642a12; *Pol.* 1254a34, b4.

6. **1161b1–2 there is neither friendship . . . inanimate things:** See 1155b31, 1157b29. We can benefit these, since things are good and bad for them. But they have no aims and desires for us to consider and to share; hence we cannot respect or advance their aims by justice or friendship.

7. **1161b3–5 For master . . . without a soul:** Cf. *Pol.* 1253b32. To be a SLAVE is to be treated purely instrumentally, not as deserving anything in one's own right. The reason for treating a slave well, insofar as he is a slave, is always derived from the interests of the master; cf. the remark on wine at 1155b29–30.

8. **§7 1161b5–6 Insofar as he is a slave, . . . insofar as he is a human being:** Though the legal status and social role of slaves imply that they count for nothing in their own right, they are nonetheless human beings, and for that reason they are possible objects of friendship, and ought not to be treated solely as instruments.

The sense of the passage would be more complicated if Aristotle were referring to those who he describes as natural slaves; see SLAVE #1. Since natural slaves lack normal human souls, it is not clear that they would be proper objects of the non-instrumental concern that is suitable for human beings with rational souls. Nothing in this passage suggests that Aristotle has his doctrine of natural slavery in mind.

9. **1161b6–7 For every human being . . . and agreement:** Given the moral importance of this claim, it is remarkable that Aristotle says so little to explain it (cf. 1155a20–1). This clause by itself leaves open the possibility that some human beings are not capable of law and agreement; but the next clause excludes that possibility.

10. **1161b8 to the extent that he is a human being:** Aristotle implies that in some way all human beings are friends to all others (not only that they can become friends).

12

12. §1–8. Friendships in families.

(a) §1. They form a distinct type of friendship because they do not rest on voluntary agreement.

1. **§1 1161b12–13 But we may . . . companions:** We set them apart because they do not clearly involve a COMMUNITY in quite the same way as the others do. See next note.

2. **1161b13–15 The friendship of citizens . . . some sort of agreement:** The contrast with the previous cases suggests that it is more natural to speak of a 'community' when some voluntary agreement is required than in, e.g., families. Aristotle discusses the sort of agreement that is needed for a political community at *Pol.* 1280a25–1281a4.

(b) §2–3. Paternal friendship.

3. **§2 1161b16–19 Friendship in families . . . from him:** On family friendships, cf. 1134b11, 1167b33; *MM* 1211b18–39. The father identifies the child's interest with his own because he regards the child as his own in something like the way his tooth or foot is his own. The natural and social relation of father to child causes the father to extend his self-concern in these ways, and (to a lesser degree) causes the child to extend his self-concern to his parents. The love of children for parents is important in education. See 1180b6.

4. **1161b19–24 But a parent . . . degree:** 'Regards as his own' translates *sunoikeiousthai*, cognate with *oikeion* (see PROPER). 'Is attached' or 'becomes close' might also be adequate. Some reference to beliefs and attitudes seems implied by the remarks about knowledge and perception. These remarks also justify 'because he regards (they regard)' in 18, 19, 29, where the Greek is simply 'as' (*hôs*).

5. **1161b26–7 And this . . . fathers do>:** In the light of this claim about mothers, it is surprising that all these friendships are said to depend specifically on paternal friendship.

6. **§3 1161b28–9 for those that . . . separate:** 'Separate' explains what makes the child other. 'Himself' insists that the child is still the father himself; John Smith's son is another John Smith. Cf. 1170b6; *EE* 1245a29–35; *MM* 1213a12.

(c) §3–4. Fraternal friendship and the types of friendship derived from it.

7. **1161b31 the same thing for both of them:** Lit. 'the same for each other', i.e., the same blood, etc. [Or 'the same as each other'.]
8. **1161a34 two of an age:** A proverb. Cf. *EE* 1238a33, Plato, *Phdr.* 240c.
9. **1162a2 the same parents:** I.e., the parents of these brothers.

(d) §5–7. Family friendships include friendships between unequals and between equals.

10. **§5 1162a4–5 The friendship of children . . . superior:** Aristotle connects family friendships with his earlier division; some involve unequals, and some equals.
11. **§6 1162a9 This sort . . . life in common:** In saying that the friendship of parents and children 'also' includes pleasure and utility, Aristotle implies that (1) it is primarily complete friendship, which is friendship for virtue, and in which (2) each has goodwill to the other for the other's own sake. It is easier to see how the familial relations he has described satisfy (2) than to see how they satisfy (1).
12. **1162a9–11 Friendship between brothers . . . similar:** Because of their similarity and their shared lives and pursuits, brothers will find it easy to take the sort of interest in each other that complete friends take in each other. The origins of the friendship are different, but the sorts of attitudes and actions expected seem to be similar.

(e) §7. Different types of friendship are found in husbands and wives.

13. **§7 1162a17–19 The friendship of husband and wife . . . among the animals:** On the natural character of couples and families, cf. *Pol.* 1252a26†.
14. **1162a20–2 Human beings, . . . in their life:** Cf. *Pol.* 1278b17–30, 1280a13. Aristotle is thinking of living well, not merely of staying alive and satisfying natural desires.
15. **1162a22 For the difference between them implies that:** [Or perhaps 'From the start . . .']. Lit. 'immediately', with a temporal or a logical sense.
16. **1162a25–7 And it may also . . . enjoyment for them:** Here again (see 1162a7–15) Aristotle refers to his threefold division of friendship. On women's virtue, cf. *Pol.* 1260a13.

(f) §8. Different friendships involve different obligations of justice.

17. **§8 1162a29–33 How should . . . a classmate:** On justice and friendship, see 1155a22, 1159b25. The remark on justice leads naturally into the discussion of disputes among friends.

13

13. §1–11. Disputes in friendships between equals.

(a) §1. Different types of friendships lead to different sorts of disputes.

1. **§1 1162a34–6 There are three . . . superiority:** Aristotle begins a long discussion of casuistical issues about friendship, and especially about the disputes that arise in it, that continues to the end of ix 3. It Is misleading to divide this discussion between two books (as the mss. do). The discussion of disputes (i) clarifies the nature of the different types of friendship (cf. note to §2 below); (ii) shows the types of character that support and undermine different friendships; and (iii) offers the sort of practical help that Aristotle has promised (cf. 1104a10–11, 1164b27–30). He begins by summarizing his previous discussion, making it clear (as he did in his discussion of familial friendships) that his threefold division is meant to apply to unequal as well as to equal friendships.

(b) §2–4. Friendships for utility easily lead to disputes.

2. **§2 1162b5–6 Accusations . . . for utility:** The discussion of disputes is a further defence of the claim of complete friendship to be complete. It avoids the conflicts and quarrels that make the others fall short of complete friendships; cf. 1156b17, 1157a20, 1159b4. This is partly because virtuous friends have more reasonable expectations of each other, partly because they are more reasonable in judging each other's success or failure in fulfilling these expectations; see 1163a21–9, 1164b1.

3. **1162b8–9 and if this is what they strain to achieve, . . . or fights:** 'Strain to achieve' (*hamillasthai*) seems to imply that each aims at this result rather than at any result that may involve competition or conflict with the other. Cf. 1169a8–11.

(c) §5–8. Disappointed expectations about reciprocal benefits are especially likely to lead to disputes.

4. **§5 1162b23 on rules:** Or 'legal' (*nomikê*, cognate with 'law', *nomos*, above).

5. **§6 1162b25–6 Friendship dependent . . . explicit conditions:** Within rule-governed friendship Aristotle distinguishes two types. One requires immediate repayment. The other allows postponement of repayment, and so involves trust in the character of the other person.

6. **§8 1162b33–4 If one party . . . accuse the other:** If we begin a new paragraph here, we make this a general comment on both kinds of friendship for advantage; it picks up the last sentence of §5. If we do not begin a new paragraph, we make this a comment specifically on the kind of friendship just mentioned in §7.

7. **1162b34–6 This happens . . . decide to do what is beneficial:** DECISIONS are concerned with what promotes ends. Ordinary people may wish for FINE things, but when they have to act on some wish, the wish that forms their decision is not their wish for the fine, but their wish for some other pleasure or good to themselves. The virtuous person is different because his wishes for what is fine are not ineffective; they are focused by deliberation on decisions to do fine actions.

(d) §9. To avoid disputes, we must make a fair return for benefits.

8. **§9 1163a2 We should, . . . willingly:** Retain *kai hekonti*.

(e) §10–11. In friendships for utility, a fair return must correspond to the benefit received.

(f) §11. A different standard applies in friendships for virtue.

9. **§11 1163a22–3 Rather, the decision . . . in decision:** Since the aim of friendships based on virtue is not some particular profit or pleasure, but the sharing of a life based on virtuous character, the important thing for measuring mutual benefits is the aim of the friend conferring the benefit. Aristotle does not suggest that fair exchange of benefits is unimportant in friendship based on virtue, but only that the basis for determining fair exchange is different.

14

14.§1–4. Disputes in friendships between unequals.

(a) §1. Disputes arise from the conflicting expectations of the superior and the inferior party.

1. **§1 1163a30–2 <The superior party . . . right in a friendship:** This analogy from business partnerships is also used in a political sphere by those who defend oligarchy as just; see *Pol.* 1280a25–40.

(b) §2–3. Sometimes these expectations are unreasonable. Reasonable expectations in rewards for public service.

2. **§2 1163b2–3 Rather, the superior . . . supplies need:** HONOUR is the reward that the magnanimous person expects for his benefits to others; see 1124b9 (though he does not benefit others only for the sake of honour, he will form friendships for honour with some people). On honour as a reward for service, cf. 1134b6.

3. **§3 1163b11–12 for distribution . . . as we have said:** On WORTH, cf. 1158b27, 1159a35, 1162b2. The point here is consistent with 1158b29. The friend's worth determines what sort of good he should get, and friends of different worth will be due different goods. But the quantity of one good should be equal to the quantity of the other, as far as this is determinable and possible; that is what prevents friendship from collapsing into entirely one-sided 'public service' (1163a29).

4. **1163b13–14 If we benefit from them in money or virtue:** This seems to mean 'if we become richer or better'. Less probably, 'if we benefit from their money or virtue'.

(c) §3–4. Sometimes honour is the only possible return for benefits. Illustration from the relation of father and son.

5. **§4 1163b18–19 it might seem:** Or 'it would seem'. Does Aristotle endorse this view? He agrees that a father is free to disown a son but a son is never free to disown his father, if the relation between father and son is simply that between creditor and

debtor. But he does not say whether he accepts the antecedent of this conditional. He alludes to a recognized practice of disowning sons in Athenian law (which, in Plato's view, allows the father too much freedom to disown; *Laws* 928e).

Book IX

1

1.§1–9. Disputes arising between friends with dissimilar expectations.

(a) §1–4. The disputes arise when aims conflict.

1. **§1 1163b32–5 In all friendships . . . and the others:** There is no break between Books viii and ix. Aristotle continues the casuistry of friendship from viii 13. Proportion in exchange: 1132b31, 1133a31, 1163b11.

2. **§3 1164a8–11 For if the friendship . . . which was unstable:** See 1156a19–24.

3. **1164a12 friendship in itself:** I.e., the type in which each loves the other in himself, not coincidentally, i.e., for what he is. Cf. 1156b7–11.

4. **§4 1164a17 pleasure in return for pleasure:** One had the pleasure of listening to the music, and the other the pleasure of anticipating payment.

5. **1164a20 common dealings:** *Koinônia*, usually rendered 'COMMUNITY'.

(b) §5–7. To settle disputes, friends must agree on the value of their services.

6. **§5 1164a22–3 Who should fix . . . received it:** Aristotle is talking about cases such as those he has just described, where people have made no explicit agreement in advance, and the question about appropriate return arises after the benefit has been given.

7. **1164a24–6 This is what Protagoras . . . collect:** See Plato, *Pr.* 328bc.

8. **1164a27 'Payment to a man . . . ' :** Hesiod, *Works and Days* 368: 'Payment to a man who is a friend should be promised and paid. Be cordial with your brother, but <make a bargain with him> before a witness. For faith and faithlessness alike have ruined men.' Hesiod supports the practice of agreeing in advance about repayment.

9. **§6 1164a27–9 But those . . . agreed to:** These people not only make an agreement in advance of the promised service, but actually exact payment in advance, and then fail to do what they have been paid for.

10. **§7 1164a30–3 And presumably the sophists . . . accused:** SOPHISTS (Protagoras is an exception) require payment in advance and then disappoint their pupils. Since they cannot fulfil their extravagant promises, they would never get paid if they agreed to defer payment until they had done what they promised to do.

(c) §7. In the best type of friendship, the value of services is fixed by the giver's intention.

11. **1164b1–2 And the return . . . and to virtue:** See 1162b6, 1163a31–3.

12. **1164b2–6 And it would . . . gods and parents:** The outlook and DECISION of the philosopher are different from those of the sophist, and so deserve the response appropriate to friends for virtue. Aristotle speaks of his philosophical colleagues in the Academy as friends (1096a13); cf. 1172a5, 1177a34. He speaks of colleagues rather than teachers; but the reference to gods and parents suggests that he has teachers in mind.

(d) §8–9. In other types of friendship, the measure must be the benefit received.

13. **§9 1164b10–11 Presumably, however, . . . before he got it:** On the right time for fixing the price, cf. 1133b1. These transactions between friends rely on principles of justice in exchange.

2

2.§1–10. Conflicts resulting from different types of friendships for different people.

(a) §1–3. The specific obligations arising from different types of friendship must usually be respected.

1. **§1 1164b23–5 Or must . . . be general:** In these cases one seems to have reasons for limiting obedience to one's father (a familiar source of quarrels; cf. 1149b8).
2. **1164b25–7 Similarly, should . . . do both:** 'Similarly' seems to refer to the second alternative just mentioned. Giving preference to friends over virtuous people, and to benefactors over companions, is similar to deferring to MEDICAL and military experts. Different people, according to their different previous relations to me, have different claims on my attention in different circumstances.
3. **§2 1164b27–8 Surely it is . . . exactly:** These casuistical questions illustrate inexactness; cf. ii 2.§3–5, and §6 below.
4. **1164b29–30 the fine and necessary:** Cf. 1126b28–30.
5. **§3 1164b30–3 Still, it is clear . . . companion:** Different spheres of activity and different relations generate distinct obligations that should not be overridden by a single obligation to, for instance, one's father.

The verb translated 'render' here (*apodidonai*) is also translated 'return' in the rest of the chapter; it may mean 'give back' or 'duly give' (cf. Plato, *Rep.* 330c; hence 'render unto Caesar', Luke 20:25), and Aristotle exploits both senses.

(b) §4–6. This rule needs to be qualified.

6. **§5 1165a2–4 As has been . . . gift to B> instead:** Aristotle's examples here show why he thinks EXACT and useful ethical rules cannot be found. The USUAL rules we can find are liable to exceptions reflecting the fine or the necessary. Cf. 1109a30–3.
7. **§6 1165a12–16 As has often . . . to Zeus:** §6 repeats §2–3, and reaffirms Aristotle's claim that lack of fixity does not preclude some definite prescriptions. Alternatively, we might attach the first sentence to §5 and the second to §6.

(c) §7–10. Different benefits are owed to different people.

8. **§8 1165a24 we should accord:** Supplied in the rest of this paragraph, on the basis of the next paragraph.

9. **1165a25–6 nor accord . . . wise person or a general:** Aristotle answers the question raised in §1; here 'wise person' (*sophos*) refers back to the doctor.

10. **§10 1165a34 the comparison:** Cf. 1109b10–13; 1126b2–4.

3

3. §1–5. The dissolution of friendships.

(a) §1. Friendships for pleasure and utility are easily dissolved.

1. **1165b6 at the beginning:** In 1164a13, or 1162b23.

(b) §1–2. Special difficulties arise if one friend is mistaken about the basis of the friendship.

(c) §3–4. If one friend sharply changes character, for the worse or the better, that may cause the dissolution of the friendship.

2. **§3 1165b13–14 But if we accept . . . still love him:** The friendship is threatened when the character changes. Only deterioration into incurable vice (cf. 1150b32) should break the friendship. The importance of shared activities and characters in the best friendship makes it unreasonable to continue a friendship with someone who has become vicious beyond recovery.

3. **§4 1165b23–4 But if one . . . as a friend:** The inferior person is not really virtuous; if he were, then could the superior person not still admire his character and share his activities? These are two developing characters (as suggested in 1157a10, 1162a9–15), one of which develops into a virtuous character while the other does not.

(d) §5. The dissolution of a friendship does not cancel all special relations.

4. **§5 1165b31–6 Then should the better . . . causes the dissolution:** Even when a friendship is justifiably dissolved, the friend's present character is not all that matters; we should still be concerned about him because of the past interactions.

4

4. §1–10. Self-love as a pattern of friendship.

(a) §1. The defining features of friendship.

1. **§1 1166a1–2 The defining . . . towards oneself:** It would be better to begin a new book here than at ix 1. Aristotle turns from casuistry to wider questions about friendship and the virtues. In c4–9 he describes the different attitudes that belong to friendship, and argues that they are both intelligible and defensible in a virtuous person. In c4, he derives the features of friendship from features of the

good person's attitude to himself. This derivation is important because it shows: (1) Self-love is sometimes good, since the virtuous person has it (ix 8). (2) The friend is another self (1161b28, 1166a31), insofar as we treat him as we treat ourselves. (3) We justify friendship by justifying the treatment of other people as other selves (ix 7, 9).

2. **1166a2–10 For a friend . . . these features:** Aristotle lists four marks of friendship: (1) A wishes and does goods or apparent goods to B for B's sake. (2) A wishes for B's life, for B's own sake. (3) A spends his time with B, and makes the same choices as B. (4) A shares B's distress and enjoyment.

> (b) §2–6. Each of these features is characteristic of the self-love of the virtuous person.

3. **§2 1166a12–13 And it would seem, . . . standard in each case:** Cf. 1113a29, 1176a15.

4. **§3 1166a13–14 For the excellent . . . whole soul:** In §3–5 Aristotle finds the marks of friendship in the virtuous person's relation to himself.

5. **1166a14–17 He wishes . . . each person seems to be:** The good person gives precedence to his reason and understanding; see 1168b30, 1178a2. Aristotle does not mean that good persons only want to think. They want their reason direct their desires and actions; hence they want to act on their virtuous decisions.

6. **1166a18–19 his rational part:** Lit. 'that by which he thinks rationally' (*phronei*). The verb *phronein* is cognate with *phronêsis*, usually translated 'PRUDENCE'; here it seems to have a more general sense.

7. **§4 1166a20–2 And no one chooses . . . by a god>:** God: 1159a3–8. Concern for myself requires concern for me as the sort of being that I essentially am. In a21 retain *ekeino to genomenon*.

8. **§5 1166a29 This . . . regrets <what he has done>:** The good person will surely be sorry if things have gone badly, if, for instance, his children (like Priam's sons; cf. 1100a5–9) have all died, or his friend was crippled in an accident. However, he will not decide he should change his principles, or that he could reasonably have made past decisions different from those he made. Hence he will have nothing to blame or reproach himself for. The major component of happiness is acting virtuously; and this does not require success in the results it aims at. See 1100b33–1101a6.

9. **1166a31–2 another himself:** Aristotle partly anticipated this description of a friend as an alter ego at 1161b18–33. He returns to it at 1170b6.

10. **§6 1166a33–b2 But is there . . . friendship to oneself:** Even if we cannot properly speak of Smith's friendship to Smith, we can speak of friendship between different parts of Smith's SOUL (cf. 1138b15) with their constituent DESIRES.

> (c) §7–10. Vicious people, however, are incapable of self-love and of friendship.

11. **§8 1166b6–7 Indeed, . . . have them:** Aristotle has contrasted (i) the many, who are base (see VICIOUS) and (ii) the utterly base and unscrupulous. Now he returns to (i). He argues that the marks of friendship (see notes to §1, 3) are absent in vicious people's attitude to themselves.

12. **1166b7–9 For they are at odds . . . best for themselves:** Aristotle compares vicious with incontinent people, but does not imply that vicious people are incontinent. See 1149a17, 1150a21, b32. If the vicious person has the wrong first principles, how can he regret his pursuit of pleasure? In 1166b7–10, 18–22 Aristotle answers that an intemperate person (a) has a conception of his good that requires him to satisfy his strongest appetites for pleasure; to do this he will plan prudently to make money, form friendships, etc. But (b) he also has strong appetites for immediate pleasures that will disrupt his more prudent plans; hence his appetite and his wish will conflict. In these cases, if the appetite is strong enough the intemperate person's initial wish gives way, and he forms a new rational plan. Since he has strong appetites and aversions, it becomes rational for him to act on them, if the pain resulting from their frustration will be greater than the pain resulting from their satisfaction. Hence he will act on his rational wish and decision; but since the rational choice he acts on is different from the one he would have acted on if he had not had such strong particular appetites, he will regret that he has to act on the choice he does act on. He will suffer conflict no less than the incontinent person suffers it, but a different conflict with different results.

[Or: 'For they . . . another. This is true, for instance of incontinent people (for they . . . harmful). And cowardice . . . themselves', implying that incontinents are included among vicious people (contrary to Book vii).]

13. **1166b12 hate . . . from life:** Read *pepraktai dia tên mochthêrian, misousi te kai.*

14. **§10 1166b22–5 Even if . . . full of regret:** Unlike the virtuous person, the vicious person does not value acting on the right decision for its own sake, but only as a means to the satisfaction of appetite. Hence he will be disturbed by failures that will not disturb the virtuous person; and these failures will multiply if his decision is liable to change in the way suggested above.

5

5.§1–4. Goodwill and friendship.

(a) §1–2. Goodwill is not sufficient for friendship.

1. **§1 1166b30 Goodwill . . . not friendship:** See 1155b32, 1157b18, 1158a7.

2. **§2 1166b34–1167a1 but goodwill . . . for contestants:** This is the wish without decision that was mentioned in 1111b24.

(b) §3. It is a beginning of friendship.

3. **§3 1167a3–4 Goodwill . . . erotic passion:** 'Beginning' renders *archê*; see PRINCIPLE.

4. **1167a7 longs for:** *Epithuei.* See APPETITE.

5. **1167a8–10 for when . . . trouble for him:** Concern for someone's good for his own sake is not enough for regarding him as a friend or other self. This requires time and familiarity (1157a10, 1162a12), which also produces the FONDNESS (i.e., affection) that is found in friendship (1126b21).

6. **1167a12 grow accustomed:** See 1156b25–9.

(c) §3–4. It is present only in the best kind of friendship.

7. **1167a12–14 It does not, . . . goodwill either:** See 1156a6–14. Goodwill is absent from incomplete friendships.

8. **1167a14–18 For a recipient . . . use to them:** Goodwill is the proper reaction to being benefited, in contrast to the calculating attitude of friendship for utility. Friendship for pleasure does not produce goodwill, because it does not imply any desire for the benefit of the other, whereas friendship for utility at least implies a desire for his benefit as a means to one's own benefit.

6

6.§1–4. Concord and friendship.

(a) §1–2. Concord requires agreement about the distribution of goods.

1. **§2 1167a32 or to make Pittacus . . . willing:** Pittacus was elected sole ruler of Mytilene (early sixth century) He resigned after ten years; hence Aristotle's 'when he himself . . .'. The concord ended when Pittacus himself dissented from his being ruler.

2. **1167a32–3 But whenever . . . in conflict:** 'Wants' might also be rendered 'wishes' (*boulesthai*, see DESIRE). Cf. Kant, *Critique of Practical Reason*, 28. Euripides' *Phoenissae* is about the bitter and uncompromising struggle (see esp. 588–624) between Eteocles and Polyneices for absolute power in Thebes. The same struggle is a theme of Aeschylus' *Septem* and Sophocles' *Oedipus Coloneus*.

3. **1167a35–b1 the common . . . party:** These terms (*ho dêmos* and *hoi epieikeis*) are often used for the democratic and the aristocratic sides in the political conflicts in a Greek city. See DECENT.

4. **1167b2–4 Concord, then, . . . <as a whole>:** On political friendship, cf. 1160a8–14.

(b) §3–4. Genuine concord is confined to virtuous people.

5. **§3 1167b4–6 Now this sort . . . same mind:** Concord, resulting from a community that aims for a common good, is a foundation of justice and of a stable friendship. This is easier for virtuous people (see 1162b6, 1164b1); for they do not seek gain at the other's expense, but they choose virtuous action, which benefits all of them. Contrast the OVERREACHING attitudes of the vicious friend with the virtuous attitude described in 1169a6–11, 28.

6. **1167b7 like a tidal strait:** Lit. 'like the Euripus'. This is a tidal strait between Boeotia and Euboea (near Chalcis, where Aristotle's mother was born, and where he lived from 323). Cf. Plato, *Phd.* 90c.

7

7.§1–7. Active benevolence and friendship.

(a) §1. A common view regards benefactors as purely selfish.

(b) §2–4. The common view is false: active benevolence realizes the capacities of the benefactor.

1. **§1 1167b25–7 Now Epicharmus . . . point of view:** Epicharmus fr. 146 Kaibel.

2. **§2 1167b28–30 However, . . . not even similar:** The active aspect of friendship was mentioned in 1159a27. Aristotle now seeks to prove what he earlier assumed, that the active aspect is valuable for its own sake. He rejects the common view that assumes that the only things we value for their own sakes are states of ourselves alone that do not essentially involve the states of another (cf. 1168b15–23). On this view, the benefactor cares only about the return he hopes for. Aristotle argues that active friendship is a NATURAL tendency of human beings, apart from any hope of reward.

3. **§2–3 1167b31–5 Benefactors, . . . acquired a soul:** Cf. 1120b13, 1134b10, 1161b18. Aristotle applies the explanation of parents' love for their children to active friendship in general. 'Product' here translates *ergon*, normally rendered 'FUNCTION'. The connexion between the two uses (which we might mark by 'work') matters in this argument.

4. **§4 1168a5–8 The reason . . . his own being:** The argument is this: (1) Being is choiceworthy for all. (2) We have being insofar as we live and act. (3) Hence we have being insofar as we are actualized. (4) The product actualizes the producer. (5) Hence the producer has his being in the product. (6) Hence the producer loves the product.

'Actuality' here translates *energeia*. Both the exercise of skill in the productive activity and the product resulting from this exercise actualize the agent's capacities, and so express his being. See also 1176a3. The product is the actuality only in a way, not without qualification *haplôs* (see UNQUALIFIED). The exercise of productive skill is the primary actuality of the producer; that is the actuality that is 'indicated' by the product. Since the agent values the exercise of his capacities, he values the product (or, in the case of friendship, the beneficiary) that is his actuality. This is a source of pleasure; see 1174b11.

This account of one's love for a beneficiary of one's benevolence does not include all the special features of friendship for a person—those that reflect his being another self valued for his own sake. These features are relevant in ix 9.

(c) §5–6. Active benevolence is both fine and pleasant.

5. **§5 1168a9–10 At the same time, . . . fine for him:** This explains the attitude of the magnanimous person (1124b9).

(d) §7. Active benevolence reflects one's own effort.

6. **§7 1168a25 more <than fathers do:** [Or 'more <than children love their mothers>'.]

7. **1168a26 children are theirs:** On mothers, see 1159a28, 1161b26.

8

8.§1–11. Self-love and selfishness.

(a) §1. A common view condemns self-love as selfish.

1. §1 1168a28–30 There is also a puzzle . . . shameful: This chapter is comple-
mentary to c7. Aristotle examines these common views: (1) Our underlying motive
for active benevolence is selfish (c7). (2) Virtue requires unselfish benevolence. (3)
Self-love is selfishness. (4) Hence actions characteristic of virtue cannot proceed from
self-love. The combination of these views implies that we cannot acquire the unselfish motive expected of the virtuous person. Aristotle agrees with (2), but rejects (4),
because he rejects (3). He therefore agrees with (1), as long as 'self-love' is substituted
for selfishness.

The puzzle discussed in c8 results from (a) the common belief that self-love is
bad (*Rhet.* 1389b35, cf. 1168b25; *Pol.* 1263b1; Plato, *Laws* 731e), and (b) Aristotle's
claim in ix 4 that the virtuous person's self-love is good. In his defence of (b) Aristotle
argues that (a) is too sweeping, because it overlooks some relevant examples, though
it is right for the examples it considers (see ETHICS #7).

2. 1168a31 go to every length: [Or 'do everything'.]

3. 1168a33 <for any . . . himself: This expansion of 'from itself' is suggested
by 'disregarding his own <interest>' at the end of the next sentence, applied to the
decent person.

[Or 'of his own accord', implying that the vicious person does nothing willingly
and spontaneously, without calculating his own selfish interest, but benefits others
only under compulsion (cf. 1167b15).]

> (b) §2–3. The demands of friendship, however, justify friendship, and
> hence love, for oneself.

4. §2 1168a35–b1 The facts, . . . not unreasonable: The 'facts' (*erga*; see
FUNCTION) that Aristotle mentions seem to be other common opinions about
friendship. He gives them the status of 'facts' because he has already discussed and
defended them.

5. 1168b5–6 since it has been said . . . to others: See c4, on self-love.

6. 1168b6–8 All the proverbs . . . shin: For the first proverb, see Euripides,
Orestes 1046 (a play in which friendship is prominent).

> (c) §4–5. The bad form of self-love results in selfishness, because it rests
> on a false view of the self.

7. §4 1168b18–19 That is why . . . contested: Goods that are contested (or
'fought over') are the goods pursued in competition. See 1169a21; *Pol.* 1271b8; Plato,
Rep. 586b–c. Since my gain, in these cases, is your loss (cf. 1167b4), self-love directed
to these goods results in OVERREACHING, and is harmful for other people, and
hence (cf. 1121a29, 1123a32; FINE #4) regarded as vicious (cf. 1169a6–11).

8. §5 1168b25 eager above all to do: The attitude of the virtuous self-lover is
non-competitive, in contrast to the competitive attitude of OVERREACHING and
excessive love of HONOUR. Cf. 1124b23–6, 1136b15–21.

[Or 'eager to excel everyone in doing'.]

> (d) §6. The good form of self-love is unselfish, because it rests on a true
> view of the self.

9. **§6 1168b31–2 And just as . . . system:** [Or 'just as a city and every other composite system, seems to be above all its most controlling part.']

Cf. 1166a17, 1178a2. A complex system is most of all its most CONTROLLING (or important) part because this part represents the interests of the whole; the direction and fortunes of the whole depend on this part. The rational part controls a human being insofar as its condition and outlook both reflect and determine the state of the whole person by the way it controls or fails to control his actions.

10. **1168b34–5 Similarly, someone is called continent . . . what each person is:** Aristotle refers to the connexion between continence, *enkrateia*, and mastery or control, *kratein*. I have mastery over my appetites when my understanding has mastery over them, since my understanding is to be identified with myself.

11. **1168b35–1169a1 Moreover, his own voluntary . . . reason:** Though Aristotle allows VOLUNTARY action on non-rational DESIRES, he thinks it is most voluntary when it results from rational desire and DECISION. For this is most of all *my* own voluntary action, in which the origin is most of all in *me*.

12. **1169a4–5 He is superior . . . guided by feelings:** Cf. 1095a6–11, 1128b15–21. Guidance by feelings does not imply impulsive or incontinent action. These are people whose non-rational desires set the ends they pursue and the DECISIONS they form; these include VICIOUS people.

[Or 'He is different from . . . '.]

13. **1169a5–6 and as much . . . seems advantageous:** Read *oregesthai tou kalou*. The virtuous person aims at the FINE (see 1162b35), since he cares about an action's being praiseworthy and advancing the common good. The vicious person cares about something's being good in itself, as certain pleasures are, in his view. But he does not care about its being fine and praiseworthy (see 1155a28–31).

(e) §7–8. Hence it leads to virtuous actions.

14. **§7 1169a8–11 And when everyone strains to achieve . . . of virtue:** In saying that people 'strain' (*hamillasthai*; cf. 1162b8) to achieve fine actions, Aristotle contrasts this attitude (aimed at the fine, not at surpassing other people) with the attitude of those who fight over 'contested goods' (§4 above). Cf. 1122b22, 1168b28. The common good is achieved when everyone strains to do fine action because it is the aim of fine action.

15. **§8 1169a17 all understanding:** Or 'every understanding'.

16. **chooses for itself what is best:** Or 'chooses what is best for itself'.

(f) §9–11. These virtuous actions include unselfish action aiming at the fine.

17. **§9 1169a18–22 It is quite true . . . fine for himself:** The recognized examples of virtuous action seemed (§1 above) to show that the virtuous person sacrifices himself in ways that are incompatible with the primacy of self-love. Aristotle answers that the virtuous person's self-love will make him want to do virtuous and fine actions; these are the actions required by the best sort of friendship and by the COMMUNITY that the virtuous person belongs to. Hence self-love is not only the paradigm

of friendship (as c4 has argued); it is also the basis for friendship, since the virtuous person's self-love will move him to the fine actions that are expected of friends. The actions that Aristotle mentions here are characteristic of the magnanimous person (1124b6–9, 23–6) displaying bravery (1116a10–5, 1117b9–10).

18. **§10 1169a32–4 It is also . . . do it himself:** This principle is followed in 1171b19.

19. **§11 1169a34–b2 In everything praiseworthy, . . . ought not to be:** The virtuous person's attitude to his friend's good is not entirely selfless. But it includes concern for the friend's good for his own sake. Since this sort of concern is fine, the virtuous person thinks it is part of his good. Hence the virtuous friend never 'sacrifices himself', if that implies sacrifice of his own interests to another's; but he aims at the friend's good for the friend's own sake no less than a 'self-sacrificing' person would. That is why the virtuous person is a self-lover, but not selfish.

9

9.§1–10. Why does the happy person need friends?

(a) §1. According to one view, the happy person is self-sufficient, and hence does not need other people.

1. **§1 1169b3–4 There is also a dispute . . . friends or not:** This is a third puzzle about self-love and friendship, following on those discussed in c7–8. This puzzle arises from Aristotle's position in c8. He has argued that the virtuous self-lover will be concerned with his friends because he is concerned with the fine. But what is fine about concern for friends? Are they not just an instrumental good, and hence not fine, but dispensable for a happy person?

2. **1169b7–8 'When the god . . . of friends?':** Euripides, *Orestes* 667 (cf. 1168b7).

(b) §2. We need friends so that we can benefit them.

3. **§2 1169b8–10 It would seem . . . external good:** Aristotle does not mean that if someone is HAPPY and BLESSED without friends, he needs friends as well. He means that someone cannot be happy without friends, so that friends are necessary for happiness, and that some of the happy person's activities are essentially shared with friends.

4. **1169b10–13 And if . . . people to benefit:** Here and in the rest of this chapter, Aristotle several times follows his common practice of incorporating a whole argument into a single Greek sentence. It is difficult to break his one sentence into several English sentences without obscuring the logical structure.

The importance of active beneficence has been discussed in c7. The role of friends in good and bad FORTUNE is discussed in c11.

(c) §3. The happy person cannot be solitary.

5. **§3 1169b18–19 tends by nature . . . with others:** Or 'naturally suited to live together with others'. On the solitary life and the political nature of human beings, see 1097b8–11, 1157b19–22.

(d) §4. To show that the happy person needs friends, we must distinguish the friendship of virtuous people from the other types of friendship.

6. **§4 1169b23 Perhaps . . . because:** Or 'perhaps <they say> that'.

7. **1169b23–4 the many . . . are friends:** The false belief underlying one side of the puzzle is exposed. As in c7 (cf. 1167b17), the objectors assume that friendship is only an instrumental good, because they recognize only friendship for advantage or pleasure. When we recognize the best sort of friendship, we see why it is a non-instrumental good.

8. **1169b26–7 for since . . . imported pleasures:** Cf. 1099a16.

(e) §5. We can observe the actions of virtuous friends.

9. **§5 1169b30–1170a4 Now if being happy . . . friend are of this sort:** The argument of these two sentences is this: (1) Happiness is activity. (2) The activity of the good person is excellent, and pleasant in itself. (3) What is our own is pleasant. (4) The actions of virtuous friends are our own. (5) Hence a good person finds pleasure in the actions of virtuous friends. (6) Hence, the blessed person needs virtuous friends.

In 1169b35 read *hai tôn spoudaiôn dê*.

Aristotle assumes that the good person enjoys his own virtuous activities, and hence enjoys his friend's too. The different uses of 'his own' (see PROPER) are important here. In b35 our friends' actions are not our own, since we do not do them ourselves. But in 1170a3–4 our friends' actions are our own, for reasons explained in 1170b5.

(f) §5–6. Friendship is a source of pleasure in virtuous activity.

10. **§5 1170a4 Further, . . . pleasantly:** This seems to begin a new argument. Aristotle still considers pleasure, as in the previous argument, but now he considers the pleasure that the virtuous person takes in his own actions (rather than in observing his friend's actions).

(g) §7. Friendship encourages virtue.

11. **§7 1170a11–12 Further, . . . Theognis says:** Theognis 35; Plato, *Meno* 95d.

(h) §7–10. Friendship realizes human capacities, through shared rational activity.

12. **1170a13 If we examine . . . <human> nature:** Cf. 1167b29. Aristotle explains how the preferences of the virtuous person, described in §5–6, are not his arbitrary inclinations, but the expression and realization of natural tendencies. Aristotle's argument from nature occupies the rest of the chapter. A simplified analysis: (1) What is good by nature is good and pleasant in itself for a good person. (2) For human beings living is perceiving or understanding. (3) Life is good and pleasant in itself. (4) What is good by nature is also good for the good person. (5) If we are perceiving or understanding, we perceive it. (6) Perceiving that we are perceiving or understanding is the same as perceiving our being alive. (7) Perceiving that we are

alive is pleasant in itself. (8) Living is choiceworthy for a good person. (9) The good person is related to his friend in the same way as he is related to himself. (10) Therefore, his friend's being is choiceworthy for him. (11) To perceive his friend's being, he must share conversation and thought. (12) Therefore, his happiness requires these activities of friendship.

13. **1170a16–17 For animals, life . . . perceiving or understanding:** On life, see 1097b33, and SOUL. Here as in 1168a5 the natural preference for life makes intelligible the preference for ACTIVITY over mere CAPACITY.

14. **1170a20–1 for it has definite order, . . . good:** Life has a definite order (lit. 'is defined'; cf. 1173a15–17) insofar as human capacities fit each other in a mutually supporting and fulfilling way. The virtuous person does not invent an order, but develops the order that is already present in the natural capacities (as complete virtue does in vi 13), whereas the vicious person perverts and destroys the natural order by misusing his natural capacities; cf. 1166b6–11.

15. **§8 1170a22–5 But we must not . . . what follows:** This parenthesis supports the claim that life is naturally pleasant, and pleasant in itself. The claim is not refuted by the experience of a life that is diverted or corrupted from its natural character. Aristotle refers forward to the discussion of pain in x 1–4 Pain prevents the full actualization of our capacities; cf. 1119a23–5, 1153b16, 1175b17.

16. **§9 1170a29–32 Now someone who sees . . . are understanding:** Self-awareness (see *DA* iii 2) is a further good that depends on the goodness of the activity we are aware of.

17. **§10 1170b5–7 The excellent . . . another himself:** On the friend as 'another oneself', cf. 1156b17, 1161b28, 1166a31–2; *EE* 1245a29–34; *MM* 1213a12–13. The best kind of friends are referred to here, since these are the ones whom the virtuous person regards as he regards himself. Since he regards his friends as he regards himself, he will want to be aware of his friends' activities as he is aware of his own. I extend my concerns and interests more widely, in a wider range of fine and virtuous activities, if I share them with a friend; hence I am better off if I have a friend than if I never have one; hence having friends is a part of my happiness.

18. **1170b10–12 He ought, then, to perceive . . . live together . . . conversation and thought:** See 1095b30, 1097b9, 1157b18.

19. **1170b14–17 If, then, for the blessedly . . . also be choiceworthy:** Since this recalls the statement in §7 of the conclusion to be proved ('an excellent friend would seem to be choiceworthy by nature for an excellent person'), the intervening text is meant to be a continuous argument.

20. **1170b17–18 What is choiceworthy . . . lack something:** Since happiness is COMPLETE and SELF-SUFFICIENT, character of happiness, taking it includes everything good and choiceworthy; cf. 1097b6, 16–20.

10

10. §1–6. How many friends are needed for a happy life?

1. **§1 1170b20 Then should . . . as possible:** Since the end of c9 has insisted that 'living together' with friends is needed, the questions naturally arise: How many

friends are needed for 'living together'? What sorts of obligations and activities are included in living together?

2. **1170b21–2 'have neither many nor none':** Hesiod, *Works and Days* 715.

(a) §2. We need only a limited number of friends for utility and pleasure.

3. **1170b25 one's life is insufficient:** Either (a) one's way of life does not provide the necessary resources or (b) a single lifetime is not long enough.

(b) §3–5. The requirements of a shared life limit the appropriate number of friends for virtue.

4. **§3 1170b31–2 For a city . . . hundred thousand:** On CITIES, see *Pol.* 1326a5–b25. If 'people' (lit. 'HUMAN BEINGS') refers to the total population of a city, Aristotle is denying that classical Athens is a city. If, however, 'people' refers to citizens (the only ones who are really parts, as opposed to necessary conditions, of a city), the number will exclude resident aliens, women, children, and slaves. A city of a hundred thousand citizens (exercising political functions) would indeed be abnormally large. See OCD, s.v. 'Population, Greek'.

(c) §4–6. We cannot have the right kind of friendship if we have too many friends.

5. **§4 1171a2–4 Now clearly you cannot . . . among them:** Cf. 1158a10.

6. **§5 1171a6–7 for many . . . their own:** Or 'to share the enjoyments and distresses of many as one's own'.

7. **§6 1171a15–17 By contrast, . . . ingratiating:** See 1127a7–10. Ingratiating people show to many people the attentions that are appropriate only to close (*oikeios*; see PROPER) friends, and so try to secure the favour due to close friends. They do not know what is required for the right sort of close friendship, and in fact all they have is the friendship of fellow-citizens, despite their efforts to make it look like something more.

11

11. §1–6. Friends in good and ill fortune.

1. **§1 1171a21–2 Do we need . . . ill fortune:** See 1169b13.

(a) §2–4. Good people want to avoid causing pain to friends.

2. **§3 1171b2–4 For a friend . . . dexterous, . . . pleasure and pain:** Cf. 1128a17. Dexterity requires someone to say the appropriate things, knowing the circumstances and the feelings of the people involved. Here would be one occasion for the PRUDENT person to display CLEVERNESS.

3. **§4 1171b6–7 That is why someone with a manly . . . his pain:** This MANLY attitude is also a sign of magnanimity, 1124b9, 1125a9.

(b) §5. But they want their friends to share their good fortune.

4. **§5 1171b18–19 We should . . . trouble to themselves:** The friend who invites help follows the principle of 1169a32–4. Presumably, however, the friend who gives the help will do something finer if his help is more difficult for him to give. Aristotle does not seem to pursue the full implications of his own views here.

(c) §6. They show proper consideration for friends in good and ill fortune.

12

12. §1. Shared activity in friendship.

(a) §1. The best friendship requires shared activity.

1. **§1 1171b32–1172a1 For friendship is community, . . . we seek:** Recapitulation of 1170a11–b19.

(b) §2. This shared activity includes the sharing of valued pursuits.

(c) §3. Virtuous friends have the best life.

2. **§3 1172a10–11 But the friendship . . . they meet:** Virtuous people's stability is contrasted with vicious people's instability. See 1156b12, 1166b6, 1167b4. When virtuous people practice their virtues, and express their characters towards each other, they benefit each other and so strengthen the friendship, while the opposite is true for vicious people.

Could someone take the virtuous person's attitude to his friend, and yet be intemperate and unjust in his attitude to everyone else? And could two people be friends on this basis, each admiring the virtue of the other as far as it goes? Aristotle might answer: (1) Vice involves perverted affections and appetites, which are not easy to restrain at will. Can such friends trust each other to restrain the vice from its normal growth (cf. 1140b12)? (2) If someone really understands the value of virtuous friendship, will he not also see the value of justice and temperance?

3. **1172a13–14 you will learn:** Theognis 35 (West, s.v. 'Theognidea'). Quoted by many authors; see, e.g., Plato, *Meno* 95d. Aristotle takes it to be so familiar that he does not name the author.

(d) §4. Transition to the discussion of pleasure.

4. **§4 1172a14–15 So much, . . . pleasure:** This is the second reference forward to a treatment of pleasure; cf. 1170a24–5.

Book X

1

1. §1–4. The right approach to pleasure.

(a) §1–2. The importance of pleasure.

1. **§1 1172a19–21 For it seems . . . pleasure and pain:** On the importance of pleasure, cf. ii 3, 1152b4.

2. **§2 1172a27–8 For some say . . . altogether base:** As in Book vii, Aristotle discusses common views about pleasure. In Book vii he concentrates on the view that pleasure is not a good. In Book x he defines his position by contrasting it with (a) hedonism (pleasure is not only a good, but the good, i.e., the supreme good), and with (b) the extreme rejection of pleasure (pleasure is not a good at all). He rejects both extreme views.

3. **1172a29–33 Others, however, . . . intermediate condition:** This second group of extreme opponents of pleasure misunderstand the practical advice that Aristotle has offered in 1103b26, 1109b1–12.

(b) §3–4. We should not commit ourselves to exaggerated and unrealistic views of pleasure.

4. **§3 1172a33–b1 Surely, however, . . . the arguments>:** In Aristotle's view, the practical aim of ethics does not justify pious frauds. These are self-defeating since the facts (*erga*; see FUNCTION) make the extreme theories incredible.

5. **1172b1–3 For if someone blames . . . make distinctions:** Someone who insincerely says pleasure is base will not be able to avoid pursuing it himself on some occasions. If he cannot live by the implications of his theory, the many will neither believe in his sincerity nor take his theory seriously. Cf. 1179a17–22.

[Or this remark about failure to live by one's theory might be aimed at both views that say pleasure is bad.]

2

2.§1–5. Eudoxus' defence of pleasure.

(a) §1–2. Eudoxus' arguments to show that pleasure is the good.

1. **§1 1172b9 Eudoxus thought . . . is the good:** EUDOXUS argues (cf. 1094a2–3): (1) All animals seek pleasure. (2) What is choiceworthy is good (*epieikes*, usually rendered 'DECENT'), and what is most choiceworthy is the supreme good. (3) Each thing finds its own good. (4) Hence, pleasure is best for all. (5) Hence, pleasure is the good. His argument looks more plausible when the ambiguity of CHOICEWORTHY is remembered.

2. **1172b12 The fact that all:** Read *to de panta*.

3. **1172b14 what is good for all, then:** Read *to dê pasin agathon*.

4. **§2 1172b19 to be avoided:** Or 'object of avoidance'. The term (*pheukton*) shares the ambiguity of *haireton* (CHOICEWORTHY).

(b) §3–4. His arguments do not show that pleasure is the good.

5. **§3 1172b26–9 This <last> argument, . . . to be the good:** This answer to Eudoxus' last argument briefly states Aristotle's position. He uses Plato's reply, *Phil.* 20d–22b, to the hedonist arguments. His assumption—that if x is the good (i.e., the

highest good), nothing can be added to x to make the result a better good than x—underlies the argument in 1097b16–20; cf. 1170b17–18; *MM* 1184a15–25†.

6. **1172b30 combined with prudence:** Here 'PRUDENCE' (*phronêsis*) may be used in the broader sense (present in Plato's *Phil.*) that extends to theoretical as well as practical reason. Cf. 1098b24; *EE* 1214a37†.

> (c) §4. A mistaken objection to Eudoxus' argument from universal pursuit of pleasure to the conclusion that pleasure is a good.

7. **§4 1172b35–6 But when some object . . . what they say:** Aristotle has rejected Eudoxus' argument for hedonism. He also rejects the extreme claim that pleasure is not a good at all.

8. **1172b36–1173a1 For if things . . . are <good>:** Aristotle endorses a universal belief about goods. [Or 'For things that seem <true> to everyone we say are <true>.']

9. **1173a2–3 desired these . . . objection:** Read *ôregeto* and *to legomenon*.

10. **1173a3 if prudent <animals>:** The sense of 'PRUDENT' may be broader than its usual Aristotelian sense; see 1172b30.

> (d) §5. A mistaken objection to Eudoxus' argument from the badness of pain to the goodness of pleasure.

11. **§5 1173a5–6 The argument . . . incorrect:** As in Book vii, Aristotle answers some arguments for the view that pleasure is not a good at all. The extreme opponents of pleasure are right to reject hedonism, but go too far in their objections to pleasure. Aristotle prepares us for his positive account in c4.

3

3. §1–13. Pleasure is a good, but not the good.

> (a) §1. A mistaken objection: pleasure is not a quality.

1. **§1 1173a13–14 Again, if . . . not a good:** Aristotle passes from arguments against pleasure that are specifically directed against Eudoxus to more general arguments to show that no pleasure is a good. This is part of his discussion of common views about pleasure; see the end of this chapter.

2. **1173a14–15 For virtuous . . . qualities either:** The opponents assume that goods are all in the CATEGORY of quality (see 1096a19–23). Aristotle answers that this is true of 'good' in 'good person', but not of 'a good' in 'a good for a person'.

> (b) §2–3. Further mistaken objection: pleasure admits of degrees, and hence is indefinite.

3. **§2 1173a15–17 They say . . . more and less:** Definiteness and goodness: 1170a29–31.

4. **1173a17–20 If their judgment . . . with the virtues:** This first argument about definiteness assumes that the experience of pleasure admits of degrees, so that we can be more or less pleased.

5. **1173a22–3 If, on the other . . . are mixed:** This second argument assumes that different types of pleasures admit of degrees, so that pleasures taken in one sort of object are pleasanter than pleasures taken in another sort of object.

(c) §4. A mistaken objection: pleasure is a process.

6. **§4 1173a31 It would seem, . . . not even a process:** Aristotle replies to Plato's a criticism of pleasure (*Phil.* 53c–54c). In 1153a7 he discussed the view that pleasure is a becoming. But now he distinguishes the generic notion of process (or change; see MOVEMENT) from the specific sort of process that is a becoming (*genesis*; see *Phys.* 225a12). According to this conception of a becoming, something's becoming is its coming into existence, as opposed to its destruction, which is its passing out of existence. Aristotle replies that pleasure is not even a process, let alone a becoming

7. **1173b2–4 It is possible, . . . pleased quickly <or slowly>:** Even if I am enjoying watching a game that happens quickly, my enjoyment itself is not quick or slow.

(d) §5–7. The relation of pleasure to pain shows that pleasure is not a process.

8. **§6 1173b7–8 They do indeed say . . . becoming>:** The view is probably derived from Plato, *Phil.* 31e (though it is not necessarily the same view; see next note).

9. **1173b11–13 This does not seem . . . becoming empty:** Aristotle assumes that pleasure is a condition of the SOUL, not a purely bodily condition, since it requires awareness (and Plato recognizes this, *Phil.* 34a). In b12 read *kenoumenos*.

(e) §8–10. The fact that some pleasures are bad does not show that pleasure is not a good.

10. **§8 1173b20–2 To those who cite . . . not pleasant:** §8–10 advance the discussion of the extreme opposition to pleasure. Aristotle's treatment of bad pleasures also clarifies his view about pleasure. He offers three accounts of bad pleasures. (1) §8: They are not pleasant, except for people in a bad condition. (2) §9: The pleasures themselves are good, but they should not be chosen when they come from bad sources. (3) §10: Pleasures differ in species, according to their sources, and those that come from bad sources are bad.

11. **1173b22–5 For if things . . . these people:** 'Pleasant to S' translates the Greek dative case, which might also be rendered 'pleasant for S'. Aristotle might mean (a) x seems pleasant to S, even if x is really not pleasant, or (b) x is really pleasant for S, even if x would not be pleasant for someone else. Cf. 1113a22–31.

12. **§9 1173b25–8 Or else . . . everything:** This second account of bad pleasures depends on the distinction between 'choiceworthy without qualification' (see UNQUALIFIED) and 'choiceworthy in these conditions'. In this reply Aristotle concedes that the pleasures themselves are good, but insists that they ought not to be chosen, since they come from the wrong sources.

13. **§10 1173b28–31 Or perhaps . . . other cases:** On the just person's pleasures, cf. 1099a7–21. This third account of bad pleasures is more restrictive than the second. Instead of saying (as the second account says) that some pleasures are good, but

ought not to be chosen because they have bad sources, Aristotle now suggests that bad sources make the pleasures bad.

(f) §11–13. Pleasure is not the only good, or the ultimate good.

14. **§11 1173b31–3 Now the difference . . . in species:** The discussion of specifically different pleasures in §10 leads Aristotle back to the question that he took up in 1172b26. There he rejected one of Eudoxus' arguments for identifying pleasure with the good, but did not decide the question. Now he decides it. In 1153b9–14 he neither endorsed nor explicitly rejected the Eudoxan position. On flatterers, see 1127a8.

15. **§12 1174a1–4 And no one . . . pain for it:** Cf. 1176b22, 1177a6; *EE* 1215b22†. Aristotle relies on the general assumption (used against a version of hedonism already in 1095b19–20) that we are concerned to exercise distinctively human FUNCTIONS.

16. **1174a4–8 Moreover, there . . . from them:** A counterfactual test (cf. 1097b3) shows that we do not always choose things for the sake of pleasure. Pleasure is not our only end, because there are some actions that we would still choose even if (contrary to fact) they did not result in pleasure. Aristotle's account of pleasure as 'necessarily following' on activity does not imply that pleasure is the highest good.

17. **§13 1174a8–11 It would seem . . . that are not>:** This conclusion from the discussion in §11–12 affirms the rejection of hedonism.

18. **1174a11–12 Let this suffice, . . . and pain:** This sentence concludes the discussion (introduced by the last words of c1) that has occupied c2–3. Aristotle does not take himself to have simply raised objections to different views. He claims to have reached positive conclusions about pleasure, which he incorporates into his own account in c4.

4

4.§1–4. Pleasure is an activity.

(a) §1. Pleasure is complete at any time.

1. **§1 1174a13–14 What, then, . . . beginning:** Aristotle signals his positive account of pleasure, anticipated at 1173a29, 1153a7–17. He relies on the distinction between processes, which are incomplete ACTIVITIES, and complete activities; see also ACTION and PRODUCTION. Since pleasure is not a process, the arguments that treat it as a process are irrelevant.

2. **1174a16–19 And pleasure . . . longer time:** Form: CAUSE. Here the form is closely connected with essence and DEFINITION; something achieves its form to the extent that it acquires the character that makes it the kind of thing that it is. The building of a temple takes time to acquire all that makes it a complete building of a temple; hence it takes time to achieve its form. An enjoyment, however, does not take time to acquire all that makes it a complete enjoyment. Though I might prefer my enjoyment to be prolonged, it is no more an enjoyment by being prolonged.

(b) §2–3. A process consists of dissimilar parts, and is not complete at any time.

3. **§2 1174a20 constructing a building:** Read *oikodomia*.

4. **1174a21 ... or, <in other ... it takes>:** Read *chronô(i) toutô(i)*.

5. **1174a21–3 Moreover, each ... from one another:** Lit. 'And in the parts and in the time they are all incomplete, and they differ in form from the whole and from each other.' The words 'they are all' must apparently refer to (a) processes such as temple-building, and 'they differ in form' must refer to (b) the parts of (a). The next sentence relies on the distinction between (a) and (b).

6. **1174a26–7 but the production ... incomplete ... of a part:** Even when any one of (b) is finished, it looks forward to a further production. This explains why the whole production (a) is incomplete at any time when it is still going on.

7. **1174a27–9 Hence ... differ in form; ... a process complete in form ... time <that it takes>:** 'Differ in form' refers to (b), and 'a process' to (a).

8. **§3 1174a29–b2 For if locomotion ... And besides ... differences in walking itself ... in different places:** Locomotion, an example of (a), is followed by examples of (b). 'And besides ...' takes walking, e.g., from London to Glasgow, as an example of (a), and its parts (e.g., walking from London to Birmingham, from Birmingham to Preston, etc.) as examples of (b). 'Traversing a line' refers to a stadium that has lines across it (like a football field). We cross the lines if we run from one end to the other.

9. **1174b2–3 Now we have ... elsewhere:** See, e.g., *Phys.* v 1–4.

(c) §4. Therefore pleasure is not a process, but an activity.

10. **§4 1174b9 for what is present in an instant is a whole:** 'Instant' translates *nun*, usually rendered 'now'; cf. *Phys.* 218a6, 220a18. An instant is unextended. Since, therefore, it is not a duration or an interval, it is not a part of time. Anything that is wholly present in an instant takes no time to come into being, and hence does not come into being at all; this is why it is a whole. There is no coming into being of pleasure because coming into being requires the parts to come into being one after the other, whereas pleasure is present as a whole all at once.

11. **1174b9–10 This also makes ... process or a becoming:** In 1173a29–b20 Aristotle considered the claim that pleasure is a process (*kinêsis*) and a becoming (*genesis*). His account explains why pleasure is not a process. Now he explains why it is not a becoming.

12. **1174b13 Nor, then <is this said> of pleasure:** I.e., it is not said to be a becoming. [Or 'Nor, then <is there any coming to be> of pleasure'.]

4. §5–11. *Pleasure completes an activity.*

(a) §5. The best activity is pleasantest.

13. **§5 1174b14–16 Every perceptual capacity ... perceptible objects:** 'Perceptual capacity' translates *aisthêsis*, lit. 'PERCEPTION' or 'sense', exercised in the ACTIVITY of perceiving. The 'object' (lit. 'perceptible' or 'thing perceived', *aisthêton*) is the special sensible (colour, sound, etc.; b27; cf. 1142a27) or common or coincidental sensibles.

(b) §6–8. Pleasure completes an activity by being a consequent end.

14. **§6 1174b23–6 But the way . . . health and the doctor . . . same way:** The doctor is the efficient CAUSE, and health the formal cause, of being healthy. The different ways of completing an activity (or 'bringing it to its goal', *teleioun*; see COMPLETE) are different final causes.

15. **§8 1174b31–3 Pleasure completes . . . supervenient end . . . youths:** Probably Aristotle here distinguishes two types of final CAUSE, which are two ways in which an activity can achieve its END: (1) Perceiving is good as an end in itself, as the activity of a desirable capacity or state; the action has the state 'present' in it insofar as that is the state it actualizes. (2) The pleasure is a further end, another good in itself, which is supervenient on our choosing the action as a good in itself. It is an extra good added to the good of the action as the 'bloom' of youth (i.e., the attractiveness of a youth that made him an object of desire and pleasure to an older man (1157a6–10) is added to his youth. See also 1153a6. A supervenient end (cf. 1104b4) is contrasted with the inherent or intrinsic end of the activity—i.e., the realization of the desirable state, which is an end in itself.

[Or one might take the state to be the formal rather than the final cause.]

(c) §9. This explains why pleasure is not continuous.

16. **§9 1175a4–6 For nothing human . . . the activity:** See 1154b20, 1170a6.

(d) §10–11. This also explains why we desire pleasure.

17. **§10 1175a10–12 Why does . . . being alive:** More literally: 'One might think all desire pleasure because they . . .'. 'One might think' goes with 'because they . . .' rather than 'desire pleasure'. Aristotle takes it for granted that people desire pleasure.

18. **§11 1175a18–21 But do we choose life . . . completes every activity:** Though Aristotle sets aside this question about pleasure and life as ends, his answer to it emerges from 1174a4 and from what he has just said. We do not choose life and its activities purely for the sake of pleasures; we choose for their own sakes the activities that constitute our living (cf. 1168a5). Nor do we choose pleasure purely for the sake of living; it is one of the desirable activities that constitute our living. See 1175b34–6.

5

5.§1–5. Pleasures differ in kind, and especially in their goodness and badness.

(a) §1–2. Different activities are completed by different pleasures.

1. **§1 1175a21–2 Hence pleasures . . . species:** Aristotle accepts the third account of pleasure that he introduced in 1173b28–31. He claims that pleasures differ in species. Just action and sunbathing are not two sources of a qualitatively uniform sensation in the way that two cows are sources of the same milk; we cannot ask how much sunbathing we would need to replace the pleasure lost by failing to do just actions. Since pleasures differ in species, Aristotle insists that the virtuous person must get the specific pleasure of virtuous action. He must enjoy it because it is virtuous; and that enjoyment will require him to value it as virtuous for its own

sake. Cf. 1099a17, 1104b3. 'Species' translates *eidos*, also translated by 'form'. See 1174a27–9.

(b) §2. The proper pleasure promotes an activity.

2. §2 1175a29–30 **This is also . . . completes:** A new paragraph. Aristotle passes from the claim that different activities have different proper pleasures to the fact that the proper pleasure has a characteristic and distinctive effect on the activity that it is proper to.

(c) §3–5. An alien pleasure impedes an activity.

3. §4 1175b12–13 **contestants:** Probably the playwrights who compete against each other for prize at dramatic festivals. Or perhaps Aristotle refers to the actors.

5. §6–11. Which pleasures are goods?

(a) §6–7. The goodness of an activity determines the goodness of the pleasure taken in it.

4. §7 1175b34–5 **Nonetheless, pleasure would seem . . . appear the same:** The pleasure of fishing, for instance, is not simply the unhindered activity of fishing itself, but a further activity (cf. 1153a12–15, 1153b10). Once we distinguish the activity and the pleasure, we can see that we do not choose life and its activities purely for the sake of pleasure.

(b) §8. The function of a species of animal determines the proper activity and the proper pleasure.

5. §8 1176a6–7 **as Heracleitus . . . than gold:** DK 22 B 9.

(c) §9–11. The human function determines the proper human pleasure, measured by reference to the virtuous person.

6. §10 1176a15–19 **But in all such . . . what he enjoys:** Cf. 1113a31–3, PROTAGORAS. The good person is the standard not only of what is a good pleasure but of what is really a pleasure.

7. §10–11 1176a21–4 **It is not pleasant, . . . corrupted people:** See 1173b20–5. Since vicious people are mistaken in their views about what is pleasant, they mistake what appears pleasant to them for what is really pleasant. They are even wrong about what is really pleasant for them; for what seems pleasant to them in their depraved condition is not what is what is really pleasant for them—i.e., what would be pleasant for them in a healthy condition.

6

6. §1–8. Happiness consists in activities in accord with virtue.

(a) §1–2. Happiness is an activity that is choiceworthy in itself.

1. **§1 1176a30–1 We have now . . . of pleasure:** This summary places the discussion of pleasure after friendship, omitting the discussion of pleasure in Book vii. However, the summary is too compressed to decide whether Aristotle is describing a treatise that includes the books common to the *EE* and *EN*. See 1179a33–5, Intro. §3.

2. **§2 1176a33–b2 We said, . . . previous <discussions>:** See 1095b31, 1153b19.

3. **1176b2–3 Some activities . . . other end:** On types of activities, see 1097a30–b11; HAPPINESS #2–3.

4. **1176b5–6 For happiness . . . self-sufficient:** A self-sufficient end (a) is pursued for its own sake; and (b) is not pursued for the sake of anything else. Here Aristotle says correctly that self-sufficiency implies (a), and that virtuous actions satisfy (a). Virtuous actions do not satisfy (b); see 1177b1–3.

(b) §3. Many suppose that pleasant amusements are the appropriate sorts of activities.

5. **§3 1176b9–10 But pleasant . . . own right>:** Aristotle deals with the claim of pleasure to be the highest good more fully than when he briefly dismissed it, 1095b19. Someone who claims that pleasure is good must also specify the relevant type of pleasure, and recognize that the value of the pleasure depends on the value of the activity that is the source of the pleasure.

When Aristotle says that people choose these amusements 'not because of other things', he means that no ulterior benefit is needed to make them seem choiceworthy to us. He does not deny that we choose them for the sake of happiness. Cf. 1097b2–5. Two reasons for thinking them choiceworthy in their own right are introduced by 'For people . . . ' and 'Moreover, most . . . '.

6. **1176b13–16 That is why . . . tyrant requires:** On witty people, cf. 1128a4, 1158a31. The people mentioned here do not have the virtue described in iv 8, but are more like the ingratiating people and flatterers of iv 6. Powerful people admired for their happiness have no more understanding of it than their imitators have; cf. 1159a12–17.

7. **1176b16–17 And so these amusements . . . in them:** On the example set by powerful people, cf. 1095b11.

(c) §4–5. But popular opinion is a poor guide; the virtuous person is the standard.

8. **§4 1176b19–21 Further, these powerful . . . bodily pleasures:** On most people's lack of relevant experience of pleasure, cf. Plato, *Rep.* 582a–583a. On 'civilized' (or 'free') as opposed to slavish pursuits, cf. 1177a7; SLAVE.

9. **1176b23–4 Hence, . . . decent people:** Cf. 1174a1.

10. **§5 1176b24 As we have . . . excellent person:** To rule out amusement as a candidate for happiness, Aristotle appeals to the excellent person as the standard for selecting the worthwhile activities and pleasures; see 1176a15.

11. **1176b27 most choiceworthy to the excellent person:** And therefore most honourable and pleasant.

(d) §6–8. Happiness must involve serious and worthwhile activities, not merely amusements.

12. **§6 1176b33–4 Rather, . . . Anacharsis says:** Anacharsis was sometimes counted as one of the Seven Sages. See DK 10 A 1.

13. **§7 1177a3–6 Besides, . . . of happiness:** The different uses of *spoudaion*, translated by 'serious' and 'EXCELLENT' are closely related here.

14. **§8 1177a8–9 even a slave, . . . happiness>:** On SLAVES, cf. 1125a1, 1161b2–8. They lack the capacity for life in accord with reason, and so are incapable of happiness; see 1099b32, 1178b27.

7

7.§1–9. Happiness: the supreme activity is theoretical study.

(a) §1–2. This is the best activity.

1. **§1 1177a13–15 The best . . . leader:** This seems to refer to the practical functions of understanding. But Aristotle's next remarks refer to STUDY, not practical thought, as the activity of reason that is to be identified with its proper virtue. Perhaps he has two points in mind: (1) The ruling functions of reason show it is our best capacity. (2) Hence the best activity of all is the best activity of the best capacity; this is the activity of study. Cf. 1178a4–8.

2. **1177a16–17 Hence complete . . . proper virtue:** Aristotle need not mean that complete happiness is exclusively this activity. If happiness is to be complete it must include this activity. The same applies to 'in accord with the supreme virtue' in a13. Cf. 1178b28–32.

3. **1177a17–18 and it has been said . . . study:** Aristotle has not explicitly said that the relevant activity is study; but cf. 1139a6–17, 1141a18–22, 1143b33–1144a6, 1145a6–11. An activity of study (*theôrêtikê energeia*) might be (1) an activity consisting wholly in study, or (2) an activity characterized by study (but not necessarily excluding activities other than study). Aristotle does not say here that the activity of understanding that constitutes happiness is exclusively concerned with study.

4. **§2 1177a18–19 This seems . . . the truth:** The rest of this chapter is a series of arguments for the claim he has just made (whatever it is): (1) Study is the single activity that best fits the criteria for happiness. (2) Hence, if happiness must be some single activity, study is the best candidate. (3) If happiness includes more than one activity, study will be the most important. These conclusions do not imply (4) study is the whole of happiness.

5. **1177a21–2 Further, it is the most continuous . . . continuous action:** Cf. 1100b11, 1175a5.

(c) §3. It is pleasantest.

6. **§3 1177a24 wisdom:** This takes up the discussion of *sophia*, introduced in vi.

(d) §4. It is most self-sufficient.

7. **§4 1177a27 the self-sufficiency that is spoken of:** I.e., the self-sufficiency that is commonly ascribed to the happy person, as in ix 9. [Or the self-sufficiency that was ascribed to happiness in i 7.]

8. **1177a28 most of all:** In 'Admittedly . . . ' Aristotle concedes that the activity of study is not wholly self-sufficient. By 'most of all' he means 'more than the other activities of the virtues'. He does not say that study, all by itself, makes someone happy.

(e) §5. It aims at no end beyond itself.

9. **§5 1177b1–2 Besides, study . . . beyond having studied:** Cf. 1176b6–7. Study is not chosen for any end wholly external to it. Aristotle's remarks here do not show that it cannot also be chosen for the sake of happiness (i.e., as a part of happiness). Cf. 1097b2.

[Or 'it is the only virtue chosen because of itself'. Neither the previous arguments in this chapter nor the following clause support this translation.]

(f) §6. It consists in leisured activity, and does not include actions aimed at some further end.

10. **§6 1177b4–6 Besides, . . . in leisure; . . . deny ourselves leisure . . . at peace:** LEISURE is not idleness or inactivity, but action that we gladly take on for its own sake. When we 'deny ourselves leisure' (lit. 'are unleisured', *ascholein*), we take on actions that we engage in reluctantly, for the sake of some further end.

11. **117b12–15 But the actions of the politician also deny us leisure; . . . it is different:** These actions 'deny us leisure' (lit. 'are unleisured'; see previous note) because of their disagreeable and instrumental character, as explained in the latter part of the sentence. Happiness for oneself and one's fellow-citizens is the aim of the just politicians. They are not simply out for their own power and wealth, but they still aim at some goal that is distinct from (i.e., not part of) political activity itself. Virtuous action has two aspects. Campaigning against racism, for instance, is (a) a just action, and hence fine and choiceworthy in itself, and (b) aimed at a result wholly external to it, the passage of a law and its success in eliminating some racism. Aspect (b) distinguishes these virtuous actions from pure theoretical study, and hence makes the virtuous person depend on external circumstances. Cf. 1140b6–7.

(g) §7. Compared with activities of other virtues, theoretical study best satisfies the conditions for happiness.

12. **§7 1177b18 and are choiceworthy . . . than themselves:** Lit. 'and are choiceworthy not because of themselves'. Aristotle has said (e.g., 1176b8) that they are also to be chosen for their own sakes. Here he says they are choiceworthy for some other end external to themselves.

[Or 'and are not choiceworthy because of themselves'.]

13. **1177b23 evidently in accord with:** Read *aponemetai, kata*.

14. **1177b24–6 Hence a human being's . . . complete span of life, . . . proper to happiness:** On a 'complete' length of life, cf. 1098a18, 1101a16.

(h) §8. This is a godlike life.

15. **§8 1177b26–8 Such a life . . . divine element in him:** Study is the activity of the most divine element or part ('element' is supplied in the next two paragraphs; the Greek has only a neuter adjective) of a human being, and hence it constitutes a life that is more than merely human; cf. *Met.* 982b28–983a11.

16. **1177b28–9 And the activity . . . the compound:** Probably Aristotle refers to the compound consisting of the understanding and the other parts of the SOUL. Less probably, he might refer to the compound of soul and body. Cf. 1178a20.

17. **1177b31–3 those who exhort . . . mortal':** Advice frequently given in Greek literature, e.g., Euripides, TGF fr. 1040; Pindar, *Isthmians* v 16.

18. **1177b33 pro-immortal:** This (*athanatizein*) is probably modelled on the terms used for supporters of the Medes (i.e., Persians) and Laconians (i.e., Spartans) (*mēdizein, lakônizein*). Aristotle does not mean that we should try to become immortal, or should pretend that we are immortal.

go to all lengths: Lit. 'do all things'.

(i) §9. It realizes the supreme element in human nature.

19. **§9 1178a2–3 Moreover, this . . . <is the person>:** I.e., 'Moreover, this <supreme element> [i.e., understanding] seems to be the person [*hekastos*; lit. 'a given one (masc.)'], if the controlling and better element <is the person>'. Less probably, one might reverse subject and predicate, or translate 'if it (i.e., understanding) is the controlling and better element in him'. See 1168b31–4. §9 adds to the claim in §8 that the life of study is (in one respect) superhuman the further claim that it is (in another respect) most truly human.

20. **1178a7 most of all:** As in 1177a28, 'most of all' marks a reservation. Aristotle does not wholly endorse the claim that theoretical understanding is to be identified with the person.

8

8.§1–13. Theoretical study and the other virtues.

(a) §1–3. The virtues concerned with action are human, not divine.

1. **§1 1178a9 <is happiest> in a secondary way:** 'Happiest' takes up the previous sentence. Or '<is happy>'.

2. **1178a10 because . . . are human:** The activities of the other virtues depend on the human and non-divine parts of the compound (see 1177b26–31), and hence are subject to some of the limitations of human beings and their external circumstances. In particular, the virtues of character need external goods more than study needs them, and hence are more vulnerable to FORTUNE.

3. **§2 1178a15–16 Moreover, virtue of character . . . feelings:** Or 'Indeed, some feelings actually seem to arise from the body; and in many ways virtue of character seems to be adapted to feelings.' A second argument to show that virtue of character is secondary in happiness, because of its dependence on the human condition.

4. **§3 1178a16–17 Besides, prudence is inseparable . . . prudence:** A third argument for the same conclusion. The claim that prudence is inseparable from (lit. 'is yoked together with'; cf. 1175a19) virtue of character was defended in vi 13.

5. **1178a23 for this much has been said:** Read *eirêtai*. Aristotle probably refers to vi 7 on *sophia*. [Some editors conjecture '*eirêsthô*' ('let this much have been said').]

(b) §4–6. Theoretical study is less dependent on external goods.

6. **§4 1178a23–5 Moreover, it seems to need external supplies . . . needs them:** Happiness and external supplies: see GOOD.

7. **1178a32–3 Similarly, the brave person . . . virtue requires:** Bravery requires me to stand firm, but if I am so feeble that I am immediately overpowered, I will never manage to stand firm. If I never find anything that would appeal to my appetites, I lack the FREEDOM or opportunity (*exousia*) to do intemperate actions, and so cannot do what temperance requires.

8. **§5 1178a34–b1 Moreover, . . . decision or action . . . on both:** Decision and action: see 1111b5, 1163a21, 1164b1. CONTROL: cf. 1100b10.

9. **1178b1 Well, certainly . . . in both:** The complete good requires virtuous action, not merely virtue; hence the next clause refers to actions.

10. **§6 1178b5–6 Insofar as he is a human being, . . . accord with virtue:** The political nature of human beings (cf. 1097b9) suggests that a human being's happiness includes not only study but also the other virtues and their characteristic actions.

(c) §7–8. Traditions about the gods support the supremacy of theoretical study.

11. **§7 1178b8–10 For we traditionally . . . ascribe to them:** See 1101b18, 1145a26; *Pol.* 1253a26†. The GODS do not suffer from the human limitations that make virtues of character necessary and praiseworthy for human beings. There is no point in praising them for not having base appetites, as we would praise the temperate person (1119a11–20); for the gods were never in danger of having them, and did not need to train themselves.

12. **1178b16 Surely it is vulgar . . . base appetites:** Or 'Surely it is vulgar to praise them <for acting temperately>, because they do not have base appetites <which are necessary for the possibility of temperance>.'

13. **1178b20 Endymion:** According to legend, his beauty did not decay with age, but the price he paid was being permanently asleep.

14. **1178b22–3 And so the human activity . . . happiness:** 'Most akin' and 'more than any others' imply a comparison between study and other human activities (cf. 1178a2–8). They stop short of identifying study with happiness.

15. **§8 1178b24–8 A sign of this . . . in study at all:** The capacity for happiness: 1099b32. Aristotle may be making the same point here, if understanding in study and in practical thought are the same capacity; cf. 1177a12–17.

16. **1178b32 And so . . . of study:** In 'some kind of' (*tis*) Aristotle stops short of simply identifying happiness with study, as in 1178b22–3.

(d) §9–10. Human beings also need external goods for happiness, but only at a moderate level.

17. **§9 1178b33–5 But we will need . . . provided:** Aristotle returns (see §6) to the place of external goods in happiness. Since we do not need a large supply of

external goods, our need for them does not conflict with the role he has ascribed to study.

18. **1179a3 discrimination and action:** Read *oud' hê krisis oud' hê praxis.* DISCRIMINATION (or 'judgment') is the ability to distinguish good from bad.

19. **§10 1179a4–6 but, we can do fine . . . accord with virtue:** §9 has recognized that we need some external goods for life and action in general. §10 considers them as resources for FINE and virtuous action. As in §6, Aristotle maintains that the happy person who gives the proper role to study in his life will not be exclusively concerned with study; he will also be concerned with fine actions that ACCORD with virtues of character. See *Pol.* vii 2–3.

(e) §11–12. Traditional views support us, but they must be tested in practice.

20. **§11 1179a9–12 Solon . . . temperately:** See Herodotus i 30.

21. **1179a13–15 And Anaxagoras . . . the many:** See DK 59 A 30. Cf. *EE* 1215b7†.

22. **§12 1179a16–17 Hence the beliefs . . . arguments:** On beliefs of the WISE, see ETHICS #5.

23. **1179a17–19 Hence we ought . . . how we live:** Lit. ' . . . from actions (or 'facts', *erga*; see FUNCTION) and lives'. We must pass the test stated in 1172a35, showing that we can apply our principles in practice. Some consistent ideals of life are so hard for a normal person to act on that they cannot be taken seriously.

(f) §13. Those who engage in study are loved by the gods.

24. **§13 1179a22–4 The person whose activity . . . the gods:** Aristotle continues the description of the godlike character of the life of study.

9

9.§1–17. Ethics, moral education, and legislation.

(a) §1–5. Since arguments alone do not make people virtuous, we must study the different means of moral education.

1. **§1 1179a33 We have now . . . pleasure also:** This summary follows the order of the *EN*; cf. 6.§1.

2. **1179a35–b2 On the contrary, . . . act on our knowledge:** Aristotle reasserts the practical aim of ETHICS (1103b26) and returns to the beginning of the *EN*. Having found what happiness is, and especially that it requires virtue of character to be acquired by moral EDUCATION (1104b11), we must now turn our attention to that. We return to explicit concern with the political community; see 1094b7, 1102a7, 1103b2, 1113b21, 1141b23, 1152b1. The right design for happiness extends beyond individuals to the city.

3. **§3 1179b4–6 Now if arguments . . . Theognis says:** Theognis 432.

4. **1179b6–7 these ought to be provided:** 'These' might refer to arguments or to rewards.

5. **§5 1179b16–18 For it is impossible, . . . characters:** This explanation suggests that the bad characters of the many make them unreceptive to moral reasoning, as though good upbringing would have made them receptive. But in b11, 'naturally obey . . .', Aristotle suggests that their nature was defective from the start; even with the right habituation they apparently could not reach complete virtue.

6. **1179b19 what we seem . . . decent:** Lit. 'through which we seem to become decent'.

(b) §6–8. Virtue requires nature, habit, and rational argument. Education forms character and habit.

7. **§6 1179b21–3 The <contribution> . . . fortunate ones:** On nature, cf. 1114b5–21, 1144b4–6.

8. **1179b23–6 Arguments . . . seed:** Arguments have some influence, but it is not always effective. On the need for a good upbringing, cf. the related but different reasons given in 1095a2, b4.

(c) §8–13. Since the formation of the right character requires legislation, states ought to be concerned with moral education, though they often neglect this task.

9. **§8 1179b32–4 for the many, . . . resistant way:** Resistance to pain: 1150a31.

10. **§9 1180a4–5 For the many . . . than to the fine:** Compulsion is distinguished from force (1179b29); see 1110a26, b1. The distinctions drawn in iii 1, iii 5, and v 8 determine the proper treatment of different offenders.

11. **§12 1180a21–2 and law is reason . . . understanding:** On the rational character of LAW, cf. *Pol.* 1287a28–32.

12. **§13 1180a24–9 And yet, . . . like a Cyclops:** On neglect of moral education, cf. 1161a8–9. Aristotle approves of Spartan concern for moral education, but not of Spartan moral education. See 1102a10–12; *Pol.* 1333b5–35. Aristotle quotes Homer, *Od.* ix 114, on the pre-political Cyclopes (also quoted by Plato, *Laws* 680bc). The context (paraphrased): 'They have no assemblies to deliberate and no rules but they live in caves. Each lays down rules for his children and wives, and <these heads of households> have no concern for one another.' (Aristotle has 'wife' instead of 'wives'.)

(d) §14–17. Legislative science is useful both for individuals and for states.

13. **§14 1180a30–2 if the community . . . decide to do it:** Aristotle offers second-best advice (characteristic of parts of the *Pol.*, e.g., iv 1) for someone who is not living in the best type of community. He advises systematic education by individuals, if the community will not do its part. In a32 read *sumballesthai <kai dran auto dunasthai>*, adding the phrase that stands in a30 in the mss.

14. **1180a33 legislative science:** 'Science' is supplied from here on. Cf. i 2, 1141b24–5.

15. **1180b6 for his children . . . to obey:** Friendship in families: 1161b19.

16. **§15 1180b7 different from:** Or 'better than'.

17. **1180b8–11 For though generally . . . on everyone:** 'Generally' translates *katholou*, translated by 'universally' in b14, 21. The patient who does not benefit is not exactly an exception to the general rule. Insofar as he is feverish he may benefit from the normal treatment; but since he has other conditions too, the normal treatment may not, everything considered, be best for him, even if it is always best for fever, considered by itself.

18. **§16 1180b16–20 Admittedly someone . . . anyone else at all:** Aristotle allows some practical success without scientific knowledge, but insists that scientific knowledge is necessary for understanding.

19. **1180b20–3 Nonetheless, . . . sciences are about:** EXPERIENCE makes someone competent in a restricted range of cases, but general competence and understanding require the grasp of the universal. The features of the virtuous person referred to in 1137a9 and 1144b3 help to distinguish the expert craftsman from the merely experienced practitioner. Here SCIENCES include CRAFTS.

9. §18–23. Who should teach legislative science, and how?

(a) §18–19. Some apparently suitable teachers lack theoretical understanding, whereas others lack practical experience.

20. **§18 1180b28–31 Next, then, . . . part of political science:** Like Plato (e.g., *Meno* 99–100), Aristotle is dissatisfied with politicians and with those who profess to offer instruction in POLITICAL SCIENCE. The practical politicians simply rely on experience, while its instructors overlook its importance.

21. **1181a1–3 Instead, those who practise . . . rather than thought:** The political activists (*politeuomenoi*) are professional politicians, who are popularly regarded as overactive busybodies; cf. 1142a2.

22. **1181a3–6 For evidently . . . friends of theirs:** This supports the claim that politicians are not guided by thought (*dianoia*), but by EXPERIENCE.

(b) §19–21. Both experience and theoretical understanding are necessary.

23. **§19 1181a9–11 Nonetheless, . . . politics:** Aristotle corrects any misunderstanding that might have arisen from the previous remarks. Though practical politicians lack political science, and cannot teach it, their experience is relevant for political science. In a11 read *sunêtheias mallon*.

24. **§20 1181a12–14 By contrast, . . . it is about:** Aristotle returns to the SOPHISTS whom he introduced in §18, and accuses them of neglecting the point about experience that he made in §19. He insists that practical experience is no less necessary in political science than in prudence as a whole; cf. 1143b7.

25. **1181a18 comprehension:** Cf. vi 10.

26. **§21 1181b3–5 And yet . . . treated:** As in §19, Aristotle tries to prevent any misunderstanding that might result from one-sided attention to what he has just said. Political science, like MEDICINE, will be practically relevant only if it rests on experience; but it does more than merely report experience.

(c) §22–3. The right approach to legislative science.

27. **§22 1181b12–15 Since, then, . . . we are able:** Predecessors: *Top.* 183b14. Aristotle does not deny that his predecessors have made particular suggestions about legislation (some are discussed in *Pol.* ii). He claims they have left the general area 'uncharted' (or 'unexamined'), with no systematic survey of the data, and no account of the proper method.

28. **§23 1181b15–17 First, then, . . . particular topics:** Aristotle announces the programme of the *Pol.*, in the order of the surviving treatise. This sentence applies to Book ii.

29. **1181b17–20 Then let us study . . . some badly:** This sentence applies especially to *Pol.* iv–vi. The 'collected political systems' are the 158 descriptions of different constitutions, compiled by Aristotle's school. (See ROT, pp. 2453–7.) Only one of them, the *Constitution of Athens*, largely survives.

30. **1181b20–2 For when we have . . . should employ:** This applies especially to *Pol.* vii–viii. After studying the experience of different political systems and practices (following the advice in §20), we will be in a better position to evaluate different systems, and to apply the ethical principles of the *EN* in an account of the best system.

31. **1181b23 having made a start:** This probably refers to the present chapter.

GLOSSARY

accord, in accord with, correspond to, kata The Greek preposition *kata* means 'according to', and includes both (a) actual guidance (I build a shed *kata* the design if I consult the design as I work); and (b) mere conformity (bodies fall *kata* the laws of nature without consulting these laws). When Aristotle speaks of action *kata* virtue, decision, etc., it is often both important and difficult to decide if he means (a) or (b) or something intermediate between them (see, e.g., vi 13).

account See REASON #4.

achievable in action See ACTION.

achievement See FUNCTION.

action, *praxis* 1. Aristotle uses *praxis* and the cognate verb *prattein* broadly for all intentional actions (translated 'do' or 'achieve in action'). What we can achieve by *praxis* (the *prakton*, usually translated 'achievable in action') is what we can achieve by our own efforts (1096b34, 1147a3). Probably a *praxis* must be VOLUNTARY. In this sense children and non-human ANIMALS are capable of action (1111a26). Such action has a DESIRE for some END as its efficient CAUSE; the desire is focused on a PARTICULAR situation by further beliefs, and it is a particular action that is done (1147a5, 1110b6) and that we are responsible for.

2. More strictly, *praxis* is confined to rational action on a DECISION. Non-human animals are incapable of this. See 1094a5,7; 1139a20; *EE* 1222b20, 1224a29 (cf. 1111b8).

3. Most strictly of all, *praxis* is confined to rational action which is its own END, and is not done exclusively for the sake of some end beyond it. It aims at 'doing well' (or 'acting well', *eupraxia*) for itself, 1140b6–7. Action may also have some end beyond it. HAPPINESS is an end beyond virtuous action, which nonetheless is chosen for its own sake: 1097b1–5, 1174a7–8. Here action is contrasted with PRODUCTION, 1139a35–b4, vi 4–5. It is a complete ACTIVITY, and not just a MOVEMENT. PRUDENCE is about *praxis* in this narrow sense, 1140b4–6.

4. Sometimes the contrast between *praxis* and *theôria* (STUDY) corresponds to the contrast between practice (i.e., actually changing something in the world) and theory (i.e., pure thought), 1178b19. *Theôria* and *praxis* are two types of energeia (ACTIVITY).

5. It is not always clear (e.g., at 1094a1) how strictly Aristotle uses *praxis*. The uses above may not mark three different senses of the word. They may be (cf. the three types of FRIENDSHIP in viii 3–6) more and less complete specimens of action.

activity, actuality, *energeia* 1. A subject's *energeia* realizes its CAPACITY; hence the *energeia* of a CRAFT, such as shoemaking, and of the craftsman, includes both the activities (involved in the exercise of the craft) and the product (the shoes) that is aimed at in the exercise (cf. notes to 1094a3, 1168a6; FUNCTION).

2. The scope of *energeia* is sometimes narrowed by contrast with *hexis*. In *DA* 412a22–8†, Aristotle contrasts 'first' activity (*entelecheia*, equivalent to *energeia*) with 'second'. Someone is in first activity in relation to his knowledge of French if he has

learnt French and can speak it on the right occasions, but at the moment is asleep or thinking about something else. He is in second activity when he is actually speaking French (1146a31). To have a SOUL is to have a first activity. In the *EN* a first activity is called a STATE. When Aristotle defines HAPPINESS as an activity of the soul, he is requiring it to include second activities, not merely states (1095b32, 1178b18–20).

3. In 1174a14 ff., *Phys.* 201a9, *Met.* 1048b18, Aristotle draws a further contrast: (a) A MOVEMENT is an incomplete activity. The degree of activity is consistent with the retention of the capacity realized in the activity, where the complete activity implies the loss of the capacity. The movement of house-building, for instance, is going on when the bricks and stones have incompletely actualized their capacity to become a house; when they completely actualize that capacity and the house exists, they no longer possess that capacity, since a house is not still capable of becoming a house. (b) A complete activity, however, does not imply the loss of the capacity that is actualized in the activity. Seeing or living, for instance, does not imply the loss of the capacity to see or live. A movement is incomplete because it aims at some end beyond itself (e.g., the building process aims at the house being built) whose achievement makes that movement impossible to continue (we cannot keep building the house when it is already built), whereas a complete activity is its own end. Hence complete activity is identical to ACTION in Aristotle's narrowest sense.

4. This complete activity is the type of activity that PLEASURE is (1153a10, 1174a14).

5. Activities of virtue; see VIRTUE.

6. Activity and FRIENDSHIP; see 1168a5, 1170a18.

agapan   LIKE

agathos   GOOD

aidôs   SHAME

aischros   shameful; see FINE.

aisthêsis   PERCEPTION

aitia, aition   CAUSE

akolasia   intemperance; see TEMPERANCE.

akrasia   INCONTINENCE

akribes   EXACT

ananke   NECESSITY

anger, *orgê*   Anger is a FEELING (1105b22) especially associated with spirit (see DESIRE). The proper treatment of anger is discussed in iv 5. See also 1103b19, 1110b26, 1111a26, 1117a6, 1130a31, 1135b29, 1138a9, 1149a24–b33, 1150a29; *Rhet.* 1378a30.

animal, *zôon*   1. Aristotle normally uses *zôon* for the genus to which insects, dogs, and human beings all belong (*Pol.* 1253a3, 8†). Sometimes he uses it for those he also calls 'the other animals' (1111b9), excluding HUMAN BEINGS (1099b33); these animals are also called 'beasts' (*thêria*, e.g., 1139a20, 1147b4).

2. Non-human animals have a SOUL defined by PERCEPTION. They live by perception and APPEARANCE without REASON (1098a2, 1139a20, 1147b4, 1149a10, 1170a16).

3. They share with human beings non-rational DESIRE (1111b12, 1178b27) but not rational desire. Hence they act VOLUNTARILY, but not on a DECISION (1111a25, b8). They are incapable of rational action; see ACTION #2.

4. They are not capable of HAPPINESS (1098b32, 1178b27) or of the VIRTUES of character (1149b31; cf. 1141a26; *EE* 1240b32), since these require decision.

5. Non-rational animals share these last two features with CHILDREN.

animate   See SOUL.

aporia   puzzle; see ETHICS.

appear, evident, apparent, *phainesthai*; appearance, *phantasia*; seem, *dokein*   1. The verb *phainesthai*, 'appear', has two constructions: (a) With the participle ('being wise, he appears so', i.e., 'he is evidently wise'), it endorses what appears (this is also the sense of the adjective *phaneron*, 'evident'; (b) With the infinitive ('he appears to be wise'), it neither endorses nor denies what appears.

2. Whenever the verb is used without either participle or infinitive expressed, it is indeterminate between (a) and (b). These cases are translated by 'is apparently'. This translation may mislead if it suggests that Aristotle is tentative or non-committal about what is apparently so; this may, but need not, be true just as what is apparent may, but need not, be misleading or dubious.

3. The condition I am in when something appears to me is *phantasia*, 'appearance' (1113b32, 1141a32). The appearance may result from PERCEPTION or from REASON (*DA* 434a5–10†), and ANIMALS who have perception without reasoning are directed by perceptual appearance (1147b5); a HUMAN BEING may act on this contrary to reason (1149a32, 1150b28).

4. When Aristotle reports what appears, or sets out the appearances (1096a9, 1145b3), only the context shows whether he endorses or rejects (e.g., 1113b1) or neither. The same applies to his use of 'seem' (*dokein*, cognate with *doxa*, 'belief'), which is equivalent to 'appear' in the *EN* (e.g., 1095a30, 1113a21; note on iv 3.§3, 34). The appearances include commonly accepted beliefs; Aristotle takes these as the material for arguments in ETHICS.

5. 'Would seem' normally translates *eoike* (sometimes 'it looks like', or 'is like'), which may, but need not, be less committal than 'seem', *dokein*.

appetite, *epithumia*   See DESIRE.

archê   PRINCIPLE

aretê   VIRTUE

argument   See REASON #3.

athlios   MISERABLE

attend, attention   Usually this renders *epimeleisthai* and cognates (e.g., 1099b20, 1114a3, 1180a25), indicating systematic practice and training. When attending is contrasted with CAPACITY or potentiality, in 1147a33, the Greek is *theôrein*; see STUDY.

autarkês   SELF-SUFFICIENT

avoid   See CHOICEWORTHY.

axia   WORTH

bad   See VICIOUS.

base   See VICIOUS.

beautiful   See FINE.

becoming, *genesis*   See note to x 2.§4.

bia   FORCE

blessed, blessedly happy, *makarios*   We might expect this to be especially closely associated with the life of the GODS (cf. *EE* 1215a10†; 1178b9), in which happiness is entirely stable and immune to the limitations of the human condition. *EN*, however, seems to use the term interchangeably with 'HAPPY'. Unless the terms are interchangeable, the argument in 1100b28–1101a21 is difficult to understand.

boulêsis, **wish**   See DESIRE.

bouleusis, **deliberation**   See DECISION.

bravery, *andreia*, **cowardice,** *deilia*   Apart from the full discussion of bravery in iii 6–9, see also 1102b28, 1103b17, 1104b8, 1119a21, 1123b31, 1129b19, 1130a18, 1137a20, 1144b5, 1166b10, 1167a20, 1169a18, 1177a32, 1178a32. *Andreia* is cognate with *anêr*, MAN, and with *andrôdês*, 'manly'. It refers to the behaviour and traits that were often thought to be the supreme display of a man's virtue, and proof of his devotion to his city. (Cf. Thucydides ii 42.) These assumptions about bravery affect Aristotle's treatment of the virtue, and especially his focus on the display of bravery in battle. (Contrast Plato, *Laches* 192c–e.) They do not, however, control his conception of bravery; see, e.g., iii 8.

capacity, capable, power, powerful, *dunamis, dunatos*   1. If x has the capacity to F, x is capable of F and x will F in the right conditions. If fire has a capacity to burn, it will burn unprotected flesh close to it; this is a non-rational capacity. If Smith has a capacity to build, he will build when he chooses to build in the right conditions for building; this is a rational capacity. See *Met.* ix 1–7, esp. 5. Hence a capacity is what is realized in an ACTIVITY.

2. Capacities include CRAFTS and branches of STUDY (1094a10, 26) and also the natural capacities from which the VIRTUES are developed (1103a25, 1106a6, 1144a23, b1).

3. A rational capacity is a capacity for contraries—e.g., we can use our medical knowledge to cure or to poison. Whether we use it well or badly depends on our choice or decision, *Met.* ix 2, 5; cf. 1129a11–17, 1144a23–8. This is the difference between a capacity and a STATE of character, which is the good use of one's capacities. Virtue requires not only capacity, but also DECISION, ii 5, 1127b14. Nor is HAPPINESS a capacity; see 1101b12.

4. *Dunamis* is also applied to power over things and people (1099b2, 1161a3 [see also FREEDOM], 1178a32).

categories, *katêgoriai*   1. Aristotle sometimes speaks of 'the figures (i.e., types) of predication', or 'the GENERA of PREDICATIONS', *genê tôn katêgoriôn*, *APo* 83b16; *Top.* 103b20. Sometimes he speaks of 'the predications', *katêgoriai*, *GC* 317b6, 9, 319a11; *DA* 402A25; *Met.* 1032a15; this is the basis for the traditional label 'categories' (listed in, e.g., *Catg.* 4; *Top.* 103b20–7; *Phys.* 200b33, 225b5–9; *GC* 317b5–11, 319a11–12; *Met.* 1017a22–7, 1028a10–13; *EN* 1096a19–29).

2. A category answers the question 'What is it?' at the most general level about items of a certain sort (e.g., this man, this white colour, etc.; *Top.* 103b27–39. The items seem to correspond to different questions that might be asked about a substance (e.g., 'What is he?' (a man); 'How big is he?' (six feet tall); etc.; *Catg.* 1b27–2a4).

3. Since the question 'What is it?' leads to these different answers, there is no one thing that it is to be something. Hence Aristotle infers that there is no one account of being, and that being is spoken of in many ways; see HOMONYMOUS. He argues in i 6 that the same is true of good.

cause, reason, responsible, *aitios*, *aitia* 1. In *Phys.* ii 3 Aristotle explains the doctrine of the four causes. Reference to an *aition* (neuter of adjective *aitios*) or *aitia* answers the question 'Why?'. Different 'why' questions about an object (e.g., a statue) can be answered by different types of explanations: (a) MATTER ('because it is made of bronze'). (b) Form, *eidos*, stating its DEFINITION and essence, and hence the species (also *eidos*) it belongs to ('because it is a bust of Pericles'); see 1174a22. (c) The efficient cause, the PRINCIPLE of MOVEMENT ('because the sculptor made it'); see 1110a15, 1139A31–2. (d) The final cause or END (*telos, hou heneka*, 'that for the sake of which'), e.g., 'to represent Pericles'.

2. Aristotle's four types of explanation include more than those we commonly call causal explanations. Sometimes (e.g., 1100a2, 1137b27), therefore, 'reason' is appropriate. 'Cause' also renders the preposition *dia* ('because of'). See 1095b7, 1155b27–1156a5.

3. In legal contexts the adjective *aitios* often indicates not only causation but also blameworthiness, and correspondingly the abstract noun *aitia* indicates both the cause and also the ground of accusation. Hence 'responsible' is sometimes apt, e.g., 1110b13, iii 5. See also CONTROLLING, VOLUNTARY.

change See MOVEMENT.

character, *êthos*, *êthikos* 1. The *EN* is about the formation of VIRTUES of character. These are the STATES resulting from (a) early habituation, to acquire the right DESIRES, FEELINGS, PLEASURES, and PAINS, 1104b11, 1179b24 (hence Aristotle connects character closely with habit, 1103a14–26); (b) the correct use of rational deliberation that marks a prudent person who makes the correct DECISION. The formation of the right character requires the EDUCATION of the non-rational parts of the SOUL (1103a3). But since they are to be trained to act according to correct REASON, training in reasoning and deliberation is also needed. It is someone's character that makes him the 'sort of' (*hoios*) person he is. Hence 'character' often translates *hoios* or the cognate *poios*.

2. The actions that are appropriate to a person's character are those said to be 'proper to him' or those he 'is the sort' to do (e.g., 1120a31, 1146a6, 12, and 'not for him', a32). All these phrases translate the Greek genitive case, i.e., 'is not of the generous (etc.) person'.

charieis CULTIVATED

child, *pais* Aristotle often mentions children together with non-human ANIMALS because they still lack REASON and rational DESIRE (1100a1; *Rhet.* 1384b23). They need primary moral EDUCATION (1104b11, 1119a33–b15).

choiceworthy, *hairetos* This includes the GOOD, the FINE, the PLEASANT, and the expedient (see 1104b30, 1155b18; *Top.* 118b27). The term is an adjective formed from the verb *haireisthai*, 'choose' (a part of *prohairesthai*, 'decide'; see

DECISION) with a verbal adjective ending, which is ambiguous between (a) actually chosen, (b) capable of being chosen, and (c) deserving to be chosen. Which Aristotle means in a particular context is not always clear.

Similar questions arise about the opposite of *hairetos*, 'to be avoided' (*pheuktos*; e.g., x 2); about *bouletos*, 'object of wish', in iii 4; about *philetos*, 'lovable', in viii 2; about *gnorimos*, 'known' in i 4; about *phoberos*, 'frightening' (1115b10–14); and about *epainetos*, 'praised' or 'praiseworthy' in iv 5 (esp. §14). See esp. 1172b9–28. Our view about this ambiguity will affect our view on the relation of GOOD #1 to choice; cf. 1097a18–b6.

city, *polis* A *polis* is a COMMUNITY of free citizens (*politai*) governed by a political system, *politeia* (or constitution); see *Pol.* i 1–2; iii 1–3, 8–9. A *polis* differs from a monarchy (1115a32) in having a political system and LAWS that assign some rights and functions to the citizens even if, as under a tyranny (1160b10), these rights and functions are temporarily ineffective. When Aristotle speaks of a *polis*, he has in mind something much smaller than most modern states; see 1094b9–10, 1170a31; *Pol.* 1276a22–30. But the *polis* is similar to a modern state insofar as it is a sovereign political unit, making alliances on its own initiative (1157a26). Cities come into being both for mutual advantage and because life in cities is itself a non-instrumental good; 1160a8–30, *Pol.* iii 9.

civilized See GENEROUS.

clever, *deinos* This is also rendered 'terrifying', e.g., 1103b15, 1115a26, 1116b35. It is used for anything remarkable or formidable, and hence is used, as Aristotle uses it, for cleverness (1144a23, 1152a10, 1158a32). Cleverness is not said to be a deliberative CAPACITY, but to be a capacity for finding what is needed to fulfil an end—which need not always require deliberation (a clever debater will be able to find the telling reply on the spur of the moment).

coincident, *sumbebekos* The term (often translated 'accident') is derived from *sumbainein*, 'come about together', which often just means 'happen' or 'turn out'. *Sumbebekota* include many things that are not, in the ordinary sense, accidents or coincidences. F is a coincident of x if (a) F belongs to x, but (b) x is not essentially F (is not F IN ITS OWN RIGHT), and x's being F does not follow from the essence of x. See note to v 8.§4; *Met.* 1025a14–16; *Top.* 102b4–9).

common, shared, *koinos*; community, *koinonia*; member, *koinonos*; share, *koinonein* 1. A UNIVERSAL is common because it is shared by the instances that it belongs to (1096a28, 1107a30, 1141b26, 1180b15).

2. 'Common good' renders *koinon* at, e.g., 1122b21, 1123a5, 1162a23.

3. People who share some common pursuits and goals are members, *koinonoi*, in a community. A *koinonia* may involve a loose and temporary connexion (as in a business transaction) or a close long-term relation (as in a family or a city); sometimes 'common dealings' represents *koinonia*, where 'community' would be misleading; see v 5, viii 9, 1164a20, 1170b11; *Pol.* 1252b12–34†. The common pursuit of a common good in a *koinonia* is the foundation of FRIENDSHIP and of JUSTICE (1129b17, 1155a22).

compel See NECESSARY.

complete, *teleios* 1. This is cognate with *telos*, 'end' (see FINAL CAUSE). It applies to something that has reached its *telos*, and hence to a mature, adult organism (1102b2; *Met.* 1072b24). Aristotle explains completeness in *Met.* v 16.

2. HAPPINESS is complete, 1097a25–b21, 1098a18, 1101a13. So is the CITY, *Pol.* 1252b27–30† (cf. 1281a1). In these contexts some prefer the rendering 'final' or 'perfect'. But the close connexion between being *teleion* and the other criteria for happiness, and its use in 1098a18, 1101a13, support the translation 'complete'. See also 1094b8, 1095b32, 1097a25–b21, 1098a18, 1099a15, 1100a4, 1101a14, 1102a1, 1103a25, 1129b26, 1153b16, 1154a1, 1156a7, 1174b15–33, 1177a17, 1178b7.

condition   See STATE.

consideration   See PARDON.

content   See FOND.

continent   See INCONTINENT.

controlling, in control, important, full, *kurios*   1. If someone is *kurios* over me, he controls me and my actions (1110a3, 6); hence the *kurios* is often a commander or ruler (1116a30, 33). To be *kurios* over an event is to be in control of whether it happens. Insofar as I am *kurios*, I am the PRINCIPLE and CAUSE of an ACTION, the action is up to me and VOLUNTARY, and I am responsible for it (1113b32, 1114a32; *EE* 1222b21†).

2. Since what controls and rules a process is the most important thing about the process, determining whether it happens, *kurios* is also used more generally to mean 'important'. Often both control and importance are suggested (1143b34, 1145a6, 1168b30, 1178a3).

3. If a property is found in degrees, the application of the term to the complete instance controls its application in partial instances. Hence the *kurios* F is F most completely, and 'F' applies to it more fully than to things that are partially F or less F. Here *kurios* is rendered 'full', e.g., at 1098a6, b14, 1103a2, 1115a32, 1176a28.

convention, conventional   See LAW.

conversation   See REASON #6.

correct, *orthos*   The verb *katorthoun*, translated 'be correct' (1098b29, 1104b33, 1106b26, 31, 1107a14, 1142b30), might also be translated 'succeed'. *Orthos* indicates success in pursuing an END or correctness in picking it (1144a20), as opposed to error (*hamartia*, 1135b18; sometimes 'fail' would also be suitable). Like 'right', *orthos* is applied to right angles and to straight lines, It is not confined to moral rightness. The virtuous person is guided by correct REASON insofar as he has the true conception of the end and its constituent ACTIONS (1142b32, see DECISION); then he does what is FINE and RIGHT.

corrective treatment, *kolazein*   Aristotle applies two terms to punishment, *timôrein* ('exact a penalty') and *kolazein*. Though they are sometimes used together (1126a28, 1180a9), Aristotle conforms to the distinction drawn at *Rhet.* 1369b12. Hence, *timôria* is concerned with satisfaction for the harm done, and so often involves revenge (1126a21, 28; 1149a31). *Kolazein*, by contrast, is forward-looking, concerned with restraining (or 'tempering'; see 1119a33, 1150a21, TEMPERANCE) and improving the offender. See 1104b16, 1109b35, 1113b23, 30, 1114a1, 1132b30, 1180a11; *EE* 1214b33†, 1230a39; *Rhet.* 1374b30; OCD, s.v. 'Punishment'.

craft, *technê*   1. See vi 4. A craft is a rational discipline concerned with PRODUCTION. Hence Aristotle sometimes speaks of it as SCIENCE (1094a1, 7), though it does not meet the strictest conditions for a science (1140b2, 34). Craft involves inquiry and deliberation, and so Aristotle often uses its methods to illustrate the procedures of VIRTUE and PRUDENCE.

2. Prudence, however, unlike craft, is concerned with ACTION (1140b3, 1153a25), not production. Moreover, it requires the correct use of a capacity, whereas a craft is a capacity that can be correctly or incorrectly used. Hence the virtuous person does not simply practise a craft, and the *EN* itself is not the exposition of craft knowledge. See 1104a5–11, 1106b5–16, 1112a34–b31, 1120b13, 1122a34, 1133a14–16, 1141b14–22, 11146b31–1147a10, 1152b2, 1167b28–1169a19, 1174a19–21, 1180b7–23. Craft and nature: 1099b20–3, 1106b14, 1140a15; *Phys.* 192b8–33.

cultivated, gracious, *charieis* The cultivated (or 'sophisticated') person may be the one who has gone more deeply into his particular craft or discipline (1102a21), or, more generally, the one who has a more discriminating view of life than the MANY have (1095a18, b22, 1127b23). In this sense being cultivated is an aspect of being civilized (see GENEROUS). See 1128a15, 31; notes to v 5.§7, viii 13.§2.

currency See LAW.

Cynics Aristotle does not mention these followers of SOCRATES by name. Their austere doctrines—virtue is sufficient for happiness; virtue is the only real good, and vice the only real evil; alleged goods outside one's control (wealth, honour, security) do not matter at all; pleasure is to be rejected as evil; and virtue consists in the complete elimination of emotions—are opposed to Aristotle's outlook, no less than to Plato's. Aristotle may allude to their views at, e.g., 1096a1–2, 1104b24–6, in iv 3 on magnanimity, and in the two discussions of pleasure.

death See 1100a10, 1115a26, 1117b9, 1124b8, 1138a9, 1169a18.

decent, *epieikēs* This is cognate with *eikos*, 'likely', and means 'plausible, reasonable, respectable' (as we say 'a likely lad' or 'a reasonable candidate for the job').

1. Hence it is used more generally for a decent person, and hence interchangeably with 'GOOD' in the right contexts, as Aristotle remarks at 1137a35. (Cf. 1102b10, 1168a33; and for the political use, which is a feature of most of Aristotle's moral terms, cf. *Pol.* 1308b27.)

2. In some contexts the term suggests someone who will do the decent thing even when the law does not require him to. This is the sort of decency (some translators use 'equity') discussed in v 10. See also 1143a20 (for its relevance to PARDON); *Rhet.* 1374a18–b22; *Top.* 141a15.

decision, *prohairesis* 1. Etymologically *prohairesis* suggests 'choosing (*hairesis*) before'. For Aristotle the 'before' has a temporal sense (1113a2–9; cf. *EE* 1226a5–9). He also recognizes a preferential sense (*MM* 1189a13–14). Many translators use 'choice' to translate it; but this is a misleading rendering, since Aristotle allows choice (*hairesis*; 1104a29–30) without deliberation or decision, and such choice does not count as *prohairesis*.

2. A decision is the result of (a) a wish, i.e., a rational DESIRE for some GOOD as an END in itself (1111b26, 1113a15); (b) deliberation, i.e., systematic RATIONAL CALCULATION about how to achieve the end (1112b15, vi 9). These result in (c) the decision, which is a desire to do something here and now, the action that deliberation has shown to be the action required to achieve the end (1112b26, 1139a21–b5).

3. Not any desire followed by deliberation results in a decision—spirit and appetite do not (1142b18). Hence the INCONTINENT's incontinent action is not the

result of his decision; his decision is correct because his rational wishes are correct (1150b30, 1152a17).

4. Deliberation and decision are not about ends, but about MEANS, 1112b14. Since MEANS include constituents of an end that can be chosen for their own sakes, the virtuous person decides on virtuous action for its own sake (1097b2–5, 1105a32, 1144a19), since he chooses them as parts of happiness, and hence as ends in themselves.

5. A virtuous person shows his virtuous decision especially clearly in emergencies that allow him no time to deliberate afresh, 1117a17–22 (cf. notes to vi 9.§2, vii 7.§8). The deliberation about this type of situation must have been done earlier, and its result is available without further lengthy deliberation.

6. The correct decision is necessary for virtue of character, and ACCORDS with a person's virtue. See 1106a36, 1110b31, 1111b4–6, note to iii 2.§1, 1117a5, 1127b14, 1134a17, 1135b25, 1139a23–6, 1144a13–22, 1145a2–6, 1157b30, 1163a22, 1178a34.

decree, *psêphisma*   From the late fifth century onwards, Athenian legal procedure distinguished (a) LAWS, *nomoi,* not confined to a particular occasion, and made by a commission of legislators, from (b) decrees, directed to a particular occasion, and enacted by a majority vote of the assembly of citizens. See note to v 7.§1; 1141b27, 1151b16, 1152a20; *Pol.* 1292a6, 32.

definition, *horismos;* **define,** *horizein:* **define, distinguish,** *dihorizein*   1. These terms are derived from *horos,* 'limit, boundary' (see note to vi 8.§9; cf. 'definition' derived from the Latin *finis*), and often *dihorizein* is translated 'distinguish' or 'determine' (e.g., 1099a25). Similarly, *horizein* is associated with limiting, bounding, and determining (1170a22).

2. Often, however, the terms indicate definition, also expressed in the account of something (see REASON #4), telling us what the essence of something is (*to ti ên einai,* or *ousia,* 'SUBSTANCE', 1107a6; *Top.* vi 4, *Met.* 1029b13–22). When we define functionally organized things, either artifacts or natural organisms, the definition specifies their FUNCTION and END (e.g., 1107a6). Aristotle seeks a definition for happiness, the virtues, friendship, etc. He is not looking simply for a verbal equivalence, a phrase that can replace the word being defined while preserving truth. Such a formula for defining happiness does not satisfy him (1095b18). He wants an account that will explain and justify the common beliefs (1098a20, b9).

3. The canonical form of definition places something in its species, *eidos* (see CAUSE), by stating its genus and the differentia of the genus that isolates the species (e.g., 'Man is a biped [differentia] animal [genus]'). Aristotle does this with virtue of character (1105b20, 1106a15; cf. 1130b8–16; *Top.* vi 5–6). Often the genus is associated with the question 'What?' (e.g., 'what is a man?'—'An animal'), and the differentia with 'what sort of?' (e.g., 'what sort of animal is a man?'—'A biped animal'). See 1098a31, 1105b19, 1106a14, 1174a13; *Top.* 128a20–9, 144a15–22.

4. Definitions are non-extensional. In cases where two definitions 'F' and 'G' apply to the same thing, x, Aristotle says that F and G are one (i.e., they both apply to x), but two in 'being', and that the definition 'F' applies to x qua (*hê[i],* lit. 'by which') F or in the respect that it is F, and the definition 'G' applies to x qua G. Hence the same road is both the road from Aix to Ghent (because it begins in Aix and ends in Ghent) and the road from Ghent to Aix (because it begins in Ghent and ends in Aix). See 1096b24, 1130a1–13, 1141b23–4; *Phys.* 191b4, 193b32, 201a29, 219b2; *Met.* 1003a21, 1004b10–17, 1035a8.

dein   RIGHT

deinos   CLEVER

deliberate, *bouleuesthui*, deliberation, *bouleusis*   See DECISION, MEANS.
Good deliberation (*euboulia*); vi 9.
Deliberation and INCONTINENCE; 1142b18–20, 1150b19–28, 1152a27–30.

demonstration   See SCIENCE.

desire, *orexis*   Aristotle normally recognizes three types of desire, corresponding to Plato's tripartition of the SOUL in *Rep.* 435 ff. (See 1138a5–13.) The three types are:

1. Rational desire, wish, *boulêsis* (see DECISION #2) is for an object believed to be good. See 1111b26; note to iii 3.§19, 1113a15, 1114a14, 1136b5, 1155b29, 1156a31, 1162b35, 1178a30.

2. Appetite, *epithumia* (sometimes rendered 'urge') is non-rational desire for an object believed to be pleasant. (See 1103b18, 1111a31, 1117a1, 1118b8, 1119a14, 1136b5, 1155b29, 1156a31, 1162b35, 1178a30.) These are one type of FEELINGS. The most striking examples of appetites are desires associated with basic biological needs, but appetite is not confined to these (e.g., 1111a31). The virtuous person has his appetites trained, but he does not lose them; he transforms them into good appetites.

3. Spirit, *thumos*, is non-rational desire for objects that appear good, not merely pleasant, because of the agent's spirited FEELINGS; see 1149a15 on the relation of spirit to reason. Aristotle regularly attributes to *thumos*, the self-assertive feelings involved with pride and (when frustrated) with ANGER. Hence 'temper' might be a suitable rendering in 1105a8, 1111b18, 1116b23, 1135b26.

On this tripartition of desire, see *DA* 414b2†, 432b4–7; *EE* 1223a27; *Rhet.* 1368b37–1369a7; *Top.* 126a3–13. While it is not so explicit in the *EN*, it is often assumed. See 1095a2–11, 1098a3–5, 1102b13–1103a3, 1111a27, 111lb10–30, 1116b23–1117a9, 1119b3–8, 1135b19–1136a5, 1136b6, 1147a31–b5, 1149a24–b3, 1166a33–b25, 1168b28–1169a6.

On the relation between THOUGHT, desire, and action, see iii 2–3, vi 2, and vii 3.

dianoia   THOUGHT

differentia   See DEFINE.

diho   THAT IS WHY

dikaiopragein   DO JUSTICE

dikaios   JUST

discipline, *methodos*   Sometimes a *methodos* is an approach, procedure, or line of inquiry (similar to English 'method'). Sometimes, however, it is the branch of study or inquiry that embodies that procedure or results from the use of it. See 1094a1, b11, 1098a29, 1129a6.

discriminate, judge, *krinein*, discrimination, judgment, *krisis*   Aristotle recognizes *krinein* as one of the functions of the senses (*DA* 418a14, 424a5, 425b21, 427a20, 428a3). Since *krinein* does not always require discursive reasoning 'discriminate' is often at least as suitable as 'judge' (cf. *Phys.* 219b4). See 1109b20–3, 1126b2–4, 1143a19–24.

discussion   See REASON #1.

disgraceful   See FINE, SHAME.

distinguish See DEFINE.

distress See PLEASURE.

divine See GOD.

do See ACTION, PRODUCTION.

do justice, *dikaiopragein*, **do injustice,** *adikein* Aristotle defines these terms narrowly to mark the distinctions he thinks significant; see 1135a8–23. They are confined (with the cognate abstract nouns 'act of injustice' and 'just act') to voluntary actions, which need not result from a just or unjust DECISION, and hence from a just or unjust CHARACTER. The passive forms 'suffer injustice' and 'receive justice' indicate voluntary action by the agent from whom we suffer or receive it. Sometimes Aristotle coins or uses terms to mark the same distinction with other virtues, indicated by, e.g., 'unjust or intemperate action' (1114a12, 1172b25).

dokein seem; see APPEAR.

dunamis CAPACITY

education, *paideia* 1. This is cognate with *pais*, 'child' (1161a17), and Greek states normally considered it appropriate for childhood (see OCD, s.v. 'Education, Greek'). Plato and Aristotle (following the SOPHISTS) are pioneers of what we regard as 'higher education'.
 2. Moral education assumes that someone has the right sort of NATURE, and it trains him by habituation, *ethismos* (1098b4, 1099b9; 1103a10, b16; 1119a27, 1121a23, 1151a19, 1152a29; 1180a3, 15) until he acquires the right habits (*ethos*; 1095a4, 1103a17, 1103b22–5, 1148b17, 34, 1154a33, 1179b21, 1180b5, 1181b22). These habits are patterns of action, acquired by training that uses pleasure and pain as incentives. But, equally important, they include tendencies to feel pleasure and pain, and to have other FEELINGS, in the right way, which is a precondition for genuine virtue. See PLEASURE #4, 1103a33, 1152b4, 1172a20, 1179b25.
 3. Childhood instruction does not provide all the habituation that forms a state of character. Training must continue with adults, to make them as virtuous as possible, 1130b25, 1180a1. This is why moral education concerns POLITICAL SCIENCE. Even if we are trained to do what the brave person does, we do not do it because of our bravery until the habituation is completed and we have become brave. (See ii 4.) We do not learn simply to repeat the actions until they become automatic or 'second nature' (cf. 1152a32). When habituation is complete, we have acquired the virtuous person's state and motive, 1105a32.
 4. The educated person will be cultivated, so that he acquires the tastes and outlook of the civilized (see GENEROUS) rather than the SLAVISH person.
 5. In the most specialized sense, the educated person is the one who has learnt enough about different branches of knowledge and methods of inquiry to understand the right demands to make of ETHICS, 1094b23; *PA* 639a5; *Met.* 1006a5.
 6. Aristotle does not say how PRUDENCE is related to education. But since education aims at producing virtue of character in those capable of it (1099b19, 1180a5–15), and virtue requires prudence, prudence must be the result of moral education. It follows that this education must include the sort of intellectual training that produces the correct deliberation (vi 10) and DECISION required for prudence.

eidos species, form; see CAUSE.

eleutheros GENEROUS

371

end, goal, aim, *telos*   1. The *telos* of a process is its final CAUSE, a state (a) that benefits some being with a SOUL; (b) that is caused by the process as efficient cause; and (c) whose occurrence, in particular the benefit it causes, explains the occurrence of the process. In this sense, cutting steak is the end of a steak knife, pumping blood is the end of a mammal's heart, and winning the game is the end of playing chess. The FUNCTION of an artifact or organism is also its end, 1097b24. See *Phys.* ii 8; 1097a18, 1110a13, 1111b16; 1113a15, b5; 1115b20, 1139a36; 1140b6, 16; 1144a32, 1151a16, 1174b33.

2. Every ACTION in the broad sense has something good or pleasant for its end (i.e., its intended goal). Every rational action based on rational DESIRE and DECISION has some good for its end, iii 4.

3. Every *praxis*, construed narrowly, has an internal end, so that it is chosen for its own sake, 1094a3, 1140b4–5. An external end makes an event or sequence of events a PRODUCTION. Internal and external ends distinguish MOVEMENTS from ACTIVITIES (in the narrow sense), and CRAFT from PRUDENCE.

4. Deliberation and decision are concerned with what promotes ends, not with ends themselves. Prudence is deliberative, but is a true supposition about the end (see DECISION #2).

5. Several things (virtue, pleasure, etc.) are ends in themselves, and not just instrumental MEANS. Only one thing, HAPPINESS #2, is a complete (*teleion*) end.

6. Sometimes *skopos*, 'target, goal', is used, sometimes in a consciously metaphorical way (1094a24, 1138b22, 1144a25). Perhaps Aristotle means that we have a *skopos* if we have a *telos* that is specified enough to let us take some definite course of action to achieve it; cf. *EE* 1214b6–14†.

energeia   ACTIVITY

enjoy   See PLEASURE.

enkratês   continent; see INCONTINENT.

enpeiria   EXPERIENCE

eoike   would seem; see APPEAR.

epieikês   DECENT

epistêmê   SCIENCE

epithumia   appetite; see DESIRE.

equal, *isos*   1. What is *isos* is neither more nor less—either because (a) it is neither more nor less than a given amount, e.g., an inch, or because (b) it is neither more nor less than the RIGHT amount. *Isos* shares the ambiguity that Aristotle points out in 'intermediate' and 'MEAN' (1106a26). In the context of the doctrine of the mean, its force is 'just right'.

2. Hence when JUSTICE is said to be about the *ison*, Aristotle means not that justice always requires numerical equality, but that it forbids having more or less than is right. Hence it forbids OVERREACHING. When Aristotle associates justice and 'equality', it is sometimes appropriate to think of fairness rather than what we would naturally call equality.

3. Different types of equality: 1131b31, 1157b36, 1158b29, 1162a35, 1168b8.

ergon   FUNCTION

erotic passion, erotic love, *erôs*, *erôtikos*   *Erôs* is one of the terms that might be translated by 'love'; see FRIENDSHIP. Sexual desire is a component of, but not sufficient for, *erôs*. The mere appetite (see DESIRE) for sexual gratification (*ta aphrodisia*, cognate with Aphrodite; see 1149b15) need not include *erôs* (see 1117a1, 1118a31, 1130a25, 1147a15, b27, 1148b29, 1149b15, 1152617, 1154a18). *Erôs* refers to the condition of those who might be said to be 'in love'. Aristotle often uses it to refer to the desire of an older male for a younger (see OCD, s.v. 'Homosexuality'). Unlike simple sexual appetite, *erôs* includes intense interest in the beloved himself, desire for his presence and company (1158a11, 1167a4, 1171a11), and friendly feelings towards him. This is why it is a source of friendship. See 1116a13, 1156b1, 1157a6–13, 1158a11, 1159b16, 1164a3, 1167a15; 1171a11, b9, 31. The verb *eran* is rendered by 'long passionately' (1155b3) and 'heart's desire' (1098a28).

error   See CORRECT.

essence   See DEFINE.

ethics, *êthika*   1. 'Ethical' is derived from *êthikos*, the adjective cognate with *êthos*, 'character'. Hence ethics is the part of POLITICAL SCIENCE that studies HAPPINESS; since virtue of character is a major component of happiness, this part of political science studies character; hence the traditional name of the *EN*. In the work itself Aristotle calls this discipline 'political science', not 'ethics' (see also *Rhet.* 1356a26–7); but 'ethics' is used at *Met.* 987b1; *APo* 89b9; *Pol.* 1261a31; *MM* 1181a25–1182a1.

2. It is concerned with ACTION, not only with knowing and STUDYING the truth, 1095a5, 1103b27 (cf. *EE* 1216b11–25†; *MM* 1182a1–7), 1179a35. Knowledge of the truth is not the end, but the means (though cf. *Pol.* 1279b11–15). This does not make the knowledge unimportant.

3. Because ethics is concerned with action, PRUDENCE and DECISION are important parts of it.

4. For the same reason, ethical truths are only USUAL (1094b21) and hence lack the EXACTNESS that would be needed for a SCIENCE in the strict sense.

5. Ethical inquiry is dialectical, as described in *Top.* i 1–4, 10–12. Hence it begins from common beliefs, what seems or APPEARS to the MANY or the WISE (i 4; *EE* i 6). Aristotle takes commonly held beliefs very seriously (1098b27, 1153b31, 1173a14, 1179a16). But he does not regard them as unrevisable; often he criticizes the many (1095a22, b16, b19, 1113a33, 1153b35, 1159a19, 1163b26, 1167b27, 1172b3). He takes common beliefs as starting points because they are known (or 'familiar') to us. See 1095b3; *Phys.* 184a16; *APo* 71b33; *Met.* 1029b3; *Top.* 141b8 (and see CHOICEWORTHY).

6. Common beliefs raise puzzles, *aporiai*, when we find apparently convincing arguments from common beliefs for inconsistent conclusions (*Top.* 145b16, 162a17). Aristotle stresses the importance of a full survey of the puzzles (*Met.* 995a27) and follows his own advice in i 10–11, ii 4, iii 4, v 9–11, vi 12–13, vii 2, 1155a32, ix 8–9, x 2–3. (Some of these are surveys of the common beliefs that also include reference to the puzzles.)

7. To solve (or 'loose', 1146b7) the puzzles, Aristotle looks for an account that will show the truth of the most and the most important of the common beliefs, 1145b5. This account will provide us with a PRINCIPLE that is 'known by nature' or 'known without qualification' (see UNQUALIFIED), not merely known 'to us' (see #5 above), because it justifies claims to knowledge.

8. A defence of a theoretical principle shows how it vindicates many of the common beliefs (1098b9). But it does not vindicate them all. Hence a proper defence

should also show why false common beliefs appear attractive and rest on explicable misunderstandings; see 1154a22, 1169b22, notes to iii 8.§1, v 9.§6, vi 5.§5.

9. Practically useful exact rules about particular cases are impossible (see #4 above). Aristotle does not intend his general principles and his account of the virtues to constitute such rules; see 1094a25, b20; 1098a20, 1101a27, 1104a1, 1129a11, 1179a34. For PARTICULAR circumstances, PERCEPTION and EXPERIENCE are needed, though some general rules will also help, 1109a30, 1126b2, 1164b27, 1165a34.

10. Since ethics is to guide action (1105b12–18), it should be addressed to those who are capable of guiding their action by it, and hence to those whose upbringing has not made them incapable of acting on ethical instructions (1095a2, b4, 1104b11, 1179b4–31).

11. These different features of ethics might be regarded as aspects of (a) the moral principles and moral deliberation of the virtuous and prudent moral agent, or of (b) the theories and arguments of the moral philosopher. Aristotle, however, does not mark a sharp distinction between (a) and (b). The *EN* is a part of political science, and hence of prudence, using dialectical method. It is both a contribution to moral theory and the account of a process of practical deliberation (see, e.g., 1168b26).

ethos HABIT

êthos CHARACTER

eudaimonia HAPPINESS

Eudoxus He was a leading mathematician and astronomer as well as philosopher (c.390–c.340 BC). His hedonist views may underlie some of the argument in Plato's *Philebus*. He is cited or alluded to at 1094a2, 1101b17, 1172b9.

exact, *akribês* 1. A CRAFT and its products (1094b14, 1112b1) are called exact when they are finished and complete in details (cf. 1141a9); the most exact craft gives accurate detailed instructions, leaving nothing to chance or guesswork, and so produces a product that has every detail right. Hence an exact statement is correct and accurate in detail, and can be applied to particular cases without any further restriction or reservation (see UNQUALIFIED).

2. It may be exact in either of two ways: (1) It is a general statement that applies to every case without the need of any qualification, e.g., 'The angles of a triangle add up to 180 degrees'.

3. (2) It is a suitably specific statement in which all the necessary qualifications have been made, e.g., 'This train runs every day, except Sunday'.

4. When Aristotle compares one discipline with another for exactness, he sometimes has just one of these aspects in mind, sometimes both. When he denies exactness to ETHICS he intends both points (1094b13, 1098a27, 1102a25, 1103b34–1104a7, 1112b1; 1141a9, 16; 1164b27). The generalizations are not true without exception, but only USUALLY true, and the exceptions cannot usefully be listed in an exhaustive and helpful qualified generalization. This lack of exactness means that ethics cannot meet Aristotle's strictest criteria for a SCIENCE.

excellent, *spoudaios* A *spoudaios* matter is a serious matter requiring us to take it seriously (*spoudazein*). Aristotle regularly uses the term as the adjective corresponding to 'virtue', and hence as equivalent to 'good'. The association with taking seriously is exploited at 1177a1–6, where 'serious' renders *spoudaios*; cf. 1125a10.

exousia FREEDOM

expect, reasonable to See REASONABLE.

experience, *empeiria* 1. Experience of PARTICULAR cases may allow us to form rules of thumb (e.g., in medical treatment) that yield some practical success. Varied PERCEPTIONS and experience are the material for reasonable induction (see INFERENCE; *APo* 100a3).

2. Experience is insufficient for CRAFT and SCIENCE (1180b20, 1181a1–6, 1181a19–b6; *Met.* i 1; cf. Plato, *Gorg.* 465a). Science and craft know why something works, and do not merely believe that it works (cf. 1095b6). They can provide a general explanation and justification, and deal successfully with unfamiliar types of cases.

3. We need experience to make reasonable decisions in cases requiring perception (1109b20). Hence experience is an important aid to PRUDENCE; 1141b18, 1142a15, 1143b11, 1147a21. Cf. 1103a16, 1154b4, 1116b3, 1158a14, 1181a19.

external goods See FORTUNE, GOODS #6.

facts See FUNCTION.

fair See EQUAL.

feeling, *pathos* 1. *Pathos* is cognate with *paschein* ('undergo, be affected, suffer'), and indicates a mode of passivity rather than activity (e.g., 1132a9, 'suffering'). Hence 'be affected' is sometimes (e.g., at 1147a14) the appropriate rendering. Usually 'feeling' is fairly close; for Aristotle regularly restricts *pathos* to conditions of the SOUL that involve PLEASURE or pain (1105b21; *EE* 1220b12; *Pol.* 1342a4; *Rhet.* 1378a19).

2. These include the DESIRES and feelings that belong to the non-rational part of the soul (1111b1, 1126b33, 1135b21, 1136a8, 1168b20, 1178a15), presumably because these appear to be passive in certain ways, as reactions to external stimuli. 'Passion' (based on the philosophical Latin rendering of *pathos* by *passio*) would also be a suitable translation, though perhaps misleading to the modern reader (since not every *pathos* is passionate).

3. A virtuous person does not lack feelings altogether (1104b24) and some feelings are both natural and necessary for a human being (1115b7, 1135b21, 1136a8, 1149b14). But he will not be controlled by his feelings; control by feelings is characteristic of the young (see YOUTH) and the INCONTINENT; 1095a4, 1128b17, 1144b9, 1150a30, 1151a20, 1156a32, 1179b13, 27; *Pol.* 1312b25–34.

fine, beautiful, *kalos* 1. What is *kalos* deserves admiration; the term is applied to aesthetic beauty (e.g., 1099b3), and its opposite *aischros* ('shameful') to ugliness (e.g., 1099b3). *Aischros* is usually translated 'shameful', but sometimes by 'disgraceful' in contexts where its cognate *aischunê* ('disgrace') and *aidôs* ('shame') are being used; see iv 9.

2. Sometimes the adverb *kalôs* just means 'well'. But often, as in 'judging finely' and 'deliberating finely', it has its narrower force (e.g., 1099a23, 1112b17, 1114b8, 1140a26, 1143a15, 1169a23, 1170b27). Doing something finely is connected with doing it RIGHTLY (1116b2, 1119b16, 1121al) and CORRECTLY (1119a29).

3. In its narrower use, *kalos* is especially connected with virtue. The virtuous person DECIDES on actions that are fine, and he acts 'for the sake of the fine'; the fineness of actions causes him to decide on them (1115b12; 1116a28, b2–3; 1117b9, 14; 1119a18, b16; 1120a12, 23; 1122b6, 1123a24, 1136b22).

4. Acting for the sake of the fine is contrasted with acting under compulsion (1116b2), and with acting only for some further end to which the fine action is merely

instrumental (see DECISION #2, 1123a25); hence the fine is contrasted with the pleasant and the expedient (1104b31, 1162b35, 1169a6; cf. 1155b19), and associated with LEISURE (*Pol.* 1333b1). Doing x because x is fine is not to be opposed to doing x for its own sake. Hence the virtuous person's concern with the fine does not conflict with his deciding on virtuous actions for their own sake (1105a32, 1144a19). He decides on them for their own sake insofar as he decides on them for the sake of the fine.

5. Concern for the fine is no narrow or exclusive concern for one's own interest (*Rhet.* 1358b38, 1389a32–5, 1389b35; *EN* 1104b31, 1169a6); when everyone concentrates on fine action, their action promotes the common good (1169a6–11). Fine action display great virtue insofar as they especially benefit others (*Rhet.* 1366b3–4; *EN* 1120a11; 1121a27–30; 1123a31–2). We find the mean, and we do what we ought to do, insofar as we do fine action (1122b6–7).

6. The *EN* is not completely clear on the relation between the fine and the non-instrumentally good (cf. *Rhet.* 1364b27, 1385b36). But it does not call an intrinsic good such as health fine, and does not suggest that if I enjoy sitting in the sun as a good in itself, it must be fine to sit in the sun. Probably Aristotle accepts the extra condition imposed in *EE* 1249b19 and *Rhet.* 1366a33 (cf. 1155a28–31) that the fine is the intrinsic good that is praiseworthy (cf. i 12, 1109b31). It must be something that we can be praised for, as a result of our VOLUNTARY action expressing CHARACTER and DECISION.

7. Actions are normally praised for being virtuous in ways that benefit others (cf. 1155a29); this partly explains why sacrificing one's life is fine (1169a18–b2). Here 'fine' might reasonably be taken to refer to the moral value of the action.

fond of, *stergein* Sometimes (cf. LIKE) *stergein* has a fairly weak sense ('be content', 1162b30). Usually, however, it indicates the FEELING associated with FRIENDSHIP and love (1126b22, 1156a15, 1157a11, 28; 1161b18, 1162a12, 1164a10, 1167a3, 1168a2, 22; 1179b30, 1180b6). Aristotle seems to think *stergein* is necessary for friendship (1126b22) but it is not clear if all the types of friendship he recognizes include *stergein*; perhaps they include it to different degrees.

force, *bia* We do something—or, more accurately, undergo it—by force whenever the origin of what we do is external to us and we contribute nothing. See 1110a1–b17, 1119a30, 1135a26–8; *EE* ii 8; *MM* i 14. Force is to be distinguished from compulsion; see NECESSITY.

form See CAUSE.

fortune, *tuchê* 1. *Tuchê* (cognate with *tunchanein*, 'happen'; hence 'chance', 'luck') is discussed in *Phys.* ii 4–6. As the *EN* understands fortune, x is a matter of fortune for S if and only if (a) x benefits or harms S; (b) S's DESIRE or DECISION does not CONTROL x. Fortune is involved not only in events entirely uncontrolled by S (if, e.g., S's uncle leaves S a legacy) but also in processes initiated by S in which something outside S's control is needed for success (e.g., S's building a house is the result of his decision, but it is vulnerable to ill fortune, since a storm might blow down the half-built house).

2. GOODS of fortune are also called 'external' goods. They affect HAPPINESS (1096a1, 1098a31–b8, 1100a5, b22; 1101a28, 1129b3, 1140a18, 1153b17). Hence they contribute to the exercise of some virtues (1124a20). Still, happiness should not be identified with good fortune. Goods of fortune are actually bad for a VICIOUS person; and a virtuous person's happiness depends primarily (though not exclusively)

on his virtuous character, which is not subject to fortune. Hence the virtuous person's primary aim will be to act virtuously, not to achieve the goods of fortune (1099b9–25, 1100b7–1101a31, 1120b17, 1124a12; *EE* viii 2).

freedom, *exousia* *Exousia* is not the legal status of a free citizen as opposed to a slave; see GENEROSITY. It is derived from *exeinai*, 'to be open, possible', and indicates the condition of someone who has open options (cf. Plato, *Gorg.* 461de). Hence 'free to' (1114a16, 1163b19), 'freedom' (1161a9, 1178a33), 'could have' (1163a13) all render *exeinai* and cognates. Since power over others leaves the ruler with more options about how to treat others, *exousia* often indicates the position of a ruler— hence 'power' (1095b21, 1158a28, 1159a19).

friendship, *philia*; love, *philein*; beloved, friend, *philos* 1. *Philia* is discussed at length in viii–ix. While 'friendship' is the best English rendering, it lacks a cognate verb, and 'love' has to be used. Aristotle's discussion reflects the fact that '*philia*' has a wider range than 'friendship' normally has. (1) *Philia* includes the love of members of families for each other. (2) It includes the favourable attitudes of business partners and associates and of fellow-citizens for each other. (3) The attitude of some *philoi* towards each other is different from what we might expect. In the best kind of friendship one virtuous person admires the other's objective merits, his virtuous CHARACTER (cf. esp. 1165b13). (4) In general, these differences reflect the smaller role of purely idiosyncratic preferences, inclinations, and choices in *philia* than in friendships we might be used to. Some *philiai* are made appropriate by my family circumstances, some by the usefulness of the other, some by his objective merits—not by my whims and inclinations.

2. Still, *philia* has aspects that make it recognizably friendship. It requires some degree of goodwill and mutual recognition (1155b32–1156a10, 1158a7, ix 5) and shared activities (1157b19). It also requires some FEELING, actual FONDNESS for the other, not mere goodwill and benevolence (1126b20–8, 1166b32).

3. Aristotle classifies different types of relations that meet the conditions for *philia* to different degrees (1158b5). He distinguishes (1) the three species with three objects (a) the good, (b) the useful, and (c) the pleasant; (2) friendships between (a) equals and (b) unequals; (3) friendships in different types of COMMUNITIES, e.g., families, clubs, cities (1161b11). The relation between these different divisions is not always clear. For instance, how many in (3) conform to (1a)? Sometimes Aristotle suggests only virtuous people are capable of (1a), 1156b7; but cf., e.g., 1161b26.

4. In some cases friendship requires concern for the good of the other for the other's own sake. The extent of this concern is considered in viii 2–3, ix 6. See Notes.

5. In some cases a friend is said to be another self (*allos autos*) or alter ego. This feature of a friend is prominent in the argument of ix 9.

6. More of the *EN* is devoted to friendship than to any of the virtues. It is a necessary component of HAPPINESS, not merely instrumental to it. (See DECISION #2; 1097b10; 1155a3–29; 1157b20, 1162a17, 1169b3, 1170b14, 1177a34, 1178b5; *Rhet.* ii 3).

7. The study of friendship is equally important to POLITICAL SCIENCE (1155a22, viii 9–11).

full, fully See CONTROLLING.

function, product, result, achievement, *ergon* The best single translation for *ergon* would be 'work'.

1. A work is a process of PRODUCTION, or a productive task to be undertaken (1109a25, 1124b25).

2. It is a product that results from such a process (1094a5–6, 1106b10, 1133a9, 1167b34).

3. It is an achievement, not involving any product (1100b13, 1101b16, 1120b13; note to iv 2.§6).

4. It is an action, more or less equivalent to ACTIVITY (e.g., 1104b5).

5. *Ergon* is contrasted with *logos* (see REASON #7); hence 'facts' (1168a35, 1172a35), 'what we do' (see note to x 8.§12).

6. It is a function, characteristic task, ACTIVITY, and END (1097b25, 1106a16, 1139a17, 1144a6, 1162a22, 1176a3; see PLEASURE). Hence a thing's *ergon* is connected with its essence (see DEFINE) and its VIRTUE. In animate beings different types of *erga* correspond to different types of SOULS.

generous, civilized, *eleutherios* This is cognate with *eleutheros* ('free'), indicating the status of a free person rather than a SLAVE (1131a28, 1134a27; see also FREEDOM). The *eleutherios* has the outlook appropriate to a free citizen (hence 'liberal' is a suitable translation).

1. A wide sense of the term is rendered by 'civilized', to indicate the contrast with boorishness and SLAVISHNESS. The civilized person has the right sort of EDUCATION, and hence is concerned with the virtues and with the sorts of PLEASURE that are appreciated only after training and cultivation (see also CULTIVATED). The civilized person avoids any narrow-minded, calculating attention to bodily needs and the satisfaction of non-rational desires; for such an attitude is characteristic of the slavish person, who cannot use LEISURE correctly, but goes in for 'degrading' (*aneleutheros*, lit. 'unfree') activities (1121b33; at 1123a16 'paltry' renders *aneleutheros*). See 1118b4, 1125a9; 1128a25, 31, 1176b20, 1179b8. (The wide and the narrow senses of *eleutherios* are perhaps both exploited in 1158a11, 1168b27.)

2. A narrower sense is rendered by 'generous', to indicate the particular virtue described in iv 1 (cf. 1115a20, 1130a19; 1178a28, b14). This is the appropriate attitude in giving money and in taking it.

3. Though Aristotle does not say so, he might have regarded these two types of *eleutherios* as HOMONYMOUS. They are clearly connected. The virtue of generosity is called *eleutheriotēs* because it is a particular manifestation of the more generally civilized character. Aristotle says less about the broader type of *eleutherios*, because it is really virtue as a whole (i.e., the appropriate non-slavish attitude to happiness) viewed in a particular way (in this respect, it is similar to general JUSTICE, 1130a10); it is especially clearly displayed in magnanimity.

genesis becoming; see note to x 2.§4.

genos See DEFINE.

gnôrimos known; see note to i 4.§3.

goal See END.

god, divine, *theos*, *theios* 1. He notices the ordinary use of 'divine', to indicate something marvellous, beyond normal human capacities, 1145a21.

2. He refers to traditional views of the gods as objects of worship, prayer, and sacrifice (1122b20, 1160a34) without endorsing these views.

3. He refers to common views of the gods influencing the FORTUNES of human beings. *Eudaimonia* ('HAPPINESS') by its etymology suggests 'having a good *daimôn*'

(divine spirit, translated 'god', 1169b8), and so suggests some belief in the role of gods (cf. 1099b9). Aristotle suggests there is something plausible in these views (1179a24).

4. Something divine, not very clearly articulated, can be seen in nature and in the natural desires and tendencies of natural organisms (1153b32, 1173a4; cf. *DA* 415a29; *Phys.* 192a16; *DC* 271a33; *PA* 658a9).

5. Aristotle rejects some common anthropomorphic views of the gods. They cannot have anything like human personalities or characters (1104b18, 1178b8). When a human being becomes a god, the change is so radical that he ceases to exist (1145a23, 1159a5, 1166a19).

6. But he is not agnostic about the divine. He recognizes a divine being that has a rational SOUL, but no FEELINGS or non-rational DESIRES; it is self sufficient (see HAPPINESS #3), and needs nothing, and hence has no need of virtues of character. The divine is unchanging, a permanent and essential feature of the universe (see 1134b28; note to vi 7.§3, 1154b26). Hence a god never passes from CAPACITY to ACTIVITY, but is always in activity. The god's activity is STUDY, and this is the object of divine PLEASURE (1154b26, cf. 1175a3).

7. These features make the god an ideal for our own pursuit of happiness. Insofar as each of us has the capacity for rational study, and insofar as the activity of this capacity is the single activity that best fulfils the criteria for happiness (x 7) we have reason to imitate the god as far as possible, and pursue study (1177b26). See HAPPINESS #7.

8. In the *EN* Aristotle does not try to describe the nature of the divine, as he does in, e.g., *Met.* xii 7–10.

good, *agathos* 1. The good aimed at by x is the result that x rationally aims at (1094a1, 1097a16). What I regard as a good is what I regard as achieving my aim. In this sense there will be many goods corresponding to my many rational aims (1097a15–22). I have a further rational aim, to satisfy each of these aims to the right extent and in the right relation to each other. When I have a conception of the right extent and relation I have a conception of my complete good, which is my HAPPINESS (1097a22–b21), discovered by REASON #1. See also CHOICEWORTHY.

2. Things are 'good for' a result insofar as someone aiming at the result has reason to aim at them. They are good for a person insofar as they contribute to aims it is rational for him to have (exercise would still be good for me even if I were irrational enough not to aim at health). Hence Aristotle contrasts UNQUALIFIED goods (good for anyone, or for people with the right aims) with goods 'for someone' (good only for those in special conditions with particular aims). See 1113a22, 1129b2, 1152b26, 1155b24, 1157b26.

3. 'A good F' (1098a8, 1106a15). A good horse is a good specimen of horses. Its goodness is determined by the FUNCTION of horses, i.e., what they characteristically do and can be expected to do. Hence a good person does well (1098a12) what persons can be expected to do, and has the VIRTUE appropriate to persons.

4. These previous three uses are related. What makes a knife a good knife (3), depends on what good (1) we want the knife to achieve, and that will depend on what the knife is good (2) for. Similarly a good (3) person will be able to achieve goods (1) that depend on what is good (2) for a person—his final good or HAPPINESS.

5. We might object that what makes a person good depends on what (if anything) a person is used for, just as what makes a knife good depends on what a knife is used for; hence if a person is not used for anything, Aristotle's account of good (3) will imply that there are no good persons. Aristotle answers this objection by arguing that

a person is not an artifact or an organ, and his goodness, VIRTUE, is not to be measured by his use, but by his own non-instrumental good, i.e., his HAPPINESS.

6. Goods of body and soul and external goods: 1098b12, 1099a31, 1129b2, 1153b21, 1178b33; *MM* 1183b19–37|. See FORTUNE.

7. Good and PLEASANT: 1111b17, 1113a34, 1140b13, 1153b7, 1155b19, 1156b15, 1157a1; 1172b9, 28; 1173b20–1174a12, 1176a15–29.

gracious   See CULTIVATED.

habit, *ethos,* **habituation,** *ethismos*   See EDUCATION #2–3.

hairetos   CHOICEWORTHY

hamartanein   be in error; see CORRECT.

haplôs   UNQUALIFIED

happiness, *eudaimonia*   1. Aristotle follows common beliefs in identifying the highest human GOOD with happiness, also identified with 'living well' or 'doing well' (1095a18; cf. 1139b3, 1140a28, 1140b7). He argues for the identification in 1097a15–b21, appealing to common beliefs about happiness in support of his account (1096a1, i 8, 1153b14, x7; see also GOD #3).

2. 'Happiness' is a misleading rendering of *eudaimonia* if we think 'happiness' means 'pleasure' or 'satisfied feeling'. If Aristotle understood it this way, the question about what *eudaimonia* is (1095a1–8) would hardly be puzzling, because it would be difficult to see any real question about the identity of pleasure and *eudaimonia*. But Aristotle thinks there is a question. A hedonist conception of the nature of *eudaimonia* (as opposed to the meaning of the word '*eudaimonia*') is worth considering. Aristotle considers it and rejects it (1175b34). He thinks the virtues he describes are necessary for *eudaimonia*; he does not mean that they are necessary to make someone pleased or contented.

3. Aristotle does not find it natural to speak of someone being *eudaimôn* for a few minutes and then ceasing to be *eudaimôn*. (Contrast: 'I was happy when I heard the news, but my mood changed when its implications began to sink in.') In these contexts 'welfare' may suggest the connotations of '*eudaimonia*' better than 'happiness' does.

4. Happiness is the COMPLETE end, the only one that is not a MEANS to any end beyond it. It is complete because it is the most comprehensive; there is no more comprehensive end for it to promote. Aristotle makes the same point in calling happiness self-sufficient, *autarkês*, because it lacks nothing.

5. Since happiness is complete, including all types of goods, and some goods depend on FORTUNE, happiness must partly depend on fortune. But its major components—the virtues—do not depend on fortune. See BLESSED.

6. Since it is complete and comprehensive, happiness includes other ends that are pursued for themselves. To find what happiness is is also to find what these ends are (1097b2, 1174a4). The task of finding them belongs to PRUDENCE, which deliberates about them (1140a28) and finds what it is RIGHT to do. The result is the virtuous person's DECISION to pursue virtuous action for its own sake (1105a31, 1144a19; see FINE, LEISURE).

7. In x 6–8 Aristotle argues that STUDY has some special place in happiness. Does he mean (a) that it is the whole of happiness, or (b) that it is the single most important component? See 1145a6, 1177a12–18, 1178a2–9; 1178b5, 28, and notes on i 7, x 6–8.

hêdonê PLEASURE

hekousios VOLUNTARY

hexis STATE

homonymous, *homônumos* 1. Two things are homonymously F if and only if they share the name 'F', but the account (see REASON) of F is different for each. If the account is the same, then they are synonymously F. See 1096b27, 1129a17, 1130a33; *Catg.* 1a1–12; *Top.* i 15.

2. Aristotle also refers to homonymy when he says that Fs are spoken of or so called 'in many ways' (*pollachôs*; 1096a23; 1125b14, cf. 1118b22; 1129a25, 1136b29, 1142b17, 1146b31, 1152b27), and when he says that some Fs are so called 'by metaphor' (lit. 'by transference'; 1115a15, 1119b3, 1137b1, 1138b5, 1149a23, b32; 1167a10).

3. He is concerned to preserve the common beliefs (see ETHICS) and the common use of names, as far as is reasonable (cf. *Top.* 110a14–22, 148b16–22). Hence he wants to avoid the assumption that one name corresponds to one nature (so that everything to which the name is truly applied is synonymous). If in fact several natures of F correspond to the name 'F', the assumption that there is only one nature of Fs will lead us to dismiss as non-Fs all those Fs that fail to fit one account, so that we wrongly dismiss many of the common beliefs (*EE* 1236a25–32; cf. 1157a25–33, 1158b5). By recognizing homonymy, we avoid this premature dismissal of the common beliefs. Aristotle puts this general principle into practice in, for instance, his discussion of JUSTICE.

4. Homonymy comes in degrees. Some homonyms are 'distant', and have only the name in common, as in the example of 'key', 1129a26–31. (The collarbone is called 'key' (*kleis*) in Greek. Similarly, the chest of an animal and a tea chest are homonymously chests.) Probably these are 'homonyms resulting from chance' 1096b27. Other homonyms, however, are connected, and have more than the name in common; they also have connected definitions. This is true of the two types of justice, v 1.

honour, price, *timê* 1. *Timê* reflects other people's judgment of someone's WORTH—of useful or FINE or GOOD qualities (1095a22–30, 1159a12–27). The English 'honour' suggests primarily the attitude of esteem and admiration. *Timê* includes this, but also includes the expression of this attitude in 'honours', i.e., the awards given to recognize worth (1123b1–24, 1124a4–25, 1134b6, 1163b5).

2. We can show how highly we estimate something's worth and how highly we honour it by how much we will pay for it. Hence 'price' or 'value' and the cognate adjectives are suitable at, e.g., 1123a15, 1133b15, 1164b17, 1165b12 (cf. 1141b2–3). This aspect of *timê* explains why a *timokratia* (lit. 'rule of honour') is a political system that restricts active citizenship by a property qualification, based on the value of a citizen's property (1160a34).

3. Aristotle rejects the single-minded pursuit of honour, since he takes happiness to include goods that depend on the agent himself, not on other people's attitude to him. See 1095b23–30, 1123b26–1124a1, 1159a17–24.

4. He also rejects the extreme view (held by CYNICS) that honour is unimportant and irrelevant to happiness. He devotes iv 3–4 to the virtues concerned with the proper attitude to honour.

horismos, horos DEFINITION

hubris WANTON AGGRESSION

hulê MATTER

human being, *anthrôpos* 1. This refers to the human species (Latin *homo*, as opposed to *vir*). Hence 'man' (understood as 'adult male') would be an unsuitable rendering.

2. Often it indicates some characteristic features of human beings as opposed to other ANIMALS (1097b25, 1148b20, 1150a2, 1170b13).

3. Sometimes it refers to human beings and their circumstances, as opposed to GODS (1100b9, 1101a21, 1141a34, 1178b33).

4. It refers to human nature in general (1110a25, 1113b18, 1115b8, 1121b14, 1178b7).

5. Some examples can be understood in more than one of these ways. Adult human beings are capable of virtue and vice because their desires are capable of being directed by DECISION; hence their VOLUNTARY actions are responsible, properly open to praise and blame. The exceptions are bestial people and those overcome by madness (vii 5; 1149b27–1150a8). See also CHILD, MAN, PERSON, POLITICAL SCIENCE, SLAVE, WOMAN.

hupolêpsis SUPPOSITION

important See CONTROLLING.

in itself, in its own right, *kath'kauto* 1. If x is F in its own right, x is F because of what x is and not COINCIDENTALLY. Virtuous friends, e.g., are good in their own right (1156b19). Something that is good in its own right is not good just as a means to something else (1096b10); it is a good for its own sake, i.e., a non-instrumental good.

2. Choosing something in its own right is choosing it without regard to conditions that make it a means to some other end, and hence implies choosing it for its own sake (1110a19, 1151b2), and hence choosing it without qualification (see UNQUAL-IFIED). Something that exists in its own right is independent of any relation to something else (1095a27, 1096a20; hence 'by himself', 1177a33).

inanimate See SOUL.

incontinent, *akratês* The incontinent—as opposed to the continent, *enkratês*—lacks 'control' or 'mastery' (*kratein*) over himself, and specifically over his non-rational DESIRES (1168b34; cf. 1138b5–14, 1148b32; Plato, *Gorg.* 491d, *Prot.* 352bc, 355b, *Rep.* 430e431d). Incontinence is fully discussed in vii 1–10. See also 1095a9, 1102b14–28, 1111b13–15, 1114a13–16, 1119b31, 1136a31–b9, 1142b18–20, 1166b6–11, 1168b34, 1179b26–9.

individual The Greek (e.g., at 1094b7) just means 'one'.

induction, *epagôgê* The Greek means 'leading on'. Aristotle uses it to refer to the process of leading us from PARTICULARS to UNIVERSALS. He refers to two types of process (which he may not distinguish sharply): (1) Sometimes he illustrates a general claim by *epagôgê*, giving a few examples to make it clear what he means. (2) Sometimes he begins with particular facts, observations, or examples, and argues from them to a universal conclusion. See 1098b3, 1139b27, 1143b4; *APo* 84b23; *Top.* i 12. In the broad sense of 'INFERENCE', induction is a type of inference. But when 'inference' is used in the narrow sense, to refer to deductive reasoning, it is contrasted with induction.

inference, *sullogismos* Inference is the exercise of REASON and of RATIONAL CALCULATION (in a wide sense) in combining propositions or beliefs to reach others. More narrowly, a *sullogismos* is the deductive form of inference commonly called 'syllogism', described in *APr* 24b18. *Sullogismos*, translated 'deductive inference' in vi 3, is required for demonstrative SCIENCE. In this sense it is contrasted with INDUCTION.

When Aristotle mentions *sullogismos* about action (1144a31) he does not refer to a syllogism in the full technical sense (since *sullogismos* about action, unlike a strict syllogism, has a particular premiss); the translation 'inference' (cf. 1149a33) avoids assuming too much. 'Practical syllogism' is a term often used by critics, but not by Aristotle, for the type of inference described in 1147a15. Aristotle does indeed speak of the conclusion (1147a27) and of a premiss (1147b9; cf. 1143b3).

intemperance, *akolasia* This term for the vice of excess opposed to temperance, is derived from *kolazein* ('punish, correct'), and so indicates someone whose desires lack the CORRECTIVE TREATMENT they need to make them subject to correct REASON (1119a33–b19, 1150a21, 1180a11).

intermediate See MEAN.

involuntary See VOLUNTARY.

isos EQUAL

judgment, *krisis* DISCRIMINATION.

justice, *dikaiosunê* 1. Aristotle treats justice as he treats some other virtues (see TEMPERANCE, GENEROSITY) that in ordinary beliefs have a wide scope; he narrows them so that each virtue is concerned with a distinctive range of feelings and actions.

2. In v 1, he narrows the scope of justice by claiming that it is HOMONYMOUS; the name is applied to general and to partial justice. In v 3–5 the types of partial justice are described; but v 6 ff. seems equally relevant to both types of justice.

3. General justice is not a distinct virtue. It is prescribed by correct LAWS of a city for the COMMON good: correct laws are concerned with all the virtues; hence general justice is the whole of virtue in relation to others (1129b25). Cf. *MM* 1193b3–18.

4. Aristotle sees, however, that some unjust actions are the result of OVER-REACHING for more than is fair and EQUAL. Since not all vicious actions are caused by this desire, the injustice resulting from OVERREACHING cannot be the whole of vice; hence, there must be another type of justice and injustice besides general justice and injustice. Aristotle takes partial injustice to result from love of gain (1130a24). It is only general justice that is correctly identified with the whole of virtue in relation to others.

5. We can see why Aristotle thinks 'general justice' is too wide to be a specific virtue; it is also wider than what we would normally describe as justice. But his partial justice seems narrower than we would expect. If, for instance, I act viciously to avoid my share of a fairly distributed burden, I am acting unjustly and unfairly in a way recognizable to Greeks and to us, but not clearly included in Aristotle's partial injustice.

6. Aristotle participates in the debate about NATURAL and conventional justice. In opposition to PROTAGORAS, he argues that not all justice depends on the laws and conventions of particular societies, but some things are just and unjust by nature. See 1094b11–22, 1134b18–1135a5.

kakos VICIOUS

kalos FINE

kata ACCORD

kath'hekaston PARTICULAR

kath'kauto IN ITS OWN RIGHT

katholou UNIVERSAL

kinêsis MOVEMENT

know See SCIENCE.

known, gnôrimos Aristotle distinguishes what is 'known to us' (or familiar to us), which is the starting point (*archê*; see PRINCIPLE) of inquiry, with what is 'known by NATURE' or 'known in itself', which is the goal of inquiry. What is known to us need not be true (i.e., it is known only from our point of view, which may be mistaken). What is known by nature may not actually be known; its nature (being a true PRINCIPLE) makes it an appropriate object of knowledge whether or not anyone knows it. See 1095b2–7, ETHICS #5.

krisis DISCRIMINATION

koinos, koinônia COMMON

kolazein CORRECTIVE TREATMENT

kurios CONTROLLING

lack See RIGHT #2.

law, convention, nomos 1. *Nomos* is cognate with *nomizein* ('think, believe, recognize', as we speak of recognizing a government) and *nomisma* ('currency'; the connexion with *nomos* is exploited in 1133a30). *Nomos* includes laws enacted by some legislator, but also includes less formally enacted rules, habits, conventions, and practices. The wide scope of *nomos* should be remembered at 1094b15, 1129b11, 1134b18; cf. *Rhet.* 1373b1–18.
   2. Aristotle regards legislation as part of the task of POLITICAL SCIENCE (1141b25). The happiness of the citizens requires virtue; and virtue requires moral education, which is best managed by legislation (1179b34). Hence moral training is the proper concern of the legislator, and a city that neglects this will undermine its political system and harm its citizens (1102a7, 1103b3, 1129b19, 1180a24; *Pol.* 1289a11, 1310a12, 1337a11). Though Aristotle insists that virtue includes more than mere conformity to law (1144a13), he thinks it will develop and flourish only in a city where it is supported by legal enforcement. He rejects the view that law should allow the maximum individual freedom; he takes this view to involve serious errors about happiness (*Pol.* 1310a28).
   3. Aristotle refers to an old debate in Greek ethics about whether principles of JUSTICE are the product of NATURE or of *nomos* (1094b16, 1129b11). The defenders of *nomos*, e.g., PROTAGORAS, maintain not merely that different laws affect beliefs about justice, but that there are no facts about justice apart from the beliefs of different societies about it. In 1129b11, Aristotle rejects this denial of objectivity for justice (see also v 7). He rejects it for other virtues also (FINE things are mentioned at 1094b14).

4. See also DECREE. On law and DECENCY, see v 10. On law and general justice, see 1129b11–25, 1130b18–29.

leisure, *scholê* The correct use of leisure is the mark of the civilized (see GENEROUS) as opposed to the SLAVISH person, and of the well-EDUCATED person. Someone is at leisure when he is free of NECESSITY in some significant area of his life; he need not devote all or most of his time and energy to securing the means for staying alive and satisfying his most immediate and basic desires (1177bl; *Pol.* 1333a30–b5, 1334a11–40). In his ethical works Aristotle addresses someone who lives in a city, a political COMMUNITY aiming at the good and not only at the necessary (*Pol.* 1252b29†, 1279a10, 1280b33), someone who has the necessities he needs. He can choose to accumulate superfluous stocks of necessities, as the slavish person does (1118a25, 1147b23), or he can choose to pursue new goals that he regards as FINE. Aristotle urges someone to choose the second option, and tells him what to regard as fine. The virtuous person is not restricted to the exclusively utilitarian calculation of expediency and instrumental value that restricts the unleisured and slavish person. This freedom is shown in BRAVERY, GENEROSITY, and magnanimity.

like, *agapan* Sometimes its sense is fairly weak; hence 'be satisfied' at 1094b7, 1171a20. Often, however, the sense is stronger, and it is closely connected with FRIENDSHIP (1156a13, 1165b5, 1167b32). It lacks the special associations of other terms of endearment (cf. FOND, EROTIC) and is readily used for non-personal objects (1096a9, b11, 1118b4).

logos REASON

lovable See CHOICEWORTHY, FRIENDSHIP.

love See FRIENDSHIP.

magnanimity See note to iv 3.§1.

makarios BLESSED

man, *anêr* This refers to an adult male human being (1149b10, 1165b27, 1171b10, 1176b23). Often this is associated with the CHARACTER expected of a 'manly' (*andrôdês*) person; the term is cognate with *andreios*, 'brave' (1109b18, 1125b12, 1126b1, 1171b6). More generally Aristotle speaks of an EXCELLENT man, where we might expect 'person' (1098a14, b28; 1101b24; 1130a2, b27; 1143b23; 1145a28, 1176a27). He evidently assumes that being a man is a necessary condition of fully manifesting the VIRTUES of a human being. See also HUMAN BEING, PERSON, WOMAN.

many, most people, *hoi polloi* The opinions of the many are accepted as the starting point, though not the unrevisable basis, of ethical argument (see ETHICS #5). *Polloi* is sometimes used in a statistical sense, rendered by 'most people' (e.g., 1150a12, 1151a5, 1152a26). But sometimes it has a more pejorative suggestion (e.g., 1095a16, 1180a4–5; *EE* 1214b34†).

The attitudes or reactions of the many are sometimes the basis for the application of particular moral terms; 1125b16, 1150b1.

matter, *hulê* See CAUSE. By a natural extension it is also applied to the subject matter of a discipline. This consists of the actions or events or states of affairs that the discipline must study (1094b12, 1098a28, 1104a3, 1137b19).

mean, *mesotês*   1. This is the abstract noun cognate with *mesos*, 'intermediate'. Being intermediate in the relevant sense is the property of actions and FEELINGS that is achieved by someone who has the relevant VIRTUE (1106b27–8). Some of Aristotle's remarks are easier to understand if we bear in mind that *mesos* does not always signify a merely quantitative relation. He connects it with the *metrion* (moderate, measured; cf. 1104a18; *MM* 1185b29), just as we speak of a 'measured response' (e.g.) when we mean that the response was appropriate or proportionate.

2. Aristotle's explanation of the sense in which virtue of character is a mean emphasizes the limits of the quantitative analogy. See ii 6 and cf. EQUAL. The point of the doctrine of the mean is indicated in 1107a1. Each virtue is a STATE, not merely a CAPACITY or FEELING; for it requires (1) training, initially directed by someone else, and (2) rational control of one's feelings and capacities by PRUDENCE. The mean Aristotle has in mind is the state in which feelings are neither indulged without restraint nor suppressed entirely, and in which external goods are neither pursued without limit nor totally rejected; in each case the right extent must be determined by reason and PRUDENCE (1107a1, 1138b18–34, 1144b21).

3. This doctrine is applied to the individual virtues of character in ii 7 and in iii 5–v 11 to show that the same principles apply to each genuine virtue, even when this does not look obvious. To show that the doctrine applies in non-obvious cases, Aristotle isolates and names means and extremes that have been overlooked (1107b2, 30; 1108a4, 1115b24, 1119a5, 1121a16, 1125b1–29, 1126b11–20, 1133b29–1134a16).

means, *ta pros to telos*   1. 'Means' is used to render Aristotle's phrase (lit. 'the things towards the end [or ends, *telê*]'). But the 'means' he refers to are not confined to instrumental means, i.e., to efficient causes of the end that neither wholly nor partly coincide with it (so that shopping for food is an instrumental means to eating dinner). They may also show us what counts as achieving the end, so that we find its components (eating the main course is 'towards' eating the meal because it is part of eating the meal).

2. This broad scope of 'means' helps us to avoid misunderstanding some of Aristotle's claims about DECISION. When he says that decision relies on deliberation, and is about means to an end, he does not refer only to actions that are purely instrumental to an end; I can also decide on something as non-instrumentally good that also promotes a further non-instrumental good by being a part of the further good. This is the relation between the virtues and happiness, 1097b2–5 (cf. 1129b17–19).

3. Similarly, we need to remember the broad scope of 'means' in examining the claim that PRUDENCE deliberates about means to living well.

medical science, *iatrikê,* **medicine**   The practice of medicine is often cited in the *EN* as an appropriate example of a CRAFT that shares some of the lack of EXACTNESS that we find in ethics, and as a rational discipline that needs to be applied to practice. The frequency of Aristotle's references to medicine may reflect the fact that his father, Nicomachus, was a doctor (see Intro. §1). It also reflects the fact that Greek medicine was the most obvious example of theory applied to practice; other crafts did not rely on any body of written theory parallel to the Greek medical writings (e.g., the 'Hippocratic' corpus, going back to the fifth century; see OCD, s.v. 'Medicine'). See, e.g., 1097a8–13, 1102a18–23, 1104a4, b17, 1105b14–18, 1114a21–18, 1127b20, 1129a19–23, 1137a12–26, 1141b16–21, 1143b25–33, 1147b8–9, 1164b24, 1181b2–6.

mesotês   MEAN

metaphor See HOMONYMY.

methodos DISCIPLINE

miserable, *athlios* A miserable person or condition is contrary to a HAPPY one (1100a9, 29, b5, 34; 1101a6, 1102b7, 1105b5, 1166b27). It appears from 1100b34 and 1101a6 that being miserable is not simply failing to be happy; some people lose happiness and are in a miserable condition without themselves becoming miserable (1100a9, b34). A miserable person is to be pitied for his bad circumstances, but also to be criticized for having managed his life badly, contrary to his interests, when it was up to him to manage it well; this is the result that the virtuous but unfortunate person avoids. Hence, Aristotle believes, a miserable person is also VICIOUS. See esp. 1166b27.

mochthêros VICIOUS

movement, change, process, fluctuation, *kinêsis*, *metabolê* A *kinêsis* may be any difference in a thing's condition between two different times. Only something absolutely stable and invariant is exempt from *kinêsis* (1154b26). More specifically, it refers to the types of change distinguished in *Phys.* v 1. In the discussion of PLEA-SURE (see notes to x 3.§4, 4.§2) Aristotle contrasts *kinêsis* (here translated 'process') with ACTIVITY #3.

Change and variation are necessary features of human life (1134b28). But the virtuous person achieves the desirable degree of stability that is compatible with these human limitations (1100b15, 1101a8, 1140b29, notes to viii 3.§6, ix 4.§5).

must See RIGHT.

nameless See VIRTUE #7.

natural virtue See vi 13.

naturalist, *phusiologos* A *phusiologos* concentrates on the material side of the study of NATURE. See *PA* 641a7; *Met.* 986b14, 989b30, 990a2. *Phusiologoi* include the 'Presocratics', the natural philosophers before and during the lifetime of Socrates. Aristotle regards them as precursors of his search for WISDOM. Among them *EN* mentions Thales, Anaxagoras (1141b 3–4), Heracleitus (1146b30 1155b4), Empedocles (1147a20, b12, 1155a7). Cf. 1154b7. *EN* uses the term only at 1147b8.

nature, *phusis* 1. Things that have a nature have an internal PRINCIPLE of change (or MOVEMENT) and stability. They include all living organisms (1140a15; *Phys.* 192b8–33; *DA* 412a11†, b15†; *Met.* v 4). Nature in general is discussed in the *Physics* (i.e., 'On Nature'). Both the material and the formal CAUSE can be ascribed to something's nature (*Phys.* 193a9–b21).

2. A thing's nature is its original constitution or tendency apart from human intervention; hence it is contrasted with LAW and EDUCATION (1094b16, 1103a19, 1106a9; 1134b18, 33; 1144b3, 1149b4, 1151a18, 1179b20).

3. A thing's nature indicates its FUNCTION and the final cause or END to which it tends. In ETHICS our task is to develop the natural tendencies so that they achieve the appropriate natural end (1097b11, 1103a25, 1152b13; 1153a12, 14, b32; 1162a16, 1170a14, 1173a4; *Pol.* i 1–2). The aspects of nature that are developed and realized include some original tendencies, but not all (1109b1–7).

4. When Aristotle discusses something 'from nature' or 'from the natural point of view' (*phusikôs*) he refers either to (a) appeals to general theories of nature (1155b2) or

to (b) appeals to human nature, especially to human psychology (1147a24, 1167b29, 1170a13). The *EN* avoids (a), but regularly relies on (b).

5. Nature and convention in ethics. See 1094b14–22, 1134b18–1135a5, PROTAGORAS.

necessity, compulsion, *anankê* See *Met.* v 5.

1. The objects of demonstrative SCIENCE are necessary truths, about necessary, not merely USUAL, states of affairs. Since these are always the same way, no matter what we do about them, we do not deliberate or DECIDE about these (1112a1, 1139b20).

2. The necessity involved in the 'mixed' actions described in iii 1 is conditional or 'hypothetical' (*Met.* 1015a20). In such cases, if I am to stay alive or to avoid some catastrophic evil, I must do something unwelcome (1110a26, 1115b8, 1116b16; 1121a34, b26). This is to be contrasted with FORCE; cf. *EE* 1225a8–19†; *MM* i 14–15. Similarly, pleasant things that are 'necessary' are those that are necessary for life or for a reasonably healthy life (1147b23). Freedom from exclusive concern with these sorts of necessities is LEISURE.

3. Necessity is also found in psychological states and in actions. Aristotle claims there is a set of beliefs, desires, and inferences that necessitates action. For, once they occur, a given action is necessary, because nothing but that action can now happen (1147a27). This is distinct from the necessity in (1), since it depends on previous particular conditions (the state corresponding to the minor premiss of the inference).

need   See RIGHT.

nomos   LAW

nous   UNDERSTANDING

observe   See STUDY.

oikeios   PROPER

old   See YOUTH.

open to   See FREEDOM.

opportunity   See FREEDOM.

orexis   DESIRE

orgê   ANGER

orthos   CORRECT

ought   See RIGHT.

ousia   SUBSTANCE

overreaching, *pleonexia* 'Greed' and 'graspingness' are more natural English, but they are unsuitable, since these motives might belong to a miser who is not necessarily unjust, whereas *pleonexia* always involves injustice (in the 'partial' sense; see JUSTICE). *Pleonexia* involves more than a mere desire to accumulate resources; it also includes a desire to have more than I am entitled to (but cf. 1136b11–12), so as to get the better of someone else (cf. Plato, *Rep.* 349b–350c). This desire results in competition for the goods that people fight over (*perimachêta*; see 1168b15–23; Plato, *Rep.* 586ab). See Hobbes' description of the law of nature: 'that . . . no man require to reserve to himself any right, which he is not content should be reserved to any one of the rest. . . . The Greeks call the violation of this law *pleonexia*; that is, a desire of more than their share' (*Leviathan* ch. 15).

paideia EDUCATION

pain See PLEASURE.

pardon, *sungnômê* This is derived from *gnômê*, 'mind' or 'judgment'. It is the exercise of judgment and consideration that finds circumstances (as we say, 'special considerations') in an action that exempt the agent from the blame USUALLY attached to that type of action. In the discussion of VOLUNTARY action, *sungnômê* is translated 'pardon' (1109b32, 1110a24, 1111a2, 1126a3, 1136a5, 1146a2, 1149b4, 1150b8). In 1143a19–24, however, Aristotle plays on the etymological connexion with *gnômê*; 'consideration' is needed. The connexion is not merely etymological; for the DECENT person's judgment often finds something pardonable in cases where the inflexible application of a rule that is only USUALLY true would result in mistaken blame.

particular, *kath'kekaston*, *kath'hekasta* Particulars include individual objects—this man or this tree—but also particular actions (1110b6, 1135a7, 1141b16, 1143a32) or situations (1109b22, 1126b3). What I actually do when I act is not just killing, e.g., but a particular token of that type—killing in a definite way at some definite place and time (cf. 1110b32–1111a21). Particulars are the objects of PERCEPTION, not of SCIENCE.

When we describe a particular we form a more specific and determinate description adding to our description of the UNIVERSAL. Hence Aristotle also speaks of particulars when he refers to more specific and determinate descriptions Hence, at 1107a29 the particulars are not particular action-tokens at definite times and places, but the specific virtues; cf. 1141b22. Here the particulars are not spatiotemporally located individuals, but simply more determinate types or general properties. In vi–vii (e.g., 1143a32; 1147a3, 26) it is not always clear which sort of particulars Aristotle has in mind.

Aristotle stresses the importance of studying particular cases or subdivisions that fall under a general account or definition. They allow us (1) to understand the general account, by seeing what it implies; (2) to apply it more successfully in practice; and (3) to test and confirm it, by showing that it fits the cases it is supposed to fit. See 1107a28, 1141b14 (PRUDENCE #2), 1180b7; *Pol.* 1260a25; *Rhet.* 1393a16.

penalty See CORRECTIVE TREATMENT.

perception, sense, *aisthêsis* The verb *aisthanesthai*, translated 'perceive', refers to the exercise of any of the five senses, each with its special object (colour, sound, etc.; see note to vi 8.§9), or of the common sense (see *DA* ii 5–iii 2). See 1103a29, 1118a1–26, 1149a35, 1174b14. Such perception is characteristic of the animal SOUL. Hence perception and non-rational DESIRE are contrasted with rational desire and DECISION (1095a4, 1098a2, 1111b18, 1139a20, 1147b5, 1149a9–10, 1170a16; cf. FEELING).

Aisthanesthai may also, however, indicate noticing or being aware of something (as in English 'I see') without any very specific reference to the five senses, and with no suggestion that everything noticed is a feature that is noticed by the senses. This sort of perception is important in applying ethical principles that are USUAL and may have exceptions in PARTICULAR cases. Actions are concerned with particulars

(1107a31, 1110b6, 1135a7, 1147a3) and perception is what makes us aware of these (1109b20–3, 1113a1, 1126b24, 1147a26). We need perception to notice the facts of the situation. Aristotle seems to believe that we also need it to notice the moral features of a situation ('This isn't harmless teasing, but wanton cruelty', or 'Giving him the book would be a kind thing to do'). Aristotle distinguishes this awareness of particulars needed by PRUDENCE (1141b14–22) from ordinary perception (1142a20–30) and calls it a type of UNDERSTANDING, though also (because of its reference to particulars), a type of perception (1143b5). The trained judgment of a prudent person can identify the perceptual features that are morally relevant.

person This corresponds to no Greek word. It is used on the many occasions when Aristotle uses the masculine definite article with an adjective or participle to refer to an agent or a possessor of a virtue or affection or state. 'MAN' would be misleading here, since it would lead to confusion with *anêr*. But no doubt the people Aristotle has in mind are primarily men; hence the translation, notes, and Introduction use masculine pronouns.

phainesthai, phaneros APPEAR

phaulos VICIOUS

philia FRIENDSHIP

phronêsis PRUDENCE

promote See DECISION.

phusis NATURE

Plato (427–347 BC). Aristotle was a member of Plato's Academy for nearly twenty years, and the *EN* reflects both what he learned from Plato and what he rejected. *EN* i 6 on the Form of the Good (cf. *MM* 1182a23–30) criticizes Platonic metaphysics. Some of the discussion of pleasure as a process or becoming may reflect Aristotle's objections to arguments in Plato's *Philebus* (see 1173a29–b7). Still, Aristotle agrees with Plato on some important principles (see 1095a32, 1104b12, 1138b5–13, 1172b28–30). Moreover, the general aim and conclusion of the discussion of virtue and happiness in the *EN* follows Plato's *Republic* quite closely. Like Plato, Aristotle maintains that the virtuous person is happier than anyone else even if he does not achieve complete happiness. Aristotle shows his familiarity with Plato himself by using the Greek imperfect tense to refer to Plato's oral remarks (1095a32, SOCRATES).

pleasure, *hêdonê* 1. This is the abstract noun corresponding to the verb *hêdesthai* ('take pleasure, be pleased') and to the verb *chairein* ('enjoy, find enjoyment'). Its opposite is *lupê* or *algos* (both rendered 'pain' or 'distress').
    2. Aristotle's way of distinguishing pleasures shows that he does not think pleasure is some introspectively uniform state, or that its different sources ('pleasant things') are merely different and interchangeable instrumental means to the same end. The pleasures of dice playing, sunbathing, and music are different in kind, not merely in origin (iii 10; 1147b24–31, 1154a7–b5, x 5; see also FUNCTION).
    3. Aristotle is not a hedonist about good, since he does not identify good with pleasure. But he rejects the extreme thesis that pleasure is not a good at all (vii 13; 1172b26, 1173b31–1174a8). The extent to which pleasure is good is explained by Aristotle's account of pleasure. It is an ACTIVITY, not a MOVEMENT or process;

and it is consequent on some other activity. The pleasure is good if and only if, and because, it is consequent on a good activity (1153a9, x 4–5).

4. Pleasure is not identical to HAPPINESS, but it is an important part of it (1095b16, 1096a1, 1098b25, 1099a7, 1153b14, 1172b26–1173a5, 1176a26, 1177a2).

5. Pleasure is the object of appetite (see DESIRE, 1111b17). Hence non-human ANIMALS have an APPEARANCE of the pleasant, though not of the GOOD (see REASON #1). Human beings are guided by pleasure insofar as they follow their FEELINGS.

6. Pleasure is important, therefore, in moral EDUCATION. Pleasure can mislead us about the good (1104b30, 1109b7, 1113a33) and destroy our conception of the good (1140b13, 1144a34). Even if we have the right conception of the good, a desire for pleasure that conflicts with this conception may cause us to be INCONTINENT. Hence moral education requires the right pleasures and pains (ii 3).

7. The virtuous person takes pleasure in being virtuous and in the actions prescribed by the virtues (1099a7–21, 1104b3, 1117a35–b16, 1119a11–20, 1120a23–31, 1166a23–9, 1170a19–b8, 1175a19). This is the natural result of his DECIDING on these actions for their own sake and because they are FINE.

8. *EN* as it stands contains two discussions of pleasure, in vii 11–14 and x 1–5. Book vii probably belonged originally to *EE*. See Intro. §3.

pleonexia OVERREACHING

poiein PRODUCE

poios CHARACTER

political science, *politikê* 'Political science' translates the adjective *politikê*; the noun understood with it is usually not expressed. Since political science is concerned with ACTION, and hence with the USUAL, it is not strictly a SCIENCE, according to Aristotle's most restrictive use of the term, but it is a rational DISCIPLINE (1094b11). Since it deliberates and DECIDES about happiness, it is the same STATE as PRUDENCE (1141b23–1142a10). It is the application of prudence to political questions about the good of a CITY. Aristotle argues that the proper concern of the state and of political science is to achieve HAPPINESS for all the citizens of the city (1094a26–b6, 1152b1–3, note to viii 9.§4–6). To discover this we must know what happiness for a human being is. That is the task of the *EN*. A human being is political by nature (note to 1097b9) because only a political community develops his nature so as to achieve his complete happiness; hence the inquiry in the *EN* is part of the inquiry continued in the *Politics* (see ETHICS).

politician, *politikos* The politician is an active participant in political affairs (1142a2, 1181a1), not a 'professor of politics' or 'political scientist'. But Aristotle thinks the 'true politician' (1102a8) will have PRUDENCE, and hence will be guided by his knowledge of POLITICAL SCIENCE and the human good. That will make him superior to contemporary politicians (1180b13–28). See also ETHICS. Since happiness requires virtue, the prudent politician wants the citizens to be virtuous (1102a7–10, 1103b2, 1180a5–12). He is concerned with moral EDUCATION, and with the motives and rewards that are part of it (1152b1–8, 1172a19–26). He seeks to punish vicious actions and to reform those who commit them, by CORRECTIVE TREATMENTS and penalties (1104b16, 1109b30–5, 1113b21–1114a3, 1180a12). See also LAW.

polloi   MANY

ponêros   VICIOUS

popular works, *exôterika, enkuklika*   Aristotle might refer (a) to his own works written for more general circulation than the lectures that have been preserved, or, less probably, (b) to other people's works. See notes to i 5.§3, 6; 1102a26, 1140a3.

praxis   ACTION

price   See HONOUR.

principle, beginning, *archê*   1. *Archê* is cognate with *archein*, meaning both 'begin' and 'rule' (cf. the use of English 'lead' and 'first'). Often an *archê* is just a beginning or starting point. On the uses of the term, see *Met.* v 1.

2. Each of the four CAUSES is an *archê*—especially the efficient cause (1110a15, 1113b20, 1114a19, 1139a31).

3. In the growth of knowledge there are two types of *archai*—the beginnings, known 'to us', and the principles, known 'by nature' (see ETHICS #5). The beginnings—the *archai* we start from—are common beliefs (1095b6, 1143b4). The *archai* we seek to discover are the principles of a theory explaining the common beliefs (1098b2, 1140b34). In ethics our knowledge of these principles provides us with a conception of the END—the good to be pursued—for deliberation and DECISION (1140b16, 1144a32).

4. 'Principle' is often used for cases where the *archê* is not a linguistic or semantic item (as we say, 'These are my principles'). It is used for causal origins, e.g., 1139a31. This ontological use of 'principles' is found in older philosophical English (as, e.g., in Thomas Reid's discussion of the 'active principle', 'animal principle', and 'rational principle' in his *Essays on the Active Powers*).

process   See MOVEMENT.

produce, production, do, *poiêsis*   Sometimes the verb *poiein* is used broadly for doing something or acting in general (sometimes where we would expect 'ACTION', e.g., 1147a28; cf. 1136b29). But its restricted use is explained in vi 4, 1140b6. It belongs especially to CRAFT, aiming at some end separate from the sequence of production itself. Insofar as a sequence of events is a production, it aims at an end outside itself, and hence satisfies the conditions for a process or MOVEMENT (1174a19–b5). This is why virtuous activity cannot be merely production, but must be ACTION. For 'product' see FUNCTION #2.

prohairesis   DECISION

proper, own, close, akin, suitable, *oikeios*   This is cognate with *oikos* ('household') and indicates the sort of closeness expected in one's relations with oneself and one's own family. Sometimes it may be rendered 'one's own'. But often (esp. in viii–ix) it indicates the recognition of closeness resulting from shared concerns and interests; hence kinship and closeness help to explain FRIENDSHIP (1155a21, 1161a16–33, 1165a30, 1169b33). On 'proper' or 'appropriate' arguments, see note to 1155b1. On actions 'proper to' the virtuous person, see CHARACTER.

pros to telos   See DECISION, MEANS.

Protagoras   Protagoras (?485–415? BC) was a leading SOPHIST (cf. 1164a20). He maintained that 'a human being is the measure of all things', meaning that 'as things appear to each person, so they are to him' (Plato, *Tht.* 152a). Aristotle rejects the Protagorean view of moral properties, by affirming that the good person, not just anyone, is the measure of what is good and bad. See 1094b16, 1113a29, 1134b24–1135a5, 1166a12, 1170a21, 1176a16.

prudence, *phronêsis* 1. The verb *phronein* indicates intelligent awareness in general (1096b17, 1152b16, 1166a19, *DA* 417b8; Plato, *Gorg.* 449e6), and the noun *phronêsis* is used in this general sense by both Plato (*Phil.* 20e–21d) and Aristotle. See 1096b24, 1172b30; *EE* 1214a32†.

2. *Phronêsis* is applied to the practical prudence described in vi 5, 1141b8–1142a30. Prudence is good deliberation about things that contribute to one's own HAPPINESS in general (1140a25–8), resulting in a correct supposition about the END (1142b33), which in turn is the PRINCIPLE of further correct deliberation (1140b11–20, 1144a31–6).

3. A good translation for *phronesis* would be 'wisdom' if that were not already needed for *sophia*. 'Prudence' (from the Latin rendering *prudentia*) is a good rendering, since it suggests good sense about one's own welfare, but it may mislead, if we identify prudence with narrow and selfish caution (Aristotle rejects this identification at 1142a6–10). The 'prudence' in 'jurisprudence' comes closer to Aristotle's use of *phronêsis*.

4. Since it is deliberative, prudence is about MEANS to ends (1144a20–9, 1145a5–6). But it is also correct supposition about the end, 1142b33. The correct understanding of Aristotle's claims about means and about DECISION explains his view of prudence too.

5. Prudence finds the right actions to be done, and hence requires a grasp of PARTICULARS, since this is needed for a successful conclusion of deliberation (1141a8–23, 1142a23–30, 1145a35). This is why prudence needs CLEVERNESS (1144a18–9, 1152a10–14), PERCEPTION, and UNDERSTANDING. Since it is concerned with action, and hence with USUAL truths, and with particulars, it cannot be SCIENCE, in the strict sense.

6. Prudence is both necessary and sufficient for complete VIRTUE of character (1107a1, 1138b18–34, 1144b14–1145a2, 1178a16–19). Since it is practical, someone cannot both have it and fail to act correctly. Hence a prudent person cannot be incontinent (1145a4–9, 1152a6–14).

psuchê SOUL

puzzle See ETHICS #6.

Pythagoreans Pythagoras (c. 530? BC) soon became a subject of legend and fable; Aristotle ascribes specific doctrines only to 'the Pythagoreans'. He attributes to them an elaborate account of reality in numerical terms, and takes it to anticipate some aspects of PLATO's Theory of Forms. See 1096b5–7, 1106b29–30, 1132b22; *MM* 1182a11–15, *Met.* 985b22–986b8, 987a13–27; DK 58 B 4.

ratio See REASON #5.

rational calculation, *logismos* This is the exercise of reason in rational INFERENCE and thought. (Greek often uses *logismos* especially for arithmetical calculation or reckoning.) Aristotle narrows the use of the term to exclude the sort of inference required in SCIENCE, involving NECESSARY truths. He confines it to the area of deliberation (see DECISION), concerned with the USUAL (1139a11).

reason, reasoning, account, argument, discussion, conversation, speech, words, ratio, *logos* 1. *Logos* is cognate with *legein* ('say'); it is what is said, or the thought expressed in what is said. It is often translated 'discussion', 'conversation', 'speech' (e.g., 1126b11, 1170b12, 1181a4).

2. *Logos* as reason belongs to HUMAN BEINGS as opposed to other ANIMALS, and to the rational part of the SOUL as opposed to the non-rational DESIRES; hence an adult human being can be guided by reason rather than by FEELING. See 1095a10, 1098a3, 1102b15, 1111b12, 1119b11, 1147b1, 1150b28, 1168b34–1169a6, 1172b10. Reason makes human beings aware of the GOOD, not merely of the PLEASANT (1170b12; *Pol.* 1253a7–18†). Awareness of the overall good requires comparison of present and future (*DA* 433b5–10†, 434a5–10†) in a single APPEARANCE, and the comparison of one desire against another to find what is good on the whole. This sort of deliberation is characteristic of reason.

3. Virtue is often said to ACCORD with CORRECT reason; see 1103b31, 1107a1, 1115b12, 19; 1117a8; 1119a20, b18; 1125b35; 1138a10, b20–34; 1144b23–8; 1147b3, 31; 1151a12, 22; *EE* 1220b19, 1222a8, b5. Here *logos* might refer to the activity of reasoning or to its product, the rule or principle discovered by the activity of reasoning, or to both the activity and the product.

4. When Aristotle speaks of reasoning, premisses, and conclusions, *logos* is translated 'argument' (1094b13, 1095a30, 1104a1, 1144b32, etc.).

5. Sometimes rational understanding of something is expressed in a DEFINITION of what it is; here 'account' translates *logos* (e.g., 1096b1, 1103b21).

6. In geometrical contexts, the *logos* is the ratio between quantities (e.g., 1131a31).

7. *Logos* is sometimes contrasted, as mere words, with actions. See FUNCTION, 1105b13, 1168a35, 1172a35, 1179a22.

reasonable to expect, *eulogos* A *eulogos* state of affairs is one that we have some good reason or argument (*logos*) for expecting, without having a conclusive reason. Similarly, a *eulogos* claim is plausible without being conclusively supported. Since ETHICS is not a SCIENCE and relies on USUAL truths, many of its arguments have to be plausible and reasonable without being certain (1097a8, 1098b28, 1120b18; *GA* 763a4).

require See RIGHT.

responsible See CAUSE.

right, must, require, need, *dein* 1. 'Ought' and 'must' would often be suitable translations. Aristotle does not distinguish *dein* and *chrênai* (translated 'ought') and the gerundive form of a verb (translated 'should').

2. What it is right for the GOOD person to do (i.e., what he ought to do) is what is CORRECT (1122b29) and what is FINE or expedient (*Top.* 110b10; *Rhet.* 1360b12†). *Dein* is used to state the rules that expound the doctrine of the MEAN, e.g., at 1106b21 (notice the connexion with 'well'). We find the mean to the extent that we do what we ought to do, towards the people to whom we ought to do it, in the circumstances in which we ought to do it, and so on. *Dein* sometimes indicates actions that are valuable for their own sakes; in these cases, it belongs to FINE actions. Hence, in the right contexts, it picks out an unqualified duty.

3. Aristotle assumes that what is right and required of us is up to us to do, and that we can justly be praised for doing it and blamed for not doing it (1111a29, 1113b34).

4. What I must have for my survival or other ends is what I need. The verb 'need' translates *dein*, but the noun, in, e.g., 1133a27, translates *chreia*. (This seems more

suitable than 'demand', since need may not be expressed in any actual demands.) When I have not got what I need, I am *endeês*, 'lacking'. (3) Sometimes it is not clear whether *dein* refers to an actual need or to a claim that I need something and hence to a demand, request, or appeal for it (e.g., 1125a10, 1162b17). To reflect the ambiguity, 'require' is used for *dein* here.

science, knowledge, scientific knowledge, *epistêmê* 1. This is a cognitive STATE of the soul, contrasted with mere *doxa*, belief. When this is the primary contrast, 'knowledge' is used (e.g., in vii 2–3).

2. But, unlike 'knowledge', *epistêmê* is found in the plural. The different *epistêmai* are the different sciences (bodies of knowledge) with their different subject matters. Hence episteme can be used both (a) for a cognitive state ('they have episteme of physics') and (b) for the propositions that we grasp if we are in the appropriate cognitive state ('physics is an episteme'). When (a) is intended (e.g., in vi 3) 'scientific knowledge' is often used to translate 'episteme'.

3. An *epistêmê* may be any systematically organized, rationally justifiable, and teachable body of doctrine or instructions. *Epistêmai*, therefore, include CRAFTS (1094a28) such as medicine or gymnastics (1180b16; cf. 1106b5, 1112b1), and exclude pursuits that proceed by mere EXPERIENCE, rules of thumb, maxims, and hunches that cannot be rationally explained and justified (1180b17; *Met.* 981a1–20; Plato, *Gorg.* 465a). For this reason 'political science' and 'legislative science' are used in the translation where the Greek has only the adjectives 'political' and 'legislative'.

4. In *EN* vi, however, *epistêmê* is often confined to knowledge of scientific laws, to necessary and invariant truths about necessary and invariant states of affairs (vi 3, 5; cf. *APo* 71b9–72a14). The knowledge must be the conclusion of a demonstration (*apodeixis*), i.e., a deductive INFERENCE in which the premises are necessary truths explaining the conclusion, and are themselves reached either by UNDERSTANDING or by further demonstration ultimately derived from understanding. In this narrower sense, sciences include mathematics and some disciplines that study the natural universe. But they do not include productive crafts or political or legislative science (which lack EXACTNESS). Hence PRUDENCE cannot be a science.

5. In trying to reach scientific knowledge, we have to begin from things that are 'known (*gnorima*) to us', so that we can progress to things that are 'known WITHOUT QUALIFICATION' or (equivalently) 'known by NATURE' (1095b2–4; *APo* 71b33–72a5). 'Known to us' means 'known as far as we are concerned' or 'known in our view', and hence 'familiar to us'. Hence in saying that something is known to us, Aristotle is not saying that it is true (cf. *Met.* 1029b8–10). At one time, it was 'known to' astronomers that the sun rotates around the earth.

'Known by nature' means 'is naturally such as to be known' or 'has a nature to be known', whether or not someone actually knows it. (Similarly, we might say someone is a 'natural marathon runner' even if she has never run a marathon.) A truth is known by nature even if no one believes it or has the concepts to express it.

seem See APPEAR.

self-sufficient, *autarkês* See 1097b6, 1134a27, 1160b4, 1169b3–8, 1170b17, 1177a27; *Pol.* 1252b29†, 1253a26†, 1256b4, 1275b21, 1280b34, 1326b3, 1328b17. A person is self-sufficient (1125a12) to the extent that his complete happiness depends on himself, and not on external conditions (cf. 1177a27–b1). CITIES are more or less self-sufficient in this sense. The virtuous person wants to make himself as self-sufficient as is compatible with the self-sufficiency of happiness. HAPPINESS is self-sufficient because it includes all the goods that can reasonably be desired within a person's life. Since these goods include the good of other people, a happy person possesses a self-sufficient good, but is not himself self-sufficient.

sense See PERCEPTION, UNDERSTANDING.

serious See EXCELLENT.

sex See EROTIC.

shame, *aidôs* See iv 9. *Aidôs* indicates modesty and restraint in behaviour; someone who has it is scrupulous in observing his standards and ideals, and prone to shame if he violates them. Aristotle associates shame closely with the sense of disgrace (*aischunê*). Though he sometimes commends shame (1115a14, 1179b11), he denies that it is a virtue. He thereby rejects a long Greek tradition (see also *EE* 1233b27).

shameful See FINE.

share See COMMON.

should See RIGHT.

sign, *sêmeion* We call x a sign of y if x is easier to notice than y (or the occurrence of x is less controversial than the occurrence of y), and noticing x makes it REASONABLE to expect y, without giving a certain proof of y. See 1104a13, b3; 1159a21; *APr* ii 27; *Rhet.* 1357a34–b21.

simple See UNQUALIFIED.

slave, *doulos, andrapodon*, slavish, *andrapodôdês* 1. In *Pol.* i 4–7, 13, esp. 1254b20–4, 1255b12, 1260a10, Aristotle distinguishes (1) slaves who have been enslaved as a result of war, or capture by pirates, from (2) natural slaves, those who are naturally suitable for slavery and incapable of the life of a free person. He maintains that natural slaves are incapable of deliberation about their overall good (and hence incapable of forming a WISH and a DECISION). This difference in their souls justifies their being treated as tools or instruments. Cf. OCD, s.v. 'Slavery, Greek'.

2. It is not always clear what kind of slave Aristotle has in mind in his remarks in *EN*. See esp. viii 11.§6–7.

3. 'Slavish' is used as a derogatory term for those who are not slaves but think and act like slaves. They care about nothing beyond the satisfaction of their non-rational desires. (They DECIDE on the courses of action that a natural slave chooses without decision.) Their narrow range of desires and concerns makes them lack self-esteem, so that they accept any humiliation to avoid pain. See 1095b19; 1118a25, b26; 1126a8, 1128a21, 1177a8, 1179b10.

4. The opposite to the slavish person is the civilized person (see GENEROUS). See note to iv 3.§29.

Socrates (469–399 BC) 1. Aristotle's specific remarks about Socrates in the *EN* can all be traced to PLATO's dialogues, but he often implies that the doctrines belong to the historical Socrates (by the use of the Greek imperfect tense; see 1095a32, 1144b19, 1145b23). He distinguishes Socrates from Plato (1127b25; *MM* 1182a15–22; *Met.* 987b1, 1086b3; *Top.* 183b7).

2. Some of the ethical doctrines ascribed to Socrates in the *EN* are familiar from Plato's *Laches* and *Protagoras*. See 1116b4, 1144b18, 1145b23, 1147b15.

3. Aristotle may allude to Socrates' view that virtue is sufficient for happiness. See 1095b31–1096a2, 1153b19–21; Plato, *Gorg.* 470e, 507c (cf. *Rep.* 354a).

softness, *malakia*   See 1150a31–b1.

sophia   WISDOM

sophist, *sophistês*   1. *Sophistês* is cognate with *sophos*, 'wise', and the sophists (who first appear in the mid-fifth century) were primarily concerned with higher education, especially for public life. See 1164a31; *Pol.* 1280b11; Plato, *Pr.* 310a–314c.

2. Sometimes Aristotle uses 'sophist' to refer to those who use fallacious arguments that seem convincing when they are not; see 1146a21; *APo* 71b10, 74a28, 74b23; *Top.* 183b2; *Phys.* 219b20; *Met.* 1004b22, 1032a6; *Pol.* 1260b34; *Rhet.* 1355b17–21.

3. He is unimpressed by the claims of sophists to give moral and political instruction; see 1164a30–3, 1180b35–1181a12.

sôphrosunê   TEMPERANCE

soul, *psuchê*   1. In *DA* ii 1, Aristotle defines the soul as the first ACTIVITY of a living body. If an axe were alive, then chopping (i.e., its characteristic activity or FUNCTION) would be its soul. In a living organism, the soul is the characteristic functions and activities that are essential to the organism and explain (as formal and final CAUSE) the other features it has. Compare 'the axe has a sharp edge for cutting' with 'animals have hearts for pumping blood' and 'human beings have senses and limbs for rational activity'. Aristotle takes the three explanations to be analogous. This conception of the soul underlies the arguments in 1097b34–1098a5, 1170a16, and 1178a9–22. (Cf. note to viii 10.§6.)

2. Since all living beings have functions, they all have souls (hence *apsuchos*, lit. 'soulless', is sometimes translated by 'inanimate' and *empsuchos*, lit. 'ensouled', by 'animate'); this broad scope of 'soul' explains some of the argument in i 7 and i 13.

3. The soul is divided into rational and non-rational parts (i 13, vi 1–2, 1144al, 1145a3, 1166a16, 1168b30, 1178a2). See DESIRE, PERCEPTION.

4. Aristotle does not regard soul and body, as Plato does, as two separable SUBSTANCES; the soul is no more separable from the body than the axe's cutting FUNCTION is separable from its MATTER (*DA* 412b6†). In the *EN*, Aristotle is careful to avoid any commitment to separable parts of the soul in which he disbelieves (1102a28 is consistent with *DA* 433a11†). Still, one part of the soul, the UNDERSTANDING that is capable of theoretical STUDY, has a special status, giving it the special place in HAPPINESS described in x 6–8 (where it is contrasted with the 'compound'; see note to x 7.§8).

Sparta   Aristotle does not admire the Spartan constitution or society (*Pol.* ii 8) or character (*EE* 1248b37–1249a5). But he admires the Spartans' attention to moral education, and especially their belief that it should be undertaken by the state, and not left to private initiative. See 11102a7–12, 1180a24–9. In this respect Spartan practice inspires the programme of education that is described in *Pol.* vii–viii.

species   See DEFINE.

speech   See REASON #1.

Speusippus   Speusippus (?407–339 BC) was Plato's nephew, and his successor as head of the Academy. Aristotle refers to his metaphysical doctrine (1096b7; cf. *Met.* 1072b31) and to his views on pleasure (1153b5). His views may be Aristotle's targets elsewhere in the discussion of pleasure. Cf. 1104b24–6.

spirit   See DESIRE.

spoudaios EXCELLENT

state, *hexis* 1. This means literally 'having, possession'; see 1105b25. This literal sense is exploited at 1146b31.

2. A *hexis* is a first actualization or ACTIVITY, and hence, in relation to complete activity, a type of CAPACITY (*DA* 417a11–b16).

3. In the *EN*, Aristotle discusses the sort of state that is disposed to do F because it includes a tendency to do F on the right occasions because the state has been formed by repeated activities, i.e., by habituation in the regular STET practise of F actions (1103a26–b25, 1104a11–b3, ii 4). Because it has been formed by training, VIRTUE is a state rather than a mere capacity or FEELING (ii 5) and it is firmer and more stable than a mere condition (*diathesis*; cf. *Catg.* 8b26–9a13).

4. A state is not merely a tendency to behave. If it were only that, two people who displayed the same behaviour on the same occasions would have the same state. Aristotle, however, denies that the same behaviour implies the same state (ii 5). Someone's state also includes his desires, feelings and DECISION. That is why 'habit' and 'disposition' may be misleading translations of *hexis*.

study, observe, attend, *theôrein, theôria* 1. *Theôrein* is cognate with *theasthai* ('gaze on') and indicates having something in clear view and attending to it.

2. *Theôria* of a question or subject is looking at it, examining it carefully and seeing the answer (1098a31, 33; 1100b19, 1104a11).

3. *Theôrein* is the ACTIVITY of the CAPACITY of knowledge. I may know Pythagoras' theorem even if I am not thinking of it; Aristotle regards that as knowing in capacity. The capacity is actualized when I consciously observe or attend to (*theôrein*) the theorem (1146b33).

4. *Theôrein* refers to the contemplative study that he identifies with HAPPINESS or with a part of it. This is study in the sense in which I 'study' a face or a scene that I already have in full view; that is why the visual associations of *theôrein* are appropriate. Aristotle is not thinking of the inquiry needed to find answers; he probably thinks of surveying the deductive structure of a demonstrative SCIENCE, seeing how each proposition is justified by its place in the whole structure (1177a26). In x 7 Aristotle explains why he thinks study is the ACTIVITY that comes closest to meeting the conditions for complete happiness.

5. *Theôria* does not actually mean 'theory' as opposed to 'practice'; but the origins of this contrast are clear in 1103b26, 1177b2. But cf. *Pol.* 1325b16–30.

substance, *ousia* This is the first category (also called 'what-it-is'; see 1096a19–25), including subjects (e.g., men, horses) as opposed to their qualities and other non-essential properties (1096a21; *Catg.* 2a10–19; *Met.* v 8). *Ousia* is also used as equivalent to 'essence' (1107a6; see DEFINE).

suffering See FEELING.

sumbêbekos COINCIDENT

sungnômê PARDON

supposition, *hupolêpsis* This is the generic term for cognitive states, including both knowledge (see SCIENCE) and belief (*doxa*). It need not, therefore, indicate something tentative or conjectural. See 1095a16, 31; 1140b13, 31; 1145b21, 26; 1147b4.

syllogism See INFERENCE.

synonymous   See HOMONYMOUS.

target   See END #6.

technê   CRAFT

teleios   COMPLETE

telos   END

temperance, *sôphrosunê*   1. The traditional rendering 'temperance' indicates correctly that the concern of this virtue is moderation in the satisfaction of bodily desires.

2. Aristotle's restricted conception of *sôphrosunê* (iii 10–11) tends to conceal the cognitive aspect of the Greek term, which sometimes indicates good sense, and the moderation resulting from it. See note to vi 5.§6 (a more probable etymology than Aristotle's derives the term from 'sound (*sôs*) mind (*phronein*)'; he is right to see some connexion with *phronêsis*, 'PRUDENCE').

3. Temperance does not require total abstinence from bodily pleasures, but the right extent of indulgence.

4. Temperance requires not merely abstinence, but abstinence without severe pain (1119a1–20). The temperate person is not merely continent (see INCONTINENT; 1104b5, 1120b35).

term   See note to vi 8.§9.

that is why, *diho*   This normally marks a transition from the exposition of Aristotle's own view to the explanation of familiar facts or commonly shared views in the light of his own view. See, e.g.,1094a2, 1103a16, 1103b22, 1105a2, 1109a24, 1116a32.

thought   See UNDERSTANDING #1.

timê   HONOUR

transfer   See HOMONYMY.

tuchê   FORTUNE

tyrant, *turannos*   A tyranny is a deviation from kingship, and, in Aristotle's view, the worst form of government altogether (viii 10.§1–2). In contrast to a king, who rules in accordance with law and tradition, a tyrant is an extra-constitutional ruler. In Greek cities, a tyrant often rose to power in times of political and constitutional crisis. To call a ruler a tyrant is to refer to his constitutional position; it is not necessarily to imply that he is a cruel or oppressive or unpopular ruler. Nonetheless, tyranny is cited as an example of arbitrary and coercive power (1110a5, 1134a35–b8). It tends to corrupt and distort FRIENDSHIPS, encouraging flattery and subservience. See 1120b25, 1122a5, 1160b27–32, 1161a30–2, b9, 1176b15; *Pol.* iv 10, v 11–12.

ugly   See FINE.

understanding, sense, *nous*   1. It is applied generally to rational thought and understanding, not distinguished from *dianoia* 'thought' (1139a26, 32, 35, b4–5; 1144b9, 12; 1168b35, 1170a19, 1178a7, 1180a20).

2. In one idiomatic use, it is fairly represented by the English 'sense'. Someone with *nous* has common sense; he understands what is going on and reacts sensibly (1110a11, 1112a21, 1115b9). (Cf. the archaic use in 1116a34, where 'notice' translates *noein*.)

3. In its most restrictive use, *nous* is confined to true rational thought and understanding not resting on further justification. At 1143a35 Aristotle describes this as theoretical *nous*, applied to the first principles of demonstrative SCIENCE; this is of necessary truths (*APo* 100b5–17).

4. Practical *nous* (1143a35) grasps the relevant features of particular cases. Probably Aristotle means that *nous* shows that what is happening is a theft, and so I can see that some general principle about trying to stop thefts applies to this occasion. See PERCEPTION. Probably the use of *nous* for good sense (in #2 above) encourages Aristotle to use *nous* to refer to this practical insight.

universal, *katholou* A universal (or 'common' property; 1096a23, 1180b15) corresponds to every natural kind (e.g., dog, human being) and to every SCIENCE (1180b15; *Met.* 980a21–981b13). Hence a science studies universals (1139b29, 1140b31). ETHICS studies them too, as far as it can, though often it can only reach USUAL truths. Universals must be grasped by REASON (1147b4; see ANIMAL), and grasp of them is an important part of deliberation leading to DECISION, since that applies universal principles to PARTICULAR situations (1141b14, 1142a20, 1144a32; 1147a2, 25).

Aristotle criticizes the Platonic Form of the Good in i 6 because he thinks it rests on the mistaken belief that a single universal corresponds to 'good' (1096a23). He insists on the recognition of HOMONYMY, to discover more than one universal corresponding to one term (1129a16).

unqualified, without qualification, simple, *haplôs* 1. The adjective *haplous* means 'simple, uniform' (i.e., not compound or complex, e.g., 1154b21). The adverb *haplôs* indicates a statement made without qualification or reservation, or a property that belongs to a subject without restriction or qualification. Hence doing F *haplôs* is simply doing F, as opposed to doing F only in certain circumstances or with certain conditions (1106a8; note to iii 1.§5). The 'simple incontinent' is the one who is just incontinent, not incontinent in a particular, limited way (1146b3).

2. Sometimes when we speak *haplôs*, we speak inexactly, and conditions or qualifications must be added to produce an EXACT statement; it is the task of dialectic (see ETHICS #5) to find these appropriate additions (*Top.* 115b3–35, 166b22, 166b37–167a20). If I say water is good to drink, that is true *haplôs*, but to be more exact I should mention the conditions in which it is and is not good to drink. Similarly goods of FORTUNE are good, if we speak without qualification, but to be exact we need to add the qualification that they are good for someone only if they are properly used. See 1095a1, 1097a33, 1098a10, 1104b25, 1105b33; 1110a9, b1; 1129b1–6, 1129b26, 1130a19, 1147b20, 32; 1148b8, 1151b2, 1156b13.

3. Sometimes, however, the *haplôs* statement is true and exact without qualification, even though it is true in some definite circumstances. Virtues, e.g., are good *haplôs* because they are good for the good person in the normal condition of a human being (1115b21, 1176a15). See 1095b3 (for 'known without qualification' see ETHICS #4,7), 1113a24, 1137b22, 1139b2, 1142b29–30, 1147b24, 1152b27, 1155b24, 1157b27; *EE* 1227a18, 1234b31, 1236a9, b27; 1237a27; 1238a3, b5; 1248b26, 1249a17.

unwilling See VOLUNTARY.

up to us See VOLUNTARY.

urge, *epithumia* See DESIRE.

usual, *hôs epi to polu* 1. A usual truth is a universal judgment that is true for most of the cases it applies to, but not for all (e.g., 'Men go gray in old age', *APr* 32b5). The state of affairs corresponding to this judgment is also called usual.

2. ETHICS is concerned with the usual, not only with the UNIVERSAL and the NECESSARY (1094b21; cf. 1110a31, 1129a24, 1161a27). That is why deliberation (see DECISION) is important in ethics (1112b8) and why PARTICULAR cases must be judged by PERCEPTION (1109b20–3, 1126b24). Since principles of JUSTICE are only usual, they must be adjusted by DECENCY (1137b14). Aristotle's casuistry reflects reluctance to offer exceptionless rules (ix 2, esp. 1164b31).

3. Concern with the usual deprives ethics of EXACTNESS, and prevents it from being SCIENCE.

4. Ethics has to offer usual truths if it is to guide action, as a practical discipline should (1103b26–1104a11). Aristotle does not say that all ethical truths (e.g., 'Bravery is finer than cowardice') are only usual. He means that those giving relatively specific practical advice (e.g., 'Stand firm in the battle line' or 'Keep promises') are only usually true. He does not try to add the exceptions to make a more complex rule with no exceptions (e.g., 'Keep your promises except in conditions A, B, C'). He might argue that such rules will be so complex as to be unlearnable and useless; he prefers the agent to use deliberation, perception and UNDERSTANDING to see what different moral principles apply to a situation, and how they affect each other. This is what the PRUDENT person can see because of EXPERIENCE and familiarity with particular cases.

vicious, bad, base, *kakos, phaulos, ponêros, mochthêros* 1. It is hard to see any clear distinction in Aristotle's uses of these terms, which are all used for the contrary of GOOD and EXCELLENT. Cf. 1165b13. (In 1148b2–4, 'vice' = *mochthêria* and 'bad' = *phaulos*. This might suggest that *phaulos* is sometimes weaker than *mochthêros*; but this is not generally true.) Like many Greek moral terms (see DECENT), these terms also have a social and political use; they are applied especially to the lower classes, the MANY, in contrast to the decent and respectable upper classes.

2. The vicious person differs from the INCONTINENT insofar as the vicious person acts on his DECISION, whereas the incontinent acts against it, 1146b22. This is what makes vice (or at least intemperance) incurable, 1150b29–1151a20.

3. A virtuous person, even if he lacks HAPPINESS, does not become MISERABLE, but vice makes the vicious person miserable, 1166b27.

virtue, *aretê* 1. If x is an F (e.g., a knife), then the virtue of x as an F is that STATE of x that makes x a GOOD F (in a knife its virtue will be cutting well, durability, etc., that make it a good knife). Hence x's virtue will reflect its good performance of the FUNCTION of Fs (see Plato, *Rep.* 352d–353e). Aristotle's conception of virtue, therefore, is wider than moral virtue. In some cases 'excellence' may be the best rendering of *aretê* (e.g., 1122b15, 1141a12). Aristotle develops his conception of a good person from excellence in a CRAFT (1098a12, 1106b8). This does not mean, however, that he has no conception of a moral virtue, or that he thinks virtues of character are just craft knowledge. He distinguishes being good at something from being a good person (1148b7).

2. Virtues are divided into virtues of thought (see UNDERSTANDING) and virtues of CHARACTER. See i 13, vi 1–2.

3. Virtue of character is acquired by habituation, ii 2–4.

4. Virtue of character requires the correct DECISION, which decides on the virtuous action for its own sake, ii 4, 1144a11–21, aiming at the FINE, 1120a12, 23–6.

Since the correct decision requires PRUDENCE, virtue of character requires prudence, vi 13.

5. Virtue includes taking PLEASURE in the virtuous action as such, 1099a15 21, ii 3, 1117a35–b16, 1120a26–7.

6. Virtue is not sufficient for happiness, 1095b31–1096a2. In i 9–10, Aristotle explains why goods of FORTUNE need to be added to virtue. But virtue is sufficient for not being MISERABLE.

7. Aristotle relies on common beliefs about how many virtues there are, and what actions and FEELINGS they deal with. But he often reforms common usage; he ascribes to each virtue a distinctive range of actions, motives, and CAPACITIES (see GENEROSITY, JUSTICE, PRUDENCE, TEMPERANCE, WISDOM). To distinguish the virtues clearly, he gives names to states of character that have not been recognized explicitly as virtues, but are shown to be virtues with the help of the doctrine of the MEAN (1107b2, 1108a16, 1125b23–8, 1126b19, 1127a13, 1128a31–2).

8. See also DECISION, DESIRE, EDUCATION, HAPPINESS, INCONTINENCE, REASON #2, SOUL, VOLUNTARY. On virtuous ACTIVITIES, see 1100b12, 1103a27, 1113b5–6, 1115b20, 1177a10, b6. On natural virtue, see 1144b1–13. On the reciprocity of the virtues, see 1144b32–1145a2.

volatile, *melancholikos*   See 1150b25.

voluntary, willing, *hekousios*, *hekôn*   1. Aristotle seems to treat these two terms as synonymous. In ordinary Greek they both suggest absence of compulsion and of reluctance, as we speak of willing helpers, volunteers, and voluntary (as opposed to compulsory) service. Aristotle, however, regards unwilling, reluctant, and non-volunteered actions as *hekousia*; that is the point of 1110a4–b17. For this reason 'intentional' has sometimes been suggested instead of 'voluntary'. But 'voluntary' is preferable in suggesting a reference to the agent's DESIRES and preferences. See 1110b12, 1111a32, 1169a1.

2. Voluntary actions belong only to agents with desire, and are those caused by desires (see esp. 1110b18–24). Since ANIMALS and children have desires, they act voluntarily, though they lack rational desire and DECISION (1111a25, b8). Hence, in Aristotle's strict use of 'ACTION' #2, not everything done voluntarily counts as an action (1139a19).

3. Aristotle seeks to identify voluntary actions, so that he can determine when praise and blame are appropriate for an agent (1109b30); he is defining conditions for holding agents responsible for their actions. Voluntary action justifies us in holding agents responsible if they are capable of DECISION (cf. 1149b30–1, 1150a1).

4. Aristotle assumes that an action is voluntary and results from decision if and only if it is 'up to us', *eph'hêmin* (1113b6). It is up to us if and only if the PRINCIPLE of the movement (i.e., the efficient CAUSE) is in us (1110a15) or (in other words) we are the cause and CONTROL what happens (1113b21–1114a7, 1114a21–31). To avoid odd results, 'in us' must be taken to mean 'in our beliefs and desires'. On 'up to us', cf. 1135a23–b2; *EE* 1225b8.

5. Apart from the main discussion of voluntary action in iii 1, 5 and v 8, see also 1119a24–33, 1128b28, 1131a34, 1132b13, 1136b5, 1138a12, 28, 1140b23, 1152a15, 1153b21, 1163a2, 1164b13, 1169a1, 1180a16.

wanton aggression, hubris   An act of *hubris* involves attacking or insulting another, but in a special way, so as to cause dishonour (see HONOUR) and SHAME to the victim (*Rhet.* 1378b23) for the agent's pleasure (1149b20). See 1115a20, 1124a29, 1125a9, 1129b32, 1148b30 (sexual assault), 1149a32.

what, what sort   See DEFINE.

wife   See WOMAN.

willing   See VOLUNTARY.

wisdom, sophia   1. *Sophia* has a fairly broad use, as *phronêsis* (PRUDENCE) has, in ordinary Greek. Any sort of expert could be called wise in a CRAFT (1127b20, 1141a9–16) or in giving practical advice (e.g., Solon and the Seven Sages [*sophoi*], 1095a21, 1098b28, 1130a1, 1137a10, 1179a20).

2. As in the case of *phronêsis*' Aristotle introduces a narrower use of *sophia* for his purposes. In this use, wisdom excludes both craft and prudence, and is confined to the best kind of knowledge (vi 7). Since neither craft nor prudence can achieve the degree of exactness needed for demonstration, neither can be SCIENCE, which alone can constitute wisdom. Hence wisdom must be concerned purely with STUDY, not with ACTION.

wish   See DECISION, DESIRE.

without qualification, *haplôs*   See UNQUALIFIED.

woman, wife, *gunê*   This refers to the adult female. Her natural differences from a MAN, leading to a FUNCTION different from a man's, are assumed in the *EN*. See 1162a19–27, 1148b31–3; *Pol.* 1259b28–1260a24, 1277b20. Greek uses the same words for 'man' and 'husband' (*anêr*) and for 'woman' and 'wife' (*gunê*). In viii 7, 10–12 Aristotle is plainly concerned with relations between husband and wife.

words   See REASON #1.

worth, *axia*   Sometimes 'value' and 'desert' might also be suitable. See 1119b26, 1123b3, 1131a26, 1133b24, 1158b27, 1159a35, 1160b33.

youth, young people, *neos*   Youths are excluded from the study of ETHICS (1095a2) because they follow their FEELINGS. A youth is older than a child, but Aristotle does not say when, for these purposes, someone stops being a youth. Perhaps he is thinking of people younger than eighteen (see OCD, s.v. 'Epheboi'). Aristotle associates the different periods of a person's life with different traits of character, and hence with tendencies to virtue and vice; hence the young and the old have their contrasting traits. See 1119a33–b18; 1121a16–30, b13, iv 9; 1154b9, 1156a14–b6, 1158a1–10 (cf. 1126b16); *Rhet.* ii 12–14; OCD, s.v. 'Age'.

APPENDIX

Supplementary Texts

The translations are adapted, where possible, from *Aristotle: Selections*, Translated, with Introduction, Notes, and Glossary, by Terence Irwin and Gail Fine, Hackett Publishing Co., 1995.

These are only a few passages from the large number that are relevant to the *Ethics*, but they may encourage readers to explore further. Since, for the sake of brevity, I have attached no notes to these passages, I have sometimes expanded the translation slightly, to make it a little easier to understand. The italicized headings give some idea of the contents, and of the relations of these passages to different parts of the *Ethics*.

[De Anima (On the Soul)]
Book II

Chapter 1
[Definition of the soul]

In the Ethics *Aristotle defines the human good as an activity of the soul. He divides the soul into parts, and takes the virtues of character and intellect to belong to the different parts of the soul. In the* De Anima *he offers an explicit account of the soul and of its relation to the body. His account relies on the views about matter and form, and potentiality and actuality, that he explains in* Met. *vii–ix.*

412a3, 5 / Let us now return and make a new start, trying to / determine what the soul is and what account of it best applies to all souls in common.

We say, then, that one kind of being is substance. One sort of substance is matter, which is not a this in its own right. Another sort is shape or form, which makes <matter> a this. The third sort is the compound of matter and
10 form. Matter is potentiality, / and form is actuality. Actuality is either, for instance, <the state of> knowing or <the activity of> attending <to what one knows>.

The things that seem to be substances most of all are bodies, especially natural bodies, since these are the sources of the others. Some natural bodies
15 are alive and some are not—by 'life' I mean self-nourishment, growth, and / decay. It follows that every living natural body is a substance and, <more precisely,> substance as compound. But since every such body is also a specific sort of body—i.e., the sort that is alive—the soul cannot be a body, since the

body <is substance> as subject and matter and is not said of a subject. The soul, then, must be substance / as the form of a natural body that is poten- 20
tially alive.

Substance is actuality; hence the soul will be the actuality of this specific sort of body. Actuality is spoken of in two ways—one corresponding to <the state of> knowing and the other to attending to <what one knows>. Evidently, then, the soul is the sort of actuality that knowing is. For both being asleep and being awake require the presence of the soul; / being awake corre- 25
sponds to attending and being asleep to the state of inactive knowing. Moreover, in the same subject the state of knowing precedes the activity. Hence the soul is the first actuality of a natural body that is potentially alive.

The sort of natural body that is potentially alive is / an organic one. . . . 412b
And so, if we must give an account common to every sort of soul, we will say that / the soul is the first actuality of a natural organic body. 5

Hence we need not ask whether the soul and body are one, any more than we need to ask this about the wax and the seal or, quite generally, about the matter and the thing of which it is the matter. For while one and being are spoken of in several ways, the actuality <and what it actualizes> are fully one.

/ We have said in general, then, that the soul is substance that corresponds 10
to the account; and this <sort of substance> is the essence of this sort of body. Suppose some instrument—an axe, for instance—were a natural body; then being an axe would be its substance, and its soul would also be this <i.e., being an axe>; and if this substance were separated from it, it would no longer be an axe, except / homonymously. In fact, however, it is <not alive, 15
but> an axe; for the soul is the essence and form not of this sort of body, but of the specific sort of natural body that has in itself a principle of motion and rest.

We must also study this point by applying it to the parts <of living things>. If the eye, for instance, were an animal, sight would be its soul. For sight is the eye's substance / that corresponds to the account, while the eye is the 20
matter of sight; if an eye loses its sight, it is no longer an eye, except homonymously, as a stone eye or a painted eye is. We must apply this point about the part to the whole living body; for what holds for the relation of part <of the faculty of perception> to part <of the body> holds equally for the relation of the whole <faculty of> perception to the whole / perceptive body, insofar as 25
it is perceptive. The sort of body that is potentially alive is not the one that has lost its soul but the one that has it; and the seed or the fruit is potentially this sort of body.

Being awake, then, is a <second> actuality, corresponding to cutting or seeing. The soul is <a first> actuality, corresponding to / <the faculty of> 413a
sight and to the potentiality of the instrument <to cut>; and the body is

potentially this. And as an eye is the pupil plus sight, so an animal is soul plus body. . . .

Since what is perspicuous and better known from the point of view of reason emerges from what is less perspicuous but more evident, we must start again and apply this approach to the soul. For the defining account must
15 not confine itself, as most definitions do, / to showing the fact; it must also include and indicate its cause. The accounts that are customarily stated in formulae are like conclusions, so that if we ask, for instance, what squaring is, we are told that it is making an equilateral rectangle equal to a rectangle. This sort of formula is an account of the conclusion, whereas the one that defines
20 squaring as the finding of the mean / states the cause of the fact.

To begin our examination, then, we say that living is what distinguishes things with souls from things without souls. Living is spoken of in several ways—for instance, understanding, perception, locomotion and rest, and
25 also the motion involved in nourishment, / and in decay and growth. And so whatever has even one of these is said to be alive.

This is why all plants as well <as animals> seem to be alive, since they evidently have an internal potentiality and principle through which they both grow and decay in contrary directions. For they grow up and down and in
30 all directions alike, not just up rather than down; they are continually / nourished, and they stay alive as long as they can absorb nourishment. This <sort of life> can be separated from the others, but in mortal things the others cannot be separated from it. This is evident in the case of plants, since they have no other potentiality of the soul.

413b / This principle, then, is what makes something alive. What makes something an animal is primarily perception; for whatever has perception, even without motion or locomotion, is said to be an animal, not simply to be alive.
5 Touch is the primary type of perception belonging / to all animals, and it can be separated from the other senses, just as the nutritive <potentiality> can be separated from touch and the other senses.

The part of the soul that belongs to plants as well as to animals is called
10 nutritive; and all animals evidently have the sense of touch. / Later we will state the explanation of each of these facts. For now let us confine ourselves to saying that the soul is the principle of the <potentialities> we have mentioned—for nutrition, perception, understanding, and motion—and is defined by them. . . .

414a12 / Now the soul is that by which we primarily live, perceive, and think, and
15 so it will be an account and a form, not matter and subject. For / substance, as we said, is spoken of in three ways, as form, matter, and the compound of both; of these, matter is potentiality, form actuality. Since, therefore, the compound of body and soul is ensouled, body is not the actuality of soul, but the soul is the actuality of some sort of body.

This vindicates the view of those who think that the soul is / not a body   20
but requires a body; for it is not a body, but it belongs to a body, and for
that reason it is present in a body, and in this sort of body. Our predecessors were wrong, then, in trying to fit the soul into a body without further
determining the proper sort of body, even though it appears that not just
any old thing receives any / old thing. Our view, however, is quite reason-   25
able, since a thing's actuality naturally comes to be in what has the potentiality for it, i.e., in the proper matter. It is evident from this, then, that the
soul is a certain sort of actuality and form of what has the potentiality to
be of this sort.

As we said, some things have all the potentialities of the soul that were
previously mentioned, while / other things have some of these potentialities,   30
and others have only one. The potentialities we mentioned were those for
nutrition, perception, desire, locomotion, and understanding. Plants have
only the nutritive part. Other things / have the nutritive part and also the   414b
perceptive part, and if they have the perceptive part, they also have the desiring part. For desire includes appetite, emotion, and wish; but all animals
have at least the sense of touch, and whatever has any perception has pleasure and pain and / finds things pleasant or painful. Whatever finds things   5
pleasant and painful also has appetite, since appetite is desire for what is
pleasant. . . .

/ Clearly, then, soul will have one single account in the same way that fig-   414b20
ure has; for just as figure is nothing apart from the triangle and the figures
that follow in order, so equally the soul is nothing apart from those <poten-
tialities> we have mentioned. Still, in the case of figures we can find a common account that fits all of them and is distinctive of none; the same is true
for / the souls we have mentioned. It is ridiculous, then, in these and other   25
such cases, to seek a common account that is not distinctive of any being and
does not fit the proper and indivisible species, if we neglect this <distinc-
tive> account. / Hence we must ask what the soul of each particular <kind of   32
thing>—for instance, a plant, a human being, or a beast—is. /   33

What is true of the soul is similar to what is true of figure; / for in both cases   28
the earlier is invariably present potentially in its successor—for instance, the
triangle in the square, and the nutritive in the perceptive. / We must consider   415a
why they are in this order. For the perceptive part requires the nutritive, but
in plants the nutritive is separated from the perceptive. Again, each of the
other senses requires touch, whereas touch is found without the other senses,
/ since many animals lack sight, hearing, and smell. Among things that per-   5
ceive, some but not all have the locomotive part. Finally and most rarely,
some have reasoning and thinking. For perishable things that have reasoning also have all the other parts of the soul; / but not all of those that have   10
each of the other parts also have reasoning—on the contrary, some animals

lack appearance, while some live by appearance alone. Theoretical intellect requires a different account.

Clearly, then, the account of each of these parts of the soul is also the most proper account of <each type of> soul.

Book III
Chapter 10
[Thought, desire, and action]

At the end of the De Anima *Aristotle discusses the part of the soul that is responsible for goal-directed movement in all animals, and for rational action in rational animals. As in EN* vi 1–2, vii 3, *and MA 7 (below), he discusses the roles of appearance, thought, and desire in the origination of action.*

433a9 / There are apparently two parts that move us—both intellect and desire, if
10 / we take appearance to be a kind of understanding. For many people follow their appearances against their knowledge and the other animals have appearance but lack understanding and reasoning. Both intellect and desire, then, move us from place to place. This is the intellect that reasons for some
15 goal and is concerned with action; / its <concern with an> end distinguishes it from theoretical intellect. All desire also aims at some goal; for the object of desire is the starting point of intellect concerned with action, and the last stage <of our reasoning> is the starting point of action.

Hence it is reasonable to regard these two things—desire, and thought concerned with action—as the movers. For the object of desire moves us,
20 and thought moves us because its starting point is the / object of desire. Moreover, whenever appearance moves us, it requires desire.

And so there is one mover, the desiring part. For if there were two—intellect and desire—they would move us insofar as they had some common character. In fact, however, intellect evidently does not move anything without desire, since wish is desire, and any motion in accordance with reasoning
25 is in accordance with wish. / Desire, however, also moves us against reasoning, since appetite is a kind of desire. Intellect is always correct, but desire and appearance may be either correct or incorrect. Hence in every case the mover is the object of desire, but the object of desire is either the good or the apparent good—not every sort of good, but the good that is achievable in
30 action. What is achievable in action / admits of being otherwise.

Evidently, then, the potentiality of the soul that moves us is the one called
433b / desire. People who divide the soul into parts—if they divide it into separate parts corresponding to the different potentialities—will find very many of them—the nutritive, perceptive, intellectual, and deliberative parts, and,

moreover, the desiring part; for the difference between these parts is greater than the one between the appetitive and spirited parts.

/ Desires that are contrary to each other arise, however, when reason and   5
appetite are contrary, which happens in subjects that perceive time. For intellect urges us to draw back because of what is to come, but appetite <urges us on> because of what is present; for the pleasant thing that is present appears both unqualifiedly pleasant and unqualifiedly good, / because we do not see   10
what is to come.

Hence the mover is one in species—the desiring part, insofar as it is desiring. In fact the first mover of all is the object of desire, since it moves us without being moved, by being present to understanding or appearance. But the movers are numerically more than one.

We must distinguish three things—the mover, its instrument, and the subject moved. There are two types of movers: / the unmoved mover and the   15
moved mover. The unmoved mover is the good achievable in action, and the moved mover is the desiring part; for the thing that is moved is moved insofar as it desires, and desire, insofar as it is actual, is a sort of motion. The thing moved is the animal. . . . / In general, then, as we have said, an animal moves   27
itself insofar as it has desire. For desire needs appearance; and appearance is either rational appearance or the perceptual / appearance that other animals   30
share <with human beings>. . . .

/ The other animals as well <as human beings> also have perceptual   434a5
appearance, as we have said, but <only> reasoning animals have deliberative appearance. For when we come to the question whether one is to do this or that, we come to a task for reasoning. And <in this case> one must measure by one <standard>, since one pursues the greater <good>. And so one is able / to make one object of appearance out of many. This is why <non-rational   10
animals> do not seem to have belief; it is because they lack the <appearance> resulting from reasoning. That is why desire lacks the deliberative part.

Sometimes one desire overcomes and moves another, but at other times the second overcomes and moves the first (like one sphere moving another), whenever incontinence occurs. By nature the <desire> / that is superior is   15
dominant in every case and moves <the agent>, and so it turns out that three motions are initiated <in the agent>. The part that has knowledge stays at rest and is not moved.

One sort of supposition and statement is universal, while another is about what is particular; for the first says that this sort of agent ought to do this sort of thing, and the second says that this is this sort of thing and I am this sort of agent. Hence the second / belief, not the universal belief, initiates motion;   20
or <rather> both initiate motion, but the first does so by being more at rest, in contrast to the second.

De Motu Animalium
(On the Movement of Animals)
Chapter 9
[Thought, desire, and action]

This further discussion of the origination of action may be compared with the preceding extract from De Anima *iii, and with the passages from* EN *that were mentioned in the introductory note.*

701a7 / How is it that thought sometimes results in action or motion, and sometimes does not? What happens would seem to be more or less the same as
10 when one thinks and deduces about immobile things. / In this latter case,
however, the goal is <a proposition that we> study; for when one has thought
the two premises, one has thought and composed the conclusion. In the
former case, by contrast, the conclusion from the two premises becomes
the action.

For example, whenever someone thinks that every human being should
walk, and he is himself a human being, at once he walks. And if he thinks
15 that no / human being should walk now, and he is himself a human being, at
once he stays where he is. And he does each of these things unless something
prevents him <from doing it> or compels him <to do something else. Take
another example:> 'I should make something good, and a house is something good.' At once he makes a house. 'I need a covering, and a cloak is a
covering; I need a cloak. What I need I should make; I need a cloak; I should
20 make a cloak.' And / the conclusion, 'I should make a cloak', is an action.

The action begins from a principle: 'To make a cloak I must first do A,
and to do A I must do B', and at once he does B. It is evident, then, that
the conclusion is the action; the premises leading to production proceed
25 through two sorts of things—through the good and through the / possible.

But in this case, as in some types of questioning, thought does not pause
to examine the obvious second premise at all. If, for instance, walking is
good for a human being, one does not linger over <the thought> that one
is a human being. And that is why whatever is done without rational calcu-
30 lation is done quickly. For whenever one is actually aware of / the object of
one's desire by perception or appearance or thought, one acts at once; for the
actualized desire actually replaces questioning or thought. 'I should drink',
says appetite. 'And this is drinkable', says perception or appearance. At once
one drinks.

This, then, is the way in which animals have an impulse towards motion
35 and action. The / last cause of motion is desire, and this results either from
perception or from appearance or thought. And among agents who desire to
701b act, some engage in action because of appetite or spirit, some / because of
wish.

410

Magna Moralia
Book I

Chapter 2
[The classification of goods]

On MM *and the other ethical works see Intro. §3. In this passage Aristotle sets out the full division of goods that he alludes to in, e.g.,* EN *i 8, 12, v 1. After this division, he discusses the character of the ultimate good, happiness, and its relation to other goods. The treatment of the ultimate good as a compound of non-instrumental goods is worth comparing with* EN *i 7 and x 6–8.*

/ Among goods some are honourable, others are praiseworthy, and others are capacities.   1183b20

What I call honourable is, for instance, the divine, the better, soul, intellect, the older, the principle, and such things. For honourable things are those that are worthy of honour, and honour is given to all the things of this kind. Virtue, therefore, is also honourable, / whenever it makes a person   25
excellent; for in that case he achieves the form of virtue.

Other goods are praiseworthy such as the virtues; for praise comes about from the actions that accord with them.

Other goods are capacities, such as ruling office, wealth, strength. For the excellent person would be capable of using these well, and the bad person /   30
badly; that is why goods of this sort are called capacities. They are certainly goods, because the value of each of them is determined by the use made by the excellent person, not by the base person. But in the case of same goods, it is sometimes luck that brings them about; for wealth, ruling office, / and in gen-   35
eral all the things that fall under the head of capacity, come about from luck.

The remaining type of goods, the fourth type, are those that preserve or produce something good, as exercise preserves and produces health, and anything else of that sort.

Goods may be divided in still another way. For instance, some goods are choiceworthy in every respect and in all circumstances, but others are not. /   1184a
Justice and the other virtues are choiceworthy both in every respect and in all circumstances, but strength, wealth, power, and such things are choiceworthy neither in every respect nor in all circumstances.

They may be divided in another way as well. Some goods are ends, but others are not. For instance, health is an end, but / the means to health are   5
not ends. And in all cases of this sort the end is better. For instance, health is better than the healthy things, and in all cases without exception the end to which the other things are means is better than they are.

Further, among ends themselves, the complete end is invariably better than the incomplete. If something is complete, then, if we have that thing,

411

10   we no longer need anything added. Something is incomplete if, / though we
have it, we still need something added. For instance, if we have only justice,
we still need many things added, but if we have happiness, we no longer need
anything added.

This, then, is the best good for us, the object of our inquiry, namely, the
complete end. The complete end, then, is the good and the end of goods.

15   / After that, then, how ought we to think about the best good? Should we
think about it on the assumption that it is also counted together with other
goods? But that is strange. For the best good is a complete end, and the complete end, to speak without qualification, would seem to be the same as hap-
20   piness; and we compose happiness from many goods. If, therefore, / in thinking about the best good you count it together with other goods, it will turn
out to be better than itself, since it is itself best. For instance, taking healthy
things and health, consider which is the best of all these. Surely health is the
best. If, then, this is the best of all, it will also be better than itself. We therefore reach a strange result. Presumably, then, this is not the way to examine
25   / the best good.

Then ought we to think of it in some such way as this, namely, in separation from itself? Is this not also strange? Happiness is composed of specific
goods, but it is strange to ask whether it is better than the goods that compose it. For happiness is not something else that is separate from these things
that compose it; it just is these very things.

30   Then would something like this be / the correct way to think of the best
good in a comparison? For instance, if one compared happiness itself, composed of these goods, with other goods that are not present in it, would that
way of thinking of the best good be correct? No, because the best good that
we are looking for now is not simple. For instance, one might say that pru-
35   dence is the best of all / goods, if they are compared one by one. But presumably that is not the way to look for the best good; for what we are looking for
is the complete good, but prudence all by itself is not complete.

Chapter 34
[Prudence and virtue]

After his discussion of the virtues of intellect, Aristotle turns, as he does in EN *vi*
12–13, to a discussion of the relation between prudence and virtue of character. He
examines the relation of cleverness to prudence, natural virtue to full virtue. He
compares his position with the views of Socrates and of later philosophers.

1197b36   / But as cleverness is to prudence, so it would seem to be in the case of all the
virtues. I mean for instance, there are virtues that arise even by nature in people of a given type. For instance certain impulses without reason, directed
towards brave and just actions, arise in one type of person, and the same

is true / in the case of the different virtues. But there are also virtues that 1198a
arise by habit and decision. These virtues that involve reason are completely
virtues. They arise later and are praiseworthy.

Natural virtue without reason, therefore, in separation from reason,
is a low degree of virtue that / falls short of being praised. But when it is 5
added to reason and decision, it makes the virtue complete. That is why,
<in the virtuous person,> the natural impulse towards virtue both co-
operates with reason and is not without reason. Nor, on the other hand,
do reason and decision constitute complete virtue without the natural
impulse.

/ That is why Socrates was mistaken in asserting that virtue is reason. 10
In his view, it is no benefit to do brave and just things, unless one acts on
knowledge and decides by reason. That is why he said that virtue was reason.
He was not correct, but people now do better, since they say that doing fine
actions things in accord with correct reason / is virtue. 15

But these people are not correct either. For someone might do just things
not by decision and not by knowledge of what is fine, but by some non-
rational impulse, and still do them correctly and in accord with correct
reason; in other words, he did them in the way that correct reason would
command. But there is nothing praiseworthy in this sort of action. / It is bet- 20
ter to say that virtue is, as we define it, the impulse combined with reason,
aiming at the fine; for this is virtue, and is praiseworthy.

Book II

Chapter 3
[How should we resolve conflicts between the virtues?]

Aristotle takes up a question about prudence and virtue that is not explicitly discussed
in EN or EE (though it is especially relevant to questions discussed in EN vi 13).
Aristotle argues that the assumption that the virtues could conflict with one another
rests on a misunderstanding of their mutual relations.

/ The following sort of thing also raises a puzzle. When it is not possible at 1199b36
the same time to do brave and just actions, which would one do? Well, in the
natural virtues we said that / we need only the impulse towards the fine to be 1200a
present without reason. But for the one who has choice, it is in reason and
the <part> that has reason. And so choice will be present if and only if he
has complete virtue, which we said involves prudence, but also requires the
natural / impulse towards the fine. 5

Nor will one virtue oppose another, for virtue by nature follows whatever
reason, instructs, so that it inclines in whatever direction reason leads. For it
is reason that chooses the better. The other virtues do not come into being
without prudence nor is prudence complete without the / other virtues. The 10

virtues co-operate appropriately with one another, following the guidance of prudence.

[Can the virtues be excessive?]

Aristotle explores another misunderstanding of the virtues. He explicates a view that he assumes without detailed explication in EE and EN.

And one will find the following no less puzzling. Do we ever find in the case of the virtues what we find in the case of the other goods, both external bodily? If these other goods / become excessive, they make people worse; for instance. If people acquire great wealth, it makes them disdainful and unpleasant. The same is true of the other goods—ruling office, honour, beauty, stature. Is this true, then, in the case of virtue as well? If, in other words, someone's justice or bravery goes to excess, will he be worse? Or is this not so?

The objector says: / 'Virtue results in honour, and when honour becomes great, it makes people worse. Hence it is clear that an increase in virtue will make people worse. For virtue is the cause of honour, so that virtue, by becoming greater, would make people worse.'

Or is this not true? For virtue, even if it has many other functions, / as indeed it has, one of its most characteristic functions is this: it is able to use these goods and others of this sort correctly when one acquires them. If, then, a virtuous person who has acquired honour or some high ruling office does not use these things correctly, he is no longer, in that case, a virtuous person. Neither honour nor ruling office will make the / virtuous person worse. Hence virtue will not make him worse either.

And altogether, since we established at the beginning that virtue is a mean, it follows that whatever is more of a virtue is more of a mean. If, therefore, virtue becomes great, it will not only not make someone worse, but it will also make him better. For the mean is the mean between excess and deficiency in feelings.

Eudemian Ethics

Book I

Chapter 1
[Happiness is the best good, but there is controversy about the nature of happiness.]

On EE and EN, see Intro. §3. The initial discussion of happiness in EE i is quite different from MM and EN. Aristotle sets out questions about happiness to the context of some views held by his predecessors. He acknowledges disputes about the nature of happiness, but he argues that there is less dispute than a superficial observer might suppose. Many of the candidates for happiness that are mentioned in these disputes are to be rejected.

/ The one who, in Delos in the presence of the god, wrote <an epigram> for   1214a1
the entrance to the temple of Leto, gave his verdict by distinguishing three
different things—the good, the fine, and the pleasant—that do not all belong
to the same subject. He wrote: / 'The finest thing is the most just, the most   5
beneficial thing is being healthy, and the pleasantest thing is the obtaining of
what one longs for'. But let us not agree with him; for happiness, being the
finest and best of all things is also pleasantest.

Now there are many views that about a given matter and a given / nature   10
involve puzzlement and need investigation. Some of these views tend only
towards knowledge, but others are about acquiring something and achieving
something in action. On the questions that involve purely theoretical philosophy, we should say whatever is appropriate for our current discipline,
when the occasion arises. But first / we should ask: What does living well   15
consists in? How it is acquired? And does everyone who called happy come
to be so by nature (just as one comes to be tall, short, or different in colour)?
Or through teaching (on the assumption that happiness is a sort of scientific knowledge)? Or through some sort of training (for people acquire many
things neither / naturally nor by learning, but by having been habituated—   20
they acquire bad traits if they have been habituated badly, and appropriate
traits if they have been habituated appropriately)? Or in none of these ways,
but in one of two other ways, either—like those possessed by nymphs or
gods—by the inspiration of something divine, as though divinely inspired,
or because of luck, since many / say that happiness is the same as good luck?   25

It is clear, then, that people achieve happiness through all of these means
or through some of them or through one of them; for practically all ways of
coming to be fall under these principles (for / one may treat all types of com-   30
ing to be from thought under the same head as the actions that proceed from
knowledge).

Now being happy, and living blessedly and finely, are most <plausibly>
to be found in three things, those that seem most choiceworthy. For some
say intelligence is the greatest good, others say this of virtue, and others say
it of pleasure. And in relation to happiness some / dispute about their rela-   1214b
tive importance, saying that one thing contributes to happiness than another.
Some assert this because they think intelligence is a greater good than
virtue, others because they think virtue is a greater good than intelligence,
and others because they think pleasure is a greater good than both of them.
And some consider that / living happily is composed of all these, some of two,   5
and others that it consists in some one of them.

Chapter 2

On these questions, then, we ought to notice that everyone who has the power to live according to his own decision sets up some target of living finely—honour, say, or reputation, or wealth, or culture—with reference to 10 which he will then do all his actions, / since failure to direct one's life towards some end is a mark of great folly. Next, one ought above all to answer first in one's mind, without being either rash or dilatory, the following questions:—First, in which of the things that belong to us does living well consist? Secondly, what are the necessary conditions for human beings to gain happi-15 ness? <These questions must be distinguished>; for / being healthy is not the same as the necessary conditions of health, and the same is also true in many other cases, so that living finely and the necessary conditions of living finely are not the same. . . .

24   / This causes the dispute about what it is to be happy and what things bring happiness into being: for some things are only necessary conditions of being happy, but some people believe they are parts of happiness.

Chapter 3

An examination of all the beliefs that just any group of people hold about happiness would be a waste of time. For many things appear to / children 30 and to the ill and the insane, but no one with any sense would go through the puzzles that they raise. What these people need is not arguments; some of them need to grow up and change, and others need correction by medical or social means (for medicine, no less than physical punishment, is a corrective 1215a treatment). Similarly we should not / examine the views of the many either. For they speak at random about pretty well everything, and especially about happiness; it is absurd to apply argument to those who need to undergo the right corrective treatment, not to be argued with.

But since there are puzzles that are appropriate to each enterprise, it is 5 clear that there are also appropriate puzzles about the / supreme way of life and the best way of living. These, therefore, are the beliefs that deserve to be examined; for refutations of one side are proofs of the arguments on the other side. . . .

1215a12   / If living finely is to be found in the things that come about because of luck or nature, it would be beyond hope for many people; for they could not 15 acquire it by practice, nor would it be up to them, / nor anything that they themselves could undertake. If, however, living finely consists in having a specific character and in specific actions of one's own, the good would be both more widely shared—because it would be open to more people to share in it—and more divine—because happiness would be available to those who acquire a specific character and engage in specific actions.

Chapter 4

/ Now most of the points that raise disputes and puzzles will be clear once we   20
determine properly what we ought to suppose happiness is. Does it consist
only in one's having the right sort of character in one's soul (as some of the
wise people thought in earlier times)? Or should we say that the right sort of
character is necessary, / but the right sorts of actions are still more necessary?   25

If different lives are distinguished, some are not even contenders for the
appropriate sort of well-being, but they are pursued for the sake of necessities. These include lives that are occupied in vulgar crafts, or in commercial
or debased pursuits—by vulgar I mean those / practised only with a view to   30
reputation, by debased I mean those that are sedentary and wage earning,
and by commercial I mean those related to markets and retail trade.

But there are three goods that are directed towards conduct suitable for
happiness, those that were also previously the greatest goods for human
beings, virtue, intelligence, and / pleasure. Hence we see that there are also   35
three lives that are lived by those who are free to decide <how to live>. These
are the lives of political activity, philosophy, / and gratification. The philos-   1215b
opher wishes to occupy himself with intelligence and study about truth, the
politician with fine actions (these are the ones that result from virtue), and
the lover of gratification with / bodily pleasures (that is why he has a different   5
conception of the happy person, as was also said before).

Now when Anaxagoras of Clazomenae was asked who the happiest person is, he said, 'None of those you think, but he would appear a strange sort
of person to you'. He gave this answer when he saw that the questioner /   10
thought it impossible for someone to be called happy without being great
and fine or rich. Anaxagoras himself presumably thought that the one who
lives painlessly and purely with a view to justice, or shares in some sort of
divine study, is blessed, as far as a human being can be.

Chapter 5

/ Now it is difficult to reach a sound judgment about many things, but espe-   15
cially difficult about this question that everyone thinks is easily answered,
indeed a question that everyone can answer. The question is this: What
aspect of life is choiceworthy, and what is it that would satisfy one's desire if
one could get it?

<Not everything in life is choiceworthy.> For many things happen that
cause people to abandon life, such as / illnesses, pains, storms. Clearly, then,   20
it would be preferable right from the start, if one were given the choice, not
to be born at all, as far as these things go anyhow. The same is true of the
life that children lead; no one in his right mind would put up with a return
to this life. And further, many things that involve neither / pleasure nor pain,   25

417

or involve pleasure but not fine pleasure, make non-existence preferable to being alive.

And altogether, if one were to collect all the things that people do and undergo, but not for their own sakes, and therefore not willingly, and one

30 were to add to these an unlimited length of time, / all that would not make us choose living in preference to not living.

But further, no one who was not altogether slavish would value living above not living, if it were for the mere pleasure of eating or of sex, and one were deprived of all the other pleasures that knowing or seeing or any other

35 sense provides to human beings. / For, clearly, anyone who made this choice

1216a would not care whether he is born a beast or a human being; at any rate / the Egyptian ox, which they honour as <the god> Apis, has more opportunities in this area than many monarchs have.

Nor, similarly, would the pleasure in being asleep make one prefer <living to non-existence>. For is someone any better off sleeping a sleep

5 without waking from one's first day of life to the one's last, / for a thousand or however many years, than he would be if he were alive as a plant? Plants at any rate seem to share in this sort of life, and so do children too; for they also, when they first come to be in their mother, continue in their natural state, but sleep the whole time.

10 Evidently, then, as far as these things go, / reflexion does not show us what it is to live well, and what the good to be found in living is.

Someone is said to have raised these sorts of puzzles to Anaxagoras, asking why one would choose to be born rather than not. Anaxagoras replied: 'For the sake of contemplating the heaven and the order in the whole uni-

15 verse'. / He, then, thought that the prospect of some sort of knowledge makes it worthwhile to choose to be alive.

But those who attribute blessedness to Sardanapallus, or to Smindyrides the Sybarite, or to anyone else who lives the life of gratification, these all appear to place happiness in enjoyment.

20 Some others, however, <namely, politicians> would choose neither / intelligence of any kind, nor the bodily pleasures, but would prefer the actions that proceed from virtue. For they choose them not only for the sake of reputation, but even if they are not going to gain a good reputation. Admittedly, most <of those called> politicians do not truly deserve to be so called,

25 because they are not true politicians; / for the <true> politician is one who decides on fine actions for their own sake, but most <of those who are called politicians> take up this life for the sake of money and overreaching.

From what has been said, then, it is evident that all ascribe happiness to three lives, the political life, the philosophical life, and the life of gratification.

30 Now among these lives the character, nature, and sources of / bodily pleasures and gratifications, are obvious, so that there is no need to inquire what

they are. The questions we should ask are: Do they promote happiness or not? How do they promote it? If some pleasures belong to living finely, are bodily pleasures the ones that belong to it? Or / ought we to possess these   35
bodily pleasures in some other way <so that they do not belong to living finely>? Are the pleasures that lead us to suppose, quite reasonably, that the happy person lives pleasantly and not merely painlessly, different <from these bodily pleasures>? But about these we must inquire later.

First let us consider virtue and intelligence. What is the nature of each? Are they parts of / the good life either themselves or the actions that result   40
from them? <These questions are reasonable>, / since all those whose views   1216b
deserve attention attribute virtue and intelligence to happiness, even if not everyone does so.

Now Socrates the elder thought that knowledge of virtue is the goal, and he used to ask what justice, / bravery, and each of the parts of virtue is. It   5
was reasonable of him to do so, since he thought that all the virtues are sci-
entific knowledge, so that at the same time one would both know justice and be just—for at the same time one has learned geometry or building and is a builder or geometer. That is why he used to inquire into / what virtue is, but   10
not into how it comes about, or from what sources.

Socrates' view, however, applies <only> to the theoretical sciences; for there is nothing more to astronomy or natural science or geometry than coming to know and contemplating the nature of the things that are the subjects of these sciences— / though indeed they may well be coincidentally   15
useful to us for many necessities of life. The end of the productive sciences, however, is different from mere science and knowledge; health, e.g., is differ-
ent from medical science, and good laws or something of that sort is different from political science. Certainly, it is fine to come to know each of / the fine   20
things; nonetheless, in the case of virtue what is most valuable is not knowing what virtue is, but knowing what its sources are. For we do not wish to know what bravery is but to be brave, nor what justice is but to be just, in the same way as we wish to be healthy rather than to know what being healthy is, and to be in a good / state rather than to know what a good state is.   25

Chapter 6

Now about all these things one should seek conviction through arguments, using the appearances as testimonies and examples. For it is best if everyone is evidently in agreement with the things that will be said; but if not everyone, then / at least everyone in some way. And this they will do this, if their   30
thought is redirected; for everyone has something of their own that tends towards the truth. From these <beliefs they begin with> we need to find some sort of proof about these matters. For if we advance from statements that are true but not perspicuous, we will reach perspicuous statements, / if   35

in each case the usual and confused statements are replaced by conclusions that are known better.

In a particular discipline the arguments that are presented philosophically are different from those that are presented unphilosophically. For this reason we should not suppose that our approach to the study of politics—the approach that makes clear not only what is so, but also why it is so—is superfluous; for that is the philosophical element in a discipline.

40, 1217a / Much caution is needed, however. For / since it seems to be characteristic of a philosopher to say nothing at random, but always to give an argument, some people often fail to notice that the arguments they give are empty and irrelevant to the enterprise. Sometimes they fail to notice this because they do not know any better, but sometimes they are giving themselves airs. / The result is that even some people who are experienced and capable of effective action are victims of <the irrelevant arguments of> these people who neither have nor are capable of having any thought about the overall design of life and actions. Their victims are taken in because they lack education; for lack of education about a given area is inability to discriminate between the arguments that are appropriate to the area and those that are / irrelevant to it.

Book II

Chapter 6
[Human agents are the origins of their own actions.]

In contrast to EN, EE *begins the account of voluntary action with a more general metaphysical discussion of PRINCIPLES* (archai). *He argues that in some way human beings are the origins of their own movements, and that this feature of human agency is manifested in voluntary action.*

1222b15 / Let us, therefore, take another starting point for the inquiry that is to follow. Every substance is naturally a sort of principle. That is why each is also capable of generating many of the same kind as itself—for instance, a human being generates human beings, and in general an animal <generates> animals, and a plant plants. But in addition to this a human being is the only animal that is also a principle of some actions— / for we would not say that any other animal acts.

All those principles that originate motions, are called controlling, and those that are most properly called controlling are those from which things cannot possibly come about otherwise than as they do. This is the sort of principle by which the god presumably originates things. In immovable principles, e.g., in mathematical <principles>, there is no controlling principle, but nonetheless we speak of it / because of a similarity. For, in this case also, if the principle were changed, practically all the things proved from it would also change, but they do not change themselves, one being destroyed by another, except by destroying the assumption and proving through it.

But a human being is a principle of a sort of motion; for action is motion. Since, / as in the other cases, the principle is responsible for the things that   30
are or come to be because of it, we ought to think about it as in the case of demonstrations. For if, given that the triangle has two right angles, it nec-essarily follows that the quadrilateral has have four right angles, it is clear that the triangle's having two right angles is responsible for this. And if the triangle changes, it is necessary for / the quadrilateral to change as well   35
(e.g., if <the triangle has> three, <the quadrilateral has> six, and if four, eight), and if <the triangle> does not change, but is as it is, it is necessary for the quadrilateral to be as it is also. It is clear from the analytics that what we have undertaken to say holds necessarily; but for now we can nei-ther say nothing nor give an altogether accurate account, but we can only say what we have said. For if nothing else is responsible / for the triangle's   40
being thus, this would be a sort of principle and cause of the things that come later.

If, therefore, some beings admit of being in contrary states, the same must be true of their principles. / For from things that are by necessity   1223a
the consequence is necessary. But the things here are capable of acquir-ing contrary states. Many of these things are those that are up to human beings themselves, and human beings themselves are principles of such things.

If, therefore, a human being is / the principle and controller of certain   5
actions, evidently these actions admit both of coming about and of not com-ing about, and it is up to him whether they come about or not. These are the actions whose being and not being are in his control. If anything is up to him to do or not to do, he is himself the cause of it, and if he is the cause of it, it is up to him.

Now virtue and vice and / the actions they produce are praiseworthy or   10
blameworthy. For blame and praise is given, not to the effects of necessity, or chance, or nature, but to whatever we ourselves are responsible for—for if someone else is responsible for something, he gets the blame or praise. Clearly, then, both virtue and vice are found whenever one is oneself / the   15
cause and principle of actions.

We should grasp, then, what sorts of actions they are of which one is one-self the cause and principle. We all agree that if something is voluntary and in accord with someone's decision, he is the cause of it, and that if something is involuntary, he is not himself the cause. Moreover, whatever he does after deciding, he clearly also does willingly. Clearly, then, both virtue and / vice   20
are among the things that are voluntary.

Chapter 8
[Involuntary action that is not forced]

After discussing force in terms similar to EN, *Aristotle argues that some actions are done in full knowledge of what we are doing, and are not forced, but are nonetheless involuntary, because some desires are compulsive (we cannot avoid having them, and we cannot avoid acting on them when we have them).*

1224a10 / We say that the forced is involuntary, and that all the involuntary is forced. And so we should first examine what it is to be forced, and how it is related to the voluntary and involuntary.

The forced and the necessary, then, and force and necessity, seem to be opposed to the voluntary and / to persuasion in the case of actions. But we

15 speak more generally of the forced and of necessity in the case of inanimate things as well; for we say that a stone travels upwards and fire downwards by force and being necessitated. Whenever these things travel in accord with their natural and internal impulse, we do not say they move by force, nor that

20 they are voluntary; we have no name for / this opposition. But whenever they move against this impulse, we say it is by force.

Similarly, in the case of animate things, including animals, we see that they both do and undergo many things by force, if something external outside moves them against their internal impulse. In inanimate things the principle is of one kind only, but in animate things there is <in some cases>

25 more than one principle; for desire and reason do not always / agree. In non-human animals, then, what is forced is simple, as it is in inanimate things; for they do not have reason and desire that are contrary, but they live by desire alone. But in adult human beings both reason and desire are present, and to adults we also attribute actions. For we do not say that a child acts, or that a

30 beast does; those who act are those who are old enough / to act on reasoning.

Everything that is forced seems to be painful; no one does something by force but with enjoyment. That is why there is most dispute about the continent and the incontinent person. For when each of them acts, he has impulses contrary to himself. Hence the continent person, they say, drags

35 himself away from the pleasant / appetites by force, because when he drags himself he suffers pain in relation to the desire that is straining in the other direction. In contrast, the incontinent person drags himself by force against his reasoning. But he seems to suffer less pain than the continent person suffers; for appetite is for what is pleasant, and he follows appetite with enjoyment. Hence the incontinent acts willingly and not by force, because he acts without pain. But persuasion is opposed to force and necessity, and the con-

1224b tinent person / leads himself towards objects that he is convinced he ought to pursue, and he advances willingly, not by force. But appetite leads us without having convinced us, since it has no share in reason. . . .

/ If, however, we add a further point to the definition, the difficulty is 5
resolved. For whenever something external moves a thing, or stops it moving, against that thing's internal impulse, we say the thing is moved by force;
but whenever this is not so, it is not moved by force. But in the continent
and the incontinent person, his internal impulse in him leads him on; / for he 10
has both impulses. And so neither of them acts by force, but, as far as these
arguments go, he does things willingly, and is not compelled to do them.
For what we call necessity is the external principle that impedes or initiates
motion against one's internal impulse— if, e.g., someone were to grab one
person's hand and strike another person, when the first person resists both
by wish and by appetite. But whenever / the principle is internal, one does 15
not act by force.

Further, both pleasure and pain are in both. For the continent person
feels pain when he has reached the stage of acting against his appetite,
and he feels enjoyment in anticipating that he will be benefited later, or
indeed he is already being benefited, by being healthy. And the incontinent person feels enjoyment at getting / the object of his appetite by acting 20
incontinently, but he feels pain in anticipation, since he thinks that what
he is bad. And so the claim that each of them does something by force has
something to be said for it, and so does the claim that each of them on
some occasion acts unwillingly, both because of desire and because of reasoning. For these are two separated impulses, and each pushes the other
out. Hence those who see this sort of force among the parts of the soul / 25
transfer the claim about force to the whole soul as well, and claim that it
acts by force.

It is indeed possible to speak of force in the case of the parts, But the
whole soul, both of the incontinent and of the continent person, acts willingly. Neither of them does anything by force, but one of the parts in them
does. By nature we have both parts. For reason is present by nature, / because 30
if no impairment prevents its growth, it will be present in us. Appetite is also
present by nature, because right from our birth it comes about and is present
in us. We define what is by nature more or less by these two things: whatever
comes about in us all as soon as we are born, and whatever comes about in
us if nothing prevents its progress—e.g., grey hair, old age, and such things.
Both the continent and the incontinent person, therefore, act, in one respect,
not in accord with nature, but / each, speaking without qualification, acts in 35
accord with nature, though not the same nature. . . .

/ But there is also another way in which people are said to act by force 1225a2
and under compulsion, in cases where reason and desire do not disagree, but
people do what they suppose to be painful and base, / and if they do not do 5
it, they face violence, imprisonment, or death. For people say that they did
these things under compulsion.

Or is this not so? Do they all do these very things willingly? One might say so, on the ground that it is open to them not to do it, but to undergo the suffering that follows.

Or again, presumably, one might accept some of these claims and reject
10   others. If it is up to him / to bring about or to prevent such circumstances, if in such circumstances he does what he does not wish to do, he does it willingly, and not by force. If, however, such circumstances are not up to him, he his action in these circumstances is forced in a way; but it is not forced without qualification, because what he decides to do is not <simply> to do this very thing that he does, but <to do it> for the sake of this end. But there is a relevant difference in these things as well. If, for instance, one person
15   were to kill another to prevent the other from touching him, / he would be laughed at if he claimed that he did it by force and under compulsion. If such a claim is to be plausible, there has to be some worse and more painful consequence that he will suffer if he does not do what he says he is compelled to do. If there is such a consequence, he will act under compulsion, neither by force nor not by nature, if he does a bad thing for the sake of a good thing, or for the sake of release from something still worse. He will act unwillingly, because these circumstances are not up to him.

20   That is why / many people also count erotic love, some types of anger, and certain natural conditions, as involuntary, on the ground that they are too strong for our nature. We pardon them as things that force nature. And it would seem to be more of a case of forced and unwilling action if one did it to avoid extreme pain than if one did it in order to avoid slight pain, and if, in
25   general, one did it to avoid pain than if one did it to / gain some enjoyment. For what is up to oneself, to which the whole thing is traced back, is what one's nature is able to bear. If there is something that one's nature is unable to bear, something that is too much for one's natural desire or reason, it is not up to oneself. That is why we also say that if some people are ecstatic and prophesy, even though they do something that requires thought, it is still not
30   up to them to say what they said, / or to do what they did.

Chapter 11
[Virtue of character makes us aim at the correct ends.]

After the discussion of decision (corresponding to EN iii 2–4) Aristotle raises a question that EN does not raise at this stage: What is responsible for our aiming at the correct end in our decision? Aristotle answers: Virtue of character. This answer should be compared with the discussion in EN vi (= EE v).

1227b12   / Does virtue make the decision unerring and the end correct in such a way that one decides for the sake of what one ought? Or does it, as some say,
15   make / reason unerring?

<It does not seem to make reason unerring>. No; what does this is continence, for this preserves reason. Now virtue and continence are not the same. We need to discuss them later, since those who believe that virtue make reason correct believe it on the ground that continence makes reason correct and continence is praiseworthy.

Let us state our view after raising puzzles. It is possible / to aim at the cor- 20 rect target, but to err in the means to it, and it is possible to aim at an erroneous target, but to get the right means to it, and it is possible for neither target nor means to be correct. Does virtue make the target correct, or the things towards the target?

We lay it down, then, that virtue makes the target correct, because the target is not the product of inference or / reasoning, but it is to be assumed as the 25 principle. For the doctor does not examine whether one ought to be healthy or not, but whether one ought to walk or not. Nor does the gymnastic trainer examine whether one ought to be in good condition or not, but whether one ought to wrestle or not. Nor, similarly, does any other <craft> inquire about the end. For as in theoretical <sciences> the assumptions are the principles, so also in the productive <sciences> / the end is the principle and assump- 30 tion; for instance, since this ought to be healthy, it is necessary for one thing to be present, if the other is to be, just as, in a theoretical science, if the triangle has two right angles, something else must be true. The end, therefore, is the principle of thought, and the last stage of thought is the principle of action.

If, therefore, either reason or virtue is responsible for all correctness, it follows that, if reason is not the cause, / virtue is responsible for the correct- 35 ness of the end, not of the means to the end. What one acts for the sake of is the end. For all decision decides on something and for the sake of something. The end for the sake of which, therefore, is the intermediate, and virtue is responsible for aiming at this end, by deciding for the sake of it. Decision, however, does not decide on the end, but on the means to the end.

/ Attaining these things one ought to do for the sake of the end is the   40 task of some capacity other than virtue. / But what is responsible for the   1228a end of the decision being correct is virtue. That is why we rely on someone's decision—that is to say, the end for the sake of which he acts, but not from his actions—when we judge what sort of person someone is. Similarly, vice makes the decision aim at the things contrary to virtue.

/ If, then, it is up to someone to do what is fine and to avoid doing what is   5 shameful, but he does the contrary, it is clear that this person is not virtuous. It necessarily follows, then, that both vice and virtue are voluntary; for there is no necessity to do what is vicious. That is why vice is also blameworthy and /10 virtue is praiseworthy; for shameful and bad involuntary actions are not blamed, nor are involuntary good actions praised, but only voluntary actions arc praised and blamed.

425

Further, we praise and blame everyone by reference to the decision, not to the actions—even though the virtuous activity is more choiceworthy than the virtue—because people do base things under compulsion as well as vol-
15   untarily, / but no one decides to do them under compulsion. Moreover, it is not easy to see what sort of decision it is, and for this reason we have to judge what sort of person someone is from his actions. The action, therefore, is more choiceworthy, but the decision is more praiseworthy.

Politics

Book I

Chapter 1
[Human beings achieve their complete good only by being members of a political community.]

In EN Aristotle affirms that a human being is essentially a political animal whose nature is fulfilled only in a political community. At the end of EN x he introduces his Politics, *which completes the project that he has begun in EN. The* Politics *begins with a statement of the distinctive features of the political community and of the ways it fulfils human nature.*

1

1252a1   / We see that every city is some sort of community, and that every commu-
nity is constituted for the sake of some good, since everyone does everything for the sake of what seems good. Clearly, then, while all communities aim at
5   some good, the community that aims most of all at the good— / at the good that most of all controls all the other goods—is the one that most of all controls and includes the others; and this is the one called the city, the political community.

It is a mistake, then, to suppose, as some do, that the character of the politician, the king, the household manager, and the slave master is the same.
10   People suppose this because they think / the difference is not a difference in kind, but only in the number who are ruled, so that the ruler of a few is a master, the ruler of more people is a household manager, and the ruler of still more people is a politician or a king—on the assumption that a large household is no different from a small city. And all they can say to distinguish a
15   king from a politician is that someone who directs things himself is a king, / whereas someone who follows the principles of political science, ruling and being ruled in turn, is a politician. These views are not true.

What we mean will be clear if the investigation follows our recognized line of inquiry. Just as in other cases we must divide the composite into

426

incomposites, since these are the / smallest parts of the whole, so also in this   20
case we must investigate the components of the city; for then we will also see
better the difference between these rulers, and the prospect of finding any
sort of scientific treatment of the questions we have mentioned.

Chapter 2

/ The best way to study this as well as other matters is to trace things back   25
to their beginnings and observe their growth. First, then, those who cannot
exist without each other have to form pairs, as female and male do for repro-
duction. And they do this not because of any decision, but from the natural
impulse that they share with other animals and with plants / to leave behind   30
another of the same kind as oneself.

Self-preservation is the basis of the natural division between ruler and
subject. For the capacity for rational foresight makes one a natural ruler and
natural master, and the capacity to execute this foresight by bodily labour
makes another a subject and a natural slave; that is why the interests of master and slave coincide.

Now there is a natural distinction / between the female and the slave.   1252b
For nature is not stingy, like a smith making a Delphic knife, in anything it
makes, but it makes one thing for one function, since the best instrument for
a particular function is made exclusively for it, not for many others. / Among   5
foreigners, however, female and slave have the same rank; the reason is that
no foreigners are natural rulers, and so their community consists of a female
slave and a male slave. Hence the poets say 'It is to be expected that Greeks
rule over foreigners', assuming that the foreigner and the slave are naturally
the same. . . .

The first community formed from a number of households for long-term
advantage is a village, and the most natural type of village would seem to be
an extension of a household, including children and grandchildren, sometimes called 'milk-mates'. That is why cities were also originally ruled by
kings and some nations are ruled by kings even at present; / they were formed   20
from communities ruled by kings—for in every household the oldest member rules as its king, and the same is true in its extensions, because the vil-
lagers are related by kinship. Homer describes this when he says, 'Each rules
over his children and wives', because they were isolated, as households were
in ancient times. And for the same reason everyone says the gods / are ruled   25
by a king; it is because we were all ruled by kings in ancient times, and some
still are, and human beings ascribe to the gods a human way of life, as well
as a human form.

The complete community, formed from a number of villages, is a city.
Unlike the others, it has the full degree of practically every sort of self-sufficiency. It comes to be / for the sake of living, but remains in being for the sake   30

of living well. That is why every city is natural, since the previous communities are natural. For the city is their end, and nature is an end; for we say that something's nature (for instance, of a human being, a horse, or a household) is the character it has when its coming to be is complete. Moreover, the final

1253a   cause and end is the best good, and / self-sufficiency is both the end and the best good.

It is evident, then, that the city exists by nature, and that a human being is by nature a political animal. Anyone who has no city because of his nature rather than his fortune is either worthless or superior to a human being. Like

5   / the one whom Homer reviles, 'he has no kin, no law, no home'. For his natural isolation from a city gives him an appetite for war, since, like a solitary piece in a game of checkers, he has no partner.

It is evident why a human being is more of a political animal than is any bee or any gregarious animal; for nature, we say, does nothing pointlessly,

10   and / a human being is the only animal with rational discourse. A voice signifies pleasure and pain, and so the other animals, as well as human beings, have it, since their nature is far enough advanced for them to perceive pleasure and pain and to signify them to one another. But rational discourse is

15   for making clear what is expedient or / harmful, and hence what is just or unjust. For this is distinctive of human beings in contrast to the other animals, that they are the only ones with a perception of good and evil, and of just and unjust, and so on; and it is community in these that produces a household and a city.

Further, the city is naturally prior to the household and to the individ-

20   ual, / since the whole is necessarily prior to the part. For if the whole animal is dead, neither foot nor hand will survive, except homonymously, as if we were speaking of a stone hand—for that is what a dead hand will be like. Now everything is defined by its function and potentiality; and so anything

25   that has lost them should not be called the same thing, but a / homonymous thing.

Clearly, then, the city is also natural and is prior to the individual. For if the individual separated from the city is not self-sufficient, but he is related to it as parts are related to wholes in other cases. Anyone who is incapable of membership in a community, or who has no need of it because he is self-sufficient, is no part of a city, and so is either a beast or a god.

30   Everyone has a natural impulse, then, / towards this sort of community, and whoever first constituted it is the cause of the greatest goods. For just as a human being is the best of the animals if he has been completed, he is also the worst of them if he is separated from law and the rule of justice. For injustice is most formidable when it is armed, and a human being naturally

35   grows up armed and equipped for prudence and / virtue, but can most readily use this equipment for ends that are contrary to prudence and virtue.

Hence, if he lacks virtue, he is the most unscrupulous and savage of animals, the most excessive in pursuit of sex and food. Justice, however, is political; for the rule of justice is an order in the political community, and justice is the judgment of what is just.

Book VII

Chapter 1
[The best political community achieves the human good.]

1

At the end of the Politics *Aristotle fulfils his promise to discuss the best form of political community and the best constitution. To show that this really achieves the human good, he begins with a summary of some of his views on happiness, and discusses some misconceptions about it. He suggests that the alleged opposition between the happy life as a life of active virtue and the happy life as theoretical study rests on some misconceptions.*

/ Anyone who is inquiring along the appropriate lines into the best political system must first determine what the most choiceworthy life is. If it is left unclear what this is, it must also be unclear what the best political system is; for those who have the best political system in their circumstances will characteristically be best off, if nothing unexpected happens. That is why we must first / agree on what sort of life is most choiceworthy for (we may say) everyone, and then agree on whether such a life is or is not the same for an individual as for a community. We may take it then, that the best life is discussed at sufficient length even in <our> popular discussions; and so we should use those now.

For certainly no one / would dispute one division of goods, at least, into external goods, goods in the body, and goods in the soul, or would deny that blessedly happy people ought to possess them all. For no one would count a person blessedly happy if he had no share in bravery, temperance, justice, or wisdom, but was afraid of / every passing fly, sank to any depth to satisfy his appetite for food or drink, ruined his closest friends for some trivial gain, and had his mind as full of senseless illusion as a child's or a madman's.

Everyone would agree with these statements, / but people disagree about how much <of each good is needed> and about large amounts of them. For they think any slight degree of virtue is quite enough, but they seek extreme abundance of wealth, valuables, power, reputation, and all such things, without limit. We will tell them, on the contrary, that it is easy / to reach a confident belief about these questions, by simply attending to the facts.

1323a15

20

25

30

35

40

429

For we see that people possess and keep external goods by having the
1323b   virtues, not the other way round. / Further, as we see, a happy life—whether
such a life for human beings consists in enjoyment or in virtue or in both—
belongs to those who go to extremes in well-ordered character and intel-
5   lect, but / possess a moderate level of external goods, not to those who have
more external goods than they can use, but are deficient in character and
intellect.

Moreover, the same point is easy to notice if we approach the question
by argument. For externals, like instruments, and everything that is useful
for some purpose, have a limit, and excess of them is bound to harm, not
10   to benefit, the / possessor. Each good of the soul, on the contrary, becomes
more useful as it exceeds (if we are to attribute usefulness as well as fineness
even to these goods).

And altogether, clearly we will say that the best condition of one thing
15   surpasses the best condition of another in proportion to / the superiority of
the first thing over the second., If, therefore, the soul is more honourable,
both without qualification and in relation to us, than possessions and the
body, it follows that its best condition must be proportionately better than
theirs. Further, these other things are naturally choiceworthy for the sake of
20   the soul, and / every intelligent person must choose them for its sake, not the
soul for their sake.

Let us, then, take it as agreed that each person achieves happiness to
the extent that he achieves virtue and intelligence, and acts in accordance
25   with them. We appeal to the god as evidence; for he is happy and blessed, /
because of himself and the character that is naturally his, not through any
external good. Indeed this is also why good fortune cannot be the same as
happiness; for chance and fortune produce goods that are external to the
30   soul, but no one is just or temperate from fortune or / because of fortune.

The next point, relying on the same arguments, is that the happy city is
also the best one, the one that acts finely. But no one can act finely without
doing fine actions, and neither a man nor a city does any fine actions without virtue and prudence. Moreover, the bravery, justice, prudence, and tem-
35   perance of a city have the same / capacity and form that belongs to a human
being who is called brave, just, prudent, and temperate.

So much, then, for a preface to our argument; for we can neither leave
these questions untouched nor go through all the appropriate arguments,
40   since this is a task for another discipline. / For now, let us simply assume that
the best life for an individual by himself, and the best common life for cities,
1324a   / is the life involving virtue that has sufficient resources to share in actions
expressing virtue. In our present line of inquiry we must leave aside objections, and consider them later, if someone turns out to be unpersuaded by
what we have said.

Chapter 2

/ Should we, however, take happiness to be the same for an individual human   5
being and for a city? We still need to answer. But the answer to this is also
evident; everyone would agree that it is the same. For those who think an
individual lives well in being rich also count a whole city blessed / if it is rich.   10
Those who honour the tyrant's way of life above all others would say that the
happiest city is the one that rules over the most people. But if anyone thinks
that virtue makes an individual happy, he will also say that the more excellent city is happier.

But now there are two questions to be investigated. First, / which of these   15
two lives is more choiceworthy—the one that involves taking part in political activities and sharing in the city, or the life of an alien, released from the
political community? Second, what political system and what condition of
the city should we regard as best (no matter whether we decide that partici-
pation in the city is choiceworthy for everyone, or only for most people, not
for everyone)? /   20

This second question—not the question about what is choiceworthy for
the individual—is the task of political thought and study; and since we have
decided to undertake a political investigation now, that first question will be
a side issue, and the second will be the main issue for this line of inquiry.

First, then, it is evident that the best political system must be the order
that guides the life of anyone at all who does best / and lives blessedly. But   25
even those who agree that the life that involves virtue is the most choiceworthy disagree about whether the active life of the citizen is choiceworthy, or
the life of someone released from all externals—some life of study, which
some people think is the only life for a philosopher—is more choiceworthy.
For practically / all those, both in the past and now, who have most eagerly   30
pursued virtue have evidently decided on one or other of these two lives, the
political and the philosophical; and it is quite important to decide which view
is correct, / since the intelligent individual, and the intelligent political sys-   35
tem no less, will necessarily order life to aim at the best goal.

Some people, however, think that ruling over one's neighbours as a master
over slaves involves one of the worst injustices, and that even rule as a citizen
over citizens, though it has nothing unjust about it, still interferes with the
ruler's well-being. Others take just about the contrary view, supposing / that   40
the only life for a man is the life of political activity, since, in their view, the
actions resulting from each virtue are open / to those who undertake political   1324b
action for the community, no less than to a private individual.

Some, then, hold this view. But still others say that only the form of political system that rules as a master and a tyrant is happy. And so in some cities
the very aim of the political system and laws is / to rule over neighbouring   5
peoples as slaves.

And so, while most laws in most cities are pretty haphazard, any city that directs its laws to any extent towards some end directs them all at domination. In this way Sparta and Crete organize both education and most of the
10   laws for war. / Moreover, all the <non-Greek> nations that have the power to overreach <at the expense of others> honour this sort of power. For in some places there are even laws that incite them to this sort of virtue. The Carthaginians, for example, so it is said, decorate soldiers with bracelets for
15   the number of / campaigns they have served in. Once the Macedonians had a law that someone who had not killed an enemy should wear a rope around his waist instead of a belt. The Scythians used to pass around a cup at feasts
20   and forbade it to anyone who had not killed an enemy. And the warlike / Iberian nations place around someone's grave a number of stakes to mark the number of enemies he has killed. Many peoples have many similar practices established by laws or customs.

   If we are willing to examine this question, however, we will find it
25   extremely strange to suppose that the / politician's task is the ability to study ways of ruling over neighbouring peoples as willing or unwilling slaves. For how could this be a politician's or lawgiver's task, since it is not even lawful? It is unlawful to rule without regard to justice or injustice, and domination
30   may quite possibly be unjust. Moreover, we never / see this in the other sciences; it is not the doctor's or pilot's task to force his patients or passengers if he fails to persuade them.

   Most people, however, would seem to think the science of mastery over slaves is political science; and they are not ashamed to treat other peoples in
35   ways that they reject as unjust and harmful among individuals. / For among themselves they seek to rule justly, but in relations with other peoples they are indifferent to justice.

   It is strange, however, to deny that some creatures are, and some are not, naturally suited to be ruled by masters. And so, if this is true, we must try to rule as masters only over those suited to be ruled, not over everyone, just
40   as we must not try / to hunt human beings for a feast or sacrifice, but only
1325a animals that are suitable to be hunted; these are the wild / animals that are suitable to eat.

   Besides, a single city even by itself—if it has a fine political system, of course—can be happy, if it is possible for a city to live in isolation somewhere, governed by excellent laws. The organization of this political system
5   will not aim at war / or at domination over enemy states, since it is assumed to have no enemies or wars.

   Clearly, then, all the ways of training for war should be regarded as fine—not, however, as the ultimate end of everything, but as promoting that
10   end. The excellent legislator's task is to consider how a city, or people, or / any other community, is to participate in a good life and in the happiness

432

available to it. However, some prescriptions of law will vary; and it is the task of legislative science, if a city has neighbours, to see what practices should be cultivated in relations with different sorts of neighbours and how to apply the suitable ones to dealings with each neighbouring city. . . .

Chapter 3

We must reply to the two sides who agree that the life involving virtue is the most choiceworthy but differ about the right way to practise it. For those on one side refuse to hold any rule over citizens, since they suppose that the free person's / way of life is both different from the life of political activity and the   20 most choiceworthy of all lives. Those on the other side, on the contrary, hold that the politically active life is the best of all, since, in their view, someone who is inactive cannot possibly be acting well, and good action is the same as happiness.

In reply we say that each side is partly right and partly wrong. The one side is right to say that the free person's way of life is better than the life of a master ruling slaves. / This is true; for employing a slave, insofar as he is a   25 slave, is quite unimpressive, since there is nothing fine about giving orders for the provision of necessities. But to suppose that every sort of rule is the rule of a master over slaves is wrong. For there is just as great a difference between rule over free people and rule over slaves as there is between being naturally free / and being naturally a slave. We have determined this suffi-   30 ciently in the first discussions. Moreover, it is incorrect to praise inactivity over activity; for happiness is activity, and, further, the actions of just and temperate people achieve many fine goals.

And yet, / someone might perhaps take this conclusion to imply that con-   35 trol over everyone is the best thing, thinking that this is the way to be in control of the largest number of the finest actions. And so, on this view, anyone capable of ruling must not resign rule to his neighbour, but must seize it from him; a father must have no consideration for his sons, nor sons for their father, nor in general one friend for another, / nor consider them at all in   40 comparison to this goal <of ruling>, since what is best is most choiceworthy, and good action is best.

Now, presumably this claim <about ruling> is true, / if brigands who rob   1325b and use force get the most choiceworthy thing there is. But presumably they cannot, and this assumption is false. For <the actions of an absolute ruler> cannot be fine if he is not as far superior to his subjects as a man is to his wife, or a father is to his / children, or a master to his slaves. And so someone   5 who deviates from virtue can never achieve a great enough success thereby to outweigh his previous deviation.

For what is fine and just for people who are similar is <holding office> in turn. For this is equal and similar treatment, whereas unequal treatment for equal people and dissimilar treatment for similar people are against nature, and nothing / that is against nature is fine. That is why, if another person is superior in virtue and in the capacity for the best actions, it is fine to follow him, and just to obey him; but he must have not only virtue but also the capacity for the actions.

If this is right, and / we should take happiness to be good action, then the life of action is best both for a whole city in common and for the individual.

However, the life of action need not, as some think, involve relations to others, and the thoughts concerned with action need not be only those carried out for the sake of the results of the action. / On the contrary, the studies and thoughts that include their own end and are carried out for their own sakes must be far more concerned with action; for <their> end is good action, and hence it is a kind of action. And in fact, even in the case of external actions, those whom we regard as acting most fully are the master craftsmen whose plans <direct production>.

Nor, moreover, are cities necessarily inactive / if their position is isolated and they have decided to live in isolation. For a city can still have activities involving parts of itself, since the parts of the city have many communities with each other. And the same is also true of any individual human being; otherwise the god and the whole universe would hardly be in a fine condition, since they have no / actions directed outside them, but only their own proper actions involving themselves.

It is evident, then, that the same sort of life must be the best one both for an individual human being and for cities and human beings in common.

Rhetoric
Book I

Chapter 5
[Happiness and its parts]

Aristotle's work on rhetoric gives advice on public speaking (in political assemblies or in courts of law). Part of this advice considers the ethical assumptions and arguments one should rely on. Aristotle is not putting forward his own ethical views; he is suggesting the best views to rely on for convincing people from their shared ethical views. His remarks on happiness and on goods give us some idea of the views that Aristotle thinks his Athenian contemporaries might find persuasive.

5

/ Practically every individual and all people in common have some target / that they aim at in their choosing and avoiding; this target, to state it in summary, is happiness and its parts. Let us then, by way of illustration, grasp what happiness is, speaking without qualification, and what things constitute its parts. / For all advice for or against <a course of action> is concerned with   10 happiness and the things relevant to it, or with their contraries. For we must do what provides happiness or some part of it, or produces a greater part at the cost of a smaller; and we must avoid whatever destroys or impedes a part of happiness or produces its contrary.

Let us, then, take happiness to be doing well with virtue; or self-sufficiency / of life; or the pleasantest life with safety; or prosperity of possessions   15 and slaves with the capacity to keep them and to use them in action. For everyone more or less agrees that happiness is one or more of these.

If, then, happiness is this sort of thing, its parts must be / good birth,   20 many friends, good friends, wealth, good children, many children, prosperous old age. They must also include bodily excellences (for instance, health, beauty, strength, size, athletic ability), honour, good fortune, and virtue. For this is the way for someone to be most self-sufficient, / by having both the   25 goods internal to himself and the external goods, since there are no other goods apart from these. The internal goods are those in the soul and body, and the external are good birth, friends, money, and honour. We also think it suitable for him to have power and good fortune, since that makes life safest. Let us, then, also / grasp in the same way what each of these <parts of   30 happiness> is.

First, then, a nation or city is well-born if <its members> are indigenous or ancient inhabitants, and if their earliest ancestors were illustrious leaders and had many descendants who were illustrious for their admired qualities. An individual is well-born on the male or / the female side if he is a legitimate   35 citizen on each side and, as in the case of a city, if his earliest ancestors were renowned for virtue or wealth or any other honoured quality and if the family has many illustrious members, male and female, young and old.

It is clear what it means to have good children and to have many children. In the case of the community, this means that its / youth are numerous   1361a and good. They are good by having bodily excellence, such as size, beauty, strength, and athletic ability; in the soul, temperance and bravery are the virtues of a youth. An individual has good children and many children if his own children, both female and male, are / numerous and have these quali   5 ties. But for females bodily excellence is beauty and size, and virtue of the soul is temperance and a love of their work that is not excessive for a free person. And we must seek to acquire each of these qualities no less for the community than for individuals, and no less for women than for men; for if the condition / of women is poor, as it is in Sparta, then happiness is lacking   10 in practically half <the community>.

The parts of wealth are a large amount of money and land; the possession of lands outstanding in number, size, and beauty; further, the possession
15   of implements, slaves, and domestic animals / outstanding in number and beauty; and all these must be our own and safely possessed, both the civilized and the useful possessions. The ones that are more useful are the productive ones, and the civilized ones are those that contribute to gratification. By 'productive' I mean those that yield a return; by 'sources of gratification' I mean those that have no result worth mentioning beyond the use of them.

20   Safety is defined / as possession in such a place and in such a way that the use of the possessions is up to us. They are defined as being our own or not our own according to whether it is up to us to alienate them. By 'alienation' I mean lending and selling. And in general wealth consists in use more than in possession; for it is the active use of possessions that is wealth.

25   / Good reputation consists in being supposed by everyone to be excellent; or in having something of the sort that is pursued by everyone, or by most people, or by the good or the intelligent people.

Honour is the sign of a good reputation as a benefactor. The people who are justly and most highly honoured are those who have conferred benefits;
30   but someone / who is capable of conferring them is also honoured. Conferring benefit refers to safety and to the causes of being alive; or to wealth; or to one of the other goods that are not easy to acquire, either not easy at all or not easy at this place or time—since many people win honour for actions that seem small, but this is explained by the places and times.

35   The parts of honour are: sacrifices; memorials in / verse or prose; privileges; grants of land; seats of honour; tombs; statues; meals at public expense; foreign customs such as prostration and stepping aside; the gifts honoured by each people. For a gift is both the giving of a possession and a sign of honour. That is why both the money-lover and the honour-lover pursue gifts,
1361b   since / gifts provide both of them with what they want; for a gift is the possession pursued by the money-lover, and provides the honour pursued by the honour-lover.

Bodily excellence is health, but health of the sort that allows us to exert
5   our bodies without falling ill; for, as / Herodicus says, there are many healthy people whom no one would congratulate as happy for their health, because they refrain from all or most human affairs.

Beauty is different for different periods of life. A youth's beauty consists in having a body that is serviceable for exertions in running and physical
10   force, and pleasant to look at for / gratification. This is why the all-round athletes are the most beautiful, since they are naturally suited both for physical force and for speed. Beauty in someone in the prime of life consists in having his body serviceable for exertions in war, and in being both pleasant and formidable to look at. Beauty in an old man is having a body adequate

for necessary exertions, and not painful to look at, because it has none of the deformities that mar old age.

/ Strength is the power to move something else as we wish. To move something we must either pull or push or raise or pin down or grip. Hence someone is strong if he is strong in all or some of these ways.

Excellence in size consists in being superior to most people in height, thickness, and width, / to an extent that makes us no slower in our movements.

Athletic bodily excellence is composed of size, strength, and speed—for the speedy person is also strong. For someone who can propel his legs in the right way and move them far and fast is good at running; if he can grip his opponent and pin him down, he is good at wrestling; / if he can repel the opponent with a blow, he is good at boxing; if he can both wrestle and box, he is a good all-round fighter; if he can do all these things, he is a good all-round athlete.

Good old age is the slow and painless onset of old age; for it is not a good old age either if we age rapidly or if we age slowly but painfully. It involves both bodily excellences and fortune; for / we will not be free of suffering and pain if we are not strong and free of disease, and we will not last long without good fortune. There is another ability, the ability to live long, that is separated from strength and health; for many people have long lives without bodily excellences. But exact discussion of this is of no use for our present purposes.

/ Having many friends and having good friends are clear enough once we have defined a friend. A friend is the sort of person who does for another's sake whatever he thinks is good for the other. Hence, whoever has many of this sort has many friends, and whenever they are also decent men, he has good friends.

We have good fortune whenever / we acquire and possess all or most of the greatest of the goods caused by fortune. Fortune causes some things that are also <of the sort> caused by the crafts, but also many things that are not subject to crafts—for instance, the <sort of> thing caused by nature, though it is also possible for some <fortunate events> to occur contrary to nature. For craft causes health, / but nature causes beauty and size. And in general the sorts of goods that result from fortune are those that provoke envy.

Fortune is also a cause of goods that happen contrary to reason. Suppose, for instance, that the other brothers are all ugly, but this one is handsome; or the other people did not see the treasure, but this one found it; or the missile hit his neighbour, / but missed him; or he always frequented the place, but <this time> was the only one who did not go, while the others went there for the first time and were killed. For all these sorts of things seem to be strokes of good fortune.

The most appropriate place to discuss virtue is the discussion of praise; hence we will define it when we discuss praise.

Chapter 6
[Different types of goods]

15   / It is evident, then, what present or future result we must aim at in advocating a course of action and what we must aim at in dissuading from it—i.e., the contrary of the former. Now, the target set for the proponent is advantage, since deliberation is not about the end, but about what promotes the

20   end, and this is what is advantageous in / action; moreover, the advantageous is good; we must therefore grasp the elementary points about what is good and advantageous without qualification.

Let us say, then, that something is good if it is choiceworthy for its own sake; we choose something else for its sake; everything, or everything that has perception, aims at it; everything would aim at it if it acquired understand-

25   ing; understanding would / assign it to an individual; his individual understanding assigns it to him, since this is what is good for each individual; its presence produces a good and self-sufficient condition in the recipient; it is self-sufficient; it produces or preserves such conditions; such conditions follow on it; it prevents or destroys the contrary conditions.

30   One thing follows on another / in two ways—either at the same time, as being alive follows on being healthy, or later, as knowing follows on learning.

One thing produces another in three ways—either as being healthy produces health, or as food produces health, or as exercising produces health, because it usually produces health.

35   Once these things are assumed, it necessarily follows that / getting a good thing and avoiding a bad thing are good; for it follows, in the latter case, that at the same time we do not have the bad thing, and, in the former case, that later we have the good thing. Moreover, getting a greater good instead of a

1362b   lesser, and a lesser bad thing instead of a greater, are good; / for we get one thing and avoid another to the extent that the one exceeds the other.

Again, the virtues must be a good thing; for these produce a good condition in their possessor, produce good results, and are active in good actions;

5   / we must say separately what and of what sort each is. Pleasure must also be a good; for all animals by nature aim at it. Hence both pleasant things and fine things must be goods; for pleasant things produce pleasure, and among fine things some are pleasant, while others are choiceworthy in themselves.

10   / The following, listing them individually, must be goods:

Happiness. For it is choiceworthy in itself and self-sufficient, and, moreover, we choose the other things for its sake.

Justice, bravery, temperance, magnanimity, magnificence, and the other such states. For these are virtues of the soul.

15   Health, beauty, and such things. / For these are excellences of the body and produce many goods. Health, for example, produces both pleasure and

life. That, indeed, is why it seems to be the best good, because it causes the two goods that most people honour more than anything else—pleasure and life.

Wealth. For it is excellence of possession and produces many goods.

A friend and friendship. For a friend is choiceworthy in himself / and moreover produces many goods.   20

Honour and reputation. For these are pleasant and also produce many goods, and usually they imply the presence of the qualities for which people are honoured.

Ability in speaking and acting. For all such things produce goods.

Further, natural aptitude, good memory, ability to learn, sharp wits, all such things. / For these abilities produce goods. The same is true of all the   25
sciences and the crafts.

Life. For even if no other good followed on it, it would still be choiceworthy in itself.

Justice. For it is an advantage for the community.

These, then, we may say, are the agreed goods.

FURTHER READING

This list is not a systematic guide to the large literature on the *Ethics*. It contains only a few books that might be useful for beginning detailed study of the *EN*. The bibliographies in these books will direct the reader to the most important papers.

A place name without a publisher's name refers to the relevant university press.

Aristotle: General

The standard English translation:

Barnes, J., ed., *Complete Works of Aristotle* (Princeton, 1984) (cited as 'ROT' for 'Revised Oxford Translation').

A selection of texts with notes:

Fine, G., and Irwin, T. H., trans., *Aristotle: Selections* (Indianapolis: Hackett, 1995).

A clear, stimulating, short account of Aristotle:

Ackrill, J. L., *Aristotle the Philosopher* (Oxford, 1981).

A fuller summary of the contents of Aristotle's works:

Ross, W. D., *Aristotle* (London: Methuen, 1923).

Books covering several aspects of Aristotle's thought, including ethics:

Shields, C., ed., *Oxford Handbook of Aristotle* (Oxford, 2012).

Shields, C., *Aristotle* (London: Routledge, 2007).

Irwin, T. H., *Aristotle's First Principles* (Oxford, 1988).

An indispensable index:

Bonitz, H., *Index Aristotelicus* (Berlin: Reimer, 1870).

An attempt to construct an index to the Oxford Translation:

Organ, T. W., *An Index to Aristotle* (Princeton, 1949).

Volume 2 of ROT contains a brief index.

The life of Aristotle:

Natali, C., *Aristotle: His Life and School* (Princeton, 2013).

Historical Background

The most convenient work of reference for historical events, dates, details of authors' lives and works, and conventions of reference to Greek texts:

Oxford Classical Dictionary, 3rd ed. (Oxford, 1996).

Short accounts of Greek philosophy:

Irwin, T. H., *Classical Thought* (Oxford, 1989).

Shields, C., *Classical Philosophy: A Contemporary Introduction* (London: Routledge, 2003).

Fragments of the Presocratics are collected in:

Diels, H., and Kranz, W., eds., *Die Fragmente der Vorsokratiker*, 6th ed. (Berlin: Weidmann, 1951) (cited as 'DK').

Graham, D. W., *The Texts of Early Greek Philosophy* (Cambridge, 2010).

Greek ethics before Aristotle:

Adkins, A. W. H., *Merit and Responsibility* (Oxford, 1960).

Dover, K. J., *Greek Popular Morality in the Time of Plato and Aristotle* (Oxford: Blackwell, 1974).

Blundell, M. W., *Helping Friends and Harming Enemies* (Cambridge, 1989).

It is especially useful to read some of Plato's dialogues, in particular the *Laches, Charmides, Protagoras, Gorgias, Republic* i–ii, iv, viii–ix, the *Philebus*, and parts of the *Laws*.

It is sometimes interesting and amusing to compare and contrast the *EN* with a work by Aristotle's pupil and successor:

Theophrastus, *Characters*, 2nd ed., ed. and trans. J. S. Rusten (Cambridge, MA: Harvard UP, 1993).

EN: Texts, translations, commentaries

Editions of the Greek text:

Aristotelis Ethica Nicomachea, ed. I. Bywater (Oxford, 1890). In the series of Oxford Classical Texts (cited as 'OCT').

Aristotelis Ethica Nicomachea, ed. F. Susemihl (Leipzig: Teubner, 1882; revised by O. Apelt, 1903).

Some English translations:

Ross, W. D. (Oxford, 2009) (revised, with notes by L. Brown, Oxford, 2009).

Crisp, R. S. (Cambridge, 2012) (2nd ed.).

Broadie, S. W. and Rowe, C. J. (Oxford, 2002) (with notes).

Reeve, C.D.C. (Indianapolis: Hackett, 2014) (with notes).

The best commentary on the Greek text:

Gauthier, R. A., and Jolif, J. Y., *Aristote: L'Ethique à Nicomaque*, 2nd ed. (Louvain, 1970).

The main English commentaries:

Stewart, J. A., *Notes on the Nicomachean Ethics* (Oxford, 1892).

Burnet, J., *The Ethics of Aristotle* (London: Methuen, 1900).

Joachim, H. H., *Aristotle: Nicomachean Ethics* (Oxford, 1951).

The best of the ancient commentaries:

Aspasius, *On Aristotle Nicomachean Ethics 1–4, 7–8*, trans. D. Konstan (London: Bloomsbury, 2014).

The most important mediaeval commentary:

Aquinas, Thomas, *In decem libros Ethicorum . . . Expositio*, ed. R. Spiazzi (Turin: Marietti, 1949).

Aquinas, Thomas, *Commentary on Aristotle's Nicomachean Ethics*, trans. C. L. Litzinger (Chicago: Regnery, 1964).

Commentaries on individual books:

Jackson, H., *EN Book V* (Cambridge, 1879).

Greenwood, L. H. G., *EN Book VI* (Cambridge, 1909).

Reeve, C.D.C., *Aristotle on Practical Wisdom: Nicomachean Ethics VI* (Cambridge, MA: Harvard UP, 2013).

Aristotle's other ethical works

Edition of the Greek text of *EE*:

Ethica Eudemia, ed. R. R. Walzer and J. M. Mingay (Oxford, 1991).

Translations of *EE*:

Inwood, B., and Woolf, R. (Cambridge, 2013).

Kenny, A. J. P. (Oxford, 2011).

Translation and notes:

Woods, M. J., *Eudemian Ethics I, II, VIII*, 2nd ed. (Oxford, 1992).

Edition of the Greek text of *MM*:

Magna Moralia, ed. F. Susemihl (Leipzig: Teubner, 1883).

Translation of *MM*:

Simpson, P. L. P., *The Great Ethics of Aristotle* (New Brunswick: Transaction, 2014).

The relation of *EN* to Aristotle's other ethical works:

Kenny, A. J. P., *The Aristotelian Ethics* (Oxford, 1978; 2nd ed., 2016).

Kenny, A. J. P., *Aristotle on the Perfect Life* (Oxford, 1992).

Aristotle's views in the *EN* are closely related to the political theory expounded in the *Politics*. English translations of this work:

E. Barker, rev. R. F. Stalley (Oxford, 1995).

C.D.C. Reeve (Indianapolis: Hackett, 1998).

On Aristotle's ethics and politics:

Kraut, R., *Aristotle: Political Philosophy* (Oxford, 2002).

The Ethics: General

A helpful general guide to the *EN*:

Hardie, W. F. R., *Aristotle's Ethical Theory*, 2nd ed. (Oxford, 1980).

Other books covering several aspects of the *EN*:

Bostock, D., *Aristotle's Ethics* (Oxford, 2000).

Broadie, S. W., *Ethics with Aristotle* (Oxford, 1991).

Aristotle's place in the history of ancient ethics:

Meyer, S. S., *Ancient Ethics* (London: Routledge, 2008).

Cooper, J. M., *Pursuits of Wisdom* (Princeton, 2012).

Annas, J., *The Morality of Happiness* (Oxford, 1993).

Irwin, T. H. *The Development of Ethics*, vol. 1 (Oxford, 2007).

White, N. P., *Individual and Conflict in Greek Ethics* (Oxford, 2002).

Collections of essays on the *Ethics*:

Barnes, J., Schofield, M., Sorabji, R., eds., *Articles on Aristotle*, vol. 2 (London, 1977).

Rorty, A. O., ed., *Essays on Aristotle's Ethics* (Berkeley, 1980).

Kraut, R., ed., *The Blackwell Guide to Aristotle's Nicomachean Ethics* (Oxford: Blackwell, 2006).

Sherman, N., ed., *Aristotle's Ethics: Critical Essays* (Lanham, 1999).

Polansky, R., ed., *Cambridge Companion to Aristotle's Nicomachean Ethics* (Cambridge, 2014).

Miller, J., ed., *Aristotle's Nicomachean Ethics: A Critical Guide* (Cambridge, 2014).

Henry, D., and Nielsen, K. M., eds., *Bridging the Gap between Aristotle's Science and Ethics* (Cambridge, 2014).

Cooper, J. M., *Reason and Emotion* (Princeton, 1998).

McDowell, J., *Mind, Value, and Reality* (Cambridge, MA: Harvard UP, 1998).

Ackrill, J. L., *Essays on Plato and Aristotle* (Oxford, 1997).

Heinaman, R., ed., *Aristotle and Moral Realism* (London, 1995).

Bibliography on the *Ethics*

Fuller bibliographies will be found in *Articles on Aristotle* and in *Cambridge Companion* (cited above).

Some of the main topics in the *Ethics*

Happiness

Kraut, R., *Aristotle on the Human Good* (Princeton, 1989).

Richardson Lear, G., *Happy Lives and the Highest Good* (Princeton, 2004).

Virtue

Crisp, R., ed., *How Should One Live?* (Oxford, 1996).

Gottlieb, P., *The Virtue of Aristotle's Ethics* (Cambridge, 2009).

Curzer, H., *Aristotle and the Virtues* (Oxford, 2012).

Foot, P., *Natural Goodness* (Oxford, 2001).

Voluntary action and responsibility

Kenny, A. J. P., *Aristotle's Theory of the Will* (London: Duckworth, 1979).

Sorabji, R. R. K., *Necessity, Cause, and Blame* (London: Duckworth, 1980).

Meyer, S. S., *Aristotle on Moral Responsibility*, 2nd ed. (Oxford, 2011).

Justice

Miller, F. D., *Nature, Justice, and Rights in Aristotle's Politics* (Oxford, 1995).

Action, practical reason, incontinence

Charles, D., *Aristotle's Philosophy of Action* (London: Duckworth, 1984).

Dahl, N. O., *Practical Reason, Aristotle, and Weakness of the Will* (Minneapolis: U of Minnesota P, 1984).

Price, A. W., *Virtue and Reason in Plato and Aristotle* (Oxford, 2011).

Natali, C., ed., *Aristotle's Nicomachean Ethics, Book VII* (Oxford, 2009).

Raz, J., ed., *Practical Reasoning* (Oxford, 1978).

Pleasure

Gosling, J. C. B., and Taylor, C. C. W., *The Greeks on Pleasure* (Oxford, 1982).

Wolfsdorf, D., *Pleasure in Ancient Greek Philosophy* (Cambridge, 2013).

Friendship

Price, A. W., *Love and Friendship in Plato and Aristotle* (Oxford, 1997).